W9-BHK-357

Sicily

THE ROUGH GUIDE

There are more than one hundred Rough Guide titles
covering destinations from Amsterdam to Zimbabwe

Forthcoming titles include
Chile • Dominican Republic • Jerusalem • Melbourne • Sydney

Rough Guide Reference Series
Classical Music • European Football • The Internet • Jazz
Opera • Reggae • Rock Music • World Music

Rough Guide Phrasebooks
Czech • French • German • Greek • Hindi & Urdu • Hungarian • Indonesian
Italian • Japanese • Mandarin Chinese • Mexican Spanish • Polish
Portuguese • Russian • Spanish • Thai • Turkish • Vietnamese

Rough Guides on the Internet
www.roughguides.com

ROUGH GUIDE CREDITS

Text editor: Geoff Howard
Series editor: Mark Ellingham
Editorial: Martin Dunford, Jonathan Buckley, Jo Mead, Kate Berens, Amanda Tomlin, Ann-Marie Shaw, Paul Gray, Chris Schüler, Helena Smith, Judith Bamber, Kieran Falconer, Orla Duane, Olivia Eccleshall, Ruth Blackmore, Sophie Martin, Claire Saunders, Anna Sutton, Gavin Thomas, Alexander Mark Rogers (UK); Andrew Rosenberg, Andrew Taber (US)
Production: Susanne Hillen, Andy Hilliard, Link Hall, Helen Ostick, James Morris, Julia Bovis, Michelle Draycott, Cathy McElhinney

Cartography: Melissa Flack, Maxine Burke, Nichola Goodliffe, Ed Wright
Picture research: Eleanor Hill, Louise Boulton
Online editors: Alan Spicer, Kate Hands (UK); Geronimo Madrid (US)
Finance: John Fisher, Katy Miesiaczek
Marketing and Publicity: Richard Trillo, Simon Carloss, Niki Smith, David Wearn (UK); Jean-Marie Kelly, SoRelle Braun (US)
Administration: Tania Hummel, Charlotte Marriott

....

ACKNOWLEDGEMENTS

Robert would like to say a big thank you to Geoff Howard for expert editing and smooth diplomatic skills; thanks as ever for advice and suggestions to Agata Scamporrino and Doriano Calandro, plus a big hug for Arthur Garbutt and family, Emma and Angelino Poggi, and his mum.

Jules Brown would like to thank Kate Hughes for all her efforts with this edition.

Kate would also like to thank Agata Scamporrino.

Thanks also to Cameron Wilson and Loretta Chilcoat for extra Basics research; Nikky Twyman for proof-reading; Maxine Burke for cartography; and James Morris for typesetting, laconic wit and biscuits.

Grateful acknowledgement is made for permission to quote from *The Leopard* by Giuseppe di Lampedusa (Harvill); *Conversation in Sicily* by Elio Vittorini (Quartet Books); and *The Day of the Owl* by Leonardo Sciascia (Carcanet Press Ltd).

....

PUBLISHING INFORMATION

This fourth edition published May 1999 by
Rough Guides Ltd, 62–70 Shorts Gardens,
London, WC2H 9AB
Distributed by the Penguin Group:
Penguin Books Ltd, 27 Wrights Lane, London W8 5TZ
Penguin Books USA Inc., 375 Hudson Street, New York
10014, USA
Penguin Books Australia Ltd, 487 Maroondah Highway,
PO Box 257, Ringwood, Victoria 3134, Australia
Penguin Books Canada Ltd, 10 Alcorn Avenue, Toronto,
Ontario, Canada M4V 1E4
Penguin Books (NZ) Ltd, 182–190 Wairau Road,
Auckland 10, New Zealand
Typeset in Linotron Univers and Century Old Style to an
original design by Andrew Oliver.
Printed by Clays Ltd, St Ives plc
Illustrations in Part One and Part Three by Edward Briant.

Illustrations on p.1 and p.379 by Henry Iles
© Robert Andrews and Jules Brown
1989, 1993, 1996, 1999
No part of this book may be reproduced in any form
without permission from the publisher except for the
quotation of brief passages in reviews.
448pp. Includes index
A catalogue record for this book is available from the
British Library
ISBN 1-85828-424-4

....

The publishers and authors have done their best to
ensure the accuracy and currency of all the information
in *The Rough Guide to Sicily*; however, they can accept
no responsibility for any loss, injury, or inconvenience
sustained by any traveller as a result of information or
advice contained in the guide.

Sicily

THE ROUGH GUIDE

written and researched by

Robert Andrews and Jules Brown

with additional research by

Kate Hughes

THE ROUGH GUIDES

TRAVEL GUIDES • PHRASEBOOKS • MUSIC AND REFERENCE GUIDES

 We set out to do something different when the first Rough Guide was published in 1982. Mark Ellingham, just out of university, was travelling in Greece. He brought along the popular guides of the day, but found they were all lacking in some way. They were either strong on ruins and museums but went on for pages without mentioning a beach or taverna. Or they were so conscious of the need to save money that they lost sight of Greece's cultural and historical significance. Also, none of the books told him anything about Greece's contemporary life – its politics, its culture, its people, and how they lived.

So, with no job in prospect, Mark decided to write his own guidebook, one which aimed to provide practical information that was second to none, detailing the best beaches and the hottest clubs and restaurants, while also giving hard-hitting accounts of every sight, both famous and obscure, and providing up-to-the-minute information on contemporary culture. It was a guide that encouraged independent travellers to find the best of Greece, and was a great success, getting shortlisted for the Thomas Cook travel guide award,

and encouraging Mark, along with three friends, to expand the series.

The Rough Guide list grew rapidly and the letters flooded in, indicating a much broader readership than had been anticipated, but one which uniformly appreciated the Rough Guide mix of practical detail and humour, irreverence and enthusiasm. Things haven't changed. The same four friends who began the series are still the caretakers of the Rough Guide mission today: to provide the most reliable, up-to-date and entertaining information to independent-minded travellers of all ages, on all budgets.

We now publish more than 100 titles and have offices in London and New York. The travel guides are written and researched by a dedicated team of more than 100 authors, based in Britain, Europe, the USA and Australia. We have also created a unique series of phrasebooks to accompany the travel series, along with an acclaimed series of music guides, and a best-selling pocket guide to the Internet and World Wide Web. We also publish comprehensive travel information on our Web site:

www.roughguides.com

HELP US UPDATE

We've gone to a lot of effort to ensure that the fourth edition of *The Rough Guide to Sicily* is accurate and up-to-date. However, things change – places get "discovered", opening hours are notoriously fickle, restaurants and rooms raise prices or lower standards. If you feel we've got it wrong or left something out, we'd like to know, and if you can remember the address, the price, the time, the phone number, so much the better.

We'll credit all contributions, and send a copy of the next edition (or any other Rough Guide if you prefer) for the best letters. Please mark letters: "Rough Guide to Sicily Update" and send to:
Rough Guides, 62–70 Shorts Gardens, London WC2H 9AB, or Rough Guides, 375 Hudson St, 9th floor, New York NY 10014. Or send email to: mail@roughguides.co.uk
Online updates about this book can be found on Rough Guides' Web site at www.roughguides.com

THE AUTHORS

Robert Andrews is a quarter Sicilian, though has lived most of his life in the UK. When not contributing to travel books and the travel pages of newspapers, he anthologizes, and has had four collections of quotations published. He is currently researching the *Rough Guide to Sardinia*.

Jules Brown first visited Sicily in 1987. Apart from this book he has also written and researched Rough Guides to Scandinavia, Barcelona, Hong Kong, Washington DC and England, and contributed as researcher and editor to guides on Portugal, Spain, the Pyrenees, Italy, Malaysia and Singapore. He is a regular contributor to the *Daily Mail* travel pages and to various Fodor's publications.

READERS' LETTERS

Thanks to all the readers who took the trouble to write in with their comments on the previous edition (apologies for any omissions or misspellings):

Yvonne Alkemade and Dick Sman, Caroline Beattie Merriman, Jennifer Book, Hilary Brooks, Peter Collins, Claudine De Vuyst, Ron and Elizabeth Elbourne, Alan Green, June Grimshaw, Peter Grunwal, Janet Guthrie, Jan and Martina Hitzger, Maggie Hodge, Hana Irfani, Andra Jepson, Herbert Kupsch, Philip Roger, David Santoro, Sotiris Soteriades, Marguerite Stratton, Dr R. Stuart, Carol Tomassin, Gioia and Alberto Tomossi, Gabriel West.

CONTENTS

Introduction x

PART THREE **CONTEXTS** **379**

LIST OF MAPS

MAP SYMBOLS

═══	Main road	⬏	Viewpoint
══	Road	⌇	Rocks
───	Minor road	∧	Mountains
-----	Path	▲	Mountain peak
▬▬▬	Railway	⌐500m⌐	Contour
─ ─	Ferry/hydrofoil route	ⓘ	Information office
▬ ▬	Chapter division boundary	⊠	Post office
✈	Airport	ⓒ	Telephone
★	Bus stop	⊞	Hospital
Ⓟ	Parking	ⅢⅢⅢ	Steps
◉	Hotel	▪▪▪▪	Wall
▣	Restaurant	●━	Gate
⋀	Campsite	■	Building
◆	Ancient monument	⊞	Church
∴	Ruins	⁺₊⁺	Cemetery
‡	Church	▨	Park
⛪	Monastery	▨	Nature reserve
⍓	Lighthouse	⠂⠄	Beach

INTRODUCTION

God first made the world and then he made the Straits of Messina to separate men from madmen.

Sicilian proverb

At the centre of the Mediterranean, but on the periphery of Europe, Sicily is a quite distinct entity from the rest of Italy. Although just 3km away across the water, it's much further away in appearance, feel and culture. A hybrid Sicilian language is still widely spoken, and many place names are tinged with the Arabic that was once in wide use on the island; the food is noticeably different, spicier and with more emphasis on fish, fruit and vegetables; while the flora echoes the shift south – oranges, lemons, olives, almonds and palms are ubiquitous. The nature of day-to-day living is somehow different here, too, experienced outdoors with an exuberance that is almost operatic, and reflected in numerous traditional festivals and processions that take place around the island throughout the year.

There's certainly an immediately separate quality in the **people**, who see themselves as Sicilians first and Italians a very firm second. The island's strategic importance meant it was held as a colony by some of the richest civilizations in the western world – from the Arabs to the Normans to the Spaniards – who looted Sicily mercilessly and made it the subject of countless foreign wars, leaving it with many fine monuments but little economic independence. Hundreds of years of oppression have bred insularity and resentment, as well as poverty, and the island was probably the most reluctantly unified Italian region in the last century, with Sicilians almost instinctively suspicious of the intentions of Rome. Even today, relations with the mainland are often strained, for many here illustrated every time they look at a map to see the island being kicked – the perpetual football.

And Sicilians do have a point. There's much that hasn't changed since Unification, and this century has brought a host of new problems, with mass emigration, both to the mainland and abroad, a high level of crime, and the continuing marginalization of the island from the Italian political mainstream. Even modernization has brought associated ills. Pockets of the island have been devastated by a tide of bleak construction and disfiguring industry, and although Sicily does now, at last, have some degree of autonomy, with its own parliament and president, little has really been done to tackle the island's more deep-rooted problems: poverty is still endemic, and there's an almost feudal attitude to business and commerce. Both European and central government aid continues to pour in, but much has been siphoned off by organized crime, which, in the west of the island at least, is still widespread.

However, this is just the background, and the island's appeal for travellers is astonishingly wide ranging. You'd do well to investigate the life – and monuments – of **Palermo**, one of Italy's most visually striking and lively cities; and the second city of **Catania**, where you may well arrive, also has a live-wire energy. But the chief pleasure is in the **landscape**: much of the island is mountainous, making for some of Italy's most dramatic scenery and providing one of its most beautiful rugged coastlines. The graceful cone of **Mount Etna**, Europe's largest volcano,

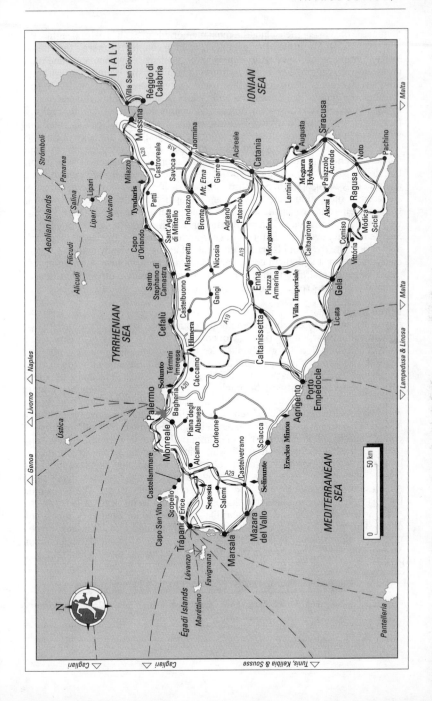

dominates the east of the island, the most memorable of Sicily's natural sights; the northern **Monti Madonie** offer strenuous walking country; or there's the simple, isolated grandeur of the interior – the island's most sparsely populated, and most undiscovered, region. The **coast** is home to much of the island's life, with any number of resorts along its northern and eastern stretches, from lively sun-worshippers' haunts like **Taormina** and **Cefalù** to simple fishing villages fronted by long beaches – out of season, at least, amazingly uncrowded. And for real soli-tude there are Sicily's **outlying islands**, where the sea is as clean as you'll find anywhere in the Mediterranean and you truly feel you're on the edge of Europe.

Sicily's diverse history has also left it with what is for many a surprising abun-dance of **archeological remains**. The island was an important power-base during the Hellenistic period, and the island's Greek relics, especially, are superb, most spectacularly at **Agrigento**, **Selinunte**, **Siracusa** and a host of remoter sites dot-ted around the countryside which stand comparison with any of the ruins in Greece itself – and are for the most part a good deal less crowded. There are also well-preserved mosaics at **Piazza Armerina** which recall the lavish trappings of Sicily's Roman governors. In terms of later architecture, too, the island is remark-ably varied, the **Arab** and **Norman** elements of its history vividly manifest, partic-ularly on the west and north coasts, and **Baroque architecture** showing its face in the elegantly restrained cities of the south east, **Catania**, **Noto** and **Módica**, all planned new towns rebuilt after an earthquake in the seventeenth century.

When to go

Any of these places can be extremely uncomfortable to visit at the height of a Sicilian summer, when the dusty **sirocco** winds blow in from North Africa, and your choice of **when to go** should take this into consideration. In **July and August**, you'll roast – and probably in the company of tens of thousands of other tourists all jostling for space on the beaches and in the museums and archeologi-cal sites. Hotel availability will be much reduced and prices will often be higher in response to demand. If you want the heat but not the crowds, there's no reason why you shouldn't go in June or September, while swimming is possible right into November, with the season starting again in April. **Spring** is the optimum time to come, though, and it arrives early: the almond blossom flowers in February and there are fresh strawberries in April, while Sicily is famous for the exuberance of its spring flowers. **Easter** is a major celebration, a good time to see some of the more traditional festivals, like the events at Trápani, Érice and Piana degli Albanesi, though again they'll all be oversubscribed with visitors. **Winter** is mild by northern European standards and is a nice time to be here, at least on the coast, where the skies stay clear and life continues to be lived very much out-doors. The interior on the other hand, especially around Enna, can get snowed under, providing skiing opportunities south of Cefalù, at Piano Battáglia, or on Mount Etna, while elsewhere in the interior can be subject to wind and rain.

AVERAGE DAYTIME TEMPERATURES (°C)											
	Jan	Feb	March	April	May	June	July	Aug	Sept	Oct	Nov	Dec
Palermo	10.3	10.4	13	16.2	18.7	23	25.3	25.1	23.2	19.9	16.8	12.6
Taormina	11	10.6	13.1	16.2	20.1	24.1	27.1	27.1	23.7	20	16	12.6

GETTING THERE FROM BRITAIN

Much the easiest way to get to Sicily is to fly, and prices for charter flights compare well with the long, overland rail option. Still, there are advantages to travelling by train, not least that you'll run the length of Italy and be able to stop off on the way.

BY PLANE

Direct flights take around two and a half hours from London either to Catania, in the east of the island, or Palermo in the west.

The cheapest way to fly is by direct **charter** flight, though you'd be advised to book some weeks in advance in high season (Easter, July & Aug). Flight-only deals to Catania or Palermo cost from around £175–230 return in high season; outside the summer months, when flights are far less frequent, you probably won't find anything under £200 return. There are daily summer departures from the various London airports (1–2 weekly in summer from Manchester), down to once or twice a week in the winter. These flights are available from one of the numerous specialist **agencies**, listed overleaf, which deal with charter flights. If you're prepared to book at the last minute, you might find some very good deals indeed, though seat availability to Sicily is limited – so if you're committed to certain dates, book ahead. Apart from the agencies, other places to check for budget flights are the classified sections in the weekend newspapers, especially the *Guardian*, the *Sunday Times* and the *Observer*; and, if you live in London, *Time Out* magazine or the *Evening*

Standard. Teletext, Ceefax and the Internet are also good sources of information; or, if you're under 26 or a student, contact the **youth/student travel specialists** STA Travel and Usit CAMPUS (see p.4), good for cheap deals.

Some agents can sell you an **open-jaw** return, flying to Catania and returning from Palermo, or vice versa – a good idea if you want to make your way across the island (or to Sicily from somewhere else in Italy), and generally no more expensive than a standard charter return. Consider a **package deal** (see p.7), too, which takes care of flights and accommodation for an all-in price.

It may also be worth looking at cheap flights to **other southern European destinations**: Naples is around seven hours by train and ferry from Messina; Lamézia (in Calabria: summer charters only) is just two hours from Messina; and even Malta is only two and a half hours by catamaran from Siracusa, three hours from Catania.

Scheduled flights with Alitalia, British Airways or Meridiana are more expensive and are routed via Italian mainland airports (usually Pisa, Milan or Rome), which could mean a total journey time of anything up to six hours if you have to wait for a connecting internal flight. However, scheduled services are very frequent (several times daily) throughout the year, and you'll also find it possible to pick up flights from a whole host of British regional airports, including Birmingham, Bristol, Glasgow, Edinburgh, Manchester, Leeds/Bradford and Teesside. Meridiana fly once a day (Mon & Thurs–Sun) from London Stansted to Palermo, via Florence. The cheapest current high-season return fares to either Catania or Palermo (booked at least 7 days in advance) are around £250–300 return, £30–40 less in low season; discounts for students and under-25s take the price down another £40 or so; Meridiana also offer a deal for under-25s, at £157 return. These are fairly restrictive tickets, though: you have to stay at least one Saturday night, the ticket is valid for one month, allows no date changes, and there's either no refund or only a partial one on cancellation; for something more flexible, you could pay anything up to £800 return. It's always worth checking for seasonal special deals, and booking tickets through a travel agent rather than the airline direct will often reduce the price considerably.

AIRLINES AND AGENCIES IN BRITAIN

AIRLINES

Alitalia, 4 Portman Square, London W1H 9PS, (☎0171/602 7111).

British Airways, 156 Regent St, London W1R 5TA; Victoria Place, Victoria Station, London SW1W 9SJ (☎0171/828 4895); 146 New St, Birmingham B2 4HN; 41–43 Deansgate, Manchester M3 2AY; 66 Gordon St, Glasgow G1 3RS; 32 Frederick St, Edinburgh EH2 2JR (all enquiries ☎0345/222 111).

Meridiana, 15 Charles II St, London SW1 4QU (☎0171/839 2222).

TRAVEL AGENCIES

Alpha Flights, 37 King's Exchange, Tileyard Rd, London N7 9AH (☎0171/609 8188).

APA Travel, 138 Eversholt St, London NW1 1BL (☎0171/387 5337).

Council Travel, 28a Poland St, London W1V 3DB (☎0171/437 7767).

CTS Travel, 44 Goodge St, London W1P 2AD (☎0171/937 3366).

Italflights, 125 High Holborn, London WC1V 6QA (☎0171/405 6771).

Italia nel Mondo, 6 Palace St, London SW1E 5HY (☎0171/828 9171).

Italy Sky Shuttle, 227 Shepherd's Bush Rd, London W6 7AS (☎0181/748 1333).

LAI, 185 King's Cross Rd, London W6 7AS (☎0171/837 8492).

Mundus Air Travel, 5 Peter St, London W1V 3RR (☎0171/437 2272).

STA Travel, 86 Old Brompton Rd, London SW7 3LQ (☎0171/581 4231); 117 Euston Rd, London NW1 2SX (☎0171/465 0485); 38 Store St, London WC1E 7BZ (☎0171/361 6161); 11 Goodge St, London W1P 1FE (☎0171/436 7779); 30 Upper Kirkgate, Aberdeen AB10 1BA (☎01224/658 222); 34 North St, Brighton BN1 1EB (☎01273/728 282); 25 Queen's Rd, Clifton, Bristol BS8 1QE (☎0117/929 4399); 38 Sidney St, Cambridge CB2 3HX (☎01223/366 966); 184 Byres Rd, Glasgow G12 8SN (☎0141/338 6000); 88 Vicar Lane, Leeds LS1 7JH (☎0113/244 9212); 14 Oxford Rd, Manchester M1 5QA (☎0161/834 0668); 9 St Mary's Place, Newcastle NE1 7PG (☎0191/233 2111); 36 George St, Oxford OX1 2BJ (☎01865/792 800); plus branches on university campuses throughout Britain. Their Web site address is http://sta-travel.com.

Travel Bug, 597 Cheetham Hill Rd, Manchester M8 5EJ (☎0161/721 4000).

Usit CAMPUS, 52 Grosvenor Gardens, London SW1W 0AG (☎0171/730 3402); 110 High St, Old Aberdeen AB24 3HE (☎01224/273 559); 541 Bristol Rd, Selly Oak, Birmingham B29 6AU (☎0121/414 1848); 61 Ditchling Rd, Brighton BN1 4SD (☎01273/570 226); 39 Queen's Rd, Clifton, Bristol BS8 1QE (☎0117/929 2494); 5 Emmanuel St, Cambridge CB1 1NE (☎01223/324 283); 20 Fairfax St, Coventry CV1 5RY (☎01203/225 777); 53 Forrest Rd, Edinburgh EH1 2QP (☎0131/668 3303); 122 George St, Glasgow G1 1RF (☎0141/553 1818); 166 Deansgate, Manchester M3 3FE (☎0161/833 2046); 105–106 St Aldates, Oxford OX1 1DD (☎01865/242 067); 340 Glossop Rd, Sheffield S10 2HW (☎0114/275 2552); plus branches in YHA shops and on university campuses all over Britain.

BY TRAIN

Travelling by **train to Sicily** from Britain does not have a lot to recommend it, except the possibility of breaking your journey. It certainly won't save any money, when you compare prices with charter flights. It can also be a real endurance test: the 2672-kilometre journey from London to Messina – across the Channel by ferry, through France and down the length of Italy – is scheduled to take 42 hours, though long delays on the Italian stretch are not uncommon. You'll need to change trains at least once, too, depending on which of the three possible routes you take. It's well worth **reserving a seat** (currently £2–10 for each train you travel on), if not a **couchette bed** (around £15), for at least part of the journey – do both well in advance.

Fares vary according to the route taken, but the cheapest ordinary second-class **return fare**, on the fastest route to Palermo (via Paris and Modane, avoiding Switzerland), will cost you £250, an extra £30 if you use Eurostar; all tickets are valid for two months. Under-26s can buy **discounted Billet International de Jeunesse (BIJ) tickets** through Wasteels (see opposite), which allow as many stopovers as you like over a two-month peri-

RAIL TICKET AGENCIES

Citalia (☎0891/715 151).

Eurostar, European Passenger Services (reservations ☎0990/186 186).

International Rail Centre, Victoria Station, London SW1V 1JY (☎0990/848 848).

Italian State Railways (enquiries ☎0171/724 0011; timetables and general information on the Web at *www.fs-on-line.com*).

Rail Europe 179 Piccadilly, London W1V 0BA (☎0990/848 848).

Ultima Travel (☎0151/339 6171).

Wasteels (☎0171/834 7066).

od; these currently cost around £170 return to Catania or Palermo. Under-26s travelling from **outside London** can also arrange discounted connecting fares to get them to London; alternatively, they qualify for reduced price tickets if they join the train at the Channel ports. Any of these tickets are available at offices in Victoria Station, London (from where all the trains depart), from youth/student agents or direct from Wasteels. Obviously, if you choose to travel the London–Paris section of the route by Eurostar, from London Waterloo through the **Channel Tunnel**, the total return fare rises considerably (£109 return, though booking 7 days in advance brings the price down to £89).

Given these prices, you might consider investing in an **InterRail** pass, which for those under 26 costs from £209 for one month's unlimited rail travel throughout Europe. The pass is zoned (Italy is grouped with Turkey, Greece and Slovenia), and gives discounts on cross-Channel services and free passage on the Bríndisi–Corfu–Patras route to Greece – though it's not actually a lot of help once you've arrived in Sicily, since the rail network isn't that extensive (see "Getting around", p.22). There's a version for over-26s too, the InterRail 26+, costing £279. The InterRail pass is available from British Rail stations and youth/student travel agencies, and you need to have been resident in Europe for at least six months to qualify.

Finally, senior citizens holding a Senior Citizen Railcard can purchase a **Rail Europe Senior Card** for £5, which allows thirty percent discounts on rail fares throughout Europe, including Italy, plus thirty percent off most ferry crossings. Specific details and tickets from British Rail stations.

For details of passes for use solely within Italy, see p.23.

Frankly, it's difficult to see why you would want to subject yourself to the rigours of getting to Sicily by **bus**, particularly since there isn't even a direct service from London. You have to use the **National Express Eurolines** (☎0990/808 080) service from London to Rome (4 weekly: £135 return, £125 for under-26s and students, £68 children), which takes 32 hours; and then take the daily Segesta bus from there to Messina (a 9hr trip), or Siracusa (12hr), or Palermo (12hr). The Segesta terminal in Rome is at Piazza Tiburtina (☎06.44.245.905), near the main Términi train station, and a one-way ticket to Palermo or Siracusa costs L65,000 (£26). About the only advantage of this route is that you are guaranteed a seat all the way to Sicily.

BY CAR: THE FERRIES AND EUROTUNNEL

The best cross-Channel options for most drivers will be the standard **ferry/hovercraft** links between Dover and Calais or Boulogne (with Hoverspeed, P&O Stena or Sea France), Folkestone and Boulogne (Hoverspeed), or Newhaven and Dieppe (P&O Stena). Crossing using Eurotunnel (24hr service, departures every 15min at peak periods) will speed up the initial part of the journey, though overall there are no great savings on time to be made since there's still a long way to go once you reach France.

From the France–Italy border, with a bit of luck it's possible to reach the Straits of Messina in a long day if you keep on the autostradas. The shortest crossing over the Straits is from Villa San Giovanni **by ferry**; or, fifteen minutes further south – at the end of the motorway – **hydrofoils** leave from Réggio di Calabria. There are a few options for those who want to cut the driving or train-journey time, using one of a number of earlier **ferry/hydrofoil crossings from the Italian mainland** to Sicily, while if you have bags of time you can even approach Sicily by travelling **via Corsica and Sardinia**.

Any travel agent can provide up-to-date cross-Channel schedules and make advance bookings (which in season, if you're driving, can be essential). For the Italian crossings, contact the companies or their agents and note that only SNAV have offices in Italy. More details on all these routes are given in the box over the page. In the low season, watch out for **special offers**

GETTING THERE BY FERRY

CROSS-CHANNEL TICKETS

Eurotunnel (☎0990/353 535). To Calais.
Hoverspeed, Dover (☎0990/240 241).
To Boulogne and Calais.

P&O Stena Line (☎0990/980 980).
To Calais and Dieppe.
Sea France (☎0990/980 980). To Calais.

AGENTS FOR FERRIES TO ITALY

Corsica Ferries, c/o Viamare, Graphic House, 2
Sumatra Rd, London NW6 1PU (☎0171/431 4560).
Grandi Navi Veloci, c/o Viamare, see above.

Siremar, c/o Serena Holidays, 40–42 Kenway Rd,
London SW5 0RA (☎0171/373 6548).
Tirrenia Line, c/o Serena Holidays, see above.

CROSSING THE STRAITS OF MESSINA

*Drivers buy their **tickets** at kiosks on the way onto the ferry; foot passengers just walk on and pay the roving ticket collector. All prices given below are for high-season one-way tickets; returns generally cost double.*

Villa San Giovanni–Messina

FS car ferries, around 25 daily, a 25min journey;
L1700 per person, cars from L27,000.

Caronte car ferries, every 20min (fewer
throughout the night), a 35min journey; cars from
L28,000, foot passengers free.

Réggio di Calabria–Messina

FS fast ferries, 19 daily Mon–Sat, 9 Sun, a
20min journey; L5000 per person, L7000 return.

Meridiano car ferries, 25 daily in summer, 15
daily in winter, a 45min journey; L12,000 per car,
including passengers, L6000 per foot passenger.

OTHER CROSSINGS FROM THE ITALIAN MAINLAND

The prices given are the cheapest one-way high-season fares (for reclining chair or deck class).

Genova–Palermo (with Grandi Navi Veloci); 6
weekly, a 20hr journey; from L144,000 per person, cars from L185,000.

Livorno–Palermo (with Grandi Navi Veloci); 3
weekly, a 17hr journey; from L124,000 per person, cars from L170,000.

Naples–Aeolian Islands/Milazzo (with
Siremar) 3–5 weekly, a 16hr 30 min journey; from
L77,000 per person, cars from L161,500.

Naples–Palermo: (with Tirrenia) 1 car ferry
daily, a 9hr journey; from around L70,000 per person, cars from L121,000; (with SNAV) 1 catamaran daily, a 4hr journey; L120,000 per person,
cars from L225,000.

CROSSING VIA CORSICA AND SARDINIA

Tirrenia run services from Genova to Cágliari and Olbia, both in Sardinia; from Cágliari, you can catch one of their ferries to Palermo or Trápani. Alternatively, in summer, you could cross to Corsica with Corsica Ferries (from La Spezia and Pisa), then make the short crossing to Sardinia, and take the Tirrenia ferry to Palermo.

Genova–Cágliari (with Tirrenia) 2 weekly, a
23hr journey; from L95,000 per person, cars from
L130,500.
Genova–Olbia (with Tirrenia) 1 daily in summer,
3 weekly in winter, a 13hr journey; from L76,500
per person, cars from L140,500; (with Grandi

Navi Veloci) 1 daily in summer, a 10hr journey;
from L72,000 per person, cars from L130,000.

Cágliari–Palermo or Trápani (with Tirrenia)
2 weekly, a 12–13hr journey; from L66,500 per
person, cars from L140,500.

on the Italian ferries if you're buying a return
ticket on your outward journey; check with the
agent.

Driving in Italy is more expensive than just
about anywhere else in Europe. On top of the
inflated fuel prices (see p.25), it'll cost around
another £35 per car to use the toll motorways

between the French border and Naples, after
which it's free until you reach Sicily.

PACKAGE HOLIDAYS

On the whole Sicily is not a cheap package-holiday
destination, but it's always worth looking at
travel-plus-accommodation package holidays.

SPECIALIST TOUR OPERATORS IN BRITAIN

Alternative Travel Group, 69–71 Banbury Rd, Oxford OX2 6PE (☎01865/513 333). Inclusive nine-day walking holidays (April/May & Sept/Oct) in the Monti Madonie, from Enna to Cefalù; costly (around £1300) but well organized.

Citalia, Marco Polo House, 3–5 Lansdowne Rd, Croydon, Surrey CR9 1LL (☎0181/686 5533). Packages to Taormina, island tours, self-catering holidays and car rental.

Interhome, 383 Richmond Rd, London TW1 2EF (☎0181/981 1294). Holiday homes across Sicily, including budget choices for four to ten people at around £70 per person, even in high season.

Italia nel Mondo, 6 Palace St, London SW1E 5HY (☎0171/828 9171). Beach holidays, island tours, offshore-island holidays, self-catering apartments and hotel reservations round the whole of Sicily.

Italian Escapades, 227 Shepherd's Bush Rd, London W6 7AS (☎0181/748 2661). Packages to Cefalù, Palermo and Taormina; tailor-made fly-drive tours of Sicily and car rental.

Magic of Italy, 227 Shepherd's Bush Rd, London W6 (☎0181/748 7575). Holidays in the Aeolian Islands, Cefalù and Taormina, or fly-drive tours throughout the island.

Ramblers Holidays, Box 43, Welwyn Garden City, Herts AL8 6PQ (☎01707/331 133). Half-board walking holidays based in Francavilla, near Taormina (one week £435–465), in western Sicily (two weeks around £750) and the Aeolian Islands and Francavilla combined (two weeks £670–690); weekly departures Feb, March–May, Sept, Oct & Dec.

Sunvil, 7 & 8 Upper Square, Old Isleworth, Middlesex TW7 7BJ (☎0181/568 4499). Holidays in the best of Sicily's resorts – Cefalù, Taormina and San Vito Lo Capo – as well as city-based stays in Catania, Palermo and Siracusa, farm holidays and fly-drives.

Many companies offer travel at rates as competitive as you could find on your own, and any travel agent can fill you in on all the latest offers. Most packages are to Taormina, the most chic resort, and to Cefalù, though you'll also see holidays in the Aeolian Islands, and special tours of the major historical sights, which take in overnight stops in several Sicilian towns.

It's obviously cheapest to go out of season, something we'd recommend anyway as the resorts and sights are much less crowded, and the weather is often warm enough to swim: in Cefalù or Taormina in winter, you could get a week's bed-and-breakfast accommodation for around £400. In high season (Easter, July & Aug) all these prices rise considerably, and you can expect to pay upwards of £500 for the same in Taormina or Cefalù, though your travel agent might come up with good, last-minute deals. Some operators organize **specialist holidays** to Sicily (see box above), particularly walking tours, and art and archeology holidays, but they don't come cheaply either: accommodation, food, local transport and the services of a guide are nearly always included, and a week's half-board holiday can cost from £750 per person, full-board as much as £1300.

If you want to rent a car in Sicily, it's well worth checking with tour operators before you leave, as some **fly-drive deals** work out very cheaply. See the box above for operators' addresses; and see pp.24–25 for more car-rental details.

GETTING THERE FROM IRELAND

There are no direct flights from Ireland to Sicily; you must either travel via London or an Italian city like Milan or Rome.

The cheapest current high-season return fares **from Dublin** to either Catania or Palermo (booked at least seven days in advance) are around IR£421 return; otherwise your best bet is to get to London and then catch a Sicily-bound plane from there. There are numerous daily flights to London with Ryanair, Aer Lingus, British Airways and British Midland. The cheapest are Ryanair's, which cost from around IR£60 for a return to Luton or Stansted, though the cost of the bus and Underground journeys across London may make the total cost greater than other fares to Heathrow. **From Belfast**, there are British Airways and British Midland flights to Heathrow, but the cheapest service is the Jersey European run to Luton, at around £85 return. From Dublin you can undercut the plane's price by travelling **by ferry and train to London** (IR£41 return), but from Belfast you'll save nothing by doing this. United Travel (see box below) are the only Irish company to operate **package tours** to Sicily: count on paying in the region of IR£599, depending on season, for a week's half-board in either Cefalù, Giardini-Naxos or Taormina, flight included.

If you're committed enough to want to take the **train** all the way, be warned that the Dublin–Palermo run takes a massive 64 hours – it really isn't worth it.

For the best **youth/student deals** from either Dublin or Belfast, and for information about rail passes, contact Usit (see box below).

AIRLINES AND AGENTS IN IRELAND

AIRLINES

Aer Lingus, 40 Upper O'Connell St, Dublin (☎01/844 4747); 2 Academy St, Cork (☎021/327 155); 136 O'Connell St, Limerick (☎061/474 239).

Alitalia, 60–63 Dawson St, Dublin (☎01/677 5171).

British Airways, Belfast reservations ☎0345/222 111; Dublin reservations ☎1800/626 747.

British Midland, Belfast reservations ☎0345/554 554; Dublin reservations ☎01/283 8833.

Jersey European Airways, Belfast reservations ☎01232/457 2004.

Ryanair, Dublin reservations ☎01/609 7800.

AGENTS

Budget Travel, 134 Lower Baggot St, Dublin 2 (☎01/661 1866). Flight agent.

Thomas Cook, 11 Donegal Place, Belfast BT1 5AJ (☎01232/554 455); 118 Grafton St, Dublin 2 (☎01/677 1721). Mainstream package-holiday and flight agent, with occasional discount offers.

United Travel, Stillorgan Bowl, Stillorgan, County Dublin (☎01/283 2555). Scheduled flights, charters and packages to Sicily.

Usit, 19–21 Aston Quay, O'Connell Bridge, Dublin 2 (☎01/602 1177); 10–11 Market Parade, Cork (☎021/270 900); Fountain Centre, College St, Belfast BT1 6ET (☎01232/324 073). Student and youth specialist.

GETTING THERE FROM THE US AND CANADA

Although there are no direct flights from North America to Sicily, you can fly to the Italian mainland from a number of cities: the main points of entry are Rome and Milan, from either of which there are plenty of connecting flights on to Sicily. Many airlines and agents also offer open-jaw tickets, enabling you to fly into one Italian city and out from another.

It might be a good idea to travel **via elsewhere in Europe** (particularly Britain or Germany), since there's a broad range of well-priced flights available from all over North America to various European cities, and there is a wider choice of options to Sicily once there. **Flying** is the most straightforward way to get from Britain to Sicily, and prices are competitive; see "Getting there from Britain" for full details. If you're interested in seeing more of Europe on the way, the long **rail** journey may be more appealing – again, there are more details under "Getting there from Britain", while in this section, under "Travelling by rail", you'll find details on the **Eurail** pass, which you'll need to purchase before you leave home.

SHOPPING FOR TICKETS

Barring special offers, the cheapest fare is usually an **Apex** ticket, although this will carry certain restrictions: you have to book – and pay – at least

21 days before departure, spend at least seven days abroad (maximum stay three months), and you tend to get penalized if you change your schedule. There are also winter **Super Apex** tickets, sometimes known as "Eurosavers" – slightly cheaper than an ordinary Apex, but limiting your stay to between seven and 21 days. Some airlines also issue **Special Apex** tickets to people younger than 24, often extending the maximum stay to a year. Many airlines offer youth or student fares to **under-25s**; a passport or driving licence are sufficient proof of age, though these tickets are subject to availability and can have eccentric booking conditions. It's worth remembering that most cheap return fares involve spending at least one Saturday night away and that many will only give a percentage refund if you need to cancel or alter your journey, so make sure you check the restrictions carefully before buying a ticket.

You can normally cut costs further by going through a **specialist flight agent** – either a **consolidator**, which buys up blocks of tickets from the airlines and sells them at a discount, or a **discount agent**, which deals in blocks of tickets offloaded by the airlines, and often offers special student and youth fares and a range of other travel-related services such as travel insurance, rail passes, car rentals, tours and the like. Bear in mind, though, that penalties for changing your plans can be stiff. Some agents specialize in **charter flights**, which may be cheaper than anything available on a scheduled flight, but again departure dates are fixed and withdrawal penalties are high (check the refund policy). If you travel a lot, **discount travel clubs** are another option – the annual membership fee may be worth it for benefits such as cut-price air tickets and car rental. Finally, **students** should be able to take advantage of discounted air fares from various travel agencies; while a couple of agencies (see box on p.11) also offer very cheap **courier** flights – though these carry severe restrictions on trip duration and the amount of luggage allowed.

Don't automatically assume that tickets purchased through a travel specialist will be cheapest – once you get a quote, check with the airlines and you may turn up an even better deal. Be advised also that the pool of travel companies is swimming with sharks – exercise caution and *never* deal with a company that demands cash up front or refuses to accept payment by credit card.

Regardless of where you buy your ticket, the **fare** will depend on the season, and are highest between June and August; they drop during the "shoulder" seasons, September–October and April–May, and you'll get the best prices during the low season, November to March (excluding Christmas and New Year, when prices are hiked up and seats are at a premium). Note also that flying on **weekends** ordinarily adds $60 (Can$80) to the round-trip fare, while **taxes** added to each fare usually run to another $35 (Can$55–65); **price ranges quoted below assume mid-week travel**.

FROM THE US

Alitalia, the national airline of Italy, fly the widest choice of routes between the US and Italy. They fly direct every day from New York, Boston, Miami, Chicago and Los Angeles to Milan and Rome. As for **American-based airlines**, Delta Airlines fly daily from New York non-stop, and also from Chicago and Los Angeles to Rome and Milan with stopovers in either New York or a European city; TWA fly daily from LA and Chicago via New York to Milan and Rome; American Airlines fly daily direct to Milan from Chicago and Miami; and Continental fly daily from Newark to Rome and Milan. If you're looking at alternatives, or specifically for a **European stopover**, other airlines with services to Italy include: Air France (via Paris); British Airways (via London); Iberia (via Madrid); Icelandair (via Luxembourg); Lufthansa

(via Frankfurt or Münich); Northwest/KLM (via Amsterdam); Sabena (via Brussels); SAS (via Copenhagen) and Swissair (via Zürich); – all of which have services to at least Rome and Milan.

Direct flights take around nine hours from New York or Boston, twelve hours from Chicago, and fifteen hours from Los Angeles; for the **connection to Sicily** add on another 1hr 15min–3hr, depending on the service, plus any time spent waiting for the connection itself.

The basic round-trip **fares to Rome or Milan** vary little between airlines, though it's always worth asking about special promotions. Generally, the cheapest round-trip fare, travelling midweek in low season, starts at around $650 from New York or Boston to Rome, rising to around $750 during the shoulder season, and to about $950 during the summer. Flights from LA work out about $200 on top of these round-trip fares; from Miami and Chicago, add on about $100. **Add-on fares to Palermo or Catania** in Sicily cost around $100–200 return, depending on season; note that these flights are with Alitalia only, from either Rome or Milan.

FROM CANADA

The only airlines to fly direct to Italy **from Canada** are Alitalia, who fly daily from Toronto and Montréal to Rome or Milan for a low-season fare of Can$1060 midweek, increasing to around Can$1320 in high season (expect to pay upwards of Can$100–200 extra for weekend travel at any time of the year); and Canadian Airlines, who fly to Rome from Toronto (daily except Mon & Sat) and

AIRLINES IN NORTH AMERICA

Air Canada ☎1-800/776-3000; in Canada ☎1-888/247-2262.

Air France ☎1-800/237-2747; in Canada ☎1-800/667-2747.

Alitalia ☎1-800/223-5730; in Canada ☎1-800/361-8336.

American Airlines ☎1-800/433-7300.

British Airways ☎1-800/247-9297; in Canada ☎1-800/243-6822.

Canadian Airlines ☎1-800/426-7000; in Canada ☎1-800/665-1177.

Continental Airlines ☎1-800/231-0856.

Delta Airlines ☎1-800/241-4141; in Canada ☎1-800/221-1212.

Iberia in US & Canada ☎1-800/772-4642.

Icelandair ☎1-800/223-5500.

Northwest/KLM ☎1-800/374-7747; in Canada ☎1-800/581-6400.

Lufthansa ☎1-800/645-3880 or 1-800/399-LUFT; in Canada ☎1-800/563-5954.

Sabena ☎1-800/955-2000.

SAS ☎1-800/221-2350.

Swissair ☎1-800/221-4750; in Canada ☎1-800/267-9477.

TWA ☎1-800/892-4141.

DISCOUNT TRAVEL COMPANIES IN NORTH AMERICA

Air Brokers International, 323 Geary St, Suite 411, San Francisco, CA 94102 (☎1-800/883-3273; www.airbrokers.com). Consolidator.

Air Courier Association, 15000 W 6th Ave, Suite 203, Golden, CO 80401 (☎303/278-8810). Courier flight broker, often with flights from New York to Milan or Rome.

Airhitch, 2472 Broadway, Suite 200, New York, NY 10025 (☎212/864-2000). Standby-seat broker: for a set price, they guarantee to get you on a flight as close to your preferred destination as possible, within a week.

Cheap Tickets, 115 E 57th St, Suite 1510, New York, NY 10022 (☎1-800/377-1000). Discounted tickets for international destinations.

Council Travel, Head office: 205 E 42nd St, New York, NY 10017 (☎1-800/2COUNCIL; in New York ☎212/822-2700). Student and youth travel organization offering discounted airfares, rail passes and travel gear. For over-26s, it acts like a regular travel agency.

Educational Travel Center, 438 N Frances St, Madison, WI 53703 (☎1-800/747-5551). Student/youth discount agent with good prices on flights to Rome and Milan.

Encore Travel Club, 4501 Forbes Blvd, Lanham, MD 20706 (☎1-800/444-9800). Discount travel club.

Halbert Express, 147-05 176th St, Jamaica, NY 11434 (☎718/656-5000). Courier flights from New York to Milan and Rome; book six to eight weeks in advance.

Last Minute Travel Club, 100 Sylvan Rd, Woburn, MA 01801 (☎1-800/LAST-MIN).Travel club specializing in standby deals.

New Frontiers/Nouvelles Frontières Head office: 12 E 33rd St, New York, NY 10016

(☎1-800/366-6387); 1001 Sherbrook East, Suite 720, Montrèal, H2L 1L3 (☎514/526-8444). French discount travel firm with summer charters to Rome. Other branches in LA, San Francisco and Québec City.

STA Travel Head office: 5900 Wiltshire Blvd, Suite 2110, Los Angeles, CA 90036 (nationwide ☎1-800/777-0112). Worldwide specialist in independent travel for students and under-26s only, with branches in the New York, San Francisco and Boston areas.

TFI Tours International Head office: 34 W 32nd St, 12th Floor, New York, NY 10001 (☎1-800/745-8000). Consolidator; other offices in Las Vegas, San Francisco, Los Angeles.

Travac, Head office: 989 6th Ave, 16th Floor, New York, NY 10018 (☎1-800/872-8800 or ☎212/563-3303). Consolidator and charter broker. Will fax current fares from their Fax Line (☎1-888/872-8327).

Travel Avenue, 10 S Riverside Plaza, Suite 1404, Chicago, IL 60606 (☎1-800/333-3335). Discount travel agent.

Travel Cuts 187 College St, Toronto, ON M5T 1P7 (☎1-800/667-2887; in the US ☎1-877/247-8881); branches all over Canada, plus an office in San Francisco (☎414/247-1800). Specialists in student fares, IDs and travel services.

Travelers Advantage, 3033 S Parker Rd, Suite 900, Aurora, CO 80014 (☎1-800/548-1116). Discount travel club.

UniTravel, 11737 Administration Drive, Suite 120, St Louis, MO 63146 (☎1-800/325-2222). Consolidator.

Worldtek Travel, 111 Water St, New Haven, CT 06511 (☎1-800/243-1723). Discount travel agency.

Montréal (Mon & Sat only) for around Can$756 in low season and Can$1070 in high season. Remember to add on another Can$150 return or so for any connecting flights to Sicily. Flights to Italy take around nine hours from the eastern Canadian cities, fifteen hours from the west. Other airlines to consider are British Airways (daily flights from Toronto, Montréal and Vancouver – via London – to Rome); Lufthansa (daily, a direct Calgary, Montréal, Toronto, Vancouver – via Frankfurt – to Milan, Rome or Venice service); and Northwest/KLM (daily from Montréal and Toronto to Milan and Rome via Amsterdam).

PACKAGES AND ORGANIZED TOURS

There are dozens of companies operating group travel and tours in Italy, ranging from full-blown luxury escorted tours to small groups sticking to specialized itineraries. However, specifically Sicilian options are less common, though the agencies listed on p.12 usually offer tours at least partly based on the island. If you're happy to stay in one (or two) places, you can also, of course, simply book a hotel-plus-flight deal, or, if you're keener to self-cater, rent a villa or a farmhouse for a week or two. Prices vary wildly, so check what

SPECIALIST OPERATORS IN NORTH AMERICA

Adventure Center, 1311 63rd St, Suite 200, Emeryville, CA 94608 (☎1-800/227-8747). Offers a "Sicilian Volcano hiking tour" starting at $835 for eight days, not including airfare.

American Express Vacations, PO Box 619008, MD 5268; DFW Airport, Texas 75261-9008 (☎1-800/241-1700). Individual and escorted programmes to Italy; they also can plan city stays, offering competitive hotel rates.

Archaeological Tours, 271 Madison Ave, New York, NY 10016 (☎212/986-3054). Fully escorted archeological tours to Sicily for fourteen to seventeen days; around $4000.

CIT Tours, 342 Madison Ave, New York, NY 10173 (☎1-800/CIT-TOUR, in Canada ☎514/845-9101 or 1-800/387 0711 in Toronto, and 1-800/361 7799 in Montréal. Specialize exclusively in tours to Italy.

Globus-Cosmos, 5301 South Federal Circle, Littleton, CO 80123 (☎1-800/221-0090). Escorted and individual tours, including a "Best of Italy and Sicily"; prices start at $1300.

Italiatour, ☎1-800/237-0517 or 1-800/845-3365. In conjunction with Alitalia, offers fly-drive tours, and escorted and individual programmes.

you are getting for your money (many don't include the cost of the airfare). Reckon on paying at least $1500 for a ten-day touring vacation without flight, and up to as much as $4000 for a fourteen-day escorted specialist package with flight.

TRAVELLING BY RAIL

If you're interested in seeing more of Europe en route to Sicily, travelling by **train** may be more appealing, though you'll have to plan ahead as rail passes usually have to be purchased before you leave home. A **Eurail Pass** (allowing unlimited free train travel in Italy and sixteen other countries) is not likely to pay for itself if you're planning to stick to Sicily alone, since the train network there is rather limited, though for anyone planning to see more of Italy on the way there or back it's ideal. It costs $554 for fifteen days, $718 for 21 days, $1260 for two months, and $1558 for three months.

If you're under 26, you can save money with a **Eurail Youthpass**, which is valid for second-class travel and is available in fifteen-day ($388), 21-day ($499), one-month ($623), two-month ($882) and three-month ($1089) increments. If you're travelling with one to four other companions, the joint **Eurail Saverpass** is available in fifteen-day ($470), 21-day ($610), one-month ($756), two-month ($1072), and three-month ($1324) increments. You stand a better chance of getting your money's worth out of a **Eurail Flexipass**, which is good for a certain number of

travel days in a two-month period. This, too, comes in first-class and under-26/second-class versions: ten days cost $654/$458; and fifteen days, $862/$599. Again, parties of two to five can save fifteen percent with the **Eurail Saver Flexipass** with travel within a two-month period for ten days ($556) and fifteen days ($732).

North Americans are also eligible to purchase more specific passes valid for travel in Italy only, for details of which see "Getting around", p.23.

RAIL CONTACTS IN NORTH AMERICA

DER Travel Services, 9501 W Devon Ave, Suite 301, Rosemont, IL 60018 (☎1-800/421-2929). Eurail and Italian passes.

Forsyth Travel Library, 226 Westchester Ave, White Plains, NY 10604 (☎1/800-367-7984). Eurail passes.

Italian State Railways, c/o CIT Tours, 342 Madison Ave, Suite 207, New York, NY 10173 (☎1-800/223-7987; in LA ☎310/338-8616). Eurail and Italian passes.

Rail Europe, 226 Westchester Ave, White Plains, NY 10604 (☎1-800/438-7245). Official Eurail agent in North America; also sells a wide range of European regional and individual country passes.

ScanTours, 3439 Wade St, Los Angeles, CA 90066 (☎1-800/223-7226). Eurail and Italian passes.

GETTING THERE FROM AUSTRALIA AND NEW ZEALAND

There are no direct flights from Australia or New Zealand to Sicily, though many airlines fly to either Milan or Rome, from where it's simple to pick up a connection. Fares are highest between mid-May and August, and at Christmas; low season is October to mid-November and mid-January to February.

Prices given below are the published airline fares to Milan and Rome. You can commonly expect to make savings of up to twenty percent on special offers at various times of the year, while booking through individual travel agents, or being a student or under 26, should bring the price down by up to another ten percent. Contact a travel agent for the lowest fares and the latest information on limited special deals.

Round-the-world fares including Italy (though not Sicily in particular) start at around A$2100/NZ$2400. If you're planning to see much of Europe by **rail** on your way to or from Sicily, see "Getting there from Britain" for route details and "Travelling by rail" below for information on European rail passes that must be bought before you leave home.

FROM AUSTRALIA

Round-trip **fares** to Rome or Milan with major airlines from the main eastern cities in Australia are around A$1600 low season, A$1900 shoulder season and A$2100 high season. Fares from Perth are approximately $100 less. The add-on one-way fare to Palermo is around A$170.

The only **direct flights** to Italy are with Alitalia (Sydney or Melbourne to Milan or Rome via Bangkok) or Qantas (from Australian capitals to Rome via Bangkok). **Indirect flights** are with – among others – Garuda (to Milan from Perth, Melbourne and Sydney via Jakarta and Zürich/Amsterdam); Malaysia Airlines and Japan Airlines (both to Rome from southeastern cities with an inclusive overnight stop in Kuala Lumpur and Tokyo respectively); Thai Airways (to Rome from Sydney, Melbourne, Brisbane and Perth via Bangkok); Singapore Airlines (to Rome or Milan via Singapore); Cathay Pacific (to Rome from Sydney, Melbourne, Brisbane, Adelaide and Perth via Hong Kong); and British Airways, who have a variety of routes via Southeast Asia. Cheapest fares are generally with Garuda to Milan or Malaysia Airlines or Thai Airways to Rome. Some airlines offer discounted tour packages, or deals on accommodation, car rental and even rail passes; check the latest details with your travel agent.

FROM NEW ZEALAND

Round-trip **fares** to Rome from most cities in New Zealand are around NZ$2000 low season, NZ$2300 shoulder season and NZ$2700 high season. Fares from Christchurch are approximately $250 higher. The add-on one-way fare to Palermo is around NZ$185.

There are no direct flights to Italy from New Zealand. Indirect flights are with Alitalia in conjunction with other carriers (from Auckland via Sydney and Hong Kong/Singapore to Rome); British Airways to Rome from Auckland via Singapore/Bangkok; Qantas to Rome from Auckland, Christchurch or Wellington; Japan Airlines to Rome from Auckland (with inclusive overnight stop in Tokyo/Osaka); and Thai Airways from Auckland via Bangkok.

TRAVELLING BY RAIL

There are a couple of European **rail passes** that can only be purchased before leaving home, though consider carefully how much travelling you are going to be doing. The rail network in Sicily itself is limited and the passes only really begin to pay for themselves if you intend to see much more of Italy and the rest of the Europe on the way.

AIRLINES AND TRAVEL AGENTS IN AUSTRALASIA

AIRLINES

Air New Zealand, 5 Elizabeth St, Sydney (☎13 2476); Quay St, Auckland (☎09/357 3000).

Alitalia, 9/118 Alfred St, Milson's Point, Sydney (☎02/9922 1555; for reservations ☎1-300/653 747); Floor 6, Trust Bank Building, 229 Queen St, Auckland (☎09/379 4457).

British Airways, Level 19, 259 George St, Sydney (☎02/8904 8800); 154 Queen St, Auckland (☎09/356 8690).

Cathay Pacific, 12/8 Spring St, Sydney (☎13 1747); 11/205 Queen St, Auckland (☎09/379 0861).

Garuda, 55 Hunter St, Sydney (☎02/9334 9944; for reservations ☎1-300/365 3300); 120 Albert St, Auckland (☎09/366 1855).

Japan Airlines, 14/201 Sussex St, Sydney (☎02/9272 1111); 12/120 Albert St, Auckland (☎09/379 9906).

Malaysia Airlines, 16 Spring St, Sydney (☎02/9364 3535; for reservations ☎13 2627); Floor 12, Swanson Centre, 12–26 Swanson St, Auckland (☎09/373 2741).

Qantas, 70 Hunter St, Sydney (☎02/9951 4294; for reservations ☎13 1211); Qantas House, 154 Queen St, Auckland (☎09/357 8900 or 0-800/808 767).

Singapore Airlines, 17 Bridge St, Sydney (☎02/9350 0121; for reservations ☎13 1011); West Plaza Building, cnr Customs and Albert streets, Auckland (☎09/379 3209 or 0-800/808 909).

Thai Airways, 75–77 Pitt St, Sydney (☎02/9251 1922; for reservations ☎13 1960); Kensington Swan Building, 22 Fanshawe St, Auckland (☎09/377 3886).

NOTE: ☎1-800 and ☎0-800 numbers are toll free, but only apply if dialled outside the city in the address.

TRAVEL AGENTS

Accent on Travel, 545 Queen St, Brisbane (☎07/832 1777).

Adventure World, 73 Walker St, North Sydney (☎02/9956 7766 or 1-800/221 931). Other branches in Adelaide, Brisbane, Melbourne and Perth.

Anywhere Travel, 345 Anzac Parade, Kingsford, Sydney (☎02/9663 0411).

Budget Travel, 16 Fort St, Auckland (☎09/366 0061).

CIT Australia, 263 Clarence St, Sydney (☎02/9267 1255); offices also in Adelaide, Brisbane, Melbourne and Perth. NZ enquiries and reservations through the Australian offices. The official Australian representative of the Italian Travel Bureau, they can help with tour packages and all Italian rail passes.

Flight Centres Australia: 82 Elizabeth St, Sydney (☎02/9235 3522), plus branches nationwide (for details ☎13 1600). New Zealand:

National Bank Towers, 205–225 Queen St, Auckland (☎09/309 6171), plus branches nationwide (for details ☎0-800/FLIGHTS).

Passport Travel, 401 St Kilda Rd, Melbourne (☎03/9867 3888).

STA Travel Australia: 855 George St, Sydney (☎02/9212 1255); 256 Flinders St, Melbourne (☎03/9654 7266); plus branches nationwide (for details ☎13 1776). New Zealand: Traveller's Centre, 10 High St, Auckland (☎09/309 0458); 132 Cuba St, Wellington (☎04/385 0561); 90 Cashel St, Christchurch (☎03/379 9098); other offices in Dunedin, Hamilton, Palmerston North and at major universities.

Topdeck Travel, 65 Grenfell St, Adelaide (☎08/8232 7222).

Tymtro Travel, 428 George St, Sydney (☎02/9223 2211).

The **Eurail Youthpass**, for under-26s only, costs A$597/NZ$698 for fifteen days unlimited travel, A$777/NZ$910 for 21 days, A$961/NZ$1124 for one month, A$1361/NZ$1592 for two months, and A$1681/NZ$1967 for three months. If you're over 26 you'll have to buy the first-class version, which also comes in fifteen-day (A$854/NZ$999), 21-day (A$1108/NZ$1296), one-month (A$1372/NZ$1605), two-month (A$1943/NZ$2273) and three-month (A$2400/NZ$2808) increments. **Eurail Flexipass** is good for a certain number of days' travel in a two-month period and also comes in youth/first-class versions; ten days cost A$705/1007 (NZ$825/

1178), and fifteen days A$929/1327 (NZ$1086/1553). A scaled-down version of the Flexipass, the **Europass** (again available in either youth or first-class versions) allows travel in France, Germany, Italy, Spain and Switzerland and costs from A$343/518 (NZ$401/606) for five days in two months to A$804/1185 (NZ$940/1386) for fifteen days in two months.

RED TAPE AND VISAS

British, Irish and other EU citizens can enter Sicily and stay as long as they like on production of a valid passport. Citizens of the United States, Canada, Australia and New Zealand need only a valid passport, too, but are limited to stays of three months. All other nationals should consult the relevant embassies about visa requirements.

Legally, you're required to register with the police within three days of entering Italy, though if you're staying at a hotel this will be done for you. Although the police in some towns have become more punctilious about this, most would still be amazed at any attempt to register yourself down at the local police station while on holiday. However, if you're going to be living here for a while you may as well do it; see p.49 for more details.

ITALIAN EMBASSIES AND CONSULATES ABROAD

Australia Level 45, 1 Macquarie Place, Sydney 2000, NSW (☎02/9392 7900); 509 St Kilda Rd, Melbourne (☎03/9867 5744); 12 Grey St, Yarralumla, ACT (☎02/6273 3333).

Britain 38 Eaton Place, London SW1 8AN (☎0171/235 9371); 32 Melville St, Edinburgh EH3 7HA (☎0131/226 3631); 111 Piccadilly, Manchester M1 2HY (☎0161/236 9024).

Canada 275 Slater St, Ottawa, ON K1P 5H9 (☎613/232-2401); 3489 Drummond St, Montréal, PQ H3G 1X6 (☎514/849-8351); 136 Beverley St, Toronto, ON (☎416/977-1566).

Ireland 63–65 Northumberland Rd, Dublin (☎01/660 1744); 7 Richmond Park, Belfast (☎01232/668 854).

New Zealand 34 Grant Rd, Thorndon, Wellington (☎04/473 5339).

USA 690 Park Ave, New York, NY (☎212/737-9100 or 212/439-8600); 12400 Wilshire Blvd, Suite 300, Los Angeles (☎310/820-0622); 1601 Fuller St NW, Washington DC, CA (☎202/328-5500).

INSURANCE

As an EU country, Italy has free reciprocal health agreements with other member states, but even if you're covered by this you're strongly advised to take out separate travel insurance in any case. This way, you're covered against things being lost or stolen during your travels. For all non-EU citizens, it's essential to have some kind of travel insurance for your trip.

Before you purchase any insurance, check what you have already. Some credit cards offer insurance benefits if you use them to pay for your holiday tickets. North Americans, in particular, may find themselves covered for medical expenses and loss, and possibly loss of or damage to valuables, while abroad, as part of a family or student policy.

For medical treatment and drugs, keep all the receipts and claim the money back later. If you have anything stolen (including money), **register** the loss immediately with the local police – without their report you won't be able to claim. Note also that very few insurers will arrange on-the-spot payments in the event of a major expense or loss; you will usually be reimbursed only after going home.

BRITISH AND IRISH COVER

Most travel agents and tour operators will offer you insurance when you book your flight or holiday. These policies are usually reasonable value; though, as ever, you should check the small print. If you feel the cover is inadequate, or you want to compare prices, any travel agent,

insurance broker or bank should be able to help. If you have a good "all-risks" home insurance policy it may well cover your possessions against loss or theft even when overseas, and many private medical schemes also cover you when abroad – make sure you know the procedure and the helpline number.

In Britain and Ireland, **travel insurance schemes** are sold by almost every travel agent or bank, and by specialist insurance companies, all of which offer two weeks' basic cover in Italy for around £20, one month for around £25. Good-value policies are issued by Usit CAMPUS (Usit in Ireland) or STA Travel (see p.4 for addresses); Endsleigh Insurance (97–107 Southampton Row, London WC1B 4AG; ☎0171/436 4451); Liverpool Victoria (County Gates, Bournemouth, Dorset BH1 2NF; ☎01202/292 333); or Columbus Travel Insurance (17 Devonshire Square, London EC2M 4SQ; ☎0171/375 0011). Columbus also do an annual multi-trip policy, which offers twelve months' cover for around £50, as do Thomas Cook (45 Berkeley St, London W1X 5AE; ☎0845/600 5454); American Express (☎0800/700 737) are slightly more expensive, at £56.

NORTH AMERICAN COVER

Canadians are usually covered for medical mishaps overseas by their provincial health plans. Holders of official **student/teacher/youth cards** are entitled (outside the US) to accident coverage and hospital in-patient benefits. **Students** will often find that their student health

---

TRAVEL INSURANCE COMPANIES IN NORTH AMERICA

Access America (☎1-800/284-8300).

Carefree Travel Insurance – US only (☎1-800/323-3149).

Desjardins Travel Insurance – Canada only (☎1-800/463-7830).

International Student Insurance Service (ISIS) - sold by STA Travel (☎1-800/777-0112).

Travel Guard (☎1-800/826-1300).

Travel Insurance Services (☎1-800/937-1387).

Worldwide Assistance (☎1-800/821-2828).

coverage extends during the vacations and for one term beyond the date of last enrolment. Bank and credit cards (particularly American Express) often have certain levels of medical or other insurance included, and travel insurance may also be included if you use a major credit or charge card to pay for your trip. **Homeowners' or renters'** insurance often covers theft or loss of documents, money and valuables while overseas, though conditions and maximum amounts vary from company to company.

After exhausting the possibilities above, you might want to contact a **specialist travel insurance** company; your travel agent can usually recommend one, or see the box opposite. Policies are comprehensive (accidents, illnesses, delayed or lost luggage, cancelled flights, etc), but maximum payouts tend to be meagre. The best deals are usually to be had through student/youth travel agencies – ISIS policies, for example, cost $60 for fifteen days (depending on coverage), $110 for a month, $165 for two months, and on up to $665 for a year.

AUSTRALASIAN COVER

Travel insurance is available from most travel agents (see p.14) or direct from insurance companies (see below), for periods ranging from a few days to a year or even longer. Most policies are similar in premium and coverage – but if you plan to indulge in high-risk activities such as mountaineering, bungy jumping or scuba diving without a certificate, check the policy carefully to make sure you'll be covered. A typical policy will cost around A$180/NZ200 for one month, A$279/NZ300 for two months.

In **Australasia** policies are issued by: AFTA, 144 Pacific Highway, North Sydney (☎02/9956 4800); Cover-More Insurance Services, Level 9, 32 Walker St, North Sydney (☎02/9202 8000 or 1-800/251 881), and at 57 Simon St, Auckland (☎09/377 5958); Ready Plan, 141–147 Walker St, Dandenong, Victoria (☎1-300/555 017), or through STA Travel (see box on p.14); 10/63 Albert St, Auckland (☎09/379 3208); and by UTAG, 122 Walker St, North Sydney (☎02/9956 8399 or 1-800/809 462).

COSTS, MONEY AND BANKS

Sicily isn't cheap, certainly compared to the other Mediterranean holiday spots. But neither is it as expensive as the rest of mainland Italy, and you'll find that food and accommodation are especially good value.

AVERAGE COSTS

If you're watching your budget – camping, buying some of your own food in the shops and markets – you could get by on as little as £20–25/US$32–40 a day; a more realistic **average daily budget** is around £35–40/US$55–65 a day; while on £45–50/US$70–80 a day you could be living pretty comfortably. Most basic things are fairly inexpensive: a pizza and a beer cost around £5–6/US$8–9.50 just about everywhere; a full meal with wine from around £12/$19; buses and trains are very cheap and distances between towns small; and hotel rooms in the cities start at around £15/US$25 a double. It's the snacks and drinks that add up: eating ice-creams and drinking soft drinks or coffee all costs around the same price (if not more) as at home. And if you sit down to do any of this it'll cost twice as much.

Of course, these prices are subject to where and when you go, and whether you're alone. You'll pay a lot more in summer for rooms and food in the big tourist spots – Éric, Cefalù, Siracusa and Taormina; and more all year round on most of the offshore islands, particularly the Aeolians and Pantelleria. The interior, too, is not as cheap as you might expect – because it's

THE EURO

Italy is one of eleven countries who have opted to join the European monetary union and, from January 1, 1999, began to phase in the single European currency, the **euro**. Initially, however, it will only be possible to make paper transactions in the new currency (if you have, for example, a euro bank or credit-card account), and the Lira will remain the normal unit of currency in Italy. Euro notes and coins are scheduled to be issued at the beginning of 2002, and to replace the Lira entirely by July of that year.

little visited, there's no competition and rarely a choice of places to stay and eat. **Out of season** you'll be able to negotiate lower accommodation prices in nearly all the small hotels and *pensioni*. However, **single accommodation** can be hard to come by: what there is tends to fill quickly and you'll often have to pay most of the price of a double room. There are no **reductions** or discounts for students or young people in Sicily: it's the one place where an ISIC card is no use at all; under-18s and over-65s, on the other hand, get into museums and archeological sites free everywhere.

MONEY AND BANKS

The most painless way of dealing with your money is probably by using **credit**, **charge** or **cash cards**, which, in conjunction with your personal identification number (PIN), give you access to cash dispensers (*bancomat*). Found even in small towns, these accept all major cards, with a minimum withdrawal of L50,000 and a maximum of L300,000–500,000 per day. Cards can also be used for cash advances over the counter in banks and for payment in most hotels, restaurants, petrol stations and some shops; for all these transactions you will pay a fee of 1.5 percent, but the rate of exchange will be in your favour. Remember that all cash advances on a credit card are treated as loans, with interest accruing daily from the date of withdrawal. To block any lost or **stolen card** in Italy, call ☎167.822.056.

A safer option is to carry your money in the form of **travellers' cheques**, available from any British high-street bank, whether or not you have an account, as well as post offices and some building societies. Most American and Canadian

banks sell American Express cheques, and they're widely accepted; your local bank will probably also sell one or more of the other brands. To find the nearest bank that sells a particular brand, or to buy cheques by phone, call the following numbers: American Express (☎1-800/673 3782), Citicorp (☎1-800/645 6556), MasterCard International/Thomas Cook (☎1-800/223 7373), Visa (☎1-800/227 6811). The usual fee for travellers' cheque sales is one or two percent, and it pays to get them in either sterling or dollars. Make sure to keep the purchase agreement and a record of cheque serial numbers safe and separate from the cheques themselves. In the event that cheques are lost or stolen, the issuing company will expect you to report the loss forthwith to their nearest office; most companies claim to replace lost or stolen cheques within 24 hours.

You'll usually – though not always – pay a small commission when you **exchange money** using travellers' cheques – again around one percent of the amount changed, although some banks will make a standard charge per cheque regardless of its denomination – usually around L6000. It's worth knowing that Thomas Cook offices don't charge for cashing their own cheques, and American Express offices don't charge for cashing anyone's cheques.

It's an idea to have at least some Italian **cash** for when you first arrive. You can buy lire over the counter in British banks; most American banks will need a couple of days' notice.

The main **banks** you'll see in Sicily are the Banco di Sicilia, the Cassa di Risparmio and the Banca Nazionale di Lavoro. **Banking hours** vary slightly from town to town, but generally banks are open Monday to Friday, 8.30am–1.20pm and 3–4pm. Outside these times you can change travellers' cheques and cash at large hotels, the airports at Palermo and Catania, and some main train stations. In Taormina and Cefalù, banks

CURRENCY

The Italian unit of **money** is the *lira* (plural *lire*), always abbreviated as L. The rate right now is around L2800 to the pound sterling/L1600 to the US$. You get notes for L1000, L2000, L5000, L10,000, L50,000 and L100,000, and coins for L50, L100, L200 and L500. It's an idea to have at least some Italian money for when you first arrive, and you can buy lire in advance from most banks.

WIRE SERVICES

Australia American Express MoneyGram (in Sydney ☎9271 8666, elsewhere ☎1-800/230 100); Western Union (in Brisbane ☎3229 8610, elsewhere ☎1-800/649 565).

Britain American Express MoneyGram (☎0800/894 887);Western Union (☎0800/833 833).

New Zealand American Express MoneyGram: Auckland (☎09/379 8243); Wellington (☎04/499 7899 or 473 7766); Western Union: Auckland (☎09/302 0143).

USA and Canada American Express MoneyGram (☎1-800/543-4080); Western Union (☎1-800/325-6000).

stay open later in summer, sometimes on Saturday as well; check the town and city "Listings" sections in the text.

If you run out of money abroad, or there is some kind of emergency, the quickest way to get **money sent out** is to use a wire service (see box, or call ☎167.220.055 or 167.464.464 in Italy to find your nearest office). This can take minutes, but note that MoneyGram can wire to Agrigento and Palermo only. Charges are on a sliding scale, from £14 for £100, to around £35 for £500. Getting money sent from your bank at home takes much longer and costs around £20 for a five-day transfer to £35 for a three-day transfer.

HEALTH MATTERS

EU citizens can take advantage of Italy's health services under the same terms as the residents of the country. You'll need form E111, available from any main post office. The Australian Medicare system also has a reciprocal health-care arrangement with Italy. However, you should also take out ordinary travel insurance – certainly if you're a non-EU citizen (see "Insurance", p.16, for more details).

Vaccinations are not required. However, cholera and typhoid jabs are a wise precaution if you intend to continue to North Africa – in which case make sure you also have an up-to-date polio booster. Otherwise, Sicily doesn't present too many health worries: the worst that's likely to happen to you is suffering from the extreme heat in summer or from an upset stomach (shellfish is the usual culprit). The water is perfectly safe to drink, though you'll probably prefer to drink bottled anyway. You'll find public fountains (usually button- or tap-operated) in squares and city streets everywhere, though look out for "*acqua non potabile*" signs, indicating the water is *not* safe to drink.

PHARMACIES

An Italian **pharmacist** (*farmacia*) is well qualified to give you advice on minor ailments, and to dispense prescriptions, and there's generally one open all night in the bigger towns and cities. They

work on a rota system, and you should find the address of the one currently open on any *farmacia* door or listed in the local paper. Condoms (*profilático*) are available over the counter from all pharmacists and some supermarkets; the Pill (*la píllola*) is available by prescription only.

DOCTORS AND HOSPITALS

If you need treatment, go to a **doctor** (*médico*); every town and village has one. Ask at a pharmacy, or consult the local *Página Gialle –Yellow Pages* – under "Azienda Unità Sanitaria Locale" or "Unità Sanitaria Locale Pronto Soccorso". The *Página Gialle* also list some specialist practitioners in such fields as acupuncture and homeopathy, the latter much more common in Italy than in many countries. If you're eligible, take your E111 with you to the doctor's: this should enable you to get free treatment and prescriptions for medicines at the local rate – about ten percent of the price of the medicine. For repeat medication, take any empty bottles or capsules with you to the doctor's – the brand names often differ.

If you get taken **seriously ill**, or involved in an accident, hunt out the nearest **hospital** and go to the Pronto Soccorso (casualty) section, or phone ☎113 and ask for "*ospedale*" or "*ambulanza*". Hospital standards vary enormously, though don't differ significantly from clinics at home. Throughout the guide, you'll find listings for pharmacists, hospitals and emergency services in all the major cities.

Incidentally, try to avoid going to the **dentist** (*dentista*) while you're in Sicily. These aren't covered by the *mutua* or health service, and for the smallest problem they'll make you pay through the teeth. Take local advice, or consult the local *Yellow Pages*.

If you don't have a spare pair of glasses, take a copy of your prescription with you; an **optician** (*óttico*) will be able to make you up a new pair should you lose or damage them.

INFORMATION AND MAPS

Before you leave, it's worth calling the Italian State Tourist Office (ENIT) for a selection of maps and brochures, though don't go mad – much of it can easily be picked up later in Sicily. Worth grabbing are any accommodation listings and town plans they may have for the area you're interested in, as well as a camping brochure (Sicilia Campeggi).

TOURIST OFFICES

Most Sicilian towns, main train stations and the two principal airports have a **tourist office**: either an APT (Azienda Promozione Turistica), a provincial branch of the state organization, or an AAST (Azienda Autónoma di Soggiorno e Turismo), a smaller local outfit. When there isn't either an APT or AAST there will sometimes be a Pro Loco office, which will have much the same kind of information, though these generally keep much shorter hours. All of these vary in degrees of usefulness, and apart from the main cities and tourist areas the staff aren't likely to speak English. But you should always be able at least to get a free town plan and a local listings booklet in Italian, and some will reserve you a room and sell places on guided tours.

Likely summer **opening hours** are Monday to Friday 9am to 1pm and 4pm to 7pm, Saturday 9am to 1pm, but check the text for more details. If the tourist office isn't open and all else fails, the local telephone office (see p.40) and most bars with phones carry a copy of the local *Tuttocittà*, a listings and information magazine which details addresses and numbers of most of the organizations you're likely to want to know about, as well as having indexed street maps for local towns and adverts for restaurants and shops.

ITALIAN STATE TOURIST OFFICES

Note ENIT is on the Web at *www.enit.it*
Australia apply to the consulate, Level 45, 1 Macquarie Place, Sydney 2000, NSW (☎02/9392 7900).
Canada 1 Placeville Marie, Suite 1914, Montréal, PQ H3B 2C3 (☎514/866-7667).
Ireland 47 Merrion Square, Dublin 2 (☎01/766 397).
New Zealand apply to the embassy, 34 Grant Rd, Thorndon, Wellington (☎04/ 473 5339).

UK 1 Princes St, London W1R 8AY (☎0171/408 1254).
USA 630 Fifth Ave, Suite 1565, New York, NY 10111 (☎212/245-5618; brochure requests 212/245-4822); 500 North Michigan Ave, Suite 2240, Chicago, Illinois 60611 (☎312/644-0996; brochure requests 312/644-0990); 12400 Wilshire Blvd, Suite 550, Los Angeles, CA 90025 (☎310/820-1898; brochure requests 310/820-0098).

MAP OUTLETS

AUSTRALIA

Hema, 239 George St, Brisbane, QLD 4000 (☎07/221 4330).

The Map Shop, 16a Peel St, Adelaide, SA 5000 (☎08/8231 2033).

Mapland, 372 Little Bourke St, Melbourne, VIC 3000 (☎03/9670 4383).

Perth Map Centre, 884 Hay St, Perth, WA 6000 (☎09/9322 5733).

Travel Bookshop, 6 Bridge St, Sydney, NSW 2000 (☎02/9241 3554).

Worldwide Maps and Guides, 187 George St, Brisbane, QLD 4000 (☎07/3221 4330).

BRITAIN

Blackwell's Map and Travel Shop, 53 Broad St, Oxford OX1 3BQ (☎01865/792 792).

Daunt Books, 83 Marylebone High St, London W1M 3DE (☎0171/224 2295); 193 Haverstock Hill, London NW3 4QL (☎0171/794 4006).

Heffers Map Shop, 3rd Floor, in Heffers Stationery Department, 19 Sidney St, Cambridge, CB2 3HL (☎01223/568 467).

Italian Bookshop, 7 Cecil Court, London WC2N 4EZ (☎0171/240 1635).

James Thin Melven's Bookshop, 29 Union St, Inverness, IV1 1QA (☎01463/233 500).

John Smith and Sons, 57–61 St Vincent St, Glasgow G2 5TB (☎0141/221 7472).

National Map Centre, 22–24 Caxton St, London SW1 0QU (☎0171/222 4945).

Newcastle Map Centre, 55 Grey St, Newcastle upon Tyne, NE1 6EF (☎0191/261 5622).

Stanfords*, 12–14 Long Acre, London WC2E 9LP (☎0171/836 1321); at Usit CAMPUS, 52 Grosvenor Gdns, London SW1W 0AG; 156 Regent St, London W1R 5TA (☎0171/434 4744); 29 Corn St, Bristol BS1 1HT (☎0117/929 9966).

The Map Shop, 30a Belvoir St, Leicester, LE1 6QH (☎0116/247 1400).

The Travel Bookshop, 13–15 Blenheim Crescent, London W11 2EE (☎0171/229 5260).

Waterstone's, 91 Deansgate, Manchester, M3 2BW (☎0161/832 1992).

*Maps by **mail or phone order** are available from **Stanfords** (☎0171/836 1321).

CANADA

Curious Traveler Travel Bookstore, 101 Yorkville Ave, Toronto, ON M5R 1C1 (☎1-800/268-4395).

International Travel Maps, 555 Seymour St, Vancouver, BC V6B 3J5 (☎604/687-3320).

Open Air Books and Maps, 25 Toronto St, Toronto, ON M5C 2R1 (☎416/363-0719).

IRELAND

Eason's Bookshop, 40 O'Connell St, Dublin 1 (☎01/873 3811).

Fred Hanna's Bookshop, 27–29 Nassau St, Dublin 1 (☎01/677 1255).

Hodges Figgis Bookshop, 56–58 Dawson St, Dublin 2 (☎01/677 4754).

Waterstone's, Queens Building, 8 Royal Ave, Belfast BT1 1DA (☎01232/247 355); 7 Dawson St, Dublin 2 (☎01/679 1415); 69 Patrick St, Cork (☎021/276 522).

NEW ZEALAND

Speciality Maps, 58 Albert St, City, Auckland (☎09/307 2217).

USA

Book Passage, 51 Tamal Vista Blvd, Corte Madera, CA 94925 (☎415/927-0960).

California Map & Travel Center, 3312 Pico Blvd, Santa Monica, CA 90405 (☎310/396-6277).

The Complete Traveler Bookstore, 199 Madison Ave, New York, NY 10016 (☎212/685-9007); 3207 Fillmore St, San Francisco, CA 94123 (☎415/923-1511).

Phileas Fogg's Books, Maps and More, 87 Stanford Shopping Center, Palo Alto, CA 94304 (☎1-800/233-FOGG in California, ☎1-800/533-FOGG elsewhere in USA).

Rand McNally*, 444 N Michigan Ave, Chicago, IL 60611 (☎312/321-1751); 150 E 52nd St, New York, NY 10022 (☎212/758-7488); 595 Market St, San Francisco, CA 94105 (☎415/777-3131); 7988 Tysons Corner Center, Maclean, VA 22102 (☎202/223-6751).

Sierra Club Bookstore, 6014 College Ave, Oakland, CA 94618 (☎510/658-7470).

Travel Books & Language Center, 4437 Wisconsin Ave NW, Washington, DC 20016 (☎1-800/220-2665).

Traveler's Bookstore, 22 W 52nd St, New York, NY 10019 – in the lobby of the Time Warner building (☎212/664-0995).

*Note: Rand McNally now has 24 stores across the US; call ☎1-800/333-0136 ext 2111 for the location of your nearest store.

MAPS

The best large-scale **road map** of Sicily is published by the Touring Club Italiano (*Sicilia*, 1:200,000), usually available from the outlets listed in the box on p.20. Otherwise, the Automobile Club d'Italia (see "Cars", p.25) issues a good, free 1:275,000 road map, available from the State Tourist Offices, while local tourist offices in Sicily often have free road maps of varying quality.

For **hiking**, you'll need at least a scale 1:100,000 map (even better, 1:50,000), though there's not much around – again, check with one of the specialist map shops listed on p.21 or with the Club Alpino Italiano, Via Fonseca Pimental 7, 20121 Milan (☎02.2614.1378). For specific towns and islands, the maps we've printed should be fine for most purposes, though local tourist offices also often hand out reasonable town plans and regional maps.

USEFUL INTERNET ADDRESSES

Italian **Web sites** have proliferated in recent years and provide a wealth of information; we've listed a few of the more useful ones for Sicily here. Other relevant Internet addresses are given on p.20 (ENIT) and p.29 (IYHA).

Alitalia
www.alitalia.it
Alitalia routes and schedules in English.

Catania
www.apt-catania.com
Comprehensive information for Catania and its surrounding area, in English.

In Italy
www.initaly.com/
Well produced, with detailed information on the whole country; the Sicily section covers history, culture, festivals, travel and services.

Italian Ministry for Arts and the Environment
www.beniculturali.it/
Museums, temporary exhibitions, performances and so on, in Italian.

Italian State Railways (FS)
www.fs-on-line.com
Timetable information in Italian and English.

Italian Yellow Pages
www.paginegialle.it

Palermo
www.aapit.pa.it
Palermo and regional information in English; wide-ranging but rather brief.

GETTING AROUND

Distances aren't especially large in Sicily, but getting around by public transport is not always as easy as it should be. The rail system is slow, few buses run on Sunday and route information can be frustratingly diffi-cult to extract, even from the bus and train stations themselves. Sicily's geography means that it's a push to get right across the island – say Siracusa to Trápani – in one day; though you'll be able to travel most of one of the coastlines easily enough. On the positive side, public transport prices are among the cheapest in Europe.

Although general points are covered below, each chapter's "Travel details" section has the full picture on transport schedules and frequencies. Note that these refer to regular working day schedules, ie Monday to Saturday; services may be much reduced, or even nonexistent, on Sundays. Note also that comments such as "every 30min" are approximations – on the railways in particular, there are occasional gaps in the schedule, typically occurring just after the morning rush hour, when the gap between trains may be twice as long as normal.

One thing to bear in mind is that travelling by train is not the best way to see all of the island. Some stations are kilometres from their towns – Enna and Taormina are two notable examples (though there are usually bus connections) – while much of the west and centre of Sicily is only accessible by bus or car.

TRAINS

Operated by Italian State Railways, Ferrovie dello Stato (FS), **trains** connect all the major towns, but are more prevalent in the east of the island than the west. On the whole the trains *do* leave on time, with the notable exception of those on the Messina–Palermo and Messina–Catania/Siracusa routes that have come from the mainland, which can be subject to delays of up to three hours – though around an hour late is more normal.

There are five **types of train**. **Intercity** trains link the main Italian centres with each other; reservations are obligatory, and a supplement in the region of thirty percent of the ordinary fare is payable. (Make sure you pay your supplement before getting on board – you'll have to cough up a far bigger surcharge to the conductor.) **Diretto**, **Espresso** and **Interregionale** trains are long-distance express, calling only at larger stations, useful for fairly quick jaunts along the coasts. Lastly there are the **Regionale** services (also called Locale), which stop at every place with a population higher than zero – usually ones to avoid. The last two categories do not permit smoking in any part of the train. Note that train **tickets must be validated** within an hour of boarding the train, ie punched in machines scattered around the station and platforms. Failure to do this may land you with an on-the-spot fine of around L50,000. In summer it's often worth making a **seat reservation** (*prenotazione*) on the main routes, something you'll be obliged to do anyway on some trains – check before you get on or you'll pay a whacking *supplemento* (around thirty percent of the ordinary fare) to the conductor. If you don't have time to buy a ticket you can simply board your train and pay the conductor, though again it'll cost around thirty percent more this way.

As well as the boards displayed at stations ("Departures" are *Partenze*, "Arrivals" *Arrivi*, "Delayed" *In Ritardo*), a timetable is useful, even if you use it only to discover exactly how late your train is. The Sicilian routes are covered by FS's little book, *In Treno Sicilia*, issued twice a year and free from most train stations, or you'll find the main Italy/Sicily routes covered in the southern regional timetables, costing L3900 and also available from most stations. Pay attention to the timetable notes, which may specify the dates between which some services run (*Si effetua dal . . . al . . .*), or whether a service is seasonal (*periódico*), denoted by a vertical squiggle; *feriale* is the word for the Monday-to-Saturday service, symbolized by two crossed hammers, *festivo* means that a train runs only on Sundays and holidays, with a cross as its symbol.

Prices are very reasonable. Tickets are charged by the kilometre; the 300-kilometre loop from Siracusa to Caltanissetta, for example, costs around L40,000, though most of the journeys you'll make will be much shorter and cheaper.

For details of Sicily's only **private railway**, the Ferrovia Circumetnea route around the base of Mount Etna, see p.226–229.

RAIL PASSES AND DISCOUNTS

The Europe-wide **InterRail** and **Eurail** passes (see p.5, p.12 and p.14) give unlimited travel on the FS network, though you'll be liable for supplements. These are the passes that are most likely to prove useful, but if you're flying to Sicily and then undertaking an intensive bout of rail travel elsewhere in Italy you might want to invest in one of the many passes exclusive to the FS system.

Travellers from the UK have a choice of three **Freedom/Euro-Domino** passes for the Italian network – three days' unlimited rail travel for £99 (£79 for under-26s), five days' for £129 (£101 for under-26s), or ten days' for £182 (£140 for under-26s). They include a 30–50 percent discount for cross-Channel ferries and for journeys to other European Channel ports.

North Americans and Australasians can buy the similar **Italy Flexi-Railcard**, valid for four days' travel within a nine-day period (US$ 209/Can$313/A$170); eight days within 21 (US$293/Can$439/A$238); or twelve days within thirty (US$375/Can$562/A$306).

Note that all the above passes should be bought before you leave home, and that you should allow at least a week for processing before you can use them; see pp.5, 11, 12 and 14 for the relevant agents.

In addition, there are two specific **Italian passes**, also available before you leave from the rail agencies listed in the relevant "Getting There" sections above, or from major train stations in Italy. The **Biglietto Turistico Libera Circolazione** is valid for unlimited travel on all FS trains, excluding "Pendolino" (a first-class inter-city service); for eight days it costs from £120/US$266/A$227; for fifteen days £146/US$332/A$284; for twenty-one days £168/US$386/A$329; and for thirty days £200/US$465/A$397. With this card you must have the station ticket office validate the first journey you make before boarding the train. The **Chilométrico** ticket, valid for up to five people, gives 3000km worth of travel on a maximum of twenty separate journeys; it costs L206,000, but you have to pay supplements on faster trains – and you're very unlikely to cover that sort of distance on a Sicilian holiday anyway.

Other **discounts** on normal fares are for large **groups** (6–24 people get a discount of 20 percent, more than 25 people get 30 percent), **children** (50 percent discount for 4–12-year-olds), and **under-4s** travel free provided they do not occupy a seat. If you're going to be spending a long time in Sicily or Italy, the **Cartaverde** for under-26s, and the **Carta d'argento** for over-60s, come into their own. Valid for one year, these cards cost L40,000, give a twenty percent discount on any fare, and are available from main train stations in Italy.

BUSES

The trains don't go everywhere and you'll have to use the **regional buses** (*autobus* or *pullman*) at some stage. Almost anywhere you want to go will have some kind of service, usually quicker and more reliable than the train (especially between the major towns and cities), but schedules can be sketchy and buses are more expensive than trains. An average journey, say Catania to Palermo, costs around L20,000.

There are two main **companies**, SAIS and AST, which between them cover most of the island; other companies stick to local routes. Nearly everywhere, services are drastically reduced, or nonexistent, on Sunday, something the timetables – and the drivers/conductors – don't necessarily make clear: always double-check. Note, too, that lots of departures (on rural routes especially) are linked to school/market requirements – sometimes meaning a frighteningly early start, last departures in the afternoon, and occasionally no services during school holidays.

Bus terminals can be scattered all over the bigger towns, though often all the buses pull up in one particular piazza, or outside the local train station – if you want the bus station, ask for the *autostazione*. **Timetables** are worth picking up at every opportunity, from the companies' offices, bus stations or on the bus. You buy **tickets** on the bus, though on longer hauls (and if you want to be sure of a place) try and buy them in advance from the companies' offices. On most routes it's usually possible to flag a bus down if you want a ride: the convention, when it stops, is to get on at the back, off at the front. If you want to get off, ask *posso scéndere?*; "the next stop" is *la próssima fermata*.

City buses are always cheap, usually charging a flat fare of L800–1300, and worth mastering in the bigger towns and cities. Invariably you need a ticket *before* getting on. Buy them in *tabacchi*, or from the kiosks and vendors at bus terminals and stops, and then validate them in the machine at the back of the bus. Checks are frequently made by inspectors who block both exits as they get on, though if you're without a ticket you'll usually get off with an earful of Sicilian and be made to buy one; some inspectors will hold out for the spot fine, though – in the region of L50,000.

A few bus services are operated by FS, the State Railways, to substitute discontinued lines. These complement the other bus services and are detailed in the train timetables and in the text.

CARS

Car travel across the island can be very quick if you use the often spectacular **motorways** or autostradas. Carried on great piers spanning the island, these link Messina–Catania (A18), Catania–Palermo (A19), Palermo–Trápani/Mazara del Vallo (A29) and – though still incomplete – Messina–Palermo (A20). The Messina–Catania and Messina–Palermo motorways are toll-roads; Messina–Catania costs around L7000 for a medium-sized car, while Messina–Palermo is around L16,000. Take a ticket as you come on, and pay on exit; the amount due is flashed up on a screen in front of you. Major credit cards are accepted; follow the "Viacard" sign. Elsewhere, roads are pretty good and well signposted, though in small towns they can be very narrow. In rural areas they can be tortuous and deteriorate into rough tracks; be prepared for a flock of sheep or a panniered horse round the next bend.

For **documentation** you need a valid driving licence, an international green card of insurance, and, if you are a non-EU licence holder, an international driving permit. It's *compulsory* to carry your car documents and passport while you're driving, and you'll be required to present them if you're stopped by the police – not an uncommon occurrence. You are also required to carry a portable triangular danger sign, available in Britain from most AA, RAC or Automobile Club d'Italia (ACI) offices, in Australia from NRMA, RACQ and RACV offices, in the US from the AAA, and in Canada from the CAA. **Rules of the road** are straightforward: drive on the right; at junctions, where there's any ambiguity, give precedence to vehicles coming from the right; observe the speed limits (50kph in built-up areas, 110kph on country roads, 130kph on motorways); and *don't* drink and drive.

If you **break down**, dial ☎116 at the nearest phone and tell the operator where you are, the type of car and your registration number. The nearest office of the ACI will send someone out to fix your car, though it's not a free service. If you need towing anywhere it will cost a fairly substantial amount, and it might be worth joining ACI to qualify for their discounted repairs scheme: write to ACI, Via Marsala 8, 00185 Roma (☎06.499.8234); alternatively, it might be easier to arrange cover with a motoring organization in your country before you leave. Any ACI office in Sicily can tell you where to get **spare parts** for your particular car: see the town and city "Listings" sections for details.

Car rental in Sicily is expensive – around £250/$400 per week for a Fiat Panda plus fuel, with unlimited mileage, from one of the major international firms (addresses are detailed in the city listings), but usually a lot less from local companies. Best of all, though, is to arrange it in conjunction with your flight/holiday – most travel agents or tour operators can provide details; as can the **rental companies** (see below for numbers) which can arrange pick-ups in Catania and Palermo. Italy is also one of the most expensive countries in Europe in which to buy **fuel**: it's around L1800 a litre for unleaded (*senza piombo*) and L1900 a litre for leaded (*super*).

Never leave anything visible in the car when you leave it, including the radio. If you're taking your own vehicle, consider installing a detachable car-radio, and always depress your aerial and tuck in your wing mirrors. When driving in cities, keep your doors locked. Most cities and ports have **garages** where you can leave your car; a safe enough option. At least the car itself is unlikely to be stolen if it's got a right-hand drive and a foreign numberplate: they're too conspicuous to be of much use to thieves.

As **parking** spaces are rare and small, good parking skills are an asset. The task is easier in early afternoon, when towns are quiet, or at

---

night; if you're hiring, it makes sense to choose a small car. If you park in a *zona di rimozione*, your car will most likely be towed away; and if you've chosen a street that turns into a market by day, you'll be stuck until it closes down.

Hitch-hiking (*autostop*) is not widely practised in Sicily and is **not recommended as a means of getting around the island**. It's very definitely not something that women should do on their own, particularly in the more out-of-the-way places; also be warned that cars will sometimes stop to offer you a lift if you're standing alone at a bus stop. If you are hitching, travel in pairs, and always ask where the car is headed before you commit yourself (*Dov'è diretto?*). If you want to get out, say *Mi fa scéndere?*.

However you get around on the roads, **watch the traffic**. Driving in Sicily is almost a competitive sport, and although the Sicilians aren't the world's worst drivers they don't win any safety prizes either. It's not as horrific as it looks at first, and if you're driving the secret is to make it very clear what you're going to do, using your horn as much as your indicators and brakes. **Pedestrians**, too, will find that far from being unable to step off the pavement – ever – you'll be able to cross quite easily by staring straight at the drivers and strolling boldly across. If in doubt, follow someone old and infirm, or put out your hand policeman-like, but *never* assume that you're safe on a pedestrian crossing – regarded by drivers as an invitation to play human skittles.

BICYCLES AND HIKING

A better way to get off the beaten track is by **bicycle**, especially on the offshore islands. However, on the Sicilian mainland, renting is virtually unheard of and, although cycling the coastal routes is all right, heading inland and up into the mountains requires a decent machine and plenty of stamina: a mountain-bike would be a good bet, though you can expect to be a real curiosity in some rural places. In the Madonie mountains, south of Cefalù, hiking itineraries published by the tourist office have brief notes for cyclists, though you should be prepared to push it some of the way. An alternative is to tour by **motorbike**, though again you'll have to bring your own. **Mopeds** and **scooters** are easier to find: virtually everyone in Sicily – kids to grandmas –

rides these, although the smaller models are not suitable for any kind of long-distance travel. For shooting around towns they're ideal, and hireable in Taormina, Cefalù and other holiday centres – check the text for details and expect to pay around L30,000 a day. Crash helmets are compulsory, though you'll see many Sicilian youths just riding with one slung over one arm.

Walking – ie serious **hiking** – was until recently a fairly rare phenomenon in Sicily, and there are no long-distance paths and few marked routes. That said, some areas have been made more amenable to walking for pleasure, including the protected coast between Scopello and Capo San Vito (see p.335 and p.348), and the Madonie mountains south of Cefalù. In the latter, rudimentary hiking routes have been established, making use of existing paths; information and rough maps are available from the tourist office in Cefalù (see p.121). We've also detailed some hiking possibilities in the text (see p.118, p.124, p.348 and p.353). Local tourist offices will also have details of the few mountain refuges (*rifugi*) for overnight stops in the Madonie and on Etna (and see "Accommodation"). For maps, see p.22.

PLANES, FERRIES AND HYDROFOILS

Hardly surprisingly, **flying** isn't a major form of transport within Sicily. Still, if you're short on time, taking a plane to the Pelágie Islands from Palermo, or Pantelleria from either Palermo or Trápani is a distinct – and not too expensive – possibility. Flights are with Air Sicilia, Meridiana or the internal arm of Alitalia, and there are tempting **discounts** available: up to fifty percent off the normal fare if you stay at least a Saturday or Sunday. Local airline and travel agents will have the latest details, and we've listed frequencies in "Travel details" for relevant chapters.

As for **ferries** and **hydrofoils** you'll use them to get to all the offshore islands: the Aeolians, Égadi and Pelágie Islands, Pantelleria and Ústica. There's also a summer hydrofoil service that runs along the northern, Tyrrhenian coast, from Palermo to the Aeolian Islands and stops at a couple of towns on the coast.

Further options are to use the catamaran service to Malta, with departures from Catania, Pozzallo and Licata (the last two on Sicily's south coast), or the ferry from Trápani to Tunis.

ACCOMMODATION

On the whole, accommodation in Sicily is slightly cheaper than in the rest of Italy. There's a whole range of places in all price categories and on average you'll pay from around £15–20/$25–30 a night for two. If you're watching your budget, a (very) few youth hostels, some private rooms and many campsites are all possibilities – for more on which see below.

All types of accommodation are officially graded, their tariffs fixed by law. In tourist areas, on the offshore islands and in big cities, there's often a low-season and high-season price, but whatever it costs the price of hotels and campsites should be listed in the local accommodation booklets provided by the tourist office and posted on the door of the room. If the prices don't correspond, demand to know why, and don't hesitate to report infractions to the tourist office. Loopholes do exist, however: in summer especially, when demand for accommodation exceeds supply, hotels are prone to add a breakfast charge to the price of the room, whether you take breakfast or not. There's nothing you can do about it; just make sure you know exactly how much you're going to be paying before you accept the room.

HOTELS

Hotel accommodation, while normally abundant in the main towns and tourist areas, tends to thin out in remoter areas, and especially inland. It's worthwhile phoning ahead to book if you're heading for a one-hotel town.

Cheapest hotel-type accommodation is a **locanda** – basic, but on the whole clean and safe, and nearly always corresponding to our category ①, ie well under L60,000 for a double room without bath/shower; in many cases you'll find prices to be cheaper than this, occasionally as little as L40,000 for a double. If you want a hot shower in a *locanda* you'll generally have to pay extra, though only around L2000–3000 per person. You'll find *locande* in most of the cities, some large towns and a few out-of-the-way places too.

More common are regular hotels, either a **pensione** or **albergo** (plural *alberghi*), the distinction between which has become obsolete since *pensioni* – the smaller, family-run establishments – have almost been edged out of business by *alberghi*, though many establishments still retain the name. All come graded with from one to five stars, and a double room in a one-star hotel usually corresponds to our price category ①: you'll be paying L40,000–50,000 without bath/shower and around L60,000 with a bath/shower. Most two-stars also fall into the ② and ③ categories, and once you're up to three-star level and beyond you will pay prices corresponding to categories ③ and ④. In resorts and especially in summer in places like the Aeolian Islands, four-star and luxury hotels can charge pretty much what they like, which means prices in the ⑤, ⑥ and ⑦ categories are the norm. For the two five-stars on the island (in Palermo and

---

ACCOMMODATION PRICE CODES

The hotels listed in this guide have been coded according to price. The **price codes** represent the **cheapest available double room in high season** (Easter & June–Aug), usually – but not always – *without* en-suite bathroom or shower. Many cheaper places will also have a few en-suite rooms, for which you'll pay more – usually the next category up in price; higher category hotels nearly always only have en-suite rooms. Out of season, you'll often be able to negotiate a lower price than those suggested here. The categories are:

① under L60,000	④ L120,000–150,000	⑦ L250,000–300,000
② L60,000–90,000	⑤ L150,000–200,000	⑧ over L300,000
③ L90,000–120,000	⑥ L200,000–250,000	

Taormina), you can count on spending between L350,000 and L700,000. That said, there are some bargains around out of the summer season, when the classier hotels drop their room rates by as much as forty percent to attract custom. Quirks in the official grading system mean that you can sometimes pay around the same in a one- or two-star hotel as in a basic *locanda*, or that the same price elsewhere gets you a bathroom included: always ask to see the room before you take it (*Posso vedere?*), and in the cheaper places check if there's hot water available (*C'è acqua calda?*).

There are few **single rooms** available and, in high season especially, lone travellers will often pay most (if not all) the price of a double. Check in the local hotel listings book, which may explicitly state (in English and Italian) that you're only liable for the price of a single room: waving the book at the offending hotel manager might have some effect. **Three or more people** sharing a room should expect to pay around 35 percent on top of the price of a double room.

In the cheaper places you might be able to negotiate a lower rate if you're staying for any length of time (ask *C'è uno sconto per due/tre/quattro notti?*).

PRIVATE ROOMS, APARTMENTS AND FARM STAYS

Certain tourist resorts, especially Taormina and the Aeolian and Égadi Islands, also have **private rooms** in people's houses for rent, which often come equipped with kitchen. Ask in local bars, shops and tourist offices, check the text for details and watch for signs saying "*cámere*" (rooms). Depending on the season and location, you'll pay anything from L30,000 to L50,000 per person a night.

For longer-term stays, you can rent holiday **apartments** in both Taormina and Cefalù and in other, more remote places, like the Aeolians or even Scopello. Although it's horrendously expensive in the summer – over L1 million a month even for a one-bedroom place – there are real bargains to be had in May or late September and during the winter: ask in the tourist offices or a local estate agency (*agenzia immobiliare*) and keep an eye out for local advertisements. Other places for rent include rural cottages or farmhouses, operated by Agriturist, Via A. di Giovanni 14, 90144 Palermo (☎091.346.046). This **agriturismo** scheme has grown considerably in recent years and you'll often find a wide range of activities

also on offer, such as horse-riding, hunting and mountain-biking, plus escorted walks and excursions; a room for two will cost from around L60,000 a night. Local tourist offices can usually tell you if there's anywhere suitable in the district, or you can buy magazines listing these properties from newsstands, and Agriturist have produced a book, *Vacanza in Fattoria* (*Farm Holidays*), written in English, which costs £19.95 and is available from travel bookshops (see p.21).

YOUTH HOSTELS, CAMPSITES AND MOUNTAIN HUTS

Official Hostelling International (HI) **youth hostels** are sparse, having dwindled to just four, in Castroreale, Érice, Nicolosi and on the island of Lípari. It's hardly worth joining just to use these (which, out of season, probably won't want to see membership cards anyway), though if you're planning to cross to the Italian mainland it's worthwhile: contact your home hostelling organization (see box opposite). There are a few unofficial hostels as well, in places like Siracusa and Trápani – all detailed in the text alongside the official places; expect to pay upward of L13,000 per person for a dormitory bed.

Camping is popular, with approximately ninety officially graded sites dotted around the island's coasts, on a few of the Aeolian Islands, on Favignana (Égadi Islands) and on Lampedusa. At the last count there were only a couple in Sicily's interior, around Mount Etna. Again, addresses, telephone numbers and rates are listed in accommodation booklets, as are their months of opening (few are open all year round), though bear in mind that these months (also detailed in the text) are flexible, and campsites generally open or close whenever they want, depending on business. If you want to be sure, it's always worth a phone call. Full details of all the campsites are contained in the book *Campeggi e Villagi Turistici in Italia*, published by the Touring Club Italiano, Corso Italiano 10, 20122 Milan (☎02/852.6245), available from bookshops; or simply get the listings booklet *Sicilia Campeggi*, which details all the Sicilian campsites, free from the Italian State Tourist Office. It's worth bearing in mind that camping isn't going to save you a great deal of money, since most of the sites are large, luxury affairs, often complete with pools, bars, shops and sports facilities. Daily rates are around L6000–10,000 per person plus the same again for a tent, and around L6000 for a vehicle. It's

YOUTH HOSTEL ASSOCIATIONS

Note: the Italian Youth Hostel Association (AIG) is on the Web at *www.hostels-aig.org/*

Australia Australian Youth Hostels Association, 422 Kent St, Sydney (☎02/9261 1111).

Britain Youth Hostel Association (YHA), Trevelyan House, 8 St Stephen's Hill, St Alban's, Herts AL1 2DY (☎01727/855 215); Scottish Youth Hostel Association, 7 Glebe Crescent, Stirling FK8 2JA (☎01786/51 181).

Canada Hostelling International/Canadian Hostelling Association, 205 Catherine St, Suite 400, Ottawa, ON K2P 1C3 (☎613/237-7884, or 1-800/663 5777 everywhere except Newfoundland).

Ireland An Oige, 61 Mountjoy St, Dublin 7 (☎01/830 4555); Youth Hostel Association of Northern Ireland, 22 Donegal Rd, Belfast BT12 5JN (☎01232/324 733).

Italy Associazione Italiana Alberghi per la Gioventù, Via Cavour 44, 00184 Roma (☎06.487.1152, fax 06.488.0492).

New Zealand Youth Hostels Association of New Zealand, 173 Gloucester St, Christchurch 1 (☎03/379 9970).

USA Hostelling International-American Youth Hostels (HI-AYH), 733 15th St NW, Suite 840, PO Box 37613, Washington, DC 20005 (☎202/783-6161).

often as cheap, certainly in Palermo, to stay in a central hotel.

By and large, **camping rough** is a non-starter in much of Sicily: it's frowned on in the tourist areas and on the offshore islands, and difficult in the interior, where there are scant water supplies and little flat land. Occasional possibilities are detailed in the text; anywhere else you're likely to attract the unwelcome attention of the local police.

In Sicily's hillier regions it's possible to stay in a staffed **mountain hut** (*rifugio*) – particularly in the Madonie and Nébrodi ranges and on Mount Etna, where overnight fees are around L15,000–20,000 per person. They're operated by the Club Alpino Italiano, Via Fonseca Pimental 7, 20121 Milan (☎02.2614.1378), which can provide lists and further information; or ask at local tourist offices and check the text.

FOOD AND DRINK

There's much to be said for coming to Sicily just for the eating and drinking. Often, even the most out-of-the-way village will boast somewhere you can get a good, solid lunch,

while places like Catania and Palermo can keep a serious eater happy for days. And it's not ruinously expensive either, certainly compared to prices in the rest of mainland Italy: a full meal with good local wine generally costs around L28,000 a head, though see below for more detailed prices.

The lists below will help you find your way around supermarkets and menus, but don't be afraid to ask to look if you're not sure what you're ordering. Also, check our lists of specialities, some of which crop up in nearly every restaurant.

THE BASICS OF SICILIAN CUISINE

Historically, **Sicilian cuisine** was held in high regard: one of the earliest of cookbooks, the *Art of Cooking* by Mithaecus, derived from fifth-century BC Siracusa; and in medieval times Sicilian chefs were much sought after in foreign courts, and accorded the same esteem as a French chef today. Contemporary cooking is still excellent, leaning heavily on locally produced basic foodstuffs and whatever can be fished out of the sea.

Primarily, Sicilian food mixes Italian staples – pasta, tomato sauce and fresh vegetables – with local specialities and products of the traditional island industries: red chillies, tuna, swordfish and sardines, olives, pine nuts and capers all figure heavily. The mild winter climate and long summers mean that fruit and vegetables are less seasonal than in northern Europe, and are much bigger and more impressive: strawberries appear in April, oranges are available right through the winter, and even bananas are grown on a small scale. Unusual and unexpected foods and fruit are a bonus too: prickly pears (originally imported from Mexico by the Spanish), artichokes, asparagus, medlars and persimmons are ubiquitous, while, in the south and west of the island, the North African influence is evident in the Sicilian version of couscous.

The Arab influence is also apparent in the profusion of sweets and desserts available in Sicily – marzipan is used extensively, while *cassata*, the most Sicilian of desserts, derives from the Arabic word *quas-at*, referring to the round bowl in which it was traditionally prepared.

The best time to sample the more unusual dishes and desserts is during a festival, since food plays a central role in Sicilian celebrations. But at any time of year you'll be able to eat dishes that – though apparently common-or-garden Italian/Sicilian – call upon 2500 years of cross-cultural influences, from the Greeks and Romans to the Arabs, Normans and Spanish.

BREAKFASTS, SNACKS AND ICE-CREAM

Most Sicilians start the day in a bar, their **breakfast** consisting of a milky coffee (cappuccino), and the ubiquitous *cornetto* – a jam-, custard- or chocolate-filled croissant, which you usually help yourself to from the counter. Bigger bars or a patisserie (*pasticceria*) will usually have a bit more choice; an *iris* is a pastry ball stuffed with sweet ricotta cheese, an *arancino* is a deep-fried ball of rice with meat (*rosso*) or butter and cheese (*bianco*) filling, and *cannoli* are pastry tubes filled with sweet ricotta cheese and candied fruit. Breakfast in a hotel (*prima colazione*) will be a limp (and expensive) affair, usually worth avoiding.

At other times of the day, **sandwiches** (*panini*) can be pretty substantial, a bread stick or roll packed with any number of fillings. There are sandwich bars in the bigger towns, though often in small villages you can go into an *alimentari* (grocer's shop) and ask them to make you one from whatever they've got on hand; you'll pay around L3000–5000 each. Bars may also offer *tramezzini*, ready-made sliced white-bread sandwiches with mixed fillings – lighter and less appetizing than your average *panino*. Toasted sandwiches (*toste*) are common too: in a sandwich bar you can get whatever you like put inside them; in bars which have a sandwich toaster you're more likely to be offered a variation on cheese with ham or tomato.

Apart from sandwiches, other prepared takeaway food is pretty thin on the ground. You'll get most of the things already mentioned, plus small pizzas, portions of prepared pasta, chips, even full hot meals, in a **távola calda**, a sort of stand-up snack bar that's at its best in the morning when everything is fresh. The bigger towns have them, often combined with normal bars, and there's always one in main train stations. Otherwise, you'll have to make do with what you can get from a **rosticceria**, something you'll find in every town on the island. The big speciality here is spit-roast chicken (*pollo allo spiedo*): half a chicken with chips will cost around L7000; anything else, like Sicilian hamburgers or hot dogs, is worth steering clear of.

You'll get more adventurous snacks in **shops** and **markets** – good bread, fruit, pizza slices and picnic food, like cheese, salami, olives, tomatoes and salads. Some markets sell traditional takeaway food from stalls, usually things like boiled artichokes, cooked octopus, sea urchins and mussels, and *focacce* – oven-baked pastry snacks either topped with cheese and tomato, or filled with spinach, fried offal or meat. In the larger cities, you'll occasionally come across an old-fashioned *focacceria* – takeaway establishments selling only bread-based snacks. For picnics, some tinned and bottled things are worth looking out for too: sweet peppers (*peperoni*), baby squid (*calamari*), seafood salad (*insalata di mare*) and preserved vegetables. You'll find **supermarkets** in most towns; look out for the "two-for-the-price-of-one" offers on things like tinned fish, meat, biscuits and soft drinks. Island-wide store chains with food halls are Standa and Upim.

Sicilian **ice-cream** (*gelato*) is justifiably famous: a cone (*un cono*) is an indispensable accessory to the evening *passeggiata*; many people eat a dollop of ice-cream in a brioche for breakfast. Most bars have a fairly good selection, but for real choice go to a **gelateria**, where the range is a tribute to the Italian imagination and flair for display. If they make their own on the premises, they'll be a sign saying *produzione propria*. You'll have to go by appearance rather than attempt to decipher their exotic names, many of which don't mean much even to Italians; you'll find it's often the basics – chocolate, lemon, strawberry and coffee – that are best. There's no trouble in locating the finest *gelateria* in town: it's the one that draws the crowds. Sitting down at a bar, on the other hand, is the place to sample a typical Sicilian *cassata*, no relation to the soapy ice-cream cake served in Italian restaurants abroad: the real McCoy is very creamy, packed with ricotta cheese, candied fruit and sometimes chocolate bits, and served with a wafer biscuit.

PIZZAS

The whole world knows about **pizza**, and, outside its home of Naples, Sicily is the best place to eat it. Here, as elsewhere in Italy, your pizza comes flat and not deep-pan, and the choice of toppings is fairly limited – none of the pineapple-and-sweetcorn variations beloved of foreign pizzerias. It's also easier to find pizzas cooked in the traditional way, in wood-fired ovens (*forno a legna*), rather than squeaky-clean electric ones, so that the pizzas arrive blasted and bubbling on the surface, with a distinctive charcoal taste. However, because of the time it takes to set up and light the wood-fired ovens, these pizzas are usually only served at night, except on Sundays and in some resorts in summer.

Pizzerias, which range from a stand-up counter to a fully fledged sit-down restaurant, on the whole sell just pizzas and drinks, usually chips, sometimes salads. A basic cheese and tomato pizza costs around L6000; something a bit fancier, between L7000 and L10,000. To follow local custom, it's quite acceptable to cut it into slices and eat it with your hands, washing it down with a beer or Coke rather than wine. You'll also get pizzas in larger towns and tourist areas in a hybrid pizzeria-ristorante, which serves meals too and is slightly more expensive. Check our list of pizzas for what you get on top of your dough.

MEALS: LUNCH AND DINNER

Full **meals** are much more elaborate affairs. These are generally served in a **trattoria** or a **ristorante**, though these days there's often a fine line between the two: traditionally, a trattoria is cheaper and more basic, offering good home-cooking (*cucina casalinga*), while a ristorante is more upmarket (tablecloths and waiters). The main differences you'll notice, though, are more to do with opening hours and the food on offer. In small towns and villages a trattoria usually best at lunchtime and often only open then – there probably won't be a menu and the waiter will simply reel off a list of what's on that day. In large towns both will be open in the evening, though there'll be more choice in a ristorante, which will always have a menu. In either, a pasta course, meat or fish, fruit and a drink should cost around L25,000–35,000 (fish pushes up the price), though watch out for signs saying "*pranzo turístico*" or "*pranzo completo*". This is a limited set menu including wine which can cost as little as L12,000, but is usually more in the region of L18,000–25,000. **Other types of eating place** include those usually found in tourist resorts, that flaunt themselves as a trattoria-ristorante-pizzeria; *távole calde*, for warmed-up snacks (see opposite); and restaurant-bars called spaghetterias, which specialize in pasta dishes and are often the haunts of the local youth.

Traditionally, a **meal** (lunch is *pranzo*, dinner is *cena*) starts with an **antipasto** (literally "before the meal"); you'll only find this in restaurants, at its best when you circle around a table and pick from a selection of cold dishes, main items including stuffed artichoke hearts, olives, salami, anchovies, seafood salad, aubergine in various guises, sardines and mixed rice. A plateful will cost around L8000–10,000, but if you're moving on to pasta and the main course you'll need quite an appetite to tackle it.

As far as the **menu** goes, it starts with soup or pasta, **il primo** – usually costing from L6,000 to L12,000, and moves on to **il secondo**, the meat or fish dish, which ranges roughly from L12,000 to L18,000. This course is generally served alone except for perhaps a wedge of lemon or tomato. Vegetables and salads (**contorni**) are ordered and served separately and often there won't be much (if any) choice; potatoes will usually come as fries (*patatine fritte*), but you can also find boiled (*lesse*) or roast (*arroste*), while salads are simply green (*verde*) or mixed (*mista*), usually with tomato. If there's no menu, the verbal list of what's available can be a bit bewildering, but if you don't hear anything you recognize just ask for what you want: everywhere should have pasta with tomato sauce (*pomodoro*) or meat sauce (*al ragù*).

Afterwards, you'll usually get a choice of fruit (*frutta*), while in a ristorante, you'll probably be offered other desserts (*dolci*) as well. Sicily is renowned for its sweets, an Arab legacy that you can't help but notice in every bar and bakery you pass, though most restaurants will only have fresh fruit salad (*macedonia*) and ice-cream (or *cassata*); sometimes there'll be *zuppa inglese* ("English soup", which, disappointingly, is only trifle), *zabaglione* or *torta* (tart, cake) too. In common with the rest of Italy, Sicily has embraced the mass-produced, packaged sweets produced by such brands as Ranieri – *tiramisù, tartufo, zuppa inglese* are the most common; some of them aren't bad, but they're a poor substitute for the real thing.

It's useful to know that you don't have to order a full meal in trattorias and most restaurants. Asking for just pasta and a salad, or the main course on its own, won't outrage the waiter. Equally, asking for a dish listed as a first course as a second course, or having pasta followed by pizza (or vice versa), won't be frowned upon.

Something to watch for is **ordering fish**,

In the guide, **telephone numbers** are only given for restaurants where it's necessary to reserve a table in advance. Outside Cefalù, Siracusa and Taormina – and not always there – the staff are unlikely to speak English, so you may have to get someone to ring for you.

which will either be served whole (like bream or trout) or by weight (usually per 100g, *all'etto*), like swordfish and tuna – if you don't want the biggest one they've got, ask to see what you're going to eat and check on the price first.

THE BILL . . . AND TIPPING

At the **end of the meal**, ask for the bill (*il conto*). In many trattorias this doesn't amount to much more than an illegible scrap of paper and, if you want to be sure you're not being ripped off, ask to have a receipt (*una ricevuta*), something they're legally obliged to give you anyway (see "Directory", p.52). Nearly everywhere, you'll pay cover (*pane e coperto*), which amounts to L1500–3000 per person; service (*servizio*) will be added as well in most restaurants, another ten percent – though up to fifteen percent or even twenty percent in some places. If service is included, you won't be expected to tip; otherwise leave ten percent, though bear in mind that the smaller places – pizzerias and trattorias – won't expect this.

VEGETARIANS – A FEW POINTERS

Some **vegetarians** might find their food principles stretched to the limit in Sicily. Fish and shellfish are abundant and excellent, while if you're a borderline case then the knowledge that nearly all eggs and meat are free range in Sicily might just push you over the edge. On the whole, though, it's not that difficult if you're committed. Most pasta sauces are based on tomatoes or dairy products and it's easy to pick a pizza that is meat- (and fish-) free. Most places can be persuaded to cook you eggs in some shape or form, or provide you with a big mixed salad.

The only real problem is one of comprehension: many people don't know what a vegetarian is.

Saying you're vegetarian (*Sono vegetariano/a*) and asking if the dish has meat in it (*C'è carne dentro?*) is only half the battle: poultry and especially *prosciutto* are regarded by many waiters as barely meat at all. Better is to ask what the dish is made with (*Com'è fatto?*) before you order, so that you can spot the offending "non-meaty" meat.

Being a **vegan**, you'll be in for a hard time, though pizzas without cheese are a good stand-by, and the fruit is excellent. Soups are usually made with a fish or meat broth. However, you'll have absolutely no success explaining to anyone why you're a vegan – an incomprehensible moral concept to a Sicilian.

DRINK

Although Sicilian children are brought up on wine, there's not the same emphasis on dedicated **drinking** here as there is in Britain or America. You'll rarely see drunks in public, young people don't make a night out of getting wasted, and women especially are frowned upon if they're seen to be indulging. Nonetheless, there's a wide choice of alcoholic drinks available in Sicily, at low prices; soft drinks come in multifarious hues, thanks to the abundance of fresh fruit, and there's also mineral water and crushed-ice drinks: you'll certainly never be stuck if you want to slake your thirst.

COFFEE, TEA AND SOFT DRINKS

One of the most distinctive smells in a Sicilian street is the aroma of fresh **coffee**, usually wafting out of a bar (many trattorias and pizzerias don't serve hot drinks). It's always excellent: the basic choice is either small, black and very strong (an *espresso*, or just *caffè*), or weaker, white and frothy (a cappuccino), but there are other varieties, too. A *caffelatte* is an *espresso* in a big cup filled up to the top with hot milk. If you want your *espresso* watered down, ask for a *caffè lungo*; with a shot of alcohol – and you can ask for just about *anything* in your coffee – is *caffè corretto*; with a drop of milk is *caffè macchiato* ("stained"). If you want to be sure of a coffee without sugar, ask for *caffe senza zucchero*. Many places now also sell decaffeinated coffee (ask for Hag, even when it isn't); while in summer you'll probably want to have your coffee cold (*caffè freddo*). For a real treat, ask for *granita di caffè* – cold coffee with crushed ice and usually topped with cream (*senza panna* if you prefer it without cream).

As for **tea**, it's best in summer when you can drink it iced (*tè freddo*) usually mixed with lemon; it's excellent for taking the heat off. Hot tea (*tè caldo*) comes with lemon (*con limone*) unless you ask for milk (*con latte*). **Milk** itself is drunk hot as often as cold, or you can get it with a dash of coffee (*latte macchiato*), and in a variety of flavoured drinks (*frappe*) too.

Alternatively, there are various **soft drinks** (*analcóliche*) to choose from. A **spremuta** is a fresh fruit juice, squeezed at the bar, usually orange, lemon or grapefruit. You might need to add sugar to a lemon juice (*spremuta di limone*), but orange juice (*spremuta di arancia*) is usually sweet enough on its own, especially the crimson-red variety, made from blood oranges. You can also have orange and lemon mixed (*mischiato*). A **frullato** is a fresh fruit shake, often made with more than one fruit. A **granita** (a crushed-ice drink) is a Sicilian speciality and comes in several flavours other than coffee. Otherwise, there's the usual range of fizzy drinks and concentrated juices; Coke is prevalent, but the home-grown Italian alternative, Chinotto, is less sweet – good with a slice of lemon. Tap water (*acqua normale*) is drinkable everywhere and you won't pay for it in a bar. But **mineral water** (*acqua minerale*) is the usual choice, either still (*senza gas* or *naturale*) or fizzy (*con gas*, *gassata* or *frizzante*).

BEER, WINES AND SPIRITS

Beer (*birra*) is usually a lager-type brew which usually comes in a third of a litre (*píccolo*) or two-thirds of a litre (*grande*) bottles: commonest (and cheapest) are the Italian brands, Peroni and Dreher, and the Sicilian Messina, all of which are fine, if a bit weak. A small (33cl) bottle of Messina beer costs about L2500 in a bar or restaurant; a larger (66cl) bottle, L3500–4500. If this is what you want, ask for *birra nazionale*, otherwise you'll be given the more expensive imported beers, like Carlsberg and Kronenberg. In some bars and bigger restaurants and in all *birrerias* you also have a choice of draught lager (*birra alla spina*), sold in units of 25cl (*píccola*) and 50cl (*media*), measure for measure more expensive than the bottled variety. In some places you might find so-called "dark beers" (*birra nera*, *birra rossa* or *birra scura*), which have a slightly maltier taste, and in appearance resemble stout or bitter. These are the dearest of the draught beers, though not necessarily the strongest.

With just about every meal you'll be offered **wine** (*vino*), either red (*rosso*) or white (*bianco*), labelled or local. If you're unsure and want the local stuff, ask for *vino locale*: on the whole it's fine, often served straight from the barrel in jugs or old bottles and costing as little as L4000–8000 a litre. You may be flummoxed by the *vino locale* not being the colour you've ordered. You'll get whatever they make – in the west, for example, it's often rosé, a tart but refreshing drink; in Marsala, it's amber.

Bottled wine is much more expensive, though still good value; expect to pay from around L12,000 a bottle in a restaurant, more like L15,000–20,000 in places like Taormina. One peculiarity is that bars don't tend to serve wine **by the glass** – when they do, you'll pay around L2000. A standard you see everywhere is *Corvo*; others to watch for are *Settesoli* (red and white) from Menfi, in the west; *Etna* (red and white) from vines grown on the slopes of the volcano; *Donnafugata* (a crisp, fruity white) from Palermo province; *Zucco* (a medium-sweet white) from Carini; *Montevagno* or *Salemi* (a tangy wine from Sicily's far west); and *Cervasuolo* (red and white) from the area around Vittória.

Sicily produces good **dessert wines**, the most famous being *Marsala*, sometimes sweetened and mixed with eggs, called *Marsala all'uovo*, but if you're heading to the offshore islands, watch out for *malvasia* (from the Aeolians) and *moscato* (from Pantelleria). In and around Taormina, the local speciality is *vino alla Mándorla*, a startlingly addictive almond wine, served ice-cold. **Fortified wine** is fairly popular too: Martini (red or white) and Cinzano are nearly always available; Cynar (an artichoke-based sherry) and Punt'e Mes are other common aperitifs. If you ask for a Campari-Soda you'll get a ready-mixed version in a little bottle; a slice of lemon is a *spicchio di limone*; ice is *ghiaccio*.

All the usual **spirits** are on sale and known mostly by their generic names, except brandy which you should call *cognac* or ask for by name. The best Italian brandies are Stock and Vécchia Romagna; for all other spirits, if you want the cheaper Italian stuff, again, ask for *nazionale*. A generous shot costs around L3000–5000. There's the standard selection of **liqueurs**, too, though at some stage try **amaro** (literally "bitter"), an after-dinner drink served with (or instead of) coffee. It's supposed to aid digestion, and is often not bitter at all, but can taste remarkably medicinal. The favourite brand is Averna (from Caltanissetta) but there are dozens of different kinds. Look out, too, for a red liqueur called

Fuoco dell'Etna, mostly sold on the east coast, whose effect – fittingly – is of a miniature volcanic explosion. Other strong drinks available, though not especially Sicilian, are *grappa*, almost pure alcohol, made from distilling the grape husks left over from the manufacture of wine, and *sambuca* – a sticky-sweet, aniseed liqueur, traditionally served with one or more coffee beans in it and set on fire at the table, though only tourists are likely to experience this these days.

WHERE TO DRINK

Bars are less social centres than functional stops, and all very similar to each other – bright, with a chrome counter, a Gaggia coffee machine and a picture of the local soccer team on the wall. You'll come here for **ordinary drinking**, a coffee in the morning, a quick beer, a cup of tea, but, at least in cities, people don't generally while away the afternoon in bars, or spend all night drinking in them (though in villages they are the venue for interminable card games). Indeed, in many places (Palermo included), it's difficult to find an average bar open much after 9pm. Where it does fit into the general Mediterranean pattern is that there are no set licensing hours and children are allowed in; there's often a telephone and you can buy ice-cream and sometimes snacks as well as drinks.

Whatever you're drinking, the procedure is the same. It's cheapest to drink standing up at the counter (there's often nowhere to sit anyway), in which case you pay first at the cash desk (*la cassa*), present your receipt (*scontrino*) to the bar person and give your order. If you don't know how much a drink will cost, there's always a list of prices (the *listino prezzi*) behind the bar or *cassa*. When you present your receipt it's customary to leave an extra L100 on the counter – though no one will object if you don't. If there's waiter service, just sit where you like: it's more expensive to sit down inside than stand up (the difference in price is shown on the price list as *távola*) and it's up to twice the basic price if you sit at tables outside (*terrazza*).

For more **serious drinking**, most people go out and eat as well, at a pizzeria or restaurant, and spin the meal out accordingly if they want a few more beers. Otherwise, the other choice is a **birreria** (literally "beer shop"), where people go just to drink, though often they sell food too. These are where you'll find young people at night, listening to music or glued to rock videos; they're often called "pubs", although they bear little relation to their British namesakes. In tourist areas, bars and

cafés (*caffè*) are more like the real European thing and they're open later, but they're more expensive than the common-or-garden bar. Other places to get a drink are the **bar-pasticceria**, which sells wonderful cakes and pastries too, and a **tàvola calda** in a train station always has a bar.

SICILIAN FOOD TERMS

Basics and snacks

Aceto	Vinegar	*Maionese*	Mayonnaise	*Patatine*	French fries
Aglio	Garlic	*Marmellata*	Jam	*fritte*	
Biscotti	Biscuits	*Olio*	Oil	*Pizzetta*	Small cheese and
Burro	Butter	*Olive*	Olives		tomato pizza
Caramelle	Sweets	*Pane*	Bread	*Riso*	Rice
Cioccolato	Chocolate	*Pane*	Wholemeal bread	*Sale*	Salt
Focaccia	Oven-baked snack	*integrale*		*Uova*	Eggs
Formaggio	Cheese	*Panino*	Bread roll/	*Yogurt*	Yoghurt
Frittata	Omelette		sandwich	*Zúcchero*	Sugar
Gelato	Ice-cream	*Patatine*	Crisps/potato chips	*Zuppa*	Soup
Grissini	Bread sticks	*Pepe*	Pepper		

Antipasti and starters

Antipasto misto	Mixed cold meats and cheese (plus a mix of other things in this list)	*Mortadella*	Salami-type cured meat with white nuggets of fat; in Sicily, often with pistachios
Caponata	Mixed aubergine, olives, tomatoes	*Pancetta*	Italian bacon
Caprese	Tomato and mozzarella cheese salad	*Peperonata*	Grilled green, red or yellow peppers stewed in olive oil
Insalata di mare	Seafood salad (usually squid, octopus and prawn)	*Pomodori ripieni*	Stuffed tomatoes
		Prosciutto	Ham
Insalata di riso	Rice salad	*Salame*	Salami
Insalata russa	"Russian salad"; diced vegetables in mayonnaise	*Salmone/tonno/ pesce spada/ affumicato*	Smoked salmon/tuna/swordfish
Melanzane alla parmigiana	Fried aubergine in tomato sauce with parmesan cheese		

Pizzas

Biancaneve	"Black and white"; mozzarella and oregano	*Margherita*	Cheese and tomato
		Marinara	Tomato and garlic
Calzone	Folded pizza with cheese, ham and tomato	*Napoli/ Napoletana*	Tomato, anchovy and olive oil (often mozzarella too)
Capricciosa	"Capricious"; topped with whatever they've got in the kitchen, usually including baby artichoke, ham and egg	*Quattro formaggi*	"Four cheeses"; usually mozzarella, fontina, Gorgonzola and Gruyère
Cardinale	Ham and olives	*Quattro stagioni*	"Four seasons"; the toppings split into four separate sec-
Diavolo	"Devil", spicy, with hot salami or Italian sausage		tions, usually including ham, peppers, onion, mushrooms, artichokes, olives, egg, etc
Funghi	Mushroom; tinned, sliced but-ton mushrooms unless it spec-ifies fresh mushrooms, either *funghi freschi* or *porcini*	*Rianata*	Fresh tomato, oregano, garlic and anchovy; a western Sicilian speciality
Frutti di mare	Seafood; usually mussels, prawns, squid and clams	*Romana*	Anchovy and olives

The first course (il primo): Soups . . .

Brodo	Clear broth	*Pasta e fagioli*	Pasta soup with beans
Minestrina	Any light soup	*Pastina in brodo*	Pasta pieces in clear broth
Minestrone	Thick vegetable soup	*Stracciatella*	Broth with egg

Pasta . . .

Cannelloni	Large tubes of pasta, stuffed	*Penne*	Smaller version of *rigatoni*
Farfalle	Literally "bow"-shaped pasta; the word also means "butterflies"	*Ravioli*	Ravioli
		Rigatoni	Large, grooved tubular pasta
		Risotto	Cooked rice dish, with sauce
Fettuccine	Narrow pasta ribbons	*Spaghetti*	Spaghetti
Gnocchi	Small potato and dough dumplings	*Spaghettini*	Thin spaghetti
		Tagliatelle	Pasta ribbons, another word for *fettucine*
Lasagne	Lasagne		
Maccheroni	Macaroni (tubular pasta)	*Tortellini*	Small rings of pasta, stuffed with meat or cheese
Pappardelle	Pasta ribbons		
Pasta al forno	Pasta baked with minced meat, eggs, tomato and cheese	*Vermicelli*	Very thin spaghetti (literally "little worms")

. . . and the Sauce (salsa)

Aglio e olio (e peperoncino)	Tossed in garlic and olive oil (and hot chillies)	*Parmigiano*	Parmesan cheese
		Pesto	Ground basil, pine-nut, garlic and pecorino sauce
Amatriciana	Cubed pork and tomato sauce (originally from Rome)		
		Pomodoro	Tomato sauce
Arrabbiata	Spicy tomato sauce, with chillies	*Puttanesca*	"Whorish"; tomato, anchovy, olive oil and oregano
Bolognese	Meat sauce	*Ragù*	Meat sauce
Burro e salvia	Butter and sage	*Trápanese*	Cold puréed tomato, garlic and basil
Carbonara	Cream, ham and beaten egg		
Frutta di mare	Seafood	*Vóngole (veraci)*	Clam and tomato sauce (fresh clams in shells, usually served with oil and herbs)
Funghi	Mushroom		
Panna	Cream		

The second course (il secondo): Meat (carne) . . .

Agnello	Lamb	*Manzo*	Beef
Bistecca	Steak	*Ossobuco*	Shin of veal
Cervello	Brain	*Pollo*	Chicken
Cinghiale	Wild boar	*Polpette*	Meatballs
Coniglio	Rabbit	*Rognoni*	Kidneys
Costolette/ cotolette	Cutlets/chops	*Salsiccia*	Sausage
		Saltimbocca	Veal with ham
Fégatini	Chicken livers	*Scaloppina*	Escalope (of veal)
Fégato	Liver	*Spezzatino*	Stew
Involtini	Steak slices, rolled and stuffed	*Tacchino*	Turkey
Lepre	Hare	*Trippa*	Tripe
Lingua	Tongue	*Vitello*	Veal
Maiale	Pork		

... Fish (pesce) and shellfish (crostacei)

Note that *surgelati* or *congelati* written on the menu next to a dish means "frozen" – it often applies to squid and prawns.

Acciughe	Anchovies	*Gamberetti*	Shrimps	*Sampiero*	John Dory
Anguilla	Eel	*Gámberi*	Prawns	*Sarde*	Sardines
Aragosta	Lobster	*Granchio*	Crab	*Seppie*	Cuttlefish
Baccalà	Dried salted cod	*Merluzzo*	Cod	*Sgombro*	Mackerel
Calamari	Squid	*Nasello*	Hake	*Sógliola*	Sole
Céfalo	Grey mullet	*Ostriche*	Oysters	*Tonno*	Tuna
Cozze	Mussels	*Pesce spada*	Swordfish	*Triglie*	Red mullet
Dattile	Razor clams	*Pólpo*	Octopus	*Trota*	Trout
Déntice	Dentex (like sea bass)	*Ricci di mare*	Sea urchins	*Vóngole*	Clams
		Rospo	Monkfish		

Vegetables (contorni) and salad (insalata)

Asparagi	Asparagus	*Cetriolo*	Cucumber	*Orígano*	Oregano
Basílico	Basil	*Cipolla*	Onion	*Patate*	Potatoes
Bróccoli	Broccoli	*Fagioli*	Beans	*Peperoni*	Peppers
Cápperi	Capers	*Fagiolini*	Green beans	*Piselli*	Peas
Carciofi	Artichokes	*Finocchio*	Fennel	*Pomodori*	Tomatoes
Carciofini	Artichoke hearts	*Funghi*	Mushrooms	*Radicchio*	Red chicory
Carotte	Carrots	*Insalata verde/mista*	Green salad/ mixed salad	*Spinaci*	Spinach
Cavolfiori	Cauliflower			*Zucca*	Pumpkin
Cávolo	Cabbage	*Melanzane*	Aubergine/ eggplant	*Zucchini*	Courgettes
Ceci	Chickpeas				

Desserts (dolci)

Amaretti	Macaroons	*Torta*	Cake, tart
Cassata	Ice-cream cake with candied fruit	*Zabaglione*	Dessert made with eggs, sugar and *Marsala* wine
Gelato	Ice-cream		
Macedonia	Fruit salad	*Zuppa Inglese*	Trifle

Cheese

Caciocavallo	A type of dried, mature mozzarella cheese	*Parmigiano*	Parmesan cheese
		Pecorino	Strong-tasting hard sheep's cheese
Fontina	Northern Italian cheese used in cooking	*Provolone*	Cheese with grooved rind, either mild or tasty
Gorgonzola	Soft, strong, blue-veined cheese	*Ricotta*	Soft white cheese made from ewe's milk, used in sweet or savoury dishes
Mozzarella	Soft white cheese, traditionally made from buffalo's milk		

Fruit and nuts

Albicocche	Apricots	*Ciliegie*	Cherries	*Melone*	Melon
Ananas	Pineapple	*Fichi*	Figs	*Néspole*	Medlars
Anguria/ coccómero	Watermelon	*Fichi d'India*	Prickly pears	*Pere*	Pears
		Frágole	Strawberries	*Pesche*	Peaches
Arance	Oranges	*Limone*	Lemon	*Pignoli*	Pine nuts
Banane	Bananas	*Mándorle*	Almonds	*Pistacchio*	Pistachio nut
Cacchi	Persimmons	*Mele*	Apples	*Uva*	Grapes

Cooking terms and useful words

Affumicato	Smoked	*Ferri*	Grilled without oil	*Pizzaiola*	Cooked with tomato sauce
Arrosto	Roast	*Al forno*	Baked		
Ben cotto	Well done	*Fritto*	Fried	*Ripieno*	Stuffed
Bollito/lesso	Boiled	*Grattugiato*	Grated	*Sangue*	Rare
Alla brace	Barbecued	*Alla griglia*	Grilled	*Allo spiedo*	On the spit
Brasato	Cooked in wine	*Al Marsala*	Cooked with *Marsala* wine	*Stracotto*	Braised, stewed
Cotto	Cooked (not raw)			*Surgelati*	Frozen
Crudo	Raw			*In úmido*	Stewed
Al dente	Firm, not overcooked	*Milanese*	Fried in egg and breadcrumbs	*Al vapore*	Steamed

Sicilian specialities: starters and pasta

Arancini	"Little oranges"; deep-fried rice balls with minced meat, cheese and peas	*Penne all'arrabbiata*	Short tubular pasta with spicy tomato sauce made with chillies (*arrabibata* means "angry")
Caponata	Sautéed aubergine, olives and tomatoes; served cold	*Peperonata*	Peppers (capsicum) sautéed in olive oil until soft and sweet, either served as antipasto or as a vegetable
Cozze alla marinara	Mussels in a rich wine-based soup		
Cozze pepata	Mussels in spicy tomato stock	*Spaghetti alla carrettiera*	"Carter's spaghetti", cooked with garlic, oil, pecorino and salt and pepper; a dish traditionally cooked by roving carters, common in Catania province
Crocchè di patate	Potato croquettes		
Insalata di arance	Orange salad; dressed with oil and parsley		
Maccu	Fava bean (like lima bean) soup	*Spaghetti alla Norma*	Spaghetti with tomato sauce topped with fried aubergine and parmesan or pecorino cheese; a special-ity of Catania, named after one of Bellini's operas
Panelle	Chickpea fritters		
Pasta con i broccoli arriminati	Pasta cooked with cauliflower, anchovy paste, pine nuts and saffron		
Pasta con la mollica	Pasta with oil and toasted breadcrumbs	*Spaghetti alla Trápanese*	Spaghetti tossed with cold puréed tomatoes, basil and garlic; a pungent dish from Trápani
Pasta con le sarde	Macaroni with fresh sardines, fennel, raisins and pine kernels; a speciality of Palermo	*Uova/funghi in tegame*	Eggs/mushrooms fried in olive oil, served at the table in a little metal pan

Sicilian specialities: main courses

Cuscus	Couscous, usually served with fish and vegetable sauce, sometimes meat; a common dish in western Sicily	*Involtini di pesce spada*	Slices of swordfish, stuffed, rolled and fried
Fritto misto	A standard seafood dish; deep-fried prawns and squid rings in batter	*Pesce spada alla Ghiotta*	Swordfish cooked in spicy tomato sauce with capers and olives; from Messina
Fritto di pesce	As above but also with other fried fish, like sardines and whitebait	*Sarde a beccafico*	Sardines stuffed with breadcrumbs, nuts, dried fruit and anchovy; a Palermitan speciality

Sicilian specialities: main courses (continued)

Scaloppine di maiale al Marsala	Escalopes of pork cooked in *Marsala* wine; the most common way of cooking meat with this Sicilian wine		although there are other regional variations
		Zuppa di cozze/ vóngole	A big dish of mussels/clams in rich wine-based soup
Stocca alla Messinese	Dried cod stewed with potatoes, olives, tomatoes, capers and celery; a speciality of Messina	*Zuppa di pesce*	As above but usually with pieces of cod, squid and prawns, and served with fried bread

Desserts and festival food

Cannoli	Fried pastry stuffed with sweet ricotta and candied peel; a *Carnevale* speciality	*Sfinci*	Fried pastry stuffed with ricotta; served at the festival of St Joseph (San Giuseppe)
Cassata	Ice-cream cake with candied fruit		
Crispelle di riso	Sweet rice fritters	*Torrone di mandorle*	Crystallized almonds and sugar, sold at markets around All Saints' Day
Pasta reale	Almond paste, shaped and coloured to form mock fruit, vegetables, even fish		

Drinks

Acqua minerale	Mineral water	*Granita*	Iced coffee/ fruit drink	*Tónico*	Tonic water
				Vino	Wine
Aranciata	Orangeade	*Latte*	Milk	*Rosso*	Red
Bicchiere	Glass	*Limonata*	Lemonade	*Bianco*	White
Birra	Beer	*Selz*	Soda water	*Rosato*	Rosé
Bottiglia	Bottle	*Spremuta*	Fresh fruit juice	*Secco*	Dry
Caffè	Coffee	*Spumante*	Sparkling wine	*Dolce*	Sweet
Cioccolata calda	Hot chocolate	*Succo di frutta*	Concentrated fruit juice with sugar	*Litro*	Litre
				Mezzo	Half-litre
				Quarto	Quarter-litre
Ghiaccio	Ice	*Tè*	Tea	*Salute!*	Cheers!

POST, PHONES AND THE MEDIA

Post office opening hours are usually Monday to Saturday 8.30am to 6.30pm; smaller towns won't have a service on a Saturday and everywhere post offices close at noon on the last day of the month. If you want stamps, you can buy them in tabacchi too, as well as in some gift shops in the tourist resorts. The Italian postal service is one of the tardiest in Europe – if your letter is urgent, consider spending extra for the express service.

Letters can be sent **poste restante** to any Sicilian post office, by addressing them "Fermo Posta" followed by the name of the town. When picking something up take your passport, and make sure they check under middle names and initials (and every other letter when all else fails) as filing is diabolical.

TELEPHONES

Public **telephones**, run by Telecom Italia, come in various forms, usually with clear instructions printed on them (in English, too). For the most common type, you'll need L100, L200 or L500 coins, or a token known as a *gettone* (L200), though these are being phased out. You need at least L200 to start a call, even to toll-free numbers (the money is refunded at the end of the call). **Telephone cards** (*schede telefóniche*) are available for L5000, L10,000 and L15,000 from *tabacchi* or newsstands. They're accepted in most Sicilian phone booths – in fact some will only take cards. Note that the perforated corner of

these cards must be torn off before they can be used. Bars will often have a phone you can use, though these often take coins only: look for the yellow phone symbol. Alternatively you could find a Telecom Italia or other office (listed in the text in the larger towns) or a bar with a *cabina a scatti*, a soundproofed and metered kiosk: ask to make the call and pay at the end. You can do the same at hotels, but they normally charge 25 percent more. Phone **tariffs** are among the most expensive in Europe; they're at their dearest on Monday to Friday between 8.30am and 1pm, but cheapest between 10pm and 8am Monday to Saturday and all day Sunday.

You can make **international calls** from any booth that accepts cards, and from any other booth labelled "*interurbano*"; the minimum charge for an international call is L2000. The cheapest way to make them is to get a Global Calling Card issued by AT&T (☎1-800/5543-3117), an MCI WorldPhone and World Reach card (☎1-800/444-333), a BT Charge Card (☎0800/345 144), or a Cable & Wireless Calling Card (☎0500/100 505). All are free, and they work in the same way – just ring the company's international operator (see box opposite), who will connect you free of charge and add the cost of the connected call to your domestic bill. Alternatively, use a special **international phone card** (*carta telefonica internazionale*) available from post offices for L12,500, L25,000, L50,000 and L100,000; all cardphones accept them, but before each call you need to dial ☎1740 and the PIN number on the back of the card. To make a **collect/reversed charge** call (*cárico al destinatario*) dial ☎172 followed by the country code (see box), which will connect you to an operator in your home country.

Mobile phones work on the GSM European standard. You will hardly see an Italian without one, but if you are going to join them make sure you have made the necessary arrangements before you leave – which may involve paying a hefty (refundable) deposit.

FAX AND EMAIL

Nearly every Italian town has a **fax office**, but the cost is fairly high: for faxes within Italy, expect to pay L3000 for the first page and L2000

COUNTRY DIRECT SERVICES

Australia Optus ☎172 1161; Telstra ☎172 1061
Ireland ☎172 0353
New Zealand ☎172 1064

UK BT ☎172 0044; Cable & Wireless
☎172 054

USA and Canada AT&T ☎172-1011;
MCI ☎172-1022; Sprint ☎172-1877

INTERNATIONAL TELEPHONE CODES

For direct **international calls from Italy**, dial the country code (given below), the area code (minus its first 0, where applicable), and finally the subscriber number.

Australia 61   **Ireland** 353   **New Zealand** 64   **UK** 44   **USA and Canada** 1

CALLING SICILY FROM ABROAD

Dial the access code (☎0011 from Australia, Canada and the US, ☎00 from Britain, Ireland and New Zealand); then ☎39 (for Italy); then the area code *including the first zero* (the major towns are listed below); and then the subscriber number. If calling **within Sicily** the area code must always be used, even when dialling locally; all telephone numbers listed in the Guide include the relevant code.

Agrigento ☎0922	**Enna** ☎0935	**Siracusa** ☎0931
Catania ☎095	**Messina** ☎090	**Taormina** ☎0942
Cefalù ☎0921	**Palermo** ☎091	**Trápani** ☎0923

ITALIAN PHONE NUMBERS

Telephone numbers change with amazing frequency in Italy. If in doubt, consult the local directory – there's a copy in most bars, hotels and, of course, telephone offices. Numbers beginning ☎147 and ☎167 are free, and ☎170 will get you through to an English-speaking operator.

for each subsequent page, plus the cost of the call; for international faxes it's about L6000 for the first and L4000 for subsequent pages, plus the cost of the call.

Internet cafés are now common in the major cities, allowing you to log on and email for between L10,000 and L15,000 an hour. Search *www.cyberiacafe.net/cyberia/guide/ccafe.htm* for a list of cybercafés. Travelling with a laptop and a modem can enable you to log in to your own service provider, but it's advisable to check before you leave whether this is possible.

THE MEDIA

You'll find the main national **newspapers** on any newsstand: *La Repubblica* is middle-to-left with a lot of cultural coverage; *Il Corriere della Sera* is authoritative and rather right-wing; *L'Unità* is the former Communist Party organ; and *Il Manifesto*, a more radical and readable left-wing daily. Sicily also has its own **local papers**, useful for transport timetables, concerts and film listings, etc. In Palermo the best is *L'Ora*; in Catania, *La Sicilia*; in Messina, *La Gazzetta del*

Sud, while *Il Giornale della Sicilia* has separate editions printed all over the island. The most widely read paper, though, is the pink *Gazzetta dello Sport*, essential reading for the serious sports fan. **English-language newspapers** can be found in Palermo, Catania, Messina, Taormina and Cefalù, at the train station and the main piazza or corso, usually a day or two late.

If the opportunity arises, take a look at Italian **TV** to sample the pros and cons of deregulation in television. The three state-run channels, RAI 1, 2 and 3, have got their backs against the wall in the face of the massive independent onslaught, led by the Euromogul Berlusconi. The output is generally pretty bland, with a heavy helping of Brazilian soaps, American sitcoms and films, and ghastly Italian cabaret shows, though the RAI channels have less advertising and mix some good reporting in among the dross.

The situation in **radio** is even more anarchic, with the FM waves crowded to the extent that you can pick up a new station just by walking down the corridor. Again, the RAI stations are generally more professional, though daytime listening is virtually undiluted nonstop dance music.

OPENING HOURS AND HOLIDAYS

Basic hours for most shops and businesses in Sicily are Monday to Saturday from 8am/9am to around 1pm, and from around 4pm to 7pm/8pm, though some offices work to a more standard European 9am to 5pm day. Everything, except bars and restaurants, closes on Sunday, though you might find fish shops in some coastal towns and pasticcerias open until Sunday lunchtime.

Other disrupting factors are **national holidays** and local **Saint's days** (see "Festivals" opposite). Local religious holidays don't generally close down shops and businesses, but they do mean that accommodation space will be tight; check the "Festivals" section at the end of each chapter. However, everything, except bars and restaurants, will be closed on the national holidays shown in the box.

PUBLIC HOLIDAYS

January 1
January 6 (Epiphany)
Good Friday
Easter Monday
April 25 (Liberation Day)
May 1 (Labour Day)
August 15 (Ferragosto; Assumption of the Blessed Virgin Mary)
November 1 (Ognissanti; All Saints)
December 8 (Immaculate Conception of the Blessed Virgin Mary)
December 25
December 26

CHURCHES, MUSEUMS AND ARCHEOLOGICAL SITES

The rules for visiting **churches** are much as they are all over the Mediterranean. Dress modestly, which usually means no shorts, and covered shoulders for women, and try to avoid wandering around during a service. Most churches open in the early morning, around 7am or 8am for Mass and close around noon, opening up again at 4–5pm, and closing at 7pm; more obscure ones will only open for early morning and evening services; some only open on Sunday and on religious holidays. One problem you'll face all over Sicily is that lots of churches, monasteries, convents and oratories are **closed for restoration** (*chiuso per restauro*). We've indicated in the text the more long-term closures, though you might be able to persuade a workman or priest/curator to show you around, even if there's scaffolding everywhere.

Museums are generally open daily from 9am to 1pm, and again for a couple of hours in the afternoon on certain days; likely closing day is Monday, while they close slightly earlier on Sunday, usually 12.30pm. **Archeological sites** are usually open from 9am until an hour before sunset (in practice until around 4pm in winter, 7pm in summer). Again, they are sometimes closed on Monday.

You can buy two useful packs called *Le Carte* (a blue pack for the independent museums, green for the state ones; L5000) from the main museums. Each pack contains a series of leaflets in English with information on and photographs of each museum's exhibits, as well as maps of their layout.

FESTIVALS AND ENTERTAINMENT

Every day in Sicily is a Saint's Day, celebrated as an onomástico or name day and, for the people called after that saint, ranking above a birthday in importance. The ones you'll notice are the *feste*, feast days for saints that have a special role for a particular locality. These are still basically unchanged in the smaller towns and villages, though some have evolved into much larger affairs spread over two or three days, and others have been developed with an eye to tourism. The ingredients are the same everywhere: people performing old songs and dances, a costumed procession, special food and sweets, and noisy fireworks to finish with.

FESTIVALS AND PILGRIMAGES

The local tourist office can tell you about events in its area. You're likely to come across a *festa* at any time throughout the year (check the "Festivals" section at the end of each chapter for exact dates), though there are certain occasions which stand out. **Carnevale** (Carnival, or Mardi Gras time) is a floating festival, five days of celebration in the period just before Lent – which means in practice some time between the end of February and the end of March. Literally the term means "farewell meat", referring to the last bout of indulgence before the abstinence of Lent, which lasts for forty days and ends with Easter. The best festivities are along the Ionian coast, at Taormina and especially at Acireale, although most Sicilian towns put on a little bit of a show.

Easter week itself is celebrated all over the island, with slow-moving processions and ostentatious displays of penitence and mourning. Particularly dramatic events take place in the west of the island, at Trápani, Marsala and the Albanian village of Piana degli Albanesi, as well as at Enna in the interior.

Other more unconventional affairs take place at Prizzi, in the western interior, and at San Fratello, on the Tyrrhenian coast. The biggest island-wide celebration is at **ferragosto**, the Feast of the Assumption on August 15, a midsummer excuse for spectacular fireworks. This is a good time to be in Messina, when the procession of the enormous Giganti on August 14 is followed by the mad scramble of the Vara at ferragosto itself, ending with fireworks over the Straits late at night; see p.183 for more.

Of the various **pilgrimages** that take place throughout Sicily, the most interesting are in September, notably at Palermo on the fourth, and at Gibilmanna and Tíndari on the Tyrrhenian coast on the eighth.

Among the biggest and best known of the **other popular festivals** are: the Epiphany celebrations in Piana degli Albanesi (Jan 6); the Festa di Sant'Agata in Catania (Feb 3–5); the Sagra del Mándorlo in Fiore, celebrating the almond blossom in Agrigento (1st or 2nd week of Feb); the Festa di Santa Rosalia in Palermo (July 11–15); and Il Palio dei Normanni, a medieval-costumed procession and joust in Piazza Armerina (Aug 13–14).

MUSIC AND CINEMA

There's a fair selection of cultural things happening throughout the year aside from the festival events. Sicily's archeological remains – particularly its Greek and Roman theatres – provide spectacular settings for **concerts**, usually classical, and there are regular events by local and visiting international orchestras in the theatres at Taormina, Segesta, Siracusa and Tíndari. The **opera** season runs from October to June, the best places to see it being the Teatro Mássimo in Palermo, or the Teatro Bellini in Catania. Smaller theatres in all the main towns and cities also have music programmes, as well as the dramatic arts. There's no specific Sicilian **rock music** scene. Radio and TV are dominated by mainstream Italian chart music, which is mostly bland Europop, slushy ballads or bad cover versions of British and American hits. Some big, international bands do come to Sicily, and, especially during the summer, some of the more enterprising local councils – in Palermo, Messina and Catania – sponsor open-air concerts in public squares or parks.

There are **cinemas** in most towns, though all English-language films are dubbed into Italian. An alternative in summer to the indoor movie houses are the open-air film shows that take place in some towns and tourist resorts, detailed in the text. Taormina hosts an important **international film festival** every year in July, with screenings in the Greek theatre.

THEATRES AND PUPPET THEATRES

Regular **theatre** is popular in Sicily: Palermo has thirteen theatres, Catania a few less, and the summer sees open-air performances in many places, including some dramatic productions in the ancient theatres at Siracusa, Tíndari and Taormina. The biggest and most famous theatrical productions are the biennial classical dramas performed at Siracusa (May and June in even-numbered years), and the Pirandello week (July) performances at Agrigento. All theatre performances will, however, be in Italian, although it's well worth getting tickets to the Siracusa and Agrigento performances anyway.

You should also try to spend at least one evening at a Sicilian **puppet theatre** (*teatro dei pupi*). A traditional entertainment, there are still some original theatres around in Palermo and elsewhere, as well as a few productions put on for tourists. Check the text for details of where to catch a performance, and see below for the full picture on who's doing what and why, once you get there.

PUPPET THEATRE: THE STORY

Popular in Sicily since the fourteenth century, the stories portrayed by the puppets, or marionettes, are always the same chivalric episodes from the lives of the Paladins, the twelve peers of Charlemagne's court. Basically, it's a tale of the clash between Christianity and Islam and, while the particular **story** unfolds in fairly incomprehensible Sicilian dialect, the **format** is straightforward and unchanged from theatre to theatre. A succession of stiff-legged knights are introduced. The main two, Orlando (Roland) and Rinaldo, always stand on the left side of the stage and strut around as the puppeteer lists their exploits and achievements; the Saracens, with baggy trousers and shields marked with stars and crescents, stand on the right. There may be a love interest, too, perhaps a jousting tournament to decide who gets the hand of Charlemagne's daughter. The main business of each performance is the succession of formal, staged **battles** between the Christian knights and the Saracen invaders. Cross-stage charges by Orlando and Rinaldo, accompanied by drums and shouts, lead to the inevitable clashes of sword and armour, the pile of Saracen dead mounting with each attack. There's often a distraction between bouts as Orlando fights a crocodile, or confronts other monsters and magicians sent to try him. But, whatever the enemy, the engagements are always coloured by great splashes of artificial blood spurted from bodies as each victim tries to outdo the shrieks and groans of the one before. The climax will be the representation of some great historical battle, like Roncesvalles, culminating in betrayal and treachery for the boys who face an untimely and drawn-out death on the battlefield.

Most Sicilians know the stories and a performance in an original theatre is accompanied by a lot of vocal audience participation. If you want more enlightenment, you can see examples of the puppets, stage scenery, handbills and other paraphernalia at the Museo delle Marionette (p.81) or the Museo Etnográfico Pitrè (p.84), both in Palermo.

POLICE AND TROUBLE

Mention Sicily to most people and they think of the Mafia. This association is one you'll forget as soon as you set foot on the island. Cosa Nostra is as invisible as it is ineradicable, and the violence that sporadically erupts is almost always an "in-house" affair.

Of more immediate concern is **petty juvenile crime**, mainly in the cities and more prevalent here than elsewhere in Italy, barring Naples. Gangs of *scippatori*, or bag-snatchers, will strike in crowded streets or markets, on foot or on scooters, disappearing before you've had time to react. As well as handbags, they whip wallets, tear off visible jewellery and, if they're really adroit, unstrap watches. You can **minimize the risk** of this happening by being discreet: don't flash anything of value, keep a firm hand on your camera, and carry shoulder bags, as you'll see many Sicilian women do, slung across your body. It's a good idea, too, to entrust money and credit cards to hotel managers. The vast majority of cases occur in Catania and Palermo, and commonly at or on the way to and from the airports. On the whole it's common sense to avoid badly lit areas at night, or deserted inner-city areas by day. Confronted with a robber, your best bet is to submit meekly: it's an excitable situation where panic can lead to violence – though very few tourists see anything of this.

THE POLICE

If the worst happens, you'll be forced to have some dealings with the **police**. In Sicily, as in the rest of Italy, they come in many forms. Most innocuous are the **Polizia Urbana** or town police,

mainly concerned with directing the traffic and punishing parking offences. The **Guardia di Finanza**, often heavily armed and screaming ostentatiously through the cities, are responsible for investigating smuggling, tax evasion and other similar crimes, and the **Poliza Stradale** patrol the autostrada. Most conspicuous are the **Carabinieri** and **Polizia Statale**; no one knows what distinguishes their roles, apart from the fact that the Carabinieri – the ones with the blue uniforms – are organized along military lines and are a branch of the armed forces. They are also the butt of most of the jokes about the police, usually on the "How many Carabinieri does it take to…?" level. Each of the two forces is meant to act as a check and counterbalance to the other: a fine theory, though it results in much time-wasting and rivalry in practice. Hopefully, you won't need to get entangled with either, but **in the event of theft** you'll need to report it at the headquarters of the Polizia Statale, the **Questura**; you'll find their address in the local *Tuttocittà* magazine, and we've included details in the various city listings. The Questura is also where you're supposed to go to obtain a Permesso di Soggiorno **if you're staying** for any length of time, or a **visa extension** if you require one.

In any brush with the authorities, your experience will very much depend on the individuals you're dealing with. Apart from **topless bathing** (permitted, but don't try anything more daring) and **camping rough**, don't expect a soft touch if you've been picked up for any offence, especially if it's **drug**-related: it's not unheard of to be stopped and searched if you're young and carrying a backpack, and there is a large, unseen network of plain-clothes police and informers on the lookout for any seemingly suspicious activity. Drugs are generally frowned upon by everyone above a certain age, and universal hysteria about *la droga*, fuelled by the epidemic of heroin addiction that is a serious problem all over Italy, means that any distinction between the "hard" and "soft" variety has become blurred. Theoretically, everything is illegal over and above the possession of a few grams of cannabis or marijuana "for personal use", though there's no agreed definition of what this means and you can expect at least a fine for this. In general, the south of Italy is more intolerant than the north, but, in any case, if found with suspicious substances you can even be

EMERGENCIES

In an emergency, note the following national emergency telephone numbers:

☎112 for the **police** (Carabinieri).

☎113 for **any emergency** service (Soccorso Pubblico di Emergenze).

☎115 for the **fire brigade** (Vigili del Fuoco).

☎116 for **road assistance** (Soccorso Stradale).

kept in jail for as long as it takes for them to analyse the stuff, draw up reports and wait for the bureaucratic wheels to grind – which can be several weeks, and sometimes months. For the addresses of the nearest **foreign consulates** (UK and US in Palermo; Irish, Australian, New Zealand, Canadian in Naples/Rome), see Palermo's "Listings" section (p.94), though bear in mind that they're unlikely to be very sympathetic or do anything more than put you in touch with a lawyer.

TRAVELLERS WITH DISABILITIES

Although most Sicilians are helpful enough if presented with a specific problem you may have, the island is hardly geared towards accommodating travellers with disabilities.

In the run-down medieval city centres and old villages, few budget hotels have elevators, let alone ones capable of taking a wheelchair, and rooms have not been adapted for use by disabled visitors. Outside, the narrow, cobbled streets, steep inclines, chaotic driving and parking are hardly conducive to a stress-free holiday either. Crossing the street in Palermo is a major undertaking at the best of times, while Taormina, the most popular resort, has great accessibility problems for anyone in a wheelchair.

However, there are things you can do to make your visit to Sicily easier. Contacting one of the **organizations** listed opposite puts you in touch with a wide range of facilities and information that may prove useful. RADAR, for instance, issues a badge enabling disabled drivers to park more freely in Italy. Indeed, if the thought of negotiating your own way around the island proves too daunting, an **organized tour** may be the way to go: it will be more expensive than planning your own trip, but accommodation is usually in higher-category hotels that should have at least some experience of and facilities for disabled travellers, while you'll also have someone on hand who speaks Italian to help smooth the way. You

should also consult the list of specialist Sicilian tour operators on p.7 (Britain) or p.12 (North America): these will at least consider your enquiries and requests, though in the end they (and you) may conclude that certain resorts and destinations are not suitable for your needs.

At all times, it is vital to be honest – with travel agencies, insurance companies and travel companions. Know your limitations and make sure others know them. If you do not use a wheelchair all the time but your walking capabilities are limited, remember that you are likely to need to cover greater distances while travelling (often over rougher terrain and in hotter temperatures) than you are used to. If you use a wheelchair, have it serviced before you go and carry a repair kit.

Read your travel **insurance** small print carefully to make sure that people with a pre-existing medical condition are not excluded. Use your travel agent to make your journey simpler: airline or bus companies can cope better if they are expecting you, with a wheelchair provided at airports and staff primed to help. A **medical certificate** of your fitness to travel, provided by your doctor, is also extremely useful; some airlines or insurance companies may insist on it. Make sure that you have extra supplies of drugs – carried with you if you fly – and a prescription including the generic name in case of emergency. If there's an association representing people with your disability, contact them early in the planning process.

CONTACTS FOR PEOPLE WITH DISABILITIES

AUSTRALIA AND NEW ZEALAND

ACROD, PO Box 60, Curtin, ACT 2605 (☎02/6282 4333); 24 Cabarita Rd, Cabarita (☎02/9743 2699).

Barrier Free Travel, 36 Wheatley St, North Bellingen, NSW 2454 (☎02/6655 1733).

Disabled Persons Assembly, PO Box 10–138, The Terrace, Wellington (☎04/801 9100).

BRITAIN AND IRELAND

Disability Action Group, 2 Annadale Ave, Belfast BT7 3JH (☎01232/491 011). Information on access for disabled travellers abroad.

Holiday Care Service 2nd Floor, Imperial Buildings, Victoria Rd, Horley, Surrey RH6 7PZ (☎01293/774 535). Holiday Care provides information on all aspects of travel.

Irish Wheelchair Association, Blackheath Drive, Clontarf, Dublin 3 (☎01/833 8241). A national voluntary organization working with disabled people and offering related services for holidaymakers.

RADAR, 12 City Forum, 250 City Rd, London EC1V 8AS (☎0171/250 3222; Minicom ☎0171/250 4119). A good source of advice on holidays and travel abroad.

Tripscope, The Courtyard, Evelyn Rd, London W4 5JL (☎ & Minicom 0181/994 9294 or 0345/585641). National telephone information service offering transport and travel advice, free of charge.

USA AND CANADA

AccessAbility Travel, 186 Alewife Brook Parkway, Cambridge, MA 02138-1102 (☎1-800/610-5640; TTY ☎1-800/228-5379). A division of FPT Travel Management Travel Group, with tours to Italy and travel information for disabled travellers.

Access First, 45-A Pleasant St, Malden, MA 02148 (☎1-800/557-2047; TTY ☎617/397-8610) Has a specialty on trips to Italy.

Jewish Rehabilitation Hospital, 3205 Place Alton Goldbloom, Montréal, PQ H7V 1R2 (☎514/688-9550 ext 226). Guidebooks and travel information.

Mobility International USA, PO Box 10767, Eugene, OR 97440 (☎541/343-1284). Information and referral services, access guides, tours and exchange programmes. Annual membership $35 (includes quarterly newsletter).

Society for the Advancement of Travel for the Handicapped (SATH), 347 5th Ave, Suite 610, New York, NY 1006 (☎212/447-284 or 212/447-0027). Non-profit travel-industry referral service that passes queries on to its members as appropriate; allow plenty of time for a response.

Travel Information Service, Moss Rehabilitation Hospital, 1200 West Tabor Rd, Philadelphia, PA 19141 (☎215/456-9603). Telephone information and referral service.

Twin Peaks Press, Box 129, Vancouver, WA 98666 (☎206/694-2462 or 1-800/637-2256). Publisher of the *Directory of Travel Agencies for the Disabled* ($19.95), listing more than 370 agencies worldwide; *Travel for the Disabled* ($14.95); the *Directory of Accessible Van Rentals;* and *Wheelchair Vagabond* ($9.95), loaded with personal tips.

Wheels Up!, ☎1-888/389-4335. Provides discounted airfare, tour and cruise prices for disabled travellers, and also publishes a free monthly newsletter.

SEXUAL HARASSMENT AND WOMEN IN SICILY

Italy has a reputation for sexual harassment of women that is well-known and well founded. Generally, it's worse the further south you go and, though things have improved radically in recent years, some women still count Sicily as the nadir of their experiences in this respect.

If you're travelling on your own, or with another woman, you can expect to be tooted and whistled at in towns every time you step outside the hotel door. You're also likely to attract unwelcome attention in bars, restaurants and on the beach. This persistent pestering does not usually have any violent intent, but it's annoying and frustrating nevertheless. There are a few things you can do to ward it off, though you'll never be able to stop the car horns and wolf whistles. Indifference is often the best policy, or try hurling a few well-chosen examples of the vernacular, like *Lasciátemi in pace* ("Leave me alone"). As a last resort, don't hesitate to approach a policeman. Obviously, travelling with a man cuts out much of the more intense hassle, though even this won't deter the more determined efforts.

Perhaps the best strategy of all for a woman alone in Sicily, where the sanctity of the family is still paramount, is to flaunt a wedding ring. As you might guess from the prominence of the Virgin Mary in all post-Norman churches in Sicily, women are certainly not absent from the Sicilian landscape, it's just that most of them are mothers. The gap between marriage and motherhood is usually very small, while unmarried women are carefully closeted indoors, their only escape being the evening *passeggiata* – needless to say, well chaperoned. Unlike the rest of Italy, in Sicily you won't even see women working in the countryside, another legacy of the Arabs.

Hardly surprising then, that women tourists, radiating freedom and independence, are assumed to be easy numbers, and that Sicilian women themselves have found it so hard to break the rigid rules governing their conduct.* The degree of freedom they enjoy varies from place to place: it's probably greatest in Messina, and smallest in the rural interior. Catania is fairly progressive, while Palermo still labours in the Dark Ages. But the town with the best track record in recent years must be Cefalù, where the women, always known in Sicily for their strong hand in ruling the family, have now extended that role into public life. In this "City of Women", practically all key posts including that of mayor, chiefs of police and magistrates, are held by young women. Other feminist activity centres on Catania, where you'll find ARCI Donna, Via di Giovanni 14, (☎091.301.650): contact them for information on the present women's movement scene.

*The problems women face are closely linked to the problems of Sicilian men, specifically to the traditional adoration of the male child that lingers on into adult life. After all, it is said that Jesus Christ himself was a Sicilian: he thought his father was God, his mother was a virgin, and he lived at home until he was 30.

FINDING WORK

With an unemployment rate of fifteen to twenty percent, higher than most other Italian regions, Sicily offers few opportunities for finding work.

However, all EU citizens are eligible to work, the two main **bureaucratic requirements** for both working and living in Sicily being a *libretto di lavoro* and *permesso di soggiorno*, respectively a work and residence permit, both available from the Questura (see "Police and trouble" p.45). For the first you must have a letter from your prospective employers saying they are prepared to take you on, for the second (which is also necessary if you want to buy a car or have a bank account in Italy) you'll need a passport, passport-sized photos and a lot of patience.

TEACHING

The obvious choice is to **teach English**, for which the demand has expanded enormously in recent years. You can do this in two ways: freelance private lessons, or through a language school.

Private lessons generally pay best, and you can charge up to L20,000–40,000 an hour, though there's scope for bargaining. Advertise in bars, shop windows and local newspapers and, most importantly, get the news around by word of mouth that you're looking for work, emphasizing your excellent background, qualifications and experience. An advantage of private teaching is that you can start at any time of the year (summer especially is a good time because there are schoolchildren and students who have to retake exams in September); the main disadvantage is that it can take weeks to get off the ground, and you need enough money to support you until then. You'll find the best opportunities for this kind of work in the tourist resorts and the bigger towns and cities.

Teaching in schools, you start earning immediately (though some schools can pay months in arrears). Teaching classes usually involves more hours per week, often in the evening, and for less per hour, though the amount you get depends on the school. For the less reputable places, you can get away without any qualifications and a bit of bluff, but you'll need to show a degree and a TEFL certificate for the more professional language schools. For these, it's best to apply in writing from Britain (look for the ads in the *Guardian* and the *Times Educational Supplement* and contact the *Italian Cultural Institute* at 39 Belgrave Square, London SW1X 8NX; ☎0171/235 1461), preferably before the summer, though you can also find openings in September. If you're looking on the spot, sift through the *Yellow Pages* (*Pagine Gialle*) and do the rounds on foot, asking to speak to the *direttore* or his/her secretary; don't bother to try in August when everything is closed. Strictly speaking, you could get by without any knowledge of Italian, but some definitely helps.

The best teaching jobs of all are with a university as a *lettore*, a job requiring fewer hours than the language schools and generally offering a fuller pay packet. Universities need English-language teachers in most faculties and you should write to the individual faculties at the universities of Messina, Catania or Palermo (addressed to "Ufficio di Personale"). That said, success in obtaining a university teaching job usually depends on you knowing someone already in place – as with so many things in Sicily.

OTHER OPTIONS

If teaching's not up your street, there's the possibility of **courier work** in the summer, especially around the resorts of Cefalù and Taormina. These are the only places where you might find **bar/restaurant work** too – not the most lucrative of jobs, though you should make enough to keep you in Sicily over the summer. You'll have to ask around for both types of work, and a knowledge of Italian is essential.

WORK, STUDY AND VOLUNTEER PROGRAMMES

BRITAIN

Central Bureau for Educational Visits and Exchanges, 10 Spring Gardens, London SW1A 2BN (☎0171/389 4004). The Central Bureau administers a number of exchanges, including LINGUA (language training opportunities).

Commission of the European Communities, 8 Storey's Gate, London SW1P 3AT (☎0171/973 1992). The information office produces a series of fact sheets on issues relating to work and study in Europe.

European Programme, The Prince's Trust, 18 Park Square East, London NW1 (☎0171/405 5799). Offers a number of "Go and See" grants to young people between 18 and with ideas for European partnerships.

ITALY

Ministero Lavoro e Previdenza Sociale, Divisone 11, Via Flavia 6, 1-00187 Roma. Job placement information.

Note: there is also *The Informer*, an expatriate magazine containing current vacancy listings; available from Buro Service, Via de Imtigli 2, 20020 Arese, Milan.

USA

(Most universities have semester abroad programmes to certain countries; the following are independent organizations that run programs in many countries, including Italy.)

American Institute for Foreign Study, 102 Greenwich Ave, Greenwich, CT 06830 (☎1-800/727-AIFS). Language study and cultural immersion for the summer or school year.

Council on International Educational Exchange (CIEE), 205 E 42nd St, New York, NY 10017 (☎212/661-1414). The non-profit parent organization of Council Travel and Council Charter, CIEE runs volunteer programmes in Italy. It also publishes two excellent resource books, *Work, Study, Travel Abroad* and *Volunteer! The Comprehensive Guide to Voluntary Service in the US and Abroad*.

Institute of International Education, 809 UN Plaza, New York, NY 10017 (recorded information only, ☎212/984-5413). Contact IIE's Publications Service to order its annual study abroad directory.

InterExchange Program, 161 6th Ave, New York, NY 10013 (☎212/924-0446). Information on work programmes and au pair opportunities.

Italian Cultural Institute, 686 Park Ave, New York, NY 10021 (☎212/879-4242); Suite 104, 1717 Massachusetts Ave NW, Washington, DC 20036 (☎202/387-5161). Publishes a directory of study courses for English-speaking students and helps with job openings.

Office of Overseas Schools, US Department of State, Room 245, SA-29, Washington, DC 20522-2902 (☎703/875-7800). Produces a list of schools for potential EFL teachers to contact.

Volunteers for Peace, 43 Tiffany Rd, Belmont, VT 05730 (☎802/259-2759). Non-profit organization with links to a huge international network of "workcamps", two- to four-week programmes that bring volunteers together from many countries to carry out community projects. Most workcamps are in summer, with registration in April–May. Annual directory costs $15.

DIRECTORY

ADDRESSES Usually written as the street name followed by the number – eg Via Roma 69. *Interno* refers to the flat number – eg *interno* 5 (often abbreviated as *int.*). Always use postal codes.

AIRPORT TAX Around L42,000, usually included in the price of your ticket.

BARGAINING Not really on in shops and restaurants, though you'll find you can get a "special price" for some rooms and cheap hotels if you're staying a few days; and that things like boat/bike rental and guided tours (especially out of season) are negotiable. In markets, you'll be taken for an imbecile if you don't haggle for everything except food. Ask for *uno sconto* ("a discount").

BEACHES You'll have to pay for access to most of the better beaches (referred to as lidos), as well as a few thousand lire to hire a sun bed and shade and use the showers all day. Elsewhere, on the offshore islands and along the south coast, they're free though not always clean. During winter most beaches look like dumps; it's not worth anyone's while to clean them until the season starts at Easter. On the other hand any beach that's remotely inaccessible should remain in a fairly pristine state. Some beaches, for instance along the north coast, are prone to invasions of jellyfish (*meduse*) from time to time. These are not dangerous, but can cause quite a sting, so take local advice.

CAMPING GAZ Easy enough to buy for the small portable camping stoves, either from hardware stores (*ferramenta*) or camping/sports shops. You can't carry canisters on aeroplanes.

CHILDREN Children are revered in Sicily and will be made a fuss of in the street, welcomed and catered for in bars and restaurants (though be warned that there's no such thing as a smoke-free environment, with chain-smoking the norm). Hotels normally charge around thirty percent extra to put a bed or cot in your room, though kids pay less on trains (see p.24). The only hazards when travelling with children in Sicily in summer are the heat and sun. Sun block can be bought in any chemist, and bonnets or straw hats in most markets. Take advantage of the less intense periods – mornings and evenings – for travelling, and use the quiet of siesta time to recover flagging energy. The rhythms of the southern climate soon modify established patterns, and you'll find it more natural carrying on later into the night, past normal bedtimes. In summer, it's not unusual to see Sicilian children out at midnight, and not looking much the worse for it.

CIGARETTES The state monopoly brand – MS, jokingly referred to as Morte Sicura (Certain Death) – are the most widely smoked cigarettes, strong and aromatic and selling for around L4200 for a pack of twenty. Younger people tend to smoke imported brands these days – all of which are slightly more expensive, at around L5200 per pack. You buy cigarettes from *tabacchi* (see overleaf).

CONSULATES Palermo holds consular agencies for British, US, Dutch, German, French, Belgian and Austrian citizens, and for people of all the Scandinavian countries. Irish, Australian, Canadian and New Zealand consulates are in Naples or Rome (see p.94).

DEPARTMENT STORES There are two main nationwide chains, Upim and Standa. Neither is particularly posh, and they're good places to stock up on toiletries and other basic supplies; branches of both stores sometimes have a food hall attached.

ELECTRICITY The supply is 220V, though anything requiring 240V will work. Most plugs are two round pins; a travel plug is useful.

ENTRANCE FEES The entrance fee for museums and sites is usually L4000–8000, although under-18s and over-60s get in free on production of documentary proof of age. Some sites, churches and monasteries, and Palermo's oratories, are nominally free to get in. But there will be a custodian around to open up and show you around, and it's expected that you hand over a tip, say L1000–2000 per person.

GAY LIFE There's not much of a gay scene in Sicily; no gay resorts and few specifically gay bars and clubs. In this respect, Sicily has much in common with the rest of the south of Italy, where attitudes towards homosexuality (male and female) are generally much less tolerant than in Rome or the industrial north. That said, there's no legally sanctioned discrimination against gays and what gay groups there are in Italy work at getting the public to accept and understand homosexuality. Also, it's worth noting that physical contact between men is fairly common in Sicily, on the level of linking arms and kissing cheeks at greetings and farewells – though an overt display of anything remotely ambiguous is likely to be met with hostility. The only contact addresses in Sicily of ARCI Gay – part of the cultural wing of the ex-Communist Party's youth section – are in Palermo, at Via Genova 9 (☎091.335.668), and in Catania, as Open Mind, at Via Gargano 33 (☎095.532.685).

LAUNDRY Coin-operated laundries are very rare, though see the "Listings" section for Palermo (p.95). More common is a *lavanderia*, a service-wash laundry, but this will be relatively expensive. Although you can usually get away with it, washing clothes in your hotel room can cause an international incident – simply because the room's plumbing often can't cope with all the water. It's better to ask if there's somewhere you can wash your clothes.

PUBLIC TOILETS Usually found in bars and restaurants and you'll generally be allowed to use them whether you're eating and drinking or not. You'll find most places to be very clean, though it's advisable not to be without your own toilet roll.

RECEIPTS Shops, bars and restaurants are all legally obliged to provide you with a receipt (*una ricevuta*). Don't be surprised when it's thrust upon you, as they – and indeed you – can be fined if you don't take it.

TABACCHI You buy cigarettes (and tobacco) in shops called *tabacchi*, recognizable by a sign displaying a white "T" on a black or blue background. Historically, tobacco and salt were both state monopolies, sold only in *tabacchi* – salt's no longer deemed so important, but cigarettes are still hard to track down anywhere else. You'll be able to buy sweets, stationery and stamps in *tabacchi* too.

TIME Sicily (and Italy) is always one hour ahead of Britain, except for one week at the end of September when the time is the same. Italy is seven hours ahead of Eastern Standard Time and ten hours ahead of Pacific Time.

WAR CEMETERIES World War II saw several fiercely contested battles on Sicilian soil; information and a list of Allied cemeteries is available from the Commonwealth War Graves Commission, 2 Marlow Rd, Maidenhead SL6 7DX (☎01628/ 34221).

WATER Safe to drink everywhere, though bottled mineral water always tastes more pleasant.

THINGS TO TAKE

A universal electric plug adaptor and a universal sink plug.

A flashlight.

Earplugs (for street noise in hotel rooms).

High-factor sun block.

Mosquito repellent and antiseptic cream.

A pocket alarm clock (for those early-morning departures).

An inflatable neck rest, for long journeys.

A multipurpose penknife.

A needle and some thread.

A towel (for cheaper hotels).

A water bottle for visiting hot, exposed archeological sites.

Photographic film – but wait until you get home to have it developed, as it costs around twice as much in Sicily.

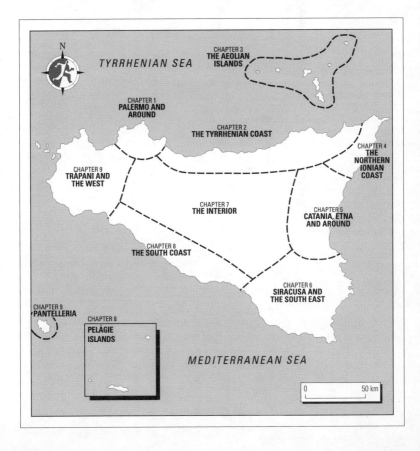

CHAPTER ONE

PALERMO AND AROUND

U nmistakably the capital of Sicily, **Palermo** is fast, brash, loud and exciting. Hub of the island since the ninth century AD, it borrows heavily from the past for its present-day look, the city showing a typically Sicilian fusion of foreign art, architecture, culture and lifestyle. In the narrow streets of Palermo's old town, elegant Baroque and Norman monuments exist cheek by jowl with Arabic cupolas, Byzantine street markets swamp the medieval warrens, and the latest Milanese fashions sit in shops squeezed between Renaissance churches and Spanish *palazzi*. And, ricocheting off every wall, the endless roar of traffic adds to the confusion. The city is probably the noisiest in Italy, and there's pollution in the air, too – a pall of yellow smog hangs over Palermo, visible on bad days from the sea or from the mountains behind.

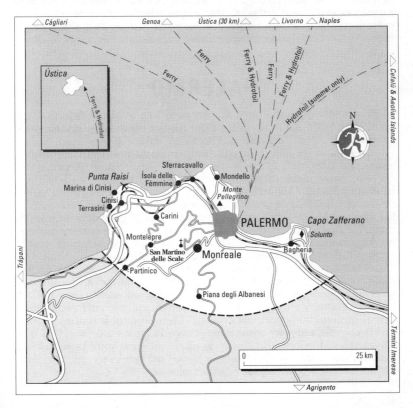

It may not be the healthiest place in the world, but it's certainly not dull, with the oppressive summer climate and frenetic street scenes redolent of North Africa or the Near East. Indeed, there's little that's strictly European about Palermo, and its geographical isolation has forced the city to forge its own identity, distinct enough to demand that you devote a fair proportion of your stay in Sicily to the capital and its environs. Easily the most populous centre on the island, with around 700,000 inhabitants, it demands at least a week of your time. Palermo has some of the island's most intriguing sights; also some of its best food and markets, cheapest hotels, and easy access to one of Sicily's finest beaches, at **Mondello**. The other obvious quick retreat from Palermo's bustle is to the heights of **Monte Pellegrino**, the mountain that looms beyond the city to the north.

More substantial targets lie just outside the city's boundaries, most warranting a day-trip. If your enthusiasm has been fired by the city's great Norman heritage, you shouldn't miss the medieval cathedral of **Monreale** and its celebrated mosaics. The **Golfo di Carini**, the curving bay to the west of Palermo, sports a couple of low-key holiday resorts, all with beaches of varying attractiveness and local popularity. Or, heading east along the coast, you can spend an unhurried afternoon at **Bagheria** and its *palazzi*, and take in the nearby Roman site at **Solunto**. Further afield, around 25km south of Palermo, **Piana degli Albanesi** survives as an Albanian Orthodox enclave in a stridently Catholic island. Further out is the offshore island of **Ústica**, possible to visit in a day, though you're likely to want to stay much longer, given the natural attractions of this craggy, black, volcanic slab.

PALERMO

In its own wide bay underneath the limestone bulk of Monte Pellegrino, and fronting the broad and fertile Conca d'Oro (Golden Shell) valley, **PALERMO** is stupendously sited. Originally a Phoenician colony, it was taken by the Carthaginians in the fifth century BC and became an important Punic bulwark against the Greek influence elsewhere on the island. Named Panormus (All Harbour), its mercantile attractions were obvious, and it remained in Carthaginian hands until 254 BC. Long considered a prize worth capturing, the city then fell to the Romans, despite a desperate counter-siege by Hamilcar Barca, directed from the slopes of Monte Pellegrino. Yet Palermo's most glorious days were still to come. The **Arabs** captured the city in 831 AD and, under them and (two centuries later) the **Normans**, Palermo flowered as Europe's greatest metropolis – famed for the wealth of its court, and unrivalled as a centre of learning.

This century, by way of contrast, has been one of social and economic decline. Allied bombs during **World War II** destroyed much of the port area, and turned parts of the medieval town into a ramshackle demolition site – a state of affairs that, half a century on, has still not been resolved, and much of Palermo nowadays seems ominously poor and decaying. Unemployment is endemic, the old port largely idle, and **petty crime** commonplace. Palermo's underworld exists on many levels and, in a city that absorbs its villains with ease, you'd be well advised to take all due precautions – avoiding the market and back-street areas after dark, and not flashing around bulging wallets or cameras.

THE MAFIA IN PALERMO

The **Mafia** problem, the most glaring symptom of decay in Palermo, is intimately connected with the welfare of the city. For years it has been openly acknowledged that a large part of the funds pouring in from Rome and the European Union, ostensibly to redevelop the city centre, are unaccounted for – channelled to dubious businessmen, or simply raked off by Mafia leaders. The subtle control exerted by the Mafia is traditionally referred to only obliquely, though it periodically erupts into the news. Mafia issues have had a higher profile than usual in recent years, following the intensification of the struggle to reassert the state's authority in the wake of a number of assassinations of prestigious figures – most notably those of anti-Mafia investigators Falcone and Borsellino in 1992 (see "The Mafia in Sicily", p.392). Since then, the arrest of leading Mafia figures – starting with the arrest of the *capo dei capi* Salvatore Riina in 1993 – has seen the tide turning against Cosa Nostra, helped by the testimony of a succession of informers.

However, the problem is deeply rooted and unlikely to disappear completely, despite the courageous efforts of various individuals. Prominent among these is **Leoluca Orlando**, the mayor of Palermo, who has attempted to combat corruption at municipal level by removing companies suspected of links with organized crime from the tenders list for new contracts. Despite reversals, including the disavowal of Orlando by his own Christian Democrat party, Orlando continued his fight at a national level, at the head of his own Rete (Network) party, and now finds himself once more as city mayor, polling consistently highly in recent elections.

Fortunately, the Mafia has little relevance for casual travellers, and the closest you'll get to it is through the screaming headlines of local newspapers. Follow the rules and you'll probably avoid having your bag snatched by Vespa-borne delinquents, many of whom are destined to be sucked into the lower ranks of the big Mafia clans.

Most areas are never anything less than perfectly safe in the daytime, however, and nothing should put you off getting around the city. There are notable relics extant from the ninth to the twelfth centuries, Palermo in its prime, but it's the rebuilding of the sixteenth and seventeenth centuries that shaped the city as it appears today; essentially a straightforward street-grid confused by the memory of an Eastern past and gouged by World War II bombs. Traditionally Palermo has been a city of rich **churches**, endowed by the island's ruling families and wealthy monastic orders, and they're still an obvious draw for visitors, from the hybrid **Cattedrale** and the nearby mosaic-decorated **Cappella Palatina**, tucked inside the Royal Palace, to the glorious Norman foundations of **La Martorana** and **San Giovanni degli Eremiti**. And that's not counting the Baroque candidates, like **San Giuseppe dei Teatini** and **Santa Caterina**. Really, though, to see Palermo in terms of an architectural tour would be to ignore much: three significant **museums** – inspiring collections of art, archeology and ethnography – splendid markets, back-street puppet theatres, and a wealth of excellent restaurants.

Arrival

Palermo's Falcone Borsellino **airport** is at Punta Raisi (international flight information on ☎091.591.275), 31km west of the city. From just outside, regular Prestia & Comandè buses (1–2 hourly, a 45min journey; 5am–last flight

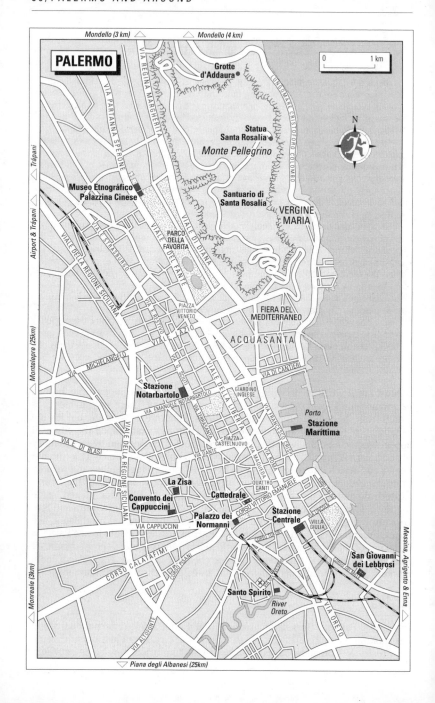

arrival) run right into the centre, stopping in front of the Politeama Garibaldi theatre on Piazza Ruggero Séttimo, and ending at Stazione Centrale, in front of the *Albergo Elena*; buy your ticket (L6500) on the bus. Note that the last departure on the return journey is at 10.30pm. Taxi fares for the same trip run to around L65,000 per car – be wary of "special offers", which are considerably less than this. Note that Catania rather than Palermo is the island's main airport, though facilities here are greatly improved since the new terminal was opened in 1994, and there are bars and money exchange facilities (daily 7.50am–1.20pm & 2.30–8pm, plus cash machines), and a **tourist office** (Mon–Sat 8am–midnight, Sun 8am–8pm; ☎091.591.698). For details of car rental at the airport, see "Listings", p.94.

Trains all arrive at and leave from Stazione Centrale (☎147.888.088) in Piazza Giulio Césare, at the southern end of Via Roma. Some (from Trápani/Álcamo) stop first in the northwest of the city at Stazione Notarbártolo; sit tight and you'll end up at Stazione Centrale.

Local, provincial and long-distance, island-wide **buses** operate from a variety of terminals all over the city, of which there are full details in the box below. Handily, though, the **main bus arrivals** are in the streets around the train station – mainly Via Balsamo and Via Gregorio – while other major termini are Piazza Marina, down by the old port, and Piazza Lolli, off Via Dante from Piazza Castelnuovo – both mostly used by AST services to and from Palermo province.

Palermo is a grand place in which to arrive by sea. All **ferry** services – from Ústica, Genova, Livorno, Naples and Cágliari (in Sardinia) – dock at the **Stazione Maríttima**, just off Via Francesco Crispi, from where it's a ten-minute walk (straight up Via Emerico Amari) to Piazza Castelnuovo and the modern city centre. There are also regular **hydrofoil** connections with Ústica and occasional summer hydrofoil services to and from Cefalù and the Aeolian Islands, again docking at the Stazione Maríttima. "Listings" has all the relevant ticket-office details.

PALERMO'S BUS TERMINALS

AST, Piazza Lolli (☎091.688.2906): for Bagheria, Capaci, Carini, Partinico; Piazza Marina (☎091.688.2906): for Castelbuono, Corleone, Lercara Friddi, Módica, Montelepre, Ragusa, Siracusa, Términi Imerese.

Cuffaro, Via P. Balsamo 13 (☎091.616.1510): for Agrigento.

Gallo, Via P. Balsamo 16 (☎091.617.1141): for Sciacca.

Prestia & Comandè, Stazione Centrale (☎091.580.457): for the airport and Piana degli Albanesi.

Randazzo, Via P. Balsamo (☎091.814.8235): for Cáccamo, Piazza Armerina, Polizzi Generosa, Santa Flavia.

Russo, Piazza Marina (☎0924.31.364): for Balestrate, Castellammare del Golfo, San Vito Lo Capo.

SAIS, Via P. Balsamo 16 (☎091.616.6028): for Caltanissetta, Catania, Cefalù, Enna, Gangi, Gela, Messina, Noto, Petralia, Rome, Piazza Armerina, Siracusa, Términi Imerese.

Salemi, Via R. Gregorio 44 (☎091.617.5411): for Castelvetrano, Marsala, Mazara del Vallo, Salemi.

Segesta, Via P. Balsamo 26 (☎091.616.7919): for Álcamo, Messina, Partinico, Trápani, Rome.

Stassi, Salita Partanna, off Piazza Marina (☎091.617.5348): for Corleone.

Verga, Piazza Verdi ☎091.418.021: for San Martino delle Scale.

Driving and parking

Driving into the city can be traumatic, something to avoid if you possibly can. Directional signs are confusing and the traffic unforgiving of first-time-around foreigners. Coming in on the A20 (from Cefalù), turn right at the first roundabout and keep straight on to reach Stazione Centrale. Otherwise, follow anything that reads "Centro" and aim/ask for Piazza Castelnuovo – around which is the best place to leave your vehicle.

Finding a **parking space** can be a real problem at any time, apart from the early morning or late evening, though you might get lucky if you drive around for long enough. If someone in a peaked cap shows you to a space, they're a contracted attendant to whom you give L1000 for every hour parked; there are car parks like this at Piazza Bellini, close to the Quattro Canti; at Piazza Giuseppe Verdi; and Piazza Marina. There are always **garages** scattered about town, a wise option if you have to leave your car in Palermo's old town area overnight; there's a list of some of the most central ones on p.95. *Never* leave anything of value, including the radio, visible in the car, and retract your aerial if you can or someone will probably snap it off.

Leaving the city by car you need Via Oreto, behind Stazione Centrale, for the Palermo–Catania (A20) and Palermo–Messina (A19) autostradas; Corso Vittorio Emanuele (westbound) for Monreale; and Viale della Libertà (northbound) for the airport and Trápani.

Orientation: some pointers

Much of the old medieval street system survives in Palermo, particularly in the area just north of the train station, which makes losing your way a distinct possibility if you don't take note of the major landmarks and thoroughfares – though our maps should be sufficient for most purposes.

On the ground the **medieval town** isn't as difficult to negotiate as it looks. It's quartered by two distinctive straight roads: **Corso Vittorio Emanuele**, which runs from the old harbour, La Cala, southwest to both the Palazzo dei Normanni and the Cattedrale; and, crossing it, **Via Maqueda**, which starts just to the west of the train station and runs northwest – both streets dating from the reconstruction of the sixteenth century. The crossroads are known as the **Quattro Canti**, the centre (if anywhere is) of the medieval town area. Parallel to Via Maqueda, and running north from Piazza Giulio Césare, **Via Roma** was a much later addition, the two parallel streets now carrying most of central Palermo's traffic. In between, and on either side of these streets, you'll find nearly all the major sights, churches and buildings. And, if you keep surfacing from the labyrinthine alleys onto the main streets, you shouldn't go too far wrong. Further north everything becomes much clearer, as most of the **modern city** is a frustrated grid-plan of large proportions. Beyond Corso Vittorio Emanuele, Via Maqueda (and its continuation, Via Ruggero Séttimo) and Via Roma strike off for the double squares of **Piazza Ruggero Séttimo** and **Piazza Castelnuovo** – a hefty 25- to 30-minute walk if you've come from the train station. East of here, down at the water, is the Stazione Maríttima, while, further north still, Palermo assumes a more European mantle. **Viale della Libertà** is the central spine of a staid, grid network of shops, apartments and office blocks, which runs right the way to the southern end of the **Parco della Favorita**.

Information and city transport

You'll be able to pick up **information** and free **maps** from small tourist offices at the **airport** (Mon–Sat 8am–midnight, Sun 8am–8pm; ☎091.591.698) and the **Stazione Centrale** (Mon–Fri 8.30am–2pm & 3–6pm, Sat 8.30am–2pm; ☎091.616.5914) opposite the main snack bar.

Palermo's **main tourist office**, however, lies in the heart of the city – on the ground floor at Piazza Castelnuovo 34, hidden behind the trees across from the bandstand (Mon–Fri 8.30am–2pm & 2.30–6pm, Sat 8.30am–2pm; ☎091.583.847 or 091.605.8351). If you haven't already got one you can get a big free map of the city and province from here (also including maps of Ústica, Mondello and Cefalù); and a booklet (*Palermo Hotels*) containing full accommodation lists and prices for hotels, campsites, rooms to rent and mountain hostels throughout Palermo province and beyond. There's also a toll-free **phone line** (☎167.234.169), with English-speaking operators, for tourist information in the city (remember to insert your coins or card in a public box – no money will be debited).

For more complete **city listings** and a rundown of **what's on where**, pick up a copy of the free monthly *Palermo & Provincia Live*, which lists useful addresses and telephone numbers, museum times, transport links, and cultural events in and around the city; it's available from tourist offices,where you may also find the weekly *News: Informazioni Turistiche*, dedicated to arts and entertainments. The local edition of the daily *Il Giornale della Sicilia*, available from newsstands all over the city, also details forthcoming events and transport timetables.

City transport

While Palermo is very much a city in which to **walk** when you can, you'll find getting around exclusively on foot exhausting and impractical, certainly for the peripheral sights. The **city buses**, run by AMAT (☎091.690.2690) are easy to use, covering every corner of Palermo and stretching out to Monreale, Mondello and beyond. There's a flat fare of L1500, the ticket valid on any bus or buses for one hour, or buy a L5000 ticket valid all day; **tickets** are available from AMAT's glass kiosks (outside Stazione Centrale or on Piazza Ruggero Séttimo), in *tabacchi*, or wherever else you see the sign "Véndita Biglietti AMAT" – validate one in the machine at the back of the bus at the start of your journey (on just the first ride with an all-day ticket). **Fare dodging** – seemingly commonplace – is punishable by L50,000 spot fines from roving gangs of inspectors who board buses at random. Don't think that tourists are exempt, though in most cases you'll just be made to buy a ticket; it has been known on rush-hour buses that *every* person aboard has had to cough up. Note that if you do buy a ticket on board, or from a kiosk on a Sunday, there's a L500 surcharge.

As far as **routes** go, the box on p.62 details the most useful ones. Note that some buses have the same number as others but run on different routes: these are distinguished either by the colour of the bus number (usually black but sometimes red), or by a stripe (or bar) through the number. Elsewhere, the text details numbers and routes where relevant. Other useful buses are the two circular **minibus** services, Linea Gialla and Linea Rossa (Yellow Line and Red Line; Mon–Sat 8am–7.30pm, Sun 8am–1.30pm), which regularly ply the most-frequented tourist

USEFUL BUS ROUTES

Circular minibuses

Linea Gialla to Stazione Centrale, Orto Botanico, La Kalsa, Via Alloro, Quattro Canti, Ballarò, Corso Tukory.

Linea Rossa to Piazza Marina, Via Alloro, Quattro Canti, Cattedrale, Via Papireto, Capo, Via Maqueda, Vucciria, La Cala.

From the ranks outside Stazione Centrale

#101 and #102 to Piazza Ruggero Séttimo/Piazza Castelnuovo.

#109 to Piazza dell'Indipendenza (for Palazzo dei Normanni and buses to Monreale).
#139 to Piazza Marina/Corso Vittorio Emanuele and Stazione Maríttima.

From Corso Vittorio Emanuele
#104 and #105 run along the Corso.

From Via Roma
#101 to Via Príncipe di Belmonte and Giardino Inglese.

From Politeama/Piazza Ruggero Séttimo
#806 to Parco della Favorita/Mondello.

TAXI RANKS

There are **taxi ranks** at:
- Piazza Giulio Césare (☎091.616.2001)
- Piazza Ruggero Séttimo (☎091.588.133)
- Piazza Giuseppe Verdi (☎091.320.184)
- Piazza Indipendenza (☎091.422.703)
- Piazza San Domenico (☎091.588.876)
- Piazza Matteotti (☎091.303.237)
- Via Malta (☎091.231.000)
- Via Roma (☎091.581.965)

destinations, including the markets. Tickets for these cost L1000 for a day's travel, available from the AMAT ticket kiosks. Other city buses run from about 6am up until around 11pm, when **night services** take over on all the main routes – generally once an hour, even out as far as Mondello. You'll find main **city bus ranks** outside the train station, in Piazza Castelnuovo/Piazza Ruggero Séttimo, along Corso Vittorio Emanuele, and along the southern stretch of Viale della Libertà.

Taxis and other transport
Other forms of city transport are few and far between. Don't be afraid of hailing a **taxi** (ranks outside the train station and in other main squares; see box above), a safe way to get around at night. They're relatively cheap: L6000 on the clock, L4000 for the first kilometre and L1300 for each kilometre after that; just make sure the meter is switched on, or for long distances (back from Mondello, say) agree on a price beforehand. As well as the numbers above, and if you want to take a taxi anywhere outside the central area or at night, call Autoradio Taxi (☎091.513.311) or Radio Taxi Trinacria (☎091.225.455).

Taking a horse-drawn carriage, a **carrozza**, would be a rather swanky way to see the city. They loiter outside Stazione Centrale: get a group together and, again, agree on a price before setting off. Don't consider getting around the city **under your own steam**: hiring a car just to see congested Palermo would be extremely misguided, and in any case one short afternoon driving here could take years off your life. Likewise, biking is for the bravest of hearts. However, we have provided addresses in "Listings" (see p.94), should you want to have your own transport once you're out of the city.

Accommodation

Palermo is the easiest Sicilian city in which to find good, cheap **accommodation**. Prices here are the lowest on the island, though in high season (July & Aug), and especially around the time of Palermo's annual festival (July 11–15), you'd be wise not to leave it too late in the day if you want the better rooms; before noon is best, or ring ahead and reserve (note that few of the cheaper places will speak English). Otherwise, just turn up and check out the options.

Hotels

Nearly all the reasonable budget **hotels** in Palermo – known variously as *alberghi*, *pensioni* or *locande* – are to be found on and around the southern ends of Via Maqueda and Via Roma, roughly in the area between Stazione Centrale and Corso Vittorio Emanuele. Here, there are often several separate places in the same block, usually cheaper the higher the floor. Beyond the corso the streets begin to widen out and the hotels get more expensive, though there are some notable exceptions. Our lists below are divided geographically and listed alphabetically, with a final section on top-of-the-range luxury hotels that are scattered across the wider city. See the **hotels map** to determine exactly where your choice of hotel is.

Something to note is that, although there are a couple of inexpensive places in and around **La Kalsa** (p.67), it's largely an area to avoid at night. Also, **women** might feel safer if they stay in hotels on the main roads, rather than side streets – though all the places listed should be safe enough, unless otherwise stated. If you're driving, **parking** near your hotel can be a real problem: we've detailed places where it's possible and it's worth trying those first.

Via Maqueda and around

Alessandra, Via Divisi 99 (☎091.616.7009, fax 091.616.5180). Modern rooms with TV and telephone in a well-maintained building; a safe choice for single women. It's at the corner with Via Maqueda, which makes the rooms overlooking that street noisy. ②.

Cortese, Via Scarparelli 16 (☎ & fax 091.331.722). The advantages of this hotel (which partly occupies the one-time home of famous eighteenth-century fraudster "Count" Cagliostro) are friendly management, clean rooms, some with views over the noisy Ballarò market (those with bathrooms fall into the next price category), and parking space outside. However, the area is not particularly salubrious: the hotel is reached down unlit side streets that can be rather intimidating at night. Follow the signs from Via Maqueda that point left down Via dell'Università. ①.

ACCOMMODATION PRICE CODES

These represent the **cheapest available double room in high season**, usually – but not always – without en-suite bathroom or shower. Out of season, you'll often be able to negotiate a lower price than those suggested here. For more information about hotels and room prices, see p.27. The categories are:

① under L60,000	④ L120,000–150,000	⑦ L250,000–300,000
② L60,000–90,000	⑤ L150,000–200,000	⑧ over L300,000
③ L90,000–120,000	⑥ L200,000–250,000	

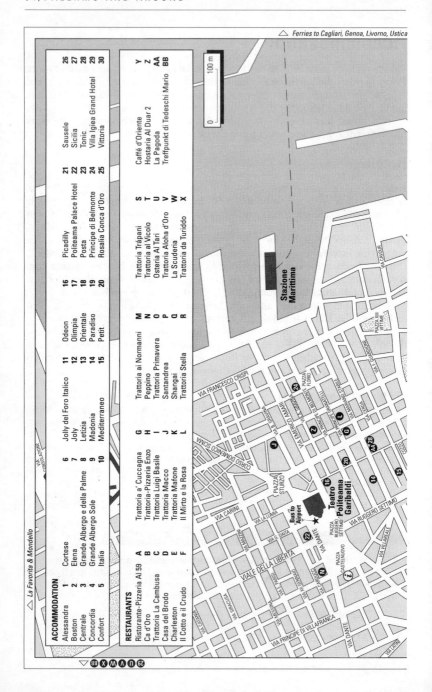

Ferries to Cagliari, Genoa, Livorno, Ustica

ACCOMMODATION

Alessandra	1	Cortese	6	Jolly del Foro Italico	11	Odeon	16	Picadilly	21	Sausele	26
Boston	2	Elena	7	Joly	12	Olimpia	17	Politeama Palace Hotel	22	Sicilia	27
Centrale	3	Grande Albergo e della Palme	8	Letizia	13	Orientale	18	Posta	23	Tonic	28
Concordia	4	Grande Albergo Sole	9	Madonia	14	Paradiso	19	Principe di Belmonte	24	Villa Igiea Grand Hotel	29
Confort	5	Italia	10	Mediterraneo	15	Petit	20	Rosalia Conca d'Oro	25	Vittoria	30

RESTAURANTS

Ristorante-Pizzeria Al 59	A	Trattoria a' Cuccagna	G	Trattoria ai Normanni	M	Trattoria Trapani	S	Caffè d'Oriente	Y
Ca d'Oro	B	Trattoria-Pizzeria Enzo	H	Peppino	N	Trattoria al Vicolo	T	Hostaria Al Duar 2	Z
Trattoria La Cambusa	C	Trattoria Luigi Basile	I	Trattoria Primavera	O	Osteria Al Tari	U	La Pagoda	AA
Casa del Brodo	D	Trattoria Macco	J	Santandrea	P	Trattoria Aloha d'Oro	V	Treffpunkt di Tedeschi Mario	BB
Charleston	E	Trattoria Mafone	K	Shangai	Q	La Scuderia	W		
Il Cotto e il Crudo	F	Il Mirto e la Rosa	L	Trattoria Stella	R	Trattoria da Turiddo	X		

La Favorita & Mondello

La Favorita & Mondello

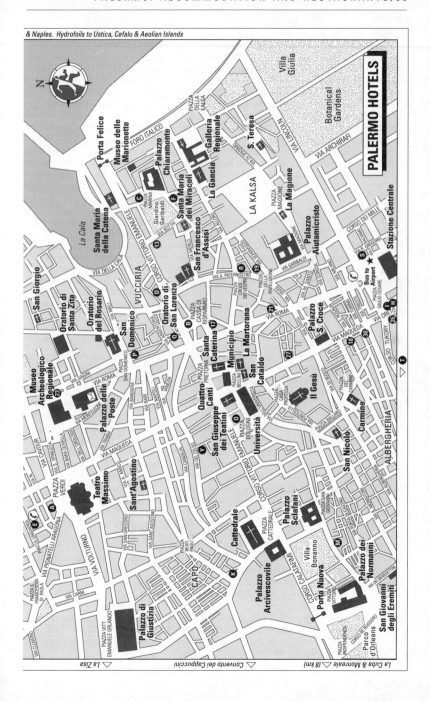

& Naples. Hydrofoils to Ustica, Cefalu & Aeolian Islands

PALERMO HOTELS

Villa Giulia

Botanical Gardens

Porta Felice
Museo delle Marionette
Palazzo Chiaramonte
PIAZZA DELLA KALSA
FORO ITALICO
Galleria Regionale
S. Teresa
Santa Maria dei Miracoli
La Gancia
Santa Maria della Catena
La Cala
San Francesco d'Assisi
LA KALSA
La Magione
PIAZZA MAGIONE
Palazzo Aiutamicristo
San Giorgio
Oratorio di Santa Zita
Oratorio del Rosario
San Domenico
VUCCIRIA
Oratorio di San Lorenzo
San Matteo
Stazione Centrale
Bus to Airport
PIAZZA GIULIO CESARE
Museo Archeologico Regionale
Palazzo delle Poste
PIAZZA CASSA DI RISPARMIO
Municipio
Santa Caterina
La Martorana
Palazzo S. Croce
San Cataldo
Quattro Canti
Teatro Massimo
PIAZZA VERDI
Sant'Agostino
San Giuseppe dei Teatini
Università
Il Gesù
Carmine
PIAZZA BALLARÒ
San Nicolò
ALBERGHERIA
Cattedrale
PIAZZA CATTEDRALE
Palazzo Sclafani
Villa Bonanno
Palazzo Arcivescovile
Porta Nuova
CAPO
Palazzo di Giustizia
PIAZZA VITT. EMANUELE ORLANDO
Palazzo dei Normanni
San Giovanni degli Eremiti
Parco d'Orleans

△ La Zisa △ Convento dei Cappuccini La Cuba & Monreale △ (8 km)

Grande Albergo Sole, Corso Vittorio Emanuele 291 (☎091.581.811, fax 091.611.0182). One of the medieval town's most alluring hotels and ideal for an end-of-holiday binge, since prices aren't too outrageous: it's bang next door to Piazza Pretoria and not far from the Cattedrale, and has a roof terrace. Rooms without a bath will save you around L75,000 and rates drop by fifty percent in low season. Prices include breakfast. Singles are available too. ④.

Mediterraneo, Via Rosolino Pilo 43 (☎091.581.133, fax 091.586.974). An uninspiring hotel, the large air-conditioned lobby furnished in 1970s style, it is nonetheless a useful base in a safe neighbourhood. Lifts ascend five storeys to rather boxy rooms without much of a view, though well equipped, with TV and telephone. Restaurant and bar; garage also available. ⑤.

Orientale, Via Maqueda 26 (☎091.616.5727). One of the most atmospheric hotels in the old town, an eighteenth-century *palazzo* with a marble courtyard and columns, and two cavernous double rooms (nos. 6 and 7, with bath) complete with a long balcony overlooking Via Maqueda. Other rooms are plain, and look down onto the courtyard and the Albergheria market. Recommended, though it can be grimy in corners and freezing in winter. No credit cards. ①.

Sausele, Via V. Errante 12 (☎091.616.1308, fax 091.616.7525). Close to the station, clean and secure, this Swiss-managed hotel represents good value and has lots of rooms, though it can be noisy at night. Take the first right off Via Oreto, south of the station. ③.

Sicilia, Via Divisi 99 (☎ & fax 091.616.8460). The spacious marble entrance that this hotel shares with the *Alessandra* is only slightly misleading: most rooms have shower and TV, though the ones overlooking Via Maqueda can be noisy. The hotel is decently furnished and pleasantly run; a good choice for women. Rooms with facilities are in the next category up. There's guarded parking available nearby (L15,000 a day). Recommended. ①.

Vittoria, Via Maqueda 8 (☎ & fax 091.616.2437). Handy for the train station but not terribly inspiring, and no en-suite facilities. No credit cards. ①.

Via Roma and around

Concordia, Via Roma 72 (☎091.617.1514, fax 091.588.614). Rather indifferently run, with rooms towards the top of this price category; only a few have bath or shower. No credit cards. ①.

Confort, Via Roma 188 (☎091.324.362). One of a choice of lodgings in this block and not a bad place to start looking. Rooms with and without shower available. No credit cards. ②.

Elena, Piazza Giulio Césare 14 (☎091.616.2021, fax 091.616.2984). Not the best or the cheapest place around, but it's right opposite Stazione Centrale, and the airport bus stops outside, so late-night arrivals need not fear walking dark old-town streets. Three- and four-bedrooms are also available. ②.

Italia, Via Roma 62 (☎091.616.5397). A friendly, family run place on the fourth floor, high above the traffic noise. There are only nine rooms, but they are reasonably sized and kept spotlessly clean, with separate bathrooms (a shower is included in the price). No credit cards. ①.

Joly, Via Michele Amari 11 (☎091.611.1766, fax 091.616.1765). A pleasant neighbourhood and clean rooms – all with bath – make this a good choice on Piazza Florio, useful for the port and Piazza Ruggero Séttimo. ③.

Olimpia, Piazza Cassa di Risparmio 18 (☎091.616.1276). A good (if noisy) location, with small rooms overlooking the piazza. Some of the rooms and bathrooms can be rather dismal; check first before accepting. It's up Via Roma from the train station and on the right just before Corso Vittorio Emanuele. There's parking available outside in the square, though a garage might be safer. No credit cards. ①.

Piccadilly, Via Roma 72 (☎091.617.0376). A higher-class hotel in an otherwise cheapish block, expensive for what you get, though there's usually space available with or without facilities. No credit cards. ②.

Posta, Via Gagini 77 (☎091.587.338). The street runs parallel to Via Roma, between Piazza San Domenico and Via Cavour, and the hotel is a good bet for women travelling on their own. Most rooms here are en suite, in the next price category up. All are modern and clean, and the service is polite. Garage parking available (L15,000). ②.

Rosalia Conca d'Oro, 3rd floor, Via Santa Rosalia 7 (☎091.616.4543). Decent rooms and a welcoming owner make this a sought-after choice in summer, especially as you're high enough up for views over downtown Palermo. It's conveniently close to Stazione Centrale, and the nine rooms fill quickly. Showers cost extra. No credit cards. ①.

Tonic, Via Mariano Stabile (☎ & fax 091.581.754). Smart, spacious hotel in the modern town, with plenty of rooms, all with private facilities. Friendly, English-speaking staff, longer-stay discounts, and parking and bike storage on request. ③.

East of Via Roma: La Kalsa

Letizia, Via Bottai 30 (☎ & fax 091.589.110). A good, clean *pensione*, on a road running between Corso Vittorio Emanuele and Piazza Marina – and really the best choice in this area. Slightly more expensive rooms with facilities available. Safe street parking, too. ②.

Paradiso, Via Schiavuzzo 65 (☎091.617.2825). Good location in Piazza della Rivoluzione in La Kalsa, but caution advisable when you're coming back at night. Ten rooms, none with private facilities. No credit cards. ①.

The modern city

Boston, Via Mariano Stabile 136 (☎091.580.234, fax 091.335.364). In the same block as the *Madonia*, but slicker, with TV in all seven rooms. No singles, and no rooms without en-suite facilities. ③.

Madonia, Via Mariano Stabile 136 (☎091.611.3532, fax 091.335.364). At the top of this category, though cheaper than average along this main street in the modern city, and with a garage available. ②.

Petit, Via Príncipe di Belmonte 84 (☎091.323.616). Small, neat rooms in a pleasant traffic-free street and close to some decent restaurants and cafés. It's one of the more attractive modern city choices, but there are only six rooms. No credit cards except American Express. ②.

Príncipe di Belmonte, Via Príncipe di Belmonte 25 (☎091.331.065, fax 091.611.3424). The same good location as the *Petit*, though with more, better and pricier rooms. ②.

Top-of-the-range hotels

Centrale, Corso Vittorio Emanuele 327 (☎091.336.666, fax 091.334.881). A few steps away from the Quattro Canti and boasting a panoramic roof terrace, this newly renovated *palazzo* pampers well enough, as you would expect with the high tab. ⑦.

Grande Albergo e delle Palme, Via Roma 396 (☎091.583.933, fax 091.331.545). Itself one of central Palermo's monuments, this magnificent building – complete with rooftop terrace – is where Richard Wagner stayed and finished composing *Parsifal* in 1882. It's also known as a meeting-place of the Mafia: Sicilian Mafia leaders met here in October 1957 to organize the operation of their heroin trade on an international basis. Glamorous in its public rooms, some bedrooms can be disappointingly basic, and overpriced at nearly L300,000 (though half that in low season). Parking available. ⑦.

Jolly del Foro Italico, Foro Italico 22 (☎091.616.5090, fax 091.616.1441). If you're looking for luxury, the *Jolly* – one of a chain – overlooks the sea and the Foro Italico, and is the only hotel in the centre with a pool. You may be able to get cheaper deals than the listed L250,000, especially outside the summer months. ⑦.

Politeama Palace Hotel, Piazza Ruggero Séttimo 15 (☎091.322.777, fax 091.611.1589). An excellent location for this modern hotel, right opposite the Politeama theatre. All the comfortable rooms are soundproofed, which deals effectively with the manic traffic outside. ⑥.

Villa Igiea Grand Hotel, Via Belmonte 43 (☎091.543.744, fax 091.547.654). At Acquasanta, 3km north of the city, this classic Art Nouveau building, originally a villa of the Florio family (the first people to put tuna fish into cans), was designed by Ernesto Basile in 1900. Still sumptuous and for the seriously wealthy only, with rooms at around L370,000 a night, or a snip at L200,000 in low season. ⑧.

Camping

There are two **campsites** outside Palermo, at Sferracavallo (see p.102), 13km northwest of the city, reachable on bus #616 from Piazza de Gásperi, at the northern end of Via della Libertà in the modern city (take #101 or #106 up this long avenue to save a walk; #101 direct from the station, #106 from Piazza Ruggero Séttimo or Viale Libertà). Given the price of Italian campsites, and the distance involved, it's probably worth sticking with a budget central hotel, though the options are listed below for the record. If you're driving and heading out of town, other campsites within range are stretched along the Golfo di Carini, to the west of Palermo (see pp.102–104).

Camping Trinacria, Via Barcarello (☎ & fax 091.530.590). Right across from the sea, with a pizzeria on the premises, and some small, basic bungalows that sleep two to four people (②).

Camping dell'Ulivo, Via Pegaso (☎ & fax 091.533.021). A fair bit cheaper than the *Trinacria*, and quite basic, though there are also similar bungalows here (②).

The City

Historical Palermo sits compactly around one set of central crossroads, the **Quattro Canti**, which is at the core of four distinct quarters. The **Albergheria** and the **Capo** quarter, the latter beyond the cathedral, lie roughly west of Via Maqueda; the **Vucciria** and old harbour of La Cala and **La Kalsa**, lie to the east, closest to the water. In the past there was little contact between the inhabitants of each quarter, which had their own dialects, trades, palaces and markets; even intermarriage was frowned upon. Today these areas, together with the more modern stretch along **Viale della Libertà**, hold all of Palermo's most enduring monuments and buildings. It's a fairly undisciplined mess, sixteenth- and seventeenth-century town planning conspiring with late nineteenth-century ambition and twentieth-century bombs to lend an eclectic look to the city – tight alleys, stately piazzas, bombsites and contemporary office blocks mixed to distraction. But each quarter retains something of its medieval character in a web-like system of streets, where decaying buildings often mask gardens or chapels containing outstanding works of art, a world away from the din of the urban assault course outside.

Given that cars, let alone buses, can't get down many of the narrow streets in the old city centre, you'll often have no choice but to walk around most of what is detailed below, although for certain specific sights don't hesitate to jump on a bus. Certainly, you'll need some form of transport to reach Palermo's **outskirts**: it's no fun at all slogging up and down the long thoroughfares of the modern city.

Around the Quattro Canti

In the heart of the old city – ten minutes' walk from the train station – is Piazza Vigliena, better known as the **Quattro Canti** or "Four Corners". Erected in 1611, this is not so much a piazza as a set of dingy Baroque crossroads that divide central Palermo into quadrants. You'll pass this junction many times, awash with traffic, newspaper vendors sitting under the ugly fountain water-spouts, and it's worth one stroll around to check the tiered statues – respectively a season, a king of Sicily and a patron of the city in each concave "corner", where, in previous centuries, the heads of convicted rebels were hung from poles. It's not a particularly promising starting point, but within a few seconds' walk are some of Palermo's most opulent piazzas and buildings, including four of the city's most extraordinary churches.

On the southwest corner (entrance on Corso Vittorio Emanuele), the early seventeenth-century **San Giuseppe dei Teatini** (Mon–Sat 7.15am–noon & 5–8pm, Sun 9am–1pm) is the most harmonious of the city's Baroque churches. The misleadingly simple facade conceals a wealth of detail inside, from the tumbling angels holding the holy water on either side of the door to the lavish side chapels. There's plenty of contrasting space, though, with 22 enormous columns supporting the dome, mostly restored after bomb damage in 1943. Outside, adjacent to the church, is the main building of the **Università**, a dull nineteenth-century restoration job replacing what was originally a convent adjoining San Giuseppe. There are generally plenty of students around here, and a couple of good bars, in the little piazza across from the entrance.

Piazza Pretoria: the Municipio and Santa Caterina

Cross Via Maqueda to **Piazza Pretoria**, floodlit at night to highlight the nude figures of its great central fountain, a racy sixteenth-century Florentine design, since protected by railings to ward off excitable vandals. The piazza also holds the restored **Municipio**, now plaque-studded and pristine, and, towering above both square and fountain, the massive late sixteenth-century flank of the church of **Santa Caterina** (closed for restoration work: when open, enter from Piazza Bellini), the antithesis of the quiet magnificence of San Giuseppe over the road. This is Sicilian Baroque at its most exuberant: every inch of the enormous interior is covered in wildly decorative, pustular relief work, deep reds and yellows filling in between sculpted cherubs, Madonnas, lions and eagles. One marble panel (first chapel on the right) depicts Jonah about to be devoured by a rubbery-lipped whale, a Spanish galleon above constructed with wire and string rigging. Given this overwhelmingly theatrical design, it's difficult to argue with Vincent Cronin's image of a " . . . frenzied mind . . . throwing out powerful and extravagant images before tumbling over the verge of madness".

Piazza Bellini: the churches of San Cataldo and La Martorana

Just around the corner from the Pretoria fountain, **Piazza Bellini** is largely a car park by day, with vehicles jammed together next to part of the city's old Roman wall and under two more wildly contrasting churches. The little Saracenic red golf-ball domes belong to **San Cataldo**, a squat twelfth-century chapel on a palm-planted bank above the piazza (Tues–Fri 9am–5pm, Sat & Sun 9am–1pm). Other

---

FRUTTA DI MARTORANA

When Palermo's religious houses were at their late medieval height, many supported themselves by turning out remarkable **sculpted confectionery** – fruit and vegetables made out of coloured almond paste. La Martorana was once famous for the quality of its almond "fruits", which were sold at the church doors, and today most Sicilian *pasticcerie* continue the tradition: in Palermo these creations are known as *frutta di Martorana*. It's always worth looking in cake-shop windows, which usually display not only fruit but also fish and shellfish made out of the same sickly almond mixture. The best time of year to see the displays is in October, before the festival of Ognissanti (All Saints).

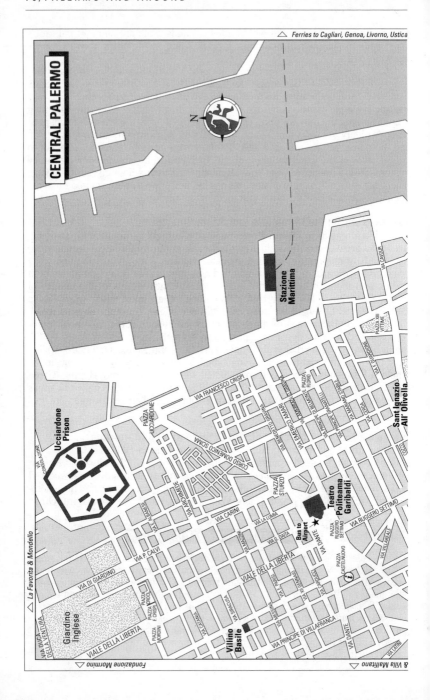

& Naples. Hydrofoils to Ustica, Cefalu & Aeolian Islands

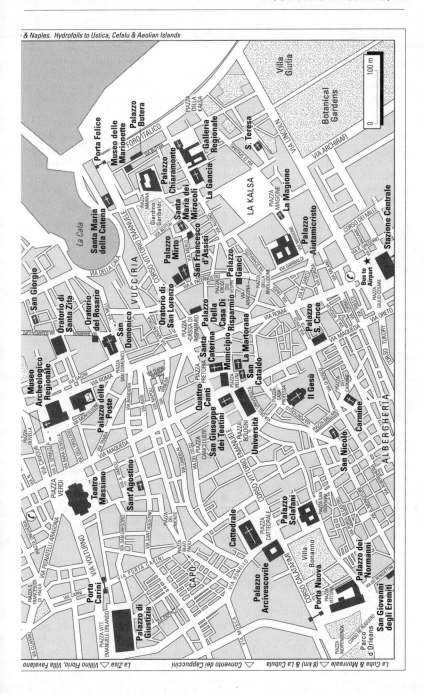

Villa Giulia

Botanical Gardens

0   100 m

PIAZZA DELLA KALSA

Porta Felice

Museo delle Marionette

Palazzo Butera

FORO ITALICO

VIA BUTERA

Palazzo Chiaramonte

Galleria Regionale

S. Teresa

VIA LINCOLN

VIA ARCHIRAFI

Santa Maria dei Miracoli

La Gancia

LA KALSA

VIA ALLORO

La Mela

Santa Maria della Catena

La Cala

PIAZZA MARINA Giardino Garibaldi

VIA DELLA CALA

CORSO VITTORIO EMANUELE

VIA BOTTAI

Palazzo Mirto

San Francesco d'Assisi

Palazzo Ganci

PIAZZA MAGIONE

La Magione

Palazzo Aiutamicristo

CORSO DEI MILLE

Stazione Centrale

San Giorgio

VIA DELLA LOGGIA

Oratorio di Santa Zita

Oratorio del Rosario

VUCCIRIA

San Domenico

Oratorio di San Lorenzo

Palazzo Della Casa Di Risparmio

Santa Caterina

La Martorana

Palazzo S. Croce

Bus to Airport

Museo Archeologico Regionale

VIA ROMA

Palazzo delle Poste

Quattro Canti

Municipio

San La Martorana

San Cataldo

Il Gesù

VIA MAQUEDA

VIA CAVOUR

VIA MARIANO STABILE

VIA PRINCIPE DI BELMONTE

VIA ROMA

Teatro Massimo

PIAZZA VERDI

Sant'Agostino

San Giuseppe dei Teatini

Università

VIA DEL CELSO

Carmine

San Nicolò

ALBERGHERIA

Palazzo di Giustizia

Porta Carini

CAPO

Cattedrale

PIAZZA CATTEDRALE

Palazzo Sclafani

Villa Bonanno

Palazzo Arcivescovile

Porta Nuova

Palazzo dei Normanni

San Giovanni degli Eremiti

Parco d'Orleans

La Zisa ▽   Villino Florio, Villa Favaloro   Convento dei Cappuccini ▽   La Cuba & Monreale ▽ (8 km) & La Cubula than the crenellations around the roof, it was never decorated, and in the eighteenth century the chapel was even used as a post office: it still retains a good mosaic pavement in an otherwise bare and peaceful interior. (San Cataldo is usually locked; get the keys from the desk at the back of La Martorana.)

The understatement of this little chapel is more than offset by the splendid interior of **La Martorana** opposite (summer Mon–Sat 9.30am–1pm & 3.30–6.30pm, Sun 8.30am–1pm; winter Mon–Sat 9.30am–1pm & 3.30–5.30pm, Sun 8.30am–1pm); it is one of the finest surviving buildings of the medieval city. A Norman foundation, it was paid for in 1143 by George of Antioch, King Roger's admiral, from whom it received its original name, Santa Maria dell'Ammiraglio. After the Sicilian Vespers, the island's nobility met here to offer the Crown to Peter of Aragon, and under the Spanish the church was passed to a convent founded by Eloisa Martorana – hence its popular name. It received a Baroque going-over and its curving northern facade in 1588, but happily this doesn't detract from the great power of the interior. Enter through the slim twelfth-century campanile, an original structure that retains its ribbed arches and slender columns. A series of spectacular **mosaics** are laid on and around the columns supporting the main cupola – animated twelfth-century Greek works, commissioned by the admiral himself, who was of Greek descent. A gentle Christ dominates the dome, surrounded by angels, with the Apostles and the Madonna to the sides. The colours are still strong, a golden background enlivened by azure, grape-red, light-green and white, and, in the morning especially, light streams through the high windows, picking out the admirable craftsmanship. Heavy Baroque marble and frescoes by the entrance do their best to dampen the effect but even here there's some respite: on both sides of the steps, two more original mosaic panels (from the destroyed Norman portico) have been set in frames on the walls, a kneeling George of Antioch dedicating the church to the Virgin, and King Roger being crowned by Christ – the diamond-studded monarch contrasted with a larger, more simple and dignified Christ.

The Albergheria

The district bounded by Via Maqueda and Corso Vittorio Emanuele, just northwest of Stazione Centrale – the **Albergheria** – can't have changed substantially for several hundred years. There are proud *palazzi* on Via Maqueda itself, notably the eighteenth-century **Palazzo Santa Croce**, at the junction with Via Bosco. But behind is a warren of tiny streets and tall, blackened and leaning buildings: it's atmospheric to wander in, and much of the central area is taken up by a street market, which conceals several fine churches too. It's a poor neighbourhood, as a stroll down shored-up **Via Ponticello**, a block before the university, proves – the bomb damage of World War II has never been made good.

This road leads directly to the church of **Il Gesù**, or Casa Professa (daily 7.30–11.30am), the first Jesuit foundation in Sicily, whose glorious Baroque swirl of inlaid marble and relief work – topped by a green-and-white-patterned dome – took over a hundred years to complete. Via Ponticello leads down to **Piazza Ballarò**, which, together with the adjacent **Piazza del Cármine**, is the focus of a raucous daily fruit and vegetable **market**, alive with the cries of vendors from early in the morning. There are some very cheap snack and drinking places here, where you can sidle in among the locals and sample sliced-open sea urchins, fried artichokes, *arancini* and beer. Above all the activity looms the bright majolica-tiled dome of the seventeenth-century church of the **Cármine**, a singular land-mark amid the dirty and rubbish-strewn alleys, with a spacious interior and adjoining cloister and convent.

San Giovanni degli Eremiti
Any of the long streets west of Piazza del Cármine lead to Via dei Benedettini, which marks the westernmost edge of the quarter. Over the busy road, behind iron gates, is the Albergheria's most peaceful haven, the deconsecrated church of **San Giovanni degli Eremiti** (Mon–Sat 9am–1pm & 3–7pm, Sun 9am–12.30pm; L4000) – St John of the Hermits. Built in 1132, this is the most obviously Arabic of the city's Norman relics, its five ochre domes topping a small church that was built upon the remains of an earlier mosque (part of which, an adjacent empty hall, is still visible). It was especially favoured by its founder, Roger II, who grant-ed the monks of San Giovanni 21 barrels of tuna fish a year, a prized commodity controlled by the Crown. A path leads up through citrus trees to the church, behind which lie some celebrated late thirteenth-century cloisters – perfect twin columns with slightly pointed arches surrounding a wild garden.

Immediately behind the church, on Corso Re Ruggero, the **Palazzo d'Orleans** is also set in its own garden: once home to the exiled Louis-Philippe of France in 1809, it's now the official residence of Sicily's president.

The Palazzo dei Normanni

Turn left out of San Giovanni and it's a few paces to the main road, where, if you turn right and veer left up the steps, you'll climb out of the clamorous traffic to gaze on the vast length of the **Palazzo dei Normanni**, or Palazzo Reale. A royal palace has always occupied the high ground here, above medieval Palermo. Originally built by the Saracens in the ninth century, the palace was then enlarged considerably by the Normans, under whom it housed the most magnificent of medieval European courts. Sadly, there's little left from those times in the current structure. The long front was added by the Spanish in the seventeenth century and most of the interior is now taken up by the Sicilian regional parliament (hence the security guards and limited access).

Entry is from Piazza Indipendenza. Of the Royal Apartments, it is now only pos-sible to visit the **Sala di Ruggero** (Mon, Fri & Sat 9am–noon; free), one of the ear-liest parts of the palace and covered with lively twelfth-century mosaics of hunting scenes. It's a brief visit, best done first, before you descend a floor to the beautiful **Cappella Palatina** (Mon–Fri 9am–noon & 3–5pm, Sat 9am–noon, Sun 9–10am & noon–1pm; free), the undisputed artistic gem of central Palermo. The private royal chapel of Roger II, built between 1132 and 1143, its intimate interior is immediate-ly overwhelming, with cupola, three apses and nave entirely covered in **mosaics** of outstanding quality. The oldest are those in the cupola and apses, probably com-pleted in 1150 by Byzantine artists; those in the nave are from the hands of local craftsmen, finished twenty-odd years later and depicting Old and New Testament scenes. As at Monreale (pp.98–100) and Cefalù (p.120), it's the powerful repre-sentation of Christ as Pantocrator that dominates the senses, bolstered here by other secondary images – Christ blessing, open book in hand, and Christ enthroned, between Peter (to whom the chapel is dedicated) and Paul. The colours are vivid, the style realistic, but even so it takes time to become accustomed to the half-light inside the chapel. Unlike the bright pictures of La Martorana, the mosaics here give a single impression – an immediate feeling of the faith that inspired their creation and more than a hint of the mastery of the work.

Aside from the mosaics, the whole chapel is a delight. There's an Arabic ceiling with richly carved wooden stalactites, a patterned marble floor and a twelfth-century Norman candlestick (by the pulpit), 4m high and contorted by manic carvings. Quite clearly, the chapel is stamped with a sense of Roger II's imperial standing. A dedicatory inscription around the cupola proclaims him to be " . . . Roger, mighty ruling king . . . " and in 1140, on Palm Sunday, it's recorded that Roger rode into the chapel on a white donkey before sitting in the royal throne at the back of the church – emphasizing his role as Christ's representative on earth.

The Cattedrale and the Capo

From the Quattro Canti, the southwestern stretch of **Corso Vittorio Emanuele** is a busy street dotted with secondhand book shops and the wrecks of run-down eighteenth-century *palazzi*. Passing the peeling Piazza Bologni, on the left, and the war-damaged shells of other churches and buildings is no preparation for the huge bulk of the **Cattedrale** (Mon–Sat 7am–7pm, Sun 8am–1.30pm & 4–7pm; free), set back in gardens on the right of the corso. This is a more substantial Norman relic than the Royal Palace. Founded in 1185 by Palermo's English archbishop Gualtiero Offamiglio (Walter of the Mill), it was intended to be his power base in the city. Yet the Cattedrale wasn't finished for centuries, and in any case was quickly superseded by the glories of William II's foundation at Monreale (see p.99).

The Cattedrale is an odd building in many ways, due to the less-than-subtle alterations of the late eighteenth century that added the dome – completely out of character – and spoiled the fine lines of the tawny stone. Still, the triple-apsed eastern end (seen from a sideroad off the corso) and the lovely matching towers are all twelfth-century originals; and, despite the fussy Catalan-Gothic facade and arches, there's enough Norman carving and detail to give the exterior more than mere curiosity value. The same is not true, however, of the inside, which was modernized by Fuga, the Neapolitan architect responsible for the dome. It's grand enough, but cold and Neoclassical, and the only items of interest are the fine portal and wooden doors (both fifteenth-century) and the royal **tombs**, Palermo's royal pantheon. As you enter, two crowded chapels to the left contain the mortal remains of some of Sicily's most famous monarchs: among others, Frederick II (left front) and his wife Constance (far right), Henry VI (right front) and Roger II (rear left) – Roger's tomb was brought back shortly after he died from the cathedral at Cefalù, where he had requested that he be laid.

Perhaps more rewarding than the rest of the overblown interior is the **treasury**, or *tesoro* (closed for repairs), to the right of the choir: a sumptuous collection that includes a jewel- and pearl-encrusted skullcap and three simple, precious rings removed from the tomb of Constance of Aragon in the eighteenth century. This was enterprising enough, but pales into insignificance beside the ingenuity required to extract a tooth from St Rosalia, also exhibited here in a reliquary, as well as the arm of St Agatha and the foot of St Mary Magdalen.

Palazzo Arcivescovile and the Porta Nuova

Over the road, at the western end of the Cattedrale, stands the **Palazzo Arcivescovile**, the one-time archbishop's palace, entered through a fifteenth-century gateway. Inside, the Museo Diocesano brings together art from the cathedral and from city churches destroyed during World War II: it's reported to be closed indefinitely, but check to see. You should be able to take a look in the courtyard anyway, and a little way up Via Bonello (left out of the palace) there's usually some activity in the open-air **Mercato delle Pulci**, an antique/junk market in Piazza Peranni.

Back on the corso, the road runs up to the Royal Palace, on the northern side of which lies the **Porta Nuova**. Erected in 1535, it commemorates Charles V's Tunisian exploits, with suitably grim and turbaned figures adorning the western side. Through the gate, the long road, now Corso Calatafimi, heads southwest to Monreale.

Il Capo

On foot, circle left around the apses of the Cattedrale and stroll up into the **Capo** quarter, one of the oldest areas of Palermo and another tight web of run-down streets, unrelieved by space or greenery. There's not much to see, save a few surviving sculpted portals in the decaying palaces, but it's an instructive tour if you've seen only grand buildings up to now. One alley, Via Porta Carini, climbs past shambolic buildings and locked and battered churches to reach the decrepit **Porta Carini** itself, one of the city's medieval gates. There are a few scrappy market stalls in the streets hereabouts, the Capo quarter's western edge marked by Via Papireto.

Better, from the Cattedrale, is to turn right at Piazza Beati Paoli for the graceful **Piazza del Monte**, tree-planted and with a couple of restful, neighbourhood bars. There's an atmosphere of faded splendour here, pell-mell on market days when the stalls spill over from the nearby goings-on down **Via Sant'Agostino**. A lively market, mainly clothes but with food too, runs all the way down to Via Maqueda and beyond to Via Roma, and just around the corner is the church of **Sant'Agostino** (Mon–Sat 7am–noon & 4–5.30pm, Sun 7am–noon), built by the Chiaramonte and Sclàfani families in the thirteenth century. Above the main door (on Via Raimondo) there's a gorgeous latticework rose window and, if you can get in through the adjacent side door, some fine **stuccos** by Serpotta. Another door leads to a quadrangle of calm sixteenth-century cloisters. Otherwise, turn the corner, and along Via Sant'Agostino, behind the market stalls, the church sports a badly chipped, sculpted fifteenth-century doorway attributed to Domenico Gagini – one of a whole dynasty of talented medieval sculptors who covered Sicily with their creations (see also the Galleria Regionale, p.82).

Along Via Maqueda and Viale della Libertà: the modern city

North of the Quattro Canti, you leave most of the interesting medieval alleys behind, and the streets off to the left of Via Maqueda gradually become wider and more nondescript as they broach the area around Piazza Verdi, site of the late nineteenth-century **Teatro Màssimo**. It's a monumental structure, all dome and columns, supposedly the largest theatre in Italy and beautifully cleaned up after years of closure (see box p.76). The majestic, heavily gilded interior is best appreciated during a performance, usually of classical music, between October and June, but a view at other times can be arranged (call ☎091.334.246 for an appointment).

THE TEATRO MÁSSIMO: THE GLORY AND THE REALPOLITIK

In May 1997, almost a hundred years to the day after its inauguration and after 23 years of closure, the Teatro Mássimo was reopened by Palermo's mayor, **Leoluca Orlando**. It had been boarded up for just over one year longer than its original construction period, during which time, in the wake of Garibaldi's liberation of Sicily from the Bourbon yoke, it had been vaunted as an emblem of the new Sicily, a monument to rival Europe's great opera houses in Paris and Vienna. Its construction was entrusted to **Giovanni Battista Basile**, whose strictly Neoclassical design was possibly influenced by Charles Garnier's contemporary plans for the Paris Opéra, and the first stone was laid in 1876. The architect did not live to see the end of the project, however, and the work was finished by his son, **Ernesto Basile**. After its inauguration, the opera house became the focus of high society and saw an illustrious procession of musical performers grace its vast auditorium, but by the time the theatre closed for radical repairs in the 1970s it was in a sorely neglected state. As the renovation became bogged down in **political and financial problems** – funding is a perennial problem for public-works projects in Italy – the likelihood of it ever reopening began to look increasingly remote. It did, however, open its doors briefly to Francis Ford Coppola, who shot the long climactic opera scene of *The Godfather: Part III* here, using the theatre's sweep of steps to great effect.

It was with a sense of triumph, therefore, that mayor Leoluca Orlando – having thrown all his influence behind the effort to bring forward the reopening, to mark the theatre's centenary – presided over the gala ceremony, at which the celebrated **Claudio Abbado** conducted and thousands attended (mostly watching from a screen outside). Inevitably, in grand Sicilian fashion, the occasion wasn't without controversy. Orlando was accused of using the event to further his political position, through hurrying up the reopening before the building was completely ready, and by having delayed the work when he was first elected mayor in the 1980s (allegedly because he knew he was about to be ousted by his erstwhile Christian Democrat colleagues and so wouldn't be around to gather the kudos). Among his detractors are the director **Franco Zeffirelli** (now a senator with Berlusconi's right-wing alliance), whose productions at the Mássimo in the 1950s ranked among the theatre's greatest moments, and **Gioacchino Lanza Tomasi**, musicologist and adopted son of Giuseppe di Lampedusa, author of *The Leopard*. But whatever political capital Orlando may have accrued from the reopening, investment in the cultural renaissance of Palermo has always been part of his agenda, and the reason for his continued support among the Palermitani. The acoustic quality of the theatre alone, so superior to that at the Politeama (which hosted the opera season during the period of closure), justifies the applause, while the spruced-up exterior injects impressive style into Palermo's cityscape – at least until the car pollution begins its blackening work once more.

The theatre marks the dividing line between old and new Palermo. Beyond here there's little that's vital, though plenty that is grand and modern. Via Maqueda becomes **Via Ruggero Séttimo**, which cuts through gridded shopping streets past the enclosed Piazza Ungheria to the huge double square that characterizes modern Palermo – made up of **Piazza Castelnuovo** to the left and **Piazza Ruggero Séttimo** to the right. Far removed from the intimate piazzas of the medieval town, these spacious expanses double as car parks and bus ranks, while dominating the whole lot is Palermo's other massive theatre, the late nineteenth-century **Politeama Garibaldi**. Built in overblown Pompeian style, and topped by a bronze chariot pulled by four horses, the theatre also houses the city's **Galleria d'Arte Moderna** (entrance on Via Turati; Tues–Sun 9am–8pm; L5000). There's some nice work here, all twentieth-century Sicilian stuff, best of which is the sculpture, including a small bronze study of an exhausted old horse (by Enrico Quattrociocchi), and Gerbino's sympathetic statuette of his greatcoated, heavily bearded father – though Michele Catti's autumnal scenes of Palermo are good, too. Watch out, as well, for the international touring exhibitions that often visit.

Along Viale della Libertà

Many of the city buses stop in between the two large piazzas. You might want to hop on one if you're heading any further north, along the wide **Viale della Libertà**, as it's about 1km to the modern city's other attractions.

At Viale della Libertà 52, the **Fondazione Mormino** (Mon–Sat 9am–1pm; free) sponsors an archeological and historical collection in the sumptuous Banco di Sicilia building. The exhibits are beautifully presented – a sixth-century BC bronze helmet, vases and coins – and there's also a fine set of old maps and prints, including a map of the Mediterranean made in the seventeenth century by a cartographer in Wapping, London. From here, you're close to the **Giardino Inglese**, one of the city's few parks, though actually not much more than a palm-planted garden. For real expanses of parkland you'll have to take the bus a couple of kilometres further north to the Parco della Favorita (p.84).

A couple of blocks east of the Giardino Inglese is Palermo's notorious **Ucciardone** prison, connected by an underground passageway to the maximum-security bunker where the much-publicized *maxi processi* (maxi-trials) of Mafia suspects were held in the 1980s. The gloomy Bourbon prison has been called "the best-informed centre in Italy for gossip and intelligence about the operations of organized crime throughout the world", not least because it's home to a good percentage of the biggest names in the Italian underworld at any one time. It's reported that Mafia affairs are conducted here almost undisturbed, by bosses whose food is brought in from Palermo's best restaurants and who collaborate with the warders to ensure that escapes don't happen – something that might increase security arrangements and hamper their activities. Following the murders of Mafia investigators Falcone and Borsellino in 1992, a large group of prisoners was transferred from here to an island prison elsewhere in Italy in an attempt to shake up the criminal intelligence network; there's even talk of a new prison being built in the city, though this is extremely unlikely to happen soon, if ever.

East to the water

On the east side of the prison, Via Cristóforo Colombo runs down to the water, past a selection of neglected Baroque *palazzi*, to the seventeenth-century **Arsenale** (closed to the public). The exterior – erected by Mariano Smirighio – is worth a look, if you fancy the stroll. To the north of here, 1km or so away, is the fairly attractive but foul-smelling port of **ACQUASANTA**, overlooking which is Ernesto Basile's **Villa Igiea**, an Art Nouveau building erected in 1899 for the wealthy Florio family. It's now a luxury hotel, and hideously expensive (see p.67), though you are free to take a drink in the bar, which gives you an excuse to poke around inside a little – if you get the chance to look, the dining room is the most fantastic of creations. Buses #721 and #731 from Piazza Croci (near the Giardino Inglese and Ucciardone prison, and reachable on #101 from the station or Politeama) run out as far as the villa.

Via Roma, the Vucciria and around

Running from the Stazione Centrale to Piazza Sturzo (below Piazza Ruggero Séttimo), **Via Roma** is a fairly modern addition to the city. Parallel with Via Maqueda, it offers a second chance for orientation if you get lost in the narrow alleys between the two. It's nothing like as interesting as Via Maqueda in its lower reaches, its buildings mostly tall apartment blocks concealing hotels, and the only real diversion is **Via Divisi**, off to the east – a narrow street whose pavements are chock-full of stacked bikes from a series of cycle shops. The rest of Via Roma is all clothes and shoe shops, and there's nowhere to linger until you cross Corso Vittorio Emanuele.

Just up from the corso is the church of **Sant'Antonio**, raised on a platform, to the side of which steps lead down into the sprawling **market** of the **Vucciria** quarter. Winding streets radiate out from a small enclosed piazza, wet from the ice and waste of the groaning fish stalls – swordfish heads stuck to the marble slabs and huge sides of tuna from which the fishmonger carves bloody steaks. There's a couple of excellent little restaurants tucked away in the alleys (best at lunchtime), some very basic bars where the wine comes straight from the barrel, and all manner of food (fresh octopus, for example) and junk on sale. This is also the place to buy great porcelain pasta bowls, espresso cups and coffee-makers. Other than early morning, when the action is at its most frenzied, lunchtime is a good time to wander around here, when the stallholders take a break for card-playing sessions conducted around packing cases, or simply fall asleep amongst their produce.

San Domenico and around

The northern limit of the market is marked by **San Domenico** (Tues–Fri 9.30am–12.30pm & 4–6pm, Sat 9.30am–12.30pm), a large church set back off Via Roma and fronted by a statue-topped marble column. The fine eighteenth-century facade, with its double pillars and slim towers, is lit at night to great effect, while inside a series of tombs contains a horde of famous Sicilians. Parliamentarians, poets and painters, they're of little interest to foreigners except to explain the finer points behind Palermitan street-naming. Outside, on the north side of the church, at Piazza San Domenico 1, you have to ring for entry to the small **Museo del Risorgimento** (Mon, Wed & Fri 9am–1pm; free), a historical collection pertaining to the nineteenth-century Italian anti-Bourbon revolt.

More worthwhile is to ring at Via dei Bambini 16 to get into the **Oratorio del Rosario di San Domenico**, behind the San Domenico church – one of many such small chapels in the old part of the city, many of which contain the best of Palermo's Baroque decoration. This sixteenth-century oratory, built and still maintained by the Knights of Malta, was adorned by the acknowledged master of the art of stucco sculpture, **Giacomo Serpotta** (see p.400), who lined the walls with allegorical figures. Born in Palermo in 1656, Serpotta devoted his entire life to decorating oratories like this, a tradition continued by his son, Procopio (some of whose work can also be seen in the Oratorio di Santa Caterina behind the main post office). Here, the somewhat dusty figures are of *Justice*, *Strength* and suchlike, resembling fashionable society ladies, who often served as models, the whole thing crowned by an accomplished altarpiece by Van Dyck. This was finished in 1628, after the artist had fled Palermo for Genova to escape the Plague.

Spacious **Piazza San Domenico** has that rare thing in Palermo, a bar with outdoor tables – the *Caffé San Domenico*, see p.88 – and it's a good place to sip a drink, close to the flower-sellers and with the sound of the Vucciria market in full swing behind you. Further up Via Roma, on the left, is Palermo's main post office, the gargantuan **Palazzo delle Poste**. Built by the Fascists in 1933, it's a severe concrete block, with a wide swath of steps running up to a colonnade of ten unfluted columns that run the length and height of the building itself. The empty pretension of the post office is put to shame by what hides behind it, around the corner in Piazza Olivella. Here, the church of **Sant'Ignazio all'Olivella** displays an opulent Baroque touch in its great chandeliers and rich side chapels; next door, the cloisters and surviving buildings of a sixteenth-century convent – once the property of the church – now house the city's excellent archeological museum.

Museo Archeologico Regionale

If you've been touring the best of western Sicily's ancient sites (or are intending to do so), the **Museo Archeologico Regionale** (Mon, Tues, Thurs & Sat 9am–1.45pm, Wed & Fri 9am–1.45pm & 3–6.45pm, Sun 9am–12.45pm; L8000) at Palermo is a must, gathering together artefacts found at all the major Neolithic, Carthaginian, Greek and Roman settlements in a magnificent collection that culminates with items from the site at Selinunte. The exhibits are displayed on two main floors, together with a top floor that is usually roped off, but can be visited in the company of one of the museum attendants, who are happy to let you in. For up-to-date information on exhibits, pick up the free illustrated booklet, in English, on the way in.

The entrance to the **ground floor** is through the smaller of two cloisters, which displays anchors and other retrieved hardware from the sea off the Sicilian coast. There are **Egyptian and Punic** remains in rooms to either side, and beyond, the larger, thickly planted cloister is devoted to **Roman** sculpture, notably a giant Emperor Claudius enthroned in the style of Zeus, on the left. Rooms at the far end contain numerous carved early Greek stelae and assorted inscribed tablets (including one from Roman Taormina recording expenses charged by the town's magistrates).

Beyond here, the material is almost entirely **Greek**, beginning with the assembled stone **lion's-head water-spouts** from the so-called Victory Temple at Himera (fifth century BC), the fierce animal faces tempered by braided fur and a grooved tongue that channelled the water, and leading on to the high spot of the museum, the adjacent **Sala di Selinunte**. This gathers together the rich **stone carvings** (or metopes) from the various temples (known only as Temples A–G) at Selinunte on the southwest coast – a vital stop if you intend to visit the site itself (see p.364); sculpted panels from the friezes that adorned the temples, they're appealing works of art, depicting lively mythological scenes. The earliest and least impressive, single panels from the early sixth century BC, sit under the windows on the right and represent the gods of Delphi, the Sphinx, the rape of Europa, and Hercules and the Bull. The reconstructed friezes opposite, from Temples C and (more fragmentary) F, catch the eye more: vivid works from the fifth century BC, like Perseus beheading Medusa with a short sword, his legs in profile but his head and torso facing directly out in archaic style. The most technically advanced tableaux are those in the frieze at the end of the room, from the early fifth-century BC Temple E, portraying a lithe Hercules fighting an Amazon, the marriage of Zeus and Hera, Actaeon savaged by three ferocious dogs, and Athena and the

Titan. There's additional interest in the female heads, three on either side of the door, taken from Temple E. The remaining rooms on the ground floor deal with mainly **Etruscan** funerary art, the most notable exhibits being several third- to second-century BC sarcophagi painted with graphic battle scenes.

You have to retrace your steps to the small cloister for the steps up to the **first floor**, which also has plenty to occupy a lengthy dawdle: lead water pipes with stopcock retrieved from a site at Términi Imerese (p.114), some 12,000 votive terracotta figures, and a few delicately carved stone heads found at Solunto (p.105). There's more Greek sculpture (including a fragment of the frieze from the Parthenon) and a reconstructed Roman mosaic pavement as well. But pick of the lot here are two rich **bronze sculptures** – the naturalistic figure of an alert ram (third century BC) from Siracusa, once one of a pair (the other was destroyed in the 1848 revolution), and a glistening, muscular study of Hercules subduing a stag, found near Pompeii.

The **second floor** holds a range of Neolithic items, including flints from Addaura, on Monte Pellegrino, and Lévanzo (p.351), shelves full of Greek and Etruscan amphorae, and frescoes from Solunto (p.105). But the most impressive sight on this floor is the room full of **Roman mosaics**, beautifully preserved, excavated from Piazza della Vittoria in Palermo: one, from the second century AD, depicts the triumph of Neptune; another, from the third century AD, shows Orpheus with a lyre, surrounded by animals.

Across Via Roma: to La Cala

There's an immediate change in style and surroundings once you cross back over Via Roma and head towards the water. The area around the docks suffered gravely during the last war, particularly the late sixteenth-century church of **Santa Zita**, on quiet Via Squarcialupo, which was badly bomb-damaged. It's since been restored, and inside you'll see some flamboyant polychrome marbling and good sculpture by Antonello Gagini. The marvellous oratory behind Santa Zita, the **Oratorio del Rosario di Santa Zita** (ring the bell 11am–noon; or ask in the church in front, San Mamiliano, Mon–Fri 9am–1pm & 3–6pm, Sat 9am–1pm), contains some of the wildest flights of Giacomo Serpotta's rococo imagination – a dazzling confusion of allegorical figures, bare-breasted women, putti galore, scenes from the New Testament, and, at the centre of it all, a rendering of the Battle of Lepanto. Take time to absorb the details of this tumultuous landscape, especially the loving care with which he depicted individual figures – the old men and women, melancholy boys perched on the ledge – and notice Serpotta's symbol on the left wall: the golden snake. Striking wealth indeed when you step outside and consider the area around.

Via Squarcialupo continues down to **Piazza XIII Víttime**, where there's a monument commemorating thirteen Palermitani shot by the Bourbons in the 1860 revolt, and some of the city's medieval walls; new excavations are currently in progress here. The whole of the area around is rather forlorn: to the south, the shored-up buildings just back from the water have ground floors given over to car-repair workshops, the rooms open to the road and stuffed full of every kind of vehicular wreckage.

The depressed inertia of these streets spreads south to the thumb-shaped inlet of the old city harbour, **La Cala**. Once the main port of Palermo, stretching as far inland as Via Roma, La Cala started to decline during the sixteenth century, when silting caused the water to recede to its current position. All the heavy work eventually moved northwest, to docks off the remodelled post-war streets (site of the Stazione Maríttima), and La Cala has been left to the few fishing-boats that still work out of Palermo. It's interesting to stroll around the marine clutter at least once, and there are excellent views over the little harbour to Monte Pellegrino in the distance.

Along Corso Vittorio Emanuele: from Quattro Canti to the water

There's a markedly different character to the quarter south of La Cala, bounded by Via Roma and the corso. Worst hit by the war and allowed to decay since, this area holds some of the poorest streets in the city, within some of the most desolate urban landscapes imaginable. Towards the water along **Corso Vittorio Emanuele**, high narrow streets peel off to the left and right, mostly dark and forbidding. One, Via A. Paternostro, cuts away to the right to the thirteenth-century church of **San Francesco d'Assisi** (daily 8am–12.30am & 4.30–6.30pm), whose well-preserved portal, picked out with a zigzag decoration, is topped by a wonderful rose window – a harmonious design that is, for once, continued inside. All the Baroque trappings have been stripped away to reveal a pleasing stone interior, the later side chapels showing excellently worked arches – the fourth on the left is one of the earliest Renaissance works on the island, sculpted by Francesco Laurana in 1468. To the side of the church, at Via Immacolatella 5, the renowned **Oratorio di San Lorenzo** contains another of Giacomo Serpotta's stuccoed masterpieces, intricately fashioned scenes from the lives of St Lawrence and St Francis. Sadly, it's likely to remain closed for the foreseeable future, as excavations are being carried out at the site.

Back on the main road, the corso runs straight down to the water, with the harbour of **La Cala** to the left, overlooked by the church of **Santa Maria della Catena**, named after the chain that used to close the harbour in the late fifteenth century. The corso ends at the Baroque gate, the **Porta Felice**, begun in 1582 as a counterbalance to the Porta Nuova, visible way to the southwest. Indeed, from here you can judge the extent of the late medieval city, which lay between the two gates.

Just before Porta Felice, turn right onto Via Butera, and at no. 1 is the engaging **Museo delle Marionette** (Mon–Fri 9am–1pm & 4–7pm, Sat 9am–1pm; L5000, ring for entrance), Palermo's definitive collection of puppets, screens and painted scenery. A traditional Sicilian entertainment, puppet theatres have all but died out on the island (though you can still see performances in Palermo, see p.94). Based around French and Sicilian history and specifically the exploits of the hero Orlando (Roland), performances nearly always depict dashing knights – Orlando, Rinaldo and friends – combating Saracen invaders, usually culminating in a great battle. With a commentary often delivered in dialect, you don't follow the lines so much as the short, sharp action – frenetic battle scenes awash with blood and cries, as Orlando single-handedly slays the enemy and saves the day. It's all great fun, and in summer the museum puts on free **shows** (the Spettácolo dei Pupi): check at the tourist office or museum for days and times. A little further down the street is the newly restored **Palazzo Butera**, whose seventeenth-century facade faces out over the Foro Italico (see overleaf). Once the home of the Spanish viceroys in Sicily, it is now open for conferences or groups of visitors (call ☎091.611.0162 to arrange an appointment).

The whole area beyond the Porta Felice was flattened in 1943, and has since been rebuilt as a fairly ugly promenade, the **Foro Italico** (sometimes known as Foro Umberto I), complete with small amusement park, from where you can look back over the harbour to Monte Pellegrino. This is one of the liveliest places in the city on summer evenings, when the locals take to the street armed to the teeth with ice-cream from one of the several *gelateria* palaces lined along here.

Piazza Marina

Double back through the gate and bear left into **Piazza Marina**, a large square that skirts around the tropical **Giardino Garibaldi** – another venue for the city's elderly card-players, who gather around green baize tables at lunchtime for a game. Reclaimed from the sea in the tenth century, subsequently used for jousting tournaments and executions, and now surrounded by decaying *palazzi* and pavement restaurants, every corner of the piazza is worth exploring. The second largest of Palermo's palaces, the **Palazzo Chiaramonte**, flanks the east side of the square: dating from the fourteenth century, the palace was the home of the Inquisition from 1685 to 1782, before becoming the city's law courts – a function it only abandoned in 1972. It's also being restored, and you can't get in, though the more determined can apply for the key at the Rettorato, the university administration office, also in the piazza. Otherwise you'll have to be content with peeking through the gates of the delicately arched inner courtyard and admiring the severe facade.

On the other side of Piazza Marina, the southwest corner is marked by the sixteenth-century church of **Santa Maria dei Mirácoli**, a lovely Renaissance structure. Via Merlo runs west of here and at no. 2 is the **Palazzo Mirto** (Mon–Fri 9am–1pm & 3–6pm, Sat & Sun 9am–12.30pm; L4000), a late eighteenth-century building that's one of the few in the city to retain its original furniture and fixtures.

La Kalsa and the Galleria Regionale

Planned and built by the Saracens, today the quarter of **La Kalsa** (from the Arabic, *khalisa*, meaning "pure") is old, shattered and – even in daylight – vaguely threatening. Its centre is a huge World War II bomb site, still lived in, but with scarred and gutted buildings on all sides; on maps, it just appears as a blank space. It goes without saying that this is one of Palermo's more notorious areas, young bag-snatchers on speeding Vespas adding to the thrills. Coming here at night would be a big mistake and, although daytime tourists are hardly strangers to the area, given the surrounding attractions, they have been known to be hit by missiles from catapults at dusk.

The Galleria Regionale

One reason for braving the district is the **Palazzo Abatellis**, Via Alloro 4, a fifteenth-century building that still retains elements of its Catalan-Gothic and Renaissance origins, notably in its doorway and courtyard. Revamped since the war, it now houses the **Galleria Regionale** (Mon, Wed, Fri & Sat 9am–1.30pm, Tues & Thurs 9am–1.30pm & 3–7.30pm, Sun 9am–12.30pm; L8000), which houses an excellent medieval art collection.

The **ground floor** contains sculpture, beginning with an incredibly intricate doorframe that once adorned a Palermitan mansion, the twelfth-century wooden carving all Arabic. Beyond lie works of the fifteenth-century sculptor **Francesco Laurana** (room 4): his white marble bust of *Eleonora d'Aragona* is a calm, perfectly studied portrait. Another room is devoted to the work of the Gagini clan, mostly statues of the Madonna, though Antonello Gagini is responsible for a rather strident Archangel Michael, with a distinct military manner. The only non-sculptural item is a magnificent fifteenth-century **fresco**, the *Triumph of Death*, by an unknown (possibly Flemish) painter. It's a chilling study, with Death cast as a skeletal archer astride a galloping, spindly horse, trampling bodies slain by his arrows. He rides towards a group of smug and wealthy citizens, apparently unconcerned at his approach; meanwhile, to the left, the sick and the old plead hopelessly for oblivion.

There are three further frescoes, this time thirteenth- and fourteenth-century Sicilian and rather crude, above the steps up to the **first floor**, which is devoted to painting. This section is unusually comprehensive, with no shortage of excellent Sicilian art, the earliest (thirteenth- to fourteenth-century) displaying marked Byzantine characteristics, including a fourteenth-century mosaic of the *Madonna and Child*, eyes and hands remarkably self-assured. Later fifteenth-century paintings and frescoes are all vivid and imaginative in their portrayal of the *Coronation of the Virgin*, a favourite theme. This floor also contains some notable highlights, not least a collection of works by the fifteenth-century Sicilian artist, **Antonello da Messina**: three small, clever portraits of SS Gregory, Jerome and Augustine (with a rakish red hat); and an indisputably powerful *Annunciation*, a placid depiction of Mary, head and shoulders covered, right hand slightly raised in acknowledgement of the (off-picture) Archangel Gabriel. There's a second view – looking down – of the *Triumph of Death*, and some important Flemish works too, such as a **Mabuse** triptych of the *Virgin and Child*, crammed with detail and surrounded by some extraordinarily ugly cherubs.

La Gancia to La Magione

There's more work by the Gagini family, sculpted fragments and reliefs, in the fifteenth-century church of **La Gancia** (summer Mon–Sat 9am–noon & 3–8pm, Sun 10am–12.30pm; winter Mon–Sat 9am–noon & 3–6pm, Sun 10am–12.30pm) – or Santa Maria degli Angeli – next door to the gallery. It's worth stopping by anyway for the interior, which is covered in understated marble decoration and boasts a ceiling of brown stars.

From here, Via Alloro runs southwest, past a succession of ailing *palazzi*, before feeding into a confusing jumble of squares, principally Piazza Aragona and **Piazza Croce dei Vespri** (marked by a cross for the French who died in the 1282 Sicilian Vespers rebellion). In Piazza Croce dei Vespri stands the huge entrance to the **Palazzo Valguarnera Gangi**, where Visconti filmed the ballroom scene in *The Leopard*; you may be able to get in by smooth-talking the porter. Close by, to the south, is **Piazza della Rivoluzione**, from where the 1848 uprising began and which is marked by an oddly elaborate fountain. From this last piazza, **Via Garibaldi** leads south, marking the end of the route that Garibaldi took in May 1860 when he entered the city (he marched north, up Corso dei Mille and into Via Garibaldi). Here, at Via Garibaldi 23, the immense, battered fifteenth-century **Palazzo Aiutamicristo** keeps bits of its original Catalan-Gothic structure.

The little street (Via Magione) around the south side of the palace leads to the lovely church of **La Magione** (Mon–Sat 8–11.30am & 3–6.30pm, Sun 8am–1pm; closed during services), approached through a palm-lined drive. Built in 1151, the simple Norman church was subsequently given to the Teutonic knights as their headquarters by Henry VI. Today, it's strikingly sparse, inside and out; the reason becomes clear as you step around the back to look at the finely worked apse.

You're standing on the very edge of the worst bits of La Kalsa here, the area (due to its proximity to the port) subjected to saturation bombing during World War II; La Magione, like many of the other historical buildings around, survives only through a combination of luck and piecemeal restoration.

Villa Giulia

Palermo's best central park, **Villa Giulia**, is just a few minutes' walk away, along Via Lincoln – an eighteenth-century garden that provides an escape from the traffic. Attractions include planned, aromatic gardens, a kiddies' train, bandstand, deer and ducks. There's also a Botanical Garden, the **Orto Botánico** (Mon–Fri 9am–6pm, Sat & Sun 9am–1pm), next door to the park, which dates from 1795 and features tropical plants from all over the world – not a bad place to finish a tour of the seedier sides of Palermo.

Out from the centre

There are several targets beyond the old centre, on the outskirts of the modern city, that warrant investigation. Some, like the **ethnographic museum**, shouldn't be missed on any visit to Palermo; others have a low-key interest for fans of the **Norman** period; while one, the **Cappuccini monastery**, is decidedly ghoulish, and for the strong of stomach only.

The Parco della Favorita and Museo Etnográfico Pitrè

To the **north**, around 3km from Piazza Castelnuovo, lies the city's grandest park, the **Parco della Favorita**: a long, wooded expanse at the foot of Monte Pellegrino, with sports grounds and stadiums – where several of the Italia 90 World Cup matches were played – at one end, and formal gardens laid out a couple of kilometres beyond. The grounds were originally bought by the Bourbon king, Ferdinand, in 1799, during his exile from Naples, and for three years he lived here in the **Palazzina Cinese** (closed to the public), a small Chinese-style pavilion. This is just inside the main entrance, beyond Piazza Niscemi, and buses #806 and #833 run right the way here, from Piazza Sturzo (behind the Politeama) or Viale della Libertà.

Next door is the **Museo Etnográfico Pitrè** (daily except Fri 8.30am–1pm & 3.30–6.30pm; L5000), a wide-ranging though poorly maintained exhibition of Sicilian folklore and culture. There's all the work traditionally associated with Sicily, perhaps most spectacularly a wealth of brightly painted carts (*carretti*) and carriages, some several hundred years old. Mostly, they're two-wheeled vehicles, from barrows to horse-drawn wagons, and in the past people's status was judged by the skill and extent of the decorations on their carts. Every available inch – sometimes including the spokes and undercarriage – is covered with geometric patterns and historical, chivalrous scenes from the story of the Paladins. There's a reconstructed puppet theatre too (with occasional performances in the summer; ask at any tourist office), and dozens of the expressive puppets, scenery backdrops and handbills lining the walls. But equally fascinating are the less-well-known aspects of Sicilian handicrafts and cultural life: whole rooms are devoted to a series of intricately sculpted and painted terracotta figures; wooden *ex voto* (votive) tablets depicting the often gruesome death of the dedicatee; and sundry dolls, games, tapestries, tools, bicycles, painted masks – even a great, flowery, iron bedstead.

Church of San Cataldo, Palermo

Cloisters of the Duomo, Monreale

Piazza Pretoria, Palermo

Window dressing, Panarea

Frutta di Martorana, Palermo

Cefalu fishing harbour

Household scene, Aeolian Islands

Convento dei Cappuccini, Palermo

Shrine to the Madonna, Taormina

Piazza Duomo, Taormina

Porto di Levante, Vulcano

Other remnants of Norman Palermo

The best Norman buildings are, with a couple of exceptions, in and around the old town area of the city. But to be thorough in tracking down the rest of Palermo's Norman relics you'll have to poke around the **southern** and **western** outskirts – built-up areas that were once rolling parkland owned by successive kings.

La Zisa, La Cuba and La Cúbula

Bus #124 runs west from the Politeama to **La Zisa** (Mon–Fri 9am–1pm & 3–6pm, Sat & Sun 9am–12.30pm; L4000) – from the Arabic *el aziz*, "magnificent" – a towering palace begun by William I in 1160, and later finished by his son William II. Built as a king's retreat along North African lines, La Zisa was at one time stocked with beautiful planned gardens and rare and exotic beasts. Apparently, a raid on the palace by disaffected locals in 1161 released some of the wild animals, something that probably came as a bit of a shock to William's neighbours. Having languished for centuries within a great private estate, La Zisa today is besieged by modern apartment blocks, but the building has been thoughtfully restored, and contains marvellous **Islamic mosaic** designs within, appropriate surroundings for an impressive collection of Islamic art and artefacts displayed here. When work is completed to restore the gardens to something like their former glory, they will make an impressive sight from the lattice-windowed rooms of the Zisa.

To the south, about 1km beyond the Porta Nuova, at Corso Calatafimi 100 (opposite Via Quarto dei Mille), **La Cuba** is the remains of a slightly later Norman pavilion that formed part of the same royal park. Later occupied by a Bourbon cavalry unit, the shell still lies within a barracks, though it has a separate entrance (Mon–Sat 9am–1pm & 3–7pm, Sun 9am–12.30pm; L4000). Frankly, there's not a great deal to see: some blind arcading on the outside, an Arabic inscription, and the traces of a water gate, which would have been used when the royal pavilion stood in the middle of an artificial lake. A room to one side holds a good model showing how the palace must once have appeared, as well as the inscription that supplied the date of the building's foundation (1180). You might catch a glimpse from the street, or from the #309, #339 or #389 buses, which run past it and continue up the corso to **La Cúbula** (on the right, at the end of Via Aurelio Zancla, between nos. 443 and 459 on the main road). This domed kiosk, once a summerhouse in the extensive grounds of La Zisa, now looks rather uncomfortable in the midst of the twentieth-century architecture that dwarfs it on all sides.

San Giovanni dei Lebbrosi and the Ponte dell'Ammiraglio

Southeast of the centre is the well-restored, eleventh-century domed church of **San Giovanni dei Lebbrosi** (Mon–Sat 9am–1pm), reachable on buses #211, #226 or #231 from the northern end of Corso dei Mille, near the station. Just off the corso, at Via Cappello 38, it's one of the oldest Norman churches in Sicily, reputedly founded in 1070 by Roger I. Its name (St John of the Lepers) derives from the building nearby, which was once a leprosy hospital.

Back down the corso, the route Garibaldi and his "Thousand" (hence Corso dei Mille) took into the city in 1860, you reach the stranded **Ponte dell'Ammiraglio**, accessible on the same bus as San Giovanni. Built in 1113 by George of Antioch, founder of La Martorana, the slender bridge once straddled the River Oreto, though the water has since been diverted and now it's surrounded by a little garden. On the night of May 27, 1860, it figured as a brief stand of the Bourbon troops as Garibaldi marched into Palermo. If you don't want to make the trek out specifically to see it, the bridge is visible from the train to Cefalù/Messina.

Santo Spirito

Last of the Norman attractions is the cemetery-surrounded church of **Santo Spirito** (daily 9am–noon), to the west of San Giovanni – take bus #246 from the station to the Cimitero Sant'Orsola. Founded in 1173, it's been restored to its original, rather severe state. Here, in 1282, began the **massacre of the Sicilian Vespers**, ostensibly sparked off when a French officer insulted a bride on her way to church. The ringing of the vesper (evensong) bell was the signal to drive the French out of Sicily; most were eventually slaughtered by the oppressed islanders.

The Convento dei Cappuccini

Of all the attractions on the edge of Palermo, the **Convento dei Cappuccini** (daily 9am–noon & 3–5pm; donation expected) is the most intriguing, reachable by taking bus #327 (from Piazza Indipendenza) southwest to Via Pindemonte and following signposts for a couple of hundred metres. For several hundred years this monastery retained its own burial ground, placing its dead in catacombs under the church. Later, responding to requests and bequests from rich laymen, many others began to be interred here, right up until 1881. The bodies (some 8000 of them) were preserved by various chemical and drying processes – including dehydration, the use of vinegar and arsenic baths, and treatment with quicklime – and then placed in niches along various corridors, dressed in the suit of clothes that they had previously provided for the purpose. Descending into the catacombs is like having a walk-on part in your own horror film. The rough-cut stone corridors are divided according to sex and status, different caverns reserved for men, women, the clergy, doctors, lawyers and surgeons. Suspended in individual niches and pinned with an identifying tag, the bodies are vile, contorted, grinning figures, some decomposed beyond recognition, others complete with skin, hair and eyes, fixing you with a steely stare. Those that aren't arranged along the walls lie in stacked glass coffins, and, to say the least, it's an unnerving experience to walk among them. Times change, though, as Patrick Brydone noted in his late eighteenth-century *A Tour Through Sicily and Malta*:

> *Here the people of Palermo pay daily visits to their deceased friends . . . here they familiarize themselves with their future state, and chuse the company they would wish to keep in the other world. It is a common thing to make choice of their nich, and to try if their body fits it . . . and sometimes, by way of a voluntary penance, they accustom themselves to stand for hours in these niches . . .*

Of all the skeletal bodies, saddest are the many remains of babies and young children, nothing more than spindly puppets. Follow the signs for the sealed-off cave that contains the coffin of 2-year-old Rosalia Lombardo, who died in 1920. A new process, a series of injections, preserved her to the extent that she looks like she's asleep – after over seventy years. Perhaps fortunately, the doctor who invented the technique died before he could tell anyone how it was done.

Eating

You can eat well and cheaply in Palermo, either snacking in bars and at market stalls or sitting down in a score of good-value pizzerias and restaurants throughout the old town. Basic foodstuffs are particularly good in Palermo: snacks like *arancini*, pastries and ice-cream, as well as more substantial pizzas are among the best you'll taste in Sicily, if not Italy. Fish is a feature on menus in more expensive trattorias and restaurants that advertise *cucina casalinga* or *cucina siciliana*; the local speciality is *pasta con le sarde*, macaroni with fresh sardines, fennel, raisins and pine kernels. It's worth noting that eating places tend to close early, especially in the central old town, where if you turn up at 10pm the waiters are likely to be packing up around you. For the most popular places, go before 8pm, or be prepared to wait in line.

Breakfast, snacks and cakes

Almost any bar or *pasticceria* is a good bet first thing in the morning, with **breakfast** pastries fresh from the bakeries. But for something more substantial than just *cornetti* head for one of the following places:

Pasticceria Alba, Piazza Don Bosco 7. Wonderful pastries.

Caffé Ateneo, Via Maqueda 170. Central café-bar, opposite San Cataldo church on the corner of Via dell'Università, bursting with *arancini*, pastries and the like.

Bellini, Piazza Bellini. The bar inside the pizzeria (see p.89) starts serving snacks, including hefty pizza slices, early. Tables outside in summer.

Bar Costa, Via Alfieri 13 (near Via Emanuele Notarbártolo, north of Piazza Boccaccio). High-class *pasticceria* in the north of the modern city, which specializes in lemon crème.

Extra Bar, Via Ruggero Séttimo 107 (corner of Piazza Ruggero Séttimo). Masses of cakes, ice-cream, and hot food at a handy central bar.

Ferrara, Piazza Giulio Césare 46. Just to the left as you exit the train station, this has a good range of fast-food snacks and complete lunches.

Magico, Corso Vittorio Emanuele 244. Cheap set lunches and substantial fast-food snacks.

Bar Mazzara, Via Generale V. Magliocco 15 (corner of Piazza Ungheria). Lampedusa is supposed to have written parts of *The Leopard* here and a few old wooden booths remain in what is otherwise a smart snack bar/*pasticceria*. Ice-cream and *arancini* also available.

FOOD MARKETS AND HEALTH STORES

Some of the best snacks are on sale in Palermo's **markets**, mostly traditional takeaway food – chopped boiled octopus (*purpu* in Sicilian), *arancini*, cooked artichokes, as well as bread, fruit and vegetables. In every market, you'll also find stalls selling *pani cu' la meuza* – bread rolls filled with sautéed beef spleen or tripe, which either come unadorned (*schiettu*, meaning "nubile") or topped with fresh ricotta and *caciocavallo* cheese (*maritatu*, "married").

Best market is the Vucciria market, off Via Roma between Corso Vittorio Emanuele and the San Domenico church, but there's also food on sale at the Ballarò market in Piazza del Cármine (p.72) and along Via Sant'Agostino (p.75). The Ballarò market, in particular, has a few very basic *hosterie* – wooden tables scattered around the market stalls – where you can accompany your snack with a beer or two.

Sicilians would argue that all their food is healthy, but there are a few specific **health food stores** springing up throughout the city. The most central is Natura, Via Bentivegna 62 off Via Roma, two blocks of north of Via Cavour (closed Wed afternoon).

Caffé Lo Nardo, Piazza S. Carlo 9–10. Unusually trendy little coffee shop deep in the backstreets, close to Piazza della Rivoluzione. Sandwiches and snacks served all day. Closed Sun.

Panineria, Via Trabia 35 (off Via Maqueda, close to Teatro Mássimo). Good sandwiches, either toasted or filled rolls; pizza slices, too.

Paninomania, Via Maqueda 158. Hot and cold sandwiches to eat at the counter or take away.

Caffé San Domenico, Piazza San Domenico. Outdoor tables close to the Vucciria market for your early-morning coffee and *cornetto*.

Pasticceria Scimone, Via Imera 8 and Via V. Miceli 18b, (both north of Via Mosca). Excellent *pasticceria* whose wares can also be eaten at *Trattoria La Cambusa* (see p.90).

Bar Spinnato, Via Príncipe di Belmonte 111. Classy *pasticceria* and bar.

Pasticceria Svizzera e Siciliana, Via M. Stabile 155. Fine uptown upmarket *pasticceria* with delightful cakes, pastries and chocolates.

Ice-cream

One of the city's prime glories is its *gelaterie* (ice-cream shops). You can buy ice-cream just about anywhere, but Palermo has some classic shops and cafés – famed all over Italy – especially worth tracking down. Many are up in the newer, northern part of the city, so check that they're still in business before trekking up there.

Da Ciccio, Corso dei Mille 73. Round the corner from the train station, one of the most central places for good ice-cream, and inexpensive.

Cofea, Via Villareale 18. Superb ice-cream.

Ilardo, Foro Italico Umberto I 12 (at the end of Via Alloro). Opposite the raucous seaside fairground, the *Ilardo* has been in business for decades serving extraordinarily good ice-cream. Closed Oct–May.

San Francesco, Piazza San Francesco. Directly opposite the *Antica Focacceria San Francesco* (see below) and run by the same people, this is a good old-town place with tables in the square, open till late.

Stancampiano, Via Notarbartolo 51. Not very central – in the modern north of the city – but well-known for its award-winning ice-cream.

Pizza places

Although you can buy slices throughout the day in bars and cafés, proper restaurants usually only serve **pizza** at night – because it takes hours to set up and light the wood-fired ovens. However, there are a couple of exceptions to this rule in Palermo; and several places do serve pizza at both lunch and dinner on Sundays. Some of the places listed below also serve other food, too: on the whole, though, the best pizzas are served in those places that prepare nothing else, save perhaps salad and the odd bowl of pasta. Since these restaurants are the cheapest option for a sit-down meal, the most popular pizza places get packed at the weekends, full of young people intent upon a night out rather than just a meal. At all of the places below, you'll be able to eat and drink inexpensively – pizza, salad and wine should rarely come to more than L20,000 a head.

Antica Focacceria San Francesco, Via A. Paternostro 58 (off Corso Vittorio Emanuele and opposite the church of San Francesco). For authentic Sicilian fast food, visit this splendid old-time pizzeria (open since 1834) with marble-topped tables and floor, cast-iron surroundings and fresh pizza slices as well as other oven-baked snacks. The only discordant note is the introduction of a microwave for reheating. See above for *gelateria*. No credit cards. No closing day.

Antica Pizzeria Belmonte, Via Príncipe di Belmonte 81. In the heart of the modern shopping district, there's nothing very old about the *Antica Pizzeria*, but it's a good place to eat – and it's close to the only central bars with a bit of life to them in the evening. No closing day.

I Beati Paoli, Piazza Marina 50. In a favourite eating-out area of Palermo, and bang next-door to another pizza choice with similar fare, this is distinguished by its monastic cellar theme. Service is brisk, and the pizzas surprisingly good considering the emphasis on *ambi-ente*. Queues start forming after about 9pm. Closed Mon in winter.

Bellini, Piazza Bellini. Housed in the old Teatro Bellini, the large pizza ovens at the back of the bar are in business most of the day. At night, sit at outdoor tables underneath La Martorana church – one of the city's more romantic locations. Arrive early to avoid the crowds. Closed Mon.

Al Galileo, Via Galileo Galilei 49 (turn right off Via Leonardo da Vinci, an extension of the western end of Via Notarbártolo). A lively joint with delicious pizzas, though not central. No closing day.

Pizzeria Italia, Via Orologio 54 (off Via Maqueda, just before Teatro Mássimo). Easily the best in central Palermo, and large queues develop quickly here. It is crowded, noisy and the pizzas are superb (though there is no local wine; only moderately priced bottles and half-bottles). No credit cards. Closed Mon Oct–May.

Naif Ristorante-Pizzeria, Via Vann'Anto 21 (corner of Via Leopardi). North of the centre, behind Via Notarbártolo (Via Leopardi runs north from this street), but a very nice place that's worth the journey. Closed Mon.

Pizza Pazza a Pezzi per i Pazzi della Pizza, Via B. Latini 25. A bit of a Palermitan institu-tion, once you've braved the name ("Crazy Pizza in Pieces for Those Crazy for Pizza") you'll discover that the pizzas are, in fact, very acceptable without being outstanding. No closing day.

Trattoria dal Pompiere, Via Bara Olivella 107 (the next parallel street north of Via Orologio). The same cheap prices as the *Italia*, but with fancier pine tables, decidedly inferi-or pizzas, and a few more non-pizza dishes. No credit cards. Closed Sun.

Trabia, Via Trabia 35. Across from the Teatro Mássimo, this is more of an adjunct to the fast-food/sandwich/take-away joint next door than a restaurant, but still a useful spot for *forno a legna* pizzas for L5000–8000, mixed salads, house wine, with barely anything else. It's open till around 11pm, and has some tables outside. No credit cards. No closing day.

Restaurants

There are several budget restaurants around Stazione Centrale, not all of them the tourist traps you might expect. Other **restaurants** are scattered all over the city and many excellent local places serving *cucina casalinga* are hidden in gloomy old-town streets: you might want to take a taxi late at night if you feel unsure about walking there. At the other end of the scale, Palermo also has sev-eral topnotch restaurants worth considering if you want to taste the very best Italian food – although prices in these are high, they're considerably less than equivalents elsewhere in Italy. **Non-Italian food** is getting more common in Palermo, though some places have a mediocre menu and a short life: check the list for some of the best current options.

ITALIAN/SICILIAN

Ristorante-Pizzeria Al 59, Piazza Giuseppe Verdi 59. *Alfresco* dining on a large covered ter-race with a central fountain, opposite the Teatro Mássimo. There's a good choice of pasta, and though the pizzas are nothing special it's a fine place to while away an evening. Moderate. Closed Wed.

MEAL PRICES

The restaurants listed are graded according to the following price categories:

Inexpensive: under L25,000	Expensive: L40,000–70,000
Moderate: L25,000–40,000	Very expensive: over L70,000

These prices reflect the per person cost of a full meal including wine and cover charge; see p.32 for more details.

Ca d'Oro, Corso Vittorio Emanuele 256–8. More often than not you end up eating in splendid isolation in this large, first-floor restaurant overlooking the main road. The waiters, you feel, would rather be somewhere else, but the food is fine and there's a good-value tourist menu. Moderate. Closed Sun.

Trattoria La Cambusa, Piazza Marina 16. Excellent old-town restaurant specializing in fish and also serving *semifreddo* – ice-cream with brittle almond topping. Moderate. No credit cards. Closed Mon.

Casa del Brodo, Via Vittorio Emanuele 175. In business for over a century, this place attracts both locals and tourists to its two small rooms. *Carni bolliti* are the specialities, though the risotto with *crema di asparagi* (asparagus sauce) or *funghi* (mushroom sauce) are also wonderful. There's a L25,000 tourist menu, which includes a selection of antipasti but not drinks. Moderate. Closed Tues.

Charleston, Piazza Ungheria 30 (☎091.321.366). If you have stacks of cash to blow, Palermo's most-celebrated high-class restaurant, the *Charleston*, serves dreamlike cuisine – with regular forays into the Italian regions to supplement its Sicilian specialities. Between mid-June and late September, the restaurant shifts to the beach at Mondello (see p.97). Meals cost in the region of L70,000 a head; reservations advised. Very expensive. Closed Sun.

Il Cotto e il Crudo, Piazza Marina. On the pricey side, but with a good choice of tasty local specialities and outdoor seating. Moderate. No credit cards. Closed Tues.

Trattoria a' Cuccagna, Via Príncipe di Granatelli 21a; off Via Roma before the Teatro Politeama. Authentic Sicilian food, including *pescespada affumicato* (smoked swordfish). The cover charge is excessive at L4000. Moderate. No closing day.

Trattoria-Pizzeria Enzo, Via Maurolico 17/19 (very close to Stazione Centrale; turn left as you exit the station). Perhaps the city's best bargain for full-blown meals, the *Enzo* serves hefty portions of pizza, pasta and basic meat and fish at absurdly low prices. Inexpensive. Closed Fri.

Trattoria Luigi Basile, Via Maurolico 11. The same excellent value as the *Enzo*, next door; the wine is good, too. Inexpensive. Closed Sun.

Trattoria Macco, Via B. Gravina 85; off Piazza Sturzo. At the top of Via Roma, this pleasant trattoria specializes in Sicilian dishes – swordfish *involtini* and spaghetti with *ricci*, for example. Good local wine. Moderate. Closed Sun.

Trattoria Mafone, Piazza Papireto 15. Reasonably priced neighbourhood trattoria behind the cathedral, with tables in the piazza. The food is excellent, especially the fish – fresh from the market. Inexpensive. No closing day.

Il Mirto e la Rosa, Via Príncipe di Granatelli 30 (off Piazza Florio) (☎091.324.353). Palermo's only centrally located vegetarian restaurant (though also serving meat dishes) with decent food on a sampling menu (*degustazione*) or fixed-price menus. Moderate. Closed Aug.

Trattoria ai Normanni, Piazza della Vittoria 25. Just off Piazza dell'Indipendenza, this is a reliable restaurant attracting mainly locals. The speciality, *spaghetti ai Normanni*, is a terrific concoction of shrimps, aubergines, fresh tomatoes and grated peanuts. Arrive early to be sure of a table outside. Moderate. Closed Mon evening.

Peppino, Piazza Castelnuovo 49. Good low prices for the address, though tourists are the main clientele. Pizzas are available too. Moderate. Closed Wed.

Trattoria Primavera, Piazza Bologni 4 (☎091.329.408). Bright and lively neighbourhood trattoria, between the cathedral and Quattro Canti, serving genuine Sicilian food. There's a short list of pastas (*alla Trapanese* is with a cold purée of fresh tomatoes, pungent garlic and basil), fresh fish (stuffed sardines) and meat (home-made sausage) served up to an enthusiastic, local clientele. Reservations advised on Saturday and Sunday nights. Moderate. No credit cards. Closed Tues.

Santandrea, Piazza Sant'Andrea (☎091.334.999). Chic and popular restaurant, a stone's throw away from Piazza San Domenico and the Vucciria market from which most of the ingredients are obtained. Menus don't exist, and dishes are seasonal and generally delicious, if somewhat pricey. The homemade desserts are fantastic and there's a good wine list. Book early if you want to sit outside. Closed Tues & Jan. Expensive.

RESTAURANTS OUT OF THE CENTRE

Some of the best of Palermo's restaurants are way out of the centre, known to locals for their classic Sicilian cookery but fairly inaccessible for most visitors. If you've got a car, or someone to drive you, try one of those listed below; always ring first to check opening times.

Trattoria Aloha d'Oro, Via Pietro Bonnano 42 (☎091.547.657). More fine home cooking at a trattoria halfway up the road to the top of Monte Pellegrino; the speciality is fish. Expensive. Closed Mon.

La Scuderia, Viale del Fante 9 (☎091.520.323). Classic Sicilian and Italian cuisine at a restaurant near the stadium at La Favorita. The food is terrific, the prices less so; advance reservations are advised. Expensive. Closed Sun evening & Aug.

Osteria Al Tari, Piazza G. le Cascino 45 (☎091.546.436). In the shadow of Monte Pellegrino, in the north of the city, this is a lovely local restaurant with authentic Sicilian food. Moderate. Closed Sun.

Trattoria da Turiddo, Via Ugo La Malfa (☎091.243.945). This fantastic fish restaurant is a long ride north of the centre by taxi – on the road to the airport, before Sferracavallo. But the trip is rewarded by a set meal (there's no menu) that encompasses plate after plate of marvellous fish and seafood. Moderate.

Shangai, Vicolo dei Mezzani 34. Not Chinese but Italian, the *Shangai* has a restaurant terrace with a bird's eye view of the Vucciria market, a great location, though the service is tired and the food mediocre. It's most easily reached by heading east along Via Vittorio Emanuele (first alley on the left past Via Roma). No credit cards. Inexpensive. Closed Sun.

Trattoria Stella, *Hotel Patria*, Via Alloro 104 (corner of Via Aragona). The hotel is no more (though you'll see the sign over the entrance), but the restaurant spills out into a lovely late-medieval courtyard, a super place to spend the evening. It's not in the most salubrious part of town, though, so keep your wits about you. Can get crowded. Moderate. Closed Mon in winter, Sun evening in July & Aug.

Trattoria Trápani, Piazza Giulio Césare; opposite the station, next to the *Albergo Elena*. This basic family-run trattoria is good for lunch, with filling food (and a minimum charge of L9000 per person). Inexpensive. Closed Sun.

Trattoria al Vicolo, Piazza San Francesco Saverio (☎091.651.2464). A good atmosphere and local specialities in a small but smart place in the Albergheria district, accessible from Corso Tukory (fifth on the right as you head west) or Piazza Cármine. Moderate. Closed Sun.

FOREIGN RESTAURANTS

Hostaria Al Duar 2, Via Ammiraglio Gravina 31. There's regular Italian food at this friendly restaurant at the north end of Via Roma, but the best bet is the superb-value *Completo Tunisino* – a huge pile of Tunisian food, which comes as several different courses and ends with couscous. Thoroughly recommended. Moderate. Closed Mon.

Caffé d'Oriente, Piazza Cancellieri (☎091.324.158). Also known as *Caffé Arabo*, this is an authentic slice of Tunisia in a sequestered nook close to the Quattro Canti (up Via Monte Vergine from Corso Vittorio Emanuele). Eat inside or in the piazza, choosing among a wide selection of rich and filling rice and couscous dishes, some outstanding salads, and marzipan sweets and *frullati* to finish. Belly-dancers do their stuff, and narghiles are on hand for a post-prandial smoke. You can also sit at the bar here – like the restaurant, open till late. Moderate. Closed Mon Oct–May.

La Pagoda, Via M. Stabile 28 (between Via Roma and Via Ruggero Séttimo). Apart from the usual pasta and pizzas there are a few unusual foreign dishes on offer here – *risotto Thailandese* for one. Closed Mon. Inexpensive.

Treffpunkt di Tedeschi Mario, Viale Lazio 49 (at the west end of Viale della Libertà). German restaurant in the north of the city steeped in Teutonic decoration, and with good food and reasonable prices. Moderate.

Drinking, nightlife and entertainment

After dark and over much of the city, Palermo's frenetic lifestyle stops, pedestrians flit quickly through the shadows, and the main roads are given over to speeding traffic and screaming police sirens. What **bars** there are in the city centre tend to close around 9pm, though **birrerias** stay open later, and in summer life continues unabated until the small hours at **Mondello** (p.96) – buses connect the city to the beach all night. Palermo's newer parts, around Viale della Libertà, see more street-life, with an energetic *passeggiata* and cruising cars blasting away like mobile discotheques. If none of this is your scene, then there is more cultural **entertainment** to be had back in the city centre. Summer in particular sees a citywide programme of music, theatre and dance performances, art events and open-air film screenings, under the umbrella title **Palermo di Scena**, during which there are usually two or three things on every night between the end of July and mid-September, for around L5000 a time. Contact the tourist office for full details, or call the toll-free information line (☎167.234.169).

To check **what's on** in Palermo, it's always worth looking in *Palermo & Provincia Live*, the events weekly *News: Informazioni Turistiche*, and *Il Giornale della Sicilia* (see p.61). In bar and shop windows, you'll also see a freesheet pinned up called *Giorno e Notte*, which details all the current eating, drinking and nightlife possibilities.

Bars and birrerias

Places to **drink** in (as opposed to a coffee stop) drift in and out of fashion and you'll have to follow the crowds to find the present favourite. They're also nearly all in the northern quarters of the city, some of them a bus- or taxi-ride away, the only central street geared up to evening drinks being the traffic-free Via Príncipe di Belmonte, which has a glitzy selection of bars and *pasticcerie*. We've listed the most accessible places below, but if you really want to bar-crawl you'll need an obliging driver and a local to show you the way – preferably the same person.

Bikers Bar, Piazza Olivella 13. Tables opposite the archeological museum make this a good spot for a snack and a pause. Open late.

Birra Messina, Via Roma at Via Venezi, just before the Teatro Biondo. Staggering home, you can get a late drink at this stand-up stall. If you need sobering up, try the sharp, fresh lemon juice – a speciality.

Bottiglieria del Mássimo, Via Spinuzza 59. Wine bar with outdoor seating near the Teatro Mássimo, centre of quite a scene on summer nights and open till late. No food.

Au Dominò, Via Príncipe di Belmonte 88. Popular place for crepes, toasted panini and beers, and open until after midnight.

Fiore, Via Príncipe di Belmonte 84. Beer, milk shakes, pizza slices and a good-humoured atmosphere.

Fusorario, Piazza Olivella 2. *Birreria* opposite the Museo Archeologico. Draught and bottled beers plus music, with tables outside; open late. Closed Aug, Sept & Tues in winter.

Il Golosone, Piazza Castelnuovo. A popular place for drinks and fancy *paste* (including *frutta di Martorana*), owned by the same people who run the *Bar Spinnato* (see p.88).

Caffé del Kássaro, Corso Vittorio Emanuele 390 (near Quattro Canti, with another entrance in Via San Salvatore). Draught and bottled beers, panini, tables outside, poetry readings and musical sessions in summer, and open late.

Liberty Pub, Via Narciso Cozzo 20. Rather a stiff atmosphere, with cocktails, beer and videos, one block north of Via Cavour; open until late. Closed Wed.

Malaluna Pub, Via della Resurrezione. Up near La Favorita, this place isn't at all bad, with live music as a further inducement to make the trip.

Di Martino, Via Mazzini 54 (corner of Via Daita). A few minutes' walk up Viale della Libertà from Piazza Castelnuovo, this has quite a loyal following. Beers are the speciality here, also mega-sandwiches, and the chance to watch the smart set at play. Outdoor seating.

Pinguino, Via Ruggero Séttimo 86. Famous *spremute*, milk shakes and a range of non-alcoholic cocktails. Closed Mon.

Villa Boscogrande, Via Tommaso Natale 91. Way out in the northeast of the city, towards Sferracavallo, this *palazzo* was the setting for parts of Visconti's film of *The Leopard*; smart and expensive. Bus #628 from Piazza de Gásperi.

Clubs

Like drinking establishments, **clubs** are almost exclusively found in the new, northern section of the city. Apart from a few fleeting exceptions, they're expensive discos, chock-full of fashion victims and – unless you're very keen – rarely worth the long journey out there. Still, for anyone determined to party in Palermo itself, here's a list of the better places, but check posters and newspapers for the current hip venues. In summer, the scene switches to Mondello (see below). Note that you may have to pay to "join" the club before they'll let you in.

Axys, Via dei Nebrodi 56 (☎091.527.265).

Biergarten, Viale Regione Siciliana 6469 (☎091.688.9727).

Il Cerchio, Viale Strasburgo 312 (☎091.688.5421).

Gazebo Club, Viale Piemonte 6 (☎091.348.917).

Grant's, Via Príncipe di Paternò 80 (☎091.346.772).

Paramatta, Viale Lazio 51 (☎091.513.621).

Live music

There's no major **rock music** venue and top British and American bands rarely make it further south than Naples, though the *comune* regularly stages open-air rock events in the summer, usually in the Giardino Inglese and other green spaces – watch for posters around the city for details.

The Teatro Mássimo on Piazza Verdi (☎091.589.575 or 091.589.070) is the first choice for performances of **classical music** (Oct–June), while the Teatro Politeama Garibaldi (☎091.605.3315), in Piazza Ruggero Séttimo, and Teatro Golden, Via Terrasanta 60 (☎091.305.217), put on a pretty fair programme throughout the year; for the Golden, take bus #103 from the Politeama, or walk west along Via Dante and turn right at Piazza Virgilio. Various local musical associations coordinate many events, among them ALEA, who have their office at Piazza G. Meli 5 (☎091.322.217), and the Associazione Siciliana Amici della Musica, at Piazza Sett'Angeli 10 (☎091.584.679).

For **jazz**, the Teatro Golden again has occasional gigs, or contact the Associazione Siciliana per la Musica Jazz (also known as Brass Group) at Via Butera 14 (☎091.616.6480), which sponsors gigs at various venues throughout the city.

Theatre and cinema

Palermo and its surroundings have a stack of other **theatres**, worth checking out if you speak Italian. In particular, the Teatro Siciliano Zappalà in Mondello, Viale Galatea 1 (☎091.684.0391) features traditional theatre productions in Sicilian dialect throughout the summer. Mainstream theatres include the Teatro Biondo, Via Teatro Biondo 11, off Via Roma (☎091.743.4341); Teatro Dante, Piazza Lolli

21, off Via Dante (☎091.581.222); Teatro della Verdura, Viale del Fante 70b (☎091.688.4137) and Teatro Libero Palermo, Vicolo Sant'Uffizio 15, at Piazza Marina (☎091.322.264).

Cinemas show the latest films dubbed into Italian, and the main central screens are on Via Emerico Amari (ABC and Nazionale). There's an English Film Club, too, which shows new releases at the Metropolitan Cinema, Viale Strasburgo 356 (☎091.688.6532; L10,000 entry, ISIC cardholders half-price.)

Puppet theatre

The best night out, though, and something you should do at least once in Sicily, is a visit to the **puppet theatre**. There are tourist performances at the Museo Etnográfico Pitrè (p.84) and Museo delle Marionette (p.81), but try to get to one of the surviving back-street puppet theatres for a genuine experience: search out G. Cuticchio, at Via Bara all'Olivella 95 (☎091.323.400), close to the Museo Archeologico; Opera dei Pupi, Vicolo Ragusi 6 (☎091.329.294), off Corso Vittorio Emanuele, close to the Cattedrale (2–3 performances weekly at 9pm); and Teatro Carlo Magno, opposite Santa Zita (daily 9pm); for shows at Monreale, see p.101. **Tickets** are around L5000–10,000 each and performances are usually confined to summer months; check timings at the theatre or the tourist office. Currently, Teatro Bradamante, Via Lombardia 25 (☎091.625.9223), has free performances on Fridays at 10pm; turn left off Viale Lazio, which is at the northern end of Via della Libertà.

Listings

Airlines Air Malta (Via Cavour 80; ☎091.611.1233); Air Sicilia (Via G. Sciuti 180; ☎091.345.004); Alitalia (Via Mazzini 59; ☎091.601.9111); British Airways (c/o Gastaldi, Via Marchese Ugo 56; ☎091.302.881); KLM (c/o Guccione, Via A. Gravina 80; ☎091.581.146); Medair (☎091.545.999); Meridiana (Via XII Gennaio 1g; ☎091.323.141); SAS (Via Cavour 80; ☎091.611.1233; Tunis Air (Piazza Castelnuovo 12; ☎091.611.1845)); TWA (c/o Gastaldi, Via Marchese Ugo 56; ☎ 091.302.881).

American Express c/o Giovanni Ruggeri, Via Emerico Amari 40 (☎091.587.144); Mon–Fri 9am–1pm & 4–7pm, Sat 9am–1pm.

Banks and exchange Banks are open Mon–Fri 8.20am–1.20pm; most branches also open 2.45–3.45pm or until after 4pm; most will exchange all travellers' cheques and accept all major credit, debit and charge cards. Central banks include: Banco di Sicilia (Via R. Séttimo 26); Cassa di Risparmio (Piazza Cassa di Risparmio 2, Via Libertà 185); and Banca Nazionale del Lavoro (Via Roma 201). There are exchange offices at Stazione Centrale (daily 8am–12.30pm & 3–7pm; cash and travellers' cheques only) and at the airport (daily 7.50am–1.20pm & 2.35–8pm).

Bike rental Via Papireto 14a (☎091.322.425); Mon–Sat 4hr for L2000, Sun 4hr for L4000.

Bookshops There's a large selection of English books from Feltrinelli, Via Maqueda 395, opposite the Teatro Mássimo (Mon–Sat 9am–8pm); from Gulliver, on the corner of Via Roma and Piazza San Domenico (also open until 8pm); and Libreria Flaccovio, Via Ruggero Séttimo 37. Libreria dello Studente, Via G. d'Alessi 1, just down the road from the Quattro Canti, has some English-language books, while Libreria Sellerio, Via La Farina 10 and Corso Vittorio Emanuele 504, was founded with the help of Leonardo Sciascia, and is worth a look, too.

Car problems ACI, Viale delle Alpi 6 (☎116 or ☎091.300.468).

Car rental Avis (Punta Raisi airport, ☎091.591.684; Via Príncipe di Scordia 28, ☎091.586.940); Eurauto (for camper vans: Via Príncipe Paternò 119, ☎091.201.529); Europcar (airport, ☎091.591.688; Via Cavour 77a, ☎091.311.949); Hertz (airport, ☎091.591.682; Via Messina 7e, ☎091.331.668); Holiday Car Rental (airport, ☎091.591.687; Via E. Amari 85a, ☎091.325.155); Maggiore (airport, ☎091.591.681; Viale A. De Gásperi 79, ☎091.517.305); Sicily By Car (airport, ☎091.591.250; Via M. Stabile 6a, ☎091.581.045).

Consulates UK, Via Cavour 117 (☎091.326.412); USA, Via Re Federico 18b (☎091.611.0020); Netherlands, Via Roma 489 (☎091.581.521). Other major consulates are in Naples or Rome, including: Australia, Via Alessandria 215, Rome (☎06.852.721); Eire, Via del Pozzetto 108, Rome (☎06.678.2541); New Zealand, Via Zara 30, Rome (☎06.440.3028).

Emergencies Dial ☎113 (general); ☎112 (police); ☎116 or 091.656.9511 (road accident); ☎115 (fire brigade); ☎091.210.111 (central police station, for lost property or theft); ☎091.288.141 (emergency first aid).

Ferry and hydrofoil companies Grandi Navi Veloci to Genova and Livorno (at the port at Calata Marinai d'Italia; ☎091.587.404); Siremar Navigazione to Ústica (Via Francesco Crispi 120; ☎091.582.403); SNAV to Naples, Cefalù and the Aeolian Islands (Via Principe di Belmonte 55; ☎091.333.333); Tirrenia to Naples, Genova, Cágliari, Tunis (at the port on Via Molo; ☎091.602.1111).

Filling stations All-night service at Agip and Mobil, Viale della Regione Siciliana (southwest up Corso Vittorio Emanuele and Corso Calatafimi and then turn right: Agip is outside the Forte Hotel Agip); also at IP, Piazza Indipendenza; Esso, Corso Calatafimi.

Garages Di Giandomenico, Via Oreto 18, behind Stazione Centrale; Central Garage, Piazza Giulio Césare 43, near station; Via Guardione 81, near Stazione Maríttima, behind Via Crispi; Via Sammartino 24, town centre, off Via Dante; Politeama, Via Parisi 6d, off Viale della Libertà near Piazza Castelnuovo; Via Archimede 88, off Viale della Libertà, also central. L15,000–30,000 a night to leave a car; usually less when arranged through your hotel.

Gay info ARCI Gay, Via Genova 7 (☎091.335.688).

Hiking Club Alpino Italiano, Via Agrigento 30 (☎091.625.4352); Club Alpino Siciliano, Via A. Paternostro 43 (☎091.581.323). For maps and details of mountain refuges, see "Maps" below.

Hospital Policlínico, Via del Vespro (☎091.655.3730). For emergency first aid, see "Emergencies".

Laundries Coin-operated laundries at Campana, Via Cuba 2 (off Corso Calatafimi; buses #309, #339 or #389 from Piazza Indipendenza); and Supersecco, Via Alfieri 25 (off Viale della Libertà, bus #806 to Viale d'Annunzio). There's a *lavanderia* on Via Dante where you can leave your clothes to be washed, though this is more expensive.

Left luggage Stazione Centrale (daily 6am–10pm; L5000 for 12hr); Stazione Maríttima (daily 7–11am & 12.30–5pm; L5000 for 12hr).

Maps Detailed maps for hiking in the Monti Madonie from the Istituto Geográfico, Via Danimarca 25 (☎091.511.401).

Newspapers English newspapers and magazines from the newsagents at the top of Via Ruggero Séttimo, junction with Piazza Ruggero Séttimo/Piazza Castelnuovo. Local listings in the daily *Giornale della Sicilia*.

Pharmacies All-night service at Lo Cascio, Via Roma 1; Di Naro, Via Roma 207; and Saladino, Via Príncipe di Belmonte 110. Other chemists operate a rota system, with the address of the nearest open chemist posted on the door of each shop.

Police The Questura in Piazza della Vittoria has an Ufficio degli Stranieri, specifically for tourists (☎091.210.111).

Post offices Main post office is in the Palazzo delle Poste at Via Roma 322; poste restante at counters #15 and #16 (Mon–Fri 8.10am–7.30pm, Sat 8.10am–1.30pm). There is a branch at the Stazione Centrale (Mon–Fri 8.10am–7pm, Sat 8.10am–noon).

Samaritans ☎091.328.692.

Supermarkets Upim, Via Roma (corner of Piazza San Domenico); Standa, Via Libertà 30 (junction with Via Archimede). Both open Mon–Sat until 8pm, and closed Mon am.

Swimming There's a pool, the Piscina Comunale, at Viale del Fante, by La Favorita (June–Nov 9am–1pm; Dec–May 9am–1pm & 3–8pm; L4000).

Telephone offices on Piazza Giulio Césare, directly opposite the train station (ASTT; open daily 9am–10pm) and Via Príncipe di Belmonte 92 (Telecom Italia; Mon 4–7.30pm, Tues–Sat 9am–1pm & 4–7.30pm).

Travel agents CTS, Via Garzilli 28 (off Via Dante, between Piazza Lolli and Piazza Castelnuovo). Mon–Fri 9am–1pm & 4–7.30pm (☎091.611.0713). Discounted tickets and ISIC cards. Transalpino has an office at Stazione Centrale (Mon–Fri 8.30am–1pm & 3–7pm, Sat 8.30am–1pm).

Women's movements ARCI Donna, Via di Giovanni 14 (☎091.301.650).

AROUND PALERMO

Any respite from Palermo's noise is welcome: take the time to get out of the city at least once. The easiest trips, to **Mondello** and **Monte Pellegrino**, can fill in a few spare hours whenever you like, though Palermitans tend to pack both destinations to the gills on summer Sundays. The other retreat, to the cathedral town of **Monreale**, demands more serious attention; you could see it in an afternoon, but consider a full day (and possibly a night) to get the most out of it and the surrounding valley. Less demanding is a jaunt west to the small family resorts that line the **Golfo di Carini**, a change in pace from the frenetic action at Mondello. Side-trips east, to **Bagheria** and **Solunto**, won't occupy more than half a day out from the city, and you could always see them as a stop on the route out of Palermo, along the Tyrrhenian coast. Travelling south from the capital, you can also make a stop at the Albanian settlement of **Piana degli Albanesi**, couched on an upland plain in thoroughly pleasant surroundings – the Easter celebrations here are justly renowned.

Bus and train services to all these places are good; details are given in the text and "Travel details", p.111. For a real change of air, though, jump on a ferry or hydrofoil to the island of **Ustica**, as little as an hour and a quarter from the city. With good, clean swimming and a lazy feel to it, you may end up staying longer than planned.

Mondello

Regular buses run the 11km to **MONDELLO**, the best route passing through Acquasanta and then skirting the coast below Monte Pellegrino as far as Valdesi. From here, a marvellous two-kilometre sandy **beach** curves round to the small resort, tucked under the mountain's northern bluff. The beach is the main attraction, though Mondello does have a tiny working harbour, a jetty from which you can try your luck fishing, and the remnants of a medieval tower. Come in the day and you can split your time nicely between the beach and **eating** on the seafront, a major occupation here. There's a line of trattorias – some with outdoor terraces – where the fish is displayed in cases, temptingly fresh. Or you can grab some excellent snack food from the waterfront stalls – *pasta con le sarde*, deep-fried vegetables, shrimps and whitebait – and then hit the beach.

Stay late and summer nights at Mondello are fun, the venue for Palermo's *passeggiata*. The bars in the main square, Piazza Mondello, are packed, the roads around blocked with cruising cars full of the local youth, and open-air discos add a bit of excitement. In winter it's more laid-back and rarely busy, but the restaurants and snack stalls are still open and it usually stays warm enough to swim until well past the end of the season.

Practicalities

From the Teatro Politeama or Viale della Libertà, buses #806 and, in summer, #833 head to **Mondello**, a half-hour ride through the city's northwestern suburbs. If the night bus fails to materialize, a taxi back to the centre will set you back around L60,000. There's a kiosk on the seafront in summer, with scraps of **tourist information** to hand out (open daily until late).

None of the **restaurants** along the front are particularly cheap, but you can put together inexpensive meals by eating from the snack stalls or buying portions of fresh, sliced *pólipo* (octopus) served at stand-up counters at the front of several restaurants.

If you do want to sit down and eat, good places along the front include *Da Calógero*, Via Torre di Mondello 22 (closed Mon Oct–June), close to the tower, where you can either stand at the counter or sit at the pine tables behind. Apart from plates of mussels and other seafood, it specializes in *ricci di mare* – black, prickly sea urchins, which you can have served with spaghetti. *Marechiaro*, at no. 26 (closed Wed), is more of a proper restaurant, with a fine antipasto table and some unusual shellfish dishes, like *zuppa di vóngole*. In the piazza, *Siciliando* (closed Wed) has reasonably priced pasta dishes and an upstairs terrace (the best places are usually reserved), while the fancier *Sympathy*, beyond the piazza at Via Piano di Gallo 18 (closed Fri), has a few tables outside and attracts a local, well-heeled crowd. Harder to find, but worth the effort, is *Opera Ghiotta*, Viale dei Lillá 4 – east of the *Mondello Palace Hotel* and behind the garage – which has excellent pizzas as well as a full menu.

If you feel like really splashing out, *Le Terrazze* (☎091.450.171) is the offshore platform in the middle of the bay, to which Palermo's swanky *Charleston* restaurant (see p.90) transfers between mid-June and late September – among the best dining experiences in Sicily, but very expensive. There are several **hotels** in Mondello, but all are impossibly full in summer and (mostly) very expensive. If you do fancy staying, ring first: the cheapest is the three-star *Conchiglia d'Oro*, Viale Chloe 9 (☎091.450.359; ④), whose prices drop at least 25 percent in low season.

Monte Pellegrino: mountain and sanctuary

North of the city, a clear landmark visible from the port area, is the massive bulk of **MONTE PELLEGRINO**, the mountain which splits Palermo from the bay at Mondello. It was occupied as far back as 7000 BC: Paleolithic incised drawings were found in the Grotta d'Addaura on Pellegrino's northern slopes and there are casts of some of the best in the Museo Archeologico in the city. Today, the mountain is primarily a target for Sunday picnickers, though it also attracts its fair share of pilgrims, coming to visit the shrine of **St Rosalia**, the city's patron saint. William II's pious niece, Rosalia, renounced worldly things and fled to the mountain in 1159. Nothing more was heard of her until the early seventeenth century, when a vision led to the discovery of her bones on Pellegrino. Pronounced sacred relics, the bones were carted around the city in procession in a successful attempt to stay the ravages of a terrible plague, a ceremony that is re-enacted every July 15 – when there's a torchlight procession to the saint's sanctuary – and again on September 4.

The **ride to the mountain** is extremely impressive (bus #812 from Piazza Sturzo or the Teatro Politeama, though the frequency is erratic), providing wide views over Palermo and its plain, the winding road climbing through a green belt of trees, cacti and scrub. It's a half-hour journey, and the bus drops you a few hundred metres before the sanctuary itself, from where you can walk or jump on the waiting minibus. The **Santuario di Santa Rosalia** is boxed in by tacky souvenir stands, cafés, and vendors flogging every kind of religious kitsch. You enter through a small chapel, built over a deep cave in the hillside where the bones of Rosalia were discovered in 1624. Inside, the water trickling down the walls is supposedly miraculous, channelled by steel plates, while fancy lighting pinpoints a bier containing a reclining golden statue of the saint. Goethe, when he came, thought it "so natural and pleasing, that one can hardly help expecting to see the saint breathe and move". Certainly the saint's expression is realistic, though she seems rather smug, too – an effect perhaps induced by the huge pile of banknotes stacked up beside her, offerings from the faithful, who can make the whole thing a bit of a scrum at times. The so-called museum of the saint's life next door is value for money, especially when you realize that most of the awful exhibits are for sale.

A small road to the left of the chapel leads to the cliff-top promontory – a half-hour's walk – where a more restrained statue of St Rosalia stares over the sprawling city. Another path, leading up from the Santuario to the right, takes you to the top of the mountain – 600m high, and around a forty-minute walk. Elsewhere, all around the trails that cover Monte Pellegrino, whole families are camped out beside their cars, eating lunch from trestle tables and studiously ignoring the "No Campfire" signs, while the kids make swings out of rope tied between the trees. It's a nice place to spend a day.

Heading back, wait until the heat drops and descend by the **Scala Vecchia**, a stepped path that twists from the road by the sanctuary all the way down to Le Falde, near the site of the city's exhibition ground, the Fiera del Mediterraneo. On the way, you can make a short diversion to the Castello Utveggio (built in 1932, now a school for management) for more marvellous views, and regain the road at the bottom to pick up a bus back to the city centre. Some people *walk up* the same route, a recipe for gut-busting if ever there was one.

Monreale

Beach and mountain are all right for an hour or two out of the city, but the major excursion is to **MONREALE**, a small hill-town 8km southwest of Palermo that commands unsurpassed views down the Conca d'Oro valley, the capital shimmering in the distant bay. Norman Lewis called the valley "the greatest and most glorious orchard and market garden in the world", noting that although "there was nothing of gold about it except the roofs of houses on nearby slopes, it frothed, bubbled and exploded with the voluptuous greenery of millions of trees and plants". This panorama from the "Royal Mountain" alone is worth making the trip for, though the real draw is not this, but the mighty Norman cathedral, hidden further in among the houses.

Bus #309 (Mon–Sat) or #389 (hourly on Sun) runs frequently from Piazza dell'Indipendenza (outside the Porta Nuova, reached by bus #109 from Palermo's train station), the journey through the western suburbs and up the valley taking around twenty minutes. Bus #309 drops you in the centre of town, from which it's a few minutes' walk to Piazza Vittorio Emanuele and the Duomo; #389 drops you right in the piazza.

The Duomo

Flanking one side of the town atop a sea-facing shelf of land, the **Duomo** (daily: summer 8am–noon & 3.30–6.30pm; winter closes 6pm) presides magisterially over the town and Conca d'Oro valley. The rather severe, square-towered exterior, though handsome enough, gives no hint of what's inside: the most extraordinary and extensive area of Christian medieval mosaicwork in the world, the apex of Sicilian-Norman art. Keep L1000 or L1500 in coins handy to switch on the lights inside if they aren't already on, though the chances are you won't be the only visitor here, as it's a regular coach stop. Bear in mind that, despite the continual influx of tourists, the same rules apply as in other Italian churches: miniskirts and shorts are frowned upon, and you may not be allowed admission if dressed inappropriately.

The cathedral and the town that grew up around it in the twelfth century both owe their existence to young King William II's rivalry with his powerful Palermitan archbishop, the Englishman Walter of the Mill. Work had started on Walter's fine cathedral in the centre of the city in 1172. Determined to quickly break the influence of his former teacher, William endowed a new monastery in his royal grounds outside the city in 1174, and its abbey church – this cathedral – was thrown up in a matter of years. Already exempt from taxes and granted other privileges, the church consolidated its position when Monreale was made an archbishopric in 1183, two years before Walter's cathedral was finished. This unseemly haste had two effects. A highly personal project, Monreale's power lasted only as long as William did: though he wanted to create a royal pantheon, he was the last king to be buried there; and later, when Roger II's tomb was removed from the cathedral at Cefalù, it went to Walter's cathedral in Palermo. But the speed with which the Duomo at Monreale was built assisted the splendid uniformity of its most famous feature, its interior art – a galaxy of coloured mosaic pictures bathed in a golden background.

The **mosaics**, almost certainly executed by Greek and Byzantine craftsmen, are a magnificent achievement, completed in perhaps only ten years. Despite the sheer size of the decorated interior (102m by 40m), the gleaming mosaics form a circular and reinforcing picture, from which it's possible to read the Testaments straight from the walls. Once inside, your eyes are drawn immediately over the wooden ceiling to the all-embracing half-figure of Christ in benediction in the **central apse**. It's an awesome and pivotal mosaic, the head and shoulders alone almost 20m high, face full of compassion, curving arms with outstretched hands seemingly encompassing the whole beauty of the church. Underneath sits an enthroned Virgin and Child, attendant angels and, below, the ranks of saints – each subtly coloured and identified by name. Interesting here is the figure of Thomas à Becket (marked "SCS Thomas Cantb", between Silvester and Laurence), canonized in 1173 (just before the mosaics were begun), and presumably included as a political show of support by William for the papacy – an organization for which Walter of the Mill's lay supporters, the nobility, held no brief. The two **side-apses** are dedicated to SS Peter (right) and Paul (left), the arches before each apse graphically displaying the martyrdom of each – respectively, an inverse crucifixion and a beheading. The **nave mosaics** are no less remarkable, an animated series that starts with the Creation (above the pillars to the right of the altar) and runs around the whole church, while the darker **aisle mosaics** depict the teachings of Jesus. Most scenes are instantly recognizable: Adam and Eve; Abraham on the point of sacrificing his son; positively jaunty Noah's-ark scenes showing the ship being built, recalcitrant animals being loaded aboard, Noah's family peering out of the hatches; the Feeding of the Five Thousand; and the Creation itself, a set of glorious, simplistic panels portraying God filling His world with animals, water, light . . . and Man.

It's difficult to keep your eyes off the walls, but it's worth roaming the whole building. Above the two thrones (royal and episcopal) are more mosaics: William receiving the crown from Christ (less graceful than a similar picture, of Roger, in La Martorana; see p.72) and the king offering the cathedral to the Virgin. Both William I and William II are buried here in side chapels, the cathedral's progenitor in the white marble sarcophagus to the right of the apse.

The southwest corner of the cathedral gives access to the **tower** (daily 9.30–11.45am & 3.30–5.45pm; L2000), an appealing diversion since the steps give access to the roof, for views of the cloisters (see below). You can then continue around the church and upwards, to leave you standing right above the central apse – an unusual and precarious vantage-point. Back inside, tickets for the **treasury** (L2000) are sold at the end of the left aisle.

The apse and cloisters

Although all its real artistic attractions are inside, the cathedral's solid exterior merits a closer look too, particularly the enormous triple **apse** (signposted "*absidi*") – a polychromatic jumble of limestone and lava, supported by slender columns and patterned by a fine series of interlacing arches. You have to circle the cathedral to see this, down a street to the left of the entrance. And it's certainly worth visiting the **Chiostro dei Benedettini**, or cloisters (Mon–Sat 9am–1pm & 3–7pm, Sun 9am–12.30pm; L4000), part of William's original Benedictine monastery. The formal garden is surrounded by an elegant arcaded quadrangle, 216 twin columns supporting slightly pointed arches – a legacy of the Arab influence in Sicilian art. Look closely at the carved capitals of the twelfth-century columns and you'll see that no two are the same: on one, armed hunters do battle with winged beasts; another has two men lifting high a casket of wine; elsewhere are flowers, birds, snakes and foliage; while around the whole facade of the arches, geometric shapes dip and dance from column to column. A single column in the southwest corner even forms a little fountain, in its own quadrangle. Entrance to the cloisters is from Piazza Gugliemo, in the corner by the right-hand tower of the cathedral.

The rest of town

After you've seen the cathedral, there's a lot to be said for just strolling the dense latticework of steep streets – especially in the early afternoon when few people are about. Several Baroque churches (mostly locked) are hidden here and there; the **chiesa del Monte**, in Via Umberto I, has stuccos by Serpotta. At some point, wander into the grounds of the new convent (built in 1747) behind the cathedral cloisters for the fine views from the **belvedere**, straight down the valley. The convent itself displays Pietro Novelli's fine seventeenth-century painting of St Benedict handing out bread to assorted monks and knights. Elsewhere, the modern **Istituto Statale d'Arte per il Mosaico** (200m south of the car park to the right, past the Carabinieri barracks) is open during term time for anyone interested in watching mosaic-restorers at work. Otherwise, it's easy to while away time in the couple of bars in Piazza Vittorio Emanuele, overlooking a fountain and palm trees.

Practicalities

Information is available from the **tourist office** (Mon–Sat 8am–2pm; ☎091.656.4270), in the cathedral square. There is only one **hotel** in Monreale itself, the expensive *Carrubella Park Hotel*, Via Umberto I 233 (☎091.640.2188;

④). A second, much cheaper option, *Il Ragno*, is situated over 10km out of the centre in Località Giacalone, at Via Provinciale 85 (☎091.419.256; ①). Alternatively, if you're really set on visiting the area, a day-trip from Palermo may be the most practical option.

For **eating**, tourism has shoved the prices up to an alarming degree, though *Le Absidi*, at Via Arcivescovado 7 (on a side street by the Duomo's apse), is bet-ter than most, with smart waiters and a reasonably priced tourist menu (no credit cards; closed Mon evening). A little further down, *Mizzica*, at Via Cappuccini 6 (closed Tues), has a bit more atmosphere, with similar fare and prices; note that the antipasti are L5000 *each*, not for all of them. In both places, the roast squid is worth sampling, and pizzas are served in the evening. Following Via Roma from the cathedral, the *Trattoria da Peppino* (closed Thurs) is tucked away down a side street off Piazzetta Giuseppe Vaglica, offer-ing decent meals and pizzas in the evenings. Further up Via Roma, at Via San Castrense 50, the *Ostaria delle Lumache* (closed Wed) is another option, lack-ing much character, while the *focacceria* next door has light snacks. Out of the centre on Via Circonvallazione (the Palermo road), *La Fattoria* (*The Farm*) is a large garden restaurant, a favourite with Palermitani on Sundays and with coach parties at just about any time, but with very low prices (try the house speciality, *pennette Caruso*); it's 3km by road from the centre, a stop on the bus route from Palermo, but far closer if you walk down the hill from the Duomo, below the main town car park. If it's quality fare you're after, though, head straight for Contrada Lenzitti, on the Via Circonvallazione towards San Martino delle Scale, where *La Botte* (☎091.414.051) has an island-wide reputa-tion for good, local food. It's a cosy place with tables on the veranda in summer and a log fire in winter; but it's not cheap, and is closed Monday to Thursday and during the whole of July and August, unless you make a telephone book-ing. If you're here on a summer Sunday, look out for evening **puppet perfor-mances** at *Munna*, Via Kennedy 10.

Around Monreale: San Martino delle Scale and Báida

Seven kilometres out of Monreale, on the road to San Martino, keep your eyes open for the finely preserved twelfth-century Norman castle on the right, known as the **Castellaccio**, topping a hill above the road. Once a fortified monastery built by William II, nineteenth-century neglect made way for the Sicilian Alpine Club, who have kitted it out as a mountain refuge, though if there's anyone at home they'll let you in to look around the castle. It's worth the twenty-minute scramble up for the views, which stretch over to the impressive white monastery at nearby **SAN MARTINO DELLE SCALE**. An ancient reli-gious settlement, it's been taken over in recent years as a summer hill resort – holiday homes and Sunday-trippers are much in evidence. But the Benedictine monks are still there, and it's worth visiting their **Abbazia di San Martino** (daily 9am–1pm & 4.30–7pm) – supposedly founded by Gregory the Great in the sixth century – to see the frescoes by Pietro Novelli, a grand fountain and sculptures by Marabitti, and the eighteenth-century marble staircase, all in the abbey; the church itself is monumental but rather bland. Ring ahead and San Martino is a pleasant place **to stay**: if not, the *Messina*, halfway between the abbey and the Castellaccio, at Via della Regione 108, also offers pizzas and cheap meals (☎091.418.149; no credit cards; ①).

You can reach San Martino from Monreale on the local #2 **bus**, or on the Virga buses that run three to four times a day from Palermo's Piazza Verdi (by the Teatro Mássimo), running through the wooded "Paradise Valley". At the eastern entrance to this, a road leads from the village of Boccadifalco (about 5km out of the capital) 2km north to **BÁIDA**, a tenth-century Saracen village (*baidha* is Arabic for "white") holding a convent built in the fourteenth century by monks from the Castellaccio. The church, too, is interesting, retaining its ochre facade from its fifteenth-century construction, together with an earlier apse, and a statue of St John the Baptist, wrought by Antonello Gagini; ask for the custodian at Via del Convento 41. Báida is a pretty village, ringed by hills, and again there are direct buses from Palermo, most convenient of which is the #462 from Piazza Príncipe di Camporeale (itself reached by #122 from Stazione Centrale, or #110 from Piazza dell'Indipendenza).

West: the Golfo di Carini and inland

If you're looking for a **beach** to while away a few hours, then the small succession of holiday resorts along the **Golfo di Carini** is perfectly adequate, and certainly less exhaustingly trendy than Mondello. In fact, given their proximity to the capital, these small fishing ports are surprisingly undeveloped. Better still, they're sheltered by the huge mass of Monte Gallo to the east and protected from the waste ejected into the sea from the city by virtue of their location, tucked safely around the corner of the headland.

The coast: Sferracavallo to Terrasini

The nearest, adjacent towns of **SFERRACAVALLO** and **ISOLA DELLE FÉMMINE** are the best bet, the latter uncomfortably close to a cement factory on one side, though it's quickly forgotten once you're inside the town. The *isola* in question is a tiny offshore islet. Both places run to pricey hotels and less-exclusive **campsites** – the closest official camping spots to Palermo: the two in Sferracavallo are listed on p.68; in Isola delle Fémmine (actually 1km west of town) the single site is only open in the summer months – *La Playa* (☎091.867.700), which lies close to a sandy beach. For a decent **restaurant**, *Ristorante Cutino*, Via Palermo 10 (closed Tues) in Isola delle Fémmine, comes highly recommended, specializing in seafood – prices are moderate. And there's similar good food on the esplanade at the *Trattoria Cardinale da Franco*, Via Lungomare Eufemia 19.

Regular local **trains** stop in Isola delle Fémmine, while bus #628 reaches here from Viale del Fante, near La Favorita (bus #101 or #107 from Stazione Centrale).

The train stops at other resorts on or just in from the coast, and there are more summer campsites around, at Capaci and Cinisi. The western promontory, **Punta Raisi**, is home to Palermo's airport, said to be controlled by the Mafia, who freight stocks of heroin, processed in factories deep in rural Sicily, out to the States.

Further west, **TERRASINI**, forty minutes out of Palermo, is typical of the small ports along the gulf, with a sandy beach, several trattorias and a clutch of expensive tourist hotels. An extra diversion is the private collection of Sicilian painted carts in the **Museo Etnográfico**, cunningly hidden away on Via Carlo Alberto dalla Chiesa (daily: May–Sept 9am–1pm & 4–8pm; Oct–April 9am–noon & 3–5pm; L2000); look out for the signposts near the main piazza, which point left from the main road as you head down to the sea: it's a right turn at the end of a cul-de-sac. On the waterfront, theatrical performances are held in the courtyard of the **Palazzo d'Aumale** in summer. If you're looking to stay on the coast, the only **campsite** for 30km or so is at **MARINA DI CINISI**: *Club Z 10* (☎091.869.3217; open all year), in Località Torre Pozzillo, with a few cabins to rent.

Inland: Carini, Montelepre and Partinico

The inland town of **CARINI** (buses and trains from Palermo), 5km from the coast, has a clutch of sixteenth-century churches, and what would be a first-rate visitable **castle** were it not in a pitiful state of decay, closed and forgotten. The battlemented fortress dates from Norman times and was subsequently held by some of Sicily's leading feudal dynasties: in 1508 a famous murder occurred here, immortalized in an anonymous contemporary poem considered to be the highest example of Sicilian popular versifying, *La Baronessa di Carini*.

Montelepre
A very minor road climbs 11km south of Carini to the small town of **MON-TELEPRE** (reachable direct from Palermo by bus). There's nothing to bring you to this backwater, except for its associations. To Sicilians, Montelepre is instantly familiar as the birthplace and home of the notorious bandit **Salvatore Giuliano** (1922–50), who hid out in the hills and caves around here, slipping into town at night to see family and friends. Not only was he hunted by the Carabinieri, but platoons of hand-picked soldiers combed the *maquis* for him and, as his ambitions and legend grew, so did his charisma, enhanced by such madcap gestures as writing to President Truman and offering the annexation of Sicily to the United States, in a last-ditch attempt to sever the island from the Italian State. As such he was a folk hero to the Sicilian people, embodying their hopes and frustrations more than any other individual in recent history. He was betrayed and killed, his body found in a courtyard in Castelvetrano, in the south, on July 5, 1950. No one knows exactly what happened or who was responsible for his death, though his cousin and deputy, Gaspare Pisciotta, chose to confess to the crime. Many doubt that he was the one who pulled the trigger, and Pisciotta himself was on the verge of making revelations at his trial that would have implicated high-ranking Italian politicians, when he too was assassinated in his cell at Ucciardone prison. Whatever the truth, there's a pungently Sicilian flavour to the affair, full of betrayal and counterbetrayal, heroes and villains, and Giuliano's legend has since grown to Robin Hood dimensions, nowhere more so than in his home territory around Montelepre. As his biographer Gavin Maxwell was told: "They should change the name of that village, really – anything else but Montelepre would do. No one can look at it straight or think straight about it now – it just means Giuliano."

Partinico
Montelepre is only one of a whole arc of villages to the southwest of Palermo where poverty and desperation have long been ingrained. Outlawry is deeply rooted, not just in its romantic guise of banditry, but in the more sinister network of mutual interests and organized criminality that bind politicians and mafiosi

together. As gripping a story as Giuliano's is that of **Danilo Dolci** and his campaign for relieving some of the burden weighing down the people of **PARTINICO**. Around 10km southwest of Montelepre on the SS113 (and 1hr by train from Palermo), this dreary and distressingly poor town is only distinguished for its connections with this social reformer, the "Sicilian Gandhi", who founded his first self-help and education centre here and campaigned tirelessly to have a dam built locally – something that was resisted at every turn by the Mafia and their political clients, who controlled the existing water supplies. For more on Dolci, and on the villages along the Golfo di Castellammare – with which Partinico properly belongs – see pp.331–333. If you're driving this way, you might relish a break at the *Mamma Rosa*, at Piazza Stazione 5 (closed Tues) – a surprisingly good, if somewhat pricey, pizzeria-**restaurant** with veranda seating, which is located outside the village next to the train station.

East: to Bagheria and Solunto

You're likely to see both **Bagheria** and the ancient ruins at **Solunto** as easy half-day trips from the capital; regular **buses** (AST from Piazza Lolli) and frequent local **trains** swing out of Palermo and cut eastwards, across Capo Zafferano, stopping in both towns. It's a considerably more pleasant journey than it was in the eighteenth century, when the road – as described by Dacia Maraini in her memoir *Bagheria* – was not only foully potholed, but lined "with the heads of bandits impaled on pikestaffs . . . dried by the sun, infested by flies, often with chunks of arms and legs with blackened blood sticking to the skin . . ."

Bagheria

It's **BAGHERIA** that provides the first spark of interest on the run out through Palermo's uninspiring eastern suburbs. Just 14km from the city, it quickly established itself as a seventeenth- and eighteenth-century summer retreat, the Palermitan nobility sitting out the oppressive heat in a series of Baroque country villas scattered across town. The whole, in the words of Maraini, evoked "the atmosphere of a summer garden enriched by lemon groves and olive trees, poised between the hills, cooled by the salt winds." Most of the villas are still privately owned, however, and you'll need to find someone in the grounds (or ring the bell) to be allowed in – this is quite acceptable, though rarely as straightforward as it sounds.

Access to the notorious **Villa Palagonia** (daily: summer 9am–12.30pm & 4–7pm; winter 9am–12.30pm & 3.30–5.30pm; L5000) is easier: it's on Piazza Garibaldi, at the end of Via Palagonia, ten minutes' walk from the train station (left out of the station onto Corso Butera, then left onto Via Palagonia). Among the travellers who have expressed shock at the eccentric menagerie of grotesque gnomes, giants, gargoyles and assorted mutants in the villa was Patrick Brydone, the eighteenth-century traveller, who wrote:

> . . . the seeing of them by women with child is said to have been already attended with very unfortunate circumstances; several living monsters have been brought forth in the neighbourhood. The ladies complain that they dare no longer take an airing in the Bagaria; that some hideous form always haunts their imagination for some time after: their husbands too, it is said, are as little satisfied with the great variety of horns.

Ferdinand, Prince of Palagonia, was responsible for all this, a hunchback who – in league with the architect Tommaso Napoli – took revenge on his wife's lovers by cruelly caricaturing them. The grounds are still amply furnished with the deformed monsters, though only 64 of the original 200 statues remain. Climbing an impressive stairway watched over by a menacing eagle that surmounts the pediment, the palace itself holds the **Salone degli Specchi** – its ceiling covered with mirrors – and some good marbling. However, the chairs with uneven legs and the cushions concealing murderous spikes, which so offended Goethe's sensibilities when he visited in 1787, are sadly no more.

From Corso Umberto, on the south side of Villa Palagonia, Via Trabia brings you to the more restrained Villa Trabia and **Villa Valguarnera** (also by Napoli), which comes as something of a relief after this madness, the latter displaying Bagheria's most sumptuous facade, pink and festooned with a royal coat of arms, Attic statues by Marabitti, and views out towards the sea. Villa Valguarnera's oval courtyard was one of the settings used in the Taviani brothers' film *Kaos*. Just when you thought you'd left the weirdness behind, **Villa Butera**, at the end of Corso Butera, has within its grounds a collection of wax figures in Carthusian apparel. Legend has it that their creator, Ercole Branciforti, had promised the erection of a Carthusian abbey in return for the granting of a prayer, and took the crafty way out when the prayer was answered.

A little further out from the centre (back to the train station and over the level crossing, 300m to the right), the **Villa Cattólica** holds a good gallery of twentieth-century art and has regular exhibitions (May–Sept Tues–Thurs & Sun 10am–6pm, Fri & Sat 10am–10pm; Oct–April Tues–Sun 10am–6pm; L5000) featuring Bagheria's most famous son, Renato Guttuso (1912–1987), whose brilliant use of colour and striking imagery made him one of Italy's most important modern artists.

Food and ice-cream

Bagheria has an excellent, unpretentious **restaurant** serving traditional Sicilian food, the *Trattoria Buttita*, at Via Stazione 8, right next to the station (closed Mon, & Sun evening). For **ice-cream** and other special desserts, the only place you need to know about is *Gelato In* on Via Libertà, off Corso Butera, one of the best around (closed Fri).

Solunto and around

You could well combine a trip to Bagheria with a tour around the Greco-Roman town at **SOLUNTO**, one stop further on the train (the station is called Santa Flavia-Solunto-Porticello). Cross over the tracks and walk down the main road towards the sea; after 300m there's a signposted left turn, from where it's another twenty minutes' walk up the hillside to the **site** (Mon–Sat 9am–2hr before sunset, Sun 9am–12.30pm; L4000), beautifully stranded on top of Monte Catalfano. Ancient Solus, a Phoenician settlement, was founded originally in the eighth century BC, resettled in the fourth century BC, and later Hellenized, finally surrendering to Rome after the First Punic War, when its name was changed to Solentum. There's a small **museum** at the entrance to the site (same opening hours and price as the site), worth a quick glance before you ascend the excavated streets, which peep out from under a tangle of thistles, dandelions and other wild flowers. The visible ruins mostly date from the Roman period, notably the impressive remains of wealthy houses that line the hillside. One, with a standing column, was built on two floors, the stairs still visible, and retains a simple mosaic floor. The main street, named Via dell'Agora, leads past more houses and shops to the *agora* itself, a piazza with nine recessed rooms at the back, clay-red-coloured. Above it, the fragmentary ruins of a theatre and a smaller odeon can be seen, deliberately sited so as to give marvellous views away to the coast. And beyond the *agora* are the remains of a water cistern and storage tanks – necessary, as Solentum had no natural springs. It was, and is, a glorious spot, looking out over the coastline: the fishing villages below are split by a small bay, and guarded at one end by the medieval **Castello di Sólanto**.

Porticello and Aspra

With your own transport you can return to Palermo along the coastal route from Santa Flavia, through **PORTICELLO** village, where there's a decent **hotel**, the *Baia del Sole*, Via Raffaello Sanzio 39 (☎091.957.590; ②), close to the beach; ring ahead, as it's popular. Past the stuck-out thumb of Capo Zafferano, it's about another 5km to **ASPRA**, from where you can see the whole of the gulf of Palermo ahead of you. From here, one road runs the 2km or so south to Bagheria; another goes west, back into the city.

South: Piana degli Albanesi

Under an hour's bus ride south out of the capital takes you to the upland plain where **PIANA DEGLI ALBANESI**, founded by fifteenth-century Albanians uprooted from their homes in flight from the Turkish invasions, sits placidly above a pleasant lake, a million miles from the manic goings-on in Palermo. The six thousand inhabitants here follow the Orthodox rite (though they acknowledge the authority of the pope), and proudly retain many of their old traditions. Piana is most spectacular at Easter, when the small town is full to the brim with people come to admire the handsome costumes – black with gold brocade on Good Friday, brightly coloured on Easter Sunday. If you can't make it then, try to come on Sunday mornings when there are traditional Orthodox services in one of the three churches lining the steeply sloping main street, **Via Giorgio Kastriota**. In truth, though, at most times of the year there's little point coming just to see the town. Apart from the street and building signs – in Albanian as well as Italian – there's little to spark your interest, save the (occasionally open) **Museo Cívico**, an ethnographical museum at the bottom of the hill filled with carts and farming equipment.

There's a bit more to the immediate surroundings. Three kilometres south of the town, the artificial **lake** lies in a beautiful setting, surrounded by mountains, a good venue for a picnic and a lazy siesta. If you want a decent walk, you could go on a bit further (4km from Piana, to the right of the lake) to the mountain pass southwest of town, **Portella della Ginestra**, scene of one of the most infamous episodes in recent Sicilian history. On May 1, 1947, when the Albanians and villagers from neighbouring San Giuseppe Jato had assembled for their customary May Day celebrations, gunfire erupted from the crags and boulders surrounding the plain, killing eleven and wounding 55, many of them children. This massacre was the work of the bandit Giuliano, whose virulent anti-Communist feelings were exploited by more sinister figures high up in the political and criminal hierarchy: only two weeks previously, the people of Piana degli Albanesi, together with most other Sicilians, had voted for a Popular Front (left-wing) majority in the regional parliament. The cold-blooded killings erased at one stroke the bandit's carefully nurtured reputation as defender of the poor and friend to the oppressed (see "Sicily's history", p.390, and Montelepre, p.103).

Practicalities

To get to Piana degli Albanesi, there are several **buses** from Palermo, from Stazione Centrale (Mon–Sat), and the last one back leaves at 7.15pm. The bus stops at the top of Piana, in Piazza Vittorio Emanuele: follow the road downhill and you'll pass all three of the town's churches, with the museum (and a tourist office in the same building) at the bottom on the right.

For **food**, the only central choice is the moderately priced *Trattoria San Giovanni*, Via G. Matteotti 34 (closed Tues), a rustic, plant-filled spot whose windows overlook the town; from the piazza, take any road to the right, cross the bridge and it's up on your right. There are a couple of bars selling panini on Via Giorgio Kastriota, and another restaurant, *La Montagnola*, lies on the outskirts, which you'll pass on the bus on the way into Piana.

Altofonte

The route to Piana takes you through crowded **ALTOFONTE**, once the extreme southerly end of Roger II's royal park and still enjoying a grand view of the Conca d'Oro bowl. The **Chiesa Madre** in Piazza Umberto gives onto the remains of the cupola-topped royal chapel from this period, though it's been considerably changed since then; ask at the sacristy if you want to see it.

Ústica

A volcanic, turtle-shaped island, a lonely 60km northwest of Palermo, **ÚSTICA** is one of the more appealing destinations away from the capital, ideal for putting your feet up for a few days. Colonized originally by the Phoenicians, the island was known to the Greeks as Osteodes, or "ossiary", a reference to the remains of 6000 Carthaginians they found here, abandoned to die on the island after a rebellion. Its present name is derived from the Latin *ustum* – "burnt" – on account of its blackened, lava-like appearance. Never a particularly attractive place to live, exposed and isolated, Ústica had a rough time throughout the Middle Ages, its sparse population constantly harried by pirates who used the island as a base. In the Bourbon period the island was commandeered as a prison for political enemies, and even as late as the 1890s the few inhabitants were nearly all exiled prisoners: Antonio Gramsci, the great theorist of the Italian Communist Party, was once interned here.

Today, tourism has rescued the island without altogether spoiling it. Though lacking sandy beaches, its greatest draw is the surrounding limpid waters, ideal for **snorkelling** and skin-diving, which attract an international meeting of scuba enthusiasts every June to September. Part of the coastline has been designated a "Natural Marine Reserve", and one of the attractions touted by the locals is "fish-watching". On land, Ústica's fertile nine square kilometres are just right for a day's ambling, and it's also easy, to take a **boat trip** to tour the many grottoes that puncture the rugged coastline.

Arrival and accommodation

Ferries and **hydrofoils** operate daily from Palermo (from the Stazione Maríttima), the cheapest passage being around L19,000 one way by ferry, or L31,000 by hydrofoil (but taking half the time); tickets from Siremar, Via Francesco Crispi 120. See "Travel details" for more detailed information.

You arrive at **ÚSTICA TOWN**, the island's only port: the town centre is reached up the flight of steps leading from the harbour. You'll emerge in the main square, which is really three interlocking squares – piazzas Cap. V. di Bartolo, Umberto I and Vito Longo. In the topmost of the three, Piazza Cap. V. di Bartolo, on the left-hand side of the church, is the Monte dei Paschi di Siena **bank** (Mon–Fri 8.20am–1.20pm) and, next door, the R&S Militello **ticket agency** (☎091.844.9002) for the ferries and hydrofoils; there's also a ticket office at the harbour, open just before sailings, and there's a **pharmacy** at Piazza Umberto I 30.

To hire a **fishing-boat** from the quay will cost from L60,000 for four people; or hire a motorboat from the *Hotel Stella Marina*, see below – prices are infinitely negotiable. The hotel also rents out **mopeds**, though these are hardly necessary as there's an efficient **minibus** service (pay on board) that plies the island's one circular road every hour or so. In any case, it doesn't take much more than two or three hours to walk round the entire island.

Accommodation

Ústica Town is where you'll find the cheaper **places to stay**, though be warned that in summer they fill up quickly, and in winter only a few remain open. However, there are plenty of opportunities to **rent rooms**, either through an agency (Agenzia Osteodes, Via Magazzino 5; ☎091.844.9210), or direct from the locals; the *Bar Centrale*, in Piazza Umberto, is a good place to ask for *cámere*.

Ariston, Via della Vittoria 5 (☎091.844.9042, fax 091.844.9335). Central hotel with eleven rooms and impressive sea views. Small apartments are also available to rent, and excursions and boat rental can be arranged. Reserve well ahead. May–Oct. ③.

Caminita Vittorio, Via Tufo 1 (☎091.844.9212). This individual rents out two little self-contained rooms (with kitchenette and bathroom) that offer sweeping views down over the town to the sea. It's just a few minutes from the square: at the church, turn right along Via Calvario and Via Tufo is the sixth on the left. No credit cards. ②.

Locanda Castelli, Via San Francesco 16 (☎091.844.9007). At the top of the town square (take a right by the church onto Via Calvario), this popular place only has four rooms, so ring ahead. No credit cards. ①.

Pensione Clelia, Via Magazzino 7 (☎091.844.9039, fax 091.844.9495). Recently refurbished, this attractive little *pensione* has a roof-terrace restaurant with sea views. ③.

Grotta Azzurra, Località San Ferlicchio (☎091.844.9048, fax 091.844.9396). This smart hotel sits over its own bay, with a pool and sun terraces cut into the rocks below. It's a 5min walk from the centre: as you climb from the port, follow the road around to the left; open mid-April to mid-September only. ⑥.

Hotel Stella Marina, Via Cristoforo Colombo 33 (☎091.844.9014, fax 091.844.9325). You'll pass this hotel on your way up from the port – nice views from some of the rooms and a restaurant that makes much of its sea-facing position. ②.

Around the island

The **town centre** is a small, bright place, built on a steep slope, its low buildings covered in murals. Most of what passes for entertainment here – chatting in the open air, having a coffee in the couple of bars, impromptu games of soccer – takes

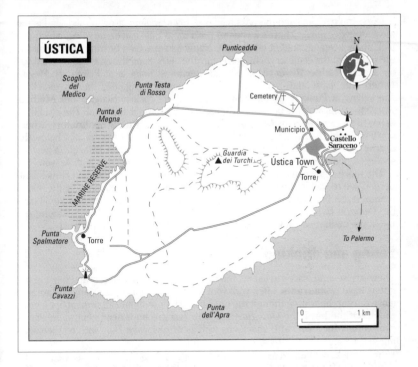

place in and around the three central squares, which merge into each other, tumbling down the hill from the church. If you want to visit the **Museo di Archeologia Sottomarina**, in the main square, contact Padre Carmelo at the church, an expert in the field who can give you a guided tour of the exhibits – a low-key assortment, mostly comprising crusty anchors, amphorae and other oddments from shipwrecks in the area.

What you don't get from the town centre, however, is a view of the water and, consequently, a sense of Ústica as an island, so perhaps the first thing you should do on arrival is climb up to the remains of the **Castello Saraceno**, above the town: from the top of the square, the path is to the left of the fancy cross at the end of Via Calvario. This easy twenty-minute walk leads to an interesting old fort, pitted with numerous cisterns to catch the precious water, and provided with rock-cut steps, which give you a good initial view of the island's layout.

From here you can see Ústica's highest point, the **Guardia dei Turchi** (244m), at the summit of a ridge that cuts the island in two, and topped by what looks like a giant golf ball – in fact a meteorological radar system. You can also climb up here from the town, in about an hour or so: take Via B. Randaccio to the right of the church, turn left at the top and then right, and you'll come to the Municipio, where you turn left along Via Tre Mulini for the summit – keep straight ahead on the cobbled path, cutting off to the left when you reach the stepped path. If you're desperately lazy, you can hire **donkeys** for the same trip at around L20,000 each, from Signor Palmisano (☎091.844.9106); ask around the town's bars.

Once you've exhausted the possibilities in town, walking around the island is the most attractive move. There's a **coastal path** for at least half of the route, which you pick up by keeping straight on past the Municipio and then bearing off the road to the right, past the cemetery. The path hugs the cliffs along the island's north side as far as the **Marine Reserve**, whose northernmost point is at **Punta di Megna** (where the path and road converge). If you're equipped, there's excellent snorkelling at Punta di Megna and at the offshore rock of **Scoglio del Médico**, where the clear water is bursting with fish, sponges, weed and coral. The road then keeps to the west coast as far as the old *torre* (tower) at **Punta Spalmatore**, where you'll find some of the island's best bathing spots; try below the *torre*, or – below the nearby lighthouse – at **Punta Cavazzi**, where there's a *piscina naturale*, a perfect, sheltered pool of seawater that can get uncomfortably crowded in high season.

The more cultivated southern coast is best seen by boat as the road runs inland here. If you're walking, veer away from the coast at Spalmatore, following the inland road past the Punta Spalmatore tourist village. After about ten minutes you'll pass the *Trattoria Baia del Sole*, a fine place for lunch (see below), and further along you rejoin the main road back across the eastern half of the island to the port.

Eating and drinking

There are several places to eat on and around the central squares, and most of the hotels have **restaurants**, often with roof terraces for sea views. Many restaurants close during the winter, though the ones listed below should all remain open year-round. Of the **bars**, the *Oasi Bar* and *John Bar* are both dead central, in Piazza Vito Longo: the *Oasi*, with snacks as well as drinks; *John Bar*, with terrace seating in the summer.

Trattoria Baia del Sole, Zona Spalmatore. In a rustic restaurant with fine sea views on the western side of the island, La Signora presents you with superb food that's all home-made – including the antipasto (preserved tuna and olives, *melanzane sott'olio*, goat's cheese) and *pasta con le sarde* (made with locally caught sardines and fennel picked from the surrounding hills). The local wine is a tart rosé, which complements the salty food well. Moderate.

Trattoria Giulia, Via San Francesco 13. The simple trattoria attached to this *locanda* is open to non-guests and specializes in couscous. Closed lunchtimes in winter. Inexpensive. No credit cards.

Trattoria Da Mario, Piazza Umberto I 21. In this very simple, box-like restaurant on the square, Mario cooks and waits on the four or five tables, dispensing things like spaghetti with fresh crabmeat, roast squid and local wine. It's excellent, and open throughout winter, too. Moderate.

Trattoria-Pizzeria Rustica, Via Petriera 21. Behind the Municipio, just out of the centre, this place serves good grilled meat and fish dishes as well as thirty different types of pizza. Moderate.

Le Terrazze, Via Cristoforo Colombo 3. A pizzeria-ristorante on the other side of the port, with terrace views of the sea and surrounding hills. Moderate. Closed Mon, Tues, Thurs & Fri in winter.

festivals

January
6 Orthodox Epiphany procession at **Piana degli Albanesi**; traditional costumes and the distribution of oranges. Similar goings-on at **Mezzojuso** to the southeast.

Easter
Holy Week Traditional Orthodox processions and celebrations at **Piana degli Albanesi**, best on Good Friday and Easter Sunday; and also at **Mezzojuso**.

April

23 Costumed processions at **Piana degli Albanesi** to celebrate St George's Day.

Last week Annual World Windsurfing Festival at **Mondello**; races, food, drink and entertainment.

July

11–15 The festival of St Rosalia in **Palermo**. A procession of the saint's relics, fireworks and general mayhem.

August

21 A colourful horseback parade, *la cunnatta*, at **Marineo**, on the Corleone road.

September

4 Pilgrimage to Monte Pellegrino in **Palermo** in honour of St Rosalia, patron saint of the city.

Last week Annual International Tennis Tournament in **Palermo**.

November

First week A week of ecclesiastical music concerts at **Monreale** cathedral.

travel details

Trains

Palermo to: Agrigento (13 daily Mon–Sat, 6 Sun; 2hr); Bagheria (2–3 hourly; 10min); Caltanissetta (8 daily Mon–Sat, 5 Sun; 1hr 40min–2hr); Capaci (hourly; 40min–1hr); Carini (hourly; 40min–1hr 10min); Castellammare del Golfo (hourly; 1hr 30min); Castelvetrano (7 daily Mon–Sat, 4 Sun; 2hr 15min); Catania (6 daily Mon–Sat, 3 Sun; 3hr 30min); Enna (6 daily Mon–Sat, 3 Sun; 2hr 15min); Isola delle Fémmine (hourly; 20–45min); Marsala (7 daily Mon–Sat, 5 Sun; 2hr 45min–3hr 30min); Mazara del Vallo (7 daily Mon–Sat, 5 Sun; 2hr 30min–3hr); Milazzo (hourly; 2hr 20min–3hr 40min); Messina (hourly; 3hr–4hr 30min); Solunto (1–2 hourly; 15min); Términi Imerese (2–3 hourly; 25–35min); Trápani (hourly; 2hr 20min).

Buses

Palermo to: Agrigento (3–4 daily; 2hr 15min); Bagheria (every 30min; 1hr); Cáccamo (2 daily Mon–Sat; 1hr 15min); Caltagirone (2–5 daily; 4hr); Caltanissetta (7–9 daily; 1hr 40min); Carini (hourly; 40min); Castelbuono (3 daily Mon–Sat;1hr 50min); Castellammare del Golfo (2 daily; 50min); Catania (hourly; 2hr 40min); Cefalù (3 daily Mon–Sat; 1hr); Corleone (hourly Mon–Sat; 1hr 30min); Enna (4–5 daily; 1hr 30min–2hr); Gela (3–4 daily; 2hr 30min–3hr 15min); Messina (1 daily; 4hr 30min); Nicosia (2–5 daily; 2hr 15min–3hr); Noto (2 daily Mon–Sat; 5hr 45min); Piana degli Albanesi (10 daily Mon–Sat, 2 Sun; 30min); Piazza Armerina (4–5 daily; 2hr 30min); San Martino delle Scale (4 daily Mon–Sat, 2 Sun; 40min); San Vito Lo Capo (2–5 daily Mon–Sat; 2–3hr); Siracusa (2–4 daily Mon–Sat, 2 Sun; 3hr 15min); Términi Imerese (6 daily Mon–Sat; 40min); Trápani (hourly; 2hr).

Ferries

Palermo to: Cágliari (1 weekly; 14hr 30min); Genoa (1 daily; 20hr); Livorno (3 weekly; 17hr); Naples (1 daily; 11hr); Ústica (June–Sept 1 daily; Oct–May 6 weekly; 2hr 20min).

Hydrofoils

Palermo to: Cefalù (June–Sept 3 weekly; 1hr 10min); Lípari (June–Sept 3 weekly; 3hr 30min); Naples (1 daily; 4hr); Ústica (June–Sept 2–3 daily, Oct–May 1–2 daily; 1hr 15min).

Ústica to: Favignana (June–Sept 3 weekly; 2hr); Naples (June–Sept 3 weekly; 4hr); Palermo (June–Sept 2–3 daily, Oct–May 1–2 daily; 1hr 15min); Trápani (June–Sept 3 weekly; 2hr 30min).

Planes

Palermo to: Genova (via Rome or Naples; 5 daily; 3hr–3hr 30min); Lampedusa (5 daily; 1hr); Milan (3–7 daily; 1hr 40min); Naples (2–3 daily; 55min); Pantelleria (2–4 daily; 35–50min); Rome (14 daily; 1hr 10min).

CHAPTER TWO

THE TYRRHENIAN COAST

P ractically the whole of Sicily's northern shore, the **Tyrrhenian coast**, is dedicated to holidaying. At its best it's an eye-catching succession of cliff and cove, sandy strips and citrus groves. But all too often these are eclipsed by a monotonous ensemble of new villas and hotel developments. In summer, the beaches can get as congested as the road that runs through the numerous small coastal towns and villages, although out of season there's plenty of room to breathe.

At any time of year, the major distraction is **Cefalù**, a beach resort *par excellence*, whose medieval cathedral contains some of the best mosaicwork you'll find on the island. Its fine beach and rocky setting provide the sort of views that attract artists in droves, and it's one of the few package-tour destinations from Britain. Consequently, you'll find hotel space difficult to come by in summer, though it's worth battling with the crowds to spend at least a day there. Cefalù aside, the Tyrrhenian coast's attractions are best enjoyed en route to Palermo or Messina. A good day's wandering can be spent in and around the old spa town of **Términi Imerese**, including a trip out to the blustery hill-top stronghold of **Cáccamo**, which has the biggest and best preserved of Sicily's Norman castles. Everywhere, too, the Tyrrhenian coast is dotted with ancient archeological remains, the most complete of which is the cliff-top site of Greco-Roman **Tyndaris** in the east.

If it's **beaches** you're after, then some of the best lie beyond the offputting industrialization around the fortified town of **Milazzo**; other more crowded ones lie around small resorts like **Sant'Agata di Militello** and **Capo d'Orlando**, which also make lively stopovers on your way through. Away from the coast, you soon leave the crowds behind in the dramatic **Madonie** and **Nébrodi** mountains. There are some good hikes in the hills between **Castelbuono** and **Piano Battáglia**, while further east you can make other inland excursions to some venerable old hill-towns, especially **Mistretta**, **San Fratello** and **Castroreale**, little-touched by the mayhem on the coast.

The Tyrrhenian coast is more accessible than much of the Sicilian seaboard. There's a good **train** service all the way along, making it easy to stop off in any of the seaside resorts that take your fancy, or at places from which regular **buses** link inland destinations, though a car is useful for continuing into Sicily's interior. **Driving** can be slow along the coast itself, especially where there's still no autostrada – specifically the 40km between Cefalù and Sant'Agata, through which the traffic files at a snail's pace along the twisting SS113. Where the A20 autostrada does exist, it's a toll-road. For a more leisurely mode of travel, SNAV operate a useful (though limited) **hydrofoil** service in summer, between Palermo and the Aeolian Islands, taking in Cefalù. There are also summer services from Capo d'Orlando and Sant'Agata di Militello (see "Travel details", p.135 for full schedules).

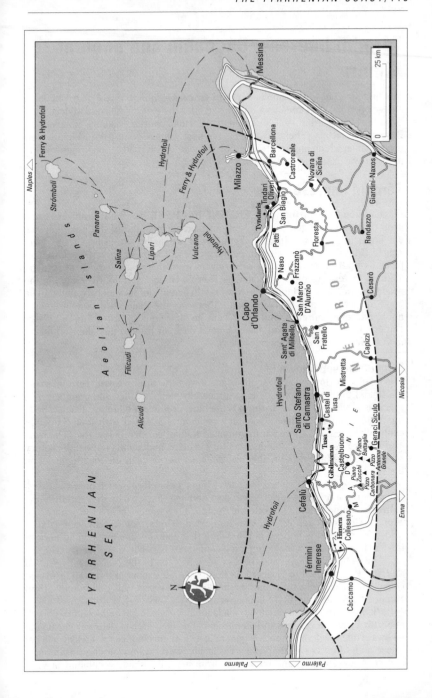

Términi Imerese, Cáccamo and ancient Himera

The first stop out of Palermo is **Términi Imerese**, though if you're driving keep an eye open for the **Chiesazza** on the left, after the exit for Altavilla Milicia. Built by Robert Guiscard in 1077, this ruin of a Norman church was once annexed to a Basilian monastery. The autostrada is the best vantage-point from which to view the remains, which appear stranded by the side of the road – don't bother working your way round to take a closer look.

Términi Imerese

Fifteen kilometres further on, **TÉRMINI IMERESE** has the magnificent backdrop of Monte Calógero, and a seafront marred by some of the only industry you'll see this side of Milazzo. Términi was originally settled by Greeks from Zancle (Messina) in the seventh century BC, and subsequently grew in importance as it absorbed the influx of survivors from the destroyed city of Himera, 13km to the east (see p.117). Later, as Therma Himeraia, it flourished under the spa-loving Romans, and today the town is still famous for its waters, reputed to be good for arthritis and pasta-making. Otherwise, the main attractions are some noble Baroque churches, and a museum holding finds from the site of ancient Himera, to the east. Términi makes a good base for trips to this site, and inland to Cáccamo – both easy bus rides away.

Términi: the upper town

The town splits into two parts, upper and lower; the **upper town**, Términi's centre, linked to its lower part by long, gracefully stepped lanes and dignified by a spacious piazza, where the **Duomo** is the most prominent building. The facade of this monumental seventeenth-century creation is adorned with four sixteenth-century statues and there's a fragment of Roman cornice below the bell-tower. The inside has a painted fifteenth-century crucifix and some eighteenth-century sculptures by **Marabitti**, notably his *Madonna del Ponte* in the fourth chapel on the right.

Beyond the Duomo extends the palm-fringed **belvedere**, which offers an excellent panorama over the lower town, port and sea that's partly disfigured by the industrial tangle below. Opposite the duomo, a few metres below the square, the **Museo Cívico** (Tues & Fri 9am–1pm, Wed, Thurs, Sat & Sun 9am–1pm & 3.30–6.30pm; free) is housed in a building that contains elements going back to the fourteenth century, including a self-contained chapel. In the latter, you can see work by Antonello Gagini and, best of all, a triptych of the *Madonna with Child and Saints*, attributed to Gaspare da Pésaro. Other rooms in this well-displayed collection hold prehistoric and archeological material (including finds from Himera), and there are more paintings upstairs.

Back across the piazza and down Via Iannelli, the small fifteenth-century church of **Santa Caterina d'Alessandria** has an old pointed arched doorway surmounted by a crude relief: the church is generally locked up, but if you're lucky you'll get to see some frescoes of the saint's life inside, with captions written in the local dialect. A few steps around the corner from here, the shady vegetation of **Villa**

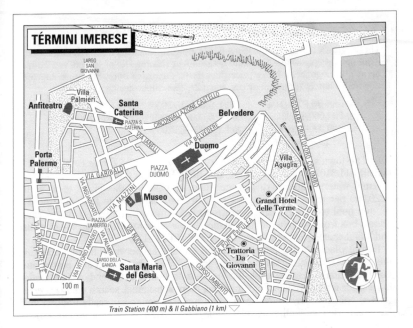

Train Station (400 m) & Il Gabbiano (1 km) ▽

Palmieri shelters the remnants of a public building from the Roman era, and there are the remains of an **Anfiteatro Romano** at the far end of the park, off Via Garibaldi – just up from the Porta Palermo, the former entrance to the city.

Although there's not much else to detain you, the steep, cracked streets below the Duomo are pleasant to explore. Below Piazza Umberto I, on Largo della Gancia, there is a fine Renaissance wooden panel hidden behind the altar in **Santa Maria di Gesù**. Dating from around 1400, it shows St George slaying the dragon.

The lower town: practicalities

Términi's **lower town** has less of specific interest, its narrow streets playing host to a congested mass of traffic, people and grocery stores. Still, it's here that you'll **arrive**, and where you'll find both of the town's hotels – including the thermal spa – and a trattoria.

The **train station** is off our map, southeast of the town centre; it has a **luggage deposit** (8am–8pm; L5000 for 12hr). Turn right outside the station, walk past Piazza Crispi and down Corso Umberto e Margherita to reach Via Roma, the stepped street that climbs to the upper town. Local and long-distance **buses** arrive and depart from immediately outside the station.

If you're going to see Cáccamo or Himera (or both), you'll probably need to **stay the night**, and the only realistic option is *Il Gabbiano*, at Via Libertà 221 (☎091.811.3262, fax 091.811.4225; ②), a nice find after the lengthy walk (turn left out of the train station, walk parallel to the lines for about 15min; the hotel is on the right). There are twenty air-conditioned and fully equipped rooms in the main building that come into the ④ category, with significant reductions outside the summer months, and twelve more modest ones with shared bath in an annexe

---

(②). The town's only alternative is the *Grand Hotel delle Terme* (☎091.811.3557, fax 091.811.3107; ⑤), dominating Piazza delle Terme at the point where Términi's thermal waters issue forth at a constant 42°C. The bill weighs in at around L220,000 per night – at this price the curative waters come free, and there's a rooftop pool too. The nearest **campsite** is 15km east of town, at Buonfornello. Take a bus from outside the train station to the *Himera*, which has a pool, a disco and small apartments available for rent (☎091.814.0175).

Eating places in Términi are similarly few and far between. In the upper town, the *Bar del Duomo*, on Via Belvedere (closed Wed), has panini and pastas, and a good selection of pastries, while the *Trattoria del Gelato*, at the end of the belvedere, is the place for ice-creams. For something more substantial, search out *Da Giovanni* (closed Sat in winter) in the lower town, a cheap, rough-and-ready trattoria in Via Nogara, buried within the network of alleys off Piazza Terme (but signposted).

Cáccamo

Buses from Términi's train station run regularly to **CÁCCAMO**, 10km south amid green hills – the first of many inland towns hereabouts worth going out of your way for. Its remarkable **castello** is the main draw, and is the first thing you see as you approach – a chalk-white array of towers and battlements dominating the town and commanding the heights above the deep San Leonardo river valley. Built in the twelfth century, but much modified since and today partly under scaffolding, the 130-roomed castle presents an imposing front nonetheless. If the gate isn't open, ring at Corso Umberto 6 (the door nearest the war memorial opposite the main entrance), from which Signor La Rosa will emerge to guide you up inside the walls, through three gateways to the main keep. One of the oldest sections contains the Sala della Congiura, the chamber where the barons' plot against William I ("the Bad") was hatched in 1160. Entrance to the castle is free, but a tip is appreciated, as you'll be reminded by the handwritten signs liberally scattered along the route.

When you've had your fill of the castle, take time to stroll around the jumble of houses and squares that make up the town. It's little more than an overgrown village, disturbed only by the weight of traffic along the one main street. At some stage you'll wind up at the secluded Piazza del Duomo behind the castle crag. Here sits an enclave of faded buildings, presided over by Cáccamo's **Chiesa Madre**, dating in part from 1090, though rebuilt during the fifteenth century, and now heavily Baroque in character. The reliefs around the sacristy door are attributed to Francesco Laurana, the Renaissance sculptor who has left his mark all over the region, particularly in Palermo. The best decoration, though, is a seventeenth-century tablet depicting St George and the Dragon over the main portal. The church forms the focus of Cáccamo's La Castellana **festa**, a medieval costumed procession around the town's streets and squares, usually taking place in September (check dates with Palermo's tourist office).

There's a good **hotel** at the back of the town, *La Spiga d'Oro*, at Via Margherita 74 (☎ & fax 091.814.8968; ③), with an attached restaurant: it's a lengthy walk up from the *castello*, though the bus from Términi stops right outside. For a **meal** right by the castle, there's the medieval-looking *A Castellana* (closed Mon), a pizzeria-ristorante. If you're heading **for Palermo**, there's a handy early-afternoon bus to the capital from Cáccamo, and there's also a lunchtime departure **for Cefalù**; otherwise the last bus back to Términi leaves at around 9pm, Monday to Saturday.

Ancient Himera

The site of Greek **Himera** is a short bus ride from Términi Imerese – if you're driving, take the Buonfornello exit from the autostrada. It was the first Greek settlement on Sicily's northern coast, founded in 648 BC as an advance post against the Carthaginians, who controlled the west of the island. The town inevitably became a flash point, and in 480 BC the Carthaginian leader Hamilcar landed a huge force on the coast nearby, with the intention of taking Himera and very probably the rest of Sicily at the same time. Pitted against the combined armies of Akragas (Agrigento), Gela and Syracuse, the invading force was demolished and Hamilcar himself perished – either assassinated by Greek spies before the battle, or killed when he threw himself onto the pyre afterwards, depending on whose version you read. The outcome of the battle marked a significant upheaval of the classical world – and, in the case of Sicily, a new balance of power, with the Greeks in the ascendant. But their glory was short-lived: in 409 BC Hamilcar's nephew, Hannibal, wreaked his revenge and razed the city to the ground, forcing the surviving citizens west to what is now Términi Imerese.

All that's left of the important Chalcidinian settlement that once stood here is one ruined monument: a massive **Tempio della Vittoria** erected to commemorate the defeat of the Carthaginians. It's a conventional Doric construction, with six columns at the front and back, and fourteen at the sides. Interestingly, the two stairwells on either side of the entrance to the cella, or sanctuary, suggest the involvement of craftsmen from Akragas in its construction, though we know that the physical labour was carried out by the captured Carthaginians themselves. Despite the paucity of the actual remains, and the proximity of the modern road and rail network, the solitary ruin does have a powerful appeal. It's said to stand on the very site of the 480 BC battle, and after the victory some of the rich Carthaginian spoils were pinned up inside.

The acropolis lay to the south of the temple, inland, and, though excavations have uncovered a necropolis and some smaller temples, much work remains to be done at the site. You can see some of the items dug up from the area in the **antiquarium** (Mon–Sat 9am–1pm & 3–6pm, Sun 9am–1pm; L4000) above the site (up a small road 100m to the west), including some of the striking lion's-head water-spouts that drained the temple's roof. There are more of these in the archeological museums in Términi and Palermo. Moderately priced **meals and refreshments** are available at *Trattoria da Peppino*, opposite the temple, though it's average fare.

Hiking and skiing in the Monti Madonie

By car, Buonfornello is also the autostrada exit you need to take for an excursion into the **Monti Madonie**: keep on the coastal SS113 and head south at Campofelice di Roccella. By **bus** (from Palermo or Términi) you can get as far as Collesano, beyond which you have to hitch or walk the 15km southeast to **Piano Zucchi**. First of the upland plains hereabouts to support a winter-sports industry, the Palermitani come here in winter to ski on the surrounding slopes. In summer, it's just as attractive to come for the pleasant hiking, and if you want more than a few hours in the hills you can **stay** at the *Rifugio Orestano*, though ring first to check for vacancies (☎0921.62.159; ②). **Meals** are also available here.

Ten kilometres further south, **Piano Battáglia** is the best base for visiting the highest of Sicily's peaks after Mount Etna, and the only other resort (apart from Etna) equipped for winter sports. It's a very un-Sicilian-looking place, with Swiss-type chalets and even alpine churches. The area is equally popular for summer picnics as it is for winter skiing. As well as **hikes** to the two highest peaks, Pizzo Antenna Grande (1977m) and Pizzo Carbonara (1979m) – see below – there's a good choice of less ambitious walks along the region's numerous paths, and one to Castelbuono (see p.125). If you want to stay at Piano Battáglia, there's a handful of **hostels** around, best of which is the *Rifugio Marini* (☎0921.49.994; ①), right in the centre of the plain. It offers full-board at around L60,000 per person (L25,000 for accommodation only) – worth taking, as there's nowhere else in the area to eat, and no shops – and also rents out **skiing equipment**. Otherwise, in the summer there are plenty of **freelance camping** possibilities in these hills.

From Piano Battáglia you can continue south along good minor roads to Polizzi Generosa (p.286) or Petralia Sottana (p.285), though without a car you'll have to walk – 16km and 25km respectively. Alternatively, you can head back down towards the coast, bypassing Collesano and following the minor road due north for Cefalù – close on a fifty-kilometre hike.

Cefalù

Despite the barrage of modern building outside the town centre, **CEFALÙ** remains a fairly small-scale fishing port, partly by virtue of its geographical position – tucked onto every available inch of a shelf of land underneath a fearsome

---

THE HIKE TO PIZZO CARBONARA FROM PIANO BATTÁGLIA

From *Rifugio Marini*, cross the plain to come out onto the road; turn right and immediately left, winding uphill to reach a small footpath ascending steeply along the main valley. Continue for an hour and round the spur, turning into the river valley. The level path enters a small wood; on leaving this you'll see a zigzag path rising on the opposite bank. Continue along this for twenty minutes and you'll find yourself looking down on Piano Zucchi; otherwise, leave the path and cut up the head of the valley to reach the open uplands, dotted with deep depressions and beechwoods. Continue in the same direction until wooden crosses mark the rounded summit of **Pizzo Carbonara** – head for it by any convenient route. On a very clear day you can see Etna's peak from here.

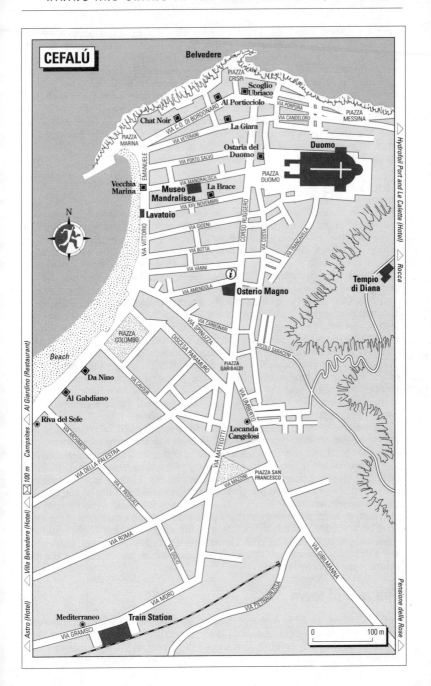

crag, **La Rocca**. Roger II founded a mighty cathedral here in 1131, and, as befitting one of Sicily's most influential rulers, his church dominates the skyline. The great twin towers of the facade rear up above the flat roofs of the medieval quarter, as the whole structure is framed by the looming cliff. Naturally, it's the major attraction in town, but most visitors are also tempted by Cefalù's fine curving sands – the main reason why the holiday companies have moved in in such great numbers during recent years. It's still not quite as developed as Sicily's other package resort, Taormina: the crowds are manageable, even in summer, and outside July and August you could do worse than make Cefalù your base for a few days, especially if you're attracted by the hiking possibilities in the hills to the south. Palermo, too, is less than an hour to the west by train.

The Duomo

It's worth making a beeline for the **Duomo** (daily: summer 8am–noon & 3.30–8pm; winter closes 7pm) first thing in the morning if you want to avoid the tour-coach hordes. Apocryphally, it was built in gratitude by Roger who found refuge at Cefalù's safe beach in a violent storm, though it's more likely that the cathedral owed its foundation to his power struggle with Pope Innocent II. Shortly after his coronation, Roger had allied instead with Anacletus, the anti-pope, whose support of Roger enhanced the new king's prestige. Roger's cathedral benefited from Anacletus's readily granted exemptions and privileges, its conception at once rich and showy, something that's obvious over 850 years later. Quite apart from the massive, fortress-like exterior, with twin towers linked by a double row of arches, inside (covering the apse and presbytery) are the earliest and best preserved of all the Sicilian church mosaics, dating from 1148.

The Duomo is accessible through a courtyard to the right of the facade. Most of the interior is thoroughly plain, all the former Baroque decoration finally stripped away after years of "restoration" – though this does have the effect of enhancing the power of the **mosaics**. They follow a familiar pattern: Christ Pantocrator, right hand outstretched in benediction, open Bible in the left, dominates the central apse; underneath is the Madonna flanked by archangels; then the twelve Apostles, in two rows of six. Though nowhere near as extensive as at Monreale (p.98), these mosaics are equally affecting and, most interestingly, display a quite different artistic tradition. Forty years older than those in William's cathedral, they are thoroughly Byzantine in concept: Christ's face is elongated, the powerful eyes set close together, the outstretched hand flexed and calming; the archangels have their heads tilted towards the Madonna. When you've seen the pictures here, and noted the two **marble thrones** on either side of the choir, head back outside and through a little gate for an exterior view of the triple apse – hemmed in by the soaring cliff. The cathedral's medieval cloisters, incidentally, are still under restoration, though if you can get in the capitals of the twin columns are expertly crafted.

The rest of town

Cefalù's ageing, tangibly Arabic, central tangle of streets provides an immediate incentive for some strolling around town. Piazza Duomo itself is always lively, especially in the early evening. Just around the corner, at Via Mandralisca 13, the **Museo Mandralisca** (daily: Easter–July & Sept 9am–7pm; Aug 9am–midnight;

Oct–Easter 9am–12.30pm & 4–7.30pm; L5000) houses a small collection of quality objects. Its two great works are the wry and powerful *Portrait of an Unknown Man*, by the fifteenth-century Sicilian master **Antonello da Messina**, and a quirky Greek *krater* (fourth-century BC) showing a robed tuna-fish salesman, knife in hand, disputing the price of his fish with the buyer.

From the museum, walk down towards the water and the little harbour off Piazza Marina. When it's quieter, say at lunchtime, this part of Cefalù repays long dawdles through its alleys with views of rows of washing stretched between houses and fishermen mending nets in the high-vaulted boathouses along Via Vittorio Emanuele, where you'll also see a relic of Saracen occupation here – the **lavatoio**, a wash house at the bottom of a curving staircase. Back past Piazza Marina, a left turn off Via C. di Bordonaro brings you to Piazza Crispi, where a **belvedere** gives onto the old Greek walls of Cefalù, mostly covered and incorporated into a sixteenth-century bastion. Frankly, though, these sights are no more than excuses to poke around this atmospheric area: each of the parallel streets off narrow Corso Ruggero is lined with attractive buildings in various stages of well-tended decay. One of the most impressive is the **Osterio Magno**, on the corner of Via Amendola and the corso, the surviving part of a medieval palace. It's usually closed, however, so ask at the tourist office if you wish to visit.

Meanwhile, the long sandy **beach** beyond the harbour beckons. It is one of Sicily's best, offering marvellous views over the red roofs of the town. If you have the time, it's also worth walking east, around the headland beyond the Duomo, to the **tourist port** where the summer hydrofoils dock. It's a pretty bay, full of fishing-boats and with some strange rock stacks inviting a clamber on the far side of the port.

La Rocca

A much more energetic pastime is to climb the mountain above town, **La Rocca** (daily 9am–noon & 3pm–1hr before sunset; free), following the steps at the side of the Banco di Sicilia in Piazza Garibaldi. A steep twenty-minute climb takes you to the so-called **Tempio di Diana**, a megalithic structure adapted in the fifth century BC by the addition of classical doorways, their lintels still in place. Keep to the left of the temple and a path continues upwards, right around the crag, through pinewoods and wild fennel. Further on, it dips in and out of a surviving stretch of medieval wall to the sketchy **fortifications** at the very top, which look down to the coasts on either side of the headland. You can then cut down to the temple and rejoin the path back into town, the whole walk taking a little over an hour – much longer if you stop and stare at the extensive views. Take water with you, as it's a strenuous climb.

Practicalities

The **train station** is south of the town centre, ten minutes' walk from the main Corso Ruggero; all local **buses** leave from the square outside the station. If you're not staying, leave your bags at the **left-luggage** office inside the station (8am–9.30pm; L5000 for 12hr). The summer **hydrofoil** service, to and from Palermo and the Aeolian Islands (see "Travel details" on p.136), docks in the tourist port to the east of town, a twenty-minute walk away around the headland. The **tourist office** is at Corso Ruggero 77 (June & Sept Mon–Sat 8am–8.30pm; July & Aug Mon–Sat 8am–8.30pm, Sun 8am–2pm; Oct–May Mon–Fri 8am–2pm & 4–7pm, Sat 8am–2pm; ☎0921.421.050), and doles out free maps, accommodation lists and local bus timetables.

Accommodation

Staying over can prove expensive in summer (if you can find space in any of the hotels), though it's easy and pleasant enough outside peak season. There's a real dearth of budget accommodation: ask at the tourist office about renting private **rooms**, or self-catering apartments, though you'll find that there's usually a minimum stay of seven nights. Note that in high season, July and August, hotel prices can rocket. From October to Easter, very few hotels remain open; of those listed below – including all the central budget choices – only the *Locanda Cangelosi* and *Pensione Delle Rose* stay open all year.

The nearest **campsites** are next to each other, 3km west of town beyond the beach, just off the SS113 (and behind the Club Med complex); both are closed in winter.

PENSIONI AND HOTELS

Astro, Via Nino Martoglio 8 (☎0921.421.639, fax 0921.423.103). A few minutes' walk west of the train station, reachable from Via Moro/Via Gramsci or Via Roma. It's close to the beach and nicely furnished, but slightly pricey (prices drop into the ③ category in winter). ⑤.

Villa Belvedere, Via dei Mulini 43 (☎0921.421.593, fax 0921.421.845). Moderately priced hotel with an excellent pool, a short walk out of town. It's quiet, though popular with tour groups. Bike rental available. ⑤.

Le Calette, Via Vincenzo Cavallaro 12 (☎0921.424.144, fax 0921.423.688). On the other side of the headland, overlooking the tourist port, this villa-style hotel is beautifully sited in its own little cove. All rooms face the sea and second-floor rooms have large balconies, though the proximity of the rail line can mean rude dawn awakenings. Otherwise, facilities are topnotch; hence the prices. ⑤.

Locanda Cangelosi, Via Umberto I 26 (☎0921.421.591). Just off Piazza Garibaldi, this is the cheapest place in town by some way, but it only has four rooms, so get there early or call ahead. It's basic, and the management isn't particularly friendly, though there is a fridge available for guests. Showers cost extra, and a couple of rooms have balconies overlooking the noisy street. No credit cards. ②.

La Giara, Via Veterani 40 (☎0921.421.562, fax 0921.422.518). Expensive for what you get, *La Giara* is at least very central, close to the Duomo, and all rooms have bath or shower. In its favour, the management is affable and there's a big terrace; avoid breakfast if you can – it's meagre and overpriced. Half- or full-board only in Aug. ⑤.

Mediterraneo, Via Gramsci 2 (☎ & fax 0921.922.5732). Handily placed right opposite the train station, this modern hotel lacks much character, but represents good value, with TVs and showers in all rooms and air-conditioning. ⑤.

Riva del Sole, Viale Lungomare 25 (☎0921.421.230). Quite good value for money, this is right on the seafront, with decent bathrooms and TV in every room. Ask for a room *con una vista del mare* and you get the sea views, though it can be incredibly noisy, and if you opt for one of the quieter rooms at the back you can at least admire the views from the roof terrace. Breakfast (with large cups of coffee) is served in a pleasant courtyard. Closed Nov. ④.

Pensione Delle Rose, Via Gibilmanna (☎ & fax 0921.421.885). Much-commended *pensione* offering the best value in town. Some rooms (without bath) have spacious terraces, and the optional breakfast is abundant, with cheese and salami as well as rolls and jam. The main drawback is its distance from the centre, a 15–20min walk along the continuation of Via Umberto I. ③.

CAMPING

Costa Ponente (☎0921.420.085). Well equipped, with a swimming pool open July and August, and beach nearby. La Spisa buses stop outside. Easter–Oct.

San Filippo (☎0921.420.184). Adjacent to the *Costa Ponente*, with minimal facilities, though there is a shop. Easter–Oct.

Restaurants

There are dozens of **places to eat** scattered around town, though many are over-priced and mundane; the best places are detailed below, most of them offering good-value tourist menus. Anyone on a tight budget, and vegetarians who will appreciate the choice, could do worse than to sample the self-service *antipasto al buffet* in the restaurants along the waterfront – you get a plateful for around L10,000. For an explanation of the restaurant price categories, see p.32.

La Brace, Via XXV Novembre (☎0921.423.570). A memorable bistro, with chic dining in a room formed by two stone arches. Don't miss the spicy *spaghetti dello chef*, the swordfish *involtini* is good too, while the *Banana La Brace* is the most alcoholic dessert you'll ever encounter. It fills up quickly, and you'll need to book in summer at weekends – the Dutch owner speaks English. Moderate–expensive. Closed Mon & mid-Dec to mid-Jan.

Chat Noir, Via Carlo Ortolani di Bordonaro 76. Less a restaurant than a late-night drinking haunt, this place serves up snacks (crêpes, salads, pastas, panini) and *frullati* alongside the cocktails and draught and bottled beers. Inexpensive.

Ostaria del Duomo, Piazza Duomo. Surprisingly, for such a central location, this is quite reasonably priced, with good antipasti and local wine. The location's the main draw, though, with tables right outside the Duomo. Moderate. Closed Nov–March.

Al Gabbiano, Lungomare G. Giardina. One of the best along the central seafront, this has a good *antipasto al buffet*, spicy *zuppa di cozze* and pizzas in the evening. There's a summer garden at the back. Moderate. Closed Wed in winter.

Al Giardino, Lungomare G. Giardina. A 15min walk west along the seafront, this lively restaurant has a summer terrace, huge pizzas and good *penne al'arrabbiata*. Inexpensive.

Da Nino, Lungomare G. Giardina. Similar food and prices to *Al Gabbiano* (and almost next door), but pizzas are also served at lunchtime in summer. On the negative side, the antipasti may have been left around too long, and service can be surly. Moderate. Closed Tues & Nov.

Al Porticciolo, Via Carlo Ortolani di Bordonaro 66 (☎0921.921.981). Atmospheric low-vaulted little ristorante attracting a smart crowd, with outdoor seating. Surprisingly reasonable prices. Pizzas also served. Moderate. Closed Wed in winter.

Lo Scoglio Ubriaco, Via C.O. di Bordonaro 2–4. At the bottom of the corso, this slick place adorned with photos and messages from stars and VIPs has a sea-facing terrace and serves pizzas as well as pasta and main dishes. The name means the "drunken rock". Moderate. Closed Tues in winter.

Vecchia Marina, Via Vittorio Emanuele 73 (☎0921.420.388). Superior fish restaurant, near the lavatoio, one of whose walls incorporates a mighty fish tank. Sicilian dishes served, and a decent wine list, too. Moderate. Closed Tues & Nov.

Listings

Banks Banco di Sicilia, on Piazza Garibaldi and Corso Ruggero; Cassa di Rispiarmo, Corso Ruggero 79; Monte dei Paschi di Siena, Piazza Duomo 15. All Mon–Fri 9am–1.20pm & 2.45–3.45pm.

Beaches Best swim spots are west of town, where there are free showers available.

Car rental Barranco, Via Umberto I 13 (☎0921.421.525); Cerniglia, Via G. Matteotti 35 (☎0921.424.200); Liberto, Via G. Matteotti 19 (☎0921.421.957).

Hiking Regular excursions around Piana Battáglia and Castelbuono. Contact the local branch of the Club Alpino Italiano for details, c/o Ferramenta Matassa, Via Spinuzza 7 (☎0921. 422.250).

Hospital Via A. Moro (☎0921.920.111).

Pharmacies Battáglia, Via Roma 13; Cirincione, Corso Ruggero 144.

Police Carabinieri at Via V. Brancati (☎0921.421.412).

Post office Via Vazzana 9 (west along Via Roma, then right towards the sea). Changes foreign currency (cash only). Mon–Sat 8.10am–6.30pm.

Scooter rental c/o Ariete Viaggi, Via Umberto I 1. L35,000–45,000 per half-day, L50,000–60,000 per day.

Supermarket Standa, Via Cannizzaro. (Mon–Sat 9am–1pm & 5–8.30pm, plus Sun 9am–1pm mid-June to Sept).

Taxis Ranks at Piazza Stazione (☎0921.422.554) and Piazza Duomo (☎0921.421.178).

Telephone offices Agenzia S. Mauro, at Via Vazzana 7, for international calls.

Travel agents Pietro Barbaro, Corso Ruggero 82 (☎0921.421.595); Turismez, Piazza Duomo 19 (☎0921.420.601).

Into the hills: Gibilmanna, Castelbuono and hiking

There are some good half-day excursions to be made into the green **Monti Madonie**, south of Cefalù, and for once the public transport services make them easily accessible. Pick up hiking itineraries from Cefalù's tourist office, together with a useful map of paths in the area.

Your first stop might be the **Santuario di Gibilmanna**, just 14km from town (buses from Cefalù's Via Umberto I), in a spot made sacred by the Arabs, who recorded miraculous deeds by the Madonna on the hillside. The sanctuary is the goal of pilgrimages, which culminate on September 8 each year, though there are usually people around throughout the summer, picnicking amid the cypress trees if not praying. Avoid the beginning of September and it can be a nice alternative to staying in Cefalù. There's one **hotel**, the *Bel Soggiorno*, a couple of kilometres below the sanctuary (☎0921.421.836; no credit cards; ②; June–Oct) and, 1km beyond it, an *agriturismo*, the *Fattoria Pianetti* (☎0921.421.890; no credit cards; half- or full-board compulsory at L70,000 and L85,000 respectively per person), an

---

ON FOOT FROM CASTELBUONO TO PIANO BATTÁGLIA

To manage this hike easily in a day, you'll have to base yourself at the snug Club Alpino Siciliano **refuge**, the *Francesco Crispi* (☎0921.672.279; L45,000 full-board per person), two hours' strenuous walk above Castelbuono, in the Milocca forest; follow the steep winding road out of town for half an hour beyond the posh *Hotel Milocca* (☎0921.671.944; ③), a fully equipped three-star with a pool, and ponies for hire.

From the refuge, keep on the jeep path, leaving the woodlands after half an hour to reach **Piano Sempria**, where there's another refuge on the right (though it's usually closed). Carry on to a small plain surrounded by four minor peaks, with crosses on each of the summits. There's a wire fence on the left, which you should climb over, and then continue over stony ground in the same direction for fifteen minutes until the large rounded peaks appear: 1km ahead (due west) is **Pizzo Antenna Grande** (1977m), topped with an antenna; further away to the left (south-west) is conical **Monte Ferro**. Take the wooded Zotofonda Valley between these two and you'll reach **Piano Battáglia** (p.118) in around three hours.

If you're intent upon other serious walks in the hills around here, get details of the local refuges from the tourist office in Cefalù before you go; there's no shortage of places to pitch a tent. If you can't get hold of the contoured 1:50,000 **maps** available from Cefalù's tourist office, or if they are *not* available, you can get one from the Istituto Geográfico, Via Danimarca 25, Palermo; photocopies are obtainable from the Ufficio Técnico in Castelbuono's town hall.

old farmhouse that also offers pony treks in summer. The *Fattoria* has a dining room (also open to non-residents), for tasty, if slightly pricey, meals and in winter a large log fire keeps everything nice and warm. The lovely surroundings offer endless opportunities for mountain and woodland walks.

Castelbuono and Geraci Sículo

Another good road (with a regular bus from outside Cefalù's train station) climbs further into the mountains, running up the green valley and dipping over the first range of hills, to **CASTELBUONO** (a 40min ride). It's a comely town, spread across the lower reaches of the surrounding mountains and sheltering behind the squat thirteenth-century keep of its **castello**: inside, there's a small stuccoed chapel, the work of Giácomo Serpotta, and a museum. The steep, crooked streets of Castelbuono – dotted with elaborate fountains and shady piazzas – encourage a stroll, and there are some fine churches, too, like the seventeenth-century **Matrice Nuova**, sitting at the back of its pretty little palm-planted square. If you're looking for **lunch**, *Ristorante Vecchio Palmento*, Via Failla 2 (closed Mon), comes highly recommended; it specializes in wild mushrooms.

There's good **hiking** country beyond Castelbuono: if you want to base yourself here, **stay** at the inexpensive *Ariston*, Via Vittimaro 2 (☎0921.71.321; no credit cards; ①), right in town. To stretch your legs, head up the road (SS286) towards Geraci Sículo and half an hour's walk gives you splendid views back over the town and castle. There's a superb hike from Castelbuono to Piano Battáglia (see box), or you could keep on the road as far as **GERACI SÍCULO** itself, 25km from Castelbuono, sitting under the brow of its hill and marked by a ruined eleventh-century castle. Buses come this way, too, from Cefalù twice a day, passing through Castelbuono, and you can complete the trans-mountain route by staying on until Gangi, another 25km (see p.285).

East to Capo d'Orlando: more routes inland

The best stretches of the Tyrrhenian coast all lie **east of Cefalù**: clean sand and stony beaches, backed for the most part by extensive groves of orange and lemon trees. The train stops at several small seaside resorts – **Castel di Tusa**, **Sant'Agata** and **Capo d'Orlando** – where there's often cheap accommodation. There are buses south, too, into the hills (the **Monti Nébrodi**) from various points on the coast; short runs worth making if only for a breath of fresh air away from the popular beaches.

Castel di Tusa

Some 25km east of Cefalù, the village of **CASTEL DI TUSA** has the remnants of a defensive castle, some good rocky beaches and a couple of places to stay – something you might want to do, as the resort is smaller and quieter than most along this stretch. There's a **campsite** here, *Lo Scoglio* (☎0921.334.345; May–Sept), though if you're looking for a roof, press on to the only **hotel** in town, *L'Atelier sul Mare*, close to the sea on Via C. Battisti (☎0921.334.295; ⑤; April–Sept). There are standard, comfortable room here, but you'll need to pay a little more (⑥) for the fifteen rooms that have been transformed into artistic installations (upside-down pyramid, bath next to bed, and so on), though you might find the experience of sleeping in an avant-garde gallery worth it. Prices are significantly lower outside the summer months.

Three kilometres up the road (there's no bus), on the way to the inland parent village of **TUSA,** are the sparse ruins of **Halaesa** (daily 9am–1hr before sunset; L4000), a fifth-century BC Sikel settlement that enjoyed some success under Rome until despoiled by the praetor Verres. You can just about make out the chequered layout of the streets, remains of the *agora*, and – at the highest point – foundations of two third-century BC temples, with lofty views down over the Tusa Valley.

Santo Stéfano and Mistretta

More frequent trains from Palermo/Cefalù stop at **SANTO STÉFANO DI CAMASTRA**, a coastal resort famed locally for its colourful ceramic work – as you can't fail to realize as soon as you get anywhere near the town. Santo Stéfano is awash with gift shops, plates, jugs and decorative pottery piled high along the sides of the roads; you can pick up some good articles – though haggle hard for the best bargains. If you're interested, there's an eclectic range of the stuff in the **Museo della Ceramica** (summer Mon–Fri 9am–1pm & 4–8pm; winter closes 7.30pm; free), towards the sea in the Palazzo Trabia, Via Palazzo. It's not the prettiest of the resorts on this coast, but Santo Stéfano does have a couple of cheap **places to stay** if you're stuck for the night – most inexpensive, the *U Cucinu*, Via Nuova 75 (☎0921.331.106; ①) – and the usual selection of **fish restaurants** and pizzerias, catering for the Italian tourists who stay here.

Just to the west of Santo Stéfano, a high viaduct flies off 16km inland to the first and biggest of the **Nébrodi** hill-villages, **MISTRETTA** – reached by bus from Santo Stéfano. This has a handsome old centre of eighteenth- and nineteenth-century buildings unspoiled by modern construction; a seventeenth-century cathedral that has the hoary look of a medieval monument; and a population largely composed of brown-suited pensioners milling around their veterans' associations. If you can, visit during the Saint's Day's **festivities** (the Festa della Madonna) on September 7–8, when the Madonna delle Luci is paraded around accompanied by two giant protectors.

Mistretta is also one of the few opportunities you'll get to find **accommodation** in the Nébrodi hills, an alternative in high season to taking your chances down on the noisy coast. There's only one choice, however: the *Sicilia*, at the top of the main corso at Via Libertà 128 (☎0921.381.463; ②; closed ten days in Sept). The hotel also operates a **pizzeria** where you can sit outside. For snacks, though, call in at the *Gran Bar*, halfway up the corso – it's an old-fashioned place perfectly in keeping with Mistretta's prevailing sepia tone.

The road from here rolls on over the range to Nicosia, 28km south (see p.283), reachable by a regular daily bus which afterwards doubles back into the mountains to the small village of Capizzi, isolated amid vernal woods and meadows.

Sant'Agata and San Fratello

Back on the coast, **SANT'AGATA DI MILITELLO** is one of the livelier Tyrrhenian resorts, busy and noisy in summer with the mainly Italian tourists it attracts. Its wide landscaped promenade supports a little funfair, there's a very long pebbled beach, and the remains of a dumpy castle have been turned into a pizzeria. The small fishing fleet working off these shores means you get excellent fish in the local restaurants and, if you want **to stay**, there's the two-star *Parimar*, Via Medici 1 (☎0941.701.888; ②). In summer, **hydrofoils** connect the town with the Aeolian Islands; there's a Covemar agency at Via Medici 383 (☎0941.701.318).

One bus a day from Sant'Agata slinks south over the mountains to Cesarò (see p.284), the first part of the meandering route taking in **SAN FRATELLO**, just 15km from the coast. This large village was once populated by a Lombard colony, introduced to Sicily by Roger II's queen, Adelaide di Monferrato, and still retains Gallic-Italian traces in the local dialect. The best time to come here is on the Thursday and Friday of Holy Week, before Easter, for the Festa dei Giudei (Feast of the Jews) – a unique Carnevale-type celebration in the post-Lent period, when the rest of the Catholic Church is in mourning. Actually, it appears to be the opposite of a Christian festival, with the locals adorning themselves in red devils' costumes, masked and hooded, complete with black tongues and horses' tails (a reminder of their traditional trade of horse-raising), all to the cacophonic accompaniment of trumpets, bells and drums. Needless to say, the ecclesiastical authorities take a dim view of these proceedings, but have been unable to stop them, making do with having the Easter Sunday church congregations in suitably contrite and sober mood.

If you're not around for the festival, make for the Norman church of **Santi Alfio, Filadelfio e Cirino**, isolated on top of a hill at the entrance to the village (follow the rough track from the cemetery) – a good place for a picnic. The church is dedicated to three brothers horribly martyred by the Romans: the first had his tongue torn out, the second was burnt alive, and the third hurled into a pot of boiling tar.

San Marco d'Alunzio and Frazzanò

Seeing any more of the coast between Sant'Agata and Capo d'Orlando, or the hills beyond, isn't really on without your own transport. Buses are too few and far between to be much good for day-trips, although regular buses do leave Sant'Agata for **SAN MARCO D'ALUNZIO**, 5km away just inland. An impressively sited village, called Aluntium by the Romans, San Marco had already been established in Greek times, and its principal point of interest, the **Tempio di Ércole**, recalls that era – an evocative shell that was converted into a Norman church by Robert Guiscard. It has since been deconsecrated, though something of its mystique remains, thanks to its imposing position high above the coast. Later religious monuments, particularly the **chiesa di Sant'Agostino**, with an interesting Renaissance sarcophagus and a *Madonna* attributed to **Antonello Gagini**, make San Marco somewhere you could easily spend a couple of hours roaming around; there are also the fragmentary remains of a **castle** where members of the Hauteville family (Sicily's Norman rulers) once resided.

A short drive along the coastal road brings you to the turnoff for **FRAZZANÒ**, 14km up in the mountains, beyond which lies the Basilian church and monastery of **San Filippo di Fragalà**, a fortress-like structure built by Count Roger in the eleventh century. With high walls enclosing a courtyard, this is sadly abandoned and falling apart, but you can tiptoe over the crumbling floors and peer into the narrow cells, examine the faded Byzantine frescoes on the walls of the church, and enjoy the views from the ramparts. If there's no one around to let you in, try round the back for an open door.

Capo d'Orlando and Naso

Occupying a headland that was the site of a historic defeat for the Aragonese king, Frederick II, at the hands of a group of rebellious barons in 1299, **CAPO D'OR-LANDO** today is a slick holiday town, though surrounded by good rocky and sandy beaches. It's the last major resort on this stretch of coast and if you're sufficiently charmed by the **swimming**, which is best on its eastern side (around the San Gregorio area), you might well want **to stay**. The cheapest choice is the 1960s-style *Nuovo Hotel Faro*, Via Libertà 7 (✆0941.902.466; no credit cards; ②), with spacious rooms and balconies fronting the sea. Turn right out of the station and walk along Via Crispi, head for the sea at Piazza Matteotti, and the hotel's a few blocks to the right. For **information**, ask at the kiosk on the seafront (summer daily 9.30am–12.30pm & 4.30–9.30pm) or the regular **tourist office** at Via Piave 71, on the corner of Via Losardo (Mon–Fri 8.30am–1.30pm & 4.30–7.30pm, Sat 8.30am–12.30pm; ✆0941.912.784). A couple of doors down from here, Meteora Viaggi sells tickets for the summer **hydrofoil services** from the town to the Aeolian Islands; see "Travel details" (p.136) for more information.

Inland from Capo d'Orlando, the oddly named town of **NASO** ("nose") sits at the end of a twelve-kilometre bus ride, where you can see (just before entering the town, up a steep lane on the left) the partly ruined **convento dei Minori Osservanti** – fifteenth-century, with an interesting tomb of the same period decorated with allegories of the six virtues. The road continues up, another 33km, to **Floresta**, lying on a grassy plain and, at 1275m, claiming the distinction of being Sicily's highest village, then down to Randazzo (p.228) and the foothills of Mount Etna.

Roman remains at Patti, Tíndari and San Biagio

East of the cape, the coast is more built-up, as the unremarkable towns merge into one long conurbation. **Patti**, however, 30km on, possesses an important relic in the shape of a fourth-century AD **Roman villa** – east of the town, close to the train station and under an autostrada viaduct. The extensive site (daily 9am–1hr before sunset; L4000) contains a few mosaics and the remains of a bathhouse. At the top of the town, Patti's **Cattedrale** has a powerful *Madonna* by Antonello de Saliba and, in the right transept, the tomb of Adelasia, much-loved first wife of Roger I, with the date of her death inscribed at the bottom, 1118.

Tíndari

The villa is one of a series of classical remains dotted along this stretch of coast. The area's most complete collection lie at **TÍNDARI**, 11km to the east (around three buses daily from Patti's main square). Originally founded in 396 BC, **Tyndaris**, as it was known, was one of the last Greek settlements in Sicily, built and fortified by settlers from ancient Syracuse as a defence against Carthaginian attacks along this coast. Almost impregnable on its commanding height, the town prospered even under Rome, when it was given special privileges in return for its loyalty.

As the bus climbs the hill to the site, though, you could be forgiven for thinking you'd come to the wrong place, since the first thing you see, glistening from its cliff-top position, is the **Santuario di Tíndari**, a lavishly kitsch temple erected in the 1960s to house the much-revered *Madonna Nera*, or Black Madonna. A plaque underneath this Byzantine icon boasts *Nigra sum, sed hermosa* ("I am black, but beautiful"); a reference to the esteem in which she has been held for a thousand years, since the icon miraculously appeared from the east, subsequently

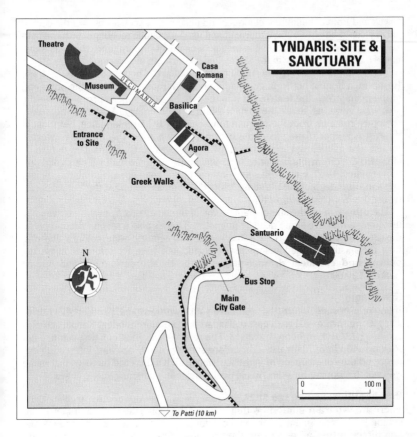

TYNDARIS: SITE & SANCTUARY

Theatre

Casa Romana

DECUMANUS

Museum

Basilica

Entrance to Site

Agora

Greek Walls

Santuario

N

Bus Stop

Main City Gate

0   100 m

▽ To Patti (10 km)

performing a series of miracles, such as producing a soft mattress in the nick of time to save a child who was hurtling to the rocks below. There's always a commotion here, with thousands of pious pilgrims thronging daily to the sanctuary to pay their respects, and especially around the Black Madonna's feast day on September 8. Buses stop in the car park over 1km from the sanctuary, from where minibuses leaving every five minutes or so shuttle up to the litter of cabins and stalls at the foot of the church (return tickets L1000).

The **archeological site of Tyndaris** (daily 9am–2hr before sunset; L4000) lies at the end of a path that starts in front of the sanctuary. Most of the visible remains are Roman, including some houses and shops along the main street, the *decumanus* – one of them (probably a *caldarium*, or bathhouse) with traces of plumbing still surviving – and an impressive **basilica** at the eastern end. Strictly an entrance to the *agora* lying beyond (in the area now covered by tourist shops), this building was subjected to restoration in the 1950s, which provoked much ire on account of the modern materials used. But it still retains a certain grandeur, undiminished by the cement, and you can clearly make out the manner of its construction, bridging

Greek and Roman building techniques and designed in such a way that the central gallery could be shut off at either end and used for public meetings, with the market traffic diverted along the side passages. Some of the sculpture that was found in the niches here is now in the archeological museum in Palermo.

The *decumanus* has streets running off it, and at the bottom of one is the **Casa Romana**, a Roman house in good condition, with mosaic floors. At the other end of the main street, the **teatro**, cut into the hill, boasts a superb prospect over the sea, with views as far as the distant Milazzo promontory. A part of the scene-structure remains from the original third-century BC Greek edifice, but most of the rest is Roman, dating from the Imperial Age when the theatre was converted for use as a gladiatorial arena. Later, the theatre was partly dismantled to furnish stone for the **city walls** that once surrounded the settlement, of which a good portion remains. You'll have seen some of them on the road up, including the ancient city's **main gate**, built on the same "pincer" design as the one at the Euryalus castle outside Siracusa (see p.240).

The **museum** on the site contains some of the best finds from the excavations, including a massive stone head of Augustus. There's also a reconstruction of the theatre's scene-building, and some eighteenth-century watercolours showing how the basilica looked before its overhaul. Ask here for information on the **operas and classical dramas** staged in the theatre during July and August (tickets L20,000).

San Biagio

If you're especially interested, and have your own transport, another short drive away along the coastal road east of Tíndari are the more modest Roman remains at **SAN BIAGIO**, right on the SS113. The recent excavation of a first-century AD **Roman villa** here (daily 9am–1hr before sunset; L4000) revealed interesting evidence on the construction of baths, but above all it's the vivid mosaics that make this worth stopping for – one in particular depicting a fishing scene at sea.

Practicalities: seeing the sites

There are two **train stations** within reach of the main sites: Patti-San Piero Patti station is the stop for Patti; for Tyndaris you can either take a bus from Patti station direct to the site or stay on the train for a few more kilometres to Oliveri-Tíndari, from where it's about a three-kilometre (uphill) walk.

Without a vehicle it's easy to get stranded in these parts. If you do stay, there's plenty of decent **swimming** to be enjoyed, and there are a couple of **campsites** at Patti and one at Oliveri. Best of these is the *Marinello* (☎0941.313.000; April–Oct), quiet and within a few steps of a good pebbly beach; it's located off the coast road between the two towns, at the end of a track. Patti also has some (fairly pricey) beachside **hotels,** and there's one very cheap place to stay in Oliveri – *La Corda*, on Via Spiaggia Mare (☎0941.313.140; no credit cards; ①).

Inland: to Castroreale

From San Biagio, two choice inland routes branch off into the **Monti Nébrodi**, the first of which, the SS185, is the only road in the province connecting the Tyrrhenian and Ionian coasts, leading to Giardini-Naxos (p.200). This is one of the finest routes on the island, climbing gently into the hills through some handsome countryside to **NOVARA DI SICILIA**. You could make a convenient lunch-break at this small town, in the *Pineta* **trattoria**, just off the main square (Largo Bertolami), which serves cheap and abundant meals. The dense woods above, with expansive views over the sea, are a favourite spot for the locals, who come out here on a Sunday, armed to the teeth with picnic hampers and portable stoves, though there are enough shady nooks and glades to find your own space. The road climbs to 1270m before descending, in sight of Etna's dramatic slopes, to Francavilla and Castiglione (see p.203).

Castroreale

Back on the coast and heading east, you can make a detour at the uninspiring Barcellona to the Peloritan hill-town of **CASTROREALE**, 8km to the south. Favoured by Frederick II of Aragon, who came here for the hunting, the town enjoys magnificent views over the hills and out to sea. At its highest point is a tower, the one remaining fragment of Frederick II's fort, built in 1324 and subsequently ruined by earthquakes. The tower, just off the end of the main Corso Umberto I, now houses a youth hostel (see below); you can enter to climb up to the top even if you're not staying.

The rest of Castroreale is creakingly medieval, and it's enough just to stroll along the quiet, sloping streets, dropping in at the couple of basic bars for a drink. If you feel like staying, however, an excellent opportunity is provided by one of Sicily's rare **youth hostels** (☎090.974.6398; April–Oct), an atmospheric location in Frederick II's fort; beds cost L13,000 per night.

To get to Castroreale by public transport, take buses from the bus station at Barcellona (7 daily Mon–Sat, 1–2 daily Sun; last departure at around 5.30pm); if you're arriving by train, hourly buses connect the *autostazione* with Barcellona's train station, some way out of the centre (tickets from the bar in the station). Alternatively, it would not be inconceivable to walk up, by following the Longano River valley inland for about three hours – the steep bit's at the end.

Milazzo

If it weren't for the industry besieging **MILAZZO** – the first major town on this coast after Términi – it wouldn't be a bad-looking place. A long plane- and palm-tree lined *lungomare* looks across the sparkling sea, while behind the town a rambling old castle caps Milazzo's ancient acropolis. Most people, though, are put off by the unsightly oil refinery that occasionally produces a yellow smog overhead, and only stop long enough to get out again, taking the first ferry or hydrofoil to the Aeolian Islands (see next chapter), for which Milazzo is the major point of embarkation. But Italian tourists know the town well, and regularly crowd the beaches and campsites strung along **Capo Milazzo**, the finger of land behind the town.

The Town

If you're in a hurry, Milazzo's easy enough to handle. You could be on an outward-bound ferry or hydrofoil within an hour of arriving; see below for all the details. But there's enough in and around town to make it an enjoyable overnight stop, before or after your Aeolian trip, with one major sight – the castle – that stands comparison with any in Sicily.

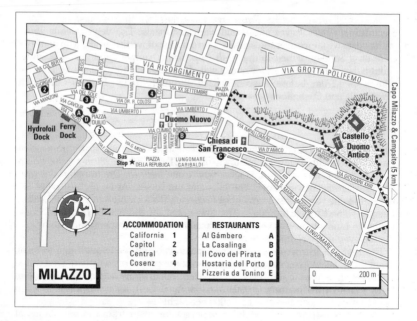

ACCOMMODATION
California 1
Capitol 2
Central 3
Cosenz 4

RESTAURANTS
Al Gámbero A
La Casalinga B
Il Covo del Pirata C
Hostaria del Porto D
Pizzeria da Tonino E

MILAZZO

0   200 m

Historically, the site's strategic importance made it one of the most-fought-over towns in Sicily. The Greeks arrived in 716 BC, after which the town was contested by successive armies, from the Carthaginians to the Aragonese. It even became a base for the British during the Napoleonic Wars, while fifty years later Garibaldi won a victory here that set the seal on his conquest of Sicily. None of this is evident from the fairly nondescript modern streets behind the port, but a fifteen-minute walk north along Lungomare Garibaldi and up through the **old town** offers a pleasing change in aspect. Here, the views open out over bay and plain, while the higher you climb, the older and more decrepit the buildings become – some churches and *palazzi* on the approach to the castle are little more than precariously balanced shells.

To appreciate the citadel's size, walk round to the north side, where the formidable defences erected by the Spanish still stand almost in their entirety. The massive walls are magnificent, pierced by a suitably imposing tunnelled gateway. The **castello** itself (guided tours hourly Tues–Sun: March–May 10am–noon & 3–5pm; June–Sept 10am–noon & 5–7pm; Oct–Feb 9am–noon & 2.30–3.30pm; free) is steeped in military history: built by Frederick II in the thirteenth century on the site of the Greek acropolis and on top of Arab foundations, it was enlarged by Charles V, and restored by the Spanish in the seventeenth century. Inside the castle walls is the **Duomo Antico** (presently closed for restoration) a central Norman keep, the old Sala del Parlamento and the remains of the Palazzo dei Giurati, later used as a prison. A museum is to be installed within these crumbling walls, but until then it's enough to admire the sheer views down to the sea.

Milazzo has a couple of other churches worth looking at. Directly opposite the castle's entrance, the Dominican **chiesa del Rosario**, together with its convent, was formerly a seat of the Inquisition, while below, in the new town, the silver-domed **Duomo Nuovo** has some excellent Renaissance paintings in the apse: four panels of SS Peter, Paul, Rocco and Thomas Aquinas; between the last of these, an *Adoration of the Child* by Antonello de Saliba; and an *Annunciation* by Andrea Giuffrè above that. You may also want to poke around Milazzo's antique, furniture and **flea market**, held on the steps below the castle on the first Saturday and Sunday of every month.

Capo Milazzo

The thin promontory north of town is the focus of most of the summertime activity. A couple of fine hotels, three or four well-equipped campsites and a decent restaurant or two are grouped around the headland of **Capo Milazzo**, 6km out of town; it's a twenty-minute bus ride away on #2 from Piazza della Repúbblica (start of the *lungomare*) or #6 from the port or Piazza della Repúbblica. There are plenty of good **beaches** all around here, but the sandiest is close to the centre of town, on Milazzo's western, less-developed side (at the end of Via Colombo).

Practicalities

Buses (including the Giuntabus service from Messina) stop right on the quayside. The **train station** is a good 3km south of the centre, but local buses run into town every twenty to thirty minutes during the day, dropping you on the quayside or further up in Piazza della Repúbblica. Buy tickets (L800) from the bar inside the train station; there's a **taxi** rank outside the station, too (about L15,000 per ride to the port).

Milazzo's **tourist office** is at Piazza Duilio 20 (July & Aug Mon–Fri 8am–2pm & 4–7pm, Sat & Sun 8am–2pm; Sept–June closed Sun; ☎090.922.2865), just back from the harbour. There's a telephone agency next door if you need to book a hotel in the Aeolians.

For **ferries** and **hydrofoils** to and from the Aeolian Islands, see the box on p.139; shipping agencies in Milazzo are listed overleaf.

Accommodation

There are plenty of reasonably pleasant **hotels** handy for the port; though, if you have a car and the inclination to get out of town, one of the nicest spots is the *Riviera Lido* (☎090.928.7834; ⑤), with its own beach on the promontory on the Strada Panoramica.

Less-exalted choices in town include the *Central*, Via del Sole 8 (☎090.928.1043; ②), a cheery little place with nice clean separate bathrooms – though the TV in reception could broadcast to Mars at that volume. The *California*, opposite, at Via del Sole 9 (☎090.922.1389; ②), is decent enough, too, and you get a room with bathroom for the price (though singles share). If these are full, next best choices are the *Cosenz*, in Via E. Cosenz (☎090.928.2996; ①), and the *Capitol*, at Via G. Rizzo 91 (☎090.928.3289; ②), which has rooms with and without bath and fluctuating prices according to season. None of these four accepts credit cards.

Of the **campsites at Capo Milazzo**, the huge *Villaggio Turistico Cirucco* (☎090.928.4746; mid-June to mid-Oct) and the *Riva Smerelda* (☎090.928.2980) both have bungalows for rent, too. The *Paradiso* (☎090.928.1633; April–Oct) is right on the headland.

Eating and drinking

Milazzo's *passeggiata* is one of the liveliest in Sicily, with baby buggies, Vespas and cars clogging Lungomare Garibaldi, and a swarm of couples and families dropping in for ice-cream at the bars along the way. One noteworthy spot for a **drink**, just downhill from the castle on Via Duomo Antico, is the *Caffè Antico*, whose outdoor terrace has distant views of the coast. More centrally, *Bounty*, on Via Crispi (beyond the pier), is lively and open late.

Of the **pizzeria-restaurants** right by the port, the *Hostaria del Porto* and *Al Gambero* are both popular and moderately priced, though neither are particularly distinguished. Local favourites for fish are *La Casalinga*, on Via D'Amico, off Lungomare Garibaldi, where the speciality is spaghetti with crab sauce (closed Sun evening Sept–July), and *Il Covo del Pirata*, Lungomare Garibaldi 47–48 (closed Wed Sept–July), which can be fairly expensive if you don't exercise restraint, though it serves pizza too. Best place for these, though, is *Pizzeria Da Tonino*, Via Cavour 27 (closed Thurs in winter), right in the centre and with low prices. Out of town, on the cape, the two places to know about are the *Villa Marchese*, on the Strada Panoramica, Contrada Paradiso (closed Mon), an excellent fish restaurant (though pricey at around L50,000 per person); and *La Baia*, for pizzas.

Getting to the Aeolians

Sailings to the Aeolians operate daily and are frequent enough to make it unnecessary to book (unless you're taking a car), although bear in mind that there is a reduced service between October and May. For schedules and prices **from Milazzo**, see the box on p.139.

The **shipping agencies** are all down by the harbour and open usual working hours as well as before all departures – Siremar for ferries and hydrofoils, SNAV for hydrofoils only, and NGI for ferries only. There's a list of the agency addresses and phone numbers below; you can pick up useful ferry/hydrofoil **timetables** from these too. If you need to leave a car in Milazzo, there's a convenient choice of **garages** (including a couple on Via G. Rizzo) – expect to pay L15,000 a day.

Navigazione Generale Italiana (NGI), Via dei Mille 26 (☎090.928.3415).
Siremar, Alliatour, Via dei Mille 45 (☎090.928.3242).
SNAV, Catalano, Via dei Mille 33 (☎090.928.7821).

festivals

February/March
Carnevale celebrated in **Cefalù** with three days of events, including a costumed children's procession on the last day.

Easter
Holy Week On the Thursday and Friday, bizarre happenings at **San Fratello**, the Festa dei Giudei, with processions and devils' costumes. Processions, too, in **Barcellona**.

May
Festival in **Milazzo** dedicated to San Francesco di Paola.

June
Start of the theatrical performances and concerts at the castle in **Milazzo** running through until August.

July
Start of the theatrical season at **Tyndaris** with events in the ancient theatre; runs through to August.

August

15 Procession of boats along the coast in honour of Madonna di Porto Salvo at **Capo d'Orlando**.

September

A medieval procession, La Castellana, in **Cáccamo**, composed of five hundred characters representing all the notables in the town's history from the eleventh to the nineteenth centuries. Check with tourist office in Palermo for dates (sometimes held in Aug).

7–8 Procession with Madonna delle Luci and her guardians at **Mistretta**.

8 Informal pilgrimage to the sanctuary of the Black Madonna at **Tyndaris**. Pilgrimage, too, at **Gibilmanna**, south of Cefalù.

October

Horse fair in **San Fratello**.

November

Historical fair held in **Sant'Agata di Militello**.

travel details

Trains

Cefalù to: Messina (1–2 hourly; 2hr 35min–3hr 30min); Milazzo (1–2 hourly; 1hr 35min–2hr 30min); Palermo (1–2 hourly; 1hr).

Milazzo to: Cefalù (1–2 hourly; 1hr 35min–2hr 30min); Messina (1–2 hourly; 1hr); Palermo (1–2 hourly; 2hr 20min–3hr 40min).

Sant'Agata di Militello to: Barcellona (1–2 hourly; 1hr–1hr 40min); Capo d'Orlando (1–2 hourly; 15min); Messina (1–2 hourly; 1hr 25min–2hr 30min); Milazzo (1–2 hourly; 50min–1hr 30min); Oliveri-Tíndari (hourly; 55min); Patti (1–2 hourly; 40min).

Términi Imerese to: Cefalù (1–2 hourly; 30min); Messina (1–2 hourly; 2hr 30min–3hr 30min); Palermo (every 30min; 30min); Sant'Agata di Militello (1–2 hourly; 1hr 10min–1hr 45min); Santo Stéfano di Camastra (hourly; 1hr 15min).

Buses

Barcellona to: Castroreale (7 daily Mon–Sat, 1–2 Sun; 30min).

Cáccamo to: Palermo (2 daily; 1hr 15min); Términi Imerese (13 daily Mon–Sat; 30min).

Castelbuono to: Campofelice (1 daily Mon–Sat; 1hr 10min); Cefalù (7–9 daily Mon–Sat, 3 Sun; 40min); Collesano (1 daily Mon–Sat; 50min); Gangi (2 daily Mon–Sat, 1 Sun; 1hr 20min); Geraci (2 daily Mon–Sat, 1 Sun; 50min); Isnello (1 daily Mon–Sat; 25min); Palermo (4 daily Mon–Sat; 1hr 30min–2hr); Términi Imerese (2 daily Mon–Sat; 1hr 30min).

Cefalù to: Castelbuono (7–9 daily Mon–Sat, 3 Sun; 40min); Gangi (1 daily; 2hr); Geraci (1 daily; 1hr 25min); Gibilmanna (3–4 daily Mon–Sat, 1 Sun; 30min); Palermo (3 daily; 1hr); Petralia (1 daily; 2hr); Términi Imerese (1 daily; 30min).

Milazzo to: Messina (hourly; 50min).

Patti to: Tíndari (3 daily; 20min).

Sant'Agata di Militello to: Cesarò (1 daily; 1hr 30min); San Fratello (1 daily; 20min).

Santo Stéfano di Camastra to: Mistretta (3–6 daily; 40min); Nicosia (1 daily Mon–Sat, change at Mistretta; 2hr 50min).

Términi Imerese to: Buonfornello (2 daily Mon–Sat; 1hr–1hr 30min); Cáccamo (14 daily Mon–Sat; 30min); Castelbuono (2 daily Mon–Sat; 1hr 5min–1hr 30min); Cefalù (1 daily Mon–Sat; 25min); Palermo (7 daily Mon–Sat; 40min).

Ferries

Ferry timetables change seasonally so, if time is of the essence, it's always worth checking with the tourist office or ferry company for the most up-to-date schedules.

Milazzo *June–Sept* to: Alicudi (6 weekly; 5hr 40min–6hr 5min); Filicudi (6 weekly; 4hr 35min–5hr); Ginostra (2 weekly; 5hr 15min); Lípari (5–7 daily; 2hr); Naples (3–5 weekly; 17hr); Panarea (1–2 daily; 4hr 15min); Rinella (8–12 weekly; 3hr 5min–5hr 35min); Santa Marina (3–4 daily; 3hr 10min–3hr 40min); Strómboli (6–8 weekly; 5–7hr); Vulcano (5–6 daily; 1hr 30min).

Milazzo *Oct–May* to: Alicudi (4 weekly; 5hr 30min); Filicudi (4 weekly; 4hr 15min); Ginostra (2–3 weekly; 6hr); Lípari (6 weekly; 2hr); Naples (2–3 weekly; 17hr); Panarea (8 weekly; 3hr 15min); Rinella (4 weekly; 3hr 5min– 5hr 35min); Santa Marina (2 weekly; 3hr 40min); Strómboli (4–5 weekly; 2hr 40min–7hr); Vulcano (6 weekly; 1hr 30min).

Hydrofoils

Hydrofoil timetables change seasonally so, if time is of the essence, it's always worthwhile checking with the tourist office or hydrofoil company for the most up-to-date schedules.

Capo d'Orlando *mid-June to Sept* to: Lípari (1–2 daily; 1hr 35min); Panarea (mid-June to Sept 1–2 daily; 2hr 5min); Strómboli (1–2 daily; 2hr 35min); Vulcano (1–2 daily; 1hr 20min).

Cefalù *mid-June to Sept* to: Lípari (1–2 daily; 2hr 30min); Palermo (3 weekly; 1hr 10min); Vulcano (1–2 daily; 2hr 30min).

Milazzo *June–Sept* to: Alicudi (1 daily; 2hr 35min); Filicudi (1 daily; 2hr); Ginostra (2 daily; 1hr 20min–3hr 45min); Lípari (hourly; 40min–1hr); Panarea (5 daily; 1hr 40min–4hr 10min); Rinella (4 daily; 1hr 35min); Santa Marina (hourly; 1hr 20min); Strómboli (5 daily; 1hr–2hr 30min); Vulcano (hourly; 40min).

Milazzo *Oct–May* to: Alicudi (1 daily; 2hr 35min); Filicudi (1 daily, 2hr); Ginostra (1 daily; 2hr 10min); Lípari (2 daily; 55min); Panarea (1 daily; 1hr 30min); Rinella (1–2 daily; 1hr 35min); Santa Marina (2 daily; 1hr 20min); Strómboli (1 daily; 1hr 5min); Vulcano (2 daily; 40min).

Sant'Agata di Militello *mid-June to Sept* to: Lípari (1–2 daily; 1hr 35min); Vulcano (1–2 daily; 1hr 20min).

CHAPTER THREE

THE AEOLIAN ISLANDS

The **Aeolian Islands**, or Isole Eolie, are a mysterious apparition when glimpsed from Sicily's northern coast – sometimes it's clear enough to pick out the individual white houses on their rocky shores; at other times they're murky, misty and only half-visible. D.H. Lawrence, on his way to Palermo by train in bad weather, thought they resembled " . . . heaps of shadow deposited like rubbish heaps in the universal greyness". The sleepy calm that seems to envelop this archipelago masks a more dramatic existence: two of the islands are still volcanically active, and all are buffeted alternately by ferocious storms in winter and waves of tourists in summer. But their unique charm has survived more or less intact, fuelled by the myths associated with their elemental and unpredictable power. Volcanoes have always been identified with the mouths of hell, and it was here that Jupiter's son, Vulcan, had his workshop. One of the islands is named after this god of fire and metalworking. Another takes its name from Liparus, whose daughter Ciane married Aeolus, ruler of the winds and master of navigation; Aeolus, in turn, lent his name to the whole archipelago. These winds were kept in one of the Aeolians' many caves, which were presented to Odysseus in a bag to bring on his travels. His curious crew opened the bag and as, a result, blew his ship straight back to port.

The more verifiable **history** of the islands is equally eventful. The first settlers exploited the volcanic resources of the islands, above all the abundance of obsidian, a hard glass-like rock that can be worked to produce a fine cutting edge and was traded far and wide, accruing enormous wealth to the archipelago. The islands were drawn more closely into the Greek ambit by the arrival in about 580 BC of refugees from the wars between Segesta and Selinus (Selinunte). Welcomed by the inhabitants, these errant Greeks organized themselves into two groups: those who cultivated the land and settled the smaller islands, and those who defended their settlements from Etruscan pirates and, in turn, preyed on other shipping. The land was held in common, and the loot divided. This system was so successful that their contributions to the sanctuary at Delphi rivalled even those of great Syracuse. Those Greeks based on the fortified citadel of Lípari later allied themselves with Carthage, whose base Lípari became during the First Punic War. For its pains, Greek Lípari was destroyed by the Romans in 251 BC and the islands became part of the Roman province of Sicily, paying a hefty tribute to Rome as well as taxes on its exports of obsidian. The islands subsequently changed hands several times before being abandoned to the frequent attacks of wide-ranging North African pirates, culminating in the terrible slaughter that took place in 1544 at the hands of Khair ed-Din, or Barbarossa, who consigned to slavery all the survivors of the massacre – a figure estimated to have been as high as 10,000. Italian unification saw the islands used as a prison for political exiles, a role that continued right up to World War II, with the Fascists exiling their political

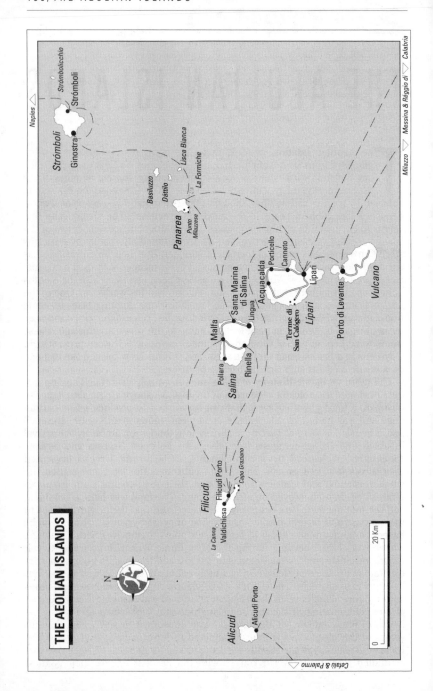

THE AEOLIAN ISLANDS

Alicudi

Alicudi Porto

Filicudi

La Canna
Valdichiesa
Filicudi Porto
Capo Graziano

Salina

Pollara
Rinella
Malfa
Lingua
Santa Marina di Salina

Panarea

Basiluzzo
Dattilo
Punto Milazzese
La Formiche
Lisca Bianca

Strómboli

Strómboli
Ginostra
Strómbolicchio

Acquacalda
Porticello
Canneto
Lipari
Lipari
Terme di San Calógero
Porto di Levante
Vulcano

Naples

Milazzo ▷ Messina & Réggio di ▷ Calabria

Cefalù & Palermo ▷

0   20 Km

opponents to Lípari. The last political detainee to be held here was, ironically, Mussolini's own daughter, Edda Ciano, in 1946.

Emigration, especially to Australia, had reduced the Aeolian population to a mere handful of families by the late 1950s, when the arrival of the first hydrofoil signalled salvation by a nascent tourist industry. Agriculture has largely been abandoned, and the economic revival today is based purely on tourism (though Lípari's pumice industry has recently expanded), with hotels sprouting on previously barren ground, and running water and electricity installed

---

GETTING TO THE AEOLIAN ISLANDS

Access is easiest and cheapest **from Milazzo** (see below), with year-round ferries and hydrofoils connecting the port with all the islands. Ferries and hydrofoils from Milazzo call first at Vulcano, followed by the main island, Lípari, which is connected by ferry and hydrofoil to all the other islands. Schedules and ticket prices from Milazzo are detailed in the table below.

There are also fairly regular hydrofoil services in summer **from Palermo, Cefalù, Capo d'Orlando** and **Messina**; check "Travel details" at the end of the relevant chapters for a general idea of the schedules, and contact local tourist office and travel agents for current information. Note that from Palermo some routes take in Filicudi and Alicudi first. From **mainland Italy**, there are connections from Réggio di Calabria (Via Messina) and Naples; from Naples, Strómboli is the first port of call. See "Travel details" (p.173) for a rundown of these services.

You'll find it useful to get hold of **timetables**, either from the tourist offices in Milazzo or Messina, or from the ferry and hydrofoil companies themselves: Siremar, SNAV and NGI are the main operators. **Ferries** (*navi* or *batelli*) take about twice as long as **hydrofoils** (*aliscafi*), but are around half the price. The hydrofoils are more prone to cancellation due to bad weather, especially in winter and particularly services to the more distant islands.

Schedules and ticket prices from Milazzo
The following table shows the frequency of services from Milazzo and gives the (rounded-up) price for the relevant **one-way** journey: return tickets are exactly double; **children** go for half-price; and tickets are a few hundred lire cheaper in the winter (Oct–May). **Taking a car** across from Milazzo to Lípari costs around L33,000 –75,000, depending on its size (small- or medium-sized cars will pay either L33,000 or L46,500); **bikes** are L8000.

	Ferries (*navi/batelli*)			Hydrofoils (*aliscafi*)		
Milazzo to:	**June–Sept**	**Oct–May**	**Price**	**June–Sept**	**Oct–May**	**Price**
Alicudi	6 weekly	4 weekly	L24,000	1 daily	1 daily	L41,000
Filicudi	6 weekly	4 weekly	L22,000	1 daily	1 daily	L34,000
Lípari	5–7 daily	6 daily	L13,000	hourly	2 daily	L22,000
Panarea	1–2 daily	8 weekly	L15,000	5 daily	1 daily	L26,000
Salina (Santa Marina)	3–4 daily	2 weekly	L16,000	hourly	2 daily	L25,000
Salina (Rinella)	8–12 weekly	4 weekly	L16,000	4 daily	1–2 daily	L25,000
Strómboli	6–8 weekly	8 weekly	L20,000	5 daily	1 daily	L31,000
Vulcano	5–6 daily	6 weekly	L12,000	hourly	2 daily	L20,000

Note that ferries and hydrofoils also call at Ginostra (Strómboli), though services to here aren't as frequent; see p.136 for details.

almost everywhere. Nonetheless, enough primitive splendour has remained for the islands to attract a procession of film crews, the movies ranging from Rossellini's *Strómboli: Terra di Dio* (1949), mostly remembered for the director's off-screen romance with the star, Ingrid Bergman, to Nanni Moretti's more recent *Caro Diario* (*Dear Diary*, 1994; shot on all the islands) and Michael Radford's *Il Postino* (1994, filmed on Salina). The islands also appeal to an increasing number of hiking enthusiasts, and there are good waymarked paths on nearly all.

The highlights

Each Aeolian island has a distinct identity, they're easy to explore using the frequent ferry and hydrofoil traffic plying between them, and all are embraced by beautiful, clean sea of a limpid quality rarely found anywhere else along the coast of Sicily. Sandy **beaches** are sparse, and the ones there are tend to be ash-black, but by renting a **boat**, easily done at every Aeolian harbour, there's access to any number of secluded coves, hidden caves and quiet snorkelling waters. **Scuba diving**, too, is increasing in popularity, with schools and rental outfits on several islands. Other attractions include a series of remarkable **archeological** sites – notably on Lípari, Panarea and Filicudi – and, quite simply, the fruits of the islands' agricultural and fishing industries. **Aeolian food** is some of the most distinctive in Italy, with capers and olives grown for centuries and flavouring most dishes, *malvasia* grapes providing one of Sicily's more ancient wines, and fresh swordfish, tuna and squid in abundance.

During the summer months at least, you'll not be alone, especially on the popular, central islands. **Vulcano**, with its mud baths, hot springs and smoking main crater, is closest to the mainland and too well-known for its own good. **Panarea**, the smallest and most attractive Aeolian, also attracts a well-heeled crowd that threatens to swamp its few hotels and beaches every August. The only two with any room are the main island, **Lípari**, and less popular **Salina** – the former sporting the most sights and facilities of all the islands, the latter making a realistic alternative base if everything elsewhere is full. For something completely different, a trip up to **Strómboli**'s seething crater is an unforgettable experience; the island itself is also becoming increasingly trendy, with the archipelago's best clubs and discos. But for a taste of what it was like twenty – or a hundred – years ago, make the effort to get out to the two wildest of the Aeolian Islands, **Filicudi** and **Alicudi**. Supporting tiny populations who make ends meet by fishing and little else, they are extremely remote (though in summer there are daily hydrofoil connections) and have very basic facilities; fine, if unsophisticated, places to come to unwind. **Out of season** on the Aeolians is a different matter altogether, and in most places that can mean up until early June and after early September. Then the islands are terribly seductive, with a slow rhythm and a refreshing absence of other tourists, though this can also mean many facilities closed and activities drastically curtailed. If the weather turns, you're in danger of being stuck here for days – the archipelago is often lashed by storms in winter and cut off from the mainland by heavy seas.

Getting around

Lípari is the hub of the Aeolian ferry and hydrofoil system, and you may need to return there to catch onward services to one of the other islands. Once there,

ACCOMMODATION PRICE CODES

These represent the **cheapest available double room in high season**, usually
– but not always – without en-suite bathroom or shower. Out of season, you'll often
be able to negotiate a lower price than those suggested here. For more information about hotels and room prices, see p.27. The categories are:

① under L60,000	④ L120,000–150,000	⑦ L250,000–300,000
② L60,000–90,000	⑤ L150,000–200,000	⑧ over L300,000
③ L90,000–120,000	⑥ L200,000–250,000	

most of the islands are small enough to be easily negotiable **on foot**, and if you're
planning on **hiking**, or climbing the craters on Vulcano and Strómboli, take
strong shoes or boots. Both Lípari and Salina are equipped with good **public
transport** links. These two islands are the only ones to which you might consider taking a car, but it's hardly necessary. A bicycle would be more apt, and you
can **rent bicycles** (around L15,000 a day), **mopeds and scooters**
(L30,000–70,000) on the islands; agencies are noted in the text. There are also
garages to store your car in Milazzo if you need to.

Accommodation

In high season (Easter, July & Aug), **accommodation** is scarce and expensive
and you'd be wise to phone in advance. In some places – Strómboli, in particular
– you often need to have booked hotels weeks in advance if you want to stay at
these times. You may also find that many places insist that you pay for **half-board**
(*mezza-pensione*), which gives you dinner, bed and breakfast. With restaurant
prices relatively high, this is usually a fairly good deal; in some cases, it's excellent, and the best options are noted in the text.

Outside high season, you should have less trouble and expense; you'll find that
many hotels and *pensioni* drop their prices by up to fifty percent from October to
March. Also, **renting apartments** or **private rooms** can turn out to be an eco-
nomical option. There's a **youth hostel** on Lípari, and **campsites** on Lípari and
Salina – but camping rough is illegal.

Prices and facilities

Prices on the islands verge on the exclusive side. **Restaurants** can be expensive,
since much of the food (as well as much of the water on some islands) has to be
imported; service and cover charges on Lípari and elsewhere can touch fifteen to
twenty percent. In many places there's not always the option of a cheap pizzeria
either, so if money is tight expect to do some self-catering.

All the islands are connected by **telephone** these days, and useful numbers are
given throughout the text; there are phone boxes at every harbourside, even in
remote areas. Unfamiliar codes and numbers belong to mobile phones, which
almost everyone sports. There are **banks** on Lípari, Salina and Vulcano (summer
only), and you can change money in travel agencies and major hotels throughout
the islands, but the rates aren't as good. **Electricity** has only slowly come to some
islands and, if you're spending any time on Alicudi, Filicudi or Strómboli, a torch
isn't a bad investment.

Lípari

LÍPARI is the busiest, the most popular and the most diverse island in the archipelago. Arriving by sea at its main town – also called Lípari – gives a pleasant foretaste of what is to come: a thriving little port, dominated by an impressive castle on an acropolis which effectively divides the town into two. The road that circles the island from here takes in several much smaller villages, some good beaches and excellent views out to its neighbouring islands, all of which are within easy reach.

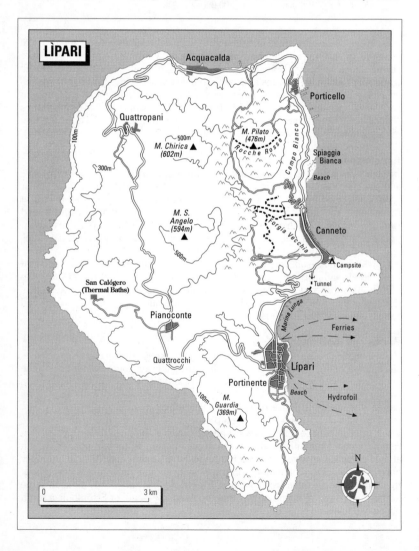

Historically, it has always been Lípari that has guided the development of the Aeolians. In classical times, after obsidian had been superseded by metals, the island's prosperity was based on its sulphur baths and thermal waters, which still attract many of the island's visitors today. Its alum too was much prized, and was found more abundantly here than anywhere else in Italy. Today, with a population of over 10,000, its economy is bolstered by an expanding pumice industry in the north of the island, though the main money-spinner is inevitably the island's natural beauty, which brings in tourists by the boatload.

Lípari Town

LÍPARI TOWN's sights are concentrated in its citadel, or **upper town**, protected by the sturdy walls of the **castello**. Most of what remains of this formidable structure is sixteenth-century Spanish in style, though it incorporates fragments of earlier medieval and even Greek buildings. Until the eighteenth century, this was the site of Lípari town, and still contains the **Duomo** (daily 9am–1pm), along with the dilapidated ruins of several Baroque churches, giving the place a forgotten, spectral air. The most impressive approach to the upper town is from Via Garibaldi, from which long steps cut right through the thick walls, bringing you up to the duomo itself: all about lie scattered the **excavations** of superimposed layers of occupation, from the Neolithic to the Roman age, a continuous record covering almost two thousand years. It's a unique sequence, providing archeologists with heaps of finds that have enabled them to date other Mediterranean cultures.

Museo Eoliano
You won't make much sense out of the wide trench exposing fragments of Bronze Age and Iron Age huts without going into the superb **Museo Eoliano** (all sections except Classica daily 9am–2pm; last entry 30min before closing; free), housed in buildings scattered around the cathedral and which contains one of Europe's most important prehistoric and classical collections.

On the right of the cathedral, the seventeenth-century bishop's palace contains the main **Sezione Archeologica** of the museum. Its displays are laid out chronologically, starting upstairs with Neolithic to Bronze Age discoveries. Here, for example, is revealed the early exploitation of obsidian, made into blades and exported all over the western Mediterranean – glass cases contain mounds of shards, worked flints, adzes and knives. These give way to finds from ancient burial sites, where you can trace the development of the various Aeolian cultures through their pottery: from the earliest, extremely plain examples to later work, adorned with motifs and other ornamentation. Downstairs covers the Iron Age to classical times, and again it's easy to follow the social and economic progress of the islands – burial techniques become more sophisticated, while the Bronze Age tools displayed here are more elaborate and more useful than anything seen previously, with scalpels, razors and fine blades all on display. There's vivid figurative work, too, like the lid of a mid-sixth-century BC *bothros*, or sacred repository of votive articles, embellished with a reclining lion.

The other principal section of the museum, the **Sezione Classica** (daily: summer 9am–2pm & 4–7pm; winter 9am–2pm & 3–6pm; last entry 30min before closing; free), on the left side of the Duomo, holds classical and Hellenic material retrieved from various necropoli. Some of this is imaginatively displayed – eighth-century BC burial urns from Milazzo are preserved in sections of lavic wall.

There are also recreations of both a Bronze Age burial ground and of the Lípari necropolis (eleventh-century BC), where bodies were either buried in a crouching position in large, plump jars or their cremated remains placed in bucket-shaped jars (situlae). Most eye-catching of all, perhaps, are the towering banks of amphorae, each 1m or so high, dredged from the ocean under Capo Graziano (p.169), many still encrusted with barnacles.

The upstairs rooms of the Sezione Classica hold the most treasured items, including shelves of **decorated vases** – some from Paestum showing a variety of satyrs, gods, queens, clowns and courtiers, from the first half of the fourth century BC. Later polychromatic works are identified as those of an individual known as the Lípari Painter (300–270 BC) and his pupils and rough contemporaries. On vases, jars and bowls, the decorations and pictures explore an extraordinary variety of themes – sacrifices, bathing scenes, mythical encounters and ceremonies. Other funerary goods here are less simple to categorize, but often more affecting: toy vases and statuettes from a young girl's grave, and delicate clay figurines of working women using mortar and pestle or washing children in a little bath.

The museum, though, is best known for what comes last in the Sezione Classia, namely the oldest and most complete range of Greek **theatrical masks** in existence. Many are models, found in fourth-century BC graves, and covering the gamut of Greek theatrical life from the tragedies of Sophocles and Euripides to satyr plays and comedies. The latter are particularly well represented, with masks of Hades and Herakles bearing unnerving, gruesome grins. One room has a good collection of small terracottas grouped in theatrical scenes, while there are also statuettes representing actual dancers and actors – nothing less than early Greek pin-ups of the period's top stars. On the way out, look out for the series of etchings by the English sea captain, W.H. Smyth, showing views of the Aeolians and other Sicilian scenes in 1823.

Having scoured the main sections of the museum, you may be daunted to discover that there's still more to come, but in truth the final two sections warrant not much more than a skip through. Across the road from the archeological section, a building houses the **Sezione delle Isole Minori**, covering the prehistory of the minor islands and including some lovely vases from Salina, finds from sites on Panarea and Filicudi, and a wealth of vulcanological material. Around the back of the archeological section, the **Sezione Epigrafica** contains a little garden of tombs and engraved stones and a room packed with more inscribed Greek and Roman tombstones and stelae. Most people head straight for the **Parco Archeologico** instead (Mon–Sat: summer 9am–7pm; winter 9am–4pm; free). Situated at the end of the road, it also has some Greek and Roman tombs, and a modern Greek-style theatre where concerts and plays are performed between July and September. There's a nice view over the rooftops and the Marina Corta from here.

The rest of town

There's little else specific to see in Lípari, though the lower town does provide occasional reminders that it wasn't just the citadel that was inhabited in classical times. A **Zona Archeologica** (usually locked), off the main Corso, preserves the remains of various buildings and houses; rather easier to appreciate is the **necropolis**, visible off Via G. Marconi, where Greco-Roman tombs stud the sunken field. The finds from here, called the Contrada Diana necropolis, are held in the Sezione Classica of the museum.

Realistically, though, all anyone does after a visit to the museum is to spend time mooching around the small, packed streets, which are a lively array of chic boutiques and souvenir emporia interspersed with *alimentari* and fishing-tackle shops. The best place to while away an afternoon is at the **Marina Corta**, where the constant coming-and-going of hydrofoils, taxis, bikes and people can be safely observed from the cool haven of parasol-covered bars. After 6pm, during the *passeggiata*, the main **Corso Vittorio Emanuele** is closed to traffic and full of perambulating people, and at some point you could also stroll up to Piazza Municipio (also called Piazza Mazzini), just north of the *castello*, for more fine sea views. A good time to be around is on August 24, when the town's main **festival** takes place – dedicated to St Bartholomew and an excuse for all sorts of high jinks.

Practicalities

Hydrofoils dock at the Marina Corta, while **ferries** dock at the Marina Lunga, a deep-water harbour, beyond which a long beach curves away to the north. Virtually everything of note lies between the two harbours, and it only takes fifteen minutes or so to cross the town on foot. The **tourist office**, at Corso Vittorio Emanuele 202 (July & Aug Mon–Sat 9am–2pm & 4–10pm, Sun 9am–2pm; Sept–June Mon–Fri 8am–2pm & 4.30–7.30pm, Sat 8am–2pm; ☎090.988.0095), will provide you with a useful hotel list, good for all the Aeolian Islands, a local bus timetable, and other brochures and leaflets. For details of ticket offices for **ferry and hydrofoil departures**, see "Listings" (p.149).

Getting around

Lípari's blue **buses** all leave from a stop by the Marina Lunga, opposite the service station. There are frequent services to every village on the island (though departures are less regular on Sundays and outside July and August); details are given where applicable in the text below; pick up a timetable from the bus operators, Urso Guglielmo, at Via Cappuccini 29 (☎090.981.1262), above the Marina Lunga. Marina Lunga is also the site of the island's only **petrol stations** (Agip and Esso), as well as two or three **scooter- and bike-rental** outfits; see "Listings" (p.149) for details. There are **taxis** available on the Marina Corta.

Lípari is not a bad place to book a **boat excursion**, since it's close enough to the main group of islands to allow a decent day-trip. You could, of course, simply use the scheduled ferry and hydrofoil services to visit the neighbouring islands, but if you're staying in Lípari and want to see Strómboli by night, or visit the offshore islets by Panarea, then one of the agencies in town (see "Listings", p.149) can oblige. Typically, you'll pay around L60,000 for an all-day trip, which lets you visit and swim off Panarea and then see the evening explosions off Strómboli. Day-trips to Panarea or Vulcano, allowing plenty of swimming, are around half that price. Alternatively, a group might bargain with one of the fishermen down at the Marina Corta for a **boat trip around Lípari** – prices are highly negotiable, depending on numbers and season.

Accommodation

There's more choice of **accommodation** in Lípari than any of the other islands, though you can still find yourself stuck for a room in high season, particularly in the cheaper range. In July and August especially, it makes sense to listen to the offers of **rooms** as you step off the boat. You'll pay around L40,000–60,000 per person in August, L30,000 at other times of the year, and, though you may be asked to spend a minimum of two nights (or a week in summer), it can still work out cheaper (and nicer) than a *pensione*, given that you'll nearly always get something with a shower, kitchen and balcony or terrace. If no one accosts you at the port, look for notices in shop windows, or ask around in the harbour bars and shops; the *Bártolo* restaurant, for example (see p.148), has rooms available, and we've detailed a couple of other good possibilities in the accommodation listings. Other budget choices include the **youth hostel**, within the castle walls, and the island's only **campsite** at Canneto, 3km north of town (see p.150). Note that all the price codes below refer to the peak summer-season prices (July & Aug); most places are up to forty to fifty percent cheaper during the rest of the year.

Carasco, Porto delle Genti (☎090.981.1605, fax 090.981.1828). Superbly sited three-star hotel with its own rocky cove, pool and sparkling views. Excellent facilities (and some good off-season discounts). March–Oct. ⑧.

Diana Brown, Vico Himera 3 (☎090.981.2584). Central location in a tiny lane parallel to Corso Vittorio Emanuele makes this apartment a good base. It's adequate, though cramped, and spotlessly clean, run by a South African expatriate usually to be found selling excursion tickets at the Viking boat kiosk on the Marina Corta. No credit cards. ③.

Enza Marturano, Via Maurolico 35 (☎090.981.2544 or 0368.322.4997). Four bright, immaculate modern rooms with views, ranged around a communal lounge/kitchen, with a terrace overlooking the corso. Call ahead if possible: otherwise, the owner usually greets the early-morning boats (and lives at Via Umberto I 13). No credit cards. ③.

Enzo Il Negro, Via Garibaldi 29 (☎090.981.3163). Nicely located rooms situated near the hydrofoil port, with a splendid roof terrace. No credit cards. ④.

Europeo, Corso Vittorio Emanuele 98 (☎090.981.1589). A useful *pensione* on the main drag, though often full, and you'll probably do better for the price in a room in a private house. It's worth paying extra for a room with shower. No credit cards. ②.

Residence Fiorentino, Via Giuseppe Franza 9 (☎090.981.2136, fax 090.988.0159). A good, friendly, family-run place for rooms, with modern facilities and kitchen; prices halve here outside July and August. Located about a 10min walk from the centre. ④.

Ostello della Gioventù, Zona Castello (☎090.981.1540, fax 090.981.1715). Lípari's youth hostel is marvellously situated in the castle: good value at L14,000 per person and with great views, though very busy in July and August – ring ahead. Note that there's a midnight curfew, but you can check in for a lunch and siesta between noon and 3pm, and the hostel often remains open all afternoon. No credit cards. March–Oct.

Residence Mendolita, Via G. Rizzo (☎090.988.0726, fax 090.981.2878). Superior apartments in attractive terraced villas south of the town centre, near the Portinente beach. They're operated in conjunction with the excellent *Filippino* and *E'Pulera* restaurants (see p.148) and the price (around L150,000 per person) is for *mezza-pensione*, with a meal in either. Out of season, you should be able to negotiate room-only rates. ⑥.

Neri, Via G. Marconi 43 (☎ & fax 090.981.1413). Down an alley off the corso after no. 85, this fine old mansion, quiet and well kept, has wrought-iron balconies and serves breakfast on a lovely terrace. Price includes breakfast; minimum of half-board in August (L125,000 per person), but again rooms are much cheaper out of season. Travellers' cheques accepted, but no credit cards. April–Oct. ④.

Oriente, Via G. Marconi 35 (☎090.981.1493, fax 090.988.0198). Rather plain on the outside, but stuffed with knick-knacks and sporting a patio garden, fully equipped air-conditioned rooms, and nice English-speaking management. ⑤.

Rocce Azzurre, Via Maddalena 69 (☎090.981.3248, fax 090.981.3247). Adjacent to its own little pebble beach, 10min south of the centre, this secluded hotel is popular with families. There's a sun terrace built over the rocks and you can arrange diving/snorkelling here, too. ⑤.

Locanda Salina, Via Garibaldi 18 (☎090.981.2332). The cheapest regular hotel in town is actually rather nice, its top double room with a balcony overlooking the harbour, and sporting an immaculate bathroom. Book ahead – there are only six rooms. Travellers' cheques accepted, but no credit cards. ②.

Tullio Cammarano, Via Francesco Crispi 135 (☎090.981.2386 or 0330.592.428). These rented rooms lie a 10min walk north of the port at Marina Lunga, towards Canneto, and right across from the sea. Check first about use of cooking facilities. No credit cards. ④.

Eating

The town's numerous **restaurants and pizzerias** – many of them open-air – come in varying degrees of expense, though some have (often poor) tourist menus at around L20,000. Even the cheaper places have exorbitant fifteen- to twenty-percent service charges that'll boost your bill. All the places below, though, are pretty good; the ones with telephone numbers require reservations in high season. For an explanation of the price categories, see p.32.

For self-catering, there's an UPIM **supermarket** (Mon–Fri 8.30am–1.30pm & 4–9pm, Sat 8.30am–1.30pm & 4–9.30pm) and various *alimentari* and bakeries on the main corso – *Il Fornaretto*, Corso Vittorio Emanuele 117, is a **bakery** with fine bread, as well as pizza slices and *calzone* to go (closed Wed afternoon & Sun).

Bártolo, Via Garibaldi 53. Cheery, touristy place, with windows open onto the street, where the *forno a legna* pizzas are worth investigating: the *arrabbiata* is with slices of *peperoni* and splashed with chilli oil for good measure. Or try the antipasto of smoked tuna and swordfish. Moderate. Closed Fri except July–Sept.

E'Pulera, Via Diana (☎090.981.1158). Romantic courtyard-garden restaurant specializing in Aeolian food – swordfish *involtini*, caper salads, home-made pasta, almond biscuits, *malvasia* wine – that's rich and filling. Super cooking, well worth the prices, and it stays open till late. It's 2min behind the *Neri pensione* (see p.147); turn left at the end of Via G. Marconi. Expensive. Closed lunchtimes & Oct–May.

Filippino, Piazza Municipio (☎090.981.1002). Lípari's top restaurant, in business since 1910. It's in the upper town and has a shaded outdoor terrace and high prices – the *zuppa di pesce* is particularly good. Very expensive. Closed Mon Oct–March, & Nov.

Il Galeone, Corso Vittorio Emanuele 220. Streetside pizza joint at the top end of the main corso, just around the corner from the ferry port. Choose from one of thirty pizzas – and from other dishes too (including a reasonable *menu turistico*), although these aren't as good. Inexpensive. Closed Wed Nov–March.

La Nassa, Via Giuseppe Franza 36. Local favourite just 5min from the Marina Corta, with excellent fresh fish and a decently priced *menu turistico*. Moderate–expensive. Closed Nov–March.

Trattoria d'Oro, Via Umberto I 32. Back-street trattoria with decent, though not sensational, food and often long waits. The L23,000 fixed-price menu includes coffee, cover charge and service. Moderate. No closing day.

Pasticceria Subba, Corso Vittorio Emanuele 92. One of the island's best, going for almost seventy years and serving up coffee, cakes and pastries from breakfast time until late in summer; nice outdoor seating. Inexpensive. No credit cards. No closing day.

Pescecane, Corso Vittorio Emanuele 223. Shares an outdoor terrace with *Il Galeone* and has similarly smart waiters who scurry across the street bearing good pizzas. There's a fairly steady takeaway trade, and a full menu too. Moderate. Closed Thurs Oct–May.

A Sfiziusa, Via Roma 29. Budget-priced trattoria back from the hydrofoil port that's good for pasta and fresh fish of the day; squid and prawns are frozen, though. Inexpensive. Closed Fri Oct–April.

Drinking and nightlife

Best **bars** for lounging around in are those with outdoor seats at the Marina Corta – *Il Gabbiano*, *Al Pescatore*, *La Vela* and *Café du Port* – where the beers and snacks are pricey but the vantage-point is the best in town. *Chitarra*, across the square beneath the church, also has harbourside seats and **live music** most nights after 10pm, as does the *Kasbah Café*, at Via Maurolico 25, which also serves pizzas and snacks in its garden (closed Mon & Nov). Lípari goes to bed fairly early, though in summer at least you can extend the night by drinking at the *Megaton Bar*, Via XXIV Maggio, on the way to the castle (open until 3am; closed Fri Oct–May); or by **dancing** at *Turmalin*, a club off Piazza Municipio, near the castle.

Listings

Banks and exchange Change money and travellers' cheques at Banca Agricola Etnea, on Via Ten. M. Amendola, just off the corso; at Banca del Sud, Banca di Roma or the Monte dei Paschi di Siena, all on the corso (all with cash machines); or at Cassa di Risparmio, on

Piazzetta Austria (cash machine). Hours are generally Mon–Fri 8.35am–1.35pm & 3–4pm, Sat 8.35am–12.05pm. There are exchange facilities at Costa-Meligunte Travel, Eoltravel and Menalda Tours, all on the corso, but the rates aren't as good. You can change also cash or American Express travellers' cheques at the post office (see below).

Bike and scooter rental From Cannizzaro Giuseppe, Via F. Mancuso (☎090.981.1408); and Da Marcello, Via Sottomonastero, Marina Lunga (☎090.981.1234). Expect to pay L10,000–20,000 per day for a bike, and around L50,000 for a scooter, excluding fuel; you'll have to leave your passport or a hefty deposit as security.

Boat excursions The main agencies are La Cava, Corso Vittorio Emanuele 124 (☎090. 981.1242); and Viking, Vico Himera 3 (☎090.981.2584), which also has a kiosk at the Marina Corta.

Boat rental Rubber dinghies for hire from Da Marcello, Via Sottomonastero, Marina Lunga (☎090.981.1234); or call at Da Maurizio, a kiosk on Piazza Marina Corta (☎090.982.2040 or 0330.833.318). L100,000–130,000 a day, plus deposit (fuel extra).

Car rental Basile, Corso Vittorio Emanuele 279 (near the petrol pumps); Cannizzaro Giuseppe, Via F. Mancuso (☎090.981.1408); and Foti Roberto, Via F. Crispi (☎090.981.2352). Around L80,000 per day.

Diving Many of the larger hotels can put you in touch with a diving school, and the Diving Center Manta Sub (☎090.981.1004) is based at the Giardino sul Mare, Via Maddalena 65; or contact Andi's Dive Centre, Via F. Crispi 92 (☎090.982.2238). Foti Roberto (see "Car rental" above) also rents out boats and scuba gear.

Emergencies Hospital (☎090.98.851); First Aid (☎090.988.5226); Vigili Urbani (☎090.988.7207); Carabinieri (☎090.988.0030).

Ferry and hydrofoil companies Covemar, Marina Corta (☎090.981.3181); NGI, Via Ten. M. Amendola (☎090.981.1955); Siremar, dockside office at Marina Corta (☎090.981.2200); SNAV, dockside office at Marina Corta (☎090.988.0266). Ferry tickets sold separately at Marina Lunga.

Pharmacy Cincotta, Via Garibaldi 60; Internazionale, Corso Vittorio Emanuele 28; Sparacino, Corso Vittorio Emanuele 95.

Post office Corso Vittorio Emanuele 207, where you can also exchange cash and American Express travellers' cheques. (Mon–Fri 8.30am–1pm & 1.30–6.30pm, Sat 8.30am–1.20pm).

Showers The barber shops in the square at the Marina Corta and on Via Maurólico have public showers.

Telephones Public phones on Via Garibaldi; outside the Upim supermarket on the corso; Piazzetta Austria; and at Marina Corta and Marina Lunga.

Around the island

Buses leave Lípari town (from Marina Lunga) approximately every hour for the **rest of the island** (every 30min in summer for Canneto), all of which is no more than thirty minutes' ride away. Buses run in two directions: clockwise to Quattropani (L2500); and anticlockwise to Canneto, Porticello and Acquacalda (L2000); buy tickets on board. If you're really pushed for time, but want to get a flavour of Lípari's island scenery, a **tour of the island** (*giro dell'isola*) by normal service Urso bus runs three times a day (currently at 9.30am, 11.30am & 5pm; L6000) from the beginning of July to the end of September.

Canneto

It's around 3km north to the nearest village, **CANNETO**, with the bus (every 30–60min, depending on the season) swooping through a tunnel to reach the bay on the other side of the headland from town. A long pebbled beach of little renown fronts the village itself, which isn't much more than a rather dreary line of buildings, and for sand and swimming you should stay on the bus until the end of the line, at the far northern end of the lungomare. From here, a stepped path runs around and down to the **Spiaggia Bianca**, an expansive sandy beach whose proclaimed whiteness is rapidly becoming a distant memory as the pumice dust that covered it gets washed away by the winter storms. Nevertheless, it's worth making a half-day's expedition for, and Canneto itself has bars, trattorias and a reasonable **hotel**, the *Odissea*, just up from the seafront on Via Nazario Sauro (☎090.981.2337; ⑤), all rooms with private bath, though not all with views. You can get a better deal, however, renting **rooms** overlooking the sea on the corner of Marina Garibaldi and Via Risorgimento (☎090.981.1298; ②). Frankly, Lípari Town is the nicer place to stay, though if you're camping you'll have to settle for Canneto. The island's only **campsite**, the *Baia Unci* (☎090.981.1909; Easter–Sept), is right at the southern end of the village (the bus from Lípari stops outside), and has its own simple bar and restaurant, and some apartments to rent. In the village, there's a small supermarket and a couple of *alimentari*, too.

Campobianco and Monte Pilato

Buses continue north of Canneto, through the Cave di Pomice at **CAMPO-BIANCO**, where the various pumice workings have left huge white scars on the hillside; the ground all around for 2km or 3km looks as if it's had a scattering of talcum powder. More uses for this volcanic debris are being found all the time, and it's presently used in such diverse products as toothpaste, light bulbs, construction materials, jeans (for bleaching) and fertilizer. Years of accumulation of pumice sediment on the sea bed below have turned the water a piercing aquamarine colour – very enticing and instantly accessible by sliding the 30m or so down the brilliant white mountains of dust formed by the quarrying. This is nothing new to the islanders and other cognoscenti, who've been doing it for years; indeed the pumice-chute was used for one of the closing scenes in the Taviani brothers' epic film *Kaos*.

Above Campobianco, a path leads up the slopes of **Monte Pilato** (476m), thrown up in the eruption from which all the pumice originally came. The last explosion occurred in around 700 AD, leading to the virtual abandonment of Lípari town and creating the obsidian flows of Rocche Rosse and Forgia Vecchia, both of which can be climbed. Although it's overgrown with vegetation, you can still make out the outline of the crater at the top, and you may come across the blue-black veins of obsidian. Despite its quite different appearance, it's almost identical in composition to pumice, and it's the presence of obsidian on Lípari that makes the island's beaches sparkle.

Porticello and Acquacalda

There's a bus-stop above the stony beach at **PORTICELLO**, from where a road (and a quicker, more direct path) winds down to the small bay, which sunbathers share with the Heath Robinson-style pumice-work machinery that connects the white hillside with the pier. Somewhere, you feel, should be someone cranking a handle on a very large wheel to set it all in motion. There's no shade here, and the pebble beach soon reaches scalding temperatures, though the water is a tempting colour. A couple of vans sell cool drinks and snacks.

There are seven or eight buses a day out here from Lípari, all of which terminate a couple of kilometres further on **ACQUACALDA**. You could walk between the two villages in about half an hour, if you wanted some aerial views of the azure waters and pumice quarries, and pick up the return Lípari bus in either place. Acquacalda itself is just a one-street village – not a very attractive one – with more pumice machinery, a long stone beach and a couple of waterfront bars. There's also a homely **trattoria** – *Da Laura* – which has a terrace overlooking the sea and Salina across the water; it's at the top of the road coming into the village from Porticello.

Quattrocchi to Quattropani

Heading west from Lípari town, you can walk to the vantage-point for one of the Aeolian Islands' most stunning vistas. Climbing the 3km through lush and fertile country, you'll know you're at **QUATTROCCHI** when Vulcano and the spiky *faraglioni* rocks, which puncture the sea between the two islands, sweep into view to the south. The curious name of this spot ("Four Eyes") is said to derive from the fact that newly wedded couples traditionally come here to be photographed, so gracing every shot of this memorable place with two pairs of eyes.

Keep on the road to **Pianoconte**, a fragmented village that has a trio of popular restaurants, best of which is probably *La Ginestra* (closed Wed), especially in the evening when they serve pizzas too.

Just before the village, a sideroad slinks off down to the old Roman thermal baths at **San Calógero**. It's a particularly nice route to follow on foot, across a valley and skirting some impressive cliffs, the baths right at the end of the road. Lengthy excavations here have unearthed a great deal of archeological material, particularly from the Mycenaean age (fifteenth century BC), and even if the spa-hotel is still closed (as it usually is) you should be able to take a look around the site, including the steamy chamber where the hot water issues, and walk down the path to the sea below.

The bus from Lípari (through Quattrocchi and Pianoconte) ends its run at **QUATTROPANI**, a dispersed settlement with a pleasing church and more fine views. There are ten buses a day here (three on Sun), though if it isn't too hot you could walk the 5km or so, round the winding road, to complete the island circle at Acquacalda, and catch the bus back from there.

Vulcano

Only a few minutes south of Lípari by ferry or hydrofoil, separated by the kilometre-wide channel Bocche di Vulcano, is the island of **VULCANO**. Closest of the Aeolians to the Sicilian mainland, it's the first port of call for services from Milazzo, and you don't have to disembark to experience the sulphurous, rotten-egg smell that hits you before you've even reached the small port – disconcerting if you're not expecting it. The island's **Gran Cratere** hangs menacingly over its inhabited northern tip, its plume of vapour a constant reminder of its silent power, though this very old volcano is in the last, smoking phase of its life and unlikely to spring anything more harmful than the nasty smell.

That said, the volcano was threatening enough to dissuade anyone from living here before the eighteenth century, since when there have been some hasty evacuations. In the last century a Scot called Stevenson bought the island to exploit the sulphur and alum reserves, but all his work was engulfed by the next major eruption. Although the volcano's last gasp of activity occurred between 1886 and 1890, its presence permeates the island, giving Vulcano a more primeval flavour

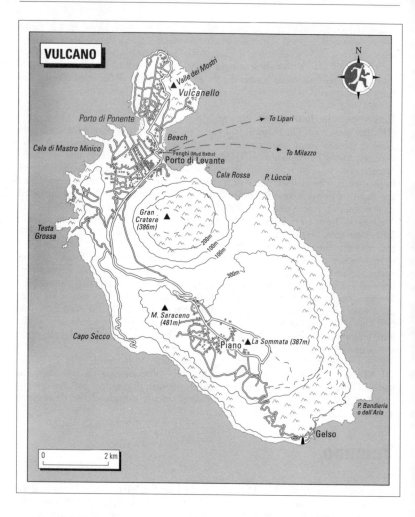

than any of the other Aeolians. Everything here is an assault on the senses, the outlandish saffron of the earth searing the eyes, as violent as the intense reds and orange of the iron and aluminium sulphates that leak out of the ground in the summer, to be washed away with the first autumn rains.

However, none of the jet-setting Italians who come to bronze themselves on Vulcano's beaches are discouraged, and numerous villas and some sprawling luxury hotels make this among the most exclusive of the Aeolian Islands. Don't let this put you off: if you can't find a place to stay here, or can't afford the prices, Vulcano still offers a good day out, with some of Sicily's stranger volcanic enticements and one of the best **beaches** in the entire archipelago.

Around the island

The ferries and hydrofoils dock at **PORTO DI LEVANTE**, a little harbour in the lee of the Gran Cratere, backed by a couple of streets of restaurants, villas and shops. This is where most of the facilities are located (see "Practicalities" p.154), while straight ahead from the landing dock and to the right you can't miss Vulcano's famed **fanghi**, or mud baths, sited below a spiky, multicoloured *faraglione*. More exactly it's one pool, containing a thick yellow soup of foul-smelling sulphurous mud, in which people come to wallow, caking every inch of their bodies with the stuff. On a busy day – with scores of people smearing each other or flopping belly up into the gloop – the scene is reminiscent of a ceremony of some deviancy during the sordid last days of Rome. This surreal performance is all part of a long tradition – specifically for skin and arthritic complaints – though the degree of radioactivity here makes it inadvisable to immerse yourself for any length of time, and unsuitable for young children or pregnant women. Avoid contact with the eyes (it stings like hell) and take off any silver or leather jewellery, which will be ruined forever, even just by coming into contact with the sand hereabouts. When you've had enough of the mud, hobble over to rinse yourself off in the nearby sea, where the water itself bubbles up hot and you need to take care in order not to get scalded. There's a fair beach here, though the smell wafting over from the mud bath precludes tucking into a leisurely packed lunch unless you have a cast-iron stomach.

Porto di Ponente and Vulcanello

A narrow neck of land separates Porto di Levante from **PORTO DI PONENTE**, a fifteen-minute walk past the *fanghi*. Here, a perfect arc of fine black sand lines a bay looking onto the towering pillars of rock that rise out of the channel between Vulcano and Lípari – the setting for some unforgettable sunsets. There are a couple of seafront cafés here, and some discreet hotels set back from the sands.

From the beach, the only road heads north through the trees to **Vulcanello**, the volcanic pimple thrown up out of the sea in a famous eruption in 183 BC, and joined to the main island by another flurry of activity a few centuries later. The walk takes less than an hour. The birth of Vulcanello excited enthusiasm in the high society of the time: it was witnessed by some of the greatest luminaries of the second century BC, and described by Pliny, Livy and Strabo. On the north side of Vulcanello, the **Valle dei Mostri** – literally the "Valley of the Monsters" – is an area of lavic rock formations, blackened and sculpted by the elements.

The Gran Cratere

Above all else, however, leave yourself time for the walk up to Vulcano's main crater, the **Gran Cratere**, just to the south of the Porto di Levante. Follow the road immediately to the left of the dock and walk up it for 500m or so (sign-posted "Al Cratere") until you're directed off the road to the left and up the slope. It only takes an hour to reach the crater, though it's a tough climb and totally exposed to the sun, so do it early or late in the day, and do it in strong shoes. The only vegetation consists of a few hardy gorse bushes on the lower slopes, nibbled at by goats whose bells echo across the scree. The first part of the path ascends a virtual black sand dune before reaching the harder volcanic crust, where the path runs above the rivulets caused by previous eruptions.

Reaching a ledge with views over all the other Aeolian Islands, you look down into the vast crater itself where vapour emissions – acrid and yellow – billow from the surrounding surfaces. It's a rewarding, if slightly alarming, climb, nerves not exactly steadied by the admonitory notices at the start of the climb that plead "Do not sit down, Do not lie down".

South to Gelso

From Porto di Levante, Vulcano's only road (and bus service) runs 8km south, past **Monte Saraceno** (481m, with views as far as Alicudi and the Sicilian coast), to the extensive **Piano**, the only plain of any size in the Aeolian Islands. A straggling road leads another 7km from here to the hamlet of **GELSO**, stranded on Vulcano's south coast. *Gelso* is Italian for "mulberry" and they're cultivated here, along with capers. Three buses daily run here between mid-June and mid-September; at other times, unless you want to do it on foot, you'll have to hitch (which is fine on the islands, unlike mainland Sicily), bike it, or hire a **boat**: fishermen at Porto di Levante will usually run you there and back for a reasonable rate, giving you enough time for lunch at one of the excellent **trattorias** (though these are normally closed in winter).

Practicalities

Disembarking from ferry or hydrofoil at Porto di Levante, walk straight ahead, between the rocks, for the *fanghi* and Porto di Ponente; or left, along the harbour in front of the *Hotel Faraglione*, to the traffic island for the crater and village. Information can be had at the peripatetic **tourist office** – little more than a desk of no permanent abode (usually June–Sept Mon–Sat 8am–2pm). The Siremar (☎090.985.2149) **ticket agency** is on the terrace, just a few metres above the traffic island, and just beyond is the NGI office (☎0368.675.461); SNAV (☎090.985.2230) operate from the Thermessa agency at one end of the *Hotel Faraglione*. There's a **bank**, Sicilcassa (summer Mon–Fri 8.30am–1.30pm & 2.45–3.45pm), at Porto di Levante, and you can also change money at the Thermessa agency.

    Buses run from the dockside to Vulcano Piano (7 daily Mon–Sat, 2 Sun). You can rent pretty much anything on Vulcano, from a scooter to a yacht, though perhaps the best bet is a **boat**, so that you can visit Gelso and the caves and bays on the island's west side. Talk to the boatmen hanging around the port, or, for self-steering boats, contact Centro Nautico Baia Levante (☎090.982.2197) or, at Porto di Ponente (by the *Mari del Sud* hotel), Da Tonino (☎0335.585.9790); expect to pay upwards of L110,000 in August (less at other times), depending on the type of boat you want. For **bikes**, Da Paolo operates from Via Porto Levante, offering mountain bikes (L6000 a day), and mopeds and scooters (around L20,000).

Accommodation

You could climb the crater and Vulcanello, and bus across the island and back all in a day-trip, but if you wanted to stay on Vulcano, in all cases ring first, and expect prices to shoot through the roof in summer.

    There are fairly reasonable rooms to let at **Porto di Levante**, though the sulphurous smell here is utterly pervasive – for the same olfactory experience you could stay in a cheap place in Lípari with bad drains. Best choice is the amenable *Casa Sipione* (☎090.985.2034; no credit cards; ②; June–Sept), at the end of a path beside the church, halfway to Porto di Ponente; otherwise, try *La Giara* (☎090.985.2229; ⑤), on Via Provinciale beyond the *Faraglione*; or the *Agostino* (☎090.985.2342; no credit cards; ③; closed Feb) in the piazzetta off the crossroads near the mud bath. The *Hotel Faraglione*, right on the harbour-front underneath the rock (☎090.985.2054; ⑤), has nice terrace views and, an outdoor *pasticceria*-bar.

On the **Porto di Ponente** side, prices are considerably higher, though there are a couple of places that are worth a call, in particular the *Residence Lanterna Bleu* (☎090.985.2178; no credit cards; ③; mid-Jan to mid-Dec) – a series of two- and three-bed apartments with kitchen, which drop in price by up to fifty percent outside July and August. *Orsa Maggiore* (☎090.985.2018; L130,000 half-board in Aug; ⑦; May–Oct), a large, modern hotel 1km from the beach at Porto Ponente, also cuts its prices by half outside summer; the bill covers half-board. Top-of-the-range, both close to the black-sand beach and comfortably equipped, are *Les Sables Noirs* (☎090.985.2454; ⑧; March–Oct) and the *Eolian* (☎090.985.2153; ⑦; March–Oct) – early-season discounts at both can be a real steal for accommodation of this standard.

Eating

Food on Vulcano is either exorbitantly priced or of poor quality, and you have to choose carefully from the battery of restaurants along the road that bends around from the port. *Da Maurizio* (Easter–Oct), just beyond the Siremar agency, has a nice shady garden and good food, though unless you stick to the tourist menu you could easily spend over L40,000. For cheaper **pizzas**, *Il Palmento* (Easter–Nov), just up from the mud baths, is not bad, but you can spend less and eat better with takeaway bits and pieces from the Italmec across the road, open until midnight in August. Most attractive spot for a **drink** is *Ritrovo Remigio*, with terrace seating overlooking the dock at Porto di Levante. There are good pastries and ice-creams here, too, and it's open until 2am or so during the summer.

Elsewhere on the island, pricier restaurants include *Baia di Ponente,* overlooking the sea at Porto di Ponente; *Belvedere*, at Vulcano Piano; and the isolated *Tony Maniaci*, at Gelso – all open in the summer (roughly end of Easter to Oct), and all worth the splurge.

Salina

SALINA's ancient name, *Didyme*, or "twin", refers to the two volcanic cones that give the island its distinctive shape. Both volcanoes are long extinct, but their past eruptions, combined with plenty of water – unique in the Aeolians – have endowed Salina with the most fertile soil of all the islands. The slopes are verdant, and the tree cover here contrasts strongly with the denuded crags of its more westerly neighbours. Look out on your wanderings for the exotic violet-flowered **capers**, and the abundant **vines** that carry the *malvasia* grape – both vigorously cultivated here and sold from houses and farms all across Salina. You'll come across these two traditional Aeolian specialities on every island, but, while caper production is still flourishing, *malvasia* wine has fallen victim to the general depletion of agriculture, and most of what you drink will have been imported from the Sicilian mainland. Only on Salina can you still taste the authentic sulphurous taste of this sweet and strong honey-coloured wine.

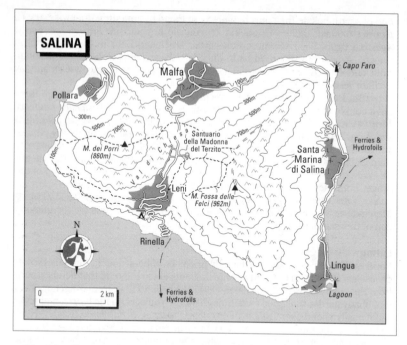

The island's central position in the archipelago makes it ideal as a base for exploring the others. It's not as in thrall to tourism as Lípari, Vulcano or Panarea, and in summer this can be a positive boon. But it sees itself as the height of sophistication compared to, say, Filicudi, and indeed Salina is big enough to support a bus service, several distinct villages, and plenty of accommodation and restaurants. Yet it's still very much part of the relaxed ebb and flow of traditional Aeolian life, ultimately dependent – as all the islands are – on the comings and goings of the ferries and hydrofoils.

Santa Marina di Salina

The main island port is **SANTA MARINA DI SALINA**, on the east coast, visually unexciting but a relaxed enough spot to persuade you to linger. Most of its identikit structures are concrete, including the long lungomare that reaches north from the harbour, fronting a stone beach from which people splash about in the sea. There's a main street, a rarity in these parts – Via Risorgimento – which runs parallel to the water, one block back, and along here are shops that sell more than just the bare necessities of life; boutiques, even. In a couple of the gift shops you can buy a decent map of the islands.

The Siremar (☎090.984.3004) and joint SNAV (☎090.984.3003) and NGI (☎090.984.3003) **agencies** are just back from the dockside, and open before sailings. **Buses** to all points on the island stop just outside the offices; there's a timetable posted on the agencies' doors. The hub of the service is Malfa (see p.158) and you may occasionally have to wait there for a short time for an onward connection, but basically there are twelve daily buses from Santa Marina to Malfa, Leni and Rinella, and seven daily to Pollara. There's also a similarly regular service to Lingua, though this is the one place you could comfortably walk to from Santa Marina. For **motorbike rental**, walk left off the dockside and, about 300m after the Agip **petrol station** on the road to Lingua, is Bongiorno Antonio (☎090.984.3308 or 090.984.3409), which has Vespas for L30,000 a day. Note that the island's only other petrol station is at Malfa.

Other services include a **post office** (Mon–Sat 8.30–noon), at Via Risorgimento 130, next to the church, where you can change cash. The nearest **bank** (indeed the only one on the island) is in Malfa (see p.158). There are a couple of **telephone** booths on the front, near the ticket agencies, a couple in the Villa Comunale by *La Cambusa* restaurant, and one by the church.

Accommodation

You can find **private rooms** if you ask around the shops and bars. A good bet is *Catena de Pasquale* at Via Francesco Crispi 17 (☎090.984.3094; no credit cards; ③); it's the street at the top end of Via Risorgimento, a ten-minute walk from the port – turn left beyond the *Carpe Diem alimentari*. Hearty, moderately priced meals are also available here.

Of the **hotels** and *pensioni*, the attractive *Punta Barone* (☎090.984.3172; no credit cards; minimum half-board in July & Aug at L105,000 per person; ③; Feb–Nov) it isn't much closer to the port, but it is right by the sea, ten minutes north up the lungomare and perched over the rocks. You're likelier to find room at *Mamma Santina*, Via Sanità 40 (☎090.984.3054; no credit cards; ③), which is signposted to the left off Via Risorgimento. Clean and friendly, the view from its wide terrace compensates for its distance from the port; you might be asked to take *mezza-pensione* in summer (L100,000 per person). Nearest to the port (left up the hill), the *Bellavista* offers comfortable rooms with verandas and views, at rates that come tumbling down by up to thirty percent outside August (☎090.984.3009; no credit cards; ⑥; April–Sept).

Eating and drinking

Self-caterers will revel in the comparative choice provided by the two or three **alimentari** along the main street. Of the two loftily named *Carpe Diem*, the further one (no. 28), is the best and makes up excellent sandwiches. For fruit and vegetables, there are usually a couple of motorized stands parked in front of the bars by the port.

Both the *Punta Barone* and *Mamma Santina* serve **meals**, those at the latter one of the better deals on the island. At *La Cambusa* (closed Tues in winter), immediately by the dock, it may take a while to get served, but when the food comes it's usually pretty good. Neighbouring *Portobello* (closed Nov & Wed in winter) is even better, serving excellent local antipasti, pasta with capers and tomatoes, slabs of swordfish, and wine by the carafe. In either, a large meal will run up to around L40,000, and from their outdoor terraces you can watch the necklace of lights come on across the water on Lípari. *Da Franco* takes more effort to reach, a good twenty-minute walk from the centre (up Via Risorgimento, left up Via F. Crispi, right at the top and keep following the signs), but it's superbly sited, open all year (except a few days in Dec) and has terrific local food and fish. You could count on spending a little more here if you pulled the stops out.

For drinking, there are a couple of shady **bars** beneath the trees near the ticket agencies, while *La Cambusa* has a pleasant terrace bar too. There's even a "pub": *Nni Lausta* at the bottom of Via Risorgimento and close to the port, which opens at 10pm or so in summer, and occasional mornings for a L6000 breakfast – out of season, the sign on the door says it's open, rather forlornly, *forse* (perhaps).

Lingua

LINGUA, 3km south of Santa Marina, makes a pleasant alternative base. There are buses, but the undulating road makes a fine stroll, weaving around the coves in between the two settlements. Lingua itself is not much more than a lungomare, backed by a tiny cluster of hotels and trattorias facing the shore of Lípari. At the end of the road is the salt lagoon from which Salina takes its name, and there's a narrow **beach**; remains of a Roman villa have been discovered in the area.

A good choice here for **accommodation** is *'A Cannata* (☎090.984.3161 half-board minimum in Aug at L85,000 per person; ③; March–Dec), set a few metres back from the sea, near the church: some of the rooms come with a terrace and wonderful views of Lípari, and the home-cooked food is exceptional (there are pizzas, too). *Il Delfino* (☎090.984.3024; half-board minimum in July & Aug at L110,000 per person; ⑥), right on the lungomare, has attractive rooms attached to its locally renowned restaurant; either side of this, the room-only rate in both hotels is more like ②. Out of season (Oct–May) you'll also be able to take your pick from a number of other options that might otherwise be full, including *La Marinara* (☎090.984.3022; ④), which has a nice garden and whose **restaurant** is also worth trying – fish, naturally, predominates; prices drop by up to fifty percent in winter. Finally, *Il Gambero* (Easter–Sept), at the end of the promenade, by the lagoon, has a shaded terrace where you can have a drink or a basic pasta meal, and there's an *alimentari* on the road above *'A Cannata*, to the left.

Malfa and Pollara

Back the other way, the island's only road climbs from Santa Marina and traces the coast north, turning west at **Capo Faro** where a "village" on the cliffs (signposted) sports a restaurant, bar and open-air pool. The road then winds in through the outlying districts of **MALFA**, easily the island's biggest town, spilling down from the wide terrace outside its peach-coloured church to a tiny mole at the bottom. There's a good beach, stony but picturesquely backed by ruined fishermen's houses. The bus stops by the church, and again, a few hundred metres below, above the harbour. The two are connected by a devilishly twisting road, across which cuts a more direct series of paths.

Malfa has the island's fanciest **hotels**, overlooking the sea, the *Signum*, Via Scalo 15 (☎090.984.4222 ⑦; April–Oct), and, at no. 8, the *Punta Scario* (☎090.984.4139; half-board obligatory in Aug at L130,000 per person; ⑤; April–Oct); both have big off-season discounts. In the upper village are a couple of **pizzerias**, and the island's **bank**, the Banca Agricola Etnea (Mon–Fri 8.30am–1.30pm; cash machine); the bus passes it (and stops opposite) on the way into and out of the village. There's a **bike rental** shop next door to the bank, with scooters (L35,000 a day) and mountain bikes (L15,000 a day); if closed, walk a couple of minutes downhill and ask at the Agip garage, where they know the owner.

Just out of Malfa, a minor road (and several buses a day) snake off west to secluded **POLLARA**, a few kilometres away, raised on a cliff above the sea and occupying a crescent-shaped crater from which Salina's last eruption took place, 13,000 years ago.

Inland: Madonna del Terzito and the peak

Trails cut right across Salina, in particular linking Santa Marina with the peak of **Monte Fossa delle Felci**, the sanctuary of **Madonna del Terzito**, Leni and the south coast at Rinella. Although the distances aren't great, climbing up from the coast at Santa Marina or Rinella is to be avoided at all costs, since the inclines are punishing. You'll do infinitely better to take the bus to the sanctuary – any between Santa Marina/Malfa and Leni/Rinella pass right by it (ask to be dropped at the *santuario*) – and start there, saving yourself the first 300m of climbing. Don't go overloaded, wear strong shoes, and take plenty of water.

Whichever route you take, the walking is very pleasant, since most of inland Salina has been zealously protected by the authorities. Pines are abundant and higher up wild flowers are much in evidence, while the scampering and slithering of geckos and snakes keep you on your toes. The paths, terraces and viewpoints are all extremely well maintained, with no vehicles allowed. Hunting and shooting are banned, too, which helps keep the bird numbers high.

The sanctuary to the peak

In the central plain of **Valdichiesa**, the road passes within 100m of the seventeenth-century sanctuary of **Madonna del Terzito**, set in the saddle between the two peaks of Salina. It's a thickly wooded location, cultivated and with fine views over the sea. A signposted track to the left of the church takes you to the summit of **Monte Fossa delle Felci**, the easternmost of the peaks and the archipelago's highest (at 962m). It's a steady climb through preserved forest and mountain parkland, which takes the best part of two hours – only in the latter stages does it become tougher, with the last 100m a clamber over rocks to reach the stone cairn and simple wooden cross at the top. The views are magnificent, naturally.

Little green signposts on the way point out alternative approaches and **descents**, from Malfa and Leni particularly, so you don't have to retrace your steps completely on the way down. You can also head straight down to Lingua or Santa Marina; though, while the tracks are never anything less than clear, the descent is very steep and soil erosion and the crumbling volcanic underlay can make getting a grip a tricky business. Count on another two hours back down, whichever descent you follow.

Rinella

Most ferries and hydrofoils also call at the little port of **RINELLA**, on the island's south coast, 15km from Santa Marina and immediately more attractive – not a bad place to base yourself for a couple of days. If you want to move straight on, **buses** meet the boat arrivals on the quayside (and call here several times a day otherwise). Notices at the port advertise **rooms** for rent and there's a **hotel**, too, *L'Ariana* (☎090.980.9075; ⑤), above the port to the left, with nice rooms and a decent restaurant. The village is also the site of the island's one **campsite**, 200m up the road from the port: *Tre Pini* (☎090.980.9155; May–Sept), which has a bar-restaurant and is easily the nicest of the two Aeolian campsites (the other is on Lípari). There are two or three other local bars and trattorias with views, too, and **bike rental** is available from the port in summer.

Rinella's only drawback is that it's at the very bottom of a remarkably winding, steep road, which makes you rather dependent on the buses. Still, you could climb at least as far as **Leni**, the little village 3km higher up the slope, whose church you can see peeking out from the shelf of land from the coast below.

Panarea

PANAREA, to the east, is the smallest island of the Aeolian archipelago, at just 3km by 1.5km, and the prettiest, surrounded by clusters of outlying islets that provide some of the best swimming hereabouts. It's almost Greek in aspect, sporting freshly painted white houses at every turn – their terraces are decked with plants and flowers, and swept narrow lanes are shaded by fruit trees. Inhabited since Neolithic times, Panarea also holds one of the region's most important archeological sites, easily accessible on the dramatic **Punta Milazzese**.

No cars can squeeze onto the island's narrow lanes to disturb the tranquillity, though heavily loaded three-wheelers are common. Indeed, Panarea's cosy intimacy has made it into something of a ghetto for the idle rich, putting it on a par with Vulcano on the exclusivity scale. In August, every room and every inch of sand is taken, as wealthy north Italians – many of whom own holiday homes here – descend for a month of high-class diversions, diving off blinding white yachts and wading knee-deep in the crystalline water while chatting on mobile phones. Nevertheless, either side of high season you can find reasonably priced accommodation if you persevere, and it's certainly worth a couple of lazy days sampling the island's pleasures.

Around the island

Panarea's population divides itself between three hamlets on the eastern side of the island – Ditella, San Pietro and Drauto – though, as they meld into one another and there are no street names as such, it's a distinction that hardly helps (or matters to) the visitor. For what the name's worth, boats dock at the port of **SAN PIETRO**, in the middle, tucked onto gentle terraces and backed by gnarled outcrops of rock. It's here that you'll find most of the accommodation, restaurants and facilities (see "Practicalities" opposite).

Make your way through the tangle of lanes, head south and it's a gentle thirty-minute stroll above the coast to the mainly stone beach below **Drauto**. Just beyond here, the path descends to a better, and popular, sand beach – the only one on the island – overlooked by the *Trattoria-Bar Alla Spiaggetta* (closed Oct–March), which serves drinks, lunch and dinner.

Steps at the far end of the beach climb up and across to the headland of **Punta Milazzese**, ten minutes further on, where a Bronze Age village of 23 huts was discovered in 1948; the oval outlines of the foundation walls are easily visible. This beautiful site, occupying a hammerhead of land overlooking two rocky inlets, is thought to have been inhabited since the fourteenth century BC, and pottery found here (displayed in Lípari's museum) shows a distinct Minoan influence – fascinating evidence of a historical link between the Aeolians and Crete that goes some way to corroborating the legends of contact between the two in ancient times. There are super views: across to Vulcano and Lípari, west to Salina, and beyond to Filicudi, where the outline of Capo Graziano is just visible.

Steps descend from Punta Milazzese to **Cala Junco**, a delightful stony cove whose aquamarine water, scattered stone outcrops and surrounding coves and caves (these others accessible only by boat, again available from San Pietro; see "Practicalities" below) make it a popular spot for snorkelling. Beyond the point, a waymarked path wends into Panarea's interior, passing below the island's highest peak, the craggy **Punta del Corvo** (421m), before descending back to San Pietro – a rewarding hike of two to three hours.

North of San Pietro, passing through **Ditella**, you'll pass evidence of volcanic activity in the steaming gas emissions (*fumarole*) on the gradual ascent to Calcara, where the track ends at the local tip. The stone beach near here (signposted "Spiaggia Fumarole") is another attractively isolated spot.

The offshore islets

Above all, be sure to make a trip out to Panarea's own archipelago, the largest islet of which is **Basiluzzo**, formerly inhabited but now only used for caper cultivation. Next down in size, and nearest to Panarea, **Dáttilo** points a jagged finger skyward and has a minuscule beach; or there's better swimming at **Lisca Bianca**, where the tranquil water is sheltered by **Bottaro** opposite. Nearby **Lisca Nera** and **Le Formiche** (The Ants) are mere wrinkles on the sea surface, though a constant hazard to shipping. You'll need to arrange **boat rental** at San Pietro (see "Practicalities").

Practicalities

San Pietro's harbourside is a line of trendy bars, restaurants with terraces, fishermen touting boat rides, and the Siremar (☎090.983.007) and SNAV (☎090.983.009) **agencies** almost next door to each other. In the warren of alleys behind are a *tabacchaio*, a little supermarket, two or three *alimentari*, a gift shop, bakery, more trattorias and a couple of pizza places.

If you're planning on going to Panarea's offshore islets, **boat rental** can be arranged at the jetty at San Pietro – not too expensive if you share it with others; expect to pay up to L130,000 for a motorboat (petrol extra at about L20,000 per day). Or look for the signs advertising "*Noleggio barche*", on display in nearly every bar, shop and restaurant. A ride to the isles and back can be arranged for around L15,000 per person: if you choose to spend some time marooned, make sure your boatman understands what time to pick you up for the return.

If you're looking for a place to **stay** in Panarea, bear in mind that the supply of accommodation in July and August does not meet the demand, and that between October and Easter almost all places are closed. It's always worth asking around for **rented rooms**, for which you can expect to pay around L60,000 per person in August, and considerably less out of season. On the harbourside, *Trattoria da Francesco* (☎090.983.023; no credit cards; ③) has ten rooms, while, up from the port, several houses on Via San Pietro also oblige; just look for the signs. If you want to be nearer Punta Milazzese and the beach, keep going as far as Drauto where the *Trattoria La Sirena* has two rooms (☎090.983.012; ③; June–Sept). The two cheapest **pensioni** are the *Casa Rodà* (☎090.983.006; ④; April–Sept) or the *Bottari* (☎090.983.268; ⑤; April–Sept), both on Via San Pietro – though with only two dozen rooms between them you'll have to move fast. In peak season, rates at all the above places rise dramatically and include compulsory half-board (an option worth considering at any time).

The two dominant **hotels** at San Pietro are the *Raya* (☎090.983.101; ⑧; mid-April to mid-Oct), on a hill to the left, with the *Cincotta* (☎090.983.014; ⑧; April–Sept) nearby. Both are superb, with wonderful terraces and facilities, and rates plummeting to more realistic levels outside the high season. If you're staying at either of these, or one of Panarea's other two or three expensive hotels, there will be a little three-wheeler at the dockside to transport you and your luggage.

For **meals**, *Da Francesco* (March–Nov) is as good and as nice as any of those by the harbour, while *Casa Rodà* has a garden-restaurant serving decent food and evening pizzas. Walking north along the path to Ditella, after five minutes or so you'll reach the *Trattoria Paulino* (April–Sept), set in a family house whose terrace has fine views of Strómboli. You can have a very unpretentious meal of pasta and salad here for about L40,000, and there's also local wine – the fish is whatever the family has caught that day – or you can just stop for a drink. For a harbourside snack, the *Bar del Porto* (May–Sept) has salads and panini.

Strómboli

The most spectacular of all the Aeolians, **STRÓMBOLI** is little more than a volcano thrust out of the sea. This most active outlet of the volcanic belt throws up showers of sparks and flaring rock at regular intervals of about twenty minutes, though only visible at night – occasionally from as far away as the Calabrian coast. It was Strómboli's crater from which Professor Lindenbrook and his colleagues emerged in Jules Verne's *Journey to the Centre of the Earth*.

Undaunted, people have always lived under the skirts of this volcano, and the communities of **Ginostra** and the straggling parishes of San Vincenzo, San Bartolo and Piscità – often grouped together simply as Strómboli – exist in a charmed world, their white terraced houses adorned with bougainvillea and wisteria, remote from the fury of the craters above. Plumbing is at best rudimentary, especially in Ginostra, on the far side of the island, which is dependent on wells for its water supply, and some houses still have no electricity at all. But despite this, Strómboli, too, has become something of a chic resort, its excellent black-sand beaches overlooked by two or three first-class hotels and some swish open-air discos.

Strómboli

The main settlement of **Strómboli** spreads between the lower slopes of the volcano and the island's beaches for a distance of around 2km. It's an utterly straightforward layout of two largely parallel roads and steep, interconnecting alleys, though the profusion of local place names keeps visitors on their toes.

Ferries and hydrofoils dock at the quayside known as **Scari**, which in summer is thick with three-wheelers and touts from the various accommodation outlets waving cards. If you haven't got a room already booked, you should succumb (see

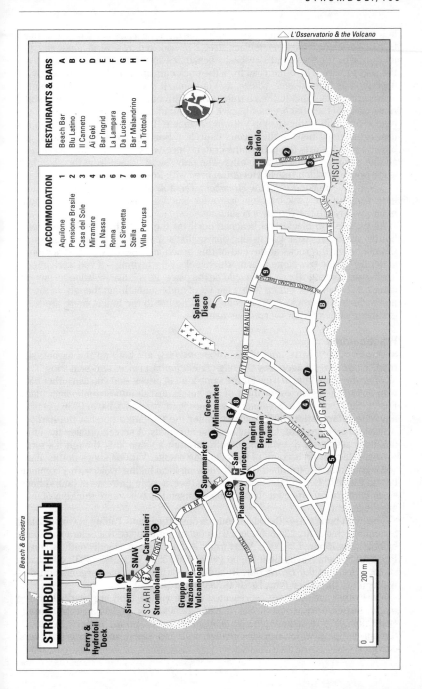

△ *L'Osservatorio & the Volcano*

△ *Beach & Ginostra*

STROMBOLI: THE TOWN

ACCOMMODATION

Aquilone	1
Pensione Brasile	2
Casa del Sole	3
Miramare	4
La Nassa	5
Roma	6
La Sirenetta	7
Stella	8
Villa Petrusa	9

RESTAURANTS & BARS

Beach Bar	A
Blu Latino	B
Il Canneto	C
Ai Gèki	D
Bar Ingrid	E
La Lampara	F
Da Luciano	G
Bar Malandrino	H
La Tróttola	I

San Bártolo

PISCITA

VIA SOLDATO LINCOLN

VIA REGINA ELENA

VIA SOLDATO GIACOMO PANETTIERI

Splash Disco

VITTORIO EMANUELE III

FICOGRANDE

VIA MARINA

VIA

Greca Minimarket

Ingrid Bergman House

San Vincenzo

Pharmacy

Supermarket

ROMA

VIA G. PICONE

SCARI

Carabinieri

SNAV

Siremar

Strombolania

Gruppo Nazionale Vulcanologia

Ferry & Hydrofoil Dock

0   200 m

below for more). From here, the lower coastal road runs around to the main beaches of Ficogrande, a long black stretch overlooked by several hotels and, further on, **Piscità**, the island's best ashy beach. It's around 25 minutes on foot from the port to here. The other road from the dock cuts up into what could loosely be described as "the village", where, as Via Roma, it runs past a few white-painted shops and restaurants to the church of **San Vincenzo**, whose square offers glorious views of the offshore basalt stack of Strombolicchio. Beyond the square, the road changes its names to Via Vittorio Emanuele III and it's another fifteen minutes or so along here to the second church of **San Bártolo**, above Piscità, just beyond which starts the path to the crater. Once you've got this far, you've seen all that Strómboli village has to offer. The only "sight", apart from the churches, is the house in which **Ingrid Bergman** lived with Roberto Rossellini in the spring of 1949 while making the film *Strómboli: Terra di Dio*. A plaque records these bare facts on the pink building, just after San Vincenzo church, on the right, before you reach the *Barbablu* restaurant.

As well as the black-sand beaches north of the dock, there's also a stretch **south of Scari**, past the fishing-boats, that's a mixture of sand and stone. Clamber over the rocks at the end of this beach and there's a further sweep of generally empty lava-stone beach, which looks very inviting – if you were intending to camp out anywhere, this would be the place. Its relative isolation means you can expect to have to put up with a fair bit of nude sunbathing; though, as there's no shade and the rocks soon become scalding hot to the touch, there are some gratifying shrieks from overzealous naturists.

Practicalities

Siremar (☎090.986.016) and SNAV (☎090.986.003) are both on the harbourside road, as are several **agencies** offering crater climbs, cruises and boat trips. They all offer the same kind of trips for the same kind of prices, and you can either book with any of the agencies, or most of the hotels, or call into Strombolania (daily: Easter–Sept 9am–noon & 3–8pm; Aug closes 9pm; ☎090.986.390 or 0336.924.528), a private **information office** agency under the *Ossidiana* hotel at the harbour, which can arrange boat, bike and apartment rentals. A screen outside the office monitors activity at the volcano mouth through a video link, though it's rarely very spectacular on account of the billowing smoke. Various shops in the village sell a good map of Strómboli (L5000) showing local hiking trails, with a commentary in English. Beyond the Strombolania office, a cabin (infrequent hours) houses an information office for the volcano – a useful stop if you're thinking of making the ascent.

The main **boat trips** offered are tours around the island, calling at Ginostra and Strombolicchio (3hr; L25,000); and trips out at night to see the Sciara del Fuoco by boat (1hr 15min; L25,000). Apart from Strombolania, a friendly outfit is run by Pippo, of Società Navigazione Pippo (☎090.986.135 or 0338.985.7883), who has a stand in front of the *Beach Bar*. In addition, various agencies organize **guided walks** up to the crater (6hr; L25,000–35,000 per person).

Most other facilities are represented in the village (and are marked on the map): **supermarket** (Mon–Sat 8.30am–12.50pm & 5–8.45pm); **pharmacy** (☎090.986.079; 8.30am–1pm & 4.30–8pm) and **post office** (Mon–Sat 8.20am–1.20pm), which can also change cash and American Express travellers' cheques.

ACCOMMODATION

If someone offers you a **room** at the dockside, check the price and location and, assuming everything is satisfactory, stick your bag in the three-wheeler that undoubtedly is standing by and off you go. Prices start at around L45,000 per person in summer. If you want to try and book in advance (and you should do so in August), the following places are all worth contacting. Most are a short distance from the sea (prices are generally higher on the coastal road), and *mezza-pensione* may be obligatory in the height of the summer season.

Pensione Aquilone, Via Vittorio Emanuele 29 (☎ & fax 090.986.080). Up an alley opposite the Greca minimarket, this is a friendly place, its plain, rather monastic cells with ill-fitting doors ranged around a rose garden and lemon grove. The beds are comfortable enough though, and the separate bathrooms are clean. *Mezza-pensione* weighs in at L90,000 per person in peak season. May–Oct. ③.

Pensione Brasile, Via Soldato Cincotta, Piscità (☎ & fax 090.986.008). Tranquil spot at the far end of town, with friendly management and clean, modern rooms with or without bath. Obligatory half-board at L80,000–90,000 per person in July & Aug. Easter–Oct. ④.

Casa del Sole, Via Soldato Cincotta, Piscità (☎090.986.017). Further down the same road as the *Brasile*, this is a cheapie in a nice old building within metres of the sea. There's no restaurant, so you can avoid half-board requirements. Kitchen facilities and sun terrace for use of guests, and five-bed rooms are available for small groups. Simple apartments are available all year; rooms only Easter–Oct. ②.

Miramare, Via Vito Nunziate 3, Ficogrande (☎090.986.047, fax 090.986.318). Small, smart hotel on the coast road, overlooking Ficogrande beach, with panoramic terraces and restaurant. April–Sept. ⑤.

La Nassa, Via Filzi, Ficogrande (☎090.986.033). Good, clean rooms near the sea at budget rates. No credit cards. April–Sept.③.

Pensione Roma, Via Roma 15 (☎090.986.088). Nearest place to the harbourside on the main street, this is nothing special, but one of the more realistically priced options with views of the sea. No credit cards. ③.

La Sirenetta, Via Marina 33, Ficogrande (☎090.986.025, fax 090.986.124). Very swish hotel with elegant restaurant and nightclub and its own pool, opposite the black sands of Ficogrande beach. Minimum three-day stay in Aug. The high room-rates drop considerably outside July–Sept. April–Oct. ⑦.

Locanda Stella, Via Fabio Filzi 14 (☎090.986.020). A cosy place with just five rooms, all raftered, two of which have private bath. ④–⑤.

Villa Petrusa, Via Soldato Panettieri 3 (☎090.986.045, fax 090.986.126). One of the furthest hotels from the port, this is also one of the nicest, with a very attractive garden. You may find space only available at the less inviting annexe 100m further along the road. No half-board requirement. April–Oct. ⑤.

EATING AND DRINKING

Assuming you're not tied to your accommodation for meals, there's plenty of choice, with most places sporting outdoor terraces and even sea views. The best **restaurant** in the village is *Il Canneto* (closed Oct–Easter), whose waiters reel off a list of daily pastas and fish: spaghetti with clams, or coloured with squid ink, followed by fresh fish, with salad, wine and coffee; the bill might touch L50,000, though you could eat for less. The creative Mediterranean cuisine at *Ai Geki* (or *Gechi*) is also considered to be good and is similarly priced, with pastas at around L15,000; this is one of the few places open all year. The food at the *Roma/Da Luciano* isn't the bargain it could be, but it does usually serve pizzas at lunchtime; much better **pizzas**, and good pasta dishes, are to be had at *La Tróttola*, a popular place where you can eat for well under L35,000 (closed Mon–Fri in winter). Higher up, past the church, *La Lampara* overlooks the sea and serves fish dishes and pizza (closed in winter). If you're staying down by the coast, or want to really splash out, the *Blu Latino*, at the *Villaggio Strómboli*, has fine food and excellent terrace views.

As far as the **bars** go, the ones down at the harbour see a lot of action during the day, particularly the *Beach Bar* and the larger *Malandrino*, where you can pick up pizzas and other snacks. At night, there's no better spot than *Bar Ingrid*, in the square by San Vincenzo church, a lively place open until 2am and doing a roaring trade in vodka shots served in curious little test tubes. If you want to bop, *Splash* is the main **disco**, tucked away above Via Vittorio Emanuele, but summer sees a handful of other places scattered around town – ask in the bars, look out for posters and follow your ears to find the scene.

Around the island by boat

Boat tours of the island set off two or three times a day from the harbour and Ficogrande beach, costing around L25,000 a person (see "Practicalities" on p.164 for how to book). The boats circumnavigate the entire island in two to three hours, calling at Ginostra (see opposite) – where you get half an hour to scramble around the hamlet – before rounding the western headland and idling slowly past the dizzy **Sciara del Fuoco**.

Even if you intend to climb the volcano (in which case you'll also see it from above), the intensely forbidding views from the water are worth the separate trip. Rising sheer out of an incredible deep-blue sea water, the *sciara* is a huge blistered sheet down which thousands of years' worth of volcanic detritus has poured, scarring and pockmarking the hillside. Menacing little puffs of steam dance up from folds in the bare slope, where absolutely nothing grows. No one docks on the pristine shoreline, since it's too unpredictably dangerous. Come at night by boat, and through the Stygian gloom you'll see orange and red flashes from the crater above as the volcano goes through its pyrotechnic paces. If ever a mountain deserved to have a pole stuck in it with a sign attached reading "Here be dragons", this is it.

Most boat trips also take in Strómboli's basalt offspring, **Strombolicchio**, a couple of kilometres out. The colours here, too, are noteworthy, this time the varied streaks of ochre, green, blue, white, brown and black rock that tumble away through the crystal water as you circle the hulking, rusting, encrusted monolith up close. You can even climb the two hundred or so precipitous steps leading up this battlemented rock to the lighthouse on its top, a lonely vantage-point.

The volcano

Guides for the **ascent of the volcano** are readily available in the village (see "Practicalities" p.164). Most ascents start at about 6pm and the climb up takes three hours; you get an hour or so at the top watching the fireworks, and it then takes another two hours to descend. Try to book in advance in summer at one of the stands or offices by the harbour, and be prepared for the hike to be postponed because of bad weather. Take note of **warning posters**, in English and Italian, and check with the Strombolania office, a good independent source of information.

Although there are signs suggesting otherwise, many people make the hike alone. It's not dangerous provided you stick to the marked paths, and it's easy enough to find your way. In hot weather you'll appreciate the value of setting out in the early morning or late afternoon. The **route** starts a few minutes' walk beyond San Bártolo church, where a fork bears left, heads through the houses and then climbs upwards to the first orientation point, *L'Osservatorio*, a bar-pizzeria (closed in winter) with a wide terrace and a view of the volcano. It's an easy forty-minute stroll to *L'Osservatorio*, but if you want to skip this bit taxis turn up hourly in summer to take people this far, leaving from San Bártolo church between 5pm and 11pm (or call ☎090.986.360 or 0337.293.942). Beyond this point, you'll need to be properly equipped, since from here on in it's a tough hike – good shoes, a sunhat and plenty of water (two litres each, minimum) are essential. If you intend to spend the night at the top (officially banned, but many do anyway), take a sweater (it gets cold and windy up there), waterproofs, groundsheet, sleeping bag, flashlight and food, and bed down in one of the lava shelters until dawn. Contact lenses are best removed on account of flying grit. Don't, under any circumstances, come down in the dark without a guide, and keep a wary eye on the weather. If it clouds over or starts to rain heavily, you're advised to stay put until it clears – even the professional guides won't go up in these conditions. Don't stray off the marked trail at any time: just follow the markers, and don't drink your water too soon – you'll need it.

On the way you'll pass the frighteningly sheer volcanic trail that channels all the lava outflows, known as the **Sciara del Fuoco**, plunging directly into the sea. At the top, the fiery explosions can vary in intensity, but it's always a fairly impressive performance, the noise alone something like an express train thundering directly below you. Ignore the warning signs at your peril.

Ginostra

There's an alternative descent from the volcano to **GINOSTRA**, the hamlet on the other side of the island. The path, skirting a desolate lunar landscape of tormented rocks and fine black dust, is steeper and more tiring than that to Strómboli, and less well marked – keep your eyes open for the red dots at all times. Not surprisingly, most people opt to arrive by boat.

However you get there, it makes an appealing destination. From the minuscule harbour – into which boats have to manoeuvre one at a time – zigzag steps climb into a supremely peaceful cluster of typical white Aeolian houses on terraces. Donkeys are tethered to posts outside houses; ancient exterior stone ovens lie idle; cultivated hedges and volcanic stone walls snake up the hillside. Picturesque though the scene is, the locals are not all overjoyed by the primitive conditions that make Ginostra so alluring to outsiders, and a campaign is currently under way to construct a heliport, a proposal fiercely opposed by environmentalists. If an air link is built, it will undoubtedly transform every aspect of life here, but until that day this remote spot retains a refreshing simplicity, with few diversions for thrill-seekers. There is a bar-restaurant, though, *L'Incontro*, at the top of the steps, and another **restaurant**, *Puntazzo*, further up the hill, near the Siremar agency (which is contactable on ☎090.981.2880), with great views. This has fairly high prices – nothing unusual there – but the local food and wine served is terrific.

If you decide to stay, seek out the tiny *Locanda Petrusa* (☎090.981.2305 no credit cards; ③; Easter–Oct), which is under the same management as *L'Incontro* and has three large rooms with their own terraces and a shared bathroom; otherwise, there's always the possibility of finding **rooms** to let if you ask around.

There are **hydrofoils** back to Strómboli twice a day in summer (once daily in winter), if weather permits. A century ago, the only route was a maintained **path** that skirted the shore and climbed the ridges and valleys en route. Years of neglect and natural assault by the elements has done for most of the path, though it still exists in part – and where it doesn't it's possible to scramble the rocks and follow the line of the coast. Experienced climbers/hikers could do the route back to Strómboli in around four hours, though if you're at all interested you'd do far better to engage the services of a guide; ask at *L'Incontro* or the *Puntazzo*.

Filicudi

FILICUDI, the bigger of the two minor, westerly islands, is the closest to the main pack, and an hour by hydrofoil from Lípari. Its small harbour is dominated on one side by a hotel complex that's closed for eight months of the year. When combined with the ungainly straggle of concrete buildings along the front, this isn't the greatest of introductions to what turns out to be many visitors' favourite Aeolian. Once you've climbed away from the port, the rest of the pretty island is relatively easily accessible on foot. Paths crisscross the slopes, lined with scraggy volcanic boulders interspersed with great flowering cacti whose pustular blooms erupt upon the ele-

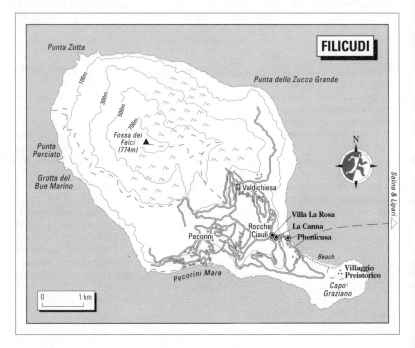

phant-ear leaves. There are no sand beaches to speak of, but the offshore waters are becoming increasingly popular with the yachting and diving set, some of whom are busy buying up the abandoned houses around the port. For the moment, though, it's still a long way from being overdeveloped (or even developed).

Around the island

The island's road runs east from **FILICUDI PORTO**, executing a sharp turn at the start of the path up to the archeological site, the Villagio Preistorico at **Capo Graziano**, where the remains of a dozen or so oval huts mark the place that gave its name to the local Bronze Age culture that immediately preceded Panarea's Punta Milazzese, from the eighteenth to thirteenth century BC. You can visit this small site (discovered in 1952) at any time; a calm but unspectacular spot from which the finds are on show at the museum in Lípari. There's a path up from Filicudi Porto's stone **beach**, too, while with a bit of determined scrambling around the southern and western sides of the cape you can reach quiet rocky coastal stretches where the swimming is sublime.

To head west, to the rest of the island, it's quicker to climb the stepped path to the left of the hotel at the port, which in ten heart-busting minutes leads to the **Rocche Ciauli** district of the island, where the road forks. Turning right (north) it's a further twenty minutes up the switchback road to the dispersed central village of **VALDICHIESA**, past stepped terraces and clusters of white houses. The church itself – set back on a terrace with splendid views – is in a terribly sorry state: paint peeling from the doors, walls riven by cracks and with a derelict campanile, inhabited by pigeons and lizards, and topped by a small dome gently subsiding beneath its own weight. It'll all come crashing down one of these days. Above church and village lie the heights of **Fossa dei Felci** (774m), reached by vague paths that climb through the terraces. Filicudi's mountain slopes are all painstakingly lined with stone terracing, a monument to former agricultural activity but now serving only to reduce soil erosion.

The road peters out shortly beyond the church, though where the road ends at the little shrine and telephone box a path leads off to the right. This cuts south, down the hillside, through abandoned houses and along walls and banks of volcanic stones, until it drops to **PECORINI**, no more than a few houses grouped around a church. Here, you meet the left (east) road-fork from Rocche Ciauli, which continues on its sinuous way, around the valley and down the little harbour of **PECORINI MARE**. A short cut, by vertiginous donkey track, starts to the side of the church up in Pecorini and takes just fifteen minutes down to the harbour. Pecorini Mare is another scrap of a hamlet with a small dockside, some engineering machinery and a Carabinieri post, from which policemen emerge every now and again to roar off in their speedboat. There's nothing else here save a "Saloon", which usually opens at 4pm and sells beer and other drinks. Then again, it may open at 3pm, or 5pm. The water either side of the dock is limpid and surprisingly warm, though the uncompromising stony beach makes lying around distinctly uncomfortable.

By boat

You could see a lot more of Filicudi by renting a **boat**, giving you the chance to explore the island's uninhabited northern and western coasts. There's usually someone at the harbour touting for custom but, if not, try asking at one of the nearby shops and restaurants; it's about L25,000 a head in high season, falling to L15,000–20,000 at other times. **Punta Perciato**, to the west, has a fine natural arch, and nearby you can visit the **Grotta del Bue Marino**, the "Seal Grotto", a wide rocky cavity 37m long by 30m wide, its walls of reddish lava barely visible in the pitch black of the interior. The last seal to have lived here was shot thirty years ago by a local fisherman. Near the island's southeast coast, the perpendicular **Canna** is a startling sight, a rugged and solitary obelisk 71m tall, the most impressive of all the *faraglioni* of the Aeolian Islands. Eduardo Taranto (☎090.988.9835) is the man to contact; or ask at *La Canna* (see below) or see any of the fishermen at Filicudi Porto or Pecorini Mare about boat trips.

Practicalities

At Filicudi Porto, the Siremar (☎090.988.9960) and SNAV (☎090.988.9984) **agencies** are on the dockside, both open before departures; next door is a **bar-***távola calda* that doubles as the **pharmacy** (Tues, Thurs & Sat 9.30–11.45am); while further along there's a **phone box**, **general store** and two or three **restaurants** – one, *Capo Graziano*, also sells home-made *gelato* (and none accepts credit cards). The port is a positive metropolis compared to the rest of Filicudi.

Accommodation and other **restaurants** are scattered around the island. If you're going to stay in summer, book in advance since it's not terribly easy to find space. The *Phenicusa* (☎090.988.9946; ③; June–Sept), overlooking the port, is the most obvious spot, and has its own restaurant (in which half-board, compulsory in July and Aug can come up to L110,000 per person). However, you couldn't do better than the relaxed *La Canna*, Via Rosa 43 (☎090.989.9956; ③), at the top of the steps to Rocche Ciauli, where eight lovely bright rooms with tiled bathrooms open onto a spacious terrace with a magnificent view down to the bay below. The price includes breakfast (good coffee and home-made bread and preserves) and dinner, which is excellent – pasta, fresh fish, local caper salads and plenty of home-produced wine and fruit – at L110,000 per person in peak season. If you ask, they'll pick you up from the dock, since the hellishly steep path up is murder with heavy luggage. Immediately above *La Canna*, at the Rocche Ciauli road junction, *Villa La Rosa* (☎090.988.9965; ③) is a bar-restaurant-grocery with rooms and a nice outdoor terrace; half-board in July and August is compulsory, at L95,000 per person. In summer, the bar becomes a late-night disco for good measure. If everywhere is full, or if you plan a longer stay, it's worth asking around for **rooms**. Up in Val di Chiesa, Aldo Ardizzone (☎090.988.9006) has a house in which he rents out rooms with spectacular views by the week: for L450,000–550,000 per person you receive full-board with fine home-cooked food, and daily guided walks with Aldo, who knows the island inside out. Vincenzo Anastasi (☎090.988.9006, or ask at *La Canna*) also has apartments for rent. Finally, there are also two **restaurants in Pecorini**: *La Sirena*, with tables overlooking the port, and *L'Invidia* (no credit cards in either). Both are open daily in summer, but only sporadically throughout the rest of the year.

Alicudi

Ends-of-the-line in Europe don't come much more remote than **ALICUDI**. Two and a half hours from Milazzo by hydrofoil, or five by ferry, there's plenty of time to have accustomed yourself to its back-of-beyond qualities by the time the boat docks. The island forms a perfect cone, a mere Mediterranean pimple, and its precipitous shores are pierced by numerous caves. Up the sheer slope behind the only settlement, Alicudi Porto, terraced smallholdings and white houses cling on for dear life, decorated with tumbling banks of flowers. Indeed, Alicudi's ancient name of Ericusa was the word for the heather that still stains its slopes purple in spring. Its rocky isolation has in the past been exploited by the Italian government, using the island as a prison for convicted Mafiosi, but now it's virtually abandoned by all but a few farmers and fishermen, giving the place a supremely relaxed pace. To say that Alicudi is as quiet as the grave would be to endow churchyards with a rather boisterous reputation.

It's this quietude that attracts tourists of course; not many, it's true, but enough for there to be some semblance of facilities in the village to cater for visitors. You'll be asked by locals if you're a foreigner, meaning *from Italy* – which is about as far-flung as can be imagined here. Life is simple, though not lived entirely in isolation. There's been electricity since the start of the 1990s, so now there's TV, too. There are two general stores, plenty of fancy boat hardware; even a car or two parked at the dock (though, since there are no navigable roads, it's not clear whether this is bravado or forward planning on behalf of the owners). You have to walk to reach anywhere and the network of volcanic stone-built paths behind the village is extremely steep and tough – all the heavy fetching and carrying is still done by donkey or mule, whose indignant brays echo across the port all day.

The Island

Things to do are simply enumerated. The most exhausting option is the hike up past the castle ruins to the island peak of **Filo dell'Arpa**, which at (675m) requires a fair bit of effort. The path runs up through the village houses from the port and there's a proper stone-built track most of the way. Unfortunately, the track looks as though it was created by a malevolent giant emptying a bag of boulders from the top and letting them fall where they will. Go in something other than very soft shoes and take plenty of water. There's absolutely no shade, and it will take at least two hours to get up – and about two inches off your legs coming back down. The only saving grace – the magnificent views aside – is that you are hardly going to get lost.

Otherwise, you'll probably get all the exercise you need clambering over the rocky **shore** to the south of the port. The path soon peters out beyond the hotel and power station, but the rocks offer a sure foothold as they get larger the further you venture. The water is crystal clear and, once you've found a flat rock big enough to lie on, you're set for more peace and quiet than you'd bargained for. The only sounds are the echoed mutter of offshore fishermen, the scrabbling of little black crabs in the rock pools and the lap of the waves.

Practicalities

From the dock, walk to the left past the beached fishing-boats and in the almost cave-like dwellings in front of you are Alicudi's facilities, in the shape of the Siremar **agency** (open before departures; ☎090.988.9795) and – in the arched terrace above – one of the **general stores** (the other one is along the path to the *Ericusa*; see p.172). The Siremar office also doubles as a telephone office (supposedly summer: Mon–Sat 9am–1pm & 4–8pm, Sun 9am–noon; winter Mon–Sat closes 7pm); though, as there's no one much to phone, it's not always open. If you're desperate to make a call, seek out Signora Russo, who has the white house with green railings and shutters directly in front of the dock.

The only **hotel** is a five-minute walk south along the shore, the *Ericusa* (☎090.988.9902; half-board minimum in July & Aug at L105,000 per person; ⑥; June–Sept), a modern, twenty-roomed place with sea views, terrace and restaurant (no credit cards, but travellers' cheques or Eurocheques accepted). The hotel also runs a row of **apartments** in front of the port (②, or ③ including kitchen). Apartment- or room-rent is always a feasible option, and, outside the summer months, the only one. It isn't usually too difficult: Signora Russo (see p.171; ☎090.988.9922) has a nice room or two (②), available with hot showers, overlooking the sea. Otherwise, ask in either of the stores; or, indeed, ask anyone. Everyone knows who's willing to rent rooms and you may get something with a kitchen if you persevere.

Unless you **eat** at the *Ericusa*, you may have to fend for yourself. Both stores sell bread, cheese, cured meats, olives, beer, ice-cream and whatever fruit and vegetables arrived on the boats. Alternatively, call in on Signora Giuseppina during the day, who lives up the hill behind the Siremar office (anyone can point you in the right direction). She cooks dinner on request – spaghetti, fresh fish, salad, fruit and wine – for around L30,000 a head, served on her lovely bougainvillea-covered terrace in the company of whoever else happens to turn up.

Incidentally, if you're staying the night, bring a **torch**. The village is asleep and pitch-black by 10pm and the steps are treacherous.

festivals

Easter
Holy week Procession of the saints in **Lípari**.

July
17 Festival of Santa Marina in **Santa Marina di Salina**, Salina.

23 Festival of St Mary of Terzito at the **sanctuary of Madonna del Terzito** on Salina.

August
10 Festival of San Lorenzo in **Malfa**, Salina.

24 Procession of San Bartolomeo's statue and relics in **Lípari Town** accompanied by fireworks. Celebrations, too, on **Alicudi**.

travel details

For ferry and hydrofoil services from Milazzo to the Aeolians, see the table on p.139; and for services from the Tyrrhenian Coast or Messina, see "Travel details", Palermo, pp.135–136 and p.205 respectively.

Ferries
Lípari *June–Sept* to: Alicudi (5–7 weekly; 3hr 45min); Filicudi (5–7 weekly; 2hr 20min–2hr 45min); Milazzo (5–7 daily; 2hr); Naples (3–5 weekly; 14hr); Panarea (1–2 daily; 1hr 40min–2hr); Salina (4–6 daily; 50min); Strómboli (1–2 daily; 2hr 45min–3hr 45min); Vulcano (3–8 daily; 25min).

Lípari *Oct–May* to: Alicudi (6–7 weekly, 3hr 15min); Filicudi (4 weekly; 2hr); Milazzo (1–2 daily; 2hr); Naples (2 weekly; 11hr 35min); Panarea (4–5 weekly; 1–2hr); Salina (1–3 daily; 50min); Strómboli (4–5 weekly; 1hr 45min–4hr 10min); Vulcano (3–4 daily; 30min).

Hydrofoils
Lípari *June–Sept* to: Alicudi (2–3 daily; 1hr–1hr 35min); Capo d'Orlando (3 daily; 1hr); Cefalù (3 weekly; 2hr 10min); Filicudi (2–3 daily; 1hr); Ginostra (1 daily; 2hr 45min); Messina (3 daily; 1hr 30min); Milazzo (hourly; 40min–1hr); Naples (1 daily; 5hr 35min); Palermo (3 daily; 3hr 30min);

Panarea (7 daily; 25–50min); Réggio di Calabria (5 daily; 1hr 20min–3hr 30min); Salina (hourly; 20min); Sant'Agata (3 daily; 1hr 30min); Strómboli (7 daily; 1hr–1hr 30min); Vulcano (hourly; 10min).

Lípari *Oct–May* to: Alicudi (1 daily; 1hr 30min); Filicudi (1 daily; 1hr); Messina (2 daily; 1hr 30min); Milazzo (8–10 daily; 40min–1hr); Panarea (1 daily; 25min); Réggio di Calabria (2 daily; 2hr); Salina (10 daily; 20min); Strómboli (1 daily; 1hr); Vulcano (9 daily; 10min).

Buses
Lípari town to: Acquacalda (10 daily Mon–Sat, 4–8 Sun; 30min); Canneto (every 30–60min Mon–Sat, 4–12 Sun; 10min); Cave di Pomice (10 daily Mon–Sat, 4–8 Sun; 20min); Pianoconte (10 daily Mon–Sat, 3 Sun; 20min); Quattrocchi (10 daily Mon–Sat, 3 Sun; 15min); Quattropani (10 daily Mon–Sat, 3 Sun; 30min).

Santa Marina di Salina to: Malfa, Leni & Rinella, Via Santuario Madonna del Terzito (11 daily; 30min); Pollara (7–8 daily; 25min); Lingua (hourly; 5min).

CONNECTIONS FROM MAINLAND ITALY

SNAV hydrofoils from Réggio di Calabria (1hr 20min–3hr 30min to Lípari; 2hr 5min to Vulcano; 2hr 40min to Rinella, Salina; 3hr to Santa Marina, Salina): June–Sept 5 daily; Oct–May Mon–Sat at 1.25pm.

SNAV hydrofoils from Naples (June to mid-July 4hr to Strómboli; 4hr 35min to Panarea; 5hr 5min to Santa Marina, Salina; 5hr 40min to Vulcano; 6hr to Lípari: mid-July to Sept 4hr to Strómboli; 4hr 35min to Panarea; 5hr to Lípari): June to mid-July daily 2.30pm; mid-July to Sept daily 8.30am & 2.30pm.

Siremar ferries from Naples (8hr to Strómboli; 9hr to Ginostra; 11hr 30 min to Santa Marina, Salina; 11hr 35min to Rinella, Salina; 12hr 35min to Lípari; 13hr 40min to Vulcano): April–June & Oct Tues, Fri & Sun 9pm; July & Aug Mon, Tues & Thurs–Sun 9pm; Sept Mon, Tues & Thurs–Sat 9pm; Nov–March Tues & Fri 9pm.

CHAPTER FOUR

THE NORTHERN IONIAN COAST

Hemmed in by the mountains, the **northern Ionian coast** is Sicily's most visually exotic strip, crammed with some of the most brilliant displays of colourful vegetation you'll see anywhere on this flower-filled island. Perhaps not surprisingly, it's crowded by an almost unbroken ribbon of development and is one of Sicily's most popular resort areas, with both Italian and foreign tourists lured by the stunning views down to a turquoise sea.

Just across the busy Straits from mainland Italy, **Messina** is for many the first taste of Sicily, and your initial impulse may be to move on quickly. Apart from its own meagre merits, however, there are some enticing spots within easy reach of here, to the mountains behind, or around the cape to the beaches on the Tyrrhenian side. Otherwise, keep on south, where you'll find some unspoiled **hill-villages** amid the woods and craggy uplands of the **Monti Peloritani**. These seem as secure today from the tourist hordes as they were in the past from piratical raids. Two or three of the villages are enlivened by impressive Norman churches built by Count Roger in the eleventh century to consolidate his grip on the island. Further down, the only road penetrating any distance inland takes in the **Alcántara valley** and its spectacular gorge, before heading up to the gnarled old town of **Castiglione di Sicilia**.

There are sandy **beaches** – and resorts aplenty– all the way down the coast, and you'd do well to avoid the area in July and August if you want a bit of elbow room. Even outside these months there's a fairly high level of saturation-tourism in the area's most illustrious resort, **Taormina**. Undeniably pretty, it was a simple hill-village as little as fifty years ago, set apart from others in the Peloritani range only by virtue of its fine ancient theatre. Now it's a high-profile, high-class tourist centre, packed in summer but still retaining enough small-town charm to merit at least a day-trip.

Messina and around

MESSINA may well be your first sight of Sicily, and from the ferry it's a fine one, stretching out along the seaboard, north of the distinctive hooked harbour from which the city took its Greek name – Zancle (Sickle). The natural beauty of its location, looking out over the Straits to the forested hills of Calabria, is Messina's best point; Shakespeare (who almost certainly never laid eyes on the city) used it as the setting for his *Much Ado About Nothing*. Yet the city itself presents a duller view from close quarters: a bland sequence of characterless new buildings lining

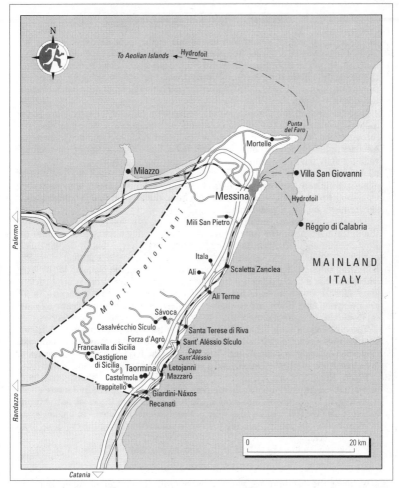

long, traffic-choked streets that are used as a racetrack by drivers who can claim to be the most reckless in Sicily. The city's unedifying appearance is not entirely its own fault: the congestion is largely the result of the surrounding mountains that squeeze the traffic along the one or two roads that link the elongated centre with the northern suburbs. Messina's modern aspect is more a tribute to its powers of survival in the face of a record of devastation that's high even for this disaster-prone island.

The greatest damage has been caused by the unstable geological belt on which Messina stands, and is responsible for a series of catastrophic **earthquakes**. The most notable of these occurred in 1783 and 1908; on the latter occasion the shore sank by half a metre overnight and 84,000 people lost their lives. The few surviving buildings, along with everything that had been painstakingly reconstructed in

CROSSING THE STRAITS

The crossing of the Straits of Messina is one of the most evocative entries into Sicily. Unless you're crossing from Réggio di Calabria, you'll be embarking 12km north of Réggio, at **Villa San Giovanni**, where two ferry services (*traghetti*) operate: the state-railway-run FS (☎090.675.234), and Caronte (☎090.41.415), a private firm inauspiciously named after Charon, the surly ferryman of dead souls over the River Styx to Hades.

If you're **driving**, the Caronte, with more frequent crossings, makes more sense: follow indications from the Villa San Giovanni autostrada exit, a straightforward run through town, stopping preferably at the first ticket kiosk (well marked) where you can park at leisure and sort out your ticket (from L28,000 for a car one way; returns valid for sixty days cost from L45,000, or a three-day return from L30,000). If you miss this kiosk there's a second after passing under the railway, but it can be a bit of a scramble here, with nowhere to park. The queue for boarding begins soon after. Outside the peak times of August and rush hour, the average wait is ten minutes; it should never be much more than 25.

Travelling **by train**, you might want to stay on it if you're crossing by night (though you'll probably be woken anyway by the clanking din that accompanies the slow dismantling of the train as it's loaded onto the FS ferry), but by day it's quicker to leave the train at Villa San Giovanni station and skip the shuttling operation. Following the signs for the ferries, descend directly from the platform to sea level, where there is a ticket office for the FS ferries, which leave from nearby (tickets about L2000). Overhead signs tell you which bay leads to the first departure, or follow everyone else. There are enough FS car ferries or train ferries leaving (about every 30min) to make it unnecessary to walk the 500m to the Caronte ferries.

The crossing on both FS and Caronte ferries takes about 35 minutes. A bar on board serves snacks, coffee and refreshments. Drivers might as well leave their vehicles (remembering to lock), though look sharp as the ferry approaches Messina, as disembarkation is a rushed affair (and a suitable introduction to driving in Messina).

From Reggio, there are at least four hydrofoil (*aliscafo*) or fast-ferry (*nave veloce*) crossings every hour from the port (walk a couple of hundred metres back from Reggio Lido station) until around 10pm. Tickets, from the kiosk at the terminal, cost L5000–6000, and journey time is a swift twenty minutes – in the marginally faster hydrofoils you're expected to keep to your seats during the crossing, in an aircraft-style cabin.

For hydrofoil and ferry tickets for the **return journey**, see "Listings", p.184.

---

the wake of the earthquake, were subsequently the target of Allied bombardments, when Messina achieved the dubious distinction of being the most intensely bombed Italian city during World War II.

Today the remodelled wide streets and low, reinforced buildings guard against future disasters of a natural kind, but make for a pretty uninspiring spectacle. The few monuments that remain – chiefly, the **Duomo** and the nearby **Chiesa Annunziata dei Catalani** – though worth investigating, won't occupy more than a couple of hours' worth of ambling. Take more time to see the treasure trove of art contained in the **Museo Regionale**, one of Sicily's best collections, that helps to make up for what the rest of the city lacks. Otherwise, Messina's pleasures are to be found in kicking around its portside promenade and absorbing the scintillating views across the Straits. If you're here in summer, you'll see the passage of the tall-masted *felucche*, or **swordfish boats**, patrolling the narrow channel, attracted to these rich waters from miles up and down the Italian coasts. You can enjoy their catch the same day in a good choice of restaurants either in town or a little way north, at **Ganzirri**, where lakeside fish restaurants provide welcome relief from Messina's motor madness. Beyond, and around the corner of **Punta del Faro**, the city's main lidos line the coast at **Mortelle**, where you can swim, eat and drink to your heart's content; the beaches, bars and pizzerias here are where the city comes to relax.

Arrival, information and city transport

It takes a good hour to reassemble **trains** from the mainland at Messina's **Stazione Maríttima**. If you're changing trains or stopping at Messina, you might as well disembark and walk 100m on to the **Stazione Centrale**, at Piazza della Repubblica, where most of the **local and long-distance buses** also arrive and depart. Note that **buses to Milazzo for the Aeolian Islands** leave from the nearby Giuntabus office, Via Terranova 8, at the junction with Viale San Martino, with a stop in Piazza Duomo. For further details of buses **out of the city**, see "Listings", p.183.

Drivers and pedestrians using **ferries** from Villa San Giovanni or Réggio di Calabria also disembark at the Stazione Maríttima, though Caronte ferries pull in further up, on Via della Libertà, ten minutes' walk north along the harbour. This is slightly more convenient for the slip road to the Palermo (A20) and Catania (A18) **autostradas**: drivers arriving off the FS ferries should head up Viale San Martino (well signposted). **Hydrofoils** (from the Aeolian Islands or Réggio di Calabria) dock at the terminal (signposted "*aliscafi*") in the port area.

Information and city transport

Messina has three different **tourist offices** with overlapping responsibilities; all should be able to hand over a town map, a hotel list (not necessarily up-to-date) and information about getting to the Aeolians. There are two close together outside the train station, on the right: the city Ufficio Informazioni Comune, on Piazza della Repubblica itself (Mon–Thurs 8.30am–1.30pm & 2.30–6pm, Fri–Sat 7.30am–1.30pm; ☎090.672.944), and, just beyond, at Via Calabria 301, the provincial tourist office (Mon–Sat 8am–2pm, plus sporadic afternoons in summer; ☎090.674.236). Most of Messina's hotels are scattered around this area, and it's just a short walk to Piazza Cairoli, where there are banks, shops and a third, local tourist office upstairs at no. 45 (Mon & Sat 8am–2pm, Tues–Fri 8am–2pm & 3–6pm; ☎090.293.5292).

Walking is the best option for getting around Messina's central core; you *could* walk to the city's museum, but it's quite a trek (about 45min from the station) along the traffic-congested shore road, and for this – or for venturing anywhere further – you'll find the **city buses** a handy resource, with frequent departures from Piazza della Repubblica, Piazza Cairoli and Via Garibaldi. There's also a circular bus #28 (Velocittà) you can pick up from Piazza della Repubblica, Via Garibaldi, or just about anywhere else in the centre; it comes round every ten minutes or so. Also from Piazza Repubblica or Via Garibaldi, take buses #76, #79 or #81 for the museum, #79 or #81 for Ganzirri, or #81 for Mortelle (other bus routes are specified in the text); hourly **night buses** take over after 11.30pm. Tickets, available from most *tabacchi*, cost L1200 (valid for 1hr 30min), and L3500 (valid all day).

Taxi ranks are found at at Piazza Cairoli (☎090.293.4880), Via Calabria, outside Stazione Centrale (☎090.673.702), and at Piazza Duomo (☎090.51.503); there's also a 24-hour radio taxi (☎090.6505).

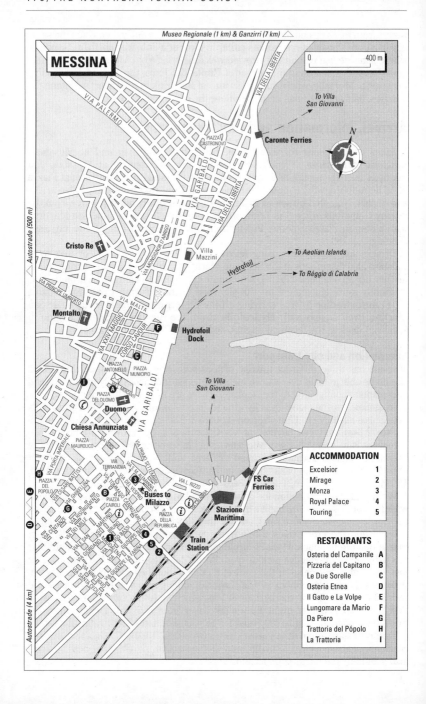

Museo Regionale (1 km) & Ganzirri (7 km)

MESSINA

0   400 m

VIA PALERMO

VIA DELLA LIBERTA

Caronte Ferries

To Villa
San Giovanni

PIAZZA
CASTRONOVO

VIA GARIBALDI

VIA DELLA LIBERTA

Autostrade (500 m)

VIA MONSIGNOR D'ARRIGO

Cristo Re

Villa
Mazzini

To Aeolian Islands

Hydrofoil

To Réggio di Calabria

VIA PRINCIPE UMBERTO

VIA MALTA

Montalto

CORSO CAVOUR

VIA XXIV MAGGIO

F

Hydrofoil
Dock

PIAZZA
ANTONELLO

C

PIAZZA
MUNICIPIO

I

A

PIAZZA
DEL DUOMO

To Villa
San Giovanni

Duomo

Chiesa Annunziata

PIAZZA
MAUROLICO

VIA GARIBALDI

VIA PRIMO SETTEMBRE

VIA PORTA IMPERIALE

VIA
TERRANOVA

H

PIAZZA
DEL
POPOLO

VIA L. RIZZO

FS Car
Ferries

E

B

PIAZZA
CAIROLI

3

Buses to
Milazzo

G

Stazione
Marittima

4

i

i

PIAZZA
DELLA
REPUBBLICA

1

5

2

Train
Station

Autostrade (4 km)

ACCOMMODATION

Excelsior	1
Mirage	2
Monza	3
Royal Palace	4
Touring	5

RESTAURANTS

Osteria del Campanile	A
Pizzeria del Capitano	B
Le Due Sorelle	C
Osteria Etnea	D
Il Gatto e La Volpe	E
Lungomare da Mario	F
Da Piero	G
Trattoria del Pópolo	H
La Trattoria	I

Accommodation

Messina's cheaper **hotels** are near the station, though they're not very scintillating choices. This is one Sicilian city where business travellers take precedence over tourists. If you're looking for comfort in pleasant surroundings at reasonable rates, move up to Ganzirri (see p.184). There's a **youth hostel** 30km west at Castroreale (see p.131), not really a viable option, and the only **campsite** you'll find in the Messina area, *Il Peloritano* (☎090.348.496; mid-June to mid-Sept), is situated inconveniently far out beyond Punta del Faro on the northern coast (bus #81 to Rodia, from Piazza della Repubblica). Otherwise, to camp you'll have to go as far west as Milazzo, or south to Sant'Aléssio, both about forty minutes away.

Excelsior, Via Maddalena 32 (☎090.293.1431). Central, modern hotel, primarily for business travellers but useful if everywhere else is full. Good low-season discounts, and singles without bath available. ④.

Mirage, Via N. Scotto 1 (☎090.293.8844). Down an alley three blocks to the left (south) of Piazza della Repubblica; rather shabby, with small rooms, but adequate. ③.

Monza, Viale San Martino 63 (☎ & fax 090.673.755). Large, old-fashioned, central hotel right next to Piazza Cairoli, and really the best budget deal in town, certainly if you get a room without bath. ④.

Royal Palace, Via T. Cannizzaro 224 (☎090.6503, fax 090.292.1075). Where the business visitors stay – and rarely leave, given the full range of facilities. ⑦.

Touring, Via N. Scotto 17 (☎090.293.8851). The flashy entrance gives way to bare but spacious rooms, each with TV and telephone. Rooms without bath are a fair bit cheaper and the communal bathrooms are fine. Try and avoid the ground floor unless you relish a night's musing about whether it's the desk clerk's TV or the hot-drinks machine that's noisier. ③.

The City

Messina's most important monument, the **Duomo** (Mon–Sat 9.30am–7.30pm, Sun 1.30–5.30pm), is symbolic of the city's phoenix-like ability to recreate itself from the ashes of its last disaster. Standing defiantly at the bottom of its spacious piazza, it's the reconstruction of a twelfth-century cathedral erected by Roger II, one of a series of great Norman churches that included the sumptuous cathedrals of Palermo and Cefalù. Formerly, the building dominated medieval Messina, and was the venue for Archbishop Palmer's marriage of Richard the Lionheart's sister Joan to the Norman-Sicilian, William II. Devastated by the earthquake in 1908, it was rebuilt in the years following World War I, only to fall victim to a firebomb in 1943 that reduced it once more to rubble. What you see today is mostly a faithful copy, which took years to complete, with few elements remaining of the original fabric.

The Romanesque facade is its best aspect, its lower part mostly authentic and dominated by a richly decorated, late-Gothic **central portal**, extravagantly pointed, with good detail, and flanked by two smaller contemporary doors. Almost everything in the undeniably grand **interior** is a reproduction, from the marble floor to the elaborately painted wooden ceiling. Two rows of sturdy columns line the nave, topped by cement capitals faithfully copied from originals, some of which survive in the Museo Regionale. The **mosaic-work** in the three grand apses holds most interest, though it pales into insignificance beside the island's other examples of the genre, and only the mosaic on the left – of the Virgin Mary with St Lucy – is original. All the same, try to find someone to switch on the lights, as the mosaics then take on a majesty that's entirely lost in the gloom that normally shrouds the cathedral's interior. There's little else here that predates the twentieth century, apart from some salvaged tombs, most handsome of which is that of Archbishop de Tabiatis from 1333, on the right of the altar and heavily graffitied. The **tesoro** (daily: summer 9am–1.30pm & 3–6.30pm; winter 9am–noon & 3.30–6.30pm; L3000) holds precious reliquaries, the bejewelled *Manta d'Oro* – a holy adornment for sacred images, of a kind more commonly used in Orthodox rites – and a collection of skilfully crafted silverware.

Back in the piazza, the detached **campanile** claims some attention, particularly when the hours strike – best of all at noon, when you get the full mechanical performance. The bell-tower, like the cathedral, is something of a fake, looking much older than its sixty years, though it can safely claim to be the largest astronomical clock in the world. On the side facing the cathedral two dials show the phases of the planets and the seasons; above them a globe shows the phases of the moon; while facing the piazza, the elaborate panoply of moving gilt figures, activated on the hour, half-hour and quarter-hour, range from representations of the days of the week and the four Ages of Man to Dina and Clarenza, the two women who saved the city from a night attack by the Angevins during the Wars of the Vespers. There's a lion, too – Messina's ancient emblem – that unleashes a mighty roar over the city at midday, quite alarming if you're not expecting it.

In front of the cathedral and its bell-tower is the **Fontana di Orione**, a fountain daintily carved in the mid-sixteenth century by Montorsoli, a Florentine pupil of Michelangelo. It depicts Orion, the city's mythical founder, surmounting a collection of cherubs, nymphs and giants, and surrounded by four figures (representing the rivers Nile, Ebro, Camero and Tiber) reclining along the balustrade.

Just back from the duomo, the truncated section of the twelfth-century **Chiesa Annunziata dei Catalani** (Sun 10am–noon) squats below pavement level, Messina's only surviving example of Arabo-Norman church-building. The blind arcading around the apses and the Byzantine-style cupola are the perfect antidote to the ugly cement facade surrounding its three portals, and the interior is suitably simple, with the transept and apse true to their original construction. In front, a martial statue by the sculptor Andrea Calamecca (Calamech) stands half-hidden under the trees, showing a proud Don Giovanni of Austria, victor of the Battle of Lépanto (the victorious Christian fleet sailed from Messina in 1535).

From here, it's a short stroll to the **harbourside**, with its combination of constant activity and compelling vistas over the Straits. It's Sicily's deepest natural harbour and a port of call for freighters and cruisers of all descriptions, as well as for frequent NATO warships. But the greatest traffic consists of ferries, endlessly plying back and forth, which – until the much-talked-about bridge across the Straits comes into being – are Sicily's chief link with the mainland.

The rest of Messina's unremittingly modern centre won't take up much of your time, though the area around **Piazza Cairoli** is the place for shopping and bustling evening promenades. You'll feel less cramped, however, when you head out north, to the city's marvellous museum and beyond.

The Museo Regionale

Messina's **Museo Regionale**, at Via della Libertà 465 (summer Mon, Wed & Fri 9am–2pm, Tues, Thurs & Sat 9am–2pm & 4–7pm, Sun 9am–1pm; winter Mon, Wed & Fri 9am–2pm, Tues, Thurs & Sat 9am–2pm & 3–6pm, Sun 9am–1pm; last entry 30min before closing; L8000), is a repository for some of Messina's greatest works of art, many of them carefully rescued from earthquake rubble, and includes what is perhaps Sicily's finest collection of fifteenth- to seventeenth-century art. Construction of a much bigger museum building next door was well under way in 1999, and the layout described below will be superseded when the collection is transferred and augmented on completion, which should be sometime in 2000. To get here by bus, take #28 or #76 from Piazza Cairoli or Via Garibaldi, or #28, #78, #79 or #80 from Piazza Repubblica. The museum lies on the left, immediately after the Regina Margherita hospital.

It's the earlier rather than the later material that claims your attention, basically the items in the first few rooms. The collection starts with some lovely Byzantine work, larded with a good helping of Gothic, well evident in a fourteenth-century triptych of the *Madonna with Child between SS Agatha and Bartholomew*, and a remarkably modern-looking wooden crucifix from the fifteenth century, with a sinuous, tragic Christ. You'll want to spend the most time in **room 4**, with marvellous exhibits of fifteenth-century art, notably an ethereal statue of the *Madonna and Child*, attributed to Francesco Laurana, and the museum's most famous exhibit, the *St Gregory* polyptych, by Sicily's greatest native artist, **Antonello da Messina** – a masterful synthesis of Flemish and Italian Renaissance styles that's a good example of the various influences that reached the port of Messina in the fifteenth century (for more on Antonello, see Palermo p.83 and Cefalù p.121). The statue of *Scilla*, the classical Scylla who terrorized sailors from the Calabrian coast (as described in Homer's *Odyssey*), is on display in **room 6**; it's an alarming spectacle, with contorted face and eyes awash with expression. Sculpted by Montorsoli in 1557, it was once adjoined to an imperious figure of Neptune in the act of calming the seas, a copy of which stands on the seafront just up from the hydrofoil terminal. Of the museum's remaining works, the most noteworthy in the suitably darkened **room 10**, are a couple of large shadowy canvases by **Caravaggio**, commissioned by the city in 1604, the best of which is the atmospheric *Raising of Lazarus*. The last room on the ground floor has a monstrous ceremonial carriage from 1742, hauled out for viceregal and other high-ranking visits. Though faded and tarnished, its gilt bodywork is still awesomely grandiose, showing an impressive array of detail. Upstairs is a collection of the silverware for which the town once excelled, mainly ecclesiastical items.

Eating and drinking

Messina has a good choice of **restaurants**, either inexpensive and fast – as befitting a port and transit point – or offering a more relaxed atmosphere. If you're here in summer, you should try and sample the swordfish, freshly caught and a local speciality; May and June are the best months for this, before the water gets too warm. Specific areas in which to look for restaurants are: behind Via Cesare

Battisti (around Piazza del Pópolo), where two or three fairly rough-and-ready trattorias have rock-bottom prices; and up Viale San Martino, where there's a bunch of more serious eating places on or around Via Santa Cecilia.

Cafés, bars and birrerias

Billé, Piazza Cairoli 7. Superb *pasticceria* with *frutta di mándorla*, ice-cream, pastries, chocolates and more. It's where the piazza joins Via T. Cannizzaro. Closed Tues.

Le Brasserie, Via Ugo Bassi 157. Large, boisterous *birreria* for carousing till late. Pasta, panini and chips also served. Closed Wed.

La Capanna 2, Via Césare Battisti 212. At the end of Via Nino Bixio, *La Capanna* is a convivial *birreria*, a focus for students from the nearby university residence block, with a range of good sandwiches and snacks available. Closed Tues.

Dolce Vita, Piazza del Duomo. Sharp little café-bar with a few outdoor tables underneath the campanile. Good snacks, sandwiches and imported beer. No closing day.

The Duck, Via Maddalena. Popular English-style pub with Stones bitter on tap and a range of German bottled beers. Rolls and chips also on the menu. Closed Mon & mid-July to mid-Sept.

Irrera, Piazza Cairoli 12. In business since 1910, serving cakes and pastries of renowned quality. No closing day.

Pisani, Via T. Cannizzaro 45. One of Messina's most famous pastry shops, especially renowned for its *pignolata* - a sugary confection covered with brown or white icing with a doughy filling. No closing day.

Restaurants

Osteria del Campanile, Via Loggia dei Mercanti 7. Nice little trattoria around to the rear side of the duomo, with a filling *maccheroni alla Norma* and surprisingly good pizzas, but terribly slow service. There are a few outdoor tables too. Inexpensive. Closed Mon.

Pizzeria del Capitano, Via dei Mille 88. Basic, reliable pizzas in this no-frills place close to Piazza Cairoli, with fast service and low prices. Beer and soft drinks only, and you can't smoke. Inexpensive. Closed Mon.

Le Due Sorelle, Piazza Municipio 4 (☎090.44.720). With only five tables, this is a small and select trattoria, but also innovative and memorable. Specialities such as *paella marinara* and *couscous con pesce* cost about L20,000 each, but are well worth the splurge. It's worth booking early. Expensive. Closed Mon.

Osteria Etnea, Via Martino 38. Unpretentiously smart, yet offering incredibly good value, this place cooks up local specialities with gusto. It's near Piazza del Pópolo. No credit cards. Inexpensive. Closed Sun.

Il Gatto e La Volpe, Via Ghibellina 154. On the corner of Via Nino Bixio, this little trattoria has an old-style brick interior and different local specialities every day. There's a L30,000 tourist menu currently on offer, excluding drinks. Moderate. No credit cards. Closed Sun & Aug.

Lungomare da Mario, Via Vittorio Emanuele 108. A good choice for a fish lunch, opposite the hydrofoil dock, though noisy if you sit outside. Moderate. Closed Wed Sept–July.

Da Piero, Via Ghibellina 121 (☎090.718.365). Although still regarded as one of Messina's best seafood restaurants, *Piero* is mainly trading on its past reputation, and locals whisper that standards have plunged of late. Make up your own mind, but be prepared to spend a (relative) fortune: the swordfish *involtini* (rolled and stuffed) are usually available between April and October, and authentic *cassata siciliana* is also on the menu. Reserve ahead in summer and at weekends, and dress up. Expensive. Closed Sun & Aug.

Trattoria del Pópolo, Piazza del Pópolo. Cheap and traditional neighbourhood trattoria where you can eat outside, if there's room, enjoying the rare calm of this corner of the city. The pasta dishes are nothing special but the meat and fish dishes are good. Inexpensive. Closed Sun & mid-Aug.

La Trattoria, Via XXIV Maggio 10 (☎090.672.569). Small and chic restaurant with a daily changing menu of fresh local dishes. It's popular, so booking is advisable. Moderate. Closed Sun.

Nightlife and entertainment

Messina by night can be extremely beautiful, especially from the high **Via Panoramica** – from which, with the city at your feet, there's a long, sparkling view across to mainland Italy. From the centre, the closest section of this route is the Viale Príncipe Umberto stretch, where there are bars and pizzerias around two floodlit sanctuaries (Cristo Re and Montalto) and plenty of scope for some pleasant evening strolling. In summer, free **classical concerts** are often held up here behind the Cristo Re (details from any tourist office).

Back down in the centre, free concerts of **jazz**, **rock and world music** are staged in Piazza Duomo in July and August, also the period when **free films** are shown in the Villa Mazzini public gardens near the hydrofoil dock – usually starting at 8.30pm. Watch out for posters giving details of all of these, or ask at the tourist office – and arrive early, as these events tend to get crowded. In summer, most evening life takes place around the lake at Ganzirri and at Mortelle, half an hour away (where there are, respectively, a better selection of fish restaurants and more open-air films – see p.184 and 185).

Ferragosto

If you're in Messina in midsummer, you might catch the festivals around the Feast of the Assumption, or **ferragosto**. Although all the villages on both sides of the Straits hold festivals around this time, with some pretty spectacular fireworks lighting up the sky on any one night, Messina's festivities are grander, beginning around August 12, when two plaster giants (*giganti*) are wheeled around town, and finally stationed near the port opposite the Municipio. These are said to be Messina's two founders, Mata and Grifone, one a white female, the other a burly Moor, and both mounted on huge steeds. On ferragosto itself, August 15, another towering carriage, the Vara, is hauled through the city centre. It's an elaborate column supporting dozens of papier-mâché putti and angels, culminating in the figure of Christ stretching out his right arm to launch Mary on her way to Heaven. This unwieldy construction is towed on long ropes, pulled by hundreds of penitents – semi-naked if they're men, all in white if they're women – and cheered on by thousands of people along the way. The whole thing is a sweaty and frenetic performance, finishing up at Piazza del Duomo, where flowers are thrown out to the crowds, many of whom risk being crushed in the mad scramble to gather these luck-bearing charms. Late at night, one of Sicily's best **firework displays** is held on the seafront near Via della Libertà.

Listings

Airlines Alitalia, c/o A. Meo & Figli, Via del Vespro 52–56 (☎090.679.940).

Airport Nearest at Réggio di Calabria, for internal services only (☎0965.642.722).

Ambulance ☎090.293.1840 or 090.384.345.

Bookshop Libreria Ciófalo, Piazza Municipio 37. Good range of guides, maps and English-language books. Mon–Sat 9am–1pm & 4–8pm.

Bus companies AST, from Via Santa Maria Alemanna (☎090.662.244), for Ali Terme, Barcellona, Forza d'Agrò, Itala and Patti; A. Cavalieri, Via Primo Settembre 137 (☎090.771.938), departures from Piazza Duomo for Réggio di Calabria airport; Giuntabus, from Via Terranova 8 (☎090.673.782), for Milazzo and the Aeolian Islands; SAIS, from Piazza della Repubblica 6 (☎090.771.914), for Palermo, Rome, the coast south to Taormina and Catania; TAI, from Viale San Martino 20 (☎090.675.184), for Capo d'Orlando, Patti and Tíndari.

Car problems ACI, Largo Bozzi 15 (☎090.52.830).

Car rental Avis, Piazza Vittorio Emanuele 35 (☎090.679.150); Maggiore, Via T. Canizzaro 46 (☎090.675.476); Sicilcar, Via Garibaldi 187 (☎090.46.942).

Ferry tickets All tickets across the Straits are on sale at kiosks at the respective terminals; for Villa San Giovanni, call ☎090.675.234 (FS) or ☎090.41.415 (Caronte).

Hospital Ospedale R. Margherita, Via della Libertà (☎090.365.6454).

Hydrofoil tickets To Réggio di Calabria and the Aeolians, on sale at the hydrofoil terminal; call SNAV on ☎090.364.044.

Pharmacy There's an all-night service on a rotating basis: consult any pharmacy window to find out current *farmacie notturne*, or call ☎090.717.589.

Police Carabinieri, at Via Monsignor d'Arrigo (☎112); road accidents ☎090.771.000; anything else, at the Questura, Via Plácida 2 (☎090.3661).

Post office Main office at Piazza Antonello, behind the Municipio on Corso Cavour. Mon–Sat 8.15am–6.30pm.

Telephones Offices at Stazione Centrale (daily 8am–9.45pm) and Corso Cavour 1 (daily 8am–10pm).

Ticket agency Travel and theatre tickets, including for Taormina's Teatro Greco and Tindari's teatro, at Lisciotto Viaggi at Piazza Cairoli 13 (☎090.719.001).

Around Messina

There are several mountain or coastal destinations not more than half an hour away from the centre of Messina by bus or car, all well worth a visit to get the most out of the city. If you're driving, you might wish to follow the high-level Via Panoramica north rather than the congested coastal road, which is the route the **bus** takes; though make a point of taking this lower road at least once, passing fishermen's houses that back onto short sandy strips, in areas that must once have justified their idyllic names of Paradiso, Contemplazione and Pace. In Pace, look out for the British cannons lining the esplanade, pulled out of the Straits where they had sunk during the Napoleonic Wars.

Ganzirri and Punta del Faro

The #79 and #81 buses make a stop in **GANZIRRI**, 10km north of Messina's centre, which (in summer especially) becomes the hub of milling crowds hanging around the excellent bars and attending the nightly **Italian pop concerts** held throughout August.

There's mussel-farming on Ganzirri's lake and you can eat plenty of fresh shellfish, swordfish or whatever else has been hauled in that day by the many boats operating around here. Most of the **trattorias** are squeezed into the wedge of land between lake and sea, and you can eat outside at nearly all of them. Prices tend to be high, but for very reasonably priced, exquisitely cooked **fish** dishes, seek out *Lilla Currò*, signposted up a lane on the right side of the lake (closed Mon). Keep going along this road (keeping right, towards Faro) for the area's best **pizzeria**, *Mito dello Stretto* (closed Thurs in winter), with a terrace right on the Straits, while further still you'll find the cosy *Mínico Il Pescatore*, which offers a good-value fixed-price menu (L38,000) of seafood dishes from Sferracavallo, west of Palermo (closed Tues). The #79 bus stops right outside.

Here, **Punta del Faro** (also called Capo Peloro) is the very tip of Sicily, the nearest point to Italy where the lighthouse (the *faro*) is dwarfed by the towering pylon supporting the massive cables that tether the island to the mainland. Here, too, was where the legendary **Charybdis** once posed a threat to sailors – along with Scylla on the opposite shore – still remembered in the locality's name of Cariddi.

For a decent **hotel** in the area, the *Donato*, at Via Caratozzolo 8 (☎090.393.150; no credit cards; ③), offers excellent value, its tastefully decorated rooms – all with bath – undisturbed by the scream of Vespas, and just 50m from the sea. It's signposted off the lake.

Mortelle and Acqualadrone

A couple of kilometres further up the road, on the Tyrrhenian coast, **MORTELLE** is the focus in summer for Messina's bronzed youth, who throng the lidos and **beaches** and fill the air with the drone of a thousand motorbikes. Apart from some sleek bars and pizzerias, Mortelle is also the site of Messina's most famous **eating** institution, *Lo Sporting di Alberto*, Via Nazionale (☎090.321.009), where you can rub shoulders with the city's elite and get down to some extremely stylish eating on the terrace overlooking the sea. Book in advance in summer (closed Mon & Nov), and dust your credit cards.

Cheaper entertainment is never far away, and in July and August you can enjoy performances of **open-air films**, nightly at 8.30pm and 10.45pm, at the Arena Green Sky (opposite the *Due Palme* pizzeria); tickets cost around L8000. Westwards from Mortelle is a succession of sandy beaches and beach towns, best of which is **ACQUALADRONE** (bus #80 from Messina's Stazione Centrale).

Inland

Inland from Messina, the ridge-top of the **Monti Peloritani** offers the best vantage-point of the Tyrrhenian and Ionian coasts and also has some good walking in the woods. To reach the ridge, take the old Palermo road from Via Garibaldi in the city (bus #73 from Via Garibaldi). On the way, you can stop off at the old monastery of Santa Maria della Valle, better known as **La Badiazza** (always open). Secluded in a deep gully, this old Benedictine monastery lies at the end of a twenty-minute walk along a dirt road leading off to the right just before Via Palermo passes under the autostrada. The monastery dates from the twelfth century, but was reconstructed after a fire in the fourteenth century and later abandoned. Today, recently restored, it has regained its fortress-like appearance and looks quite capable of withstanding a corsair raid.

You can wander through the pinewoods around here, but they are thicker further up the SS113 (Via Palermo); from there you can take a left turn at the crossroads at **Colle San Rizzo** (where the bus stops), then it's another 10km south to reach the panoramic **Monte Antennamare** sanctuary, a shabby building in a sublime spot (1124m high). Back at Colle San Rizzo, you could make a round-trip of it by descending north to Castanea, another wooded area favoured by hunters, and down to the Tyrrhenian coast at Sparta, on the Messina road.

The coastal route to Taormina, and the hills

There's no shortage of beaches on the coastal strip **south of Messina** if you delve in between the closely packed houses that line this stretch. They're nothing special near the city, but once beyond the suburbs there are a few low-key seaside resorts that would do for an hour or two if you are desperate for a swim. Along the coast, it's best to take the **train** that traces the shoreline pretty much all the way: on a clear day there are sparkling views across to Calabria, while the ragged cliffs on the other side are covered with acres of prickly pears. The slower buses, on the other hand, stick to the back-streets of the successive towns and villages – a largely unedifying ride and excruciatingly slow. This is also true for **drivers**, though the toll autostrada (the A18) is a fast alternative, plunging through some fairly dramatic scenery as it cruises above the sea. You don't have to stick with the coast all the way, though: there are some short trips to be made **into the hills** on the way. There are good **bus services** from some of the coastal resorts for these, and there should be no difficulty in hitching, or even walking, if you've the time.

Mili San Pietro to Ali Terme

Messina's ungraceful suburbs extend almost as far as the autostrada turnoff at Tremestieri. Shortly beyond, a minor road leads off inland from Mili Marina to **MILI SAN PIETRO**, a nondescript little place 2km up the road. (From Messina, take bus #28 from Piazza Cairoli or anywhere central, heading south along Viale San Martino to the terminus in the ZIR industrial zone, changing there onto the #8.) As the village swings into view, the grey cupolas of the monastery-church of **Santa Maria** are just visible below the road on the right. The Basilian monastery of which this was a part was founded by Count Roger in 1082, but is now abandoned – irreverently occupied by assorted farmyard animals and permeated by their pungent rural smells. The church survives – just – its exterior displaying some nice interlaced blind arcading on one wall and a semicircular apse. But the inside is derelict and not particularly interesting, although it's said to contain the burial place of Roger's son, Jordan; ask at the church in the centre of the village for the key.

Further down the coast by 7km or 8km, **Scaletta Zanclea** is a popular resort with an impressive eleventh-century **castle** at its highest point, containing some heraldic knick-knacks. The key is kept at the *comune*. The next village down, Itala Marina, has an inland parent, **Itala**, 2.5km up the road from the coast, just beyond which – over the bridge on the road to Croce – is the church of **San Pietro e Paolo**. Built by Roger in 1093, in thanksgiving for a victory over the Arabs, this church has features in common with Santa Maria in Mili San Pietro, and provided the model for the church near Casalvécchio Sículo built eighty years later (see opposite). This domed, red-brick construction has been restored and is still in use; indeed the best time to see it is before the 11am service on Sunday morning – otherwise, contact the priest at no. 26, on Itala's main street, for the key.

If you're stuck for **somewhere to stay** along this stretch, **ALI TERME** – a village known since antiquity for its sulphur baths – has three hotels, the antique but inexpensive *Terme Granata Cassibile* (☎0942.715.029; ①); the *Terme Marino Giuseppe* (☎090.715.031; ③), a bit classier; and *La Magnolia* (☎0942.716.377; ③), smaller, more modern and on the seafront.

Santa Teresa di Riva and Sávoca

Ten kilometres south of Ali Terme, **SANTA TERESA DI RIVA** is the first recognizable resort on this stretch, with an extensive beach and a few trattorias. Though the town itself is nothing to shout about, it's a useful jumping-off point for the foothills of the **Monti Peloritani: buses** leave from here for Sávoca and Casalvécchio Sículo; ask the driver of the Messina–Catania bus to put you off on the seafront (Lungomare Santa Teresa), and Sávoca is signposted to the left, the bus-stop for the village one block back from the sea on the corner of a crossroads.

Sávoca

It's a winding four-kilometre run up to **SÁVOCA**, a peaceful village, evocatively sited: houses and three churches perch on the cliffsides in clumps, with a tattered castle (originally Saracen) topping the pile. Two pincer-like streets, Via San Michele and Via Chiesa Madre, reach around to their respective churches, the grandest the square-towered thirteenth-century **Chiesa Madre**. Sitting on a tiny ridge between two opposing hills, it's a fine vantage-point from which to look down the valley to the sea and across the surrounding hills. Spare a glance, too, at the house next door, lovingly restored and displaying a fifteenth-century stone-arched double window. It's one of many in the village that have had a face-lift as outsiders move in to snap up run-down cottages as second homes. These days, Sávoca is within the Taormina commuter belt and most of the people who live here work elsewhere – something that's to its advantage: during the day the streets and hillside alleys are refreshingly empty, the medieval atmosphere still intact.

Signs in the village point you to the **Cappuccini monastery**, whose *catacombe*, or catacombs (daily: summer 9am–1pm & 4–7pm; winter 9am–1pm & 3–5pm; donations requested) contain a selection of gruesome mummified bodies. These are the remains of local lawyers, doctors and the clergy: two hundred to three hundred years old, they stand in niches dressed in their eighteenth-century finery, the skulls of less-complete colleagues lining the walls above. An added grotesque touch is the green paint with which the bodies have been daubed, the work of vandals and hard to remove without damaging the cadavers. Ask the custodian and you'll probably be shown the church **treasury** as well, which has a small collection of liturgical books and seventeenth- and eighteenth-century bibles; it's appreciated if you leave a small donation on the way out. More offbeat delight is at hand in the village's *Bar Vitelli*. An appealing eighteenth-century wood-panelled, stone-flagged building, it (and the village) was used as the scene of Michael Corleone's betrothal to Apollonia in Coppola's film *The Godfather*. A few words of Italian might nudge the woman behind the bar into recounting her memories of the shoot – she's something of an expert on all the *Godfather* films. There are numerous mementos of other episodes in the bar's past inside, and tables under the pergola outside.

Sávoca has a popular **ristorante**, *La Pineta*, with a panoramic terrace, near the bar, and a *paninoteca* for snacks below the Capuchin monastery, but nowhere to stay – a shame really, but you could easily see the village (and the rest of the route, described below) on a day-trip from Taormina or Messina, provided you time the buses right.

Casalvécchio Sículo

The only road beyond Sávoca (and the same bus from Santa Teresa) careers another 2km along the ridge to **CASALVÉCCHIO SÍCULO**, which if anything has even better views of the valley from its terraces. There's not much to detain you here, except the quiet village atmosphere, but walk through Casalvécchio and, after about 500m, a rough road drops away to the left (signposted), snaking down into a lush, citrus-planted valley. It's about a twenty-minute hike to the Norman monastery of **Santi Pietro e Paolo**, gloriously sited on a high bank above the river. Built in the twelfth century, its battlemented facade and double domes are visible from a distance through the lemon groves and, though considered Sicily's best example of Basilian (Greek) architecture, the church betrays a strong Arabic influence, particularly in the polychromatic patterns of the exterior. If it's locked, there should be someone around in one of the adjacent buildings with a key.

Either head back up to the main road and wait for the return bus to pass, or continue downhill for a longer **walk**, beyond the monastery to the River Agrò. It's about another hour's tramp, alongside the wide (and mostly dry) river bed to Rina, back towards the sea. The main (SS114) coastal road is signposted from Rina, and in another twenty minutes, through a small tunnel, you're back in Santa Teresa, on the Messina–Catania bus route.

Forza d'Agrò and Sant'Aléssio

The only other worthy diversion into the hills is just a few kilometres south, where the turnoff at **Capo Sant'Aléssio** gives the first views of Taormina. The cliffs here support a sturdy castle and, though you can climb up to it, you can't get in – it's been for sale for years.

Four kilometres inland of here, atop a corkscrew road, is **FORZA D'AGRÒ** (reached by AST bus from Messina and Taormina) – like so many Sicilian villages, a breezy place defiantly crumbling all around its mostly elderly inhabitants and with little left of the Norman **castello** that crowns it. It's a memorable clamber up to the top: the streets become ever more perilous, and the stone cottages increasingly neglected and held together by rotting spars of wood. One push, it seems, would bring the whole lot down. The lower parts of the village are better maintained, but not much – hi-fi stores and clothes shops are tucked into tiny cottage interiors, and a couple of churches are locked and decrepit.

Still, it's close enough to Taormina to attract the tour buses, which deposit their passengers in the village square, where there are couple of bars to help idle the time away. And there's a fine, moderately priced **restaurant** too, known to both tourists and locals: *L'Abbazia*, where specialities include mixed vegetable grill made with local mushrooms, aubergine, peppers and radicchio, which you can eat on a terrace with great views (closed Wed). There's even **somewhere to stay** if you are so inclined, the *Souvenir* (☎0942.721.078; ②) on Via Belvedere – not at all bad value (but no credit cards).

Sant'Aléssio Sículo

If you're energetic enough, you can make the descent on foot from Forza d'Agrò back down to the main coastal road and Capo Sant'Aléssio, where you can pick up the Messina–Catania bus. One kilometre north of the cape, there's a train station at **SANT'ALÉSSIO SÍCULO** village, a small resort with a wide beach and a few cheap accommodation possibilities. There's a **campsite** here, *La Focetta* (☎0942.751.657; June–Sept), and another close to Sant'Aléssio, the *Forza d'Agrò Mare* (☎0942.971.158; May–Sept), at Località Buzzurratti.

Taormina

TAORMINA, high on Monte Tauro and dominating two grand, sweeping bays below, is Sicily's best-known resort. The whole town is devoted to – and dependent on – the topnotch international tourism that flaunts through its streets from April to October. You'd be wrong, though, to avoid Taormina because of this: it's certainly expensive to stay here, but the veneer of exclusivity is only skin-deep, and at heart the small town still can't seem to believe its good luck. Certainly there's enough left of its hill-village charm to make it a worthy stop, especially if you hole up at one of the cheaper nearby beach resorts. And, although Taormina itself has no beach, the outstanding remains of the classical theatre and the sheer beauty of the town's site amply compensate. Among many passing travellers besotted by Taormina, Goethe and D.H. Lawrence are the two big names touted by the tourist office; Lawrence was so enthusiastic about Taormina's prospect and climate that he lived here (1920–23), in a villa at the top of the valley-cleft behind the theatre.

Despite the intrusion of contemporary tourists, Taormina retains much of its late medieval character. The one main traffic-free street is an unbroken line of fifteenth- to nineteenth-century *palazzi* and intimate piazzas; its churches are unobtrusive and attractive; and there's an agreeably crumbly castle and rows of flower-filled balconies. The downside is that at Easter and between June and August it can get supremely crowded: the narrow alleys are filled shoulder-to-shoulder with tourists, while the beaches below town simply seethe. April, May or September are better, but to avoid the crowds completely come between October and March, when it's usually still warm enough to swim and the spring brings with it flamboyant displays of all kinds of flowering plants.

Locally, there are several good walks to be done, including a trip up to the neighbouring village of **Castelmola** and the mountain behind it. Most people, though, are content with the excellent **beaches** that punctuate the coastline below Taormina; all the details are given in "Around Taormina" (see p.199). You'll not avoid the crowds in any of these places, but it's worth noting that the nearest town to Taormina, Giardini-Naxos, might be a more realistic base for your beach-going – cheaper and less pretentious than Taormina in every way.

Arrival, information and getting around

Trains pull up at Taormina-Giardini station, where there's a left-luggage office (6am–10pm; L5000 per piece for 12hr) on the water's edge, way below town. It's a *very* steep thirty-minute walk from here up to Taormina: turn right out of the station and, after 300m, turn left through a gap in the buildings, signposted *"Centro"*. Much better (certainly if you have luggage) is to arrive by bus – from Messina or Catania – or take one of the fairly frequent local buses up the hill, roughly every 45 minutes from outside the train station. Taormina's **bus terminal** (information on ☎0942.625.301), where they all stop, is on Via Luigi Pirandello. Alternatively, a **taxi** ride from the train station to the town costs L20,000–30,000, and around L100,000 from Catania airport. If you have a car, you'll be charged in peak season at least L15,000 to leave it for 24 hours, or L4000 for two hours, in one of the main **car parks** (assuming there's space), either at Lumbi at the top of town (signposted off the Taormina Nord autostrada junction), or at Mazzarò (see p.199), alongside the cable car off the coast road.

The main street, **Corso Umberto I**, runs right through town, from Porta Messina to Porta Catania at the other end. The useful English-speaking **tourist office** is in the crenellated Palazzo Corvaja, off Piazza Vittorio Emanuele (April–Oct Mon–Sat 8.30am–2pm & 4–7pm, Sun 9am–1pm; Nov–March closed Sun; ☎0942.23.243). Pick up a free map, accommodation listings and bus and train timetables, and programmes for summer events in the theatre.

Getting around

You'll walk nearly everywhere in town, though there is a **minibus service** (L1500) from the bus terminal linking the more far-flung parts of Taormina, including the Lumbi car park. The most useful service is the one from the terminal to Madonna della Rocca, which passes several of the main hotels; it operates from 6am to midnight, half-hourly from March to October and hourly the rest of the year. **Taxi** ranks are in Piazza San Pancrazio and Piazza Vittorio Emanuele, where prices are posted; as a general guide, it's about L12,000 to Madonna della Rocca.

The **cable-car** service between Taormina and the beach at Mazzarò, next to the Lumbi car park, is useful and fun, operating until about 1.30am in summer, 8.30pm in winter (tickets L3000, or L5000 return); alternatively, a regular bus from the bus terminal runs down to Mazzarò daily from 6.45am to 7.45pm.

Accommodation

Finding a bed between June and September is a time-consuming business without a reservation. Only a handful will be both available and affordable, so start looking early. Late arrivals can usually persuade the tourist office to ring round for available rooms, though this way you don't get to see them first.

It's worth bearing in mind that in the frantic summer months, everywhere (these places included) can more or less charge what they like, often by simply slapping on an obligatory breakfast charge: it's a good idea to take the first reasonable place you're offered and check the rest later. If everywhere is full, or you prefer to be nearer the beach, you'll have to try Giardini-Naxos (p.200) or Mazzarò (p.199).

Hotels

Camere, Via Bagnoli 66. Cheap rooms in an unmarked apartment block – very few rooms but with incredible views from the roof terrace, and one room has a small kitchen. No credit cards. ②.

Continental, Via Dionisio I 2a (☎0942.23.805, fax 0942.23.806). At the top of town and, consequently, with sweeping views across to Etna and the bay from the impressive bar-roof terrace. Rooms are modern; lower prices in low season. ⑤.

Cundari, Via Nazionale 9 (☎0942.53.287). This is a good-value choice if you want to stay around the train station rather than in Taormina itself. Take a note of the bus times at the station and you're just ten minutes away from the centre of town. No en-suite rooms. ②.

Diana, Vico di Giovanni 6 (☎0942.23.898). This little *locanda* has just four rooms (only a couple with bath/shower) and some of the cheapest prices in town. No credit cards. ①.

Elios, Via Bagnoli Croce 98 (☎ & fax 0942.23.431). A smartish two-star *pensione* with nice rooms, all with shower, and a view-laden roof terrace, but occasionally fierce management. ④.

Pensione Grazia, Via Iallia Bassia 20 (☎ & fax 0942.24.776). A budget option in a street behind the public gardens. Basic, but clean rooms, and friendly. No credit cards. April–Oct. ②.

Il Leone, Via Bagnoli Croce 126 (☎ & fax 0942.23.878). Around 300m from the bus station, the balconies here overlook the bay below, making this one of the better budget places. Small, plain apartments also available for lets. ②.

Moderno, Via Nazionale (☎0942.51.017). This ramshackle villa run by a chatty woman from Emilia-Romagna is right opposite the train station, so expect some noise. No credit cards. ②.

President Hotel, Via Dietro Cappuccini (☎0942.23.500, fax 0942.625.289). Unbecoming modern hotel but good value and with views. Small apartments (without kitchen) also to let across the road. ④.

Residence, Salita Dente 4 (☎0942.23.463, fax 0942.23.464). Tucked into one of the town's central, medieval streets, the cheapest rooms here are good value, though they don't have the views that the more expensive rooms with bath enjoy. Low-season rates are two price categories down. ④.

San Domenico Palace, Piazza San Domenico 5 (☎0942.23.701, fax 0942.625.506). Taormina's finest hotel, stunningly situated and occupying a fifteenth-century convent. Views and facilities are unsurpassed – there's a heated pool and tennis courts – and prices ridiculous (L440,000–700,000 per night), though it does appear at discounted rates on high-class packages from the UK. ⑧.

Svizzera, Via L. Pirandello 26 (☎0942.23.790, fax 0942.625.906). Just up from the bus terminal, the orange-pink hotel sports a pleasant shady terrace and some good views over the coast north of town. Rooms are fine, and should be booked in advance. Half- or full-board only from mid-July to mid-August from L120,000 per person. ④.

Victoria, Corso Umberto I 81 (☎ & fax 0942.23.372). Housed in one of the main corso's converted *palazzi*, close to Piazza IX Aprile, this has been refurbished and now has showers in every room. Central, smart and reasonable value, with off-season prices plummeting. ④.

Villa Belvedere, Via Bagnoli Croce 79 (☎0942.23.791, fax 0942.625.830). Large cliff-side hotel in an attractive turn-of-the-century building, with gardens and a pool below. Rooms at the front are easily the best, though you're paying more for the views and terrace. Out of season, prices halve; in summer, it's around L200,000 a night. ⑤.

Villa Fiorita, Via L. Pirandello 39 (☎0942.24.122, fax 0942.625.967). A three-star rating, comfortable, airy rooms with expansive views, a garden and – more importantly – a swimming pool, which isn't bad at all for these prices. It's close to the cable-car station (and only just creeps into this category, with uniform prices all year). ⑤.

Villa Greta, Via Leonardo da Vinci 44 (☎0942.28.286, fax 0942.24.360). Delightful *pensione* managed by a friendly family, who also offer decent half- and full-board rates. The comfortably furnished rooms have shower and terrace, with superb views over town and bay; the little restaurant (see p.197) has an outdoor terrace. It's a steep 10min walk above Taormina on the Castelmola road; the bus passes right outside. ④.

Apartments

It can also be worth enquiring at the tourist office about **furnished apartments**, usually rented out by the month only in summer, but for negotiable periods out of high season. There are dozens all over town, all with bathroom and kitchen facilities, and off-season prices start at around L160,000 a week – though in summer you're talking about well over L1 million a month. There are some nice, reasonable apartments for rent called *Cormoran*, at Via Don Bosco 29 (☎0942.21.130), between the corso and the Circonvallazione; and others at Salita dei Gracchi 4 (☎0942.447.678), off the main corso by Piazza IX Aprile; information from the tourist office. *Il Leone* and the *President Hotel* also have apartments to let; check above for details.

Campsites

The nearest **campsite**, *San Leo* (☎0942.24.658), on the cape below town (next to the *Grande Albergo Capo Taormina*), is open all year, but it's only worth it if you're desperate to be close to town; you can reach it on any bus running between Taormina and the train station. Otherwise, head further afield to sites at Letojanni (p.200) and Giardini-Naxos (p.201).

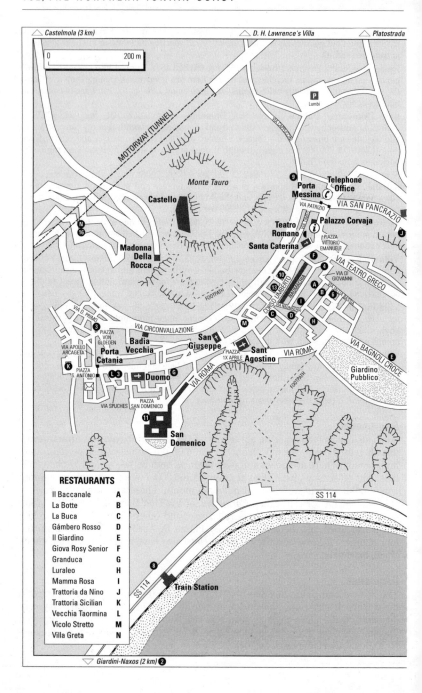

Castelmola (3 km)

D. H. Lawrence's Villa

Platostrada

0   200 m

MOTORWAY (TUNNEL)

Monte Tauro

Castello

Madonna
Della
Rocca

Porta
Messina

Telephone
Office

VIA SAN PANCRAZIO

VIA PATRIZIO

Teatro
Romano

Santa Caterina

Palazzo Corvaja

PIAZZA
VITTORIO
EMANUELE

VIA TEATRO GRECO

VIA DI
GIOVANNI

VIA CIRCONVALLAZIONE

VIA D. PRIMO

PIAZZA
VON
GLOEDEN

Badia
Vecchia

San
Giuseppe

VIA APOLLO
ARCAGETA

Porta
Catania

PIAZZA
S. ANTONIO

Duomo

PIAZZA
1X APRILE

Sant'
Agostino

VIA ROMA

VIA ROMA

VIA BAGNOLI CROCE

Giardino
Pubblico

VIA SPUCHES

PIAZZA
SAN DOMENICO

San
Domenico

FOOTPATH

SS 114

RESTAURANTS

Il Baccanale	**A**
La Botte	**B**
La Buca	**C**
Gámbero Rosso	**D**
Il Giardino	**E**
Giova Rosy Senior	**F**
Granduca	**G**
Luraleo	**H**
Mamma Rosa	**I**
Trattoria da Nino	**J**
Trattoria Sicilian	**K**
Vecchia Taormina	**L**
Vicolo Stretto	**M**
Villa Greta	**N**

SS 114

Train Station

Giardini-Naxos (2 km)

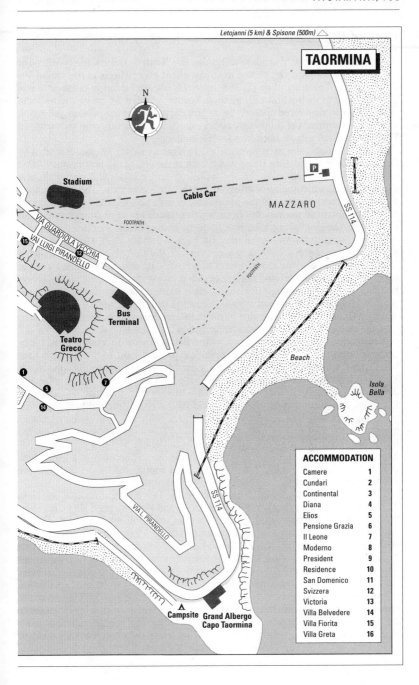

Letojanni (5 km) & Spisone (500m)

TAORMINA

N

Stadium

Cable Car

MAZZARO

P

SS 114

FOOTPATH

VIA GUARDIOLA VECCHIA

VAI LUIGI PIRANDELLO

15

12

Bus
Terminal

FOOTPATH

Teatro
Greco

1

5

7

14

Beach

Isola
Bella

VIA L. PIRANDELLO

SS 114

Campsite **Grand Albergo
Capo Taormina**

ACCOMMODATION

Camere	1
Cundari	2
Continental	3
Diana	4
Elios	5
Pensione Grazia	6
Il Leone	7
Moderno	8
President	9
Residence	10
San Domenico	11
Svizzera	12
Victoria	13
Villa Belvedere	14
Villa Fiorita	15
Villa Greta	16

Around the town

Whenever you come, you shouldn't miss the **Teatro Greco** (daily 9am–1hr before sunset; L4000), signposted from just about everywhere, at the end of Via Teatro Greco. Vincent Cronin (in *The Golden Honeycomb*) thought the theatre was " . . . deluged to distraction with multiple beauty . . . sited by connoisseurs", and certainly it's a considered choice, the theatre carved out of the hillside and giving a complete panorama of southern Calabria, the Sicilian coastline and snow-capped Etna – a glorious natural backdrop for the audience.

Despite its name, the existing remains are almost entirely Roman. Founded by Greeks in the third century BC, it was rebuilt at the end of the first century AD, a period when Taormina enjoyed great prosperity under Imperial Roman rule, and the reconstruction completely changed the theatre's character. The arched apertures, niches and columns of the impressive Roman scene-building, for example, must have obscured the views of Etna, which presumably were a major reason for the theatre's original siting. Likewise, Imperial Roman drama was strictly gladiatorial, so the stage and lower seats were cut back to provide more room and a deep trench was dug in the orchestra to accommodate the animals and fighters. Still, it all adds to the interest, and you'll want to scramble up and down the seats of the *cavea*, as well as poke around the high-vaulted rooms on either side of the scene-building – all of which is best done in the early morning or near closing time if you want to avoid the high-season crowds. You can't fault the acoustics either, and in summer (July & Aug) the theatre hosts an **international arts festival** including film, theatre and music; tickets and information from the tourist office.

A **museum**, close to the entrance, with relics of Roman Taormina, is currently being restored, and may yet reopen, though at present some of the contents have been transferred to the **Badia Vecchia**, near where Via Circonvallazione meets Via Leonardo da Vinci (summer daily 9am–1pm & 4–7pm; winter Mon–Fri 9am–1pm & 4–6pm, Sat 9am–1pm; L2000) – though this, too, may be closed for long-term renovation work. One of the old town's most graceful buildings, this surviving remnant of a fifteenth-century abbey, with the swallow-tailed battlements and twin Gothic windows characteristic of Taormina, holds everything that hasn't been squirrelled away by the museums at Catania and Réggio Calabria, or kept back in the vaults. Frankly, at present this doesn't amount to a great deal, though the temporary exhibition may have been augmented by the time you see it, if it hasn't been transferred back to the antiquarium at the theatre.

There's little else that's vital in town and, really, Taormina's attractions are all to do with strolling along the flower-decked streets and sheer-stepped alleys, and window-shopping in the converted ground floors of Corso Umberto's fifteenth-century *palazzi*. If you have dropped in to Taormina's tourist office, you will already have seen the fine fourteenth-century **Palazzo Corvaja**, decorated with inlaid black and white lava and encompassing an attractive courtyard staircase. You can usually get into the main hall, where the Sicilian "parliament" met in 1410 to choose a successor to the Aragonese line, and there are concerts and exhibitions held inside throughout the year (details from the office itself). A little way up the corso, the church of **Santa Caterina** has been built almost on top of a small, brick-built odeon, known as the **Teatro Romano** (originally used for musical recitations): peer down at it through the railings from outside and then enter the church to take a closer look at bits of the theatre exposed in the floor of the nave.

A few other vestiges of Roman and medieval Taormina can be taken in during your wanderings through town. Heading south, back along the corso, turn off a side street to the left (Via Naumachia) to find, on the left, the niched wall of **La Naumachia**, a Roman water cistern and gymnasium. It's a long (122m), refreshingly shop-free expanse – though a restaurant and barber's have staked their pitch here. Bang in the middle of Corso Umberto I, **Piazza IX Aprile** is identifiable by its restored twelfth-century **Torre dell'Orologio**, a clock tower you can walk right through. The views here, from a terrace overlooking Etna and the bay, are splendid, and the inviting outdoor cafés here make much of their position – though be warned that they are expensive places to sit and drink. Both churches in the square, low-key and unassuming, indicate how small-scale Taormina was until fairly recently. Squat fifteenth-century **Sant'Agostino** is now a library, while **San Giuseppe** tops the steps at the back of the piazza – its seventeenth-century facade curiously decorated with plaques depicting skull and crossbones.

Through the clock tower is the oldest part of Taormina, and the narrow corso is awash with stately *palazzi*, now neatly displaying antiques, shoes, clothes and local lace in their lower windows. The battlemented **Duomo**, originally built in the thirteenth century, though restored since, isn't of vast interest. Typically subdued in design, it is fronted by a pretty seventeenth-century fountain. Steps to the right lead to a patchy, enclosed Roman mosaic, badly faded, just above Piazza del Duomo.

Head the other way, behind the square and cathedral, and a street drops down to the impressive convent of **San Domenico**, now a luxury hotel and containing a contemporary cloister (which you can't get into) and a restored church hall adjoining it (which hosts the odd concert). Though you'd never know to look at it, the convent was badly bombed during World War II, when it was commandeered as the headquarters of Field Marshal Kesselring.

At some point, it's worth fetching up at the **Giardino Pubblico** (dawn–dusk) on Via Bagnoli Croce. Endowed by an Englishwoman, the shady gardens are furnished with a diverting collection of curiosities (memorials, bits of artillery, a submarine). It's an ideal place for a sit-down or picnic, looking down to the bay from its benches, and there's a bar (March–Oct) perched on the edge of the drop, with outstanding views.

Out of the centre: D.H. Lawrence's villa and the castello

A left turn out of the easternmost town gate, Porta Messina, leads you down Via Cappuccini and Via Fontana Vecchia, before dropping down to Piazza Franz Pagano. Follow the road around and a left fork – Via David Herbert Lawrence – announces that you've reached the villa in which **D.H. Lawrence** lived for three years in the 1920s. It's on the right-hand side of the road, a pink-and-cream-coloured building, now a private house, and marked by a simple plaque reading: "D.H. Lawrence, English author, lived here 1920–1923".

This is of fairly specialist interest (after all, there's nothing to see except the back of a house) and, for a more rewarding walk, consider hiking up to the tumbledown medieval **castello** above Taormina, where the panoramas take in the town and theatre as well as the coastline. There's a very steep path that leads up from the Circonvallazione, past the cliff-top cross of **Madonna della Rocca**, the climb taking around half an hour.

Eating, drinking and nightlife

As with accommodation, so with eating and drinking: there are few bargains in Taormina and unless you're careful you'll go through money like water. Many **restaurants** offer a limited-choice *pranzo turístico*, usually around L20,000–25,000 a head, but these rarely include a drink. The quality of the food can sometimes be a bit of a lottery, too, especially in peak season, when every place is run off its feet. The restaurants listed below may not be the very cheapest in town, but they do offer consistently good value. A good alternative for lunch is to buy some fast food Sicilian-style at a **rosticceria** like *La Fontana* on the corner of Via Timeo and Via Patrizio, just up west from the Porta Messina, where you can load up with delicious takeaway *arancini, caponata, parmigiana, lasagne*, etc. See also "Listings" for **market** and **supermarket** shopping; and p.32 for an explanation of the restaurant price categories.

Taormina's **nightlife** may seem dauntingly exclusive at times, but it isn't really – just dauntingly dear and in fact rather tame. Be prepared to pay heavily for drinks in the few **discos** and video-bars, all of which are as good, or bad, as each other. At some point you'll probably want to sit and **drink** in one of the pavement cafés. Again, though, they're not cheap – in Piazza IX Aprile, the prime spot, a small beer will set you back around L5000–6000, and a cappuccino not much less. In summer, ask in the tourist office about **performances** in the Teatro Greco, enabling you to appreciate the auditorium for the purposes for which it was designed. Ticket prices start at L7000 for film, L15,000 for theatre, L20,000 for music and ballet. The local *comune* also stages a season of events in the Giardino Pubblico, including traditional dance, song and puppet shows (admission free); get details from the tourist office and on posters around town. The favourite entertainment at Taormina is also free: joining the town's swanky *passeggiata* along the corso. Alternatively, if you've overdosed on Taormina's glitzy glamour, take a bus down to Giardini-Naxos for a waterfront stroll – by no means the worst way to spend an evening.

Restaurants

Il Baccanale, Piazzetta Filea 3. Just off Via Bagnoli Croce, in the old centre, you can sit outside this rustic little place and enjoy decent Italian and Sicilian specialities, including grilled sardines. Moderate. Closed Thurs in winter.

La Botte, Piazza Santa Domenica 4. An accommodating restaurant that promises *cucina tipica Siciliana*, and there's outdoor seating in summer. A wood-fired oven produces better pizzas than in most competing places; or circle the impressive antipasto table along with the local clientele. Moderate. Closed Mon in winter.

La Buca, Corso Umberto I 140. Either eat in the cavern-style dining room or in the attractive terrace garden beyond. There's a decent list of pastas and a memorable *zuppa di pesce*, but pricey house wine. Moderate.

Gámbero Rosso, Via Naumachia 11. Outdoor tables on the steps and others, off the main thoroughfare, round the back. Choosing one of the pricey fish dishes pushes the prices up considerably, but there is a pizza menu too. Moderate. Closed Thurs in winter.

Il Giardino, Via Bagnoli Croce 84. Though the food here can be sometimes mediocre, this family-run trattoria opposite the Giardino Pubblico avoids the hard sell of the places in the centre. Good-value meals (a L20,000 tourist menu is offered) and amiable service, and tables outside. Moderate. Closed Thurs.

Giova Rosy Senior, Corso Umberto I 38. One of the town's best restaurants, but with a surprisingly modestly priced menu given the upmarket pretensions; the stuffed squid makes a tasty change. Steer clear of extras, and go easy on the wine, and you could eat very well for under L60,000 inclusive. Outside eating on the terrace. Expensive. Closed Thurs in winter.

Granduca, Corso Umberto 170. A restored fifteenth-century *palazzo*, whose dining room looks out over the bay below town. A fine, if slightly forbidding, place for a quality repast. Cheaper pizzas also available. Expensive.

Luraleo, Via Bagnoli Croce 27. Touristy, but they serve good antipasti and risotto, with an outdoor eating area. Moderate. Closed Wed in winter.

Mamma Rosa, Via Naumachia 10. Straightforward pizzeria-ristorante, with fine pizzas and cheap local wine. Fairly good value for Taormina. Moderate. No closing day.

Trattoria da Nino, Via Pirandello 37. About as cheap as it gets in Taormina; basic but good Italian dishes – pastas, grills and salads – in a little trattoria on the road to the bus station. Inexpensive. Closed Fri Sept–July.

Trattoria Siciliana, Salita Ospedale 9. Outside the Porta Catania, across from the post office, this is a pleasant place to eat, raised above the square on a terrace. It's well thought of locally for its Sicilian specialities, including fresh tuna, though you can eat more simply and less expensively, too. Closed Wed. Moderate.

Vecchia Taormina, Vico Ebrei 3. Probably Taormina's best pizzeria, so expect a crowd. Inexpensive. No credit cards. Closed lunchtime & Wed.

Vicolo Stretto, Vicolo Stretto 6. Reached up the slimmest of alleys off the corso, by Piazza IX Aprile (and easy to miss), this wonderfully chic restaurant has a good spaghetti with *zucchini* and other tasty Sicilian dishes. Expensive. Closed Mon in winter.

Villa Greta, Via Leonardo da Vinci 44. This attractive *pensione* dining room is open to non-guests and has alfresco terrace seating in summer. Grilled fish is the speciality and the wine's from their own vineyard. Moderate. No closing day.

Bars and cafés

Arco Rosso, Via Naumachia 7. A rarity: a proper little bar, tucked just off the corso, which sells good local wine by the glass or bottle, doesn't charge the earth for it, and sees its fair share of locals, too. Closed Wed.

Charlies, Corso Umberto I 135. A good ice-cream and *frappé* bar, next to Piazza IX Aprile. No closing day.

Cantina dei Duchi, Via Spuches 8. Small, select Sicilian pub with wine, beer and panini available until 2am. Weekends are liveliest outside summer. No closing day.

Marrakech, Piazzetta G. Garibaldi. Elegant tearoom and late-night café with Arab-type decor, one of a cluster of sophisticated drinking holes at this end of town (between Piazza San Domenico and the corso), this one with outdoor seating. Closed Wed.

Mediterraneo Café, Via di Giovanni. Trendy bar and crêperie which has DJs playing hip-hop, drum'n'bass and jazz until late. Fruit vodkas a speciality. No closing day.

Mocambo, Piazza IX Aprile. Seats on the corso in Taormina's most prestigious spot, and comfy armchairs and sofas inside this rather genteel teashop-cum-*gelateria*.

Caffé Shaker, Piazza Vittorio Emanuele. At the less exclusive end of town, near the Porta Messina, this is still a pleasant place to sit and watch the antics of the taxi drivers. Closed Sun.

Wunderbar Caffé, Piazza IX Aprile. Best billet in town for the see-and-be-seen brigade, with outdoor seats beneath the clock tower. But even a coffee here runs into thousands of lire, so sip slowly.

Festivals and nightlife

Festival time is always fun in Taormina, since it's not difficult to pack the narrow central streets with revellers. Main annual occasions are the **Sfilata del Carretto Siciliano**, a parade of traditional, decorated Sicilian carts in May; **Taormina Arte**, from July to October, with theatrical, film and musical performances at the theatre; and festivals and parades at both **Christmas** and **Carnevale**.

In summer particularly, Taormina enjoys late hours, with people milling around the streets until long after midnight. There are several **bars and birrerias** open into the small hours, for example *Time Out* at Via San Pancrazio 19, scene of a lively crowd and offering panini and chips as well as beers in its pleasant garden.

If you're looking for a **disco**, most are only open in the summer and charge L15,000–20,000 for entry (usually including your first drink). Those listed below are among the best.

Bella Blu, Via Guardiola Vecchia. Smart, fashionable, expensive.

La Giara, Via La Floresta. As above, with a terrace.

Le Perroquet, Piazza San Domenico. Taormina's main gay club.

Séptimo, Via San Pancrazio. Closed Mon–Fri & Sun in winter.

Tout Va, Via L. Pirandello 70. A former bordello. Closed Mon–Fri in winter.

Listings

Airport SAIS buses run six times daily (three on Sun) to Catania airport from the bus terminal, calling at the train station.

Banks and exchange At the Banco di Sicilia, Corso Umberto I 91 (Mon–Fri 8.30am–1.30pm & 2.45–3.45pm). Also, an exchange office at Silvestri's, Corso Umberto I 145 (Mon–Wed, Fri & Sat: March–Oct 9am–1pm & 4–8pm, plus Sun 9am–1pm; Nov–Feb 9am–12.30pm & 4–7.30pm); CST, Corso Umberto I 101; Centro Raccolta Valuta, Corso Umberto I 224 (Mon–Sat 9am–1pm & 4–8pm), and Farida, Corso Umberto I 181. The post office also changes cash and American Express travellers' cheques; see below.

Bike rental Push-bikes available from Etna Rent, in Giardini-Naxos (see p.201).

Car rental Avis, Via S. Pancrazio 6 (☎0942.23.041); California, Via Bagnoli Croce 86 (☎0942.23.769); Italia, Via Pirandello 29 (☎0942.23.973); Sicily on Wheels, Via Bagnoli Croce 90 (☎0942.625.657); Tauro, Viale Apollo Arcageta 12 (☎0942.24.700). From L80,000 a day.

Excursions and travel agents For trips around Etna, Alcantara and further afield to Siracusa and Piazza Armerina, contact: SAT, Corso Umberto I 73 (☎0942.24.653); CST, Corso Umberto I 101 (☎0942.23.301); SAIS, Corso Umberto I 222 (☎0942.625.179); or the tourist office. Prices start at L25,000 per person.

First aid Call ☎0942.53.745, or ☎0942.625.419 at night.

Laundry Coin-operated machine wash at Piazza San Domenico. L10,000 for 7kg.

Market There's a daily indoor morning market (Mon–Sat) off Via Cappuccini, for fruit and veg, and a weekly Wednesday market at Parcheggio von Gloeden, below town, for household items.

Newspapers English-language papers from shops along the corso and in the news kiosk at the train station.

Petrol stations Agip, Esso and IP on Via L. Pirandello.

Pharmacy There are English-speaking pharmacists at the British Pharmacy, on the corner of Piazza IX Aprile (☎0942.625.866), and Ragusa, on Piazza Duomo (☎0942.23.231).

Police Carabinieri, at Piazza Badia 4 (☎0942.23.105).

Post office Piazza Medaglia d'Oro S. Ten. Buciunì, just outside the Porta Catania. Mon–Sat 8.30am–6.30pm; closes at noon last day of month.

Scooter rental Available from California, Italia, Sicily on Wheels, and Tauro – see "Car rental" above. From L30,000 a day.

Supermarket Standa supermarket outside the Porta Catania (and to the right) on Viale Apollo Arcageta.

Telephones Make telephone calls from inside the Avis rent-a-car office, Via S. Pancrazio 6 (Mon–Sat 8.30am–12.30pm & 4.30–7.30pm, Sun 9am–12.30pm), or at Rubino Nunziata, Piazza Sant'Antonio 1.

Around Taormina: the coastal towns and beaches, and Castelmola

The **coastline below Taormina**, north and south, is immensely appealing – a mixture of grottoes, rocky coves and good sand beaches – although much of it is either sectioned off as private lidos (which you have to pay to use; around L10,000 a day) or simply gets very packed in summer. Little communities – not quite villages – have developed around the bay to the north; easiest to reach, on foot or by cable car, are the small, stony stretches around **Mazzarò**. For decent expanses of sand you'll have to travel to **Giardini-Naxos**, around a fifteen-minute bus ride south of Taormina, very much a separate town, with its own holiday trade and nightlife. Indeed, rooms here are plentiful, and you might well want to stay in one of the numerous *pensioni* right on the beach, rather than up in Taormina.

For an alternative day out from Taormina, away from the crowded streets, it's an idea to head **inland**, up into the hills surrounding the nearby village of **Castelmola**.

North: Mazzarò, Spisone and Letojanni

The closest beaches to Taormina are the extremely popular pebbled coves at **MAZZARÒ**, easily reached by a **cable-car** (*funivia*) service – L3000 each way (L5000 return), every fifteen minutes from Via L. Pirandello in Taormina (until after 1am in summer, 8.30pm in winter). There's also a steep **path**, which starts just below the cable-car station.

Whichever way you arrive, the water here is remarkably clear and you can rent pedal boats to explore the local grottoes. Of the two beaches, the southernmost is usually the most packed, fronting its much-photographed islet, the **Isola Bella**, while the little bay to the north (Spiaggia Mazzarò) is emptier and shelters a very reasonable restaurant, the *Trattoria Il Barcaiolo*, whose terrace looks out over beached fishing-boats. If you're still searching for a bed, there are a dozen small **hotels** here, too, ranged along the main road and above the beaches, though get the tourist office to ring for you first from Taormina: cheapest are *La Conchiglia*, in Piazzale Funivia (☎0942.24.739; ②), near the cable-car station, and *Villa Moschella*, Via Nazionale 240 (☎0942.23.328; ③; mid-March to Sept). Recommended, though devilishly expensive in summer, is the *Villa Sant'Andrea*, Via Nazionale 137 (☎0942.23.125; ⑧), right on the beach, with the water lapping under the balconies. Expect to pay over L500,000 for a room here in peak season, and about half that in low season.

Spisone and Letojanni

The beach bars and restaurants at **SPISONE**, north again, are also accessible by path from Taormina, this time from below the cemetery in town (off Via Guardiola Vecchia). It's around half an hour's walk, though there are also buses that make the trip from Taormina's bus terminal, passing Isola Bella and Mazzarò on the way.

From Spisone, the coast opens out and the beaches get wider. **LETOJANNI**, 5km from Taormina, is a little resort in its own right, with some rather more ordinary bars and shops, and a few fishing-boats on a sandy beach. There's a superb **restaurant** here, *Da Nino*, at Via L. Rizzo 29 (☎0942.36.147; closed Tues in winter), attracting fans from Taormina and beyond – a great place to eat fish, well worth the steepish prices.

In summer, Letojanni gets as busy as anywhere else on this stretch, but it would-n't be a bad place **to stay** out of season: *Da Nino* has ten rooms with or without bath (② out of season; otherwise ③), and there are several other cheapish *pensioni* nearby. If you want to stay along the seafront, try *Da Peppe*, Via Vittorio Emanuele 345 (☎0942.36.159; ④, but cheaper outside July & Aug; March–Oct), which also has a good restaurant over on the beach, Peppe himself presiding from behind a bushy beard. There are also two nearby **campsites**: *Paradise International* (☎0942.36.306; April–Oct), about 1km north up the coast, and the larger but equal-ly well-equipped *Eurocamping Marmaruca* (☎0942.36.676), 3km away in the same direction. Regular buses head back to Taormina, passing Spisone and the Isola Bella, and trains link the village with Taormina-Giardini station.

South: Giardini-Naxos

Roomier and better for swimming are the sands **south of Taormina**, principally at **GIARDINI-NAXOS**. The wide, curving bay – easily seen from Taormina's ter-races – was the launching point of Garibaldi's 1860 attack on the Bourbon troops in Calabria and, equally significantly, the site of the first Greek colony in Sicily. An attractive and obvious stop for ships sailing between Greece and southern Italy, there was a settlement here by 734 BC, named Naxos after the Greek island from which the colonists came, though it was never very important. The **excavations** (daily 9am–1hr before sunset; L4000) lie right on the cape, Capo Schisò, the entrance in between two restaurants. The remains are very low-key – a long stretch of ancient, lava-built city wall, two covered kilns and a sketchy temple – but it's a pleasant walk through the lemon groves and there's a small but mildly interesting **museo archeologico** on the site, which houses some of the finds and stays open until 11pm Thursday to Saturday in summer. To visit the site, walk or take the bus from Taormina to Naxos/Recanati and follow the signs ("*Scavi*").

Giardini itself, the sprawling town backing the beach, is an excellent alternative to Taormina as a source of accommodation and food. Prices tend to be a good bit cheaper, and in high season, if you've arrived by train, it's probably worth trying here first; again, though, starting early in the day is a good idea. The **beach** itself is among the most popular in the whole of Sicily, large parts of it partitioned off and maintained by private lidos, where you can rent sun loungers, umbrellas and water-sports gear. Nearly all have associated bar-restaurants, too, so provided you've come with enough cash there's little incentive to leave the sands all day.

Around the cape, the next bay south is largely taken up by the holiday village of **Recanati**. This is the end of the line for buses from Taormina and, though the beach here is fairly long, it's not at all an attractive target. Almost without excep-tion, every building is either a package-tour hotel or a block of holiday apart-ments, and it's a long walk to Giardini for a decent bar or restaurant.

Getting there, accommodation and practicalities

Buses run every thirty minutes to Giardini from Taormina's bus terminal, the last one at 11.45pm in summer, and 9.45pm the rest of the time. Last one back to Taormina is at 11.15pm in summer, 7.45pm in winter, from the stop outside the bar-restaurant *Da Angelo*, opposite the Chiesa Immacolata, on Via Tysandros by the seafront. **Taxis** back to Taormina cost around L20,000.

Via Tysandros runs right the way around the bay, with the **tourist office** at no. 54 (July–Sept Mon–Fri 8.30am–2pm & 3.30–6.30pm, Sat 8.30am–2pm & 4.30–7.30pm; Oct–June closed Sat & Sun; ☎0942.51.010), and an **exchange office** at no. 78. Beyond the tourist office, Via Tysandros becomes Via Schisò, curving round as far as the headland and fishing harbour, while Via Naxos runs behind, and parallel to, much of Via Tysandros/Via Schisò.

If you're looking for a **place to stay**, you could do worse than start at the tourist office, which recommends centrally located, budget hotels. Good initial choices include: *La Sirena*, Via Schisò 36 (☎0942.51.853; ②), at the far end of the road, next to the pier; *Villa Palmar*, Via Naxos 23 (☎0942.52.448; ②); or *Otello*, Via Tysandros 62 (☎0942.51.009; ②). A grade up, there is the central, German-run *Villa Moro* at Via Naxos 47 (☎0942.51.839; ③), and *Del Sole*, Via Naxos 98 (☎0942.51.159; ④). But there are loads of other possibilities, from *pensioni* to smart hotels, and if these are full, or don't appeal, just take a walk along the seafront and see which of the others have room, as well as looking out for "*camere*" signs above the trattorias. Another option if you intend to stay in the area for some time is to take a **furnished apartment**. Like Taormina, they're cheaper in winter and rented by the month only in summer, but the prices here are a good bit more realistic – ask in *Immobiliare Naxos* (☎0942.51.184), Via Vittorio Emanuele 58; they speak English.

The **campsite**, *Maretna* (☎0942.52.794; mid-March to mid-Oct) is fairly central, off Via San Giusto, but is poorly equipped and has almost no shade; get off the bus from Taormina at the Chiesa Immacolata, cross the train tracks and turn left. A better choice would be to catch any bus for Catania, getting off after about five minutes (ask for San Marco, near Calatabiano) and walk a couple of kilometres towards the sea: two campsites sit within a few minutes of each other on Via San Marco, the best being the *Almoetia* (☎095.641.936), equipped with restaurant, a market and plenty of shade, and the prices aren't bad.

You can **rent bikes** in Giardini-Naxos from Etna Rent, Via Casarsa 27, a turning off Via Dalmazia (☎0942.51.972), with prices at around L15,000 per day, or L87,000 a week.

Restaurants and bars

Giardini's **pizzerias** and **restaurants** are consistently better value than Taormina's. Of the cheaper places, best is the friendly ristorante-pizzeria attached to the *Lido Europa* (opposite the Chiesa Immacolata, on Via Tysandros), and there are fine pizzas, a big antipasto table and fresh pasta at the moderately priced *Fratelli Marano*, Via Naxos 181. The *Arcobaleno*, Via Naxos 169, also serves pizzas and has plenty of grilled fish specials, while *Polli all'Inferno*, next door at no. 173, is a good (takeaway) spit-roast chicken joint. For something more upmarket, but still reasonable, try *Da Angelina*, at the end of Via Schisò by the pier, where you can eat excellent home-made pasta and large servings of *zuppa di cozze/pesce* at outdoor tables overlooking the bay; and *La Conchiglia*, Via Naxos 221, which has Sicilian meat specialities, including *agnello* (lamb) and high-quality pizzas.

Of the **bars** along the front, *Café Chantal*, Via Tysandros 116, sees late-night drinking in kitsch pink surroundings; and the *Bar Pancrazio*, nearby, is also popular with a young crowd, who hang out in the glass-fronted pavement section. Drinks are cheap, English is spoken, and ice-cream and panini are available too. The *Bar Nettuno* also does decent snacks at no. 68, and find time for the ice-cream and *granite* at the *Bar Europa*, Via Naxos 195, which closes at about 11pm.

Inland: Castelmola and Monte Vénere

After taking in Taormina's castle, you could always just continue to follow the road (or the marked path) further up to **CASTELMOLA**, 5km above and seemingly sprouting out of the severe crag beneath it. It's around an hour's climb on foot to the village, making it best tackled in the morning or evening, but there are regular buses, too, which you could use to or from Taormina. It's a tiny place, with just one cobbled road, some lean-to houses and the remnants of a long-demolished castle, though modern building has destroyed some of the place's charm, as do the view-seeking tourists with cars who make drink-stops here in summer. There's a fine **bar** in the Lilliputian piazza, with a yellowing newspaper cutting chronicling the visit of Earl Mountbatten (a cousin of the Queen, and Prince Philip's uncle) in the mid-1950s. Most of the bars in town serve a splendid *vino alla mándorla* (almond wine), the sweet local brew. The *Bar Turrisi* also specializes in frankly phallocentric decor, probably intended to give tourists a shock or a smirk – you have been warned. Among the **restaurants** here, most highly recommended is *Il Maniero*, occupying a tower once part of the castle on Salita Castello, with phenomenal views. It might be worth phoning first, as it quickly fills up (☎0942.28.180; closed Wed & Feb).

If you fancy spending the night up here, or using this as a base instead of Taormina, there is one cheap **hotel**, the *Panorama di Sicilia*, Via de Gaspéri 44 (☎0942.28.027; ②), and one expensive one, the *Villa Sonia*, Via Porta Mola 9 (☎0942.28.082; ⑤).

Another couple of hours' walk beyond are the heights of **Monte Vénere** (885m) – take the path behind Castelmola's cemetery – where usually the only other people around are the shepherds. **Returning to Taormina**, through Castelmola, you can vary your route back. At the crossroads just out of Castelmola, a road leads off around Monte Tauro and across the other side of the valley: keep bearing right and you'll eventually end up on Via Fontana Vecchia, which finishes up in town – around a two-hour stroll. Less of a hike is the path (signposted "Taormina"), which leads steeply down behind the castle, entering town on Via Cappuccini.

The Alcántara Valley

Buses from Taormina-Giardini train station (and twice daily from Taormina itself) motor a few kilometres south and then turn inland to coast through the pretty **ALCÁNTARA VALLEY**. It's an hour's ride all told, east into the green hills beyond Taormina, and the bus stops at several small towns, many crowned with ruined medieval castles. The first places you reach, **TRAPPITELLO** and **Gaggi**, are uninviting dormitory suburbs for Taormina and Giardini. But, if you're going by car (the last bus back to Taormina is at about 4pm), Trappitello at least has the attraction of one of Sicily's best rural **restaurants**, inside the Azienda Sant'Antonio farm (closed Thurs), just outside town and above the road to Gaggi (on the right). All the food and wine is reared, grown and made on site: there's usually ravioli stuffed with wild boar and celery, and if you stick to the grand self-service antipasti and the fresh pasta rather than the roast meats, it works out fairly reasonably. There's a supermarket here, too, if you want to take back some home-made cheese and wine.

The Gola di Alcántara

On the other side of Gaggi, the valley is immediately more attractive, the road snaking into the hills and the railway line carried over a viaduct which crosses the Alcántara River (the name, Alcántara, is a corruption of the Arabic word for bridge). For the most part it's fertile, green countryside, with gentle hills supporting a profusion of citrus groves, olive trees and wild flowers, while the road runs over and alongside the river past isolated farms.

Twenty minutes beyond Gaggi, get the bus driver to let you off at the **Gola di Alcántara**, a vast geological cleft in the hillside. The deep, grey-green gorge, with a silent frog-filled river at the bottom, invites a splash around, and there's a bar and restaurant above if you want them. There are steps down from the main road (beyond the official entrance) or a lift (L3500 return) on the site, which also rents out thigh-length boots for some serious gorge-wading (L10,000). These (or at least some strong, gripped plastic shoes) are essential to get beyond the first swirling, rocky pool, though the boots are fairly useless for some stretches, as the water can reach neck-level. Take a waterproof bag with you in any case to avoid your things getting wet (there's nowhere to leave them), and you can use it to carry a change of clothes. Inside the gorge, it can get very hairy indeed, with biting insects, freezing waterfalls and soaring stone walls providing the obstacles; that said, it is enormous fun, and it takes about an hour to clamber as far up as you can get. The last bus back to Taormina leaves at 3.45pm Monday to Saturday, 2.25pm on Sunday.

Francavilla and Castiglione

You could walk from the gorge, or pick up the next bus on to **FRANCAVILLA DI SICILIA**, 4km away, alongside the river and overlooked by the few surviving walls of its hillside castle. There's a path up to the ruins, and although much of the town is newly built there's a fair amount of interest in the couple of old central streets, and in walking up to the convent that peers over town and river. You might want **to stay** in Francavilla, both for the scenery and the fact that it has the area's only hotels: the *Centrale* (☎0942.981.052; ②) on the main road through town (shared bathrooms only), and the smarter *D'Orange Alcantara* (☎0942.981.374; ⑤), on the way in from the Gola di Alcántara, the latter used in the summer by package tourists holidaying around Taormina.

There's a **train station** in Francavilla, for local trains back to Taormina or west to Randazzo (see p.228), while the bus keeps on to **CASTIGLIONE DI SICILIA**, 5km above. This is an old and decrepit mountain settlement, the numerous church spires and the solid, rock-built castle making an inviting target as the bus inches up the switchback road. It's easy to spend a couple of hours just wandering the quiet streets, which meander up as far as a small piazza at the top of town containing a bar and a barber with a sign in English offering "fashion" haircuts. The town was a formidable medieval stronghold as the doughty castle remains attest.

If you're heading back to Taormina, you can either hang around for the return bus to Giardini (it leaves from outside the bar at Via Regina Margherita 174, back down the hill from the piazza), or – better – walk down the hill to Francavilla, an easy hike, and pick up a bus or train from there. (Castiglione's train station, incidentally, is miles away, impractical for visiting the town.) The walk takes around an hour, and at the bottom of the crag, on the way into Francavilla, you cross a sturdy medieval bridge. Just beyond here, at the back of the factory at the side of the road, is the sad ruin of a **Byzantine church**, one of several in the area left to rot.

Beyond the Alcántara valley: some day-trips

There are a handful of **round-trip** alternatives from Taormina if you want to make a day of it. Infrequent buses from Castiglione head to Catania (p.206), or two a day go on to Randazzo to the west, from where it's an hour by local train back to Taormina-Giardini. Alternatively, it's around 9km through Castiglione to Linguaglossa (p.229), where you can pick up the round-Etna railway – a journey described in the next chapter. One last possibility for those with their own transport is to return to Francavilla, from where the SS185 climbs up into the Monti Peloritani and to Novara di Sicilia, and then down to the Tyrrhenian coast. Both town and route are covered on pp.130–131.

festivals

January
1–6 New Year celebrations in **Taormina**. Puppet shows, folk-singing and concerts, ending on Twelfth Night.

February & March
Carnevale Carnival celebrations in **Taormina** and **Giardini-Naxos**: processional floats, fireworks and music for three days.

May
Last week Sfilato del Carretto: puppet shows, a parade of painted carts and folk-singing in **Taormina's** most traditional festival.

July
21–30 International Film Festival in **Taormina**, with screenings in the Greek theatre.

31 onwards Dance, drama, film and music; all performances held in the Greek theatre in **Taormina**; runs until October.

August
12–14 Procession of the *giganti* in **Messina**.

15 Ferragosto procession and fireworks in **Messina**.

December
20 onwards Christmas celebrations in **Taormina**. Puppet shows, folk-singing parades and concerts.

travel details

Trains
Messina to: Catania (every 40min; 1hr 40min); Cefalù (10–16 daily; 2hr 45min); Milan (3–4 daily; 15–17hr); Milazzo (1–2 hourly; 40min); Naples (2–3 daily; 6hr 30min); Rome (6–7 daily; 8–9hr); Palermo (up to 15 daily; 3hr 30min–6hr); Taormina (every 40min; 1hr).

Taormina to: Catania (2 hourly; 50min); Francavilla di Sicilia (3–6 daily; 25min); Messina (every 40min; 1hr); Randazzo (1–2 daily; 1hr 20min); Siracusa (hourly; 2hr 30min).

Buses
Messina to: Ali Terme (1–2 hourly Mon–Sat, 4 Sun; 45min); Barcellona (10 daily Mon–Sat; 1hr); Capo d'Orlando (12 daily Mon–Sat; 1hr 15min–1hr 50min); Catania (fast service 1–3 hourly Mon–Sat, 13 Sun; 1hr 35min; regular service 7 daily Mon–Sat, 1 Sun; 3hr–3hr 30min); Catania airport (11 daily Mon–Sat, 5 Sun; 1hr 45min); Forza d'Agrò (1 daily Mon–Sat; 1hr 30min); Giardini-Naxos (13 daily Mon–Sat, 2 Sun; 2hr); Itala (8 daily Mon–Sat; 50min); Letojanni (14 daily Mon–Sat, 4 Sun; 1hr–1hr 30min); Milazzo (fast service 1–2 hourly Mon–Sat, 1 Sun; 50min; regular service 11 daily Mon–Sat, 4 Sun; 1hr 20min); Palermo (4 daily Mon–Sat, 2 Sun; 3hr 15min); Patti (7 daily Mon–Sat; 1hr 15min); Randazzo (4 daily Mon–Sat; 2hr 15min); Rome (4 daily; 9hr); Sant'Aléssio (14 daily Mon–Sat, 4 Sun; 1hr 15min); Santa Teresa di Riva (1–2 hourly Mon–Sat, 4 Sun; 1hr 10min); Scaletta (hourly

Mon–Sat, 4 daily Sun; 35min); Taormina (13 daily Mon–Sat, 4 Sun; 1hr 15min–1hr 45min); Tíndari (2 daily Mon–Sat; 1–2hr).

Taormina to: Castelmola (5–6 daily; 20min); Castiglione (2 daily Mon–Sat; 1hr 15min); Catania (hourly; 1hr–1hr 45min); Catania airport (2 daily Mon–Sat, 3 Sun; 1hr 15min–2hr); Forza d'Agrò (2–3 daily; 30min); Francavilla di Sicilia (4 daily Mon–Sat, 1 Sun; 55min); Giardini-Naxos (1–2 hourly; 15min); Gola di Alcántara (4 daily Mon–Sat, 1 Sun; 1hr); Isola Bella (roughly every 30min in summer, hourly or less in winter & Sun; 10min); Letojanni (roughly every 30min in summer, hourly or less in winter & Sun; 25min); Mazzarò (roughly every 30min in summer, hourly or less in winter & Sun; 12min); Messina (14 daily Mon–Sat, 3 Sun; 35min–1hr 20min); Recanati (every 15–30min in summer, less in winter & Sun; 25min); Spisone (every 30min in summer, hourly or less in winter & Sun; 15min); Trappitello (4–7 daily; 40min).

Taormina-Giardini train station to: Bronte (3 daily Mon–Sat; 1hr 40min); Castiglione (6 daily Mon–Sat; 55min); Cesarò (3 daily Mon–Sat; 2hr 20min); Francavilla di Sicilia (6 daily Mon–Sat; 40min); Gola di Alcántara (9 daily Mon–Sat; 25min); Randazzo (3 daily Mon–Sat; 1hr 20min).

From Santa Teresa di Riva to: Messina Casalvécchio Sículo (5 daily Mon–Sat, 3 Sun; 20min); Sávoca (5 daily Mon–Sat, 3 Sun; 15min).

Ferries
Messina to: Villa San Giovanni (FS every 45min, Caronte every 20min, every 40–60min at night; 35min).

Hydrofoils and fast ferries
Messina to: Lípari (4 daily June–Sept, 1 daily Oct–May; 1hr 30min); Panarea (2 daily June–Sept; 2hr 5min–3hr 30min); Réggio di Calabria (every 20min; 20min); Rinella (1 daily; 2hr 15min); Santa Marina Salina (4 daily June–Sept, 1 daily Oct–May; 2hr 10min–2hr 35min); Strómboli (2 daily June–Sept; 1hr 30min–3hr 15min); Vulcano (4 daily June–Sept, 1 daily Oct–May; 1hr 20min–3hr 10min).

CHAPTER FIVE

CATANIA, ETNA AND AROUND

Bang in the middle of the Ionian coast, **Catania** is Sicily's second largest city and a point of arrival for most of the island's foreign visitors, who land at the airport just outside. But unlike other stops on the mostly pretty, indented shoreline, Catania is by no means a prime tourist destination: there's heavy industry here, a large port and some depressing suburbs, glimpsed as you edge in on the train. Still, it's a lively city with a uniformly grand architecture bestowed upon it after the late seventeenth-century earthquake that wrecked the whole region. Making full use of the local building material (lava), the eighteenth-century architect Giovanni Vaccarini gave the city a lofty, noble air. Despite the neglect of many of the churches and the disintegrating, grey mansions, there's still much of interest. Delving about reveals lava-encrusted Roman relics, surviving alongside some of the finest Baroque work on the island; and the **university**, the first in Sicily, adds a youthful feel to the streets.

Excursions from the city take in the villages around the town of **Acireale**, small-scale resorts with good swimming from the rocks and fresh fish in the trattorias. But the most rewarding expedition is to drive or take a bus a few kilometres north to **Mount Etna**, Europe's highest volcano. Still active, its massive presence dominates the whole of this part of the coast. The towns and villages around, like Catania, are built from the lava it periodically ejects. A road and a small single-track railway, the **Circumetnea**, circumnavigate the lower slopes, passing through a series of hardy towns, like **Randazzo**, almost foolishly sited in the shadow of the volcano and surrounded by swirls of black volcanic rock. Reaching the top, or at least the lower craters below the summit, is possible too, either on foot or by mountain bus – both are heady experiences.

CATANIA AND THE COAST

First impressions don't say much at all for **CATANIA** – on an initial encounter possibly the island's gloomiest spot. Built from black-grey volcanic stone, the central streets can feel suffocating, dark with the shadows of tall grimy Baroque churches and *palazzi*. The influence of Etna is pervasive: in the buildings, in the brooding vistas you get of the mountain at the end of Catania's streets – even the city's main thoroughfare is named after the volcano.

But fight the urge to cut and run, as Catania is one of the most intriguing of Sicily's cities, with a **history** to match. Some of the island's first **Greek colonists**, probably Chalcidinians from Naxos, settled the site as early as 729 BC, becoming

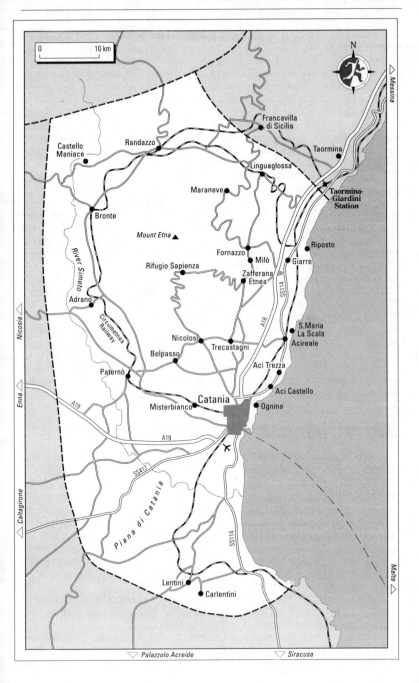

so influential that their laws were eventually adopted by all the Ionian colonies of Magna Graecia. Later, the city was one of the first to fall to the **Romans**, under whom it prospered greatly and, unusually for Sicily, Catania's surviving ancient relics are all Roman. In the early Christian period Catania witnessed the martyrdom of **Agatha**, who, having rejected the improper advances of the praetor, Quintianus, was put to death in 252. She was later canonized (becoming the patron saint of Catania) and it was her miraculous intervention that reputedly saved the city from complete volcanic destruction in the seventeenth century. Even with the saint's protection, Catania has had its fair share of disasters: Etna erupted in 1669, engulfing the city in lava, and the **earthquake** of 1693 devastated the whole of southeastern Sicily.

Given these repeated catastrophes, the **modern city** is overshadowed in terms of historical monuments by Palermo. Still, there are some remarkable Baroque churches – dating from the eighteenth-century rebuilding of the city – and the stumpy remnants of its medieval castle. Catania is also Sicily's only large urban centre outside the capital: first and foremost, a businesslike, commercial city, with the island's busiest market and some of its best traditional food. While drivers usually choose to see the volcano from the prettier towns and villages roundabout, if you're travelling by public transport you'll have to leave for Etna from Catania itself.

Catania is a major transport terminus, not only for buses and trains south to Siracusa, but also for travel west, including services to Enna, Agrigento and Palermo. Before moving on, it's worth taking day-trips out to the nearby towns and villages: there's a diverting **coastal route north**, through small bathing resorts, to Baroque **Acireale**; while **south** of Catania you can make a quick escape to the good beaches fronting the gulf, behind which lies the flat and mostly uninhabited **Piana di Catania**, the fertile plain that traditionally fed the city. At the plain's southern extremity sits **Lentini**, close to the site of one of the earliest Greek colonies to be founded in Sicily.

Arrival, information and city transport

The **airport**, Fontanarossa, is 5km south of the city and is the entry point of most charter flights to Sicily (for flight information, call ☎095.730.6266 or 095.730.6277). To get into the city, take the Alibus (every 20min 5.30am–midnight; L1300) from right outside, which runs to the central Piazza Stesicoro (on Via Etnea) and to Stazione Centrale in around twenty minutes; tickets are available from the *tabacchi* on the first floor of the departures hall. A taxi from the rank outside the airport will cost around L35,000 for the same journey. Note that buses to and from Siracusa, Taormina, Ragusa, Agrigento, Enna and Palermo make a stop at the airport; and there are direct services, too, from the airport to Messina and Milazzo (for the Aeolian Islands). Timetables are posted near the tourist office in the arrivals hall.

Catamarans from Malta dock on the Molo Vecchio, just off Via Dusmet, from where it's a short walk to Piazza del Duomo; bus #4/27 also runs past the dock into the centre and terminates at Stazione Centrale.

All main-line trains use **Stazione Centrale** in Piazza Giovanni XXIII (information on ☎095.531.625), northeast of the centre, which has **left-luggage** facilities (6.30am–10.30pm; L5000 per day). You could walk into the city from here, though if you're aiming for Piazza del Duomo or Via Etnea it's quicker to jump on a bus; see "City transport" below. All other **buses**, both regional from Catania province and island-wide, also stop at various points in Piazza Giovanni XXIII, across from Stazione Centrale. It's a very large square-cum-parking-lot, bisected by fast-moving traffic, so keep your wits about you. Night arrivals would do well to take a taxi into the centre (around L10,000–12,000), since the station area isn't the most salubrious in town.

For arrivals and departures on the narrow-gauge Etna train, the **Stazione Circumetnea** is at Corso delle Province 13 (for information ☎095.374.842 or 095.534.323), at the junction of Corso Italia and Via della Libertà, around 1km north of the main station. There are more details about the round-Etna train on p.226.

For all **departure information**, including full details of getting to the airport, bus companies, ferry and catamaran operators, and "travel agents", see "Listings", pp.220–221.

Information

There's a small **tourist office** (June–Sept daily 7am–9.30pm; Oct–May Mon–Fri 9am–1pm & 4–7pm; ☎095.730.6255) inside Stazione Centrale on platform #1: usually very helpful, with accommodation listings and free maps. The main office is at Via D. Cimarosa 10 (Mon–Sat 9am–7pm, Sun 10am–6pm; ☎095.730.6211 or 095.730.6233, fax 095.316.407), signposted off Via Etnea and down Via Pacini. There's also an **information office** at the airport (daily 8am–10pm; ☎095.730.6266 or 095.730.6277), again with free maps, accommodation lists and bus timetables.

City transport

You'll need little more than a map and your own two feet **to get around the city**. Most of the sights are confined within a small area, the centre of which is Piazza del Duomo – just a twenty-minute walk from the train station. From here, Via Etnea steams off north, lined with the city's most fashionable shops and cafés; fish market and port lie behind to the south; the best of the Baroque quarter, to the west.

You'll rarely need to use the AMT **city buses** (information ☎095.736.0450) in Catania itself, though they'll save you a walk into the centre from the station – and you'll have to jump on one to get to the airport and the campsites. There are **stops** immediately outside Stazione Centrale: buses #1/4, #4/7 and #4/8 run into the centre, along Via VI Aprile and Via Vittorio Emanuele to Piazza del Duomo. Other central pick-up points are Piazza del Duomo itself and Piazza Stesicoro (where you can catch the buses already listed); and Piazza Borsellino (below Piazza del Duomo), where there's a stop for the airport Alibus and for #4/27 and #5/38 (for the campsites). **Tickets** (L1300) are valid for two journeys within ninety minutes and are available from *tabacchi*, the newsagents inside Stazione Centrale, or the booth outside it. The same outlets also sell a Biglietto Turístico (L3500), valid for one day's unlimited travel on all local AMT bus routes.

There are **taxi** ranks at Stazione Centrale, Piazza del Duomo and Via Etnea (Piazza Stesicoro). To call a cab, ring CST (☎095.330.966); there's also an all-night service, Taxi Auto Púbblico (☎095.386.794).

Finally, if you're planning to **rent a car** on arrival, consider renting from agencies in the city to avoid the surcharge on airport rentals; see "Listings" (p.220) for addresses and numbers. Also note that **parking in the centre** is extremely difficult – another good reason to rent in Catania itself on the day you leave.

Accommodation

Finding a vacant hotel room in summer, particularly August, can be very difficult; it's always as well to reserve in advance if you possibly can. There's a shortage of rock-bottom choices, although as long as you plan ahead you'll be able to stay very centrally. That said, you should know that parts of central Catania have a reputation for petty crime and violence – be careful if you're out on your own at night. If you're happy with security at your hotel, leave your valuables there before going out.

Campsites are all a bus ride out of the city: there's one to the north, while buses #4/27 from Stazione Centrale or Porta Uzeda, and #5/38 from Piazza Borsellino, head to the long beach south of Catania where there are three more big campsites, along Viale Kennedy. All have bungalows available, too (two-berth ④ in summer, ① in winter; four-berth ⑤ summer, ① winter), though you'll need to reserve well in advance.

Hotels

Central Palace, Via Etnea 218 (☎095.325.344, fax 095.715.8939). Catania's top hotel, in prime position on the main drag, with the best eating, drinking and shopping opportunities all close at hand. Come outside July and August, and you should be able to negotiate some decent room discounts too. ⑦.

Europensione, Piazza dei Mártiri 8 (☎095.531.152, fax 095.531.007). A practical one-night stop, not too far from the train station, with comfortable, spacious rooms and separate, spotless bathrooms – it can be extremely noisy, though. No credit cards. ①.

Ferrara, 2nd floor, Via Umberto I 66 (☎095.316.000, fax 095.313.060). A fair old walk from the train station or the duomo, but near some good eating and drinking places. It's looking a little shabby these days, though the rooms with balconies bring a bit of street-side cheer. Prices fall to ① in winter. No credit cards. ②.

Gresi, 3rd floor, Via Pacini 28 (☎ & fax 095.322.709). One of the best places in town, close to the Villa Bellini, kept spick-and-span and cheerily run, though a little overpriced and the plumbing can be idiosyncratic. There's a welcome lift. No credit cards. ②.

Holland International, Via Vittorio Emanuele 8 (☎095.533.605). On the first floor of an ageing *palazzo*, on the way into town from Stazione Centrale (at the eastern end of the street). It could do with a lick of paint, but is otherwise clean and welcoming, with a Dutch owner who knows the region well. There's a comfortable, if eccentrically decorated lounge overlooking Piazza dei Mártiri and, less pleasingly, a midnight curfew. In summer, rooms with bath could just nudge into the next price category. No credit cards. ①.

Moderno, Via Alessi 9 (☎095.326.250, fax 095.326.674). In a quiet cul-de-sac off Via Crociferi, this swish hotel is as well placed as anything in the city centre. Facilities are much as you'd imagine at the price – including welcome heating in winter – though there are some bargain singles available. ④.

ACCOMMODATION PRICE CODES

These represent the **cheapest available double room in high season**, usually – but not always – without en-suite bathroom or shower. Out of season, you'll often be able to negotiate a lower price than those suggested here. For more information about hotels and room prices, see p.27. The categories are:

① under L60,000	④ L120,000–150,000	⑦ L250,000–300,000
② L60,000–90,000	⑤ L150,000–200,000	⑧ over L300,000
③ L90,000–120,000	⑥ L200,000–250,000	

Roma, Via della Libertà 63 (☎095.534.911). Functional, well-appointed rooms (including singles), close to Stazione Centrale; a useful fall-back for late-night arrivals. No credit cards. ②.

Royal, Via Antonio di San Giuliano 337 (☎095.313.448, fax 095.325.611). Good location with views, west of Via Etnea where the street starts to climb in steps. ④.

Rubens, Via Etnea 196 (☎095.317.073, fax 095.321.277). Best budget choice if you want to stay on the main Via Etnea, though with only seven rooms (all without bath) it's always busy. ①.

Savona, Via Vittorio Emanuele 210 (☎095.326.982, fax 095.715.8169). Well placed, close to Piazza del Duomo on a brightly lit main road. Prices can be relatively high, especially in summer, but it makes a safe, clean, central base. No credit cards. ②.

Camping

Jonio, Via Villini a Mare 2, Ognina (☎095.491.139). Smaller-scale than most of the local sites, and quite a way north of the city centre, at Ognina (see p.222). From Stazione Centrale, take bus #4/48.

Villagio Souvenir, Viale Kennedy 71 (☎095.341.162 or 095.355.440). The cheapest and smallest campsite south of the city, more open in aspect than its counterparts. June–Sept.

Internazionale La Plaja, Viale Kennedy 47 (☎095.340.880). Popular, monster-sized campsite, near the beach, with a disco. Horse-riding also available.

Villagio Turístico Europeo, Viale Kennedy 91 (☎095.591.026). Similar setup to *La Plaja*, though rather functional. Mid-June to mid-October.

The City

You could see the whole of central **Catania** in a busy day's strolling, but the city really deserves more of your time if you can spare it. In any case, you'll need the extra time to get around the restrictive opening hours of the city's attractions – and, besides, there's vigorous street activity in the swarming markets and along the main Via Etnea well worth staying to enjoy.

Something to be aware of as you potter around the crumbling back-streets of the Baroque town is the high incidence of **petty crime**. Catania has a well-deserved reputation for thievery and, while the main streets are safe enough, don't flash money and cameras around too obviously in the more run-down areas or the markets, and avoid badly lit roads at night.

Around Piazza del Duomo

Catania's main square, **Piazza del Duomo**, at the bottom of Via Etnea, is a handy orientation point: from here, most things of interest are only a few minutes' walk away. It's also one of Sicily's most engaging piazzas, rebuilt completely in the first half of the eighteenth century by the Palermitan, Giovanni Battista Vaccarini, who was made Catania's municipal architect in 1730. He surrounded the square with elegant buildings, like the **Municipio** on the northern side, finished in 1741, providing some relief from the grandeur by adding the central **elephant fountain**: an eighteenth-century lava elephant supporting an Egyptian obelisk on its back. This has become the city's symbol and features an inscription, *Agatina MSSHDE-PL* – apparently an acronym for "The mind of St Agatha is sane and spontaneous, honouring God and liberating the city".

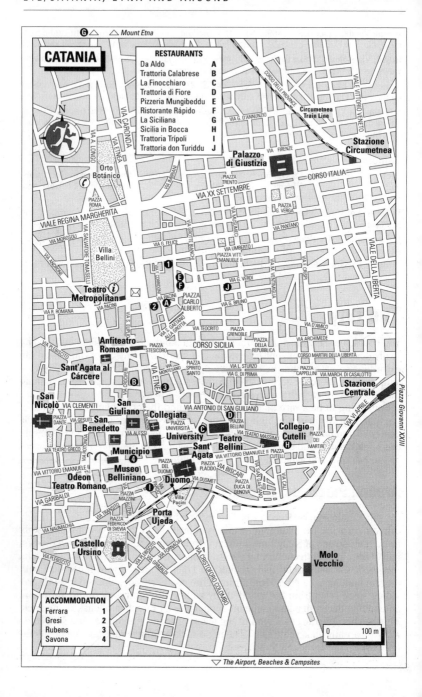

CATANIA

RESTAURANTS

Da Aldo	A
Trattoria Calabrese	B
La Finocchiaro	C
Trattoria di Fiore	D
Pizzeria Mungibeddu	E
Ristorante Rápido	F
La Siciliana	G
Sicilia in Bocca	H
Trattoria Trípoli	I
Trattoria don Turiddu	J

ACCOMMODATION

Ferrara	1
Gresi	2
Rubens	3
Savona	4

0   100 m

▽ *The Airport, Beaches & Campsites*

The Duomo

Cross over to the piazza's eastern flank for Vaccarini's grandest project, the **Duomo** (closed noon–5pm). Originally founded by Count Roger in the eleventh century, only the marvellous medieval apses, beautifully crafted from volcanic rock, survived the 1693 earthquake. They are viewable through the gate at Via Vittorio Emanuele 159. Vaccarini's heavy Baroque touch is readily apparent from the imposing facade, on which he tagged granite columns filched from Catania's Roman amphitheatre.

The interior is no less grand, adorned by a rich series of **chapels**: the Cappella di Sant'Agata (to whom the duomo is dedicated) is to the right of the choir, and houses the relics paraded through the city on the saint's festival days; next to it, entered through a fine sixteenth-century doorway, is the Cappella della Madonna, with a Roman sarcophagus which holds the ashes of the Aragonese kings – Frederick II, Louis and Frederick III. It's worth looking in the sacristy too, for a fresco depicting the disastrous 1669 eruption of Mount Etna, completed only eight years after the event, while a wander through the rest of the church reveals the uncovered medieval foundations and ancient columns. The tomb of the composer Bellini, a native of the city, is set in the floor before the second column on the right as you enter, inscribed with a phrase from his opera, *La Sonnámbula*.

Along Via Vittorio Emanuele II

Via Vittorio Emanuele II cuts across the piazza, its eastern arm running towards the sea. Opposite the duomo, the church of **Sant'Agata** (Mon–Sat 8am–5pm) is another of Vaccarini's creations, though this time the pale grey Rococo interior dates from after his death: capitals, iron balconies, even the chandeliers and aisle lights, are a profusion of ruffs, curls and spidery ornamentation. The church entrance is just off the main road, on Via Raddusa. Slightly further on is the little **Piazza Plácido**, with an eighteenth-century church of the same name and a house, at Via Vittorio Emanuele 140, that was the home of early nineteenth-century Catanese erotic poet Domenico Tempio. It's now desperately neglected, though you can still make out the fairly raunchy figures of men and women playing with themselves, and supporting the balcony above the blackened doorway. Further east, past the **Collegio Cutelli**, now a school but distinguished by Vaccarini's round courtyard, Via Vittorio Emanuele ends in **Piazza dei Mártiri** – marked by a statue of St Agatha atop a Roman column, looking over the harbour.

From the market to the Castello Ursino

Back in Piazza del Duomo, head for Catania's noisome open-air **market** – at its best early in the day – either by walking down through the towering late seventeenth-century **Porta Uzeda** and bearing right, or by going south across the piazza and nipping down the steps behind a marble fountain. This takes you right into the action – usually over by the early afternoon, but until then almost frightening in its intensity. A medieval warren of narrow streets spreads around the fish **market** (the Pescheria), slabs and buckets full of twitching fish, eels and shellfish, some of which – mussels and sea urchins – you might be offered, cut open, to try. There are endless lanes full of vegetable and fruit stalls, too, as well as bloody butcher's tables and one or two excellent lunchtime trattorias.

The roads wind from here through a dilapidated neighbourhood to an open space (Piazza Federico di Svevia) punctured by the **Castello Ursino**, once the proud fortress of Frederick II. Originally the castle stood on a rocky cliff, over the beach, but following the 1669 eruption, which reclaimed this entire area from the sea, all that remains is the blackened keep. The **Museo Cívico** (Tues–Sat 9am–1pm & 3–6pm, Sun 9am–1pm; free) is housed inside and makes excellent use of the gloomy interior. Wooden walkways run the breadth of the castle, looking down into the foundations and basement rooms, while the walls of the central chambers are hung with retrieved mosaic fragments, stone inscriptions and tombstones. Emerging into the interior courtyard you'll find more stacked funerary bits and pieces, columns and inscriptions, while the first floor – reached by external staircase – is used for temporary exhibitions. The interior of the musem is presently undergoing restoration, but when reopened you'll be able to visit its principal treasures, five cases of hand-picked and extraordinarily delightful items, ranging from a Greek terracotta statuette of two goddesses being pulled in a sea carriage by mythical beasts, to a seventeenth-century French pistol, inlaid in silver and depicting rabbits, fish and cherubs.

Beyond the spruced-up gardens fronting the castle, the houses hereabouts are in a fairly ruinous state and you might as well head back towards the centre (following Via Auteri). It's easy to miss **Piazza Mazzini**, straddling Via Garibaldi, an arcaded square, that must have been much prettier once, constructed from 32 columns, presently scaffolded, which originally formed part of a Roman basilica.

SPAGHETTI ALLA NORMA

Spaghetti alla Norma – cooked with tomato and aubergines/eggplant (*melanzane* in Italian) – is served in most local restaurants. Here's how to prepare it:

Ingredients (*serves 4*)
2 aubergines/eggplants, cut into 1/2 inch(1cm) slices
2 tablespoons (30ml) olive oil
2 cloves of garlic, peeled and crushed with the back of a knife
1 tablespoon tomato purée
1lb (454g) fresh plum tomatoes, chopped roughly (use tinned if unavailable)
10oz (300g) spaghetti
grated hard ricotta cheese
2 tablespoons chopped basil leaves
salt
black pepper

Spread aubergine/eggplant slices on a plate, sprinkle with salt and leave for thirty minutes; this removes the bitter oils. Wash the slices under cold water, dry, and then fry on both sides in a large frying pan until golden brown (use a low heat). Put to one side.

Gently fry the garlic cloves in 2 tablespoons of olive oil for two minutes, then add chopped (or tinned) tomatoes, 1 tablespoon tomato purée, and a pinch of salt and pepper, and sauté for thirty minutes, or until the sauce reduces slightly. Add half the chopped basil leaves to the sauce and stir.

Cook the spaghetti in boiling water until *al dente*, drain and place in bowls. Spoon the tomato sauce on top of the spaghetti, add slices of fried aubergine and top with grated ricotta and the remainder of the basil leaves. Eat with a robust red wine.

Via Crocíferi and the Teatro Romano

Just north of Piazza Mazzini is perhaps the most interesting section of the city – a tangle of churches, narrow eighteenth-century streets and archeological remains that begins as you cross over Via Garibaldi and walk up to Via Vittorio Emanuele II. Everything close by is big and Baroque, and even the narrow **Via Crocíferi** – which strikes north from the main road under an imposing arch – is lined with some arresting religious and secular buildings, little changed since the eighteenth century. The street is closed to traffic while restoration work continues; excavations along here have revealed sections of Roman mosaic paving. Amble up Via Crocíferi and you can peer in the courtyards of the *palazzi* (one with a plantation of banana trees) and poke around the churches – best of which is **San Giuliano**, about halfway up on the right, which has a facade by Vaccarini and an echoing elliptical interior.

Back at the bottom of the street, opposite San Francesco church, the house where the composer Vincenzo Bellini was born in 1801 is now open as the **Museo Belliniano** (Mon–Fri 9am–1.30pm, Sun 9am–12.30pm; free), an agreeable little collection of photographs, original scores, his death mask and other memorabilia. Bellini composed his first work at 6, and was only 34 when he died in Paris; his body was transported back to Sicily to be buried. He notches up several tributes around the city, including a piazza, and Catania's main theatre and park all named after him, as well as the ultimate accolade – a pasta dish, *spaghetti alla Norma*, named after one of Bellini's operas (see box for the recipe).

To the west, along Via Vittorio Emanuele, is the **Teatro Romano** (Mon–Sat 9am–1pm & 3–7pm, Sun 9am–1pm; L4000), at no. 266, a surprisingly large chunk of Roman hardware to have survived the city's eighteenth-century refit. Built of lava in the second century AD, on the site of an earlier Greek theatre (it is marked "Teatro Greco" on some maps), much of the seating and the underground passageways are preserved, though all the marble which originally covered it has disappeared; adjacent, there's a smaller **Odeon**, which was used for music and recitations, built between the second and third centuries AD. If the gate is locked you can get a view of it by walking around the block and doubling back on the higher Via Teatro Greco.

San Nicolò

The other way down Via Teatro Greco, west, leads to **Piazza Dante**, a pretty crescent of houses, some of whose ground floors contain little workshops – of cabinetmakers, metalworkers – open to the pavement. Opposite is the unfinished facade of **San Nicolò**, its grim eighteenth-century exterior studded by six enormous, lopped columns. The biggest church in Sicily (105m long), it's currently being restored but there's usually someone around in the early morning to show you the stark interior: undecorated save for the sculpted choir stalls and a meridian line drawn across the floor of the transept, embellished with zodiacal signs. The custodian will probably show you the sacristy, too, but it's doubtful whether you'll be able to climb up to the dome – a shame, as it used to provide one of the best views over the city.

The church is part of the adjoining Benedictine convent, also under restoration and with equally impressive dimensions – it's the second largest convent in Europe after Mafra in Portugal. Officially you can't get in, but there's a gate to the left of the church, through which are the remains of some **Roman walls** and, behind, the massive conventual buildings: from here, you can at least see part of the Baroque exterior, rich in sculpted ornamentation. If you can persuade a workman to open the gate into the convent itself, there are two lovely courtyards beyond, the first containing an overgrown cloistered garden.

Along Via Etnea

Most of the other city sights are ranged around the long and busy **Via Etnea**, which runs north from Piazza del Duomo and out of the city. Following its full length would eventually lead you right to the foothills of Mount Etna – and from the street's northern end there are much-trumpeted views of the peak in the distance. Mostly, you'll be concerned with the southern stretch of Via Etnea, the liveliest section lying between Piazza del Duomo and the Villa Bellini: an out-and-out shopping street, good for browsing and a coffee at one of the popular brightly polished bars.

The west side

Nearly all the notable buildings and churches are on the **west side** of Via Etnea. Past the Municipio, the first square off the street (Piazza dell'Università) holds the main building of the **University**, founded by the Aragonese kings in the fifteenth century. The earthquake postponed its completion until the 1750s, and Vaccarini – again – was responsible for the attractive courtyard.

Further on, **Piazza Stesicoro** marks the modern centre of Catania, an enormous square split into two by Via Etnea, and a useful point to pick up buses. The western side is almost entirely occupied by the sunken, black remains of Catania's **Anfiteatro Romano** (currently closed, though viewable), dating back to the second or third century AD. Although much is still concealed under the surrounding buildings, it's the grandest of Catania's Roman remains. Built from lava blocks, the amphitheatre could hold around sixteen thousand spectators – quite a formidable size – and from the church steps above the square you can see the seating quite clearly, supported by long vaults. When open, there's access down into the **vaults**, where you can wander the black corridors under Piazza Stesicoro. A diagram here shows the original dimensions of the theatre – it's quickly clear that the section you're walking through represents only one tiny excavated corner.

Much more modest is the little twelfth-century church of **Santo Cárcere** (Tues–Sat 4–7pm, Sun 9.30am–noon), above its own square nearby (reached from Via Cappuccini). With strong defensive walls, it was built on the site of the prison where St Agatha was confined before her martyrdom at the hands of the Romans, and a custodian will let you into the third-century **crypt** – now bright with electric candles. More sinister is the chapel's medieval stone doorway, topped by evil, grinning, sculpted heads and apelike creatures.

Back on Via Etnea it's not far to the **Villa Bellini**, just beyond the post office: a large, ornamentally laid-out public garden that provides a welcome touch of greenery and even the occasional concert from the bandstand in the summer. The stand-up drinks bar here is where the local police hang out, whiling away time between meal breaks – on the bar are pinned rather touching photos of the regulars, posing stiffly in uniform on horseback or motorbikes. There's more seclusion, too, in the **Orto Botánico** (Mon–Sat 9am–2pm), a botanical garden at the northern end of the park, across from Piazza Roma.

The east side

There's precious little on the **east side** of Via Etnea worth the legwork. Mostly modern, the gridded shopping streets march off from the Villa Bellini towards the station and the sea. Further south, the area around **Piazza Carlo Alberto** is worth exploring, a long rectangular square that hosts the Fera o Luni **market** (daily except Sun), replete with fruit and vegetables, household gear and clothes. This is a good area to eat, particularly at lunchtime, though (the market aside) there's little else of interest in the shabby back-streets around.

Once beyond Via Antonio di San Giuliano, you're back in the old-town area of Catania, and the only real draw here is **Piazza Bellini**, a strange conglomerate of buildings from some diverse architectural periods. A wide flight of steps leads up to a crumbling church, there's a Fascist-built office block and – overshadowing the lot – the bulky **Teatro Mássimo Bellini**. Finished in 1890, its elaborate facade leans over the square and during the opera and concert season (winter & spring) you can usually take a quick look inside before the performances begin; programme details are available from the box office inside.

Eating, drinking and nightlife

You'll rarely do better for **eating** than in Catania: fresh fish is a speciality, and there are some good restaurants about, from budget places in the markets to expense-account jobs in the modern city. The presence of students means that the **bars** and **nightlife** are fairly lively too, while Catania hosts one of Sicily's best religious **festivals** every February.

Markets, snacks and fast food

Catania's two main **markets** are in Piazza Carlo Alberto (see opposite) and in the streets through the Porta Uzeda (see p.213), great places to wander and munch from a variety of fresh-fruit stalls, stand-up cafés and snack bars. Outside these areas, and at other times, there's an abundance of places to get **breakfast** and other **snacks**, the best of which are listed below. Around San Martino's Day (November 11), the Catanese make *crispelle* – fritters of flour, water, yeast and ricotta or anchovies – and the Festa di Sant'Agata in February (see p.219) also sees a whole panoply of food stalls selling traditional sweets and snacks. During summer, kiosks along Via Umberto I offer a thirst-quenching Catanian speciality: soda water and crushed lemon with or without salt (*seltz e limone con/senza sale*).

Astoria, Via S. Euplio 30. Near the Villa Bellini and tourist office (parallel to Via Etnea), you can sit down here and sample a choice selection of *cannoli, arancini*, ice-cream, pastries and exotic teas. It's one of the few in town with outdoor tables, too, and thus not a bad place for a beer in the early evening. Closed Sun.

Al Caprice, Via Etnea 30–36. Wide choice of snacks, sandwiches and *tavola calda* meals (grilled meats and chicken), with indoor seating and waiter service. It also advertises itself as a Gelateria Catanese, and has two dozen different varieties. No closing day.

Centrale, Via Etnea 123. A busy *tavola calda*, at Piazza Stesicoro, with a full range of snacks.

Café Charmant, Via Etnea 19. Half a dozen tables overlooking Piazza dell'Università; the smart staff nip out with coffee, snacks and ices. No closing day.

Étoile d'Oro, Via Dusmet, through the arch in Piazza del Duomo and right. The only place in Catania open 24hr, and at night a magnet for a real cross-section of the city, including police, mafiosi and assorted lowlifes. Snacks (usually freshly cooked) and drinks always available. No closing day.

Café Fontana, Largo Paisello 14. Esplanade café in the modern square opposite the tourist office, named for the *modernista* fountain hidden under the steps at the far end of the square. A rare, relatively calm place to sit outside during the day for a drink and snack. Closed Sun.

Friggitoria Stella, Via Monsignor Ventimiglia 66. A good place to sample *crispelle* as well as other traditional fried snacks – this back-street establishment has been going for years and is well thought of locally. Closed Sun.

Savia, Via Etnea 302. Opposite the main entrance to the Villa Bellini, this is one of Catania's finest stand-up café-bars, open since 1899 and always busy with folk digging into *arancine*, pastries and the like. Closed Mon.

Spinella, Via Etnea 300. Next-door rival to the *Savia*, though smaller and less frantic; snacks, pastries and ice-cream. Closed Wed.

Restaurants

The consistently best deals are found in **restaurants** in and around either of Catania's two markets, though these won't necessarily be open at night. It's surprisingly difficult to find a central pizzeria, but with many places cooking good-quality Sicilian and Catanese dishes – *spaghetti alla Norma*, see p.215, is the local pasta – you shouldn't have too hard a time. For an explanation of the restaurant price categories, see p.32.

Da Aldo, Piazza G. Sciuti. A popular place at lunchtime for quick grills (*cucina alle brace*); it's first left off Via Pacini, down Via al Carmine, coming from the Carlo Alberto market. Inexpensive. No credit cards. Closed Sun.

Trattoria Calabrese, Via Penninello 34. A quiet – often morgue-like – place to eat, down the steps at the top end of Via Crocíferi, with a reasonable tourist menu. Inexpensive. No credit cards. Closed Sun lunchtime.

La Finocchiaro, Via E. Reina 13 (☎095.715.3573). Very good central restaurant – just off Piazza dell'Università, set back in a courtyard. Help yourself from the antipasto table; this, and the pasta, meat and (fewer) fish dishes are all thoroughly Sicilian in execution – which means vegetarians could do themselves well here. Moderate. Closed Wed.

Trattoria di Fiore, Via Coppola 24. Close to Piazza Bellini and patronized by locals, it offers good basic cooking. Try the *spaghetti alla zucca* (with pumpkin sauce). Inexpensive. No credit cards. Closed Mon.

Pizzeria Mungibeddu, Via Corridoni 37. On the outskirts of the Fera o Luni market (Piazza Carlo Alberto) – just off Via Pacini – this back-street pizzeria is good for takeaway food or meals at one of the few tables. Inexpensive. No credit cards. Closed Sun.

Ristorante Rápido, Via Corridoni 17. A bustling market trattoria (though rather more sepulchral at night) usually with fresh tuna and a bargain *pranzo completo*. It's an excellent place, and a popular lunch spot with the locals, who share the tables and natter away. Inexpensive. No credit cards. Closed Sun.

Sicilia in Bocca, Piazza Pietro Lupo 16–18 (☎095.746.1361). Not far from the Teatro Mássimo Bellini, and off Via Ventimiglia, this is a lively and attractive place, where you can watch the crustacea twitch as you choose your fish amidst earnest conversation as to their individual merits. Good antipasti. Moderate. Closed Wed.

La Siciliana, Viale Marco Polo 52a (☎095.376.400). Renowned as one of eastern Sicily's best restaurants, though it's way up in the north of the city – take bus #7/22 up Via Etnea from Piazza Stesicoro. The pasta dishes and desserts, particularly, are marvellous, but a full meal costs around L80,000 a head. You'll need to reserve a table and dress up. Very expensive. Closed Sun evening & Mon.

Il Solaio, Via Crociferi 48. Smart little pizzeria with a couple of tables outside and a menu of "normal" or "super" (50cm) pizzas, from L7000 to L25,000. Closed Mon. Inexpensive. No credit cards.

Trattoria Trípoli, Via Pardo 30. Down in the fish market behind Piazza del Duomo, off Via Garibaldi: it's one of two opposite each other, this one without a menu in the window and run by a friendly woman who dives out of the door to drag you in and then dishes up set meals, including wine, which are unbeatable value. *Spaghetti alla Norma* and fried fish are specialities; eat with the market in full swing in front of you. Inexpensive. No credit cards. No closing day.

Trattoria don Turiddu, Via Musumeci 50. There's no menu: just choose your main course at the entrance (usually fish), help yourself to antipasti, and tuck in alongside the regular local clientele. Moderate. Closed Sun & Aug.

Nightlife: bars, pubs and clubs

Catania's student population ensures a fair choice of youthful **bars and pubs** – some with live music – which stay open late; rather a novel experience for Sicily. In addition, the *comune* operates *café concerto* periods during the summer, when the old town streets and squares between Piazza dell'Università and Piazza Bellini are closed to traffic between 9pm and 2am. The bars here all spill tables out onto the squares and alleys, and live bands keep things swinging until the small hours. Drinks are relatively pricey (L6000–8000 for a beer), but it's one of the nicest evening diversions in Sicily.

La Cartiera Pub, Via Casa del Mutilato 8. Young, studenty Catanese bar, off the northeastern side of Piazza Bellini, with various beers on tap and in bottles. Sells food as well. Closed June–Sept.

La Collegiata, Via Collegiata 3. This large pub-pizzeria on two levels overlooks Piazza dell'Università; the terrace is a pleasant place for a night-time drink, with the floodlit churches of Via Crocíferi as a backdrop.

Guliven's, Via Crocíferi 69. Pub-*panineria* on a nice street, with outdoor tables by the steps of the adjacent church, and karaoke thrown in.

Irish Pub, Piazza Scammacca 4. Cocktails, foreign bottled beers (including, of course, Guinness), sandwiches and salads in a nice old-town square.

Nievski's, Via Alessi 15–17. Down the steps from Via Crocíferi, this intriguingly describes itself as a *"pub alternativo"*, a billing it lives up to. It sells trattoria food, too, and is the centre for all kinds of concerts and events. Closed Mon.

The Other Place Pub, Via E. Regina 18. Amazingly, exactly like a pub, with a youthful crowd spread at tables across two floors. It's just off Piazza dell'Università, and there are tables (and pizzas served at them) outside in summer. Closed Mon.

Picasso, Piazza Ogninella 4, & **L'Altro Picasso**, Piazza Scammacca 1b. Adjacent old-town bars with interior art displays, at their best during *café concerto* season, when the tables here offer the best ringside view of all the action.

Pierrot, Via Antonio di San Giuliano 190. On the east side of Via Etna, this American-style bar comes complete with banks of TVs playing rock videos, and serves pasta, pizza, sandwiches and beer.

La Sonnámbula, Via Teatro Mássimo 39. A decent pub, close to Piazza Bellini.

The arts . . . and the Festa di Sant'Agata

To check out all the options, a free monthly **arts and entertainment guide**, *Lapis*, is available from and posted outside bars and cafés; it's in Italian, but comprehensive and comprehensible. For more general information about what's on where, get a copy of Catania's daily newspaper, *La Sicilia*, which has city entertainment listings, available from kiosks all over the centre.

As far as cultural entertainment goes, there are occasional open-air jazz and classical **concerts** held in the summer in the Villa Bellini; and the Catania **festival** runs from November to April, with gigs in the Teatro Metropolitan, Via S. Euplio (☎095.322.323), parallel to Via Etna, next to the Villa Bellini, and Teatro Nuovo, Via Re Martino 195–7 (☎095.493.775; bus #448 from Piazza Stesicoro).

The Cine-Club Ariston, Via Balduino 15a (☎095.441.717), holds foreign **film seasons** (in the original language) from November to June; bus #2/01 from Piazza Stesicoro to Via Giuffrida. Of the city's **theatres**, the Teatro Mássimo Bellini (☎095.730.6111; see p.217) is the most famous: the opera and concert season starts in October and runs through until June. You'll have to go elsewhere to see plays: either to the Teatro Stábile Verga, Via Giuseppe Fava 35 (☎095.363.545), or, for more alternative productions, to Teatro Musco, Via Umberto I 312 (☎095.535.514), and Teatro Nuovo (see p.219) – though all performances are in Italian. You might be able to make more of a **puppet-show** performance, but this involves leaving Catania and heading out to Acireale (see p.222), an easy evening's excursion.

The Festa di Sant'Agata

One of Sicily's best festivals, the **Festa di Sant'Agata**, takes place in Catania between February 3 and 5. A golden statue of the saint is paraded through the streets, there are fireworks in Piazza del Duomo, special stalls in Via Etnea selling festival nougat and sweets, and the highlight of the event is the procession of the *Cannaroli* – long candles, up to 6m high, carried for hours at a time by groups representing different trades. A prize goes to the group which holds out the longest.

Listings

Airlines Air France, Corso Mártiri della Libertà 188 (☎095.532.050); Alitalia, Corso Sicilia 111 (☎095.252.111), and at the airport (095.252.419); Air Malta, Corso Mártiri della Libertà 188(☎095.539.983); Lufthansa, at the airport (☎095.346.151); TWA, Corso Mártiri della Libertà 38 (☎095.534.961).

Airport Fontanarossa (☎095.730.6266 or 095.730.6277). Take the Alibus from Stazione Centrale; departures every 20min, 5am–11.40pm; L1300.

American Express Collect mail at La Duca Viaggi, at Via Etnea 63 (☎095.316.155) or Piazza Europa 2(☎095.375.508). No facilities for cashing cheques; Mon–Fri 9.30am–1pm & 4.30–8pm, Sat 9am–12.30pm.

Banks Banco di Sicilia at Corso Sicilia (Mon–Fri 8.30am–1.30pm & 2.45–3.45pm); at the airport Banca Etnea Agricola (Mon–Fri 8.30am–1.30pm & 2.50–3.50pm).

Bookshops English-language books at English Book Vaults, Via Umberto 36 (☎095.325.385).

Bus terminals AST, Piazza Giovanni XXIII, opposite Stazione Centrale (☎095.746.1096), for services to Acireale, Carlentini, Etna (Rifugio Sapienza), Francoforte, Lentini, Nicolosi, Sortini and Zafferana Etnea; there are timetables pinned to posts and a ticket office at Via L. Sturzo 220, on the east side of the square. Etna Trasporti, Via d'Amico 181, at the back of Piazza Giovanni XXIII (☎095.532.716), to Acireale, Caltagirone, Carlentini, Gela, Giardini-Naxos, Lentini, Licata, Piazza Armerina, Ragusa and Taormina; Fratelli Scionti, Stazione Centrale (☎095.354.704), to Augusta; SAIS, Via d'Amico 181 (☎095.536.168), to Agrigento, Enna, Caltanissetta, Messina, Taormina, Nicosia, Noto, Pachino, Palermo and Siracusa.

Car problems Automobile Club d'Italia, Via Sabotino 1 (☎095.533.324).

Car rental Avis, at the airport (☎095.340.500) and Via S. Giuseppe La Rena 87 (☎095.347.116); Eurodollar, at the airport (☎095.340.252); Hertz, at the airport (☎095.341.595) and Via P. Toselli 16 (☎095.322.560); Holiday Car Rental, at the airport (☎095.578.368); Maggiore/Budget, at the airport (☎095.340.594) and Piazza G. Verga 48 (☎095.536.927).

Catamaran tickets Virtu Ferries, La Duca Viaggi, Piazza Europa (☎095.384.855), and Tropical Travel, Piazza Giovanni XXIII 3 (☎095.532.207) for catamaran services to Malta; L195,000 return in summer, L155,000 return in winter.

Club Alpino Italiano Via Vecchia Ognina 169 (☎095.387.674), off Viale della Libertà – for climbing advice, information and maps of Mount Etna.

Emergencies Ambulance ☎113; police ☎112.

Exchange There's an exchange office, Agenzia Cambio, at Via S. Maria del Rosario 2, off Piazza dell'Università (Mon–Fri 8.30am–1pm & 3.30–6.30pm, Sat 8.30am–1pm); one inside Stazione Centrale, and another at the airport (daily 8am–9pm), where there's also an exchange machine.

Gay information Open Mind, Via Gargano 33 (☎095.532.685). Daily 5–8pm.

Hospital Casualty at the following hospitals: Ospedale Generale Garibaldi, Piazza S. Maria di Gesù 7 (☎095.759.1111); Santa Marta e Villermosa, Via Clementi 36 (☎095.317.699); and S. Tomaselli, Via Passo Gravina 185 (☎095.759.1111).

Pharmacies Caltabiano, Piazza Stesicoro 34 (☎095.327.647); Croce Rossa, Via Etnea 274 (☎095.317.053); Europa, Corso Italia 105 (☎095.383.536); Fonzo Dr Franca, Via Vittorio Emanuele II 54 (☎095.531.400). The last three are open all night.

Police In emergencies, ☎112; Carabinieri, Piazza Giovanni Verga 8 (☎095.537.822); Vigili Urbani, Via Veniero 7 (☎095.531.333). The Questura is in Piazza S. Nicolella (☎095.736.7111).

Post office Main post office and poste restante at Via Etnea 215, close to the Villa Bellini. Mon–Sat 8.30am–7.30pm.

Supermarket SMA supermarket at Corso Sicilia 50. Closed Wed afternoon.

Swimming Piscina Comunale at Viale Kennedy (near the campsites; bus #4/27 or #5/38 from where the station or Piazza Borsellino).

Telephones Telecom Italia at Corso Sicilia 67 (daily 8am–8pm). Telephone offices also at the airport (daily 8am–8pm), and at Via A. Longo 54 (daily 8am–9.45pm), next to the botanical gardens.

Travel agents La Duca Viaggi, Via Etnea 63–65 (☎095.316.155); Elisea, Corso Sicilia 31 (☎095.312.321); Etnea Viaggi, Corso Sicilia 109 (☎095.327.080); Munzone Mineo, Piazza dei Mártiri 4 (☎095.539.983); Viaggi Wasteel, Piazza Giovanni XXIII (☎095.531.511).

North of the city: the coastal route

Although all the good sandy beaches are to the south of Catania, it's the coast **north of the city** that's the most popular holiday area. The lava streams from Etna have reached the sea many times over the centuries, turning the coastline into an attractive mix of contorted black rocks and sheer coves, excellent for swimming. Consequently, what was once a series of small fishing villages, stretching from **Ognina** as far as **Acireale**, is now a fair-sized strip of hotels, lidos and restaurants, idle in the winter but swarming in summer with trippers from the city. It's an appealing coastline, easily reached by AST bus from outside Catania's Stazione Centrale and, while some of the villages – like **Aci Castello** – are really only worth a visit when the summer is well under way, Baroque Acireale warrants a day-trip from Catania at any time.

It's an area that has taken well to imaginative interpretation. The nineteenth-century Sicilian novelist, Giovanni Verga, set his masterpiece *I Malavoglia* in and around the village of **Aci Trezza**; and some of the better known of the Homeric myths have been ascribed to this locality. The prefix "Aci", given to a number of settlements here, derives from the local River Aci, said to have appeared following the death of the herdsman Acis at the hands of the giant, one-eyed Polyphemus.

Ognina, Aci Castello and Aci Trezza

Bus #3/34 from Catania's Piazza del Duomo runs right the way to **OGNINA**, a small suburb on the northern outskirts of Catania. Built on lava cliffs formed in the fifteenth century, it's an easy break from the city: there are a few restaurants here, overlooking the little harbour, as well as a campsite.

To go any further north continue on the #3/34 bus or take one of the frequent AST buses, which run up the coast to Acireale, stopping first in **ACI CASTELLO**, 9km from the city. Here, as the name suggests, there's a **castle** (Tues–Sun: summer 9am–1pm & 4.30–7.30pm; winter 9am–1pm & 3–5pm), a lofty thirteenth-century building that rises above the sea in splinters from a volcanic rock crag. It was the base of the rebel Roger di Lauria in 1297 and is remarkably well preserved, despite many volcanic explosions and the destruction wrought by Frederick II of Aragon, who took the castle from Roger by erecting a wooden siege-engine adjacent. In town, there are a couple of small trattorias, handy for lunch, while the ragged coastline to the north is popular for sunbathing and swimming: in summer, a wooden boardwalk is built over the lava rocks here and you pay a small fee to use the changing rooms and showers.

Aci Castello marks the beginning of the so-called Riviera dei Ciclopi, named after the jagged points of the **Scogli dei Ciclopi** that rise from the sea just beyond the town. Homer wrote that the blinded Polyphemus slung these rocks (broken from Etna), at Ulysses as he and his men escaped from the Cyclops in their ships. The three main sharp-edged islets present an odd sight (the largest sticking some 60m into the sky) and it's a good half-day's diversion to get off the bus at Aci Castello, and walk the couple of kilometres north along the rough coast to **ACI TREZZA**. Here, right opposite the rocks, on the lungomare, is a fine **restaurant**, *I Faraglioni* – in a posh four-star hotel, but with great views and food. If you want to **stay** in the area, *I Malavoglia*, Via Provinciale 3 (☎095.276.711, fax 095.276.873; ③), is friendly and in a leafy position, or there's a **campsite** at Aci Trezza, *Camping Galatea*, right on the coast, at Via Livorno 150 (☎095.277.279; June–Sept).

Acireale

ACIREALE, 16km north from Catania, is marvellously sited, high above the rocky shore and the surrounding lemon groves, something best appreciated from the public gardens at the northern end of town: from here you can look right back along the Riviera dei Ciclopi. Known since Roman times as a spa centre, Acireale's sulphur baths (Terme di Santa Vénera) are still in use, though visitors these days are more likely to be attracted by the town's striking examples of Sicilian Baroque in the crowded central streets. This, the fourth successive town on the site, was rebuilt directly over the old lava streams after the 1693 earthquake. As in Catania, the result is a planned town centre, which relies on a few grand buildings, a handsome square and some long thoroughfares for its effect.

All the finest buildings are right in the centre, on and around Piazza del Duomo. The restored **Duomo**, with its extravagant tiled spires, still retains a good Baroque portal; it's the bigger of two churches in the open square. Over the way, facing the piazza from Via Romeo, is the long **Municipio**; a little further down, in

Piazza Vigo, the church of **San Sebastiano** sports an elaborate balustraded facade, decked out with a barrage of statues; and straight up from Piazza del Duomo is the grand **Palazzo Musmeci**, in Piazza San Domenico. It won't take long to whip around this compact enclave of decorative Baroque work and once you've done that there's little else to detain you in town, though you might derive some small interest from the art and historical collections in the **Pinacoteca Zelantea** (Mon & Wed 9am–12.15pm; free), just off Piazza San Domenico.

A visit to Acireale really pays dividends if you come at Carnevale (see p.43), when it hosts one of Sicily's best **festivals**, flower-decked floats and fancy-dress parades clogging the streets for five noisy days. There's more traditional entertainment, too, in Acireale's surviving **puppet theatre**: check out the Teatro dell'Opera dei Pupi, which comprises Turi Grasso, at Via Nazionale 95 (☎095.764.8035), and Cooperativa E. Magri, at Corso Umberto 113 (☎095.606.272); or contact the tourist office (see below) for details.

Practicalities

You can get to Acireale by **train**, though the station is well to the south of town, near the sulphur baths, and it's a long walk into the centre along Corso Vittorio Emanuele. It's better to arrive by **bus**, either locally from Catania or stopping off on the SAIS Catania–Messina route: local buses stop along the main Corso Umberto or at the ranks outside the public garden, at the end of the corso; the Messina buses pass Piazza del Duomo. If you need information, the **tourist office** is at Corso Umberto I 179 (Mon–Fri 9am–1pm & 4–7pm; ☎095.604.521). With Catania so close, you shouldn't need **to stay** in Acireale, and there are no budget choices in the centre, though if you're stuck the *Albergo delle Terme*, at Via de Gaspéri 20 (☎095.601.166; ③), is relatively good value – turn right out of the station, and right again under the tracks at Via Santa Caterina. Around festival time, everywhere in town will be full.

Santa Maria La Scala

There's hardly anywhere decent to get a meal in Acireale. Your best bet – and something that's worth doing anyway if you've got the time – is to stroll the couple of kilometres downhill to the tiny hamlet of **SANTA MARIA LA SCALA**, huddled around a miniscule harbour full of painted fishing-boats. There's also a tiny church, a beach of lavic, black rock at the southern end of Santa Maria, and three or four **trattorias** overlooking the small bay. The one at Via Scalo Grande 46 (no name, but opposite a "Pepsi" sign, the only street, is a simple place where you're offered spaghetti and then a choice of charcoal-grilled fish or seafood from a tray. It's a good deal; though for something a little more elaborate, *Al Mulino* – at the southern end of the hamlet, away from the harbour – has an outdoor terrace and more grilled fish.

The walk to Santa Maria takes half an hour from Acireale – down Via Romeo (to the side of the Municipio), across the busy main road and then down the steep rural path to the water: you might find yourself passing a flock of sheep on the way or a donkey being led up or down. You might even fancy the **campsite** nearby, too; *Camping La Timpa* (☎095.764.8155), Via Floristella 25, next to the sea.

South: across the Piana di Catania

There's a real paucity of places to stop south of the city, certainly compared to the good day-trips to be made to the north. Partly, this is down to geographical factors, much of the land a vast, largely uninhabited plain – the **Piana di Catania**. Known to the Greeks as the Laestrygonian Fields after the cannibal Laestrygones who was reputed to live there, it's a fertile region, rich agricultural land full of citrus trees and other crops. You'll head across here on the way to Siracusa, or taking the autostrada to Enna, and it's a pretty enough ride through the windmill-dotted flat fields, but the only features of interest lie on the very fringes of the plain. Closest to Catania are the good sand **beaches** which line the wide Golfo di Catania, reached by taking buses #4/27 or #5/38 from the city; there are also three big campsites here that front the sea (see p.211).

Lentini

Half an hour or so south of Catania, **LENTINI** has a long pedigree that puts it among the earliest of the Greek settlements in Sicily, and the first of all the inland colonies. Established in 729 BC as a daughter city of Naxos, Lentini (Leontinoi) flourished as a commercial centre for two hundred years, before falling foul of Hippocrates of Gela. Later, the city was absorbed by Syracuse, sharing its disasters but never its prosperity. It was Leontinoi's struggle to assert its independence, by allying itself with Athens, that provided the pretext for the great Athenian expedition against Syracuse in 415 BC. Another attempt – this time an alliance with the Carthaginians during the Second Punic War – resulted in the Romans beheading two thousand of its citizens, a measure that horrified the whole island, as no doubt it was intended to do. By the time Cicero got round to describing the city, Lentini was "wretched and empty", though it continued as a small-scale agricultural centre for some time, until the great earthquake of 1693 completely demolished it.

Some of the ancient city survives today as an extensive archeological site, a few kilometres out of the modern town (see below), and Lentini itself has a good collection of finds in the town's **Museo Archeológico** (Mon–Sat 9am–5pm, Sun 9am–noon; free), in Piazza del Liceo, though some of the best artefacts have been appropriated by the museums at Catania and Siracusa. All the same, you'll see plenty of examples of the local pottery, a graphic reconstruction of the ancient city's south gate and plans of the site itself.

That's if you can be bothered to come, of course. Lentini does little on any length of acquaintance to dispel first impressions of a noisy, sprawling modern town with few redeeming features. The long main Via Garibaldi curves round into what remains of the old town, principally the **Duomo** (often locked) at the head of a reasonably attractive double square. The museum is tricky to find – and defies directions; there are no signposts and no tourist office, so you'll have to be very persistent.

Practicalities

From the **train station**, on the edge of town, buses #3 or #4 run into the centre, to Piazza del Duomo, while #1 or #2 go to Carlentini for the Zona Archeologica. Buy tickets in the station bar. **Buses** from Catania drop you just off Via Garibaldi, from where it's a ten-minute walk to the duomo. Frankly, it's barely worth bothering with Lentini at all – you can reach Carlentini directly from Catania much quicker.

Carlentini and the Zona Archeológica

The Zona Archeológica is a twenty-minute walk south of the nearby upper town of **CARLENTINI**, which you can reach directly by bus from Catania with either AST or, less regularly, Etna Trasporti. Again, there's no real point in getting out at Carlentini itself, though it, too, has a fairly pleasant central square with bars: most buses also stop in Piazza San Francesco on the outskirts of Carlentini, closer to the zone, as do buses #1 or #2 from Lentini's train station. From Piazza San Francesco, there are regular buses back to Catania, the last one at 7.30pm.

The **Zona Archeológica** (Mon–Fri 9am–1pm; free) is then a five-minute signposted walk away, spread over the two hills of San Mauro and Metapíccola. The first of these is the more interesting, holding the ancient town's acropolis and substantial remains of a vast necropolis nearby, from which most of the museum's contents come. You'll see the pincer-style **south gate** immediately, part of a well-conserved system of fortifications that surrounded the ancient town. After about 600 BC, Leontinoi expanded over the opposite hill of Metapíccola, though the remains here are very scanty: the foundations of a Greek temple and some scattered huts belonging to an earlier native village, mentioned by Thucydides. Together, the hills make a good couple of hours' rambling, while a dirt road to the side of the main entrance climbs around the perimeter fence to allow views over the whole site and down to Lentini in the valley below.

MOUNT ETNA

One of the world's largest volcanoes, **MOUNT ETNA**, dominates much of Sicily's eastern landscape, its smoking summit a familiar feature when travelling in this area. The main crater is still dangerously active: throughout much of 1992, the volcano was in a continual state of eruption, destroying local roads and threatening the villages that skirt its base; activity continued intermittently in 1997 and 1998, causing planes to deviate from their normal flight paths. Earlier eruptions, stretching right back into antiquity, have done far worse – devastating Catania, repeatedly ripping up the cultivated fields and farms, with the lava flows even reaching the sea on several occasions. Yet the volcano remains a remarkable draw for travellers, and really demands that you set aside at least a day to see it.

If you're pushed for time you'll have to make do with the glimpsed views of its peak and hinterland from the **Circumetnea railway**, a circular route from Catania to Riposto that provides one of Sicily's most fascinating rides. It passes through some intriguing settlements: medieval **Randazzo** is the only place you might want to stop over, but there's interest in the towns of **Paternò** and **Adrano**, both of which have fine castles, while **Linguaglossa** is the base for Etna's ski resorts. If you're driving, you can follow exactly the same route as the railway, around the volcano, a minor but perfectly adequate road sticking close to the line.

There are interesting villages, too, on the **southeastern** side of Etna, worth stopping in for their proximity to the lower craters: **Nicolosi** is an important ski-centre and within walking distance of craters blown open in the seventeenth century. But skirting the foothills of the volcano can only be second-best to **the ascent** to the top, a trip worth every effort to make (and one made easier by taking the cable car). Although you're not allowed to reach the main crater itself, getting to the ones just below is possible and (usually) not at all dangerous.

The Circumetnea railway: Catania to Riposto

The **Circumetnea railway** (Ferrovia Circumetnea) is a private line, 114km long, which runs around the base of the volcano through fertile vegetation – citrus plantations, vines and nut trees – and past (often through) the strewn lava of recent eruptions. It's a marvellous ride, across Etna's foothills with endless views of the peak, starting in Catania and circling Etna as far as Riposto on the Ionian coast. There's only 30km between Catania and Riposto if you go on the direct coastal route, which means that you can circumnavigate the volcano and get back to Catania on the same day: if you make the entire trip, allow around five hours to Riposto, plus another half an hour back to Catania on the FS main line. InterRail/Eurail passes are not valid on the Circumetnea, and **tickets** for the route (not including the FS coastal trip back to Catania) cost L9800 one way, L19,600 return: buy them on the train, or visit the Circumetnea office in Catania, at Via Caronda 352 (☎095.541.111); see "Travel details" at the end of the chapter (p.235) for schedules.

Something to note is that **accommodation** in the towns around Etna is scarce, so if you're going to stop over anywhere, plan (and ring) ahead; see the text for details of hotels.

Catania to Bronte

The first part of the route runs out through Catania's grim suburbs, **Misterbianco** the first stop. Soon, though, the first of the citrus and olive groves are visible and, by the time you reach **PATERNÒ**, you're well within sight of Etna's southern slopes. A lively town in the valley of the River Simeto, Paternò clusters around its main street, Via Vittorio Emanuele, its train station at one end and a medieval **castello** at the other. Founded by Count Roger in 1073, the castle is largely thirteenth-century (though much restored) and is worth a look for the view from the terrace at the top – the reason the Germans used it as an observation post during World War II. They proved hard to dislodge and four thousand people died here during the subsequent aerial bombardment. If you're lucky, you'll find the doors open, in which case don't hesitate to poke your nose inside, and, if at all possible, have a wander.

There's one **hotel** in Paternò, the *Sicilia*, near the station at Via Vittorio Emanuele 391 (☎095.853.604, fax 095.854.742; ②), though it's rather grumpily run and often full. Hotel and station are about a twenty-minute walk to the old centre, at the other end of Via Vittorio Emanuele.

Biancavilla and Adrano

Ten kilometres further on, **BIANCAVILLA** was founded by Albanian refugees in 1480. The area around is devoted to growing oranges, and small sideroads from here run up through the orchards and onto the higher, southwestern slopes of Etna – a nice little diversion if you're coming this way by car.

ADRANO, close by, is one of the more interesting stops hereabouts, built over the site of ancient Adranon, a town founded by Dionysius the Elder – parts of the Greek lava-built **walls** are still visible in town, though they're barely distinguishable from later fortifications. Much more impressive is the **castello**, another of Count Roger's creations and, like that at Paternò, squat, solid and battlemented. Inside there's a small **museum** (closed for restoration), with finds from local sites, including early Bronze Age pottery. Take a look, too, in the **Chiesa Madre**, next to the castle, which has some good artwork inside, though the exterior is disfigured by an unfinished modern campanile. The old centre of Adrano provides a fairly pleasant wander, with its shady gardens and faded churches; sit-down bars offering snacks face the gardens. For **lunch**, wander further down the road to Piazza Duca degli Abruzzi, where the cosy and rustic *Hostaria Bellini* is tucked away next to the derelict Teatro Bellini (closed Mon); the emphasis here is on local ingredients.

If you're driving, there are a couple of possible side-trips from Adrano. Around 8km west, near Cárcaci, the **Ponte dei Saraceni** is a fourteenth-century bridge that arches over the River Simeto (at the end of the first road on the right after Cárcaci; keep to the right). And southwest of town, on the SS575 (before it meets the SS121 to Catania), is **Eurelios**, a massive solar-energy centre at the foot of a volcanic plateau on the same river. It's one of the biggest in Europe, completed in 1982, and there are **free guided tours** (daily except Monday 9am–1pm & 2–6pm).

Bronte and around

Between Adrano and Bronte are some of the best views of Etna, as the railway line and road climb ever closer to the lava flows that have marked the landscape further north. **BRONTE** lies about halfway along the Circumetnea route, its rather shabby, amorphous aspect belying its noble past. Founded by Charles V in 1535, many echoes of its original layout survive, particularly in the town's numerous battlemented and pointed campanili that top its ageing churches. The town gave its name to the dukedom bestowed upon Nelson, the English admiral, in 1799, and his ducal seat (the Castello Maniace, see below) is a few kilometres north of town. Otherwise, Bronte's sole claim to fame these days is as the centre of Italy's pistachio-nut production, the plantations around town accounting for 85 percent of the country's output. It's also a handy jumping-off point for an extended trip into the interior of Sicily, buses heading to Cesarò, from where a fine route cuts west into the Nébrodi hills – covered in Chapter Seven.

Back on the Circumetnea, beyond Bronte the pistachios give way to walnuts and chestnuts, and the train passes the huge lava flow of 1823 which came close to destroying the town. A little further on, **Maletto** is the highest point on the Circumetnea line. From here, a very minor road leads west to the **Castello Maniace**, founded as a convent in 1174 on the site of a victory over the Arabs by George Maniakes, when he was attempting to regain the island for Byzantium. The 1693 earthquake destroyed much of the building, but the estate was given to Lord Nelson as part of his dukedom, granted by King Ferdinand in gratitude for British help in repressing the Neapolitan revolution of 1799, which had forced the Bourbon court to flee to Palermo. Nelson never got round to visiting his Sicilian estate, though his family only relinquished control of the property in 1978; it's now owned by the *comune*.

You can visit Maniakes' walled castle (daily 9am–6pm; free) and the lava-built church, and the custodian will probably show you round the granary, now used for conferences. Impressively restored to a plain, almost spartan appearance, the same restraint is evident in the well-tended garden, English in style but for the presence of palm trees. This, or the grounds outside the gates, would make a pleasant **picnic** spot. On the other side of the river lies the only part of the estate still owned by Nelson's descendants, the English cemetery, its most celebrated occupant the Scottish author William Sharp (1855–1905), who wrote under the name of Fiona Macleod and was a regular visitor here.

Maniace is a stop on the Bronte and Cesarò **bus** route, with three passing in each direction daily (except Sun).

Randazzo

Closest town to the volcano's summit as the crow flies, **RANDAZZO** is imbued with Etna's presence, the dark medieval town built entirely of lava. Despite the dangerous proximity, it has never been engulfed – though an eruption in 1981 came perilously close; the lava flow is easily visible on the road out of town. Randazzo was also one of the main forward positions of the German forces during their defence of Sicily in 1943 and everything in town was bombed to bits. But the churches and buildings from the wealthy thirteenth- to sixteenth-century period have been meticulously restored, and there's some pleasant rambling to be enjoyed around the dingy lava-clad streets.

In medieval times three churches took it in turns to act as cathedral, a sop to the three parishes in town whose inhabitants were of Greek, Latin and Lombard origin and had little in common. The largest, **Santa Maria**, in the main Corso Umberto, is the modern-day holder of the title, a severe Catalan-Gothic structure incorporating chunks of volcanic rock. More interesting is the church of **San Martino**, further up the road on the northern edge of town, which features a four-teenth-century campanile, cracked and moss-ridden. Across the square, the blackened tower that forms part of the old city walls is all that survives of Randazzo's castle. From the fifteenth century until about twenty years ago, it did duty as a prison; nowadays it holds the town's **museum** (Mon–Fri 9am–1pm & 4–7pm, Sat 9am–1pm; L2000), a small collection of puppets and historical knick-knacks.

Practicalities

Arriving in Randazzo on the **Circumetnea train**, walk straight down the road in front of you to reach the central Piazza Loreto; the medieval town is down Via Umberto and away to the left. The **bus station** is a couple of blocks back from Piazza Loreto, towards the Circumetnea station (down Via Vittorio Véneto). There's a regular **FS train station** too, from which you can catch frequent trains to the coast, at Taormina-Giardini, an hour away. It's another block over from the bus station.

If you wanted to break the journey around Etna, Randazzo is the best place to get **lunch**. Choices narrow down to two, both off Piazza Loreto; *La Veneziana*, Via dei Romano 8a (closed Sun evening and Mon), has excellent rustic dishes, specializing in mushrooms; and the *Trattoria Romana* (no credit cards; closed Mon), a small place offering a limited selection of no-frills, authentically prepared pastas and meat dishes – try the herb sausage. In the evening, Randazzo has a lively *passeggiata* up and down Corso Umberto, a street with some nice, old-fashioned bars (like the *Arturo*). However, the only **accommodation** is uninspiring: the tatty *Motel Scrivano* (☎095.921.126; no credit cards; ②) behind the Agip petrol station on Via Regina Margherita, off Piazza Loreto.

East to Riposto

The lava flows around Randazzo are quite clearly defined, and you'll pass through the midst of great rivers of volcanic rubble cluttering the slopes. Occasionally, all that survives of a former orchard or vineyard is the wall, visible through the wreckage. Naturally, the views of Etna are magnificent this close to the summit – just 15km away.

Linguaglossa

Road and rail stick close together around the northernmost stretch of the route, passing the station at Castiglione di Sicilia (a good 5km from the town itself; see p.203) and, shortly after, running into **LINGUAGLOSSA**. It's the main tourist centre on Etna's northern slopes, but for all that a quiet town during the summer, with locals' bars lining the cobbled streets and extensive pine forests out of the centre, good for a ramble. It's a different story in winter when Linguaglossa becomes a busy **ski centre**, although all the equipment, ski schools and ski lifts are out of town, 15km further up the mountain, at Piano Provenzana (see p.231); information from the helpful Linguaglossa **tourist office**, in Piazza Annunziata (Mon–Sat 9am–12.30pm & 4–7pm, Sun 9am–12.30pm; ☎095.643.094), which has a little museum behind it displaying local artefacts, from flora and fauna to lava and a few pickled snakes (same hours as office; free).

If you're going **to stay** in town in summer, there should be no problem finding space; try the *Happy Day*, Via Maraneve 9 (☎ & fax 095.643.484; ④), 300m left out of the station, or, on the same road, *Villa Refe* at no. 42, which offers cooking facilities (☎095.643.926; ③). And there's a campsite, the *Clan dei Ragazzi* (☎ & fax 095.643.611), though again it's out of town, 10km up the road to Piano Provenzana (see p.231).

Giarre-Riposto

Back on the train, after a fairly uneventful forty-minute ride – all the best views of Etna have been and gone – the Circumetnea route ends on the coast at the twin town of **GIARRE-RIPOSTO**. There's no reason to linger here longer than the time it takes to change stations for your onward transport: it's a sprawling, largely modern town, split between gridded Giarre and, down the long, main Corso Italia, the shabby port area of Riposto. To switch onto the main FS line for **trains** to Taormina or Catania, change at Giarre; for **buses** to Taormina, Messina and Catania, keep going straight uphill to the piazza in front of Giarre's grand **Duomo**.

It would be hard luck indeed to get stuck here for the night; if you do, head for the inexpensive *Sicilia* (☎095.779.2552, fax 095.779.2832; American Express credit cards only; ②), at Via Gallipoli 444, near the mainline station. At the bottom of Corso Italia, around Piazza San Pietro, there are a few bars, a couple of trattorias and views over the working boatyard. Much more attractive, if you're driving, is to head up the coast, 3km north, to Fondachello, where there are two seaside **campsites**, signposted from just about everywhere on this stretch of coast; *La Zagara*, Via Spiaggia 127 (☎095.770.0132; June–Oct), pleasantly sited among trees, and *Mokambo*, Via Spiaggia 211 (☎095.938.731; April–Sept), which has a wide range of facilities. Both also have bungalows available for rent (book ahead in summer; two-berths at ②, four-berths at ③).

The volcano: its foothills and the ascent

Although the Circumetnea route takes in some fairly adventurous scenery, you get little impression of Etna as an active volcano except for the odd lava flow. This can only really be gleaned by making the effort to roam around the **northern and southeastern foothills**, much closer to the summit than the towns on the Circumetnea route – though without your own transport the effort can be considerable. Still, it's not impossible to get around the foothills and craters by public transport, and there are buses from Catania that link some of the villages, notably **Zafferana Etnea** and **Nicolosi**.

The major attraction, though, is a trip to the **summit** of what, at 3323m high, is a fairly substantial mountain – the fact that it's also an active volcano only adds to its fascination. Etna was just one of the places that the Greeks thought to be the forge of Vulcan, a fitting description of the blustering and sparking from the main crater. The philosopher Empedocles studied the volcano closely, living in an observatory near the summit. This presumably terrifying existence was dramatized by Matthew Arnold in his *Empedocles on Etna*:

> *Alone! –*
> *On this charr'd, blacken'd melancholy waste,*
> *Crown'd by the awful peak, Etna's great mouth.*

Certainly, it all proved too much for Empedocles, who in 433 BC jumped into the main crater in an attempt to prove that the gases emitted would support his bodyweight. They didn't.

Of the scores of recorded **eruptions** since that of 475 BC (described by Pindar), some have been disastrously spectacular: in 1169, 1329 and 1381 the lava reached

---

ETNA TOURS AND EXCURSION BUSES

Tours are most easily taken from Taormina and are usually full-day affairs, including transport there and back, an accompanied trip up to the craters, and protective clothes and boots – around L75,000 per person, plus another L20,000–25,000 for lunch if you want it. Departures depend on weather conditions and generally don't take place at all from September to April. Always check exactly what you're getting for your money: some operators charge extra (about L6000) for the obligatory guides to reach the higher craters. If this is too pricey, then inexpensive excursion buses leave throughout the year for various points in the foothills, where you can at least get a taste of the volcano, though this is very much a second-best option.

- Of the **agents**, try La Duca Viaggi, at Via Don Bosco 39 in Taormina (☎0942.625.255), or SAT (☎0942.24.653) at Corso Umberto 73, also in Taormina, and at Corso Umberto 73. Otherwise, try the **tourist offices** in Catania, Taormina and Giardini-Naxos.
- Ferrovia Circumetnea, Corso delle Province 13, Catania (☎095.531.402), operate a bus on Sunday in winter to the hill-resort and ski-base of Piano Provenzana (Jan–April 7am; return 3pm) for around L10,000 return.
- AST operate a daily 8am bus (all year) from Catania's Piazza Giovanni XXIII (outside Stazione Centrale) to *Rifugio Sapienza*, the trip taking one to two hours. The return bus is at around 4pm; tickets around L10,000 return.

the sea, while in 1669, the worst year, Catania was wrecked and its castle surrounded by molten rock. In the twentieth century, the Circumetnea railway line has been repeatedly ruptured by lava flows, the towns of the foothills threatened and roads and farms destroyed, and in 1979 nine tourists were killed by an explosion on the edge of the main crater. This unpredictability means that it's no longer possible to get close to the main crater. An eruption in 1971 destroyed the observatory supposed to give warning of such an event; another in 1983 brought down the cable car which provided access – not the first time this had happened. The eruption that started on December 12, 1991, and which continued for much of 1992, engulfed the outskirts of Zafferana Etnea. At one stage the American navy joined Italian forces in an attempt to stem the lava flow by dropping reinforced concrete blocks (so-called "Beirut-busters", used to defend military camps) from helicopters into the fissures. Local villagers, on the other hand, preferred to place their faith in parading statues of the Virgin Mary before the volcano. The flow did finally cease, though whether due to divine intervention or geological exhaustion no one is quite clear. The more recent eruptions in 1997 and the summer of 1998 were high, but not life-threatening.

Apart from the cable car (which isn't always open), access to the summit is by 10km of rough track. Despite the lurid tales of past eruptions, you'll not be in any danger, provided you heed the warnings as you get closer to the top.

Approaches: around the northern and southeastern foothills

If you're short on time and don't have your own transport, the easiest way to see the volcano and climb its slopes is by **organized tour** from either Catania or Taormina or by special **excursion bus** (see box opposite). Otherwise, with your **own transport** there are several approaches to the craters: some of the best scenery is on the **north side** (signposted "Etna Nord"), from the road that leads up from Linguaglossa. By **public transport**, the only practicable routes into the foothills are on the **south side** of Etna ("Etna Sud"), frequent buses running out of Catania to the nearby villages.

The north side

From Linguaglossa (see p.229) a tortuous fifteen-kilometre road corkscrews up past the skiing pistes of **Piano Provenzana**; the settlement of Mareneve beyond doesn't exist any more, despite still being marked on most maps. In the summer, a daily bus from Catania unloads its passengers at Piano Provenzana, giving them plenty of time for lunch and the opportunity to reach some of the craters higher up by jeep – a trip that will take around three hours and cost around L35,000. Otherwise the walking around here is especially good, and you'll have no trouble **staying** either at the pricey *Le Betulle* (☎095.643.430; ④), or the *Rifugio Nord Est* hostel (☎095.647.922), which includes breakfast in the L25,000-a-head price and is the base for excursions. There's also a **campsite** in the pinewoods 5km below Piano Provenzana: the *Clan dei Ragazzi* (☎ & fax 095.643.611), which has reasonable chalets available where you can get full-board for L70,000 per person. If you're coming to ski, you'll need to book accommodation here or in nearby Linguaglossa well in advance.

A lower, more direct road leads south from Linguaglossa past various old lava flows – of 1852, 1950 and, near Fornazzo, of 1979 – to **MILÒ**, 15km away; here, there are impressive views of the Valle del Bove above (see p.234 for more views of this, from the top). Maps show a road from Milò which climbs northwest, up the volcano to the *Rifugio Citelli*, and back towards Linguaglossa, but frequent landslides often make this route impossible. You should be able to get some of the way up though, for more striking views of the summit and the coastline below.

The south side

Most pleasant of the villages on the south side is **ZAFFERANA ETNEA**, an hour from Catania by bus and surrounded by vineyards and citrus groves. Parts of the outskirts were damaged by lava in April 1992, when the village became the operational centre of the effort to halt the flow from the volcano. The centre, however, was untouched and it retains an eighteenth-century air to its buildings and churches, making for a leisurely stop, say for a coffee in the bar on the corner of the elegant central piazza. The previous eruption to threaten Zafferana occurred in 1792, halted on that occasion – according to local tradition – due to the intervention of Our Lady of Divine Providence, whose name was again invoked by God-fearing locals during the last volcanic ructions.

Zafferana is acquiring a reputation as a low-key hill-resort and the population of around seven thousand practically doubles at weekends and holidays as the trippers arrive. Certainly, there's some good walking to be done in the green hills behind the village, and if you fancy a longer stay here there's a choice of **hotels**; try the comfortable *Primavera dell'Etna*, Via Cassone 67 (☎095.708.2348, fax 095.708.1695; ③), set in its own grounds, or the *Villa Pina*, Via dei Gerani 19 (☎ & fax 095.708.1024; no credit cards; ② including breakfast). Currently, one bus daily from Monday to Saturday leaves Zafferana for *Rifugio Sapienza* (see opposite), running along a scenic road that cuts due-west, twisting further up towards the main craters on Etna.

The other easily reached village from Catania is **Trecastagni**, whose main church, the **Chiesa Madre**, is a fine Renaissance building, probably designed by Antonello Gagini and affording marvellous views over the coast from its elevated position. Frankly, though, you're hardly likely to come here for just these; better, if you're driving, to look upon Trecastagni as a coffee-stop.

Nicolosi

NICOLOSI, a tidy little town just to the west of Trecastagni, has been developed as a winter ski resort and, though rather bland in itself, is probably the best target in the foothills, with several hotels and some good places to eat; there are frequent AST buses from Catania. At around 700m, it's pretty brisk in Nicolosi even in summer, and the area around boasts some good walking possibilities. Best of these, certainly if you're going no further, is the hike up to the **Monti Rossi** craters, around an hour each way. Formed in the eruption of 1669, they're the most important of the secondary craters that litter the slopes of the volcano.

Nicolosi is the last main stop before the steeper slopes begin – a good place to pick up information. There's a small **information office** at Via Garibaldi 63 (daily: summer 8.30am–1pm & 4–7.30pm; winter 8.30am–1pm; ☎095.911.505), on the main road that runs through town. The **hotels** in Nicolosi are a fairly expensive bunch, though there are some exceptions: try the somewhat dingy *Monti Rossi*, Via Etnea 177 (☎095.791.4393; ①), or, across the road, the *Gemmellaro*, at no. 160 (☎095.911.373, fax 095.911.071; ④), again, cavernous and dreary, but some of the big rooms have views of Etna. They're both some way out of town, about 2km up the hill: the same road has a recommended **restaurant**, *Il Buongustaio*, specializing in local mushrooms and sausage. The *Monti Rossi* also has a traditional wood-fired **pizza** oven, which warms the place up in the evenings. If you're **camping**, *Camping*

Etna (☎095.914.309) is on Via Goethe, signposted from town. There's also a **youth hostel** at Via della Quercia 7 (☎095.791.4686, fax 095.791.4701; L25,000 per person), with a helpful warden, and a supermarket just across the street.

The ascent

Although there are regular buses to Nicolosi from Catania, only one (early morning, from outside Catania's Stazione Centrale) continues to the mountain refuge/hotel that marks the end of the negotiable road up the south side of Etna. It's a bizarre ride. **Beyond Nicolosi**, the green foothills give way to wooded slopes, then to bare, black and grey seas of volcanic debris, spotted with the hardy, endemic plants, the yellow-green Spino Santo and Etna violets – the only things to grow on the heights of the volcano. Everywhere, the slopes are dotted with earlier, spent craters – grass-covered on the lower reaches, and no more than black pimples further up.

Rifugio Sapienza

At **RIFUGIO SAPIENZA**, 1400m below the summit, the road ends in a car park (L2000), below which are several small, extinct volcanoes and craters that you are free to wander around and into. Further up there's a row of souvenir shops, flogging ashtrays made of lava, glittery lava Virgin Marys and the like, several restaurants and the *Rifugio Sapienza* itself (☎095.911.062; L30,000 per person). In 1983 and 1985, small-scale eruptions led to the evacuation of guests from the refuge: good photographs inside show it surrounded by the lava streams, the sky glowing red. If you've arrived with your own transport and it's late, this is the best place to **spend the night**, though it's wise to ring ahead and book. Otherwise, arriving on the early-morning bus, you'll have enough time to reach the top and get back for the return bus to Catania – it leaves around 4pm from the refuge. Failing that, it's not impossible to cadge a lift down with someone.

Up the volcano

If you choose to take the **cable car** (*funivia*) close to the *Rifugio Sapienza*, weather depending, it'll cost L32,000 return per person up to the *Rifugio Montagnola*, from where **jeeps** with a guide will take you to the Torre del Filósofo (April–Oct, weather allowing; L15,000 one way, L30,000 return). Otherwise, you can walk. It really depends on finances and time: **walking** up from the *Sapienza* will take around four hours, and from the *Montagnola* two hours at least, the return obviously much less. However you go, take warm clothes, good shoes or boots and – especially if you wear contact lenses – glasses to keep the flying grit out of your eyes; it's not an easy climb. Weather conditions higher up are often different from those at the *Rifugio Sapienza*, so the cable-car station comes equipped with two television screens, which show pictures from the crater area and the cable-car stop, helping you to decide whether to go onwards and upwards. Padded jackets are available for rent if you're using the cable car or jeep (L4000 – from the operators and guides).

The volcano is a lunar landscape, the ground under your feet alternately black, grey or red depending on the age of the lava. The more recent stuff lies in great folds, earlier minor craters signposted as you climb; below, the red roofs and green fields of the lower hills stretch away to the sea. Even in winter, the snow on the southern side tends to lie only in patches, partly melted by the heat of the rocks (see footnote overleaf). On the way up, the minibus makes a short stop at the **Valle**

del Bove, an enormous chasm almost 20km in circumference, its lava walls 900m high. A massive rent in the side of the volcano, its sunken flank comprises a sixth of the entire surface area of Etna – only one of many mind-boggling photo opportunities on this trip.

Depending on weather conditions, you should be able to reach the so-called **Torre del Filósofo**, a tower said to have been the home of Empedocles, but more likely a memorial built by the Romans to celebrate the emperor Hadrian's climb to the summit. Most tours stop at this point (2900m) though there is a path up to the highest point of unguided access, taking another thirty minutes or so to reach. Beyond, from the turnaround point for the minibus, you look up to the summit, smoke puffing from the **southeast crater** immediately above. Though there's only a rope across the ground to prevent you from climbing further, it would be foolish to presume that nothing serious would happen to you if you did – gaseous explosions and molten rock are common this far up. Higher still is the **main crater**: depending on the weather conditions you'll see smoke from here too, and, if you're lucky, spitting explosions. If you've walked, you'll be glad of the **bar** set up in a wooden hut at the minibus stop, one of the more peculiar places in the world to get a cappuccino.

Over on the northern side of the volcano, where hollows in the ground are filled year-round with snow, the ice used to be cut, covered with ash and then transported to the rest of the island, the mainland and even Malta, for refrigeration purposes – a peculiar export that constituted the main source of revenue for the Bishop of Catania, who owned the land until comparatively recently.

festivals

January
15 Festival of San Mauro in **Aci Castello**.
17 Festival of Sant'Antonio in **Nicolosi**.

February
3–5 Festa di Sant'Agata in **Catania**: boisterous street events, fireworks and food stalls, and the procession of the saint's relics.

February/March
Carnevale Five days of floats, flowers and traditional music in **Acireale** – one of Sicily's best annual events. Smaller-scale affair at **Paternò**.

March/April
Easter Good Friday procession in **Acireale** in traditional costume. Easter Sunday ceremony in **Adrano**, the Diavolata – a symbolic display showing the Archangel Michael defeating the Devil.

May
9–10 Traditional high jinks at **Trecastagni**: a pilgrimage by athletic souls who, barefoot and shirt-less, run the main road linking Catania to the sanctuary at Trecastagni; as well as costumes, painted carts, etc.

July
19–26 Festival commemorating St Vénera in **Acireale**.
24 Pesce a Mare festival at **Aci Trezza**: if the tourist office is to be believed, "a fisherman pretends to be a fish and excitedly the local fishermen catch him". Unmissable.

August
15 Procession of the *vara* in **Randazzo**: an 18-metre-high column with decorative figures representing the Assumption.

November
11 San Martino's Day celebrations in **Catania**.

December
Christmas week Display of eighteenth-century cribs in **Acireale**.

travel details

Trains
Catania to: Acireale (every 40min; 15min); Caltagirone (9 daily; 2hr); Caltanissetta (6 daily; 2hr 30min); Enna (9 daily; 1hr 30min); Gela (9 daily; 2hr 40min); Giarre-Riposto (every 40min; 30min); Lentini (hourly; 30min); Messina (every 40min; 1hr 30min); Palermo (6 daily; 3hr 15min); Siracusa (hourly; 1hr 30min); Taormina (every 40min; 1hr).

Randazzo to: Taormina (3–5 daily; 1hr).

Circumetnea trains
Catania to: Paternò, Adrano, Bronte, Maletto, Randazzo (9 daily; 2hr 10min).

Randazzo to: Linguaglossa, Giarre-Riposto (6 daily; 1hr 15min).

Buses
Bronte to: Castello Maniace (Mon–Sat 5 daily; 20min).

Catania to: Acireale (every 30min; 30min); Adrano (1 daily Mon–Sat; 1hr 15min); Agrigento (9 daily Mon–Sat, 4 Sun; 2hr 50min); Augusta (11 daily Mon–Sat, 3 Sun; 50min); Caltagirone (6 daily Mon–Sat, 4 Sun; 1hr 30min); Enna (7 daily Mon–Sat, 4 Sun; 1hr 30min); Fornazzo (for Milò, 6 daily Mon–Sat, 2 Sun; 1hr 15min); Gela (7 daily Mon–Sat, 2 Sun; 2hr); Giardini-Naxos (14 daily Mon–Sat, 6 Sun; 1hr 25min); Lentini (every 30–60min Mon–Sat, 6 Sun; 30min); Messina (fast service hourly Mon–Sat, every 2hr Sun; 1hr 35min: regular service 12 daily Mon–Sat, 6 Sun; 3hr 10min); Nicolosi (hourly; 40min); Nicosia (5 daily Mon–Sat, 2 Sun; 2hr 30min); Noto (5 daily Mon–Sat, 1 Sun; 2hr 15min); Pachino (5 daily Mon–Sat, 1 Sun; 3hr); Palermo (hourly; 2hr 40min); Piazza Armerina (7 daily Mon–Sat, 2 Sun; 2hr); Ragusa (8 daily Mon–Sat, 4 Sun; 3hr); Rifugio Sapienza (1 daily; 2hr); Siracusa (11 daily Mon–Sat, 4 Sun; 1hr 15min); Taormina (14 daily Mon–Sat, 6 Sun; 1hr 40min); Trecastagni (10 daily Mon–Sat, 6 Sun; 40min); Zafferana Etnea (hourly Mon–Sat, 5 Sun; 1hr).

Catania airport to: Agrigento (8 daily Mon–Sat, 6 Sun; 2hr 40min); Enna (5 daily Mon–Sat, 2 Sun; 1hr 10min); Messina (by autostrada 11 daily Mon–Sat, 9 Sun; 2hr); Milazzo (1 daily Mon–Sat June–Sept; 2hr).

Lentini to: Catania (every 30–60min Mon–Sat, 6 Sun; 30min); Ragusa (2 daily Mon–Sat; 2hr 15min); Siracusa (9 daily Mon–Sat, 1 Sun; 40min).

Randazzo to: Bronte (3 daily Mon–Sat; 30min); Cesarò (3 daily Mon–Sat; 1hr); Giardini-Naxos (4 daily Mon–Sat; 1hr 20min); Maletto (3 daily Mon–Sat; 20min); Messina (4 daily Mon–Sat; 2hr 15min).

Catamarans
From Catania to: Malta (5–6 weekly July & Aug, 2 weekly June & Sept to mid-Oct; 3hr).

CHAPTER SIX

SIRACUSA AND THE SOUTHEAST

S icily's **southeast** corner is dense with interest, an area whose historic towns and vigorous scenery merit as much time as you can give them. This has always been one of the island's wealthiest enclaves, reflected in the opulence of its building styles, and especially in **Siracusa**, whose long and glorious history outshines all other Sicilian cities. With its streets displaying examples of the architecture of almost every age, Siracusa has managed to survive the earthquakes that have repeatedly afflicted the area, none so destructive as that of 1693, which affected the whole of the region as far north as Catania. This upheaval did, however, produce one positive and lasting effect: where there were ruins, a confident new generation of architects raised planned towns, displaying a noble but vivacious **Baroque style** – of which **Noto**, **Ragusa** and **Módica** are the most outstanding examples.

In contrast to the refinement of its cities, much of the southeastern landscape is rough and wild, cut through by the **Monti Iblei** and riven by unexpected and often spectacular ravines, or *cave*. Wedged in one of these, **Pantálica**, west of Siracusa, is Sicily's greatest necropolis. Nearby **Palazzolo Acréide** has the best of the classical digs outside Siracusa, while there are several other sites along the coast, often beside uncrowded expanses of sand.

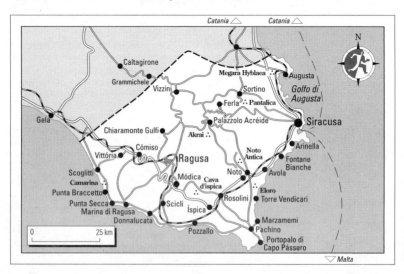

SIRACUSA AND AROUND

Once **Siracusa** was the most important city in the western world. Now, with most of Sicily's business activity located elsewhere and all political power centred on Palermo, the port's only status is that of a mere provincial capital. Although Siracusa retains the intimacy of a small town at its heart, it's charged with historical resonance. There's no shortage of things to see, and it's a useful base for visiting any of the other places mentioned below, all on bus routes and few more than 45 minutes from the city.

Like Siracusa, **Augusta**, to the north, is a port centred on an offshore islet, but the similarity ends there. The coast between the two, the **Golfo di Augusta**, has Sicily's greatest concentration of industry, a petrochemical nightmare of immense proportions that utterly overwhelms what's left of the old Greek city of **Megara Hyblaea**. Inland, the high mountainous area around **Pantálica**, occupied since the thirteenth century BC, has preserved its ancient necropolis from twentieth-century intrusions, while the nearby town of **Palazzolo Acréide** shelters the site of Greek **Akrai**. You have to head south, though, for the biggest draw in Siracusa's hinterland: the town of **Noto**, whose charms vie with those of the provincial capital but are dedicated to the perfection of just one artistic style, the Baroque.

The coast around here has plenty of good **beaches**, trailing off into a humdrum series of small resorts dotting Sicily's southern cape, **Capo Pássero**.

Siracusa

More than any other Sicilian city, **SIRACUSA** (ancient Syracuse) has a past that is central not just to the island's history, but to that of the entire Mediterranean region. Its greatest splendour belongs to antiquity. Syracuse established its ascendancy over other Sicilian cities for more than five hundred years and at its height was the supreme power in Europe, with at least three times its present population. Its central position on the major trade routes ensured that even after its heyday the port continued to wield influence and preserve its prestige.

All this is reflected in a staggering diversity of monuments, spanning the Hellenic, early Christian, medieval, Renaissance and Baroque eras – the styles are often shoulder-to-shoulder, sometimes in the same building. Combined with its inspired location, this distracting medley makes Siracusa one of the most enjoyable towns in Sicily in which to spend time.

A brief history

The **ancient city** grew around Ortygia, an easily defensible offshore island with two natural harbours on either side, fresh springs and access to extensive fertile plains over on the mainland, from which important trade routes weaved inland. These natural advantages couldn't help but attract settlers, and around 733 BC Corinthian colonists arrived here, apparently at the behest of the Delphic oracle. It wasn't until the beginning of the fifth century BC that the city's political position was boosted by an alliance with Greeks at Akragas (Agrigento) and Gela. With the crushing victory of their combined forces over the Carthaginians at Himera in 480 BC (see p.117), and the transfer of Gela's tyrant, **Gelon**, to Syracuse, the stage was set for a century of expansion and the beginning of the city's long supremacy on the island. The grandest monuments you'll see here are from this period, and more often than not were built by slaves provided from the many victories won by Syracuse's bellicose dictators.

Inevitably, the city's ambitions provoked the intervention of Athens, who dispatched one of the greatest fleets ever seen in the ancient world. This **Great Expedition** was scuppered in 413 BC by a mixture of poor leadership and astute defence: "to the victors the most brilliant of successes, to the vanquished the most calamitous of defeats" commented the historian Thucydides. But Syracuse earned the condemnation of the Hellenic world for its seven-year incarceration of the vanquished Athenians in appalling conditions in the city's notorious quarries, some still visitable today.

Throughout this period Syracuse was in a state of constant tension between a few overweening but extremely capable rulers, and sporadic convulsions of democracy. Occasionally the tyrants displayed a yearning for cultural respectability that sat uncomfortably beside their shrewd power-seeking. **Hieron I** (478–466 BC), for instance, described by the historian Diodorus as "an utter stranger to sincerity and nobility of character", invited many of the luminaries of the age to his court, including **Pindar**, and **Aeschylus** – who possibly witnessed the production of his last plays, *Prometheus Bound* and *Prometheus Released*, in the city's theatre. **Dionysius the Elder** (405–367 BC) – "cruel, vindictive and a profane plunderer of temples" and responsible for the first of the **Euryalus** forts – comically harboured literary ambitions to the extent of regularly entering his poems in the annual Olympic Games. His works were consistently rejected, until the Athenians judged it politic to give him the prize, whereupon his delirious celebrations were enough to provoke the seizure which killed him. His son **Dionysius II** (367–343 BC) dallied with his tutor **Plato**'s "philosopher-king" theories until megalomania turned his head and Plato fled in dismay. Dionysius himself, recorded Plutarch, spent the end of his life in exile, "loitering about the fish market, or sitting in a perfumer's shop drinking the diluted wine of the taverns, or squabbling in the streets with common women".

Rarely, the rulers themselves initiated democratic reforms – men such as **Timoleon** (343–337 BC), who arrived from Corinth to inject new life into all the Sicilian cities, and **Hieron II**, who preserved Syracuse's independence from the assertions of Rome by a novel policy of conciliation, abandoning expansion in favour of preserving the status quo. His long reign (265–215 BC) saw the construction of such monuments as the **Ara di Ierone II**, and the enlargement of the **Teatro Greco** to more or less its existing proportions.

With the death of Hieron, Syracuse, along with practically every other Sicilian city, sided with Carthage against Rome in the Second Punic War. For two years the city was besieged by the Romans, who had to contend with all the ingenious contrivances devised for its defence by **Archimedes**, though Syracuse eventually fell in 211 BC, an event that sent shock waves rippling around the classical world. Syracuse was ransacked, and Archimedes himself – the last of the great Hellenic thinkers – was hacked to death, despite the injunctions of the Roman general Marcellus.

Syracuse languished under Roman rule and shared in the general despoliation of Sicily carried out by the governor Verres. Its trading role still made it the most prominent Sicilian city, and it became a notable centre of early Christianity, as attested by its extensive **catacombs**. Syracuse briefly became the capital of the Byzantine empire when Constans moved his court here in 663 AD, but otherwise the city was eclipsed by events outside its control and played no active part against all the successive waves of Arab, Norman and other medieval conquerors. The **Castello Maniace**, erected by Frederick II, survives from this period, along with some other important vestiges of fourteenth- and fifteenth-century building that help to give Ortygia its lavish appearance today. The 1693 earthquake laid low much of the city, but provided the impetus for some of its Baroque master-pieces, notably the creations of the great Siculo-Spanish architect Giovanni Verméxio, who contributed an imposing facade to the **Duomo** – a building that encapsulates the polyglot character of modern Siracusa.

Modern Siracusa: orientation

Siracusa today has kept the same general arrangement as it had two and a half millennia ago, with the city divided between its ancient hub, the island of Ortygia, and the four mainland quarters of Achradina, Tyche, Neapolis and – further west – Epipolae. You'll spend much of your time on **Ortygia**, still the heart and soul of Siracusa, and predominantly medieval and Baroque in appearance. Across the Ponte Nuovo, the main bridge linking the island with the mainland, the modern city is centred on **Achradina**, now, as in Greek times, the busy commercial cen-tre, traversed by the main street of **Corso Gelone**. North of Achradina, the old residential quarter of **Tyche** holds Siracusa's **catacombs** and its celebrated **Museo Archeológico**, while **Neapolis** is the site of a **Parco Archeológico**, con-taining remains of the Greek city's theatres and some extensive quarries. Spread over the ridge to the west of town, **Epipolae** holds the old defensive walls and the solid remnants of the **Euryalus fort**.

Arrival, getting around and information

The **train station** (☎0931.67.964) is on the mainland at the end of Via Francesco Crispi; there's a **left-luggage** office here if you need to dump your bags (L5000 for 24hr). The **bus station** is on Piazza della Posta (also known as Riva della Posta), just over the Ponte Nuovo in Ortygia; AST have their office and operate their city and regional buses from here (☎0931.462.711). You'll find the SAIS ticket office and regional buses at Via Trieste (☎0931.66.710), round the corner from Piazza della Posta. For departure points and destinations out of Siracusa, see "Listings".

Although much of Siracusa is easy enough to see on foot, you can always avail yourself of the orange AST **city buses** when the sightseeing begins to take its toll. The main stops on Ortygia are in Piazza della Posta, Piazza Archimede, and Piazza Pancali/Largo XXV Luglio; on the mainland, they are along Corso Umberto. One ride costs L600, and relevant routes are specified in the text (tick-ets and information from the Piazza della Posta office). As for **taxis**, there are ranks in Piazza Pancali (☎0931.64.323), on Corso Gelone (☎0931.69.302) and Via Ticino (☎0931.64.323), and at the train station (☎0931.69.722).

For free maps, accommodation listings and other information, the main **tourist office** is on Ortygia, at Via Maestranza 33 (summer Mon–Sat 8.30am–2pm & 4.30–7.30pm, Sun 8.30am–2pm; winter Mon & Sat 8.30am–2pm, Tues–Fri 8.30am–2pm & 4.30–7pm; ☎0931.464.255, fax 0931.67.803). There's another office on the mainland, at Via San Sebastiano 43–45 (summer Mon–Fri 8.30am–1.30pm & 3.30–6.30pm, Sat 8.30am–1pm; winter Mon–Sat 8.30am–1.30pm; ☎0931.67.710).

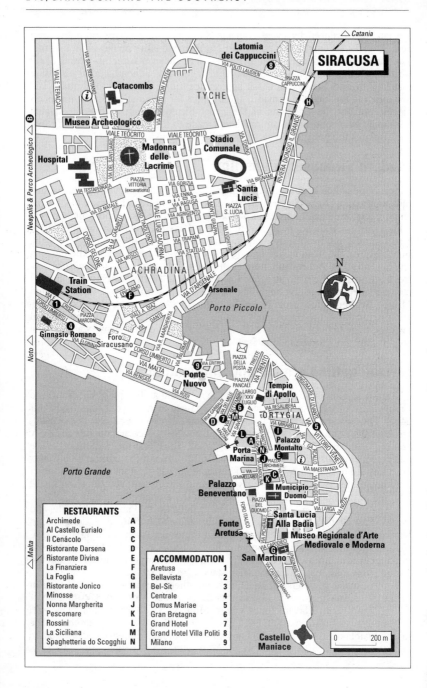

△ Catania

**Latomia
dei Cappuccini**

SIRACUSA

PIAZZA
CAPPUCCINI

VIA SAN SEBASTIANO

VIALE TERACATI

VIALE AUGUSTO VON PLATEN

VIA POLITI LAUDIEN

8

H

Catacombs

TYCHE

Museo Archeologico

VIALE TEÓCRITO

VIALE TEÓCRITO

VIA DEL SANTUARIO

**Stadio
Comunale**

VIA LORENO

Hospital

**Madonna
delle
Lacrime**

PIAZZA
VITTORIA
(excavations)

VIA GORIZIA

VIA BIGNAMI

**Santa
Lucia**

VIA TESTAFERRATA

VIA ENNA

VIA RAGUSA

PIAZZA
S. LUCIA

VIA DI NATALE

CORSO GELONE

VIA CARABELLI

VIALE LUIGI CADORNA

CORSO TIMOLEONE

VIA AGRIGENTO

VIA MONTE GRAPPA

VIA RIGHETTI

VIA TRAPANI

VIA STATELLO

VIA MOSCO

ACHRADINA

VIA EPICARMO

**Train
Station**

F

Arsenale

VIA CRISPI

CORSO UMBERTO I

PIAZZA
MARCONI

VIALE A. DIAZ

VIA DANTE

Porto Piccolo

N

1

4

Ginnasio Romano

VIA FLORINA

**Foro
Siracusano**

CORSO UMBERTO I

VIA MARGHERITA

VIA MALTA

9

VIA ERITREA

PIAZZA
DELLA
POSTA

VIA TRIESTE

VIA TRENTO

**Ponte
Nuovo**

PIAZZA
PANCALI

LARGO
XXV
LUGLIO

**Tempio
di Apollo**

VIA BENGASI

VIA RODI

RIVA GARIBALDI

6

ORTYGIA

VIA RESALIBERA

VIA MIRABELLA

7

D

M

VIA SAVOIA

VIA MAZZINI

5

I

Porto Grande

A

**Porta
Marina**

N

J

**Palazzo
Montalto**

PIAZZA
ARCHIMEDE

E

VITTORIO VENETO

VIA MAESTRANZA

VIA GEMMELLARO

VIA ARCHIMEDE

K

C

Municipio

**Palazzo
Beneventano**

PIAZZA
DEL
DUOMO

FORO ITALICO

Duomo

VIA LARGA

VIA NIZZA

**Fonte
Aretusa**

**Santa Lucia
Alla Badia**

VIA PICHERALI

VIA CAPODIECI

**Museo Regionale d'Arte
Mediovale e Moderna**

G

LUNGOMARE DI ORTIGIA

VIA CASTELLO MANIACE

San Martino

**Castello
Maniace**

0   200 m

N

RESTAURANTS

Archimede	**A**
Al Castello Eurialo	**B**
Il Cenácolo	**C**
Ristorante Darsena	**D**
Ristorante Divina	**E**
La Finanziera	**F**
La Foglia	**G**
Ristorante Jonico	**H**
Minosse	**I**
Nonna Margherita	**J**
Pescomare	**K**
Rossini	**L**
La Siciliana	**M**
Spaghetteria do Scogghiu	**N**

ACCOMMODATION

Aretusa	**1**
Bellavista	**2**
Bel-Sit	**3**
Centrale	**4**
Domus Mariae	**5**
Gran Bretagna	**6**
Grand Hotel	**7**
Grand Hotel Villa Politi	**8**
Milano	**9**

△ Neapolis & Parco Archeologico **B**

△ Noto

△ Malta

> ### ACCOMMODATION PRICE CODES
>
> These represent the **cheapest available double room in high season**, usually
> – but not always – without en-suite bathroom or shower. Out of season, you'll often
> be able to negotiate a lower price than those suggested here. For more informa-
> tion about hotels and room prices, see p.27. The categories are:
>
> ① under L60,000   ④ L120,000–150,000   ⑦ L250,000–300,000
> ② L60,000–90,000   ⑤ L150,000–200,000   ⑧ over L300,000
> ③ L90,000–120,000   ⑥ L200,000–250,000

Accommodation

Siracusa's **accommodation** choices aren't spectacular, and in high season you
should check in early or reserve in advance. In summer, be prepared to pay
another L5000 or so for obligatory breakfast tacked onto the official prices. Most
of the city's cheaper hotels are on the mainland, within walking distance of the
train station, where there's no problem parking; there are only three hotels on
Ortygia and you should reserve in advance if you want to stay there.

Hotels

Archimede, Via Francesco Crispi 67 (☎0931.462.458). Friendly and comfortable, this good-
value hotel specializes in large, comfortable bathrooms, and all rooms come equipped with
electric fans. ②.

Aretusa, Via Francesco Crispi 75 (☎ & fax 0931.24.211). Halfway between the station and the
Foro Siracusano, this is the most reasonable of the modern hotels in this part of town. Rooms
with bath are more expensive. American Express cards only. ②.

Hotel Bellavista, Via Diodoro Siculo 4 (☎0931.411.355, fax 0931.37.927). Way to the north
of the centre, but handy for the Museo Archeológico and Neapolis, this comfortable hotel has
a sun terrace. ④.

Pensione Bel-Sit, 4th floor, Via Oglio 5 (☎0931.60.245). Adequate accommodation, within
walking distance of the Neapolis, though less handy for the bars and restaurants of Ortygia.
From Foro Siracusano, head up Corso Gelone and take the second left down Via Brenta. All
rooms with bath and there's a lift. No credit cards. ③.

Hotel Centrale, Corso Umberto 141 (☎0931.60.528). On the west side of Piazzale Marconi,
very basic, but very friendly, with good prices; you can even try bargaining them down a little out of season. Also a home for pigeons, which can be noisy. No credit cards. ①.

Domus Mariae, Via Vittorio Veneto 76 (☎0931.24.858 or 0931.24.854, fax 0931.24.859). On
Ortygia, efficiently run by nuns and with views to the sea, the fairly swish rooms all have
bathrooms and air-conditioning. There's a solarium and a chapel, too. ⑤.

Gran Bretagna, Via Savoia 21 (☎0931.68.765). This is the most feasible option if you want to
be at the heart of things in Siracusa. It's got loads of character: the rooms, which vary enormously, are frescoed or have walls festooned with framed works of art. On the other hand the
hotel is often full, and some travellers have expressed irritation, not least with the midnight
curfew. More expensive rooms with bath also available. There is a restaurant on the ground
floor, which is mediocre; breakfast included in the price. ②.

Grand Hotel, Viale Mazzini 12 (☎0931.464.600, fax 0931.464.611). This veteran establishment enjoys a prime position in Ortygia, overlooking the Porto Grande. Access to a private
beach, lavish furnishings and all the refinements, as you'd expect when the bill comes to a
cool L350,000 per double room. ⑧.

Grand Hotel Villa Politi, Via M. Politi 2 (☎0931.412.121, fax 0931.36.061). North of the centre, in Tyche, this luxury hotel has attracted the rich and famous in the past. It's next to the
Latomia dei Cappuccini, a splendid spot for a splurge. ⑧.

Hotel Milano, Corso Umberto 10 (☎0931.66.981). Nearest to Ortygia, on the mainland, the *Milano* is cheap enough, but check the bathrooms before accepting: some are less than adequate. Single rooms here tend to be noisy, windowless boxes. No credit cards. ①.

The youth hostel and campsites

Albergo della Gioventù, Viale Epipoli 45 (☎0931.711.118). The youth hostel is out at Belvedere on the Epipolae ridge, just beyond Euryalus castle. Open all year, it's a clean and relaxed place, with a maximum of four beds per room, serving breakfast and sometimes other meals. Buses #11 and #25 run up here in around 20m from Piazza Pancali, the last one leaving at around 9.30pm. L25,000 per person.

Agriturist Rinaura (☎0931.721.224). The nearest campsite to Siracusa is 5km away, just off the Noto road, turning right after the junction for Arenella. It has a few cabins available for rent but is otherwise in a fairly shabby state, and lies 2km from the sea. If you bus it (#21, #22 and #23 from Corso Umberto or Piazza della Posta), you'll have to walk the last kilometre to the site. Open all year.

Fontane Bianche (☎0931.790.333). Posher than the *Agriturist*, and near an excellent beach, this site is much further south – 24km from Siracusa, at the resort of Fontane Bianche, though with regular bus connections. May–Oct.

Ortygia

The ancient nucleus of Siracusa, **ORTYGIA**, best conserves the city's essential spirit. Here the artistic vestiges of over 2500 years of history are concentrated in a space barely 500m across, 1km in length and all within the ambit of an easy stroll through quiet streets and alleys. Although parts of Ortygia have been badly neglected in the past, sensitive maintenance in recent years has rescued many of the island's monuments from irreversible damage, helping to restore the old town's lustre.

Across the narrow ribbon of water severing the island from the mainland, the **Tempio di Apollo**, at the back of Piazza Pancali, is a case in point. This dignified old ruin is thought to have been the first of the great Doric temples built in Sicily, though not much survives of its seventh-century or early sixth-century BC fabric apart from a couple of columns, fragments of others and part of the south wall of its cella. The high arched window in this wall dates from a Norman church that incorporated part of the temple into its structure, and you can make out a dedication inscribed to Apollo on the reconstituted stereobate. However, to get a complete picture of the original temple you'll have to see the scale model in Siracusa's museum (p.247).

Around Piazza Archimede

Corso Matteotti leads up from Piazza Pancali to Ortygia's central **Piazza Archimede**, its centrepiece a twentieth-century fountain depicting the nymph Arethusa (the symbol of Ortygia) at the moment of her transformation into a spring. The square has a couple of bars with outdoor seating, from which you can survey the Catalan-Gothic *palazzi* around its sides, a common architectural style in Ortygia.

Take a look, too, around the corner from Piazza Archimede, down the claustrophobic Via Montalto, where the **Palazzo Montalto** is sadly shored up and undergoing some radical restoration. You can still admire its facade, graced by immaculate double- and triple-arched windows, and with an inscription dating the building's construction to 1397. This is one of the few surviving examples of the style favoured by the powerful Chiaramonte dynasty, more of which can be seen from the derelict courtyard at the back, where a loggia still stands.

Piazza del Duomo: the Duomo

Ortygia's most impressive architecture, though, belongs to its Baroque period, and nowhere does this reach such heights as in the city's loveliest square (though it's presently undergoing maintenance work), the elongated **Piazza del Duomo** – a largely traffic-free space surrounded by a range of seventeenth- and eighteenth-century buildings, best of all the **Duomo** itself (8am–noon & 4–7pm). To get an idea of the great age of this cathedral, walk round to the side on Via Minerva to see not just the battlemented west wall added by the Normans, but also the stout Doric columns that form the skeleton of the structure, part of an earlier Greek temple. Although these bones were fleshed out by later builders, they still provide the church's main proportions and set a tone of dark antiquity.

The site was already a sacred one when the Greeks started work on an Ionic temple to Athena here in about 530 BC, though this was abandoned when a new temple was begun in thanksgiving for the victory over the Carthaginians at Himera. The extravagant decoration that adorned this building spread its fame throughout the ancient world, and tantalizing details of it have come down to us through Cicero, who visited Syracuse in the first century BC and listed the temple's former contents as part of his prosecution of the Roman praetor and villain Verres, who appeared to have walked off with a good proportion of them – part of the booty he plundered from many Sicilian temples. The doors were of ivory and gold, and its walls painted with military scenes and portraits of various of Syracuse's tyrants – claimed to be the earliest examples of portraiture in European art. On the temple's roof stood a tall statue of the warrior-goddess Athena carrying a golden shield which, catching the sun's rays, served as a beacon for sailors out at sea.

Although all this rich decoration has vanished, the main body of the temple was saved further despoliation thanks to its conversion into a Christian church, which was elevated to cathedral status in 640 AD. A more drastic overhaul was carried out after the 1693 earthquake, when the Norman facade collapsed and was replaced by the present formidable Baroque front, with statues by Marabitti. This is in sharp contrast to the more muted **interior** in which it is still the frame of the ancient temple that is prevalent. The aisles are formed by the massive Doric columns, while the cella walls were hacked through to make the present arched nave. There's also evidence of the temple in the apse at the end of the north aisle, where you can make out the columned end of the cella wall. This apse is actually the one Byzantine element in the building, and stylistic boundaries are further fudged by the presence here of a good statue by the Renaissance artist Antonello Gagini, *Madonna of the Snow*. Other statues by the Gagini clan line the north aisle, where the distorted pillars give some inkling of how close the entire structure came to toppling when the seventeenth-century earthquake hit Siracusa. The duomo's south aisle shows more characteristic Baroque effusion in the series of richly ornate chapels, though the first one – actually the baptistry – is from an earlier age. Enlivened by some twelfth-century arabesque mosaics, it contains a Norman font that was cut from a block still marked with a Greek inscription, and is supported by seven bronze lions.

The rest of the square

Across from the duomo, on the corner of Via Minerva, the **Municipio** displays the foundations of the first Ionic temple that occupied this site in its basement, and there are more fragments from it in two ground-floor rooms (ask at the gate).

Opposite here, **Palazzo Beneventano** has an attractive eighteenth-century facade, while further down the piazza the southern end is marked by the late seventeenth-century church of **Santa Lucia alla Badia**, finishing point of the procession of Santa Lucia in December. The church's upper storey was a later, mid-eighteenth-century addition; the whole building is currently closed.

Palazzo Bellomo and San Martino

Siracusa's tradition of architectural hybridism is again apparent in the **Palazzo Bellomo**, Via Capodieci 14, an interesting mixture of thirteenth- and fifteenth-century features, with a courtyard that has some thirteenth-century arcading and a Spanish-style stairway leading up to the loggia. This and the next-door Palazzo Parisio are the ideal surroundings for the superlative **Museo Regionale d'Arte Medioevale e Moderna** (Mon–Sat 9am–1pm, Sun 9am–noon; L8000), a small but select display, with mainly sculpture on the ground floor – including some medieval and Renaissance tombs, and the inevitable examples of Gagini expertise – and some exceptional paintings on the first floor. Most famous of these is the *Annunciation* by Antonello da Messina, rescued from a state of advanced decay in a church at Palazzolo Acréide (see p.258), and subjected to some pretty rigorous and controversial restoration. The debate arose over the decision to transfer the painting from wood to canvas, and the whole story of how this was done is meticulously illustrated and explained here, a useful appendage (if you read Italian), though your attention will be principally taken up by the painting itself, still an absorbing image despite the considerable damage. You can also find here Caravaggio's *Burial of St Lucy*, a local favourite.

In nearby Via San Martino, take a look at the church of **San Martino** – one of Siracusa's oldest churches. Originally a sixth-century basilica, it was rebuilt in the fourteenth century and smartened up with a good-looking rose window and Gothic doorway. If you can get in (it's currently closed for restoration), its dusky interior is a treat – plain stone columns leading to a tiny mosaic half-apse with a fifteenth-century triptych to the right of the choir.

The Fonte Aretusa and medieval Ortygia

Walk east down Via Capodieci to the seafront, where the **Fonte Aretusa** spreads serenely below the small piazza Largo Aretusa. Mentioned in the original Delphic directions that brought the first Greek settlers here, the number of myths associated with this freshwater spring underlines the strong sentimental links that continued to bind the colonists to their motherland. This was where the nymph Arethusa rose after swimming across from the Peloponnese, having been metamorphosed into a spring by the goddess Artemis to escape the attentions of the predatory river god Alpheus, all in vain, though, for the determined Alpheus pursued her here to mingle with her in a watery form. Other legends declared that the spring's water would stain red at the time of the annual sacrifices at the sanctuary of Olympia, and that a cup thrown into the river there would rise here in Ortygia. More recently, and less apocryphal, Admiral Nelson took water supplies on board here on his way to the Battle of the Nile. Now that the spot has been planted with papyrus, and filled with bream below the water and ducks above, it's a compulsory stop on the evening *passeggiata*, and the piazza's furnished with a nice selection of cafés.

At the end of the dangling limb of land south of here sits the stout **Castello Maniace**, a defensive bulwark erected around 1239 by Frederick II, but named after the Byzantine admiral who briefly reconquered Syracuse from the Arabs in

NEIL SETCHFIELD

Cooked onion stall, Catania

ALAN McARTHUR

Seafood market, Siracusa

ALAN McARTHUR

Ortygia, Siracusa

Duomo, Piazza Amerina

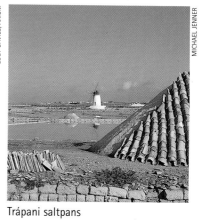

Trápani saltpans

Villa Imperiale mosaic, Casale

La Scala, Caltagirone

Valle dei Templi, Agrigento

Baroque balcony, Siracusa

Festival of St Lucy, Siracusa

Il Cretto, Rúderi di Gibellina

Fallen *telamon*, Valle dei Templi

Norman castle, Erice

Segesta theatre

1038. Unfortunately the solid square keep still retains its military function as a barracks and access isn't allowed.

Back below the Fonte Aretusa is a small garden; from here the main procession of promenaders takes off, extending all the way along the tree-lined **Foro Vittorio Emanuele II**, with rows of bars on one side and the odd millionaire's yacht on the other. The vast, still pool of the **Porto Grande** spreads out beyond, dotted with fishing-boats, liners and tankers. At the end of the avenue, to the right, the **Porta Marina** is a remnant of the city's medieval walls, a fifteenth-century gateway surmounted by a curlicued Spanish heraldic device.

If you've walked around the sights in a fairly disciplined order, it's well worth taking a couple of hours to do some aimless wandering around the less immediately obvious parts of Ortygia: typically, you'll run across a clutch of good-looking *palazzi* from different epochs, spread all over the island. The best of these are from the spate of building that took place under the aegis of the Aragonese, such as the **Palazzo Gargallo** (in Via Gargallo, north off Via Maestranza), with a Catalan outer stair, and the **Palazzo Migliaccio** in Via Picherale (off Piazza del Duomo, close to the Fonte Aretusa), its white marble terrace adorned with black lava chevrons. But look out too for the later Baroque constructions, notably in **Via Maestranza** itself and **Via Vittorio Véneto**, on the eastern side of the island. Connecting this last street with Largo XXV Luglio, **Via Resalibera** is also worth a stroll, squeezing the occasional church between its tangled rows of houses, or a solitary bar – usually just a room full of wine barrels and old men, both half full of the stuff.

Achradina

Modern development in the central mainland quarter of **ACHRADINA** makes it difficult to picture the ancient city that Plutarch wept over when he heard of its fall to the Romans. Much of the new building dates from World War II, when Siracusa was bombed twice over – once by the Allies, then, after its capture, by the Luftwaffe in 1943. But you're likely to be staying in one of the hotels scattered around this part of town, or will pass through on the way to the archeological museum and park, so you could well drop in on some of these lesser sites en route.

You'll certainly become familiar with the rather shabby park area known as the **Foro Siracusano**. Site of the old town's *agora*, it holds a few paltry columns in a landscaped garden, and is not improved by the grotesque war memorial towering above, a Fascist monument from 1936. On Via Elorina, to the west, there's a much more interesting relic, the little-visited **Ginnasio Romano** (Mon–Sat 9am–1pm; free). This was never actually a gymnasium but a small Roman theatre, probably built in the first century AD when the ancient city's much grander Greek theatre was requisitioned for blood sports. A well-tended lawn surrounds the rectangular *cavea*, with the remains of a portico behind it. This once enclosed a small shrine, part of which is still visible. These days the theatre's orchestra is flooded from an underground cistern, hindering further excavation, though if anything enhancing the appeal of this forgotten mossy site.

Eastern Achradina

Over on the eastern edge of Achradina, close by the crowded huddle of boats in the **Porto Píccolo**, you'll find a much less recognizable ruin, the **Arsenale**, by the railway line, which is fenced off to the public. As its name suggests, it was a provisions centre, where ships were refurbished, hoisted up from the port by devices that clamped into the ground – and the slots that engaged them are about the only thing to look at here. Adjacent is another low-key sight, the **Edificio Termale**, a Byzantine bathhouse claimed to be the very same one in which, in 668 AD, the Emperor Constans was assassinated, knocked on the head by a servant wielding a soap dish. It's under a modern block of flats and about the only thing visible are a few piles of stones.

North: Santa Lucia

Via Fuggetta leads up to the modern city's most pleasant square, Piazza Santa Lucia, a huge space planted with an arcade of trees around three sides. It takes its name from the church of **Santa Lucia** (daily 9am–noon & 4–6pm), lying at its northern end, built in 1629 and supposedly marking the spot where St Lucy, Siracusa's patron saint, was martyred in 304 AD. Today the church has been methodically stripped of all the treasures that once made it an essential item on tourist itineraries, though it does retain its fine wooden ceiling and Norman tower. You can still visit Giovanni Verméxio's octagonal chapel of **San Sepolcro** outside in the piazza – ask inside the church. The mortal remains of the saint were originally preserved below this chapel, before being carried off to Constantinople by the Byzantine admiral Maniakes in 1038, and later shipped to Venice as part of the spoils plundered by the Venetian "crusaders" in 1204.

The real disappointment, though, is the lack of access to the extensive network of **catacombs** lying beneath this site, closed to the public until they can be made safe. After the ones in Rome, these constitute the largest system of subterranean tombs in Italy and are the oldest in Sicily.

Tyche

The entire district of **TYCHE**, which stretches north from Santa Lucia, is riddled with more of these catacombs, on account of the Roman prohibition of Christian burial within the city limits (Siracusa having by then shrunk back to its original core of Ortygia). The warrens were hewn out of the rock and often followed the course of underground aqueducts, disused since Greek times. All are now inaccessible, apart from those below the **Basilica di San Giovanni** (daily except Tues 9am–12.30pm & 2–5.30pm), which lies opposite the tourist office at Via San Sebastiano, off Viale Teócrito, and has been in ruins since 1693. Fronted by a triple arch, the church's nave is now open to the sky and the interior overgrown, but you can still admire the seventh-century apse and a medieval rose window. Once the city's cathedral, it was built over the crypt of St Marcian, first bishop of Siracusa. Steps lead down to the pillar where he was flogged to death in 254; his tomb is here too, along with a modern altar marking the spot where St Paul is supposed to have preached, stopping in the city as a prisoner on his way to Rome.

It's an unnerving experience walking through the gloomy, labyrinthine system of **catacombs** (tours L4000) underneath the church. Numerous side-passages lead off from the main gallery (*decumanus maximus*), often culminating in *rotonde*, or round caverns used for prayer; other passages are forbiddingly dark and closed off to the public. Entire families were interred in the thousands of niches hollowed out of these walls and floors, anxious for burial close to the tomb of St Marcian. Most of the treasures buried with the bodies have been pillaged, though the robbers overlooked one – an ornate sarcophagus unearthed from just below the floor in 1872 and now on show in Siracusa's archeological museum.

Just behind the archeological museum in Viale Teócrito the small **Museo del Papiro** (Tues–Sun 9am–1pm; free) is worth a visit to see papyrus art, ancient and modern, and the video.

The Museo Archeológico

Aside from the catacombs, the **Museo Archeológico** (Mon 3.30–6.30pm, Tues–Sat 9am–1pm & 3.30–6.30pm; first and third Sun every month 9am–12.30pm; L8000) forms Tyche's main attraction, just round the corner on Viale Teócrito. From Ortygia, buses #4, #5, #12 and #15 for the museum leave from Largo XXV Luglio and run up Corso Gelone and along Viale Teócrito. Purpose-built in the grounds of the Villa Landolina, and a bit of a maze, the museum contains Sicily's most wide-ranging collection of antiquities, worth a prolonged browse to view the almost indescribable wealth disgorged from archeological sites throughout the province and beyond. Near the entrance, an explanatory diagram colour-codes the three main sections into which the exhibits are arranged: prehistoric (section A); items from Syracuse, Megara Hyblaea and the Chalcidinian colonies (B); and finds from Gela, Agrigento, Syracuse's subcolonies and the indigenous Sikel centres, including copious material from the sites of Pantálica and Castelluccio (C). The information in English on the cases peters out after a while; the leaflet provided by Le Carte (see "Basics", p.42), on sale at the desk, is useful.

The museum's most celebrated exhibit is the **Venus Anadiomene**, also known as *Landolina*, after the archeologist who discovered her in 1804. *Anadiomene* means "rising from the sea", which describes her coy pose: with her left hand she holds a robe, while studs show where her broken-off right arm came across to hide her breasts. Probably Roman-made in the first century AD, from a Greek model, the headless statue has always evoked extreme responses, alternately exalting the delicacy and naturalism of the carving, and condemning her "immodest modesty", her knowing sensual attitude that symbolized the decline of the vigorous classical age and the birth of a new decadence. By the statue's feet, the dolphin, Aphrodite's emblem, is the only sign that this was a goddess.

Among the earlier Hellenic pieces, the museum also has some excellent *kouroi* – toned, muscular youths, one of which (in section B), from Lentini, is one of the most outstanding fragments still extant from the Archaic age of Greek art – around 500 BC. Of the same period, from the colony of Megara Hyblaea, there is a striking image of a mother/goddess in the act of suckling twins, its absorbed roundness expressing a tender harmony as close to earth and fertility rites as the *Venus Landolina* is to the cult of sensuality. The huge burial urns (pithoi) from the seventh century BC are impressive; look out also for the gruesome theatrical masks and the finely worked fourth-century marble sarcophagus from the catacombs below San Giovanni. It held a Roman official and his wife, both prominently depicted and surrounded by reliefs of scenes from the Old and New Testaments.

Santuario della Madonna delle Lácrime

Opposite the museum, across Viale Teócrito, stands the monolithic **Santuario della Madonna delle Lácrime** (daily 7am–12.30pm & 4–7pm), completed in 1994 to house a statue of the Madonna that allegedly wept for five days in 1953 (*delle Lácrime* means "of the tears"). Designed to resemble a giant teardrop, the monument is the latest and most prominent addition to the city's skyline and, some would say, the least harmonious. Typically for Siracusa, the newest architecture appears next to some of the oldest: just to the south, in Piazza della Vittoria, fenced-off (but visible) **excavations** have revealed extensive Greek and Roman houses and streets.

Neapolis and the Parco Archeológico

NEAPOLIS was the district containing most of the ancient city's social and religious amenities – theatres, altars and sanctuaries – and was thus never inhabited. Today it's encompassed by Siracusa's large **Parco Archeológico** (Tues–Sun 9am–2hr before sunset; L4000), reachable on foot in about twenty minutes from Foro Siracusano, or on buses #4, #5, #6, #8, #11, #12 or #15 from Piazza della Poste to Corso Gelone/Viale Teócrito. The entrance is hidden behind a tawdry circus of souvenir stalls and ice-cream stands, catering to the bus loads of tourists which arrive every few minutes in the summer.

On your way to the ticket booth, you'll pass the ruined base of the **Ara di Ierone II**, a 200-metre-long altar erected by Hieron II in the second half of the third century BC. Built in honour of Zeus Eleutherios, "the giver of freedom", it commemorated the achievements of Timoleon, who liberated the city from tyranny and decline, and was the biggest construction of its kind in all Magna Graecia. It was also the venue for some serious sacrificing: Diodorus records that 450 bulls were led up the ramps at either end of the altar to be slaughtered in the annual feast. Now railed off to the public, little is left standing above plinth level, though the sheer dimensions of the structure still retain their impact.

The Teatro Greco

At the end of the lane is the ticket office and the entrance to the **Teatro Greco**, Siracusa's most spectacular monument. One of the biggest and best-preserved Greek auditoriums, there's been a theatre on this site since at least the fifth century BC, though it was frequently modified and added to at different periods. Most of what you see today is owed to Hieron II, who expanded it to accommodate 15,000 people, in nine sections of 59 rows (of which 42 remain). The inscriptions around the top of the middle gangway on the west side of the theatre – faint but still visible – date from the third century BC, giving the names of the ruler and his family, with Zeus Olympios in the middle.

Most of the alterations carried out by the Romans were made to adapt the arena for gladiatorial combat, and included extending the orchestra by cutting back the first rows of seats. They also installed some marble-faced seats for privileged spectators, and the seventeenth row was removed, possibly to segregate the classes. Nowadays the theatre is used for a milder form of entertainment: concerts and Greek dramas, the latter performed, as in antiquity, in May and June in alternate (even-numbered) years – though not staged early in the morning, as were the original performances; ask at the ticket office for details.

Walk up through the theatre and the high terrace above contains a large artificial grotto, the **Nymphaeum**, fed by water from an ancient aqueduct, where a number of statues were found, now in the museum. To the left of here, the **Via dei Sepolcri** (Street of the Tombs) is deeply rutted by the carts that plied to and fro, and is flanked by more votive niches. It's closed to the public but you can see a fair way up the street from the fence.

Below the Greek theatre, in the trees behind the stage, sits a smaller structure, known as the **Teatro Lineare** due to its simple, straight design. Nearby are the scant remains of one of the site's most venerated spots, the **Santuario di Apollo**, which once contained a huge bronze statue of the god before this was carried off to Rome by the Emperor Tiberius.

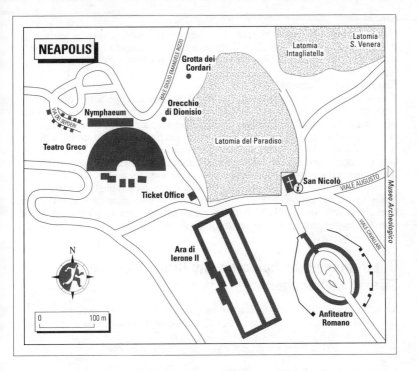

The Latomie del Paradiso and Grotta dei Cordari

At the entrance to the theatre, another path descends to the largest of Siracusa's huge *latomie* (pits), from which the rock for the city's multifarious monuments was excavated. These wide, vertically walled **quarries** also provided a harsh but effective prison for the 7000 Athenian prisoners of war, following the fiasco of the Great Expedition. Most were probably kept in the lusciously overgrown Latomia dei Cappuccini, across on Siracusa's eastern seafront in Tyche – now a garden for the Capuchin monks and closed until the collapsing walls can be bolstered. But here in Neapolis, the **Latomia del Paradiso** is well worth a look in its own right, mainly for the remarkable cavern known as the **Orecchio di Dionisio**. Over 60m long and 20m high, it owes its name (Ear of Dionysius) to the painter Caravaggio, who noted its resemblance to a human ear, while the association with Dionysius derives from a story that the tyrant used the cavern's acoustic qualities to over-hear the conversations of suspected conspirators. In fact, Dionysius probably had far more efficient means of extracting information, though the sound-enhancing effect is still there and can be tested by anyone.

A second cave, the geometrically shaped **Grotta dei Cordari**, was used as a work space by the ancient city's ropemakers, who found that the damp air in the cave prevented the rope strands from breaking under stress: inside, it's possible to see the grooves worn into rock by the twined rope – though the cave remains closed indefinitely to visitors. There are two other quarries here, the **Latomia**

Intagliatella, with a tall rocky pillar in the centre amid the lemon trees, and the niched **Latomia di Santa Vénera**, from where a precipitous passage leads off to the **Necrópoli Grotticelle**. This Greco-Roman burial ground includes one grave with a Doric pediment, dubiously imagined to be the tomb of Archimedes.

The Anfiteatro Romano

Keep hold of your ticket for the **Anfiteatro Romano**, through a gate on the right as you leave the park: a large elliptical arena built in the third century AD to satisfy the growing lust for circus games. One hundred and forty metres long – one of the largest of its kind anywhere – it's encircled by a parapet inscribed with the names of some of the leading citizens of the time, though you're unlikely to get near enough to see this as the interior is out of bounds. The rectangular tank in the centre of the arena is too small to have been used for aquatic displays, and is more likely to have been for draining the blood and gore spilled in the course of the combats. But not before the spectators had had their fill: at the end of the contests the infirm, ill and disabled would apparently attempt to suck warm blood from the bodies and take the livers from the animals, in the belief that this would speed their recovery.

Out from the city: Epipolae, the Ciane River and Siracusa's beaches

If you're beginning to wilt under the combined onslaught of heat and crowds, Siracusa offers some good possibilities for **half-day trips** out of the centre. Each is a bus ride away, or, in the case of the River Ciane, a boat ride – though this last would also make a decent walk, once you get off the main road.

Epipolae and the Castello Eurialo

The outlying area of **EPIPOLAE**, 7km west of the city, holds ancient Siracusa's inland military and defensive works. To get here from the centre, take bus #9, #11 or #12 from Ortygia or from Corso Gelone outside the Parco Archeológico, to the village of **Belvedere**, a twenty-minute ride.

These heights were first fortified by Dionysius the Elder in about 400 BC, after the Athenians had come so close to taking the city by occupying them a few years previously. Constantly modified and extended over a couple of centuries, what remains today consists of a great wall, which marked the city's western limit, and the **Castello Eurialo** (daily 9am–1hr before sunset; free), just before the village on the right. The Euryalus castle is the major Greek fortification in the Mediterranean that is still standing, most of it dating from Hieron II's time, when **Archimedes**, as his General of Ordnance, must have been actively involved in its renovation. Despite the effort and ingenuity that went into making this site impregnable, the castle has no very glorious history: ignored altogether by the attacking Carthaginians, it surrendered without a fight to the Roman forces of Marcellus in 212 BC.

Assailants had to cope with three defensive trenches, designed to keep the new artillery of the time at bay, as well as siege-engines and battering rams. The first of the trenches (approached from the west, where you come in) was just within range of catapults mounted on the five towers of the castle's most impressive remain, the **keep**, while in the trench below the keep you can see the high piers supporting the drawbridge that once crossed it. All around here, long galleries burrow beneath the walls into the keep, serving as supply and escape routes, and also enabling the defenders to clear out by night the material thrown in by attackers during the day. Chambers were also dug out of the rock for use as storerooms and stables.

Behind the keep is a long, wedge-shaped fortification, to the north of which is the main gateway to the western quarter of the city. This, the **Epipolae gate**, was built indented from the walls, allowing the defenders to shower attackers with missiles, and is reminiscent of the main gate at Tyndaris (p.128), a city that shared the same architects. The longest of the underground passages surfaces here, stretching 180m from the defensive trenches. From the gate, you can stroll along Dionysius' extensive walls, looking down over the oil refineries and tankers off the coast north of the city, and back over Siracusa itself, Ortygia clearly visible, pointing out into the sea.

Ciane and the Olympieion

Just south of the city, the **Ciane River** offers a good rustic excursion. The river's source is only 10km inland, forming a pool said to have been created by the tears of the nymph Cyane when her mistress Persephone was abducted into the underworld by Hades. The pool and the river banks are overgrown by thickets of papyrus, apparently the gift of Ptolemy Philadelphus of Egypt to Hieron II, making this the only place outside North Africa where the plant grows wild. Indeed, there's still a thriving papyrus industry in Siracusa, gift shops on Ortygia selling painted scrolls and pictures.

You can get to the pool from Siracusa **by car**, taking the road for Canicattini Bagni at the end of Viale Paolo Orsi, and following the signs for about 5km. But if you want to make the trip **on foot**, following the lush river banks along a good path, take the #21, #22 or #23 from Piazza della Posta, getting off where the SS115 crosses the Ciane River (immediately after the Ánapo River, which runs parallel). It takes just over an hour from the main road, and this route allows you to drop in on the scant but evocative remains of the **Olympieion**, or Tempio di Giove Olimpico, a Doric temple built in the first half of the sixth century BC, of which only two columns and the stylobate remain. The hillock the ruin stands on was a vital strategic point in classical times and was often occupied by Siracusa's enemies when the city was under attack. The pestilential air of the Lysimelia marshes below saved the day on more than one occasion, infecting the hostile armies with malaria.

In summer, a **boat service** operates off the Porto Grande's Molo Zanagora, the most laid-back way to see both temple and pool; it costs around L50,000 to rent the boat, or – if there's a large group of you – L6000 per person. The whole trip takes around two hours.

The beaches

Since the coast north of Siracusa has become an evil depository for noxious chemicals, the city's main **beaches** all lie to the south. **Bus #23**, from Piazza della Posta in Siracusa, goes direct to **ARENELLA**, the first of the beach resorts and the only sandy stretch in the area, though most of it consists of private lidos and all can get horribly crowded. You might prefer the less populous stretches of rock further south, where the inlets create clear pools that are good for snorkelling. You can walk to these easily enough from Arenella, or else drive down the coast (or take bus #21, also from Piazza della Posta) to **OGNINA** and walk back a little way.

If you want to be sure of beautiful surroundings, though, it would be worth heading down a bit further south, to Fontane Bianche, 20km south of Siracusa; see p.260 for details.

Eating and drinking

There's no shortage of opportunities to spend money in Siracusa, either in the many sit-down bars with outdoor seating, or at a choice of **trattorias** and **restaurants**. Prices here are higher than in much of the rest of Sicily, but there's a great deal to be said for paying a little more to sit outside in a medieval street or courtyard and while the evening away over a beer or a pizza. On the whole, Ortygia has the best choice of eating places, many offering tourist menus at around L20,000 excluding drinks; every restaurant listed below, except *Al Castello Eurialo, Ristorante Jonico* and *La Finanziera*, is on the island. **Bars** are rather more widely scattered, though again, most of the best are on Ortygia: Via Capodieci, in particular, is worth strolling down, featuring several little café-bars.

Inexpensive and moderate restaurants

Al Castello Eurialo, Viale Epipoli 286. A ristorante-pizzeria out at Belvedere that attracts crowds of Siracusani every night during the summer. It's by the entrance to the castle, 2min walk from the youth hostel. Take buses #9, #10 or #11 from Ortygia, a 20min ride. Moderate. Closed Sun.

Archimede, Via Gemmellaro 8. Signposted off the Piazza Archimede. Provides good basic dishes, especially fish, and game when in season, to visitors and locals alike. Wash it all down with Corvo. Inexpensive. Closed Sun.

Il Cenácolo, Via del Consiglio Reginale 9–10. Signposted everywhere, this restaurant is north of Piazza del Duomo down Via Landolina and off to the right, 100m or so down, set back in a little square. It's worth the effort to find since you can sit outside and you can find a tourist menu for as low as L10,000. The pizzas are good and the house speciality – pasta with *melanzane* – is a splendid dish. Inexpensive. Closed Wed.

Ristorante Divina, Via Dione 6 (entrance on Via dei Montalto). Hidden up an alley off Piazza Archimede, the upmarket interior incorporates a stone arch in the dining room. There's well-prepared fish on the menu, as well as decent pizzas, though the wine's a bit pricey. The tourist menu costs L25,000. Moderate. Closed Wed.

La Finanziera on Via Epicarmo, off the southern end of the Corso Gelone and useful if you want a pit-stop on the mainland. Very fresh ingredients, good antipasti and friendly staff. Inexpensive.

Nonna Margherita, Via Cavour 12. Ortygia's finest pizzeria, the wood-fired ovens here produce excellent pizzas, snappily served and best accompanied by beer. You may have to wait for a table. Inexpensive. Closed Mon.

Pescomare, Via Landolina 6. Just off Piazza del Duomo (the northern end), here you can eat succulent giant clams and other excellent fish and shellfish meals in an atmospheric, plant-filled old courtyard. It tends towards the pricey, though. Moderate–expensive. Closed Mon.

MEAL PRICES

The restaurants listed are graded according to the following price categories:

Inexpensive: under L25,000	Expensive: L40,000–70,000
Moderate: L25,000–40,000	Very expensive: over L70,000

These prices reflect the per person cost of a full meal including wine and cover charge; see p.32 for more details.

Rossini, Via Savoia 6, close to Largo Porta Marina. Gaily decorated througout in red and green (even the cacti are ornamented), it almost feels like Christmas. Everything is very fresh and carefully prepared. Moderate. No credit cards. Closed Tues.

Spaghetteria do Scogghiu, Via Domenico Scina 11. Close to Piazza Archimede, this popular place has a long list of excellent, very reasonably priced spaghetti, and a shorter menu of fish and meat dishes to follow. Service is fast and evenings can be rowdy. Inexpensive. No credit cards. Closed Mon.

La Siciliana, Via Savoia 17. A no-frills pizzeria, close to the *Gran Bretagna* hotel, with a wood-fired oven and a choice of over fifty tasty pizzas from around L7000. The local wine is a madeira-coloured white. You'll not eat for less in town. No credit cards. Inexpensive. Closed Mon.

Expensive restaurants

Ristorante Darsena, Riva Garibaldi 6 (☎0931.66.104). Overlooking the fishing-boats at the northwestern end of Ortygia, this fish restaurant is a popular Sunday lunch spot, with a conservatory-like dining room. The *spaghetti alla vongole*, with fresh clams, is excellent, or you can eat more expensively from the fish and shellfish on display at the front of the restaurant. Expensive. Closed Wed.

La Foglia, Via Capodieci 39 (☎0931.66.233). Family run and describing itself as a Mediterranean-vegetarian restaurant, it has some interesting soups and salads; stuffed sardines, and pasta are perfect. The attractive decor, emboidered tablecloths and pictures by local artists make for an intimate atmosphere; the menu will be recited by the artist/proprietor. Though pricey, it's worth it. Expensive. Closed Tues.

Minosse, Via Mirabella 6 (☎0931.66.366) in a narrow street off the Corso Matteotti, and once visited by the pope, as is advertised by the photographs on the walls. The food comes in ample portions; try the seafood mixture (*insalata di mare*), and the service comes with deference. Expensive. Closed Mon.

Ristorante Jonico, Riviera Dionisio ll Grande 194 (☎0931.655.40). Siracusa's best restaurant, perched above the sea in the Santa Lucia district, north of Ortygia, has a menu written entirely in dialect, but the owner speaks enough English to guide you through the superb Sicilian specialities – pasta with fresh tuna, or, a specifically Siracusan dish, spaghetti with dried breadcrumbs, olive oil and parsley. Grilled fish and local desserts complete the meal, which – if you eat your way through the menu – will cost around L70,000, though you could eat well enough for around L60,000. It's best to reserve a table before trekking out here: take bus #3 or #7 from Piazza della Posta to the *Villa Politi* hotel, from where it's a 3min walk, or it's a 25min walk up the Riviera from the Foro Siracusano. Expensive–very expensive. Closed Tues.

Bars and cafés

Bar Bel Caffè, Corso Gelone 48. Announced by the smell of fresh bread, this bar on the way to Neapolis has its own bakery for fresh rolls, *arancini*, pizza and cakes.

Bar Ortygia, Largo Aretusa 2–3. A large bar-*gelateria* right by the fountain with pop videos, cocktails, good ice-cream and snacks. Seats outside in the square, too.

Bar del Ponte, Piazza Pancali 23–24. On the corner with Via Trento, at the end of the Ponte Nuovo on Ortygia, this makes a good breakfast-stop – pastries, *frutti di martorana,* and large pizza slices.

Les Crepes, Via del Castello Maniace 9. An intimate "pub" with wooden tables and an assortment of bottled beers.

Bar Viola, Corso Matteotti 51. A smart bar, set apart from other buildings on this main Ortygia street, serves famous ice-cream (with optional extra cream), cakes, sweets and pastries. Closed Mon.

Lungo la Notte, Lungomare Alfeo. Just off the Arethusa fountain, a modish bar attracting a posh clinetele, but magnificently sited overlooking the harbour. It's only open in the evening.

Minerva, Piazza del Duomo 20. Opposite the duomo, a good place for coffee or cocktails, with tables outside.

Spizzica, Via del Castello Maniace 8. In a prime position close to the Arethusa fountain, it does a mean *latte di mandorla,* as well as food.

Voglia Matta, Corso Umberto 34. A superb *gelateria* near the Ponte Nuovo, with an incredible range of ice-cream, and usually busy with customers.

Entertainment: puppet shows and concerts

If you're looking for other evening diversions in Siracusa, look for posters or enquire at the tourist office about **puppet shows**, in which you can follow the swashbuckling adventures of Orlando and his pals – a bit touristy perhaps, but good for a laugh. The performances generally take place in summer only, in piazzas or small theatres on Ortygia. Fans can also visit the collection of puppets, props and various related articles at Via Giudecca 17, off Via Maestranza, the stock in trade of the Vaccaro family, Siracusa's puppeteers; it's usually open in the evenings, and mornings in summer too.

The tourist office can also fill you in on the possibility of seeing **Greek plays** at the Teatro Greco (even-numbered years May & June) in the Parco Archeológico, one of Sicily's finest venues; tickets start at around L30,000 on weekdays and L40,000 weekends, though look out for special reductions on specified days. If you miss these, there are **other performances** every year throughout July and August too: jazz, opera and ballet, attracting some big names, with seats at around L30,000.

Listings

Banks Banca di Roma, Corso Gelone 120, changes travellers' cheques and cash.

Boat trips Daily in summer around the city's harbours on the boat *Selene*: departures from Ortygia's Molo Zanagora, Foro Vittorio Emanuele. (☎0931.62.776) L10,000 per person.

Buses AST, at Piazza (or Riva) della Posta, for buses to Lentini, Catania, Cómiso, Íspica, Módica, Noto, Pachino, Palazzolo Acréidé, Ragusa, Sortino and Vittória; SAIS, in Via Trieste, for Agrigento, Catania, Messina, Noto, Pachino, Palermo and Taormina.

Car problems ACI, Foro Siracusano 27 (☎0931.66.656).

Catamarans Tickets to Malta (L155,000–195,000 return) available from various travel agents, including: Maritime Service, close to the dock at Viale Mazzini 8 (☎0931.463.866), and Sliema Viaggi, Via San Sebastiano 49 (☎0931.463.699).

First aid Call ☎0931.68.555 or ☎113.

Hospital Ospedale Civile, Via Testaferrata (☎0931.461.042).

Market Food market every morning from Monday to Saturday, at Via Trento near the Tempio di Apollo.

Pharmacies La Madonnina, Corso Gelone 1 (☎0931.21.284), and Scariolo, Via le Tisià 50 (0931.39.643), which is open all night.

Police The Questura is in Via San Sebastiano (☎0931.402.111).

Post office The main post office is at Piazza delle Poste 15. Mon–Fri 8.30am–5.30pm, Sat 8.30am–1pm.

Supermarkets Linguanti, Corso Umberto 1; or Famila, at Viale Teracati 34, which takes credit cards.

Telephones The main Telecom Italia office is at Viale Teracati 42, close to the Parco Archeológico (8am–10pm). At night (8pm–8am), use the phones at the *Bar Bel Caffè*, Piazza Marconi 18.

Travel agent Zuccalà, Viale Pipoli 136 (☎0931.740.732).

North: the coast to Augusta

The coast **north of Siracusa**, the **Golfo di Augusta**, has been defaced by some of the ugliest industry you'll see in Sicily, filling the air with acrid fumes and the sea with chemicals. These mammoth plants employ one tenth of Siracusa's population, but the scale of this industrial zone – the largest concentration of chemical plants in Europe – has effectively obliterated the coast from any other point of view. Oil tankers hover offshore, while people living in some of the coastal villages have been evacuated and their houses destroyed, their places taken by a mesh of pipes and containers that will seem all too close if you're travelling this route by train. It casts a foul shadow (and smell) over the area's ancient sites: the Bronze Age tombs of Thapsos on the besieged peninsula of Magnisi are closed off now, and the extensive remains of **Megara Hyblaea** are hidden behind a barrage of alien development, though you can still fight your way through to visit them. Beyond, **Augusta** thrives as an industrial port but preserves a fine Baroque centre, with beaches to the north just out of reach of the emissions.

Megara Hyblaea

You'll have to see the site of **Megara Hyblaea** with your own car (25min out of Siracusa), unless you want to walk from Megara Giannalena station. It's a fair hike, though if you're very careful you could reduce it to 1km by walking along the rails and climbing up at the road bridge – however, this isn't a particularly safe or desirable option.

Although the earliest settlers here were Neolithic, it was as a Greek colony that the town prospered, after the Sikel king of Hybla had granted Greeks from Megara (near Athens) this tract of land alongside his own. By the mid-seventh century BC, the population had done so well out of trade and their high-quality pottery that they were able to found some minor colonies of their own, including Selinus (see p.362), though their city was eventually submerged by Syracusan ambitions and destroyed by Gelon in 482 BC. In the middle of the fourth century BC, the site was resettled and the town flourished again, until it was finally levelled by the Romans in the same avenging campaign that ended Syracuse's independence in 214 BC.

Most of the ruins you'll see at the **site** (open all year; free) belong to the fourth-century revival, but the fortifications were erected a century later, interrupted by the Romans' arrival. Various buildings – temples, baths, the marketplace – lie confusingly scattered over a wide area, though this is considered to be the most complete model of an Archaic city still surviving. Your best bet to make head or tail of it is to spend some time in the excellent **Antiquario** (daily 9am–1hr before sunset; free), where illustrations and diagrams put it all into context. However, the best finds, including a statue of a goddess suckling twins and a *kouros*, are in Siracusa's Museo Archeológico (see p.247).

Augusta and its beaches

Despite **AUGUSTA**'s superficial resemblance to Siracusa – its old centre detached from the mainland on its own islet, surrounded by two harbours – the port has never attained the same importance and didn't even exist until 1232.

Frederick II, who founded the town, characteristically stamped his own personality on it in the form of a castle, though everything else of the medieval town was entirely destroyed by the 1693 earthquake. What's left is a handsome – though crumbling – Baroque centre with several restaurants and a decent hotel; a relief after the rampant industrialization all around.

You can't miss the **castello** that dominates the causeway leading onto the island, though you're unlikely to get inside: used for years as a prison, it's now awaiting conversion into a war museum. The **Villa Comunale** below is a shady public garden through which all traffic is channelled, including the promenaders who overflow into here from the long and narrow main street, Via Príncipe Umberto. On both sides of the gardens are views out to sea: on one side over the port and tankers; on the other, to the headland. A few blocks down Via Príncipe Umberto is a piazza holding the eighteenth-century Duomo (now shored up by scaffolding) and a solemn **Palazzo Comunale**, its facade crowned by Frederick II's imperial eagle.

The beaches: Monte Tauro and Brúcoli

If you've got time to explore the **coast to the north**, you'll come across resorts with some decent swimming and a couple of **campsites**. The nearest of these is *A'Massaria* (☎0931.983.078; May–Oct), in **MONTE TAURO**, reachable by hourly bus from Augusta's Villa Comunale. Much nicer, though, is the *Baia del Silenzio* (☎0931.981.881; May–Oct), a little further on and overlooking a pretty bay: take the Brúcoli bus (also from the Villa Comunale), get off at the signpost before the town and walk the 2km to the site. **BRÚCOLI** itself is a small resort with a restored fifteenth-century castle and ominous "Bathing prohibited" signs that are studiously ignored by locals and tourists alike. You, too, might chance a swim here: it's far enough round the point to be safe from the Gulf's contaminated waters.

Practicalities

From the **train station** it takes fifteen minutes on foot to reach the castle and causeway to the town centre. Walk through the gardens to the top of the main street and there's a **hotel**, the *Kursaal Augustaeo*, Piazza Castello 1 (☎0931.521.782; ①), here in the square below the castle, offering clean, decent-sized singles and doubles. It's housed in the old cinema building, and the style is very Art Deco. The ground floor also has a bar-*rosticceria*.

Augusta has a poor selection of **places to eat.** If you want to sit outside, try *The Company* in Piazza Castello, with a wide-ranging menu of inconsistent standard, but including a set-price choice for L20,000. On a left turn off Via Umberto, at Via San Lorenzo 20, the *Pizzeria Poiana* has fairly regular pizzas; otherwise, take your choice among a crop of drinks bars, mostly on or around Via XIV Ottobre (parallel to Via Umberto), where you can find panini and chips to go with your beers, plus music: try *Horizon* or *Cyborg*. The same road, incidentally, behind the Duomo, holds Augusta's daily morning **market**, where you can pick up bread, fruit and veg. For breakfast, the bar-*pasticceria* at the bottom of Via Umberto is a good bet, opposite the Villa Comunale.

Inland: Pantálica and Palazzolo Acréide

These are two separate day-trips you can make **inland from Siracusa**, both destinations lying in the folds of the **Monti Iblei**. It's a dramatic landscape, crossed by dry-stone walls and dotted with small villages springing the odd surprise – a crumbly church or an inviting trattoria. Whatever time you spend at the necropolis of **Pantálica** will be mainly taken up by wandering the deep gorge through which the Ánapo River runs. Weekend picnickers are drawn from all over the region by the refreshing walks, though the chief interest is the presence of several thousand tombs hollowed out of the valley sides. **Palazzolo Acréide** is a mainly Baroque town with a compact Greek and Roman site lying just outside, one of the most interesting of the province's classical sites.

Pantálica

Around 40km west of Siracusa, **PANTÁLICA** is Sicily's greatest necropolis, first used between the thirteenth and the tenth century BC by Sikel refugees from the coast. After the eighth century BC, this plateau is thought to have been the site of Hybla, whose king invited Megarian Greeks to colonize first Thapsos and then Megara Hyblaea; there are visible remains from this era, but the fascination of the place derives from the five thousand or so tombs hewn out of the gorge below. Several skeletons were found in each tomb, suggesting that a large population of a few thousand people once lived in the vicinity.

The plateau rises between the River Ánapo and its northern tributary, the Calcinara, and can be approached on foot from either end of the gorge. The **approaches** are from the villages of Sortino or Ferla, of which the first is nearer to the gorge (5km as opposed to 9km from Ferla). Both places are linked to Siracusa by **bus**, though Sortino has far more connections, with a last departure back to Siracusa at 6.30pm from Sortino. As there is nowhere to stay in either village, you might be forced to fall back on a **day-excursion** by coach from Siracusa, for which tickets start at around L40,000 per person: ask at the travel agency Zuccalà (see "Listings", p.254) for details.

Getting there: from Sortino

Buses to **SORTINO** (daily except Sun) leave Siracusa from Piazza della Posta and the journey takes around an hour; the earliest departures are at 7.15am and 9.30am. You're dropped on, or close to, the central Piazza G. Verga and signs throughout the sprawling village point you through the streets towards Pantálica. Your best bet is first to find an **alimentari** and get a sandwich made up: there's nowhere on the way to buy anything to eat or drink. Even without the sun, you'll get through a litre of **water** walking both ways: in high season, take as much water as you can carry. Once you're clear of Sortino (about 5min), the road drops steeply downhill, passing the roofless fifteenth-century ruin of Santa Sofia after 1km, and then climbing across the valley to the gorge. It takes around an hour to reach the end of the road and the entrance to the gorge – about twenty minutes from the entrance, you'll have your first view over the rock-cut tombs. If you're driving, you can park just before the site entrance.

The site

At the **entrance** (always open; free) an obvious path leads through the gorge, around the **northern cemetery**, down to the river and up the other side. You'll soon see the **tombs,** first just dotting the walls of the valley in clusters and finally puncturing the whole cliff face; at times the tombs are very close to the path. They were dug out of the vertical cliff walls, and the sheer number of them creates an eerie impression. In some were found the traces of several separate skeletons, probably of the same family, and others show evidence of habitation, though much later, when the Syracusans themselves were forced to flee inland from barbarian incursions. The atmosphere is primeval and almost sinister – for Vincent Cronin, even something terrifying: "Here is Sicily of the stone age, intent on nothing higher than the taking of food and the burial of its dead." The free play of nature in this ravine embodied for Cronin Sicily's own particular contribution to the man-made wonders bestowed later by the island's conquerors, and as such – symbolized by a honeycomb he came across in one of the caves – the object of the quest described in his book, *The Golden Honeycomb*.

From the Sortino side it takes thirty minutes to walk through this stretch of the gorge: there are superb views from the higher reaches and the path and rock-cut steps remain good all the way. Once across the river and up the other side of the gorge, the road begins again and runs west, all the way to Ferla (see below). Even if you're planning to return to Sortino, continue along the road for a while. It climbs up past the remains of a Villagio Bizantino (there's nothing to see) and a lookout point across the section you've just walked; after 25 minutes or so, on top of the plateau, a sideroad leads off to the left to the rectangular foundations of a building from ancient Hybla: the **Anaktoron**, or prince's palace, with a few stretches of walling nearby. There's a signposted path, below the Anaktoron, leading back into the gorge, to the **south cemetery**, a 1.5-kilometre walk with more visible rock tombs at the end as your reward.

Returning to the road, you can then either head on to Ferla (around 8km to the west), or **return to Sortino**. If the latter is your plan, reckon on it taking three hours from the Anaktoron back to Sortino, aiming for the last return bus to Siracusa at 6.30pm. Note that buses from Sortino's Piazza G. Verga also run to Lentini and Carlentini (see p.225) and (four times daily) to Catania.

Ferla

FERLA is prettier than Sortino, possessing a good **trattoria** (closed Sun) with a terrace at the back, in its Piazza San Sebastiano, a stately church – overrun with weeds – nearby, and surroundings planted with fruit trees. That said, it's trickier to see the gorge from here by public transport, since there's only one bus from Siracusa (Mon–Sat) at 2.00pm, returning at 6.40pm, and there is nowhere to stay.

If you do come by bus, ask to be let off at the site's entrance at the bottom of the hill, immediately after crossing the river and before reaching Ferla. The lower road to the gorge is closed to all private traffic but there's a free **minibus service** that does the whole route in about an hour. It leaves the entrance every ninety minutes or so on weekdays (every 45 minutes at weekends), making stops along the way – a useful help if you're short on time or energy. Coming by car from Ferla, along the upper road, you'll find the basic *Ristorante Pantalica*, which sells a map of Pantálica.

Palazzolo Acréide

Lying on a hill some 18km south of Ferla, **PALAZZOLO ACRÉIDE** is the modern successor of the Greek colony of Akrai, founded in the middle of the seventh century BC by Syracuse in its first drive inland. The remains of the ancient town lie just outside the modern settlement, a twenty-minute walk. Both occupy the higher slopes of a promontory once strategically commanding routes inland, now somewhat stranded from the main road and rail links crossing the province. It's a good excursion, though, enabling you to wander the town's knot of small Baroque streets before visiting the site.

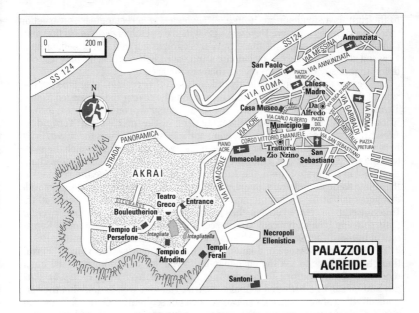

Palazzolo's main square, **Piazza del Pópolo**, is the heart of the Baroque town, two sides dominated by the handsome church of San Sebastiano and the town hall. From here lanes radiate down past opulent facades and gargoyled balconies, eventually leading to a trio of fine Baroque churches, the Chiesa Madre, San Paolo and the Annunziata. But the main focus of interest in this part of town – at least for anyone curious about the roots of Sicilian culture – is the **Casa-Museo di Antonino Uccello** (daily 9am–1pm; free), tucked away in an old house at Via Machiavelli 19. The fruit of one man's thirty-year obsession to root out and preserve the traditions of rural Sicily, this varied collection of 5000 objects constitutes eastern Sicily's most important documentation of folk art, showing trousseaux, ceramics, olive presses, puppets, reconstructions of houses and stables, and anything else judged by Uccello to be in danger of extinction. There's lots more that's not on display, kept upstairs in the workshop where the restorations are attempted – try and take a peek.

Akrai: the ancient city

Syracuse chose the site of **Akrai**, its first inland colony, well; it dominated the trade routes into the interior, particularly the Via Selinuntina to Akragas. The city thrived during the peace and security that characterized Hieron II's reign in the third century BC, though it declined under the Romans, later re-emerging as an important early Christian centre, as shown by the number of rock-cut tombs in the area – only to be eventually destroyed by the Arabs.

Of the ancient city's visible remains at the **Zona Archeológica** (daily 9am–1pm & 3pm–7pm; L4000), most complete is the small **Teatro Greco**, built towards the end of Hieron's reign and modified by the Romans. A perfect semicircle, the theatre held six hundred and retains traces of its scene-building. Behind the theatre to the right is a small **senate-house**, or *bouleuterion*, a rectangular construction that was originally covered. Beyond is a 200-metre stretch of *decumanus* that once connected the two gates of the city (Porta Siracusana and Porta Selinuntina). Crossed at regular intervals by junctions and paved in lavic rock, it's in better condition than many of the more recent roads in the area.

The rest of the site isn't as clearly defined and other remains give little impression of their former grandeur. You'll have a job identifying the excavated Roman **Tempio di Persefone**, above the theatre, an unusually round chamber, formerly covered by a cupola. Equally fragmentary is the much older **Tempio di Afrodite**, sixth- or fifth-century BC, lying at the head of what was the *agora*. From here you can look straight down into one of the two quarries from which the stone to build the city was taken. Later they were converted into Christian burial chambers, and in the first of them, the **Intagliata**, you can plainly see the recesses in the walls: some of them catacombs, others areas of worship, the rest simply rude dwellings cut in the Byzantine era. The narrower, deeper quarry below it, the **Intagliatella**, has more votive niches and a relief cut from the rock-face, over 2m long, that combines a typically Greek scene – heroes banqueting – and a Roman one of heroes offering sacrifice. It's thought to date from the first century BC.

There are more niches and chambers in a lower quarry, the **Templi Ferali**, though you'll have to ask the custodian to let you see this, along with the much more interesting **Santoni** further down (a 15min walk from the site). If it's a slack day and he can't be bothered to make the trip, you may well be told that they are "closed". It's a shame, since these twelve rock-cut sculptures are of a fertility goddess Cybele, a predominantly eastern deity whose origins are steeped in mystery. Certainly there's no other example of so rich a complex relating to her worship, and the local name tagged to these sculptures – *santoni*, or "great saints" – suggests that the awe attached to them survived until relatively recently. Carved no later than the third century BC, the rough, weathered images are protected in individual locked shelters; they represent the Magna Mater seated, attended by priests, lions and other deities.

Practicalities

Buses from Siracusa pull up in the main square, Piazza del Pópolo, across from which – next to the church – the *Bar Canguro* is handy for snacks and drinks. There are plenty of good **places to eat** in town, including the **trattoria**, *Da Alfredo*, at Via Duca d'Aosta 27 (closed Wed), just down from the piazza, or try the less expensive *Trattoria Zio Nzino*, Via Ortocotogno 5, left off Corso Vittorio Emanuele (closed Fri). Apart from the tasty ricotta-filled ravioli, there's not much in the trattoria that doesn't have meat in it. Even if you fancied a quiet alternative to staying in Siracusa – and Palazzolo can be dead as a doornail at night – there's only one **hotel**, the relatively expensive, modern *Senatore*, Largo Sen. Italia (☎0931.883.443, fax 0931.883.444; ③).

South: to Fontane Bianche and Ávola

It's not until you reach **FONTANE BIANCHE**, 20km south of Siracusa, that the coast comes into its own: the wide arc of sand here provides some of the best swimming on this part of the coast. Buses #21, #22 and #24 do the journey here from Siracusa in about half an hour, as do AST buses leaving every forty minutes or so from Piazza della Posta (last one at around 8pm). Along with a number of bars and trattorias, this popular resort has a good **campsite**, *Fontane Bianche* (see p.242), or you might be tempted by the **hotel** of the same name across the road at Via Mazzarò 1 (☎0931.790.611, fax 0931.790.571; ⑤). In either case, you get the beach; however, don't expect a lot of action here outside the period from June to September.

Slightly inland of here, and about 4km to the north on the SS115, the nondescript town of **Cassíbile** is known to Italians as the place where, in an olive yard on September 3, 1943, generals Bedell-Smith and Castellano signed the armistice that took Italy out of the Axis alliance in World War II.

Ávola

The main road (and railway) continues on another 10km south to **ÁVOLA**. This agricultural town has an old Baroque centre, partly reconstructed on a hexagonal design after earthquake damage. An idea of its erstwhile proportions can be gleaned in the huge central Piazza Umberto, the square and long main Corso Vittorio Emanuele lined with forlorn *palazzi*, slowly crumbling away. There's a small **Museo Cívico** at Piazza Umberto 17, containing finds from Thapsos, Pantálica and the pre-earthquake town – if you're lucky, you'll get in, though it's been closed for "renovations" for as long as anyone can remember.

The **train station** is at the top of the corso; **buses** drop you halfway down, on Piazza Vittorio Véneto, with Piazza Umberto another five minutes' walk down the corso. Glinting in the distance is the sea and the seaside settlement of **ÁVOLA MARINA**, a two-kilometre walk straight downhill from the square. Most **eating places** down here are seasonal, though one of the best is open all year, *La Ola*, a large bar-restaurant with a very good-value tourist menu (closed Tues in winter): turn left when you reach the water and it's about 250m along.

If you're driving, you can reach the magnificent gorge and nature reserve of the **Cava Grande** by taking the main road north out of Ávola for about 15km, past the signpost marked "Convento di Ávola Vecchia". Look out for signs for the belvedere along this road, where you can park and either just admire the circling birds of prey, or follow the footpath down to the pool below; here the path will take you alongside the River Cassabile for most of the gorge's 11km (allow 3hr for the return trip).

Noto

Six kilometres beyond Ávola, and the same distance inland, **NOTO** represents the apogee of the wholesale renovation that took place following the cataclysm of 1693, a monument to the achievement of a few architects and planners, whose vision coincided with the golden age of Baroque architecture. Although there existed a town called Noto, or Netum, in this area for centuries, what you see today is in effect a "New Town", conceived as a triumphant symbol of renewal.

Noto was flattened on January 11, 1693, and a week later its **rebuilding** was entrusted to a Sicilian-Spanish aristocrat, Giuseppe Lanza, Duke of Camastra, on the strength of his work at the town of Santo Stéfano di Camastra, on the Tyrrhenian coast. Lanza visited the ruins, saw nothing but "un montón de piedras abandonadas", and quickly decided to start afresh, on a new site 16km to the south. In fact, the ruins weren't abandoned; the city's battered population was already improvising a shantytown, and even held a referendum when Lanza's intentions became known, rejecting the call to relocate their city. But partly motivated by the prestige of the undertaking, partly by the need to refurbish the area's defences, Lanza ignored the local feeling, even pulling down their new constructions and the old town's remaining church. With the help of the Flemish military engineer Carlos de Grunemburg, Lanza devised a revolutionary new plan, based on two quarters – one for the political and religious establishment, the other for the people – which were to be almost completely separated from each other. The best architects were to be used: Vincenzo Sinatra, Paolo Labisi and the master craftsman Rosario Gagliardi – not innovators, but men whose enthusiasm and experience enabled them to concoct a celebration of the latest architectural skills and forms. Their collaboration was so complete that it's still difficult to ascribe some buildings to any one person. Within an astonishingly short time the work was completed, a new city, planned with the accent on symmetry and visual harmony, from its simple street plan to the gracious curves of its buildings. It's easily the most harmonious post-earthquake creation and, for a time, in the mid-nineteenth century, the new Noto replaced Siracusa as the region's provincial capital.

This century has seen a deterioration of the town, mainly due to the traffic that thunders through. The local Iblean stone, so workable and suitable for delicate carving, is also highly fragile; but it was not until 1987 that belated restoration work was begun. Heavy traffic was diverted round the outskirts of town and corroded ornamentation subjected to a thorough cleaning. Many of the buildings (including the duomo) are still under scaffolding – a shame in a city where the visual aspect is so important – but it's still worth the visit.

Around the town

The centre is best approached through the monumental **Porta Reale**, built in 1838 and topped by the three symbols of the town's allegiance to the Bourbon monarchy: a dog, a tower and a pelican (respectively, loyalty, strength and sacrifice). The **Corso Vittorio Emanuele**, which leads off from here, runs through the heart of the lower, patricians' quarter and is lined with some of Sicily's most captivating buildings. All are a rich honey colour – starting with Vincenzo Sinatra's formal-looking church of **San Francesco** (1704), to the right, its facade rather dulled by the more flamboyant **Convento del Santíssimo Salvatore** next door. Part of this convent houses the **Museo Cívico**, on the corner, containing finds from Greek coastal sites and material from Noto Antica, but it's been closed for years and is unlikely to open in the near future.

A little way up is what is arguably Sicily's finest piazza. Perfectly proportioned, the tree-planted **Piazza del Municipio** is the elegant heart of the town and contains its noblest buildings. Unfortunately, the imposing twin-towered **Duomo** is now closed, due to the collapse of its dome in March 1996. This was precipitated by a heavy thunderstorm, but was really the cumulative result of inadequate repair work in the past and the soft quality of the stone. Completed in 1776, it's said to have been inspired by models of Borromini's churches in Rome, but now it's a good example of the inadequacy of the Italian bureaucratic system; with delays in even the first stages of the restoration work, no one can venture a guess as to when it will be back to its former glory. Opposite, the **Municipio** (or Palazzo Ducezio) is again the work of Vincenzo Sinatra, flanked by its own green spaces,

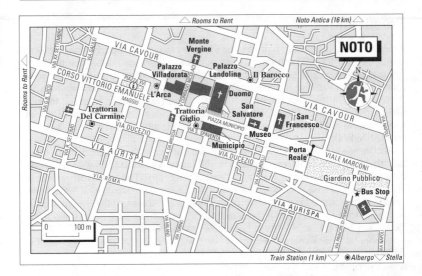

the arcaded building presenting a lovely, convex front of columns and long stone balconies. To the west of the duomo, on Via C. Nicolaci, the **Palazzo Villadorata** (also presently undergoing restoration and scaffolded) is an eccentric piece of work. Onto a strictly classical front six extravagant balconies were grafted, supported by the last word in sculpted buttresses – a panoply of griffins, galloping horses and bald and bearded figures with fat-cheeked cherubs at their bellies.

There's a lot more pleasure to be had out of Noto by straying off into the side streets on either side of Corso Vittorio Emanuele, or down the corso to Piazza XVI Maggio and Noto's food **market** (Mon–Sat 8.30am–1.30pm). Don't leave without visiting the upper part of town, filled with massive monastic houses and the dwellings of Noto's poorer eighteenth-century citizens. They had their own church, Gagliardi's **Santíssimo Crocifisso**, in Piazza Mazzini. Never completed, the church preserves some treasures from the old town, including a magnificent pair of Romanesque lions and the only statue in Sicily actually signed by the master-sculptor Francesco Laurana, *Madonna of the Snow*, carved in 1471 (behind the altar on the right-hand side).

Noto Antica

If you've got a car, you could venture out to see the sparse remains of **NOTO ANTICA**, 16km northwest of town, up the SS287. Until finally abandoned in 1693, the town had several times been a significant historical stronghold – one of the few Sicilian towns to resist the looting of the Roman praetor Verres and the last bastion of Arab Sicily before the Normans arrived. After passing the convent of Santa Maria delle Scale, turn left and pass through the gate of a castle. The visible remnants of the old town are confined to bits of wall and the bric-a-brac held in a makeshift museum at the **Éremo della Madonna della Providenza**. There should be someone around to let you in: it's free, but not very exciting.

Practicalities

From Siracusa, it's around half an hour's journey to Noto by hourly buses or (less frequently) by train. The **bus** will drop you at the Giardino Pubblico at the eastern end of town, close to the Porta Reale; the **train station** is ten minutes' walk away down Via Príncipe di Piemonte; the FS bus for Pachino (see opposite) leaves from outside Noto's train station. Get free maps and information from the **tourist office** in Piazza XVI Maggio, behind the Hercules fountain (April–Sept Mon–Sat 8am–2pm & 3.30–7pm, Sun 9am–2pm; Oct–March Mon–Sat 9am–1.30pm; ☎0931.836.744).

Accommodation possibilities in Noto are limited, with one hotel that's often full: the fairly basic *Albergo Stella*, Via F. Maiore 44 (☎0931.835.695; no credit cards; ②), on the corner of Via Napoli, east of the centre. The tourist office should also be able to advise you about the availability of **rented rooms**, which may have private bathrooms and cooking facilities. If you want to contact the owners directly, try the friendly and cheerfully furnished *L'Arca*, in the centre of the town at Via Rocco Piri 14, off Corso Vittorio Emanuele (☎0931.894.202, fax 0931.573.360); *Al Canisello*, at Via Cesare Pavese 94 (☎0931.835.793); or the rooms at Via Francesco Giantommaso 14 (☎0931.835.554) are both about a fifteen-minute walk from the centre. Expect to pay around L80,000 for two people. Alternatively, you could stay at Noto Marina, a small coastal resort 8km to the southeast, where there are several holiday hotels, though these may be booked up in summer; again, the tourist office should be able to find out about vacancies.

If you want a **meal**, *Trattoria Giglio*, in the corner of Piazza del Municipio, is a cheap and cheerful place for lunch; and the small *Trattoria del Carmine*, Via Ducezio 9, serves popular *cucina casalinga* – also excellent value. Behind the duomo, at Via Cavour 8, *Il Barocco* is a second-best choice, but offers a tourist menu for L18,000. Just down the steps from the *Giglio*, behind the Municipio at Via Silvio Spaventa 7–11, *Costanzo* is a famous **bar**-*gelateria*, known for its locally made sweets and pastries.

The coastal route to Sicily's southern cape

Trains no longer run south from Noto, and if you're travelling **down the coast** you'll have to take the regular SAIS bus from Siracusa/Noto to Pachino, or there is the FS service from Noto's train station (currently only 1 daily, at 6.16pm). It's quite easy to reach Eloro by foot from Noto Marina, to which there are frequent buses; otherwise there are morning bus departures for Eloro every two hours from Noto. If you have a car, though, you'll be able to stop off at some of the more remote beaches along the way.

Eloro and Torre Vendícari

First stop out of Noto, 8–9km to the southeast, are the seaside ruins of Helorus, or **Eloro** (Mon–Sat 8am–1hr before sunset; free). This Syracusan colony, founded in the seventh century BC at the mouth of the Tellaro River, is still being excavated, but the small site can be viewed quite easily even when closed, through the fence. It has some city walls, a small theatre and a sanctuary dedicated to Demeter and Kore, with the remains of a *stoa*, or portico. It's all very ramshackle, but made all the more attractive by its position right on the rocky shore. The broad expanse of sand alongside also offers **good swimming**, though access is tricky from the site: best option for drivers is to take the next road along that leads directly to the beach.

If you're driving, there's another secluded **beach** 5–6km further south, at the **Torre Vendícari**, an abandoned Norman tower overlooking a crescent of sand that's hidden behind some disused saltpans. It's signposted off the new road running down the coast to Pachino: turn left over a narrow railway bridge and keep an eye open for the tower.

Pachino and the cape

The lowlands south of here are best reached from the area's main town, **PACHINO**. It's a pleasant enough place, with an outsized central piazza that's lined with bars, and there are regular local buses from here to various coastal resorts. One, **MARZAMEMI** (4km northeast), is a resort-cum-fishing port with an old Arab feel to it and a couple of **hotels**: the *Celeste*, Via del Porto 7 (☎0931.841.244; ②), and *La Conchiglietta*, Via Regina Elena 9 (☎0931.841.191; ②); out of season, prices should drop at both of them. The bay here is littered with the submerged hulks of Greek, Roman and Byzantine ships that foundered on their way round the cape.

Seven kilometres south of Pachino is the larger town of **PORTOPALO DI CAPO PÁSSERO**. In summer it's a fairly lively place, with several bars and discos along the main street and three or four reasonable **hotels**, including *El Condor*, Via Vittorio Emanuele 38 (☎0931.842.016; ②). You might be able to persuade someone to row you over to the little islet lying just offshore, complete with a seventeenth-century castle. Otherwise, there's a pleasant day's moseying around to be done in the area: the flat land here is market-garden country, the fields and greenhouses sheltering tomatoes, strawberries and artichokes; the coast – when you can get to it along dusty, unmade tracks – rough and seaweed-scattered, and often edged with high bamboo. Along the road that leads to the cape, there are two **campsites** (both with cabins and adjacent beaches). The first of these is only a kilometre away, the *Capo Pássero* (☎0931.842.333; two-berth bungalows at L90,000, four-berth ones at L130,000) though it can get fairly crowded; if you can face the hike, you'd do better to go a bit further, to the southeastern point of **Isola delle Correnti**, where the clean and well-equipped *Captain* campsite (☎0931.842.595; two-berth cabins at L44,000, four-berth ones at L64,000; July–Sept) sits in happy isolation behind its own unspoiled sandy bay. You're on the southernmost tip of Sicily here, with nothing between you and Africa.

RAGUSA AND THE BAROQUE SOUTHEAST

Aside from the much-vaunted Noto, the best of the Baroque in Sicily's southeast is in the **province of Ragusa** – less visited, but providing surprising pockets of grandeur amid the bare hills and deep valleys of the region. The most congenial base for any exploration of the area is **Ragusa**, a busy provincial capital not especially interesting in itself but with two or three hotels and a pleasant, atmospheric old town. From here, it's easy to reach the other Baroque towns by train or bus: **Módica** to the south, **Cómiso** and **Vittória** to the west, with smaller examples closer to the coast – like **Scicli** or **Íspica**. This last town is at the end of one of the best **walks** in the region, through the **Cava d'Íspica**, a gorge lined with rock-cut tombs. The **coast** south of Ragusa has a string of small-scale holiday towns and a couple of ancient sites, interspersed with good **beaches**.

Ragusa

The 1693 earthquake destroyed many towns and cities that were then rebuilt in a different form, but the unique effect on **RAGUSA** was to split the city in two. The old town of Ragusa Ibla, on a jut of land above its valley, was comprehensively flattened, and within a few years a new town emerged, on the higher ridge just to the west. Unlike Noto Antica, Ibla was stubbornly rebuilt, though retaining its medieval appearance, while its new neighbour, known simply as Ragusa, developed along planned lines. Rivalry between the two was commonplace, until 1926 when both towns were nominally reunited, a move which proved to be the kiss of death for Ragusa Ibla. Rapidly depopulated, all the business and industry was relocated to the prosperous upper town, where oil is the latest venture – derricks scattered around modern Ragusa's higher reaches. Ibla meanwhile still survives, a short walk out of the modern centre, an anachronistic appendage to its younger relative.

Ragusa: the upper town

It's in the **upper town** that you'll arrive, buses and trains dropping you a five-minute walk from the exposed **Ponte Nuovo**. The bridge spans a huge cleft in

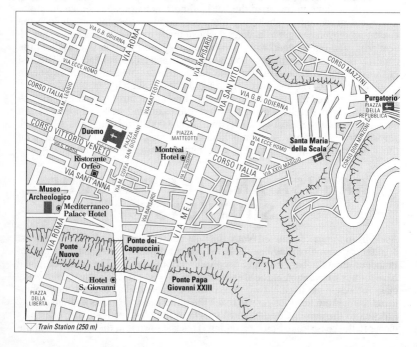

the ridge, and what there is of interest lies across the far side of this. Via Roma runs right into the heart of modern Ragusa, the gridded town slipping off to right and left on either side of the steeply sloping Corso Italia. Just around the corner, above Piazza San Giovanni, stands the **Duomo**, conceived on an imposing, symmetrical scale. Finished in 1774, its tapered columns and fine doorways are a fairly sombre background to the vigorous small-town atmosphere around.

Close by, underneath the Standa supermarket at the Ponte Nuovo, there's an important **Museo Archeológico** (daily 9am–1.30pm & 3–6.30pm; L4000). Aside from the usual exhibits – prehistoric flints to late Roman mosaics – the museum deals mainly with finds from the Greek site of Camarina (sixth-century BC), on the coast to the southwest (p.272). Especially interesting are the necropolis reconstructions, amplified by photos, and a restored potter's kiln (from a site at Scornavacche), the neat little terracotta figures found around it displayed in separate cases.

As far as Ragusa goes, that's about it. Although the new Baroque town received its share of good-looking buildings (like the few grand *palazzi* down Corso Italia), most of the architects' efforts seem to have gone into keeping the streets as straight as possible, and the town's most striking vistas are where this right-angled order is interrupted by the gorge, exposing the bare rock on which the city was built (best appreciated from the motor-free **Ponte dei Cappuccini**). Otherwise the liveliest scenes in this predominantly commercial town are around Piazza San Giovanni and the main streets at *passeggiata* time. Via Roma is packed shoulder to shoulder with milling people by 6pm, the cars forced off the roads for an hour or two while everyone circulates among the bars and cake shops.

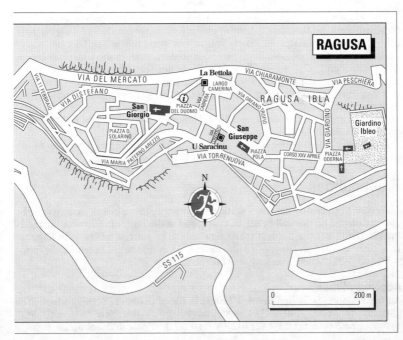

Ragusa Ibla

It's in **RAGUSA IBLA**, the original, lower town, that you'll probably while away much of the day. The locked and shuttered buildings of its stepped streets give the impression of a ghost town, and it's much the most interesting part of Ragusa despite the evident abandonment. From the new town, head down Corso Italia and the narrow Via XXIV Maggio, and from the terrace by the restored fifteenth-century church of **Santa Maria della Scala** (which features the remains of an unusual exterior pulpit), Ragusa Ibla lies beyond and below. It's a mighty view, the weather-beaten roofs straddling the outcrop of rock, rising to the prominent church dome of San Giorgio, which fronts the town like the prow of a ship.

Walking, it'll take about another twenty minutes to descend to Ragusa Ibla itself, following the steps from Santa Maria down beneath the winding road, to the **Chiesa del Purgatorio**. Although there are quicker routes into the centre, it's an idea to follow Via del Mercato, which hugs the edge of the spur on which the town rests, so that you can look out over the grey valley before cutting back through Largo Camerina. This is the best approach for entering Piazza del Duomo, for the first excellent views of **San Giorgio**, stridently placed at the top of the square. One of the masterpieces of Sicilian Baroque, the church was designed by Rosario Gagliardi – one of Noto's chief architects – and took nearly forty years to complete. The sloping piazza, split by six palms, ends in broad steps which lead to the church set slightly at an angle. Its three-tiered facade, sets of triple columns climbing up the wedding-cake exterior to a balconied belfry, is an imaginative work, though typically not matched inside. As with Gagliardi's other projects, all the beauty is in the immediacy of the powerful exterior.

The whole town – deathly quiet at lunchtime – is ripe for aimless wandering. Gagliardi gets another credit for the elegant rounded facade and bulging balconies of **San Giuseppe** in Piazza Pola, a few steps below San Giorgio, while Corso XXV Aprile continues down past abandoned *palazzi* to the **Giardino Ibleo** (daily 8am–8pm). The violet-strewn flowerbeds here set off the remains of three small churches, abandoned in the grounds; and to the right of the garden's entrance there's the surviving Gothic portal of the shattered old church of San Giorgio Vecchio, the badly worn stone centrepiece depicting a skeletal St George killing the dragon. The shady benches and fountains in the gardens make a good picnic or siesta spot.

If you can't face the long and winding walk back to the upper town, bus #1 or #3 makes the trip every thirty minutes from Piazza Pola.

Practicalities

All **buses** stop outside the **train station** in the upper town: bus departure schedules are posted on the wall by the bus park; and in the *Bar Salinitro* over the road (at Via Dante 94) the barman *is* the timetable. The **tourist office** is in Ragusa Ibla, in Piazza del Duomo (daily except Mon 9.00am–1.00pm & 3–7pm; ☎0932.621.421), where you may well find English spoken.

Accommodation

Accommodation is limited to a few **hotels** in the upper town, none of which are particularly good value. The most convenient is the *San Giovanni*, Via Traspontino 3 (☎ & fax 0932.621.013; ②), just off the Ponte dei Cappuccini; rooms have TV and central heating (those with bath fall into the next category up), and there's a bar downstairs. Near the station, you might want to save a walk and dive into the nearest hotel, in which case you can try the uninspiring, 1950s-style *Jonio*, 50m to the right from the station at Via Risorgimento 49 (☎0932.624.322, fax 0932.654.530; ③). However, in the centre of the new town, the *Montreal* is not much more expensive and far better equipped, at Via San Giuseppe (☎ & fax 0932.621.133; ④). And if you want to treat yourself, the spanking new *Mediterraneo Palace* beckons just over the Ponte Nuovo on the way into town from the station, at Via Roma 189 (☎0932.621.944, fax 0932.623.799; ⑤). It has superb views and marble everywhere, though you'll be rubbing shoulders predominantly with business types.

The nearest **campsites** are on the coast at Marina di Ragusa (see below), 24km south: *Villa Nifosi* (☎0932.39.118) on Via del Mare, and, nearer the sea on Lungomare Andrea Doria, *Baia del Sole* (☎0932.39.844) – both open all year. There are buses every hour in summer from Ragusa.

Eating and drinking

There's rather more choice when it comes to eating and drinking. For a really good, inexpensive **place to eat** in the new town, the *Ristorante Orfeo*, at Via Sant'Anna 117 (closed Sat & Sun), is a good bet; try the stuffed sardines and bean soup, washed down with the local wine. For **pizza**, visit *La Grotta*, Via G. Cartia, off Via Roma (closed Wed), which has draught beer and cheap prices. Fuller and marginally pricier meals can be found at one of the handful of trattorias in Ragusa Ibla, best being the *U Saracinu* (closed Wed) at Via del Convento 9, very close to the church of San Giorgio, and *La Bettola* in Largo Camerina (closed lunchtime & Mon), where you can sit outside in summer.

Ragusa also has some surprisingly good **bars**, mostly along Via Roma and the surrounding streets. *Caffè Roma*, Via Roma 158, has Art Deco fittings, a designer crucifix above the till, and good cakes and savoury snacks. The equally swish *Caffè Trieste*, Corso Italia 76–78, does a decent line in savouries, too, and has a full range of pastries, as well as the same designer crucifix.

South: Módica and around

The wild countryside continues to impress as you head beyond Ragusa. The route to **Módica**, half an hour's drive to the south, is a case in point. As the bus swirls down past Ragusa Ibla and climbs through some rugged hills, all the vegetation seems to have been pulled into the valleys below, the tiered slopes bare and rocky – the effect only spoiled by the siting of an asphalt works right on the top, disfiguring the stark hills. Beyond Módica, the train ambles south towards the coast, passing other small Baroque towns like **Scicli**, before reaching **Íspica**, base for an exploration of its gorge.

Módica

MÓDICA is an enjoyable place to spend half a day. A powerful medieval base of the Chiaramonte family, the **upper town** (Módica Alta) is watched over by the magnificent eighteenth-century facade of **San Giorgio**, a worthy rival to the church of the same name in Ragusa Ibla. It's thought that Gagliardi was responsible for this too: the elliptical facade is topped by his trademark, a belfry, while the approach is characteristically daring – twin flights of stairs zigzag up across the upper roads of the town, ending in a terrace before the church. From here, or better still from the tight streets above San Giorgio, you can look back over the grey-tiled roofs and balconies of the town, built up two sides of a narrow valley. The **lower town** (Módica Bassa) lies in the valley cleft, traced by the main Corso Umberto I and home to *palazzi* whose balconies are buttressed by gargoyles, twisted heads and beasts – and to a crop of battered churches.

It's worth making the journey from Ragusa to Módica by **bus** if you can – the train route isn't half as spectacular. Buses pull up on Corso Umberto I, and just down the street, on the left, a side street flanking San Pietro church leads up to the steps which rise to San Giorgio. To get into the town centre from the **train station**, walk to the right and, at the ornamental fountain, bear left for the corso.

Practicalities

Módica would make a good alternative to **spending the night** in Ragusa. The Corso Umberto I has the *Motel di Módica* (☎0932.941.022, fax 0932.941.077; ②), an adequate lodging with prices dropping one category in winter. The alternative is the *Hotel Bristol* (☎0932.762.890, fax 0932.763.330; ④) at Via Risorgimento 8, more expensive but good value for what you get; the snag is the location, just over 2km south of the centre in the Sacro Cuore district, on the road in from Íspica (you might want to take a taxi if you're not driving).

Back in town, if you're looking for **somewhere to eat**, try *La Contea*, Via Grimaldi 15 (opposite San Domenico church), a moderately priced restaurant with (unusual inland) fish on the menu. Módica's best restaurant is *Fattoria delle Torri* at Via Nativo 32 (signposted off Corso Regina Margherita) in Módica Alta: a cool interior with marble-topped tables and choice local dishes. The wine list is enormous, all bottled, and nothing under L18,000; you should book if you're coming in the evening (☎0932.751.286; expensive; closed Mon). Alternatively, there's a good, basic trattoria, *L'Arco*, at the bottom of town, beyond the fountain, next to the Esso petrol station on Piazza Corrado Rizzone (closed Mon), offering a wide choice but no menu.

Scicli, Pozzallo and Íspica

SCICLI, just 10km south (buses and trains from Ragusa and Módica), is dramatically pitched against the bottom of a knobbly bluff, its air of faded grandeur reinforced by the almost exclusively geriatric population; indeed the only sounds you're likely to hear are the prayers for the dead seeping out of shuttered windows. Perhaps because it's off the tourist track, Scicli's profusion of pale-yellow eighteenth-century churches, balconied *palazzi* and spacious, empty squares is being allowed to slip into terminal neglect, though it still retains the graceful lines and tones typical of the region's post-quake towns.

Just off the main piazza, the crumbling **Palazzo Beneventano** features some spectacularly ugly eighteenth-century exterior decoration: manic grinning faces with lolling tongues and bald heads tucked under the balconies and clinging to the walls. From the *palazzo*, it's worth the trek uphill to the terrace by the empty church of **San Matteo** (now fenced off) to enjoy grand views over Scicli below. Take Via Matrice and then, to the right of Via San Matteo, the cobbled steps, which in turn become an overgrown path; you'll see an abandoned shell of a chapel on your way. At the church, the track leads to the remains of a lookout tower; walk a little way beyond here, to the top of the ridge, and you're standing right above a series of abandoned **cave-dwellings** that litter the hills around, used from Neolithic times until fairly recently. From the vantage-point you can make out bricked-up entrances, caves and doorways in the tree-dotted cliffs below.

The **tourist office** (Mon–Sat 8.30am–12.30pm & 3–7pm; ☎0932.839.211) is situated on the ground floor of the municipal palace in Via Mormina Penna. You'll find a decent **place to eat**, *Al Ritrovo*, at Via Belfiore 5, off Via Stelvio (closed Mon), which offers a good local tourist menu at L25,000.

Pozzallo

From Scicli the train forges a devious route south, to the coast at **POZZALLO**, a small port with a nice beach and a tangled industrial complex close by. British troops, led by Montgomery, landed here in 1943, joining with the Americans, who had landed further west, to take Gela – the first European ground to be recaptured by the Allies in World War II.

If you need a **place to stay** in Pozzallo, the central Corso Vittorio Veneto holds the reasonable *Villa Ada* (☎ & fax 0932.954.022; ③), with TVs in the rooms and a restaurant. There's also a fully equipped **campsite** called *The King's Reef*, a little way out in Contrada Scaro (☎0932.657.611; April–Sept). In summer, **catamarans to Malta** leave from Pozzallo's port; tickets, costing up to L195,000 return (less outside the peak season), are available from Via Studi 80, off Via Lungomare Raganzino – see "Travel details" (p.274) for frequency and journey time.

Íspica

Another ten minutes on, **ÍSPICA** lies at the head of a wide gorge riddled with more Neolithic tombs and cave-dwellings, later used by Sikels, Greeks and early Christians to bury their dead. The gorge, the **Cava d'Íspica**, stretches for 12km to the northwest, and the whole length can be walked without too much hardship. Rock-cut **dwellings** and **tombs** are scattered along the entire route, but you'll see the most impressive set at the other, northwestern, end of it. If you have transport and want to head directly to these, they're roughly halfway between Módica and Íspica, 6km up a minor road signposted off the main SS115. Currently much of the official **site** is closed, though the main part of the northwest end remains open (Mon–Sat 8.30am–7.30pm, Sun 8.30am–1.45pm & 3–6.45pm; L4000). A torch would be useful.

Cómiso, Vittória and the southern coast

Cómiso and **Vittória**, situated to the west of Ragusa, are strictly for passing through, only of interest to lovers of Baroque or students of small-town life. Both are on the main train line from Ragusa to Gela and could be seen in half a morning each. The coast is considerably more difficult to see without your own transport; to be frank, you're not missing a great deal if you move on to pastures new.

Cómiso

The journey to **CÓMISO** is worth making by bus or car if you can, crossing a barren 600-metre-high plateau that looks away to the distant sea and down to the massive domes dominating the town's skyline. Although the Chiaramonte and other noble families filled Cómiso with a wealth of architecture during the Middle Ages, it is the Baroque spirit which infuses the place, most prominent in the two major churches, the **Chiesa Matrice** and the nearby **Santíssima Anunziata**. Both are post-1693 products and overwhelm everything else within reach of their ponderous shadows. A relief, then, to wander up Via Virgilio (or, from the Anunziata, Via degli Studi) to gaze on a much more modest affair, the thirteenth-century church of **San Francesco**, to which a rich Renaissance chapel was added in 1517 to house the tombs of the powerful Naselli family. You can see their restored **castello** near the centre of town, at the end of Via San Biagio.

Cómiso was the birthplace of both the painter and sculptor **Salvatore Fiume** (1915–97) and his friend, the writer **Gesualdo Bufalino** (1920–96). The main body of Fiume's paintings, chiefly figurative in style, can be seen in the Vatican museums, but he also designed sets for opera houses and worked on architectural projects. Bufalino's career was a more curious one. He began his first book in 1950, having spent three years in a Palermitan sanatorium, but declined to let it be published until 1981, when he was finally satisfied with it. After that he picked up steam and wrote several novels and short stories, including the respected *Night's Lies*, which won Italy's most prestigious literary Strega prize in 1988.

Vittória

Another ten minutes beyond Cómiso by train, **VITTÓRIA** lies at the centre of a rich wine district. Founded in 1607 by Vittória della Colonna, daughter of the Spanish viceroy and wife of the Count of Módica, it differs from other hillside towns in the region in its location on the plain west of the Iblean mountains – a setting reflected in its flat and regular street plan. You can confine your visit here to the two principal squares, Piazza del Pópolo and Piazza Ricca, the first graced by the curved facade of the church of **Madonna della Grazia** and the later Neoclassical Teatro Comunale. The smaller Piazza Ricca lies in the lee of the church of **San Giovanni Battista**, its interior dripping with gilt.

Along the coast

The coast – and the start of the so-called "riviera", which extends as far as **GELA** (p.304) – is only 10km southwest of Vittória, at Scoglitti. Three kilometres south of here, just beyond the mouth of the River Ípari, lie the desolate remains of ancient **Camarina**, a Syracusan colony founded in 599 BC, several times devastated in the conflicts with nearby Gela and eventually destroyed by Rome in 258 BC. Only reachable by bus from Ragusa, this dispersed area lies on a headland overlooking beaches on either side, though an **Antiquarium** (daily 9am–2pm & 3pm–1hr before sunset; free) marks the site's centre, containing everything that hasn't already been appropriated by Ragusa's museum. Behind the antiquarium is all that's left of a fifth-century BC **Tempio di Atena**, surrounded by the rubble of city walls. West of it lie the various ruins of the Hellenistic-Roman city, accessible from separate entrances along the road, each keeping the same hours as the antiquarium.

At the bottom of steep cliffs south of here is a swish Club Med complex, while 5km further down the coast, at **PUNTA BRACCETTO**, are a clutch of **campsites**, most open only in the summer, though the *Baia dei Coralli* (☎0932.918.192) stays open all year round. Carry on down to the next point, **PUNTA SECCA**, to see another minor archeological site, Byzantine **Caucana**. There are traces of a fourth- to sixth-century harbour here, and the remains of a basilica, though nothing very thrilling. You might be more engaged by one of the area's most fashionable sandy **beaches** nearby.

The coast stretches further east dotted by a series of minor resorts and attendant bars and hotels. None of it is overdeveloped, and some of the small towns – **MARINA DI RAGUSA** and **Donnalucata** – are quite appealing, if rather dismal out of season. Marina di Ragusa is probably the best target, with frequent buses running from Ragusa in summer. There are campsites here (see "Ragusa", p.269), as well as some decent ice-cream bars and a couple of popular "pubs".

Without your own transport, the only way to reach the coast is **by bus**, from Ragusa to Marina di Ragusa or Camarina, or from Scicli to Donnalucata. There's a coastal road that connects them all, though there is little or no transport service between.

festivals

April
Last Sunday St George's Day celebrations in **Ragusa Ibla**: statues paraded through the streets and a costumed procession.

May
1 Procession in **Siracusa**, with the statue of St Lucy carried around town.

May /June
Classical drama festival at **Siracusa**, even-numbered years only, events taking place in the Greek theatre.

August
First Sunday Boat race (*palio*) round Ortygia island in **Siracusa**, in which the five traditional quarters of the city compete with raucous enthusiasm.

27–29 Festivities in **Ragusa** to mark the city's patron St John the Baptist; more processions and statues.

29 Start of Madonna delle Lacrime festival (devoted to the "weeping" Madonna) in **Siracusa**; runs until September 3.

Last Sunday Festival of St Corrado in **Noto**.

December
13 Festival of St Lucy in **Siracusa**: a procession to the church of Santa Lucia.

travel details

Trains
Ragusa to: Cómiso (11 daily; 30min); Gela (11 daily Sat–Sun, 8 Sun; 1hr 20min); Íspica (7 daily; 1hr 10min); Licata (6 daily Mon–Sat, 3 Sun; 1hr 40min); Módica (11 daily Mon–Sat, 6 Sun; 25min); Noto (8 daily Mon–Sat, 5 Sun; 1hr 30min); Pozzallo (8 daily Mon–Sat, 5 Sun; 1hr); Scicli (8 daily Mon–Sat, 5 Sun; 35min); Siracusa (8 daily Mon–Sat, 5 Sun; 2hr 20min); Vittória (10 daily Mon–Sat, 7 Sun; 40min).
Siracusa to: Augusta (17 daily; 30min); Catania (17 daily; 1hr 30min); Gela (3 daily; 4hr); Lentini (17 daily; 50min); Messina (15 daily; 3hr); Módica (9 daily Mon–Sat, 6 Sun; 2hr); Noto (12 daily; 40min); Ragusa (8 daily; 2hr 20min); Taormina (16 daily; 2hr 30min).

Buses

Módica to: Íspica (13 daily Mon–Sat, 4 Sun; 20min); Pachino (2 daily Mon–Sat; 1hr); Palermo (3 daily Mon–Sat, 2 Sun; 4hr 30min); Pozzallo (11 daily Mon–Sat, 2 Sun; 30min); Ragusa (hourly Mon–Sat, 2 Sun; 20min); Scicli (9 daily Mon–Sat; 20min); Siracusa (8 daily Mon–Sat, 4 Sun; 2hr).

Noto to: Eloro (3 daily; 20min); Siracusa (12 daily Mon–Sat, 4 Sun; 40min).

Pachino to: Marzamemi (4 daily Mon–Sat; 10min); Portopalo di Capo Pássero (9 daily Mon–Sat; 15min); Ragusa (2 daily; 1hr 30min); Siracusa (11 daily Mon–Sat, 3 Sun; 1hr 30 min).

Ragusa to: Agrigento (2 daily Mon–Sat; 2hr 30min); Camarina (2 daily Mon–Sat; 40min); Catania via airport (8 daily Mon–Sat, 5 Sun; 2hr); Catania via Lentini (3 daily Mon–Sat; 3hr 10min); Gela (4 daily Mon–Sat; 1hr); Íspica (hourly Mon–Sat, 4 Sun; 40min); Marina di Ragusa (hourly June–Sept; 30min); Módica (hourly Mon–Sat, 2 Sun; 20min); Noto (6 daily Mon–Sat, 1 Sun; 1hr); Palermo (3 daily Mon–Sat, 2 Sun; 4hr); Pozzallo (9 daily Mon–Sat, 3 Sun; 1hr); Scicli (10 daily Mon–Sat, 2 Sun; 40min); Siracusa (6 daily Mon–Sat; 2hr 15min).

Siracusa to: Augusta (hourly Mon–Sat; 40min); Ávola (12 daily Mon–Sat, 4 Sun; 40min); Caltagirone (1 daily Mon–Sat; 2hr); Catania (hourly Mon–Sat, 4 Sun; 1hr 15min); Catania airport (9 daily Mon–Sat, 6 Sun; 1hr); Eloro (3 daily; 1hr); Ferla (1 daily Mon–Sat; 1hr 30min); Lentini (11 daily Mon–Sat; 55min); Noto (11 daily Mon–Sat, 4 Sun; 40min); Pachino (11 daily Mon–Sat, 3 Sun; 1hr 30min); Palazzolo Acréide (10 daily Mon–Sat; 1hr); Palermo (6 daily Mon–Sat, 2 Sun; 4hr 10min); Piazza Armerina (1 daily Mon–Sat; 2hr 30min); Ragusa (6 daily Mon–Sat; 2hr 15min); Rome (1 daily; 12hr); Sortino (7 daily Mon–Sat; 1hr).

Sortino to: Carlentini (1 daily; 40min); Catania (4 daily Mon–Sat; 1hr 30min); Lentini (1 daily; 40min); Siracusa (7 daily Mon–Sat; 1hr).

Catamarans

Pozzallo to: Malta (6–14 weekly June–Oct; 1hr 30min).

Siracusa to: Malta (2 weekly July–Aug ; 2hr 30 min).

CHAPTER SEVEN

THE INTERIOR

. . . for the last five hours all they had set eyes on were bare hillsides flaming yellow under the sun . . . They had passed through crazed-looking villages washed in palest blue; crossed dry beds of torrents over fantastic bridges; skirted sheer precipices which no sage and broom could temper. Never a tree, never a drop of water; just sun and dust.

Giuseppe di Lampedusa, *The Leopard.*

Sicily's slow cross-country trains and the limited-exit motorway (the A19) do little to encourage stops in the island's vast and mountainous **interior**, but it's only here that you really begin to get off the tourist trail. Intensely rural, there are just two or three decent-sized towns, bunched together almost in the dead centre of the island. Outside these, much of the land is burnt dry during the long summer months, the cracked fields and shrivelled plantations affording a meagre living to the sparse population. Unlike other parts of Italy, those who cultivated the land here (if it was cultivable) actually travelled to work from their towns and villages rather than living on site. Now thoroughly depleted by mass emigration, the countryside is empty and you're unlikely to see many signs of life outside the small hill-top towns. But these towns, though often moribund, occasionally possess an exuberance and vitality that's in startling contrast with the stillness of the interior's rolling hills.

Travelling in the interior can get monotonous, as much of the land is given over to extensive cornfields – a feature of the Sicilian landscape since Greek times. But there are compensations for coming this far off the beaten track. Some of the minor inland routes give fascinating glimpses of a life that's all but disappeared in the rest of Sicily (indeed Italy), and there are some of the finest routes and views on the island, as well as some of its most curious towns. **Enna** is as central as you can get, a blustery mountain settlement dominating the dry hills below and making a good starting point for trips to the untouched towns and villages of the **northeastern interior**, of which **Nicosia** is the main attraction. The biggest town in the region, **Caltanissetta**, is also the most disappointing, largely modern and devoid of life. But, with your own transport, the region beyond it – the little-visited **western interior** – makes an absorbing journey, stretching to **Corleone**: an agricultural centre that, like so many in the neighbourhood, is tainted by its Mafia associations.

Although the Arabs settled the centre of the island, leaving their mark in a number of place names and warren-like towns, the Greeks and Romans tended to leave Sicily's interior alone. Nevertheless, the **southern interior** boasts some unexpected ancient gems, not least **Piazza Armerina** and its fabulous Roman mosaics, and the nearby excavations at **Morgantina**. And there's interest, too, in ceramic-studded **Caltagirone**, a handy departure point for the Baroque towns of the southeast (for which, see p.265).

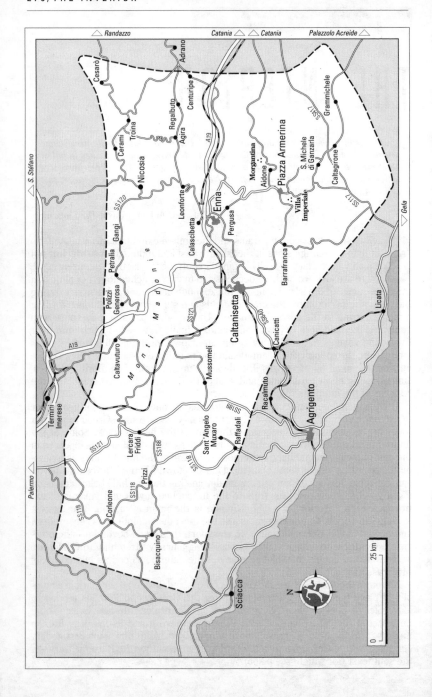

ACCOMMODATION PRICE CODES

These represent the **cheapest available double room in high season**, usually – but not always – without en-suite bathroom or shower. Out of season, you'll often be able to negotiate a lower price than those suggested here. For more information about hotels and room prices, see p.27. The categories are:

① under L60,000   ③ L90,000–120,000   ⑤ L150,000–200,000   ⑦ L250,000–300,000
② L60,000–90,000   ④ L120,000–150,000   ⑥ L200,000–250,000   ⑧ over L300,000

Practicalities

Getting around the interior can be tricky. Public transport is patchy at best, though you can easily reach all the important centres – Enna, Caltanissetta, Piazza Armerina and Caltagirone – by bus or train. It's more difficult to travel into the mountains: most accessible are the hilltop towns of the northeast, with **buses** running out of Enna and along the two major routes. Virtually impossible to reach without your **own transport** are the towns and villages west of Caltanissetta. You should plan ahead if you want to stay the night anywhere, as good **accommodation** is scarce; most of the options are detailed in the text, but it's worth noting that there are *no* official **campsites**.

ENNA AND THE NORTHEASTERN INTERIOR

Despite its stranded mountain-top position and the frontier feel of the town, there's no great effort involved in getting to **Enna** these days: there are regular buses and trains from Catania and Palermo. But without your own transport you'll usually have to be prepared to spend the night, certainly if you intend to move further into the **northeastern interior** to some of the least-developed parts of the island. Fairly frequent **buses** leave Enna for towns along the eastbound **SS121**, which eventually runs right the way to Catania. From **Leonforte**, first stop on this route, there are buses north to **Nicosia**: like Enna, a good place to base yourself. Nicosia sits in the middle of a second route, the **SS120**: running east to **Cesarò** and on into the foothills of Etna, though, this is fairly hard to travel by public transport; or west to **Polizzi Generosa**, an easier choice, as all the towns on this stretch are connected by bus. A few places along the SS120 (east and west) can also be reached from towns on the Tyrrhenian coast, cutting across dramatic tracts of the Nébrodi and Madonie mountains.

You may be able to help matters by hitching some of the way between towns in the northeast, but don't count on it, and it's certainly not to be recommended if you're on your own: traffic is scarce and strangers are viewed with suspicion. If you do get stuck, it's of some comfort to know that some towns at least have good, cheap hotels.

Enna

From a bulging V-shaped ridge almost 1000m up, **ENNA** lords it over the surrounding hills of central Sicily. One of the most ancient towns on the island, Enna has only ever had one function: Livy described it as "inexpugnabilis" and, for obvious strategic reasons, Enna was a magnet for successive hostile armies, who in turn besieged and fortified it. The approach to this mountain stronghold is still formidable, the road climbing slowly out of the valley and looping across the solid crag to the summit and the town. Enna remains medieval at heart, as any foray into its densely packed streets shows, and even the modern development echoes the town's defensive past, its office buildings and apartment blocks rising like so many watchtowers from a distance.

The very distinct hill-town atmosphere here is worth staying overnight for. Summer evenings in Enna are among the most enjoyable in Sicily, watching the sun set from some of the finest vantage-points imaginable. Come in winter and you should expect snow, the wind blowing hard through the streets, white slopes blending with the anaemic stone buildings.

The Town

Despite the numerous wars that have touched the town over the years, most of Enna's remains are medieval and in good nick, prize exhibit being the thirteenth-century **Castello di Lombardia** (daily 9am–1pm & 3–5pm; free) dominating the easternmost spur of town. Built by Frederick II, it's a mighty construction with its strong walls complete, guarding the steep slopes on either side of town. Six surviving towers (out of an original twenty) provide lookouts and the tallest, the Torre Pisana, takes in magnificent views of Enna itself, some rugged countryside in all directions and, if you're lucky, Mount Etna. The main courtyard is used as an open-air theatre in the summer, and there's plenty of room elsewhere to lounge about with a picnic.

A road to the side of the castle climbs a little way further to the **Rocca di Cerere**, an exposed outcrop where some scattered foundations are presumed to be the remnants of a temple erected by Gelon in 480 BC. Enna was the centre of the Greek cult of Demeter, the fertility goddess (her Roman counterpart was Ceres, hence the rock's name), and the most famous of the myths associated with the goddess – the carrying off of her daughter, Persephone, to the underworld – is supposed to have taken place just a few kilometres away, at Lago di Pergusa (see pp.281–282).

Attractive chunks of the **old town** survive intact too, though much worn by the brisk winds that scurry across the squares and streets, even in summer. Tightly packed houses hug the two ridges that divide Enna, occasional gaps revealing swirling drops down into the valleys. Though it's fun to wander through the crumbly southern and eastern sections of Enna, virtually all the accredited sights lie stretched out along and around the better-preserved **Via Roma**, which decends from the castle. It's a narrow street, interrupted by small piazzas, one of which fronts the hemmed-in **Duomo** (daily 9am–1pm & 4–7pm), dating in part from 1307. Rebuilt several times since, its long medieval wall, which has Gothic touches, is hardly complemented by the duomo's thin Baroque facade, while the spacious sixteenth-century interior, whose every surface is encrusted with ornamentation or draped with red velvet hangings, features huge supporting alabaster columns, the bases of which are covered with an amorphous, writhing mass – manic heads with human hands and snake bodies, snarling mouths and dome-like pates.

Outside, the **Museo Alessi** (Tues–Sun 9am–1pm & 4–7pm; L3000) fields the impressive contents of the cathedral's own treasury, including a tall eighteenth-century wooden cabinet which opens to reveal a silver throne. Some of the

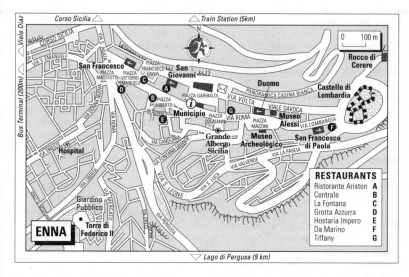

handiwork on display is remarkable: a seventeenth-century gold and crystal crown is decorated with minute scenes from the life of Christ, picked out with studded jewels. There's a rich collection of local church art too, downstairs, and cases of old coins on the floor above. A second museum, equally good, lies at the back of the Piazza Mazzini, opposite the cathedral – the **Museo Archeológico**, or Museo Varisano (daily 9am–1pm & 3–6.30pm; L4000), which covers Neolithic to Roman times, all the exhibits dug up in the locality, including a fine series of painted Greek vases.

Via Roma continues down past the Catalan-Gothic **Palazzo Pollicarini**, opposite the *Grande Albergo Sicilia*. The *palazzo* has now been turned into apartments, but if you peek into the courtyard you can see the typical medieval Catalan exterior staircase climbing up to the first floor. Just to the west of here, in Piazza Coppola, the tower of the church of **San Giovanni** is crowned by a little cupola. It's one of the few surviving relics of the Arab occupation of Enna, though the winding central streets suggest an Eastern influence too. The Arabs spent twenty years trying to gain entrance to the town and eventually resorted to crawling in through the sewers in 859.

The eastern extremity of Via Roma is marked by the sloping, rectangular **Piazza Vittorio Emanuele**, focal point of the evening *passeggiata*. Off here, a long cliff-edge promenade looks out to the little rust-coloured village of Calascibetta (p.281) over the valley; there's a good bar (with outside tables) at the top of the square. The plain, high wall of the church of **San Francesco**, which flanks the piazza, has a massive sixteenth-century tower, previously part of the old town's system of watchtowers, which linked the castle with all Enna's churches.

One of the watchtowers, the **Torre di Federico II**, still stands in isolation in the **Giardino Pubblico** (Mon–Sat 9am–1pm; free), in the largely modern south of the town. An octagonal tower, 24m high, it's a survivor of the alterations to the city made by Frederick of Aragon, who added a (now hidden) underground passage connecting the tower to the castle. There should be someone around to let you in for more views from the top of the tower.

Practicalities

All long-distance and most local buses use the **bus terminal** on Viale Diaz in the new town – turn right out of the terminal, right again down Corso Sicilia, and it's around a ten-minute walk to Piazza Vittorio Emanuele. If you possibly can, arrive by bus: Enna's **train station** is 5km below town, a long but and dauntingly steep walk, though a local bus runs roughly hourly to the town centre (only at selected times on Sunday, when you may have to take a taxi); for train information, call the station (☎0935.500.910), or there are timetables at the tourist offices and at Agenzia Viaggi Coppola, Via Sant'Agata 64 (☎0935.501.169).

You can reach everywhere in Enna itself very easily on foot, though #5 **buses for Pergusa** (7am–9.30pm every 30min) leave from Piazza Matteoti, outside San Francesco church; you'll need a ticket (L1000) before you get on, bought from *tabacchi* and valid for one hour. **Taxi** ranks are along Viale Diaz, near the bus terminal, on Via Pergusa and at Piazza Vittorio Emanuele; alternatively, call ☎0935.500.905.

Information, as well as a good free **map** of Enna, is available from the **tourist office** at Via Roma 413 (Mon–Fri 9am–1pm & 3.30–6.30pm; ☎0935.528.828, fax 0935.528.229), just around the corner on the main road; and a smaller office in Piazza Colaianni (Mon–Fri 8am–4pm, Sat 9am–1pm; ☎0935.500.875), right in front of the *Grande Albergo Sicilia*.

Accommodation

There's only one **hotel** in Enna, and if it's full (or too expensive) you'll have to take a bus to nearby Pergusa instead, where there are several cheaper possibilities. (If you're coming to Enna from Piazza Armerina, you'll pass through Pergusa first.) The dead central *Grande Albergo Sicilia* is in Piazza Colaianni (☎0935.500.850, fax 0935.500.488; ④), and its brutalist exterior hides a rather nice Art Deco lobby and decent rooms with bath, TV and views over town; breakfast is included in the price.

Eating and drinking

There's considerably more choice when it comes to **eating and drinking**. For pizzas and regular Italian dishes, *Da Marino*, Via Lombardia 2 (no credit cards; closed Mon) near the castle, is an accommodating place with friendly service. *Tiffany*, Via Roma 487 (closed Thurs), just down from the cathedral, is also friendly and serves pizza. There are a couple of moderately priced trattorias, including the little back-street *Hostario Impero*, Via Ree Pentite 17, off Via Roma at Piazza Umberto, and the more adventurous *Grotta Azzurra* (closed Sat & winter), down the hill on Via Colaianni (between Piazza Matteotti and Piazza Vittorio Emanuele); follow the signs up the alley.

Moving up a notch, *La Fontana*, Via Vulturo 6, is close to Piazza Francesco Crispi and the belvedere. This has good home cooking and friendly service, some good meat specialities and even a couple of outdoor tables; a full meal runs to around L35,000, though you could eat for less. Considerably more costly, but worth every lira, is the *Ristorante Ariston*, Via Roma 353 (closed Sun), which specializes in fresh pasta and good Sicilian dishes; expect to pay around L50,000–60,000 a head for a full meal with wine. For a little less, you could eat at the *Centrale*, Piazza VI Dicembre 9 (closed Sat in winter), also well thought of for its local dishes.

The **market** in Enna is held on Tuesday (8am–2pm) at the end of Viale Diaz, below the Torre di Federico II. And for takeaway **spit-roast chickens**, there's a shop (closed Mon) – marked *"pollo alle brace"* – at Via Pergusa 24, just around the corner from Piazza Matteotti.

For a good **bar**, try the chrome-trimmed *Extra Bar*, Via Roma 391, which deals in tasty snacks as well as drinks. There are many other appealing *pasticcerie*-bars in town, most stretched along Via Roma; one of the nicest is the *Caffè Roma*, Via Roma 312, down by Piazza Vittorio Emanuele, which serves wine by the glass and has tables at the back.

Listings

Banks Banco di Sicilia, Via Roma 367; Banca d'Italia, Piazza Garibaldi 4; Cassa Centrale di Risparmio, Piazza Vittorio Emanuele 18.

Bus companies SAIS at the bus terminal (☎0935.500.902); services to Calascibetta, Caltanissetta, Catania, Catania airport, Centúripe, Leonforte, Messina, Nicosia, Palermo, Piazza Armerina.

Car problems ACI, Via Roma 200 (☎0935.26.299).

Cinema Supercinema Grivi, Piazza Ghisleri, near Piazza Umberto.

Hospital Ospedale Umberto I, Via Trieste (☎0935.45.111).

Pharmacies Librizzi, Piazza Vittorio Emanuele 20 (☎0935.500.908); Termine, Via Roma 315 (☎0935.500.650).

Police Questura at Via San Giuseppe 2 (☎0935.522.111).

Post office Via A. Volta, off Piazza Garibaldi.

Telephones Telecom Italia, Piazza Scelfo, off Piazza Vittorio Emanuele. Daily 8am–8pm.

Around Enna: Calascibetta and the Lago di Pergusa

Close to Enna, on a lower hill to the north across the valley, the small town of **CALASCIBETTA** hints at what Enna would be like without the tower blocks. Once a Saracen town, it was fortified by Count Roger in his successful attempt to take Enna in 1087, and the brooding atmosphere in its tangled streets seems straight from that age. Tightly packed red-stone buildings are perched above a sheer drop on the eastern side, rising to the restored Chiesa Madre at the very top. There are frequent buses to Calascibetta from Enna's bus terminal (or every couple of hours from Enna's train station); the trattoria halfway up the steep road there is very good.

Lago di Pergusa

Nine kilometres south of Enna, the **Lago di Pergusa** is the legendary site of Hades' abduction of Persephone to the underworld. The story has it that Persephone, surrounded by nymphs, was gathering flowers on the lush banks of the lake when Hades emerged from a chasm beneath the water and spirited her away. Demeter searched in vain for her daughter, and her grief at the loss of Persephone prevented the corn from growing. To settle the matter, Zeus ruled that Persephone should spend half the year as Queen of the Underworld, living for the other six months in Sicily with her mother as one of the island's goddesses. In her gratitude, Demeter, as goddess of grain and agriculture, made the corn grow again – a powerful symbol in a traditionally fertile land.

Today, the lake is encircled by a motor-racing track, and despite the wooded banks beyond the water it's difficult now to imagine a less romantic spot. Mary Taylor Simeti's journal, *On Persephone's Island*, labels the lake "a brilliant example of the Sicilians' best efforts to ruin their landscape"; and certainly, it's not worth coming here for any glimpse of the truth behind the legend, though it is a possible base near Enna. Alongside the lake there are several modern **hotels**: the best value on the Enna road is the *Miralago* (☎0935.541.272; no credit cards; ②), offering decently equipped rooms with bath. Overlooking the lake, on Via Autodroma Pergusa, the *Riviera* (☎ & fax 0935.541.267; ②) has decently priced rooms and a swimming pool; when there are no race meetings, it's a peaceful place. If you don't want to go back into Enna, there are plenty of places to **eat,** including the pizzeria at the *Miralago*, or try the *Trattoria Al Carretino* (closed Wed), opposite on the main road, whose local pasta speciality (*Cavatelle al Carretino*) is excellent.

For **buses to Pergusa** from Enna, see "Practicalities" (p.280); the last bus from Enna to Pergusa is at around 9.30pm; from Pergusa to Enna, it's at 10pm.

The SS121: Enna to Centúripe

Out of Enna, and beyond Calascibetta, it's around forty minutes by bus to **LEONFORTE**, in many ways typical of the many small towns you'll come across east of Enna, with its roots firmly in the seventeenth century. Its attractive central square sprouts bars in profusion, and besides the impressive duomo there's also great interest in the domineering Palazzo Baronale, whose bulky facade is recognizable from way outside town. However, the most notable sight here is **La Gran Fonte**, less a fountain than a range of 24 water-spouts set in a sculpted facade of embossed roses and figures, built in 1651. It's about 300m on foot down from the Chiesa Madre (or follow the signs at the western end of the village if you're driving), overlooking the hills on the edge of town. The fountain has recently been restored, and is a good place to fill water bottles; there's even a little, adjacent bar with outdoor seats offering fine views. If you were going to stop anywhere along the SS121, this is perhaps the place; there are a couple of reasonable trattorias up in the town centre.

The bus from Enna steers a course further east through attractive **NISSORIA**, whose central leafy street is lined with bars occupied by old men shooting the breeze across the moving traffic. It's another 7km on to **AGIRA**, again, well sited on the brow of a hill. From a distance, its buildings form a perfect cone, with the ruins of its medieval castle prominent atop the peak, though much neglected. If you've got your own transport, you could pause here for **lunch** at the *Ristorante al Capriccio*, Via Vittorio Emanuele 323, the main road through town, where there's a panoramic view, or for a quick pizza and drink try *Al Muretto* on the same road at no. 343. Agira's also the only place for an **overnight stop** on this route, at the tidy *Albergo Aurora*, Via Annunziata 6 (☎0935.691.416; no credit cards; ②), which only just fits into this price category. There are several daily buses from here north to Troina – useful if you want to get to the SS120 (see opposite).

The SS121 continues through tiny Regalbuto and eventually to Catania, a journey that strikes through land fiercely contested during the short Sicilian campaign of World War II. The hills between Agira and the western slopes of Etna saw most of the heaviest fighting. Just out of Agira, close to the **Lago di Pozzillo**, there's a poignant **war cemetery** sited on a gentle hillside, the resting place of 490 Canadian soldiers killed in July 1943.

Centúripe

Some 20km on, a minor road in remarkably good condition leads south for 8km through orange and olive groves and then sharply uphill to **CENTÚRIPE**, which faces Etna across the Simeto River valley, giving it a strategic importance that accounts for the struggles for control of this isolated outpost over the centuries. Various medieval campaigns destroyed the town, while the last great battle in August 1943 dislodged Hermann Goering and his forces. Most of the damage has since been made good, rather to the detriment of Centúripe, which is an uneasy mix of new building and an untouched central piazza. A terrace not far from here – reached by an avenue of imposing pines – is the best vantage-point for the outstanding views that earned for Centúripe the tag "balcony of Sicily". Here, and from various other points, you look down over the switchbacked roads and stepped terraces all the way to the SS121 to the north or the autostrada to the south, the latter accessible directly from Centúripe by a similarly superbly engineered road. For all its strategic attractions, though, Centúripe is not a place to aim for unless you're driving; after gazing at the views you'll exhaust the town's possibilities in around two minutes flat – perhaps ten, if you stopped for a drink at one of the three bars in the central square.

The towns beyond Centúripe, on and off the SS121, are covered in the section on the Circumetnea railway; see p.226.

Across the mountains: the SS120

Before the Palermo–Messina coastal road was constructed, traffic between the two cities passed inland, on a long mountainous route that took in some of the island's most impressive scenery. Today, free of the traffic that clogs the coast, **the SS120** makes an attractive trans-island alternative, across some of the remoter stretches of the Madonie and Nébrodi mountains. Make sure you reserve accommodation in advance, though, as the few hotels that there are tend to fill up quickly.

Nicosia

The biggest town on this stretch, and best base for excursions east and west, is **NICOSIA** (reachable by buses from Leonforte, Palermo, Términi Imerese and Santo Stéfano Mistretta), a basically medieval, convoluted mass of cracked *palazzi* topped by the remains of a Norman castle. In the cramped centre, the chatter-filled Piazza Garibaldi is the site of Nicosia's lovely old cathedral, **San Nicola** (daily 8–10.30am), a stately construction with a fourteenth-century facade and bell-tower, and a sculpted Gothic portal.

Behind the cathedral, Via Salomone rises steeply to the former Saracen district of the town, a jumble of streets occupying one of the four hills on which Nicosia is built. At the top, **Santa Maria Maggiore**, founded in 1267 but rebuilt after an eighteenth-century landslide, has the bells from its campanile piled up outside – they fell down after another earthquake and the sound of them is now electrically reproduced. Inside, amid "No Spitting" notices, there's an impressive marble polyptych by Antonello Gagini and a throne used by Charles V when he passed through here in 1535, on the way back from his Tunisian crusade. The views from outside encompass the town's other three promontories, on the highest of which sits the ruined **castello**.

Buses leave Nicosia from Piazza Marconi, at the bottom of Via Vittorio Emanuele. There is only one **hotel** here, the rather dark and dingy *Albergo Patria*, Via Vittorio Emanuele 11 (☎0935.646.103; ③), with its own restaurant. If you're driving, you can reach one of the two out-of-town hotels: *Pineta*, in the San Paolo neighbourhood (☎0935.647.002; ③); and *Vigneta* (☎0935.646.074; ②), in Contrada San Basilio. Both are somewhat characterless, modern places, though comfortable enough, and well indicated on the SS120 as you head into town. Having your own transport will also enable you to seek out *La Cirata* **restaurant**, about 5km towards Enna on the SS117 (☎0935.640.561; closed Mon & Nov), for dishes based on the produce of the surrounding mountains; it's a vast place, catering mainly to passing coach groups and quite pricey, but better than nothing – which is what you'll get in town unless you go to the *Patria*'s restaurant, which is rather plain and unexceptional. For a nightcap or ice-cream at any time, the **bars** in Piazza Garibaldi are worth a visit: try the *Diana* or its grander, untitled neighbour.

East to Cesarò

The towns to the **east of Nicosia** are set in a bare landscape astride the Monti Nébrodi, dominated ever more dramatically by the giant silhouette of Etna. There's no bus to the first stop, **CERAMI**, 21km away, which lies at the foot of a massive rock topped by the remains of a castle. But you can reach the next town east, **TROINA**, by bus from Agira, a tortuous thirty-kilometre ride to what, from a distance, appears like a silver thimble perched on a hill, 1120m high. Troina played a prominent role in the reconquest of Sicily from the Arabs, when it became one of the first cities to be taken by the Normans. Count Roger withstood a siege here for four months in 1064 that nearly put paid to his Sicilian adventures, a victory he commemorated by founding the convent of **San Basilio**, now in ruins near the present Capuchin convent. But it's the journey to this wind-blown village that's the real event.

CESARÒ, 20km further east, stands at the crossroads with the SS289, which runs north to the coast. Well within the lee of Etna, it's endowed with some remarkable views over to the volcano. Climb up to the cemetery above town, and from behind the battered castle fragments Etna is framed between gentle hills. It's difficult to reach Cesarò from the west by public transport; only possible if the early-morning bus from Nicosia still runs. However, there are buses from Sant'Agata on the Tyrrhenian coast and from Giardini-Naxos on the Ionian, the latter route taking you through Randazzo (p.278) and the volcano's foothills. If you're stuck for a bed, Cesarò has a couple of **hotels**: the most central is the *Nébrodi*, Via Margherita 30 (☎095.696.107; ①), with rooms with or without bath, and a restaurant.

West to Polizzi Generosa

The towns and villages on the western stretch of the SS120 are easier to see by bus, linked up by several daily services from Nicosia. **SPERLINGA**, only fifteen minutes away, is one of the most interesting. The name derives from the Latin *spelonca* (grotto), a reference to the numerous cave-dwellings, some hundreds of years old, that pit the sandstone slopes on which the town stands. Sprouting above is a formidable battlemented **castello**, its storerooms, cellars and stables hewn out of the rock. The lookouts above give onto a ruckled brown landscape that's typical of this part of Sicily, described by Giuseppe di Lampedusa as "a sea suddenly petrified at the instant when a change of wind had flung the waves into a frenzy". On a wall in the castle, you can make out an old Latin inscription referring to the time when Sperlinga was the only town in Sicily to open its doors to the Angevins, bloodily expelled from other Sicilian towns during the thirteenth-century Wars of the Vespers: barricading themselves inside the castle, the French held out for a year before surrendering. If the castle's closed, ask at the tourist office on the main street, or at the Municipio.

Half an hour on, just inside Palermo's provincial boundary, **GANGI** forms a symmetrical mound on its hill-top, the shape of a tortoise's shell. The town produced two seventeenth-century artists, each known as Zoppo di Gangi ("Cripple of Gangi"), one of whom has an excellent *Last Judgement* in the church of **San Nicola** – identifiable by its incomplete fourteenth-century campanile. From Gangi you can take a bus along the minor SS286, north to Castelbuono and down to the coast at Cefalù, with departures at 5.55am and 12.45pm Monday to Saturday, or 7.25am on Sunday; note that the 12.45pm service does not stop at Cefalù. If you want to stay, the only **hotel** is the modern *Miramonti*, Via Nazionale 19 (☎0921.644.424; ③), on the main road below town.

Petralia Sottana and Petralia Soprana

A better target than Gangi, if you want to combine some exploring with an overnight stop, is 14km on. The two towns of Petralia are actually quite separate, on opposite sides of a hill. It's the lower town, **PETRALIA SOTTANA**, that holds more of interest and the only accommodation. There are several weathered medieval churches here, strung along the lively main street, Corso Agliata. Particularly evocative is the **Chiesa Matrice**, whose crumbling bell-tower looks down upon an elegant piazza. The sacristy holds a tenth- or eleventh-century Islamic bronze candelabra unique in Sicily – which is kept locked away: short of bribing the sacristan, your only chance to see it will be at a religious ceremony. If you're **staying** here, try the stylish *Madonie*, Corso Agliata 81 (☎0921.641.106; ③), which is excellent value and has a great third-floor **restaurant**. Other good trattorias in town include *Petra Leium*, at Corso Agliata 113 (closed Fri evening), which features local mountain dishes and offers a generous tourist menu; and *Saxum*, just up from the war memorial (closed Wed), a ristorante-pub with outdoor seating. The town is something a centre for hikers and skiers in the Monti Madonie running south from here (see p.118); for information on **hikes**, contact the local Parco delle Madonie agency at Corso Agliata 16 (☎0921.684.011), or the Club Alpino Italiano, at Corso Agliata 154 (☎0921.642.558), who also conduct escorted treks. Note that the nearest bank is 18km away at Piano Battáglia.

It's 3km across to the upper town, **PETRALIA SOPRANA**, quieter and older than its neighbour, at an altitude of nearly 1150m. This was the birthplace of the craftsman Fra Ùmile da Petralia (1580–1639), whose wooden crosses are to be found in churches all over southern Italy. From the edge of the village you get a long view over the Madonie and Nébrodi mountains and, if you're westward bound, a last dim sight of Etna.

Polizzi Generosa and Caltavuturo

Minor roads connect the Petralias with the lovely Madonie mountain region to the north centred on Piano Battáglia (p.118), though there's no bus this way. The service along the SS120 branches off for **POLIZZI GENEROSA**, half an hour west and right in the heart of the Madonie mountains. Stop here to see the grand old **Chiesa Matrice**, containing the area's greatest work of art: a triptych of the Madonna and Child flanked by saints; attributed to a mysterious fifteenth-century Fleming known only as the "Maître au Feuillage brodé", it's reckoned to be his best work. There's a great **restaurant** just up from here in Piazza Castello – *U Bagghiu* (closed Tues), with a little *cortile* (courtyard) to which the dialect name refers, where you can dine under a pergola shaded by apple and fig trees. If you just want an ice-cream or home-made pastry, the *Pasticceria Al Castello* close by will serve.

From Polizzi, two buses a day cross the autostrada and head to **CALTAVUTURO**, a predominantly Baroque town despite its Saracen castle and Arabic name. Nearby, smaller **SCLÁFANI BAGNI** also attests to its former importance as a fief of the Scláfani family by notching up two fourteenth-century castles and a cathedral. These, though, are minor diversions, and you might as well sit tight in Polizzi Generosa and await the onward bus to the Tyrrhenian coast, or to Palermo, an hour and a quarter away.

CALTANISSETTA AND THE WESTERN INTERIOR

With twice as many inhabitants as Enna, **Caltanissetta** is easily the largest town in the interior, though there's little else that's remarkable about it. Beyond lie the rolling expanses of Sicily's **western interior**, the rural heart of the island. The towns and villages you'll pass through are uniformly poor and raddled; at times, positively ghostlike. Many, like **Corleone**, have names that have become familiar through their Mafia associations, but few are worth even a coffee-stop. The only place that merits more than a cursory glance is the village of **Sant'Ángelo Muxaro**, whose 3000-year-old tombs dot the hill below.

Access **by public transport** is very awkward: you can get to Caltanissetta easily enough, but otherwise you're unlikely to be able to see much more of the region than what you can glean from a bus window on the fast route between Agrigento and Palermo. From Caltanissetta, the railway line meanders northwest (ultimately to Palermo), past a series of empty upland plains occasionally pocked by unexpected crags and gullies, one of the most desert-like of Sicilian journeys.

Caltanissetta and around

Despite the modern sheen that marks out **CALTANISSETTA** from other inland towns, this provincial capital is immersed in the same listless torpor that you find anywhere else in Sicily's interior. Consequently, it's not exactly the most exciting place to end up, though it is near enough to Piazza Armerina (p.292) to make it a convenient base for day-trips there; the bus timetables, for once, are kindly disposed. If you're heading for Enna by train from the south coast, you might also be changing transport here as it's better to arrive in Enna by bus. But there's little else to entice you: Caltanissetta's one worthy attraction is the **Museo Cívico** (daily Mon–Sat except last Mon of month 9am–1.30pm & 3–7.30pm; L4000), on Via Napoleone Colajanni, close to the train station, which contains some of the earliest of Sicilian finds, including vases and Bronze Age sculpted figures. Otherwise, with time to kill, you could strike out to one of Sicily's stranger castle sites. The **Castello di Pietrarossa** lies at the town's western extremity, though within easy walking distance from Caltanissetta's centre, Piazza Garibaldi. Improbably balanced on an outcrop of rock, the castle – of Arab or Norman origin – looks like it should have fallen down years ago, and you get the feeling that no one would notice if it did.

Back in the centre of town, take a spin round the sagging walls of the seventeenth-century **Palazzo Moncada**, off Corso Umberto I; an aristocratic mansion, belonging to one of Sicily's great feudal dynasties, it's undergoing belated restoration. For some views and fresh air in this traffic-drowned town, it's best to stroll down Viale Regina Margherita (a continuation of Corso Umberto I), where there's a park and belvedere.

As well as these meagre attractions, the outskirts of Caltanissetta hold a restored twelfth-century abbey, the **Badia di Santo Spírito**, which drivers en route to Enna might find worth a stop. Lying about 3kim north of town, on a left turn off the SS112 (signposted "Santa Caterina Villarmosa"), the abbey was founded by Count Roger and – a rare thing in Sicily – is purely Norman in form. On the outside, the plain structure is only enlivened by three tiny apses at the back, though the interior has more distraction in the form of a fifteenth-century fresco over the central apse and a twelfth-century font. Seek out the parish priest if the church is locked; he lives nearby.

Practicalities

Train travellers **heading to Enna** would be advised to take a bus instead from Caltanissetta, as Enna's train station is a long way out of town (see p.280). To get to Caltanissetta's **bus station**, head up Via Kennedy from the tourist office, turn right at Piazza Don Sturzo, left at Via Salemi: the bus station is at Piazza Repubblica, off Via Turati, which begins at the end of Via Salemi (it's about a 25min walk in all).

If you're **staying** in Caltanissetta, the realistic choice is the *Plaza*, Via Gaetani 5 (☎0934.583.877; ④), off Corso Vittorio Emanuele. The only central alternative – though quite cheap for its four-star rating, with a pool – is the dearer *Hotel San Michele* on Via Fasci Siciliani (☎0934.553.750; ⑤), off Via della Libertà, near the Campo Sportivo at the end of Via Rosso di San Secondo. The **tourist office** (Mon–Fri 9am–1pm; ☎0934.421.089) is on Viale Testasecca, or else try the larger and more efficient office located above a bank at Corso Vittorio Emanuele 109 (Mon–Fri 9am–1pm & 4–8pm, Sat 9am–1pm; ☎0934.530.411).

One of the best places for a **meal** in Caltanissetta is *Le Siciliane*, on Piazza Trento (up Via Rosso di San Secondo and right at the second set of lights). Expect to pay less than L30,000 for a full spread at this superb restaurant; **pizzas** are also available (closed Wed). Closer to the centre, at Via Palmieri 10, *L'Archetto* is an informal pizzeria/ristorante that does a couscous paella (closed Tues). For **snacks**, the *RaiR* bar on Corso Umberto I has great almond biscuits (the local speciality), *cannoli* and other ricotta delights, as well as *arancini* and pizza slices (closed Tues).

CALTANISSETTA

Out of town, the village of **SAN CATALDO** (7km west) has *U'Anzalone*, an inexpensive and very traditional *osteria* specializing in such local delicacies as snails, tripe and calves' hooves; it's on the main corso. This would be a good place to visit during the Easter celebrations, during which the trial and crucifixion of Christ are re-enacted. Ask for details from Caltanisetta's tourist office.

Towards Agrigento: Canicattì and Racalmuto

Buses run southwest down the SS640 from Caltanissetta, reaching Agrigento in around an hour and a quarter. It's more fun to do the same journey by **train**, though, steering out of Caltanissetta through wooded hills and up through almond- and olive-planted slopes into higher, craggy country.

At **CANICATTÌ** the line splits, trains running south to Licata (p.307) on the coast, or continuing for another hour southwest to Agrigento (p.309). Canicattì itself is intriguingly referred to by Italians as their equivalent of Timbuktu, a reference to the town's supposed remoteness. It's actually just a dull market town, not all that remote and barely worth venturing off the train for.

The train route to Agrigento (or a 5km diversion off the main road by car) also runs through **RACALMUTO**, a similarly minor fly-blown town, though distinguished by the fact that it was the birthplace of **Leonardo Sciascia** (1921–89), perhaps the greatest of all modern Sicilian writers; he's buried here, too. Since much of his work was devoted to exploring the peculiar nature of this island and its people, it's apt that his book *Death of an Inquisitor* uncovered an Inquisitional punishment once practised in his own home town that could only be Sicilian: in Racalmuto's Piazza San Francesco, he wrote, was a corner known as "*lu cuddaru*, the collar . . . in memory of an instrument frequently used by the Holy Office to punish blasphemers . . . it was attached to a wall or post: so that, naked from the waist up, and conveniently smeared with honey, the venial blasphemer could be exhibited there for several hours". It's probably best not to curse too loudly if you get lost in the town's one-way traffic system.

Into the western interior

Unless you're driving, the only part of the **western interior** you'll see much of is along the train or bus route between Agrigento and Palermo. The quickest route between the two places – and the way that the direct Agrigento–Palermo bus runs – is following the **SS189**. But if you've the time, you might consider driving along the less-used **SS118**, which passes through some of the remoter inland towns and villages. Either way, there are several short detours you can make that are worth doing. Both the routes below are described heading north from Agrigento.

The SS189

Around 40km north of Agrigento, a sideroad off the main **SS189** turns east up to **MUSSOMELI**. On the other side of the town is the extraordinary, crag-perched castle of **Castello Manfredónico**, erected in the fourteenth century by the powerful Chiaramonte family. It makes a vivid impression on the unsuspecting traveller, tilting over its tall rocky base as if lashed by a strong wind.

About 10km west of the SS189, **Monte Cammarata** (1578m) was a key point of the Axis defences in World War II, an impregnable redoubt that was expected to seriously delay the American advance to Palermo in 1943. In the event it was taken without a shot being fired, apparently due to pressure exerted on the Italian soldiers by Calógero Vizzini (Don Calò), head of the island's Mafia. As a reward for his services, Vizzini was appointed mayor of his home town of **VILLALBA**, 20km northeast of Mussomeli. It's a shabby place, little more than a village really, typical of the area in its poverty and long-standing subjection by absentee landlords. Indeed, the sole function of the countless obscure villages that dot this landscape has always been to house the labour for the great feudal estates, watched over by complacent, self-interested priests.

Back on the main road, halfway between Agrigento and Palermo, **LERCARA FRIDDI**'s claim to fame is as the birthplace of the Sicilian-American gangster Lucky Luciano, freed from a thirty- to fifty-year prison sentence (convicted on 62 counts of "compulsory prostitution") in the US, to be sent to Sicily. Like Don Calò, Luciano was enlisted by the Americans in their Sicilian campaign, which was fully backed by the Mafia in its anxiety to end the Fascist rule.

A few kilometres north of Lercara, you pick up the SS121, which winds across the entire length of Sicily from Catania and finishes its run in Palermo. Twenty-five kilometres north of the junction at **BAGNI DI CEFALÀ** –

signposted just off the SS121 – are some eleventh-century Arab baths, flowing with thermal waters, which the locals use for washing clothes, though you can swim here too. There are few other examples of Arab architecture in such good condition in Sicily.

The SS118: Sant'Ángelo Muxaro and Corleone

Taking the alternative **SS118**, a minor road that wriggles all the way to Palermo, turn off 30km north of Agrigento at Raffadali for **SANT'ÁNGELO MUXARO**, another 15km along. This small agricultural centre in the middle of the steeply sloping Plátani River valley boasts a number of local *tholos* (tombs) hollowed out of the rock in dome-shaped caves. The earliest date from the eleventh century BC, but most are from around the eighth to the fifth century BC, and in design recall Minoan and Mycenaean examples. You'll spot them as you approach the bare hillside on which the village stands: the road leads up past a ramshackle brick wall, beyond which a path heads along the sheer rock to the "beehive" caves. At the bottom, the largest is known locally as the **tomba del Príncipe**: later converted into a Byzantine chapel, it's half-hidden by overhanging trees and

---

CORLEONE AND THE MAFIA

Mario Puzo chose the name Corleone for his central character in *The Godfather* with good reason: for over fifty years it's been the stamping ground of some of the most feared – and respected – Mafia leaders. Many of the so-called *capo di tutti capi* (literally "boss of all the bosses"), who have held sway over an international network of crime and corruption, came originally from the town, including **Luciano Liggio** (imprisoned in 1974) and his effective successor **Salvatore Riina**, who was captured by the Carabinieri in early 1993. Recognized by most Mafia families, and by the authorities, as the present *capo di tutti capi*, Riina's arrest came as a complete surprise – informed on by his driver, a native of San Giuseppe Iato, to the northwest of Corleone, Riina was picked up as he was being driven through Palermo. He was the most-wanted man in Italy, allegedly responsible for ordering at least 150 murders, 40 of which he's said to have committed himself; the authorities also hold him responsible for the murders of anti-Mafia investigators Giovanni Falcone and Paolo Borsellino, both killed in Palermo in 1992.

Once he was under arrest, the political fallout began, since it became clear that for over twenty years Riina had lived with his family openly in Corleone, registering his children at local schools and hospitals, and coming and going pretty much as he pleased. This, it's said with some justification, could only have been the case if Riina had enjoyed some variety of high-level protection; and, if so, who had been responsible for shielding one of the Mafia's most notorious leaders? The arguments that this arrest in particular have provoked will doubtless continue to rumble on. Meanwhile, at the time of writing, Riina is firmly ensconced in prison and declining to say anything; his wife and family have disappeared behind closed doors in Corleone; and his driver – also under arrest – doubtless fears the revenge of Riina's associates. More members of the Corleonese clan have been put away since Riina's arrest, which may yet end the hegemony of this sleepy inland town, though one Bernardo Provenzano – known as "the Tractor" on account of his brutal methods – remains at loose, and may be behind a regrouping of the Cosa Nostra after its recent setbacks.

you may have to backtrack to get inside. Like all the others, it's empty now, the finds scattered in various museums around Europe.

You can get to Sant'Ángelo by **bus** from Agrigento with the Lattuca line, leaving from outside Agrigento's Astor cinema on Piazza Vittorio Emanuele (daily at 9am & 2pm); the last bus back leaves at 4pm. The route takes you through depressed villages, in a landscape given over to grain cultivation and the almonds for which the region is famous.

Corleone

The best countryside begins past Alessandria della Rocca, the road climbing up to 1000m at Prizzi, from where there are occasional bus services down to **CORLEONE,** a fairly large town for these parts, squeezed between a couple of rocks with a craggy column at its centre. The only tourists who pass this way come on the scent of the Mafia. Especially in the immediate postwar years, statistics showed the town to have one of the highest murder rates in the world, with 153 violent deaths (out of a population of 18,000) in the four years between 1944 and 1948. One of the men who met a violent end in this period was the trade union leader **Plácido Rizzoto**, who took advantage of the Mafia's internal preoccupations to do the unthinkable and manoeuvre into power a left-wing town council. Two years after his disappearance in 1948, the fire brigade hauled out his dismembered corpse from a ninety-foot crevice near Corleone, along with sackfuls of other bodies of Mafia victims. His killers were eventually acquitted for lack of evidence, the most common end to murder charges brought against mafiosi.

The town's notoriety has been fuelled since it lent Mario Puzo's fictional Godfather, Don Corleone, his adopted family name (though it is also the real-life name of Sicily's most notorious Mafia clan). Fact and fiction finally merged completely in January 1993 when Corleonese clan leader, **Salvatore Riina** (see box) – the alleged supreme Sicilian Mafia boss – was arrested on the outskirts of Palermo, having apparently lived in Corleone with his family for over twenty years. When all's said and done, though, there's little to see here, just some rather old-fashioned bars clustered around a small town centre. However, the town does have one of the area's few **hotels**, the modern and clean *Belvedere* (☎091.846.4964; ③), on the southern approach road to the town, with views over Corleone from some rooms. Further up the hill, there's a **trattoria** under the same management, *A'Giarra*, a popular place for pizzas and local dishes, with outdoor tables.

Ficuzza

From Corleone, regular buses run through the hills to Palermo, 60km away. If you're driving, though, you could make a stop at **FICUZZA**, around 25km north, backed by the wooded heights of Rocca Busambra (1613m), which is crisscrossed by a network of mountain paths. The tiny hamlet was once a hunting centre and it's still dominated by Ferdinand III's hunting lodge, the stately **Palazzina Reale** (daily 10am–7pm; free). There's not a great deal of interest inside – Mussolini's troops burnt most of the palace – though the Sala da Pranzo survives, decorated with hunting scenes, as does the queen's bidet. You could have **lunch** in one of the trattorias in the piazza, before heading on to the hills around Piana degli Albanesi, 25km from Palermo (p.106).

THE SOUTHERN INTERIOR

The **southern interior** has a tamer feel than any of the other inland areas. Journeys here are easy on the eye, through intensely cultivated slopes to a succession of small country towns, which hold most of the region's population. Sights are confined to the lively main towns of **Piazza Armerina** and **Caltagirone** and their surroundings – aside from Enna, the only two places in the whole interior that you might pick as specific destinations. Close to the first is easily the region's biggest draw, the lavish Roman mosaics at the **Villa Imperiale**, which features high on any list of Sicily's top attractions. Caltagirone, on the other hand, is one of the unsung towns of the region, plastered with assertive Baroque buildings and emblazoned with the ceramics for which it is renowned. Other brief diversions might take in the extensive Greek ruins of **Morgantina** and the planned eighteenth-century settlement of **Grammichele**.

The southern interior is also well served by **public transport**. Regular buses run to Piazza Armerina from Enna and Caltanissetta, and Caltagirone and Grammichele are accessible by train and bus from Gela or Catania.

Piazza Armerina

Less than an hour from Enna, **PIAZZA ARMERINA** lies amid thickly forested hills: a quiet, unassuming place, mainly seventeenth- and eighteenth-century in appearance, with a skyline pierced by towers and houses huddled together under the joint protection of castle and cathedral. It's a thoroughly pleasant place to idle around, though few who come to Piazza Armerina bother to do so, given the enticement of the Imperial **Roman villa**, which stands in rugged countryside at Casale, 5km southwest of town. Hidden under mud for seven hundred years, excavations in 1950 revealed a rich villa, probably a hunting lodge and summer home, decorated with multicoloured mosaic floors that are unique throughout the Roman world in their quality and extent.

The Town

Given that seeing the villa and the mosaics might well entail spending the night in Piazza Armerina, you're going to have at least some time to spare for the town, one of the prettiest in the interior and small enough to cover in a morning's stroll. A score of dilapidated, but graceful, churches and *palazzi* line the narrow streets and squares of the hill-top old-town area, which centres around sloping **Piazza Garibaldi**. From here, Via Cavour winds up to **Piazza del Duomo** and the elegant seventeenth-century **Duomo** itself, with its cool blue and white interior, built at the town's highest point. The earlier (fifteenth-century) campanile sports blind Catalan-Gothic windows, a nice contrast to the Baroque antics of the rest of the church. What really sets off this handsome, view-laden square is the simple facade of the eighteenth-century **Palazzo Trigona** adjacent, its spruced exterior crowned by a spread-eagle plaque.

Narrow alleys lead down from the terrace of Piazza del Duomo into the older parts of town: an endearing jumble of cobbled flights of steps and faded grandeur, oddly adapted to the modern age. Just behind the cathedral, on a spur off Via Cavour, the seventeenth-century church and former convent of **San Francesco**

is now in use as a hospital; at the bottom of a steep street nearby, Via Castellina, the surviving medieval town wall has had a rough arch hacked through it for traffic access; and there's someone living in the adjacent watchtower. The other way, down Via Floresta (to the side of Palazzo Trigona), leads to the closed and tumbledown **castello**, built at the end of the fourteenth century and surrounded by once-rich *palazzi* in a similar state of decay. Best route, though, is down the steep **Via Monte**, once the medieval town's main street.

The town is compact enough for you to get out fairly easily into the fields and slopes beyond. It's only a kilometre's walk to the twelfth-century Norman church of **Sant'Andrea**, north of town and still impressive despite its simple proportions. Another kilometre or so down the same road, through orchards and gardens, is the sixteenth-century church and convent of **Santa Maria di Gesù**, a low building, gently set amid green hills.

Practicalities

Most **buses** will drop you off in Piazza Sen. Marescalchi in the lower, modern town on the main road (Viale Generale Muscara). The old town is further up the hill, centred around Piazza Garibaldi, off which is the **tourist office**, Via Cavour 15 (summer Mon & Sat 8am–2pm, Tues–Fri 8am–2pm & 4.30–7.30pm; winter daily 8am–2pm; ☎0935.680.201), which can provide a map, bus timetables and endless brochures and information about the mosaics.

For **bus information and tickets** to Aidone, Caltagirone and Dittaino (the nearest train station to Piazza Armerina, 35km north), ask in the *Bar della Stazione* in Piazza Sen. Marescalchi, or the AST office next door. There's a **taxi** rank in Piazza Generale Cascino, while **banks** are found either along Via Generale Ciancio, which runs between piazzas Generale Cascino and Marescalchi, or in Piazza Garibaldi in the old town.

Accommodation

There are only three **hotels** in Piazza Armerina itself, and of those one is currently closed for restoration and another is way out of the centre and decidedly pricey. This is one place where it pays to plan ahead.

Until the *Selene*, Viale Generale Gaeta 30 (☎0935.682.254; ①), in the lower town, reopens, the only central choice is the rather unattractive and noisily sited *Villa Romana*, Via A. de Gasperi 18 (☎ & fax 0935.682.911; ②), which only has a few rooms without bath at the lower price; it's on the southern edge of town, at the signposted route to the mosaics. Piazza's top hotel is the *Hotel Park Paradiso* (☎0935.680.841, fax 0935.683.391; ④), 1km beyond the church of Sant'Andrea and thus only really of use if you're driving; it's signposted from just about everywhere in town (and province come to that).

All of which suggests that you **phone ahead** to secure a room at the *Mosaici da Battiato*, in Contrada Paratore (☎0935.685.453; no credit cards; ②), 4km out of town, at the turnoff to the mosaics, which are just 1km from the hotel. A friendly place, it has over twenty smart rooms with bath, an outdoor terrace, and a grill-restaurant where you can eat very well for under L26,000; try the *pasta alle sarde* and anything from the grill. Taxis here won't be prohibitively expensive, while the bus to the mosaics passes right by. Immediately across the roundabout from here, a little way down the road to the Villa Imperiale, *La Ruota* (☎0935.680.542; March–Oct) has space for **camping**, though it's not an official campsite.

Eating and drinking

In town, *La Tavernetta*, Via Cavour 14 (closed Sun), isn't bad value for money, or alternatively there's a tourist menu at *Da Pepito*, Via Roma 140 (closed Tues & Dec), opposite the park – this has some specifically Sicilian dishes, too, that are well worth trying. The trattoria *Al Goloso* (closed Wed), on Via Garao near Piazza Garibaldi, is also good value. Between Piazza Europa and the duomo, Via Mazzini holds the *Centrale da Totò* (no credit cards; closed Mon), with fine staple dishes and decent prices. In the lower town, the *Italia*, at Piazza Generale Cascino 25 (no credit cards; closed Thurs), is fairly soft on the wallet and offers standard fare.

Out **at the Villa Imperiale**, best place to eat is at the *Mosaici* hotel, though as tour groups are liable to descend for lunch avoid these times if you want peace and quiet. *La Ruota*, across the way, also has a decent, moderately priced restaurant (closed evenings in winter) in addition to its ceramic shop.

Casale: the Villa Imperiale

Built on terraces in the rolling countryside that surrounds Piazza Armerina, the **Villa Imperiale** (daily 9am–1.30pm & 3–7.30pm; L4000; ☎0935.680.036) at the otherwise virtually uninhabited hamlet of **Casale**, is a confusing swatch of rooms and corridors, built and decorated with pictorial mosaics on a sumptuous scale. There are conflicting theories about its function, though the most convincing explanation of its siting in the middle of deserted slopes and woods is that the villa was an occasional retreat and hunting lodge; a theory supported by the many mosaics of animals and birds, including two specific hunting scenes. Dating from the early fourth century AD (though built over an earlier structure), it was used right up until the twelfth century when a mudslide largely covered it until comprehensive excavations began in the 1950s. It's been covered again, more recently, to protect the mosaics, a new roof and walls added to indicate the original size and shape, while walkways lead visitors through the rooms. If you're here in summer, try coming early or late in the day in order to avoid the heat and crowds, as it's rather like being in a greenhouse.

Getting there

From Piazza Armerina, a **bus** (Line B) leaves Piazza Sen. Marescalchi for the Villa Imperiale at 9am, 10am, 11am, 4pm, 5pm and 6pm; the return service is on the half-hour, starting at 9.30am. Otherwise you'll have to **walk**: head down Via Matteotti or Via Principato and follow the signs – it takes around an hour on foot and is an attractive walk. If you're pushed for time, or there's a group of you, you might consider taking a **taxi**, from Piazza Generale Cascino in Piazza Armerina, which costs around L30,000 to take you to the site, wait for an hour and bring you back. Drivers might want to park just out of sight of the official entrance to avoid the L2000 parking fee. As for food, you can either take your own or there's a bar-restaurant at the site.

Coming **from Caltanissetta**, currently the 8.10am (Sun 10.10am) bus gets to Piazza Armerina at 9.35am, returning at 3.35pm. **From Enna**, there's a bus at 8.15am (arriving 8.50am), or 11am (arriving at 11.55am); the return bus leaves from Piazza Armerina at 4pm or 5.15pm. Bear in mind that you'll still have to get from Piazza Armerina itself to the site.

The Villa Imperiale

It's immediately clear from the extent of the uncovered remains that the villa belonged to an important owner, possibly Maximianus Herculeus, co-Emperor with Diocletian between 286 and 305 AD. There's considerable evidence to support this view, not least what's left of the villa's palatial structure. It's made up of four separate groups of buildings, built on different levels of the hillside and connected by passageways, doors and courtyards. Nearly all of what you see would have been occupied by the family it was built for, and, though the modern structural additions give an effective idea of what the villa actually looked like when in use, the remains are by no means complete: the slaves' housing, presumably fairly extensive, and other outbuildings, are still to be excavated properly. Yet it's not the building that's the main attraction – although there are few enough surviving examples of such splendid Imperial Roman wealth – so much as the unrivalled interior decoration. The floors of almost the entire building are covered with bright **mosaics** of excellent quality, stylistically belonging to an early fourth-century Roman-African school, which explains many of the more exotic scenes and animals portrayed. Their design also contains several hints as to their period and patron, though given their extent they're likely to have taken fifty or sixty years to complete.

What's left of the villa's **main entrance** gives one of the best impressions of its former grandeur, the approach leading through the remains of a columned arch into a wide courtyard. Today's site entrance, though, is through the adjacent **thermae** (or baths): a typical arrangement of dressing/massage rooms and

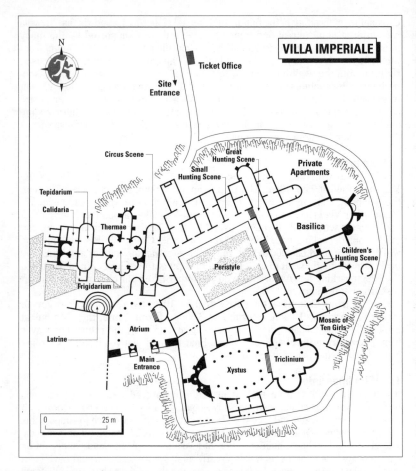

plunge-baths around an octagonal **frigidarium**, its central mosaic a marine scene of sea nymphs, tritons and little cherubs rowing boats and spearing fish. A walk-way leads out of the baths and into the villa proper, to the massive central court-yard or **peristyle**. This is where guests would have been received and the vestibule displays a badly fragmented mosaic depicting a formal welcome by an attendant holding an olive branch. The corridor around the four sides of the courtyard is covered with a series of animal-head medallions, snarling tigers, yapping dogs and unicorns. Just off here, a balcony looks down upon one of the villa's most vivid pictures, a boisterous circus scene showing a chariot race. Starting in the top right-hand corner, the variously coloured chariots rush off, overtaking and crashing at the turns, until finally there's victory for the green faction. The next room's mosaic shows a family attended by slaves on their way to the baths. Period detail – footwear, hairstyles and clothes – helped archeologists to date the rest of the mosaics.

Small rooms beyond, on either side of the peristyle, reveal only fragmentary geometric patterns, although one displays a **small hunting scene**, an episodic adventure ending in a peaceful picnic in the centre. Another room contains what is probably the villa's most famous image, a two-tiered scene of **ten girls**, realistically muscular figures in Roman "bikinis", taking part in various gymnastic and athletic activities. One of the girls sporting a laurel wreath and a palm frond is clearly the winner of the competition.

The peristyle is separated from the private apartments and public halls beyond by a long, covered corridor, which contains the best of the villa's mosaic works. The **great hunting scene** sets armed and shield-bearing hunters against a panoply of wild animals, on sea and land. Along the entire sixty-metre length of the mosaic, tigers, ostriches, elephants and even a rhino, destined for the games back in Rome, are pictured being trapped, bundled up and down gangplanks and into cages. The caped figure overseeing the operation is probably Maximianus himself. Much of the scene is set in Africa, Maximianus's main responsibility in the Imperial Tetrarchy, while an ivy-leaf symbol on the costume of the attendant to his right is that of his personal legion, the Herculiani.

Family apartments and public halls beyond are nearly all on a grand scale. A large courtyard, the **xystus**, gives onto the **triclinium**, a dining room with three apses, whose mosaics feature the labours of Hercules. One bloody scene portrays his fight against the giants, who writhe and wail with contorted faces, all stuck by arrows. A path leads around the back to the **private apartments**, based around a large basilica, with mosaics echoing the spectacular scenes of the main building: a **children's circus**, where the small chariots are drawn by colourful birds, and a **children's hunt**, the tiny tots being chased and pecked by the hares and peacocks they're supposed to snare.

Aidone and the site of Morgantina

Fifteen kilometres northeast of Piazza Armerina, there's more classical interest in the extensive remains of the Greek city of **Morgantina**, at its height in the fourth century BC. The site's hard to reach without your own transport (and little visited in any case), though there are several **buses** daily from Piazza Armerina (from Piazza Sen. Marescalchi) to **Aidone**, a fifteen-minute ride. The site is a long, hot walk away, another 5km beyond the village, along the minor SS288. If you're driving, turn off the SS117 for Aidone at the crossroads known as Madonna della Noce, where there's a large **restaurant-pizzeria**; it's then a gorgeous seven-kilometre ride through the trees to the village.

Aidone
AIDONE itself is a charming little spot, its quiet central square and most of its inhabitants laid-back to the point of being comatose. There are a couple of nice bars, a crumbly church and – signposted in the upper part of the village – a **Museo Archeológico** (daily 9am–1.30pm & 3–7.30pm; L4000), an indispensable preliminary to seeing the site itself. Housed in an ex-Capuchin monastery, the museum gathers together all the removable bits and pieces from the ancient city: ceramics, statuettes and third-century BC busts, as well as some domestic artefacts, all imaginatively displayed, while aerial photos and plans of the excavations provide a useful idea of Morgantina's layout.

Morgantina

The **site of Morgantina** (daily 9am–1.30pm & 3pm–1hr before sunset; L4000; ☎0935.87.955) occupies two dusty hillsides. The only life here is the tapping of the archeologists, the buzzing flies and the occasional jangle of a herd of goats. There's a car park close to the west hill (the first you reach), though it's best to continue down the rough track to a second car park near the main entrance under the east hill, opposite which is a **bar-restaurant**, which can dish up a decent plate of spaghetti, grilled meats and local wine at the drop of a hat.

After its demise, the city became buried and forgotten for almost two thousand years, and even after the site's discovery it wasn't identified as Morgantina until 1957. To date, only a fifth of the city has been excavated, but the finds have shed much light on the island's pre-Hellenic Sikel population, who inhabited central Sicily from the ninth century BC. In the sixth century BC Chalcidian Greeks settled here and lived in harmony alongside the Sikels until the city became the centre of a revolt led by the Sikel leader Ducetius, who destroyed it in the late fifth century BC. Swiftly rebuilt on a grid-plan with walled and towered defences, Morgantina reached its apogee in the fourth and third centuries BC under the protection of Syracuse, and many of the surviving buildings date from this period. A couple of hundred years later the city was in decline and soon after was abandoned altogether: "Once Morgantina was a city; now it no longer exists," the historian Strabo wistfully recorded at the end of the first century BC.

From the main entrance a path (straight ahead) leads directly onto Morgantina's most distinctive ruin, the **agora**, bounded by the three stepped sides of an uncompleted polygon, the steps used as seats for public meetings. The small **teatro** to its right was built in the third century BC but reconstructed in Roman times. There are **performances** of Greek plays here in August; check with the site office (☎0935.86.777) or the tourist office in Enna (see p.280) for details. You can find an (almost indecipherable) inscription to Dionysus on the upright of a seat in the fifth row from the top, along the third wedge of seats from the right as you face them. Immediately in front is a Roman building, behind which (next to the *agora*) is a fourth-century BC **santuario** of Demeter and Kore. Many votive objects, including lanterns and cups, were found here, most buried in two *bothroi* (sacred trenches), having been produced in a small furnace, since excavated at the bottom end of the sanctuary area. On the level ground behind the *agora* is a granary and square slaughterhouse, beyond which stretches the long **east stoa**. The stumps of its columns run all the way down its 100-metre length. Further up the hillside stand the ruins of some Hellenic **houses**, with two mosaic-laid floors. One of which, the so-called "House of Ganymede", has a damaged illustration of the youth Ganymede being carried away to Olympus by Zeus's eagle to become the cupbearer of the gods. Excavations on the **west hill**, a twenty-minute walk across the site, are less revealing, but you'll come across the fairly substantial remains of houses, some with mosaics, roads and walls, in what was once a residential area of the ancient city.

South to Caltagirone

Around 16km south of Piazza Armerina, the minor SS124 breaks east off the Gela road and heads for Caltagirone, passing through fine farming country, at its best around the village of **SAN MICHELE DI GANZERIA**. There's no particular reason to break your journey here, though you might be tempted by *Pomara*, at Via

Vittorio Veneto 84 (☎0933.976.976, fax 0933.977.090; ③), a surprisingly fine hotel for the sticks, and the village's couple of pizzerias. The bus from Piazza Armerina also comes this way, though diverting first to the even tinier **Mirabella Imbaccari**, just to the north. All told, it's just under an hour from Piazza Armerina to the heights of Caltagirone.

Caltagirone

There were settlers in **CALTAGIRONE** well before the Greeks, making it one of the most ancient of Sicilian towns, but the present name derives from the Arabic (*kalat*, "castle" and *gerun*, "caves"). Nothing from these periods survives, and the dominant impression of the town is Baroque. Its central swath of monumental buildings date from the rebuilding after the 1693 earthquake that flattened the area. Well before that, though, Caltagirone had acquired a reputation for the excellence of its **ceramics**, an industry given an added dimension with the arrival of the Arabs, who introduced local craftsmen to the glazed polychromatic colours – in particular, blues and yellows – which have subsequently become typically Sicilian in execution. Up until the great earthquake, the town supported a population of around 20,000, of whom perhaps fully five percent were actively engaged in the tiled decoration of churches and public buildings. The Baroque rebuilding saw a further burst of creative construction; later, in the nineteenth century, came the principal period of ceramic figurative work (excellent examples are on display in the town museum); while today, Caltagirone's traditional industry is flourishing again, with over seventy ceramicists displaying work at galleries across the town.

The Town

The old **upper town** has great public edifices, decorative churches and public gardens spread across three hills, the effect lightened by tiled decoration found in nooks and crannies everywhere; with the recent renovations, a good selection of shops and general activity, there is an upbeat feel to a town that once seemed on the way down.

Most effective decorations are the ceramic flowers and emblems flanking both sides of the **Ponte San Francesco** on the way into the centre from the train station. The grandest statement, though, is undoubtedly made by the 142 steps of **La Scala**, which cut right up one of Caltagirone's hills to the sorely neglected church of Santa Maria del Monte at the top. The risers in between each step are covered with a hand-painted ceramic pattern, no two the same. It's a tough climb, but the views from the top are magnificent, across town to the distinctive spire of the Sicilian Baroque church of San Francesco all'Immacolata, with the plain stretching away into the distance beyond. The staircase was originally conceived at the turn of the seventeenth century as a road between the Santa Maria del Monte church, then the town cathedral, and the Senatorial Palace below; the steps were added once it was clear that the incline was too steep, but the majolica tile risers are a much more recent addition, in place only since 1954. On July 24 and 25 every year, the steps are lit by thousands of coloured paper lamps as part of the celebrations for the feast of St James (San Giácomo).

On either side of the staircase, all the way up, are some of the **workshops** and galleries of today's ceramicists, all worth venturing inside even if you're not planning to buy anything. If you're interested in tracing the development of the industry, there's a **Museo della Cerámica** (Tues–Sun 8am–6pm; L8000) stuffed full of

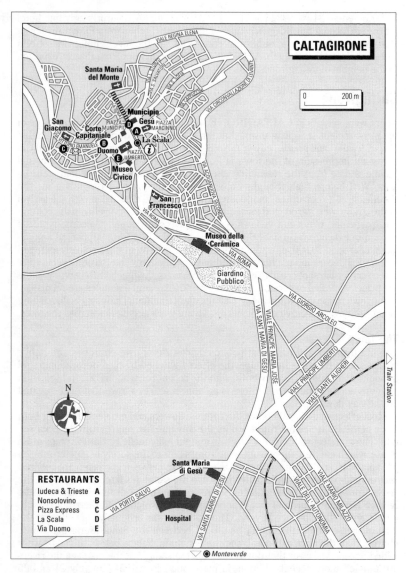

CALTAGIRONE

Santa Maria del Monte

Municipio

San Giacomo

Corte Capitaniale

Duomo

La Scala

Museo Civico

San Francesco

Museo della Cerámica

Giardino Pubblico

VIA REGINA ELENA
VIA CIRCONVALLAZIONE DI LEVANTE
PIAZZA MUNICIPIO
PIAZZA MARCINNO
PIAZZA UMBERTO
VIA VITTORIO EMANUELE
VIA ROMA
VIA AQUILA NUOVA SECONDA
VIA GIORGIO ARCOLEO
VIA PRINCIPE UMBERTO
VIALE PRINCIPE MARIA JOSÉ
VIA SANT MARIA DI GESÙ
VIALE DANTE ALIGHERI
VIALE PRINCIPE UMBERTO
▷ Train Station

N

Santa Maria di Gesù

Hospital

VIA PORTO SALVO
VIA SANTA MARIA DI GESÙ
VIALE MARIO MILAZZO
VIALE DELL'AUTONOMIA

RESTAURANTS

Iudeca & Trieste	A
Nonsolovino	B
Pizza Express	C
La Scala	D
Via Duomo	E

0   200 m

▽ ◉ Monteverde

ceramicware, in the large public garden off Via Roma; while the **Mostra Mercato Permanente** on Via Vittorio Emanuele, just to the right at the bottom of *La Scala*, is the best place to see modern ceramics made by local artists.

The upper town also holds several more striking buildings. Beyond Piazza Umberto and the restyled **Duomo** is the length of the seventeenth-century **Corte Capitaniale**, a sturdy, low building decorated by the Gagini family and used today for temporary exhibitions. Back below Piazza Umberto, the solid square-built block with grilled windows and spike-studded metal doors was once an eighteenth-century Bourbon prison and now houses the **Museo Cívico** (Tues & Sat 9.30am–1.30pm, Wed & Fri 4–7pm, Sun 9.30am–12.30pm; free). This has a small but rather good display of modern ceramics, while the rest of the collection is the usual, diverting, load of local curios and junk – architectural fragments, barrowloads of paintings by the Vaccaro family who renovated the cathedral in the nineteenth century, and a gilded, sixteenth-century processional cart.

Practicalities

Buses nearly all stop first in Piazza Municipio in the upper town, where you should get off if you're only looking around for the day. If you're planning on staying, stay on until the new town, a couple of kilometres below, which is home to the **train station** and Caltagirone's only accommodation. When **leaving town**, Pitrelli buses to Ragusa depart from Viale Príncipe Umberto 215, and AST services leave from outside the Metropol cinema further up the road – though again they should all call at Piazza Municipio in the upper town on the way. There's a helpful **tourist office** (daily 9am–1pm & 3.30–7.30pm; ☎0933.53.809) in the upper town, down an alley (Via Volta Libertini) just off Piazza Umberto, which has a brochure and map in English about Caltagirone.

Accommodation in the centre is rather limited, but *La Scala 2* (☎0933.51.552, fax 0933.57.781; ①) has **rooms** to rent right in the main square at Piazza Umberto I 1; book in advance in summer. The hotel *Monteverde* (☎0933.53.682, fax 0933.53.533; ②), just south of the town at Via delle Industrie 11, is comfortable with a good restaurant as well, and if you're driving it's a better bet than the expensive and ugly *Villa San Mauro*, at Via Porto Salvo 18 (☎0933.26.500; ④).

Among **places to eat** in the upper town, *La Scala* (closed Wed), at the bottom of the eponymous staircase, must be unique for the mountain stream running through; it's not cheap, but it's a good place to splash out, and the coffee here is excellent. The *Nonsolovino*, on Via Vittorio Emanuele at Piazza Municipio (closed Mon), offers an average tourist menu at L25,000. *Iudeca & Trieste* on Discesa Collegio, in front of the Gesù church, is a good *távola calda*, with a raised outdoor terrace; there's another *távola calda*/bar – with quieter outdoor seating – at Via Duomo 2, opposite the cathedral. *Pizza Express* (no credit cards) at Via Vittorio Emanuele 121 serves, amongst others, fresh-fish pizza every Friday. There's a daily food **market** in the mornings on Piazza Marcinnò, behind and below the Gesù church.

Around Caltagirone: Grammichele and Monte San Mauro

Just ten minutes **east** of Caltagirone by train, **GRAMMICHELE** is worth an expedition, if you're architecturally minded, to view one of the most ambitious of the new towns built after the 1693 earthquake. The best place to appreciate Grammichele's hexagonal design would be from the air – failing that, position yourself at the dead centre of the town's imposing central piazza to see the six radial streets reaching out, each bisected by secondary piazzas. The shape's no longer entirely perfect, due to a surfeit of new streets around the station at the southern edges of town, but it makes for an intriguing couple of hours' stroll, with more chances than you might think for getting lost, since all the streets in each segment correspond exactly to their neighbours in dimension and appearance. Despite the grand design, Grammichele still manages to appear a mite tatty. It's a predominantly rural-looking town and the impressions are all pastoral ones – be prepared to meet a donkey in the road, or see chickens cooped up in a basement, and farms near the train station. The best **place to eat** is *La Tavernetta*, a barn-like trattoria at Via Garibaldi 100: walk straight up from the train station, along Corso Vittorio Emanuele, over the piazza, and it's down the first street on the right. There are numerous bars surrounding the square.

If you're driving or travelling by train **south** of Caltagirone, you might ask someone to point out the hill of **Monte San Mauro**, halfway to Niscemi, which was the scene of the one battle that could be called a separatist uprising in Sicily. At the end of 1945, Concetto Gallo, lawyer, landowner and commander-in-chief of the Separatist army (EVIS), much reduced by desertion, led 58 men in a last stand against a force of five thousand Italian troops commanded by three generals. Gallo's inevitable defeat signalled the effective end of the Separatist movement in Sicily.

festivals

March/April
Easter Holy Week celebrations in **Enna**; including processions, special Masses and the parade of saintly relics. Running all week from Palm Sunday to Easter Sunday, the best day is Good Friday, when thousands march in silent procession dressed in the white-hooded costumes of the medieval fraternities. More costumed processions can be seen at **Caltagirone**, **Troina** and at **Caltanissetta** (best days Maundy Thursday and Good Friday), with processional carts (the *misteri*) and monks. **Prizzi**, in the western interior, is a good place to be on Easter Sunday, when giant statues of Christ and the Virgin Mary are taunted by masked figures representing Death and the Devil, to whom onlookers are forced to give money. The **motor racing** season starts at the Autodromo di Pergusa, around the **Lago di Pergusa**, running until September.

May
Sagra del Lago Throughout the month at **Lago di Pergusa**, with folk events and fireworks, singing competitions and games.

Penultimate Sunday Festa dei Rami at **Troina,** in which laurel branches are carried to the tomb of St Silvester.

July
Estate Ennese Beginning of a series of concerts and opera in the open-air theatre at the castle in **Enna**. Runs until end of August.

24–25 Festival of San Giácomo in **Caltagirone**, when the La Scala steps are illuminated.

August
13–14 Il Palio dei Normanni in **Piazza Armerina**, a medieval pageant commemorating Count Roger's taking of the town in the eleventh century. Processional entry into town on the thirteenth, ceremonial joust on the fourteenth, along with costumed parades and other festive events.

September
Festival of Madonna dell'Alto in **Petralia Sottana**, with a nocturnal procession on horseback and a maypole dance known as the Ballo della Cordella.

December
Annual exhibition of terracotta sculpted cribs in **Caltagirone**.

travel details

Trains
Caltagirone to: Catania (9 daily; 1hr 50min); Gela (10 daily; 40min); Grammichele (10 daily; 15min). **Caltanissetta** to: Agrigento (9–10 daily; 1hr 20min); Canicattì (10 daily; 30min); Gela (9 daily; 2hr); Licata (9 daily; 1hr 20min).

Enna to: Caltanissetta (11 daily; 1hr); Catania (9 daily; 1hr 20min); Palermo (6 daily; 2hr 20min).

Buses

Agira to: Troina (Mon–Sat 5 daily, 1 Sun; 55min).

Caltagirone to: Catania (6 daily Mon–Sat; 1hr 10min); Gela (5 daily Mon–Sat; 1hr 25min); Piazza Armerina (3 daily Mon–Sat, 1 Sun; 45min); Ragusa (4 daily Mon–Sat; 1hr 30min).

Caltanissetta to: Agrigento (10 daily Mon–Sat, 7 Sun; 1hr 15min); Caltagirone (1–2 daily; 2hr 10min); Canicattì (9 daily Mon–Sat, 7 Sun; 35min); Catania (9–10 daily; 1hr 35min); Enna (4 daily Mon–Sat; 40min); Piazza Armerina (1 daily; 1hr 20min).

Cesarò to: Giardini-Naxos (2 daily Mon–Sat; 2hr 30min); Messina (2 daily Mon–Sat; 3hr 30min); Nicosia (1 daily; 1hr 30min); Randazzo (3 daily Mon–Sat; 1hr 10min); Sant'Agata (1 daily; 1hr 30min).

Enna to: Agira (2–3 daily; 1hr 5min); Calascibetta (11 daily Mon–Sat; 20min); Caltanissetta (4 daily Mon–Sat; 40min); Catania (8 daily Mon–Sat, 4 Sun; 1hr 20min–2hr); Gela (4 daily Mon–Sat, 3 Sun; 1hr 40min); Leonforte (11 daily; 40min); Palermo (hourly; 1hr 50min); Pergusa (12 daily Mon–Sat, 3 Sun; 30min); Piazza Armerina (7 daily Mon–Sat, 5 Sun; 40min); Regalbuto (2–3 daily; 1hr 30min).

Leonforte to: Catania (9 daily; 1hr 50min); Enna (11 daily; 40min); Nicosia (2–5 daily; 45min).

Nicosia to: Agira (2–5 daily; 1hr 10min); Catania (2–5 daily; 2hr 35min); Gangi (2–6 daily; 45min); Leonforte (2–5 daily; 45min); Mistretta (2 daily Mon–Sat; 55min, continuing on to Santo Stéfano di Camastra); Palermo (2–4 daily; 3hr 15min); Petralia Soprana (2–5 daily; 1hr 20min); Petralia Sottana (2–5 daily; 1hr 30min); Polizzi Generosa (3–5 daily; 2hr); Sperlinga (2–6 daily; 15min).

Piazza Armerina to: Aidone (7 daily Mon–Sat, 3 Sun; 15min); Caltagirone (3 daily Mon–Sat, 1 Sun; 1hr); Enna (6 daily Mon–Sat, 5 Sun; 40min); Gela (3 daily; 1hr); Palermo (3–4 daily; 3hr).

Polizzi Generosa to: Caltavuturo (2 daily Mon–Sat; 35min); Cefalù (1 daily Mon–Sat; 1hr); Palermo (3–5 daily; 1hr 15min); Términi Imerese (3 daily Mon–Sat; 1hr 30min).

Troina to: Agira (5 daily Mon–Sat, 1 Sun; 55min).

CHAPTER EIGHT

THE SOUTH COAST

The long south coast, from Gela to Sciacca, should be one of the most attractive parts of Sicily. Sparsely developed, there are good beaches and some low-key Mediterranean ports and resorts which are barely known to Italians, let alone other tourists. Nevertheless, sporadic but spectacularly ugly industrial development along the coast conspires to put off many people. The sea is heavily polluted in some areas, particularly around Gela, a large port and petrochemical town. But to give this coast a miss would be to ignore some of the most important sights on the island. Gela itself retains its extensive Greek fortifications, while further west the hill-top town of **Agrigento** overlooks a series of splendid ancient temples, unrivalled in extent and preservation outside Greece.

Northwest of Agrigento, isolated sandy **beaches** pan out, and with a car you can reach some of the better stretches at the end of several minor roads and tracks that branch off from the SS115. One of the best lies just below another Hellenic site, **Eraclea Minoa**. **Sciacca** is more accessible, a fishing port and summer resort, and from here you can make a couple of diversions into the tall and craggy mountains that back this part of the coast. Or you might consider heading out to the **Pelágie Islands**: barren spots in the Mediterranean, closer to Africa than Europe, but connected by regular ferry with **Porto Empédocle**, near Agrigento.

Regular **train** and **bus** services link the coastal towns and villages, while there are less frequent services to the inland towns; these are detailed in the text. **Hotel** accommodation is limited outside the major towns, but there are plenty of opportunities to **camp**, either in sites or freelance among the dunes.

Gela

GELA couldn't present a worse aspect as the train edges into town, through a mess of futuristic steel bubbles and pipes – the city is known locally as "Beirut". There are fine dune-backed beaches in the vicinity, but there must be serious doubts about the cleanliness of the water and there's often a chemical tang to the air. It was not always so. Gela was one of the most important of Sicily's Greek cities, founded in 688 BC, and under Hippocrates in the fifth century BC it rivalled even ancient Syracuse as the island's political hub. Its artistic eminence attracted literary stars, most notably the dramatist Aeschylus, who left his mark on the city (literally) when felled by a tortoise dropped by an eagle, which – the tale relates – mistook his bald head for a stone on which to dash its prey. However, Gela's heyday was short-lived. Hippocrates' successor, Gelon, transferred his power and half the city's population east to Syracuse in 485 BC, the deep-water harbour there being more to the tyrant's liking. Gela was subsequently smashed by the Carthaginians and the Mamertines, its walls razed in the third century BC and abandoned to the encroaching sands. Modern Gela was the first Sicilian town to be liberated by the Allies in 1943, but otherwise – beyond an excellent archeological museum and a fine set of Greek defensive walls – is almost entirely without interest.

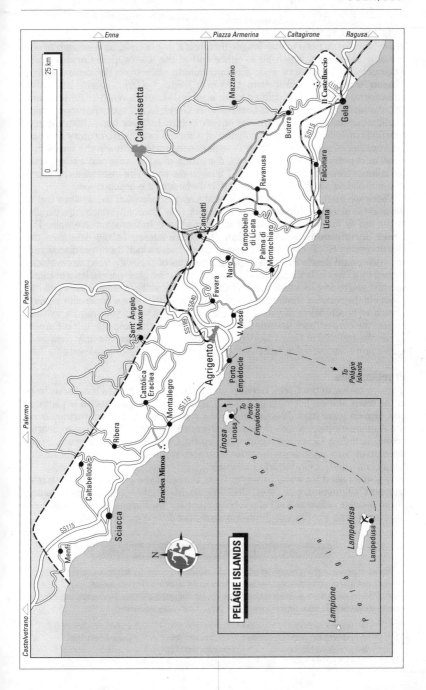

Gela's Greek remains

There's really no need to stay longer than half a day in Gela, time enough to see the only two sights, which lie at either end of the town's main Corso Vittorio Emanuele. At its eastern end, a twenty-minute walk from the centre, Gela's **Museo Archeológico** (daily 9am–1.30pm & 3–8pm; L4000) is notable largely for its important collection of painted vases upstairs. Mainly seventh- to fifth-century BC, the black and red jugs and beakers were Greek Gela's speciality: most major world museums tend to feature one or two, but the bulk are here. Other impressive finds include an animated sculpture of a horse's head (sixth-century BC) and the remains of necropolises from Geloan dependencies. Outside the museum a small **acropolis** has been uncovered, consisting of a few walls and a single temple column from the fifth century BC, though the small site loses all its romance to the brooding, dirty industrial plant that dominates the beach below.

There are more archeological remains at **Capo Soprano**, at the western end of town. Head along the corso and take a left fork (Via Manzoni), which runs parallel to the sea as far as the red gates of the site, a three- to four-kilometre walk. The **Greek fortifications** here (daily 9am–1hr before sunset; L4000) date from the fourth century BC. Preserved by the sand dunes under which they were discovered, the walls stand nearly 8m high in parts, made up of perfectly fitted stone blocks topped by a layer of brick and now covered in protective glass panels. It's a beautiful site and you're free to wander around the line of the walls: in some places you can make out the remains of watchtowers and gateways, while waves crash onto a duned stretch of beach below. If you've come this far out of town, you may as well nip around the corner (back towards the centre and left, by the hospital), to Via Europa, to see the remains of Gela's fourth-century BC **public baths**, the only ones from Greek times discovered in Sicily and still equipped with their original seats.

Practicalities

If you're taking in the Greek remains on a flying visit, it's best to leave your bags at the **train station** left-luggage office. There's a map of town posted at platform one. **Buses** leave from directly outside the station (tickets and information from the Autolinee office, across the square): there are regular departures to nearby towns, including Licata and Agrigento, Vittória, Caltanissetta and Siracusa. From the station, turn right down the main road and, at the junction, bear right for the town centre and Corso Vittorio Emanuele.

You won't need (or want) to stay in Gela, though if you get stuck, the *Sole* isn't bad, on Via Lungomare 32 (☎0933.912.785; ①). More information can be obtained at the **tourist office** at Via Palazzi 66, further up Via Europa and then right, on the corner with Via Francia (Mon–Sat 9am–1pm & 4–7pm; ☎0933.823.107).

ACCOMMODATION PRICE CODES

These represent the **cheapest available double room in high season**, usually – but not always – without en-suite bathroom or shower. Out of season, you'll often be able to negotiate a lower price than those suggested here. For more information about hotels and room prices, see p.27. The categories are:

① under L60,000	④ L120,000–150,000	⑦ L250,000–300,000
② L60,000–90,000	⑤ L150,000–200,000	⑧ over L300,000
③ L90,000–120,000	⑥ L200,000–250,000	

Inland: to Butera

Northeast of Gela, the scenic SS117 swoops towards Caltagirone/Piazza Armerina, following the line of the fertile Gela valley; by car, you can be in either within the hour, the road taking you through rolling cornfields and vineyards.

Around 8km out of Gela, at a small road junction, a forlorn Norman keep – **Il Castellúccio** – sticks out on a hillock, in the middle of land keenly contested at the start of the Allied landings in Sicily in 1943. Defensive concrete pillboxes still stud the dirt-brown hillsides on either side of the keep.

Butera

From Il Castellúccio, a minor road runs 7km west to join the rather more direct SS191 from Gela, which runs to **BUTERA** in twenty winding kilometres. An important sixteenth-century town, under the control of the Barresi princes, Butera today idles along in its lofty, remote way, pulling in the occasional stray driver to Caltanissetta, another 50km north. It's a pretty little place, with the drive up alone revealing why Butera was once coveted by medieval overlords – the town sits on a impregnable crag, overseeing a patchwork of walled fields, burnt hillsides, bare peaks, regimented rows of vines and tomato plantations.

All traffic (including buses from Gela and Caltanissetta) pulls into Piazza Dante, the main square, from where Via Aldo Moro leads up in five minutes to the **Castello dei Normanni**, a yellowing pile of which one battlemented wall and the central keep survive, incongruously tucked between modern apartment blocks. From the terrace beyond are tremendous views, to Gela and the coast.

Back in Piazza Dante, you can get a drink while contemplating the next move. *La Lanterna* has outdoor seats, and doubles as a pizzeria-restaurant, while both *Big Ben* and the adjacent *Britannia* are as oddly named a pairing as you'll come across in Sicily.

Along the coast to Agrigento

The long empty coastline to the west of Gela is dotted by more pillboxes left behind after the war. Following the SS115 from Gela, there's a decent sand **beach** at **MANFRIA**, just off the main road, although you won't get to stop here if you're travelling by train as it loops inland soon after Gela and doesn't stop until **FALCONARA SICULA**, a few kilometres beyond. There's little at either place apart from their respective beaches, though Falconara does boast a fourteenth-century castle – the private property of Palermitan aristocrats – and a local **campsite**: the *Due Rocche* (☎ & fax 0934.349.006), which has a **hotel** attached, the *Lido degli Angeli* (☎0934.349.054; no credit cards; ②).

Licata

Ten kilometres further along the coast, the port of **LICATA** is the only other worthwhile coastal stop before Agrigento. The lower town splits into two distinct halves: pavement cafés line the two wide corsos that form an L-shape at the heart of town, while behind here the narrow criss-crossed alleys of the old town reach back to the harbour. There's a lido and **beach** just up from the harbour, perfectly adequate for most purposes, though as Licata is still a working port, full of maritime hardware, it's hardly the most attractive of locations. Indeed, the best aspect of town is from above: from the main Corso Roma, you can climb up to the top of the town for a view over the harbour, and then work your way round the hill to reach an imposing sixteenth-century **castello**. Other strolls can take in the lively old-town **market** (over by 2pm), held in the cobbled square in front of the church, and some of Licata's good *palazzi*, the most prominent the gargoyle-studded **Palazzo Canarelli** on Corso Roma. The **Museo Cívico** in Piazza Linares, off Corso Umberto (Tues–Sat 9am–12.30pm & 4–7pm; free), displays a good deal of local prehistoric material.

Buses pull up on Corso Roma, right in the centre; the bar at no. 36 posts timetables and sells tickets for departures to Agrigento, Gela, Catania and Palermo. The **train station** is five minutes' walk away: go back down the corso to the church, turn right down Via Giovanni Amendola, left at the bottom and then take the fifth right, down a little street called Via Stazione.

There are a couple of **hotels**, though neither are terribly alluring. The cheapest is the *Roma*, Corso Serrovira 54 (☎0922.774.075; no credit cards; ②); walk down Corso Roma to Piazza Progresso, turn left down Corso Umberto, and after 200m take a left again onto Corso Serrovira. It would be nicer to stay at the *Al Faro*, Via Dogana 6 (☎0922.775.503; ④), where breakfast is included in the price, by the port and near the lido, which also has its own decent restaurant – the surroundings, though, are nothing special. Other **meals** are served at the lido itself, Lido Giummarella, which has pizzas at night; or at the occasionally funereal *Ristorante Calveri*, Via N. Sauro 19 – on the right, down Corso Umberto – where moderately priced fish is dished up by rather indifferent staff.

Palma di Montechiaro and Naro

If you're heading straight for Agrigento, it's quicker to pick up a direct bus at Licata than stick with the train, which swoops inland to Canicattì before doubling back to the coast. If you're driving, though, there are a couple of stops you could make along the way.

From Licata, it's 20km to shabby **PALMA DI MONTECHIARO**, which lies just off the SS115; the Agrigento–Licata bus passes this way too. This was once the seat of the Lampedusa family, the last of whom – **Giuseppe Tomasi di Lampedusa** – wrote the acclaimed novel, *The Leopard*. He died in 1957 (*The Leopard* was published a year later), though the palace in Palma had lain derelict for a long time before that. Today, the only echoes of the great feudal family recorded in the novel are to be found in Palma's imposing seventeenth-century **Chiesa Matrice**, built by one of Lampedusa's ancestors and approached by a wide flight of crumbling steps, and the ruined site of the **Castello di Palma**, a few kilometres to the west of town at the end of a small track.

North of Palma, the road climbs 17km up to medieval **NARO**, whose thirteenth- and fourteenth-century buildings may merit a look if you have time on your hands; there are SAIS **bus** services here from Agrigento (4 daily, last one returning at 6pm). The best of the buildings are the Chiaramonte **castello** at Naro's highest point, and the nearby ruins of the old cathedral; other churches in this walled and battlemented town are emphatically Baroque. Architecturally harmonious though Naro is, the real attraction is less the end destination and more the drive itself, from Palma and Agrigento, which is rewarded by extensive sweeping views down to the coast.

Agrigento

No one comes to **AGRIGENTO** for the town, though its worn medieval streets and buildings soak up thousands of tourists every year. The interest instead focuses on the substantial remains of Akragas, Pindar's "most beautiful city of mortals", a couple of kilometres below. Strung out along a ridge facing the sea, its series of Doric temples are the most captivating of Sicilian Greek remains and are unique outside Greece.

In 581 BC, colonists from nearby Gela and Rhodes founded the city of Akragas between the rivers of Hypsas and Akragas. They surrounded it with a mighty wall, formed in part by a higher ridge where they placed the acropolis (and where, today, the modern town stands). The southern limit of the ancient city was a second, lower ridge and it was here, in the so-called Valle dei Templi (Valley of the Temples), that the city architects erected their sacred buildings during the fifth century BC. They were – and are – stunning in their effect, reflecting the wealth and luxury of ancient Agrigento: "Athens with improvements", as Henry Adams had it in 1899.

But, as so often, Agrigento's Hellenic pre-eminence was no buffer against the cruel tide of Sicilian history. Conquered and sacked by successive waves of Carthaginians, Romans (twice), Saracens and Normans, the ancient city lost its status and many of its finest treasures. In a way, Agrigento never really recovered and despite the undoubted modern pulling power of the temples which fills the town with tourists throughout much of the year, there's little sense of purpose here. Ugly modern suburban building and road flyovers on the coast below town lack all sense of proportion and are creeping ever closer to the temples themselves. Meanwhile, government statistics show Agrigento to be one of Italy's poorest towns. Consequently it comes as no surprise to learn that the Mafia has an undue local influence; the speculative building projects aside, Agrigento crime families are generally reckoned to be heavily involved in trafficking cocaine from South America.

Arrival, orientation and information

Come by public transport, and you'll **arrive** in the centre of town. While you could easily jump on a bus straight down to the archeological park, the Valle dei Templi, it's a long day's sightseeing. Given the good accommodation possibilities in Agrigento, you may as well track down a room first and give yourself time to see the town as well – no mean attraction itself. The resort of **San Leone**, 6km south of Agrigento, with several hotels and restaurants, two campsites and a decent beach, is another reason to stick around for a while.

Trains, buses and information

Trains arrive at the edge of the old town at Stazione Centrale (☎0922.25.669) – where the facilities even extend to automatic toilets, a beautiful garden, a left-luggage office (8.30am–9pm; L5000 per item) and an exchange office (see "Listings", p.316) – don't make the mistake of getting out at Agrigento Bassa, 3km north of town. **Buses** – including those to Porto Empédocle, for ferries to the Pelágie Islands – use the terminal in Piazza Roselli, near the post office a few minutes' walk to the north; see "Listings" (p.316) for company and departure details. If you're **driving** into Agrigento, be warned that the one-way system in the old town is a complete nightmare. Some of the hotels are signposted, but it's a matter of pure luck whether

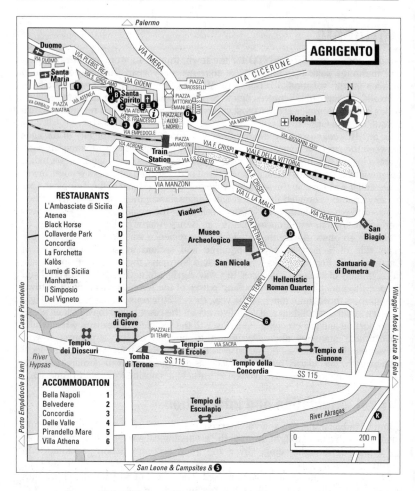

AGRIGENTO

RESTAURANTS

L'Ambasciate di Sicilia	A
Atenea	B
Black Horse	C
Collaverde Park	D
Concordia	E
La Forchetta	F
Kalòs	G
Lumie di Sicilia	H
Manhattan	I
Il Simposio	J
Del Vigneto	K

ACCOMMODATION

Bella Napoli	1
Belvedere	2
Concordia	3
Delle Valle	4
Pirandello Mare	5
Villa Athena	6

or not you'll actually be able to park anywhere near where you're staying. If you do park some distance from your hotel, don't leave anything visible in the car.

For getting around, **city buses** leave from Piazza Marconi, outside the train station, to the temples and the beach at San Leone. You need to buy city bus tickets (L1000) before your journey from kiosks or *tabacchi*, not on the bus; plan ahead, since most outlets are closed on Sundays. **Taxi** ranks are at Piazzale Aldo Moro (☎0922.21.899) and outside the train station (☎0922.26.670).

The old town stretches west of the three main interlocking squares, piazzas Marconi, Aldo Moro and Vittorio Emanuele. Via Atenea is Agrigento's principal artery, running west from Piazza Aldo Moro, with the **tourist office** at its eastern end, at Via Cesare Battisti 15 (Mon–Sat 9am–1.45pm & 5–7pm; ☎ & fax 0922.20.454); the staff are helpful, will give you hotel listings and free maps, and you should find English spoken here, too.

Accommodation

Finding **accommodation** in Agrigento shouldn't be a problem, except perhaps in peak season, when you should arrive early to look for a room. Even the cheapest hotels in Agrigento have two stars – there are no *pensioni* – but that doesn't mean they're particularly swanky. This is one town where paying a little extra for a better room with bath is probably worth it. All the budget choices are in the old town, above the temples, and the options are reviewed below. Tour groups tend to stay at one of the grander hotels a few kilometres east of town at **Villaggio Mosé**, on the coast road into Agrigento. The hotels themselves, three- and four-star palaces, are fine (and expensive), but it's a horrible traffic-choked suburb lined with stores, garages, furniture shops and apartment blocks.

Hotels

Villa Athena, Località Templi (☎0922.596.288, fax 0922.598.770). The only hotel actually in the Valle dei Templi – you pass it on the way down by bus – is well sited but expensive. It's also surprisingly small, so ring ahead if you fancy a night of pampered comfort. ⑦.

Bella Napoli, Piazza Lena 6 (☎ & fax 0922.20.435). At the western end of the old town, this is a reasonable budget choice, though it can be noisy. It's off Via Bac Bac and if you're lucky you'll be able to park in the square outside. ②.

Belvedere, Via San Vito 20 (☎ & fax 0922.20.051). On the east side of the main squares, across from the old town. Room 30 has an enormous balcony (though not much of a view), and is worth snapping up if it's available. ②.

Collaverde Park, Passeggiata Archaeológica (☎0922.29.555, fax 0922.29.012). Close to the archeological zone, with English-speaking staff and beautiful gardens, it's reasonably priced for the location. ③.

Concordia, Piazza San Francesco 11 (☎0922.596.266). A few minutes' walk behind the train station, this is good value, central, and has a trattoria next door. It's modern, and the rooms are on the small side, though they come with big, fluffy towels (try to avoid the windowless basement rooms, unless you want something really cheap), and there's a coffee bar in the lobby. ①.

Della Valle, Via Ugo La Malfa 3 (☎0922.26.966, fax 0922.26.412). Smart new hotel en route to the temples, with good gardens and restaurant; out of season, prices drop considerably. ⑥.

Pirandello Mare, Via Giovanni XIII, San Leone (☎0922.412.333, fax 0922. 413.693). A smart hotel with comfortable rooms, close to the beach in San Leone, the small resort 6km south of town; prices are at their highest in July and August. Take bus #2 from outside the train station. ③.

Camping

The nearest **campsites** are 6km south of town at the coastal resort of San Leone: both are near the beach, and open all year round. Take bus #2 from outside the train station (every 30min until 9pm), and the sites are a one-kilometre hike along the coast at the other end.

Internazionale San Leone (☎0922.416.121). The first site you reach, and the most comfortable.

Nettuno (☎0922.416.268). Further along from the *San Leone*, and cheaper.

The Town and around

It would be a mistake not to scout around the modern **town of Agrigento**. Modern only in comparison with the temples, it's thoroughly medieval at its heart, the main street, **Via Atenea**, starting at the eastern edge of town, above the train station. After the mean streets of some Sicilian towns, this long drag is something of a revelation, flaunting a run of quality jewellers, boutiques, bookshops and *pasticcerie*

– closed to traffic in the late afternoon, it's a positive pleasure to window-shop here. The streets off both sides revert to type, however, harbouring ramshackle *palazzi* and minuscule *cortili* (courtyards), and, while just ambling around here is entertainment enough, there are a couple of specific buildings worth seeking out. North of Via Atenea, **Santo Spírito**, at the end of Via Foderà, was built for Cistercian nuns in 1290, and although the attached convent is still being restored someone should appear with the keys to show you the church, in return for a small tip; inside, early eighteenth-century florid monochrome stuccos by Serpotta sprawl over the walls and trompe l'oeil domed ceiling. Upstairs there's a small **folk museum** (daily 9am–1pm; free) with some decorative nineteenth-century pictures of angels and saints inlaid with mother-of-pearl just before the entrance; the museum itself contains local artefacts, including Toby jugs. From here there are marvellous views of the temples across the fields. Back downstairs, if you ring the bell marked "*monastero*" and ask for "*dolci di mandorla*", a nun will bring you a tray of almond cakes; they're expensive, chewy, and worth the experience.

Via Atenea cuts right through the oldest part of town, at its most grand at the western end, around the **Municipio**, in Piazza Sinatra, housed inside a seventeenth-century convent. The narrowest and steepest of the streets spread up the hill from here, passing the church of **Santa Maria dei Greci**, built over a Greek temple of the fifth century BC. The flattened columns are visible in the nave and outside, viewable from an underground tunnel in the flower-filled courtyard, the stylobate and column stumps are incorporated into the church's foundations. Inside are visible the remains of Byzantine frescoes; if the church is closed, you can get a key from the guardian at Via Santa Maria dei Greci 15, opposite. Just up from here, Via Duomo leads past a line of decrepit *palazzi* to the massive **Duomo**, set on a terrace at the top of the hill and fronting a spacious piazza below.

Caos and the Casa Pirandello

Just **out of Agrigento** (at the end of the flyover leading out towards Porto Empédocle; bus #1 hourly from the train station), the suburb of **Caos** was the birthplace of **Luigi Pirandello**, and the inspiration for the Taviani brothers' film, *Kaos*, which was based on four of his short stories. One of the greats of twentieth-century Italian literature, Pirandello is best known for his dramatic works, such as *Six Characters in Search of an Author* and *Henry IV*, though his 1934 Nobel prize was awarded as much for his novels and short stories. He had a tragic life: his wife was committed to an asylum having lapsed into insanity following the ruin of her family and the birth of their third son, and for much of his life Pirandello was forced to write to supplement his frugal living as a teacher. His drama combines elements of tragedy and comedy with keenly observed dialogue. The nature of identity and personality, reality, illusion and the absurd are all recurring themes. Pirandello's ideas – and innovations – formed the blueprint for much subsequent twentieth-century drama.

His house, signposted "Casa Natale di Luigi Pirandello", has been converted into a **museum** (Mon–Fri 9am–1hr before sunset, Sat & Sun 9am–1pm; L4000). Although Pirandello left while still young, to study in Berlin and later live in Rome, he spent time here every summer. You can see the study where he wrote, crammed with foreign editions of his works. As well as a couple of murals he painted, there are stacks of photos, including one sent by George Bernard Shaw. After seeing the house, with its bamboo and daub interior, you can wander down through the grounds to a windswept pine, under which the writer's ashes are interned, though the pine, unlike all its pictorial representations, is now completely denuded, and the views he once enjoyed over the sea are now ruined by a patch of industrial horror.

The Valle dei Templi

A road winds down from Agrigento to the **Valle dei Templi**, buses (#1, #2 or #3) from outside the train station dropping you at a car park between the two separate sections of archeological remains, the eastern and western zones. You'll pass Agrigento's Museo Archeológico on the way and, if you're intent upon doing the ancient site and museum in one go, you'll need a full day here: take a picnic, or use the bar-*távola calda* at the car park (closed Sat) – where, incidentally, you'll find English newspapers on sale.

The eastern zone

The **eastern zone** is unenclosed and is at its crowd-free best in the early morning or late evening, when there's often a spectacular sunset. A path climbs up to the oldest of Akragas's temples, the **Tempio di Ércole** (Herakles). Probably begun in the last decades of the sixth century BC, it's a long structure, nine of the original 38 columns re-erected, everything else scattered around like a half-finished jigsaw puzzle.

Retrace your steps, back over what remains of a deep wheel-rutted Greek street, and the main path continues up past the site of the city's ancient necropolis to the **Tempio della Concordia** (Concord), dated to around 430 BC. Perfectly preserved and beautifully sited, with fine views to the city and the sea, the tawny stone lends the structure warmth and strength. It's the most complete of the temples, and has required less renovation than the others, mainly due to its conversion in the sixth century AD to a Christian church. Restored to its (more or less) original layout in the eighteenth century, the temple has kept its simple lines and slightly tapering columns, although sadly it's fenced off to keep the crowds at bay and is presently scaffolded at one end. Circle the temple at least once to get a decent view, and stand well back to admire its elegant proportions.

The path continues, following the line of the ancient city walls which hug the ridge, to the **Tempio di Giunone** (Juno, or Hera), an engaging structure, half in ruins, standing at the very edge of the spur on which the temples were built. A long altar has been reconstructed at the far end of the temple; the patches of red visible here and there on the masonry denote fire damage, probably from the sack of Akragas by the Carthaginians in 406 BC.

All the temples in the eastern zone are **illuminated at night** to great effect, something well worth trudging down to see or at least viewing from the town. You'll catch them floodlit from January to March and October to December between 9pm and 11pm; in April to September, between 9.30pm and 11.30pm.

The western zone

The **western zone** (daily 8.30am–7pm; L4000), back along the path and beyond the car park, is less impressive, though still archeologically engaging – a vast tangle of stone and fallen masonry from a variety of temples. Most notable is the mammoth pile of rubble that was the **Tempio di Giove** (Jupiter, or Zeus). The largest Doric temple ever known, it was never completed, left in ruins by the Carthaginians and further damaged by earthquakes and the removal of stone to build the port of Porto Empédocle to the south. Still, the stereobate remains, unnaturally huge in scale, while on the ground, face to the sky, lies an eight-metre-high *telamone*: a supporting column sculpted as a male figure, arms raised and bent to bear the temple's weight. **Other scattered remains** litter the area, not least piles of great column drums marked with a U-shaped groove, which enabled them to be lifted with ropes.

Beyond, behind the excavated gates and walls of the Greek city, is the earliest sacred site, the Sanctuary of the Chthonic Deities, marked by two altars (one square and fire-reddened, the other round), dating from the seventh century BC, before the official foundation of the colony. This is also the site of the so-called **Tempio dei Dioscuri** (Castor and Pollux), rebuilt in 1832, its columns and corner-work actually made up of unrelated pieces from the confused debris on the ground.

The Museo Nazionale Archeológico

The road that leads back to town from the car park, Via dei Templi, runs past the excellent **Museo Nazionale Archeológico** (Wed–Sat 9am–1pm & 2–5.30pm, Mon, Tues & Sun 9am–1pm; L8000). Since the bus passes by outside, you could always start here first before the temples, though it's better to make a separate visit if you can. It's an extraordinarily varied collection, devoted to finds from the temples, the ancient city and the surrounding area, and can occupy a good couple of hours when you combine it with seeing the remains of the residential area of the old city, just over the road.

Unusually for an archeological museum, there's much here that's of artistic merit as well as historical interest; it's also clearly and attractively laid out. You could skip most of the initial local prehistoric and Bronze Age finds, though look out for the gold signet rings, engraved with animals in **room 1. Room 3** features an outstanding vase collection, beguiling sixth- to third-century BC pieces, one of which depicts the burial of a warrior. Among the other objects here there's a tiny candlestick-holder engraved with a galloping horse. But it's the finds from the temples themselves that make this collection come alive: in **room 4** there's a series of sculpted lion's-head water-spouts, a common device for draining the water from the roofs of the city's temples, while **room 6** is given over to exhibits relating to the Tempio di Giove. Some useful model reconstructions help to make sense of the disjointed wreckage on the ground, although the prime exhibit is a reassembled *telamon* stacked against one wall: all the weather damage can't hide the strength implicit in this huge sculpture. Rooms beyond hold coins, inscriptions and finds from local necropolises; typical is an alabaster child's sarcophagus in **room 11** showing poignant scenes from his life, which was cut short by illness. The last couple of rooms contain finds from the rest of the province, one of which, in **room 15**, is the equal of anything that's gone before: a fifth-century BC *krater* displays graphic red figures hacking and slicing away in the Battle of the Amazons, amply demonstrating the famed Geloan (from Gela) skill as masters of vase-ware.

In the grounds of the museum, take time to look at the Gothic doorway of the adjacent church of **San Nicola**. There's an invigorating view from the terrace outside over the temple valley, while just beyond is a small odeon (third-century BC) used for public meetings, during which the participants stood rather than sat in the narrow rows. Nip over the road on the way out of the museum, too: the **Hellenistic-Roman quarter** opposite (daily 9am–1hr before sunset; free) contains rows of houses, inhabited (on and off) until the fifth century AD, many with mosaic designs still discernible.

Other archeological remains

You could see everything already described in four or five hours, but without your own transport the archeological park's remaining sights mean a lot of extra walking. The quickest way to reach the most distant is to climb over the wall to the side of the Tempio di Concordia and scramble down through the field to the road. Here, at the end of a dusty track, stands the undersized **Tempio di Esculapio** (Asclepius), with solid walls instead of a colonnade. Nearby, back along the main road and close to the crossroads, is a large two-storeyed Roman tomb (75 BC), the **Tomba di Terone**, mistakenly named by historians after the Greek tyrant Theron. The road then heads up, past the car park and museum, where a right fork followed by another right turn (Via Demetra) leads to the tiny church of **San Biagio**, a three-kilometre walk. A Norman chapel, this was built over the visible remains of a temple, contemporary with the ones below on the ridge. It's currently closed for restoration, but hang around and a custodian will lead you down the cliff behind the chapel to the eerie **Santuario di Demetra** (be prepared to tip). A stone-built chambered shrine hides two dingy caves that stretch 20m into the hillside. The thin corridor between building and caves was a sort of vestibule with niches for water so that worshippers could wash themselves. It's the most ancient of Agrigento's sacred sites, once devoted to the cult of Demeter and Persephone and in use even before Akragas was founded. It's at its best as the sun sets, with shadows flitting across the dark and silent caves, a mysterious and evocative place.

Eating and drinking

There's a fairly good choice of **restaurants** in Agrigento, nearly all on or just off Via Atenea, most offering some kind of *menu turistico*. In the cheaper places, though, you're usually better off picking out the specialities from the menu since prices in town – perhaps surprisingly for a tourist spot – aren't too bad. For an explanation of the price categories, see p.32. You'll find **pizzerias** in the town centre, and also at Villagio Mosé, east of town, below the temples, or to San Leone; for these, you'll really need your own transport.

Agrigento's **bars**, too, are an attractive lot for the most part. Alongside a couple of particularly youthful late-night drinking places, the regular bar-cafés along Via Atenea – most with good cakes and pastries – buzz during *passeggiata* time, when the whole street is packed, though you'll find them closed by about 9pm. There are outdoor seats at the little bars in Piazzale Aldo Moro, a nice place to sit in the early evening.

Restaurants

L'Ambasciate di Sicilia, Via Giambertoni 2. Fairly standard food in folksy surroundings, though things improve dramatically if you can get a table on the outdoor terrace – providing one of the few good views in town. The house pasta and fresh fish are the things to choose; you may be (un)lucky and get the Sicilian folk-music accompaniment. Moderate. Closed Sun.

Atenea, Via Ficani 12. Best of the budget restaurants, family-run and set in a quiet courtyard. Tasty pasta, meat and fish dishes with no frills in a simple, friendly trattoria. No credit cards. Inexpensive. Closed Sun.

Black Horse, Via Celauro 8. Welcoming place, though the temple paintings are a trifle lurid, with fine food – especially the fish – that attracts as many locals as tourists. There are a couple of outdoor tables on the steps off Via Atenea too. There's a tourist menu at L13,000. Inexpensive–moderate. Closed Sun.

Concordia, Via Porcello 6. Basic local restaurant with blaring TV. The speciality is the mixed grilled fish, not at all bad value, and there's local wine and large pasta portions. The street is opposite Via Atenea 61. Inexpensive.

La Forchetta, Piazza San Francesco 11. Small, wood-panelled trattoria, next door to the *Concordia* hotel, with a couple of good speciality pastas and local wine, though meat can be stringy. There's an unadvertised *menu turístico* at L20,000, if you're looking to save money, though you'll do better choosing from the menu. Moderate. Closed Sun.

Kalòs, Piazzetta San Calógero, off Piazza Aldo Moro (☎0922.26.389). Rather pink and flowery and can be a little noisy as the balcony overlooks the nightlife of the square. Nevertheless it's worth it for the food, arguably the best in the centre of town. Try the swordfish and white shrimps on rocket and thyme with an expert, tart dressing. You get a complimentary drink too. Expensive. Closed Sun.

Lumie di Sicilia, Via Lipari 8. You can't beat the pasta, pizza and drink *combinazione* at this trendy little eatery; not the greatest food in the world, but a welcoming place equipped with bentwood furniture in the secluded garden and, rather incongrously, baseball-capped waitresses. It's along an alleyway at Via Atenea 144. Inexpensive–moderate. Closed Wed.

Manhattan, Salita degli Angeli 9. Up the steps to the right at the beginning of Via Atenea, this trattoria/pizzeria/*paninoteca* attracts a young crowd for its excellent sandwiches with American names. Moderate. Closed Sun.

Il Simposio, Via Atenea Piano Lo Presti 19, signposted opposite Via Atenea 141. Pizzas on offer include "Pizza Viagra" (with seafood); there's a piano bar at weekends. Inexpensive. Closed Mon.

Del Vigneto, Via Cavaleri Magazzeni 11 (0922.414.319). You'll need a car to eat at this restaurant, way outside town beyond the temples, but it's a cracker, serving excellent regional dishes and locally made wine. Reservations advised in summer. Moderate–expensive. Closed Tues & Nov.

Bars

La Galleria, Via Atenea 123. A large video screen dominates this "American Bar" and there's loud music playing. You can simply sit and drink at the tables or tuck into pasta and ice-cream. Closed Sun.

Caffeteria Nobel, Viale Vittoria 11 (an extension of Via Crispi, which runs west from Piaza Marconi). A good place for an ice-cream or a drink after viewing the temples in the evening.

La Preferita, Via Atenea 68. Excellent bar-*pasticceria* with *arancini*, pizza slices and other savouries; a good breakfast stop.

Listings

Banks and exchange Banco di Credito Siciliano, Via Atenea 15; Banco Populare Sant'Angelo, Piazza Vittorio Emanuele 23; Banco di Sicilia, Piazzale Aldo Moro 1. There's an exchange office in the bowels of the train station (Mon–Sat 5.25am–7.30pm, Sun 6.05am–8.05pm).

Buses The bus terminal at Piazza Roselli is little more than a bus park, with timetables posted on stands in front of the various companies' stops. Services include: Autoservizi Cuffaro to Palermo; SAL to Licata, Palma di Montechiaro and Porto Empédocle; SAIS to Caltanissetta, Catania and Naro; Salvatore Lumia to Castelvetrano, Marsala, Mazara, Montallegro, Ribera, Sciacca and Trápani; Fratelli Camilleri to Raffadali. The only company with an actual office is SAIS, at Via Ragazzi del'99, just off the piazza. Otherwise, you can buy tickets on the bus.

Hospital Ospedale Civile San Giovanni, Via Giovanni XXIII (☎0922.401.344).

Police Carabinieri at Piazzale Aldo Moro 2 (☎0922.596.322).

Post office The circular building in Piazza Vittorio Emanuele (8.10am–7.40pm).

Telephones Make calls from Telecom Italia, Via Atenea 96 (9am–12.30pm & 4.30–8pm).

Travel agents For tickets to the Pelágie Islands and other services: Bellavia, Via Atenea 138 (☎0922.26.333); Edrega Viaggi, Via Atenea 21 (☎0922.594.155); Trasportaereo, Via Imera 23 (☎0922.596.333).

The Pelágie Islands

The remote **PELÁGIE ISLANDS** (Isole Pelágie) are little more than dry rocks, even further south than Malta and bang in the middle of the Mediterranean. Throughout history they've been neglected, often abandoned or uninhabited, and only occasionally has their strategic importance been recognized. In 1943 the Allies bombed the main island, Lampedusa, prior to springing into Sicily; and Colonel Gaddafi of Libya nearly gave a repeat performance in 1987 when he retaliated against the American bombing of Tripoli by targeting missiles at the US base on Lampedusa. Italian troops were mobilized and Sicily was on a virtual warfooting for three days, though in the event the missiles dropped into the sea short of the island.

The largest island, **Lampedusa**, attracts Italians in ever-increasing numbers, and it's pretty jam-packed in July and August, but it does offer good scuba diving and snorkelling in the wonderfully clear waters. The smaller, volcanic **Linosa**, reached only by ferry, is much quieter, generally hotter and less breezy than Lampedusa. The tiniest islet, **Lampione**, is uninhabited and not on the ferry route at all.

Getting there

Most visitors get to the islands by **ferry from Porto Empédocle**, just 6km southwest of Agrigento. It's as ugly, depressing and dirty a town as you could ever wish to visit, a large oily port dominated by its enormous cement works; however, the ferry doesn't leave until midnight, so if you've bought your tickets in advance you don't have to come here until the evening. Buses leave for the port from Agrigento every half an hour or so from outside the train station (a 10min journey; L2500), dropping you in Piazza Italia, one block from the waterfront; the last bus from Agrigento leaves at 8.30pm. A taxi will cost you around L20,000.

There are daily ferries in summer, six weekly in winter, calling at Linosa (5hr 45min) and Lampedusa (8hr 15min). Get **tickets** from the Siremar office (☎0922.636.683 or 0922.636.685) in Porto Empédocle, right on the quayside, or from travel agents in Agrigento (see opposite); one way in high season is around L49,000 to Linosa, around L62,000 to Lampedusa; returns cost double the amount. It's worth reserving either a **couchette** for L25,000 or a reclining chair for L6000, at least for the outward journey – or you can bend yourself round a couple of chairs in the TV lounge, where it's dark and quiet. Returning, it's possible to indulge in eight hours' hard sunbathing on a hard seat on deck. Bring your own **food** if you can, as that on board is expensive and unimaginative.

If you have your own car, there's no point in taking it across: use the Stagno **garage** (☎0922.636.029; from L5000 to L10,000 per day, depending on the size of the car) down at the port, at one end of Via Roma. If it's full, you should be able to leave your vehicle inside the port itself, preferably near the Dogana (customs) or anywhere else where it's likely to be watched over by official eyes; enter by the eastern entrance and drive through.

The alternative to the sea crossing would be to **fly from Palermo** direct to Lampedusa (1hr). Contact Air Sicilia (☎091.625.0566) or Alitalia (☎091.702.0313), who both operate twice-daily flights, either directly or through travel agents (see "Listings" in Palermo, p.95). You can get a one-way fare from around L175,000, but ask around first, for special weekend deals offering cheap returns, or even occasional promotional offers, which can cut the fares down to around L140,000 return. There are currently deals for three people travelling together, valid for certain months, which bring the price down to L80,000 return per person.

Linosa

Northernmost of the islands, **LINOSA** is the tip of a submerged volcano, with four extinct craters to poke around, some laval beaches and not much else in the way of sights. A haven for pirates in the sixteenth century, the small island (five square kilometres) wasn't really settled properly until the mid-nineteenth century, though even now the only village has just a few hundred inhabitants, rather fewer cars and a minimal road system. In sharp contrast to Lampedusa, it exudes tranquillity; the sunbathing is less hectic and commercial, and the water is just as crystal clear. If you take the tracks that lead away from either side of the port, you can clamber around the cliffs and coves, and reach the couple of black-sand beaches. About the only exciting events to disturb this quiet island were when the government in Rome regularly sent their latest star Mafia prisoner to be detained on the island pending trial – a practice that has been suspended since the tourist trade picked up.

There is one **hotel** in Linosa village, the *Algusa* (☎0922.972.052; ③), all of whose rooms come with a shower. You should really make a reservation in advance if you want to stay; alternatively, there's an unofficial **campsite** near the port.

Lampedusa

LAMPEDUSA, 50km south of Linosa and 205km from Porto Empédocle, is the last inhabited vestige of Italy. Originally a fragment of the African continent, and lying further south than Tunis, it's much bigger than Linosa and is the centre of more activity. Around 5000 people live here, mostly in the town of the same name, the majority making their living from fishing and tourism; increasing numbers of tourists, the vast majority of whom are Italian, arrive every year, especially in July and August.

Historically, however, Lampedusa has been as neglected as the other Mediterranean islands off Sicily. In 1667 it passed into the hands of the **Tomasi** family (as in Giuseppe Tomasi di Lampedusa, of *The Leopard* fame), one of whose descendants attempted to sell the island to Queen Victoria in 1839 when it still had only twenty or so inhabitants. The queen lost out on the sale, at a cost of twelve million ducats, to Ferdinand II, the Neapolitan king, who was no doubt aghast at the prospect of losing such a scraggy but strategically important island.

The island is long, thin, flat and dry, the main attraction being the **beaches** and the sea. For years the pristine water has offered some of the best swimming and diving in the Mediterranean, with an abundance of fish life; you might also see dolphins, or even, in March, the **sperm whale migration**. But a myopic attitude for most of this century has meant that Lampedusa has been practically stripped of its natural vegetation – the resulting soil erosion accounting for the arid, uncultivable state of the land. Recently, however, a programme of reforestation in a couple of the shallow valleys has been started, thus encouraging the regrowth of pine and mastic trees, and germander (from the mint family). At Cala Galera, look out for the Phoenician juniper, and carob and wild olive trees, all survivors of the original blight. Rare plants, too, can be seen here, including the *caralluma europa*, a cac-

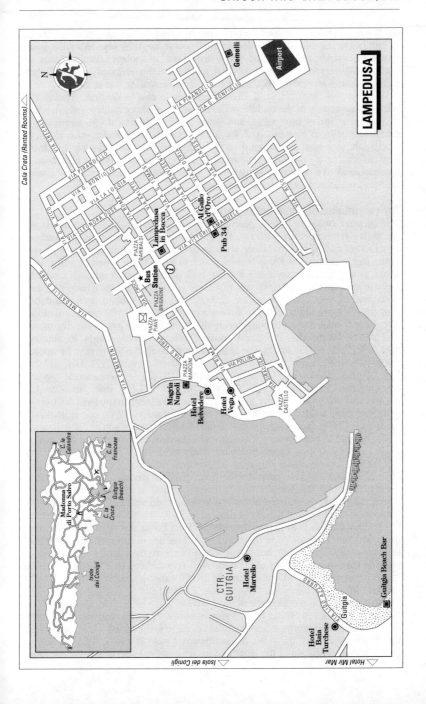

tus-like plant with star-shaped flowers, and the *centaurea acaulis*, from the centaury family. During mid-May, the flowers really come into their own as squills, irises, crocuses, orchids, echinops and thyme are all part of a vibrant display. Along the roads you'll see more common tall cacti, which rival the telegraph poles in height; poles that only arrived in 1963, when the telephone system was installed.

After the sun, sea and sand, there's really little else to do here. That said, a religious sanctuary in the middle of the island, an offshore nature reserve where turtles come to lay their eggs, and some good cliff-walks do go some way to diverting you from your tan. And, for the views of the cliffs and grottos alone, it's worth taking a boat trip around the island; consider too a day-trip to Linosa. Remember that it's a small, exposed island, so evenings are cooler here than on the mainland (it's not really somewhere you'd want to holiday in winter), when the wind whips across the barren landscape.

Arrival, information and getting around

The **airport** (☎0922.971.446) practically sits in the town, and most hotels and campsites arrange courtesy buses for guests. Arriving by ferry at the **harbour** (Porto Vecchio), it's a ten-minute walk up to town, or a twenty-minute walk west to the larger harbour of Porto Nuovo, which is home to the pleasure and fishing-boats, as well as the main beach and the bulk of the hotels. A minibus meets the ferry in summer, and will take you wherever you want to go for a couple of thousand lire, or you can take a taxi (L5000); if you've booked accommodation, though, it's more likely that you'll have a courtesy bus. If you haven't arranged anywhere to stay, it's worth considering the offers that you get as you disembark.

If you're lucky, the Pro Loco **tourist office** (erratic hours in summer; ☎0922.971.390) on Via Roma, the main street through the town, may be open. If not, try the travel agent, 35° Parallelo, at Via Anfossi 4 (☎0922.971.906), and then any of the others in "Listings" (see p.323); the environmental agency, Legambiente, Via V. Emanuele 27 (☎ & fax 0922.971.611; daily 9am–2pm), is friendly and will be able to give you information in English on the Isola dei Conogli and excursions around the island. Town and island **maps** are on sale at bookstalls for around L7000, including one that details the fish species you're likely to see.

From June to September it's also possible to **visit Linosa** for the day, only an hour away by Ústica Lines hydrofoil (daily at 9.30am, returning at 6.45pm; L27,000) – tickets from Agenzia Marrittima Strazera, Lungomare Rizzo 1 (☎0922.970.003). If you fancy trying your hand at **diving**, it's not difficult to arrange, either independently (see "Listings", p.323) or through hotels, many of which offer equipment, excursions and boats at reduced rates; a complete set of equipment costs around L76,000 a day.

The **bus station** is in Piazza Brignone, off Via Roma and right in the centre of the town; hourly buses go to the south coast beaches in summer. The town itself is easily coverable on foot, but if you want to explore the island you're better off **renting transport** from any of the numerous rental shops (see "Listings on p.323 for addresses); a bike will cost around L10,000 a day, a scooter between L20,000 and L25,000, and a mini-moke or car about L40,000.

You can do a complete circuit of the island in a day by bicycle, and even in the hottest months a refreshing breeze always blows. The cliff road along the north coast is rough and stony, as are the roads that cross the island – they deteriorate the further west you go – but the south coast road is easier. Take provisions (there are no shops along the way) and insect repellent (the ground is jumping).

If you're thinking of taking a **boat** around the island, you'll find numerous offers littering the quayside at the port; try Selvaggia Balestra (☎0922.971.018), in front of trattorias *Lampara* and *Arrogosta* on the harbourside. A small motorboat costs from L90,000 per day or, if you fancy a day-trip, reckon on paying about L20,000 per person (L35,000 with lunch thrown in).

Accommodation

Outside July and August there'll be no problem finding somewhere to stay in one the many **hotels**, bearing in mind that the season runs from Easter to November. During July and August, however, booking is essential and you're likely to find that there's a minimum stay of three nights and that full- or half-board is compulsory; we've indicated where this is the case.

HOTELS

Baia Turchese, Via Lido Azzurro (☎0922.970.130, fax 0922.970.098). Spacious, comfortable and only 30m from the beach. The pastel-coloured rooms are all air-conditioned, but if you want a view you'll have to pay more. They'll give you umbrellas and sun loungers to take down to the sand. Half-board from L154,000 per person in July & Aug. ③.

Belvedere, Piazza Guglielmo Marconi 4 (☎0922.970.188). Not as luxurious as the *Baia Turchese*, but it offers adequate accommodation overlooking the harbour. You're more likely to find room-only rates here and singles are cheap. ②.

Martello, Salita Medusa (☎0922.970.025, fax 0922.971.696). A modern hotel near the harbour, it has a restaurant complete with panoramic sea views. It's easy to arrange diving and boat trips from here as there's a diving club associated (see "Listings", p.323). Half-board from L140,000 per person in July and Aug. ③.

Mir Mar, Contrada Guitgia (☎0922.535.666). The cheapest hotel on the island and one of the few places where you can get a room only in summer. It's right on the beach; rooms are basic, but all have showers. No credit cards. ②.

Vega, Via Roma 19 (☎0922.970.099). One of the few hotels in the town itself, at the harbour end of the main street. Smaller than most of the other hotels, it provides good and friendly service. ③

SELF-CATERING AND CAMPING

There are numerous options for **rented rooms**, either in the town itself or along the coast; again, to be sure of a room in July and August, you need to book ahead. From Easter to November, try Emanuele Billardello at Via Eleonora Duse 52 (☎0922.970.697 or 0368.330.5837), who offers accommodation in this street (from L800,000 for a room for four in July and Aug, half that in low season). Mikael Apartimenti, Via Tacceri 24 (☎0922.970.408, or 0922.973.135 out of season) remains open all year, and offers rooms in town from L45,000 per person in August, L30,000 in low season.

For something different, there are modern versons of traditional **dammusi**: shepherd's huts found only in Sicily and North Africa, these small, stone buildings with domed roofs are purpose-built to stay cool in summer. You can find them at Cala Creta; contact Licciardi, the car-rental agency on Via Siracusa (☎0922.970.678), or Complesso Borga, at Cala Creta itself (☎0922.970.408, fax 0922.970.950).

There are two official **campsites**: *La Roccia* (☎0922.970.055), at Cala Greca, 3km from the town, with its own beach; and the slightly nearer *Lampedusa*, at Cala Francese (☎0922.970.720). Both are open from June to September.

Lampedusa Town

The gridded system of streets in the upper part of the town funnels down to the harbour, awash with fishing- and pleasure boats, from where a gentle walk westwards brings you to the popular beach, **Spiaggia della Guitgia**, around which the main cluster of hotels is sited. The town's activity centres on Via Roma, which turns pedestrian in the evenings for the *passeggiata*. Lining the pavements are the usual souvenir shops selling beach paraphernalia and fruits of the sea, especially sponges; look out for the hand-crocheted Arab caps you'll see the women making in between serving customers.

Around the island

There'll be no difficulty in finding spots to **swim** away from the port (though in season you'll never be alone on the beaches), and there are plenty of opportunities for diving on an organized trip or just snorkelling privately; you'll find there's good fish-watching only a few metres away from the beaches. If you don't fancy the main beach, and don't want to trek too far, then try **Cala Croce**, the next bay west of Spiaggia della Guitgia; or the rockier **Cala Francese**, a ten-minute walk east of town. Less busy are the rocks, up the east coast at **Cala Calandra** – but watch out for tar spots – and the craggy inlets that punctuate the south coast. There's nowhere to swim on the north side of the island, unless you do it from a boat – it's mostly sheer cliffs, which tier down like a wedding cake.

A further 7km west along the south coast, you'll come across the **Isola dei Conigli** (Rabbit Island). If you've got your own transport, leave it at the top of the cliff (there's usually an ice-cream van marking the spot, and it's well signposted); the spot's also reachable by hourly bus. Clamber down and you'll find fine, white sand – another popular stretch of beach, but note that there are no facilities here, so bring your own umbrella and picnic. Just offshore is the little island itself, which you can reach either on foot or by swimming, depending on the tide. A **nature reserve** (open at all times; free), it's the only place in Italy where you can see the turtle *Caretta Caretta* laying its eggs. During summer evenings, the turtles deposit between 100 and 150 eggs in deep holes, from which the babies stagger out after sixty days. The nests are individually fenced off, but that doesn't help protect them from the peregrine falcons, who also nest here. Trips to the island are advertised along Via Roma, back in town, or contact Legambiente (see "Arrival, information and getting around" on p.320).

There's not a great deal to see inland, apart from a stream of boy-racers zapping around on scooters. Off the main road west out of town, the church of the **Madonna di Porto Salvo** can be appreciated for its scenic location, its white steeple set in a little wooded valley, flowers and bougainvillea abounding in the garden in front. There's a story attached to the church, relating to a sixteenth-century Italian slave, captured by Saracans, who was shipwrecked on the island and made his way to the sanctuary here; afterwards, he used the image of the Madonna on the sail of his makeshift raft and made his way safely back to Liguria. There's a pilgrimage here every September.

Lampione

Lampedusa is also the starting point for trips to the third island, **LAMPIONE**, a mere speck of land to the west. Starkly vegetated and uninhabited, the island offers wonderful offshore fishing – you should be able to persuade someone to take you in their boat from Lampedusa Town, or contact the Mediterranee Immersioni Club diving centre (see "Listings" opposite); it's around a two-hour crossing.

Eating and drinking

There's no shortage of eating places; prices tend to be a little higher than on the mainland, though you'll still find plenty of inexpensive tourist menus. Fish, of course, is a speciality, along with couscous, either as a main dish or an antipasto (see p.32 for price codes). At night the whole of the Via Roma becomes one long café, with chairs and tables sprawling on the pavements; the *Café Royal* does great ice-cream. Other places to try are the *Bar del Amicizia*, Via Vittorio Emmanuele 34, where you can get a deliciously light *latte di mandorla* or *granite*; or, if you're heading to the beach, stop at the *Trattoria e Bar del Porto*, for a snack and a full-bodied *tè freddo*. Most places are closed in winter but open every day in season.

Pub 34, Via Vittorio Emanuele 34. A friendly "pub" offering Tex-Mex, daily specials, and a range of drinks. There's a tourist menu at L25,000, too, and a pleasant rear garden.

Al Gallo d'Oro, Via Vittorio Emanuele 45. Cheap, cheerful and friendly, with a good tourist menu of fish. Inexpensive.

Gemelli, Via Cala Pisana 2 (☎0922.970.699). Off the Via Bonfiglio, on the airport side of town, and worth the few minutes' walk for Arab specialities as well as *bouillabaisse*, paella and *crespelle di pesce* (fish pancakes). A quiet spot, where oil lamps on the tables and Arab decoration add to the ambience. Booking essential in Aug. Expensive.

Guitgia Beach Bar and Spaghetteria, Via Lido Azzurro. If you're on the beach, use this as a pit stop for good sandwiches (try the unleavened bread). At night, sit under bamboo thatch by candlelight and enjoy the lapping of the waves. Standard food, but excellent location. Inexpensive–moderate.

La Lampara, Via Madonna. Watch the evening *passeggiata* of mobile phones and Vespas along the harbourside as you sample the local fish, spicy couscous and sweet tomatoes. Moderate.

Lampedusa in Bocca, Via G. Mazzini 38 (☎0922.970.877). A somewhat oppressively pink atmosphere, but with a wide range of local dishes; try *orecchiette al gambero* (pasta with crayfish) and *calamari ripieni* (stuffed squid). Booking advised. Expensive.

Pizzeria Magria Napoli, Via della Grotte. Just up from the harbour at the edge of the town, it offers the full range of pizzas, a tourist menu at L25,000 and funky music. Inexpensive.

Listings

Banks Banco di Sicilia, Via Roma 129, has an ATM.

Bike rental OK Il Prezzo é Giusto, Via Roma.

Car rental Licciardi, Via Siracusa, first street north of the Porto Vecchio (☎0922.970.768).

Diving centres Lo Verde Diving, Via Roma 118 (☎0922.971.986); Mediterranee Immersioni Club (☎0922.971.526), on the lungomare and behind the hotel *Martello*, which also does excursions to Lampione and Linosa.

Ferry tickets Siremar (☎0922.970.003) at the harbour.

Pharmacy Sanfilipo, on Via Roma (8.30am–1pm & 5–9pm).

Police Carabinieri (☎0922.970.112).

Post and telephone office At Piazza Piave, just west from the bus station.

Supermarket Standa at Via Terranova in the upper part of the town; Sarina, Via Riso.

Travel agents Agenzia Marittima Raccomandataria, Lungomare Luigi Rizzo (☎0922.971.964); La Pelagie, Via Roma 155 (☎0922.970.170); 35° Parallelo, Via Anfossi 4 (☎0922.971.906).

Eraclea Minoa

Back on the Sicilian mainland, frequent buses travel to Sciacca from Agrigento in around two and a half hours. With your own transport, you could branch off towards Palermo along a couple of inland routes (see pp.289–291) or keep to the coast and drop in on the other important Greek site on this stretch, **ERACLEA**

MINOA. According to the historian Diodorus, this was originally named Minoa after the Cretan King Minos, who chased Daedalus from Crete to Sicily and founded a city where he landed. The Greeks settled here in the sixth century BC, later adding the tag Heraklea. A buffer between the two great cities of Akragas, 40km to the east, and Selinus (Selinunte), 60km west, Eraclea was dragged into endless border disputes, but flourished nonetheless: most of what's left dates from the fourth century BC, the city's most important period, three hundred years or so before it fell into decline.

It's an almighty effort to **reach the site** without transport of some description. Catch any bus running between Agrigento and Sciacca, and ask the driver to put you off at the turning, 5km west of Montallegro, on the SS115; the site is another 4km from there, with the beach another 1km below. **Heading on** west from the site turnoff, you should be able to flag down a bus en route to Sciacca.

The site

The **site** (daily 9am–1hr before sunset; L2000) sits on a ridge high above a beautiful arc of sand, with the mouth of the River Plátani on the other side. It's one of the most attractive of all Greek sites in Sicily, occupying a headland of which only around a third has so far been excavated. What there is to see is the fruit of successive (and continuing) excavations by foreign universities, who, together with the local *comune*, have landscaped the remains to good effect. Don't stray too far off the paths, though; signs at the entrance warn of snakes in the undergrowth.

Apart from the city **walls**, once 6km long and with a good part still standing, the most impressive remains are of the sandstone **theatre**, disconcertingly wrapped in a protective plastic covering. This was designed to protect the theatre, whose seats – made of very soft stone – had degenerated badly over the years, as a photograph in the small museum shows. Unfortunately, the plastic merely created a greenhouse effect over the stone, leading to further deterioration: funds permitting, the eventual plan is to restore the theatre completely.

Above the theatre, excavations have also revealed tombs and traces of a Greco-Roman temple, while below are the ruins of a grand house, with fragments of Roman mosaics. Many of the finds are held in a small on-site **museum** (free), which one of the custodians should open up for you.

The beach

While you're here, you'll be hard put to resist a trip down to the **beach**, one of the best on Sicily's southern coast, backed by pine trees and chalky cliffs. If you've been forced to come under your own steam, on foot from the main road, then you should make for here first and find a place to stay. At the foot of the road from the site, a couple of bar-restaurants sit right on the beach; at one, *Lido Gabbiano*, you can rent **rooms**, as well as chairs and sunshades. A couple of hundred metres back up the road, an apartment house also offers *camere*; there's a **campsite** nearby with cabins, *Camping Eraclea* (☎0922.847.310; two-bed cabins at L475,000 per week full-board; May–Oct), and a supermarket and the *Costa Bianca* pizzeria-restaurant, all within easy walking distance of each other.

Sciacca and around

Just over 30km further up the coast from Eraclea Minoa, **SCIACCA** comes as a welcome surprise after the ugly industry around the southern coast's other towns; it's a working fishing port with a good-looking upper town that's virtually untouched by tourism. In ancient times a spa town for nearby Selinus, it enjoyed great prosperity under the Arabs, from whom its modern name is thought to derive (the Arabic *xacca* meaning "from the water"). The town was at the centre of a feud between Catalan and Norman families that simmered on for a century, resulting in the deaths of a good half of the local population. Despite the destruction, Sciacca preserves some notable buildings, which infuse its agreeable Mediterranean air with more than a passing historical interest and make for some pleasant strolling through the weaving streets.

The upper town is still walled, entered through one of five grand gates, the westernmost of which, **Porta San Salvatore**, leads onto the **Chiesa del Cármine**, whose facade is lent a skewwhiff air by an off-centre Gothic rose window. Past the church, up Via Gerardi, the fifteenth-century **Palazzo Steripinto** is even more ungainly, its embossed exterior only partially offset by some slender arched windows.

From here, Sciacca's main street, **Corso Vittorio Emanuele**, runs right the way down to the lovely **Piazza A. Scandaliato**, a large terrace with some good cafés, enhanced by wide views over the port and distant bays. The most enduring Arab legacy in town is the street layout and, back from the piazza, above the **Duomo**, a Moorish knot of passages and steep alleys leads up to the rather feeble remains of the fourteenth-century **Castello Conti Luna**, which belonged to one of the feuding families that disrupted medieval Sciacca. A little way down from here, the twelfth-century church of **San Nicolò** (Sat evening) is a tiny construction with three apses and some elegant blind arcading.

From Piazza Scandaliato, steps lead down the cliff-side to the lower town and **port**, whose most distinctive feature is a steepled modern church. Just north of the church you'll see steps, each riser decorated with contemporary ceramic tiles, some depicting sea life, some just patterned, and each one different. You might well come down here to eat (see p.327), but it's worth at least an hour of your time to stroll among the dockside clutter. Fishing vessels lie tied up at the quayside, lorries unload salt by the bucketful for the anchovy and sardine processing, and repairmen, foundry workers and chandlers go about their business, breaking off work for a drink in one of the scruffy portside bars.

Practicalities

Buses pull up on Via Figuli at the Villa Comunale (the town gardens), at the eastern end of Sciacca. For bus tickets to Agrigento or Trápani, you need to cross the gardens to the *Bar Lorenzo* on Viale della Vittória. The **tourist office** is 300m to the west at Corso Vittorio Emanuele 94 (Mon–Sat 9am–2pm & 3–7.30pm; ☎0925.86.247), and there's another office at no. 84, on the first floor – both have maps, public-transport timetables, hotel lists and information in English. You might also try the travel agent Maratur, Corso Vittorio Emanuele 23 (☎0925.84.110), where English is spoken and you can find out about scuba-diving and boat trips.

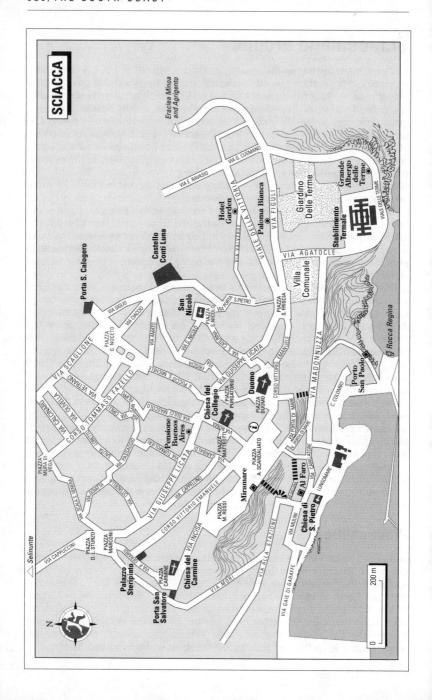

There are three **hotels** in the centre of town. Close to the Villa Comunale, there's the *Paloma Bianca*, at Via Figuli 5 (☎0925.25.130; ②); there's the *Hotel Garden*, Via Valverde 2 (☎ & fax 0925.26.299; ②), both around the same price; or, if you fancy a thermal cure, you could go for a room at the plush *Grand Hotel delle Terme*, Viale Nuove Terme 1 (☎0925.23.133; ③), on the cliffs beyond the Villa Comunale, set in its own park and with superb views out to sea. There are also a couple of **campsites**, closest of which is the *Mimose* (☎0925.991.167; June–Sept), 4km to the west of town at Contrada Foggia, right on the sea and with a trattoria-bar at its entrance; city bus #3 drops you 1km before the site. Eight kilometres to the east, the grander *Baia Makauda* (☎0925.997.254; June–Sept) is accessible from the bus to Agrigento, though this too involves a walk.

The best places to eat are the fish **restaurants** at the port, down the steps from the main piazza. When you reach the modern church, turn left (a sign points to "Trattoria") and you'll find *Al Faro*, Via al Porto 25 (no credit cards; closed Sun), with moderate prices and local wine. Further along the quayside in a westerly direction, at Largo San Paolo 1, *Porto San Paolo* (☎0925.27.982; closed Wed), is pleasantly decorated in marine style and has a terrace that overlooks the sea. You can get a good pizza for L11,000 and a full meal for L40,000. Try the seafood risotto in saffron sauce or the lobster *fettuccine*; it's advisable to book in summer. The *Miramare*, in the upper town's main Piazza Scandaliato (closed Sat), has fine views of the sea from its terrace, and serves fish specials and pizzas.

Around Sciacca

A couple of kilometres **east of Sciacca**, on bus routes #1 or #4, at **Il Castello Incantato**, Via Ghezzi, just out of Sciacca (Tues–Sat 10am–noon & 4–8pm; free), you'll find a garden full of thousands of stone heads. Carved in naive style over a period of fifty years by one Filippo Bentivegna, their faces are serious, beautiful and disturbing. After being rejected by his girlfriend, beaten up and left for dead on the streets of America, he returned home to Sciacca and devoted his life to carving these heads, symbols of his imaginary enemies, until his death in 1967. The eccentric artist would walk the streets of Sciacca with a short stick and a sceptre, and liked to be addressed as "Your Excellency".

Inland from Sciacca, you can sweat off a few kilos in the vaporous caves at **Monte San Calógero**, 8km north of town. Recent finds have shown that the site has been used since antiquity, and bus #5 runs here in ten minutes, every ninety minutes from Sciacca.

Further inland you can visit the cloud-swathed village of **CALTABELLOTTA**, 20km northeast of Sciacca, magnificently perched on three jutting fangs of rock, from which tremendous views stretch out on all sides. On the highest of these pinnacles, you can pass through the solitary surviving entrance of the Norman castle that once stood here, and climb up some rock-cut steps to the very top, from which the village below appears as a patchwork of grey roofs. The castle itself, ruined by an earthquake, was where the Angevins and Aragonese signed the peace treaty ending the Wars of the Vespers. Immediately below sit the Norman **Chiesa Madre** and the Gothic **Chiesa di San Salvatore**, both wonderfully sited against a rocky backdrop. SAIS buses to Caltabellotta run from Sciacca three times a day (Mon–Sat), the last one back leaving in the mid-afternoon – an impressive ride, past sparkling fresh streams and jagged outcrops of rock.

Along the coast : Ribera and Menfi

Along the coast from Sciacca, the road carries on northwest to Selinunte and Castelvetrano (see p.366). It's a journey you can make by FS bus from the town of **RIBERA**, 25km east of Sciacca, known as the *"città d'arancia"* for the expansive orange groves that surround it. The bus calls at Sciacca's abandoned train station (beyond the port) – so you don't need to stop in Ribera – and at **MENFI**, planned in the eighteenth century but devastated by an earthquake in 1968. Today Menfi presents a very mean aspect: lacerated churches on derelict central streets, a jumble of untidy prefab housing – still being used – and bland rebuilding on the outskirts.

festivals

February
First/second week Almond-blossom festival, the Sagra del Mandorlo in Fiore, at **Agrigento**: events take place in the Valle dei Templi – costumes, music and processions.

February/March
Carnevale at **Sciacca**, with participation of the entire town in five days of parades and competitions.

March/April
Easter Holy Week processions at **Agrigento**.

June
27–29 Sagra del Mare at **Sciacca**: a statue of St Peter is paraded on a boat at sea; there's a big fish fry-up and maritime-themed games at the port.

July
First/second Sunday Festival at **Agrigento** in honour of St Calógero.
Pirandello week Plays and concerts held at Pirandello's house at **Caos**, near Agrigento.

September
22 Pilgrimage and religious procession at **Lampedusa**, in honour of the Madonna di Porto Salvo.

travel details

Trains
Agrigento to: Caltanissetta (10 daily; 1hr 30min); Canicattì (10 daily; 45min); Enna (5 daily; 2hr 40min); Palermo (10 daily; 2hr).

Gela to: Caltagirone (11 daily; 1hr); Canicattì (10 daily; 1hr 30min, change at Canicattì for the 10 daily service to Agrigento); Licata (10 daily; 30min); Ragusa (9 daily; 1hr 30min); Vittória (8 daily; 40min).

Buses
Agrigento to: Caltanissetta (9 daily Mon–Sat, 7 Sun; 1hr 15min); Canicattì (7 daily; 40min); Catania (9 daily Mon–Sat, 5 Sun; 2hr 50min); Gela (3 daily; 1hr 30min); Licata (every 30–60min; 1hr); Montallegro (for Eraclea Minoa, hourly Mon–Sat,

2 Sun; 30min); Palermo (4 daily; 2hr); Palma di Montechiaro (every 30–60min; 30min); Porto Empédocle (every 30min until 8.30pm; 20min); Ribera (for Eraclea Minoa, hourly Mon–Sat, 2 Sun; 1hr); Sant'Angelo Muxaro (3 daily Mon–Sat; 1hr); Sciacca (11 daily Mon–Sat, 3 Sun; 2hr); Trápani (4 daily Mon–Sat; 3hr 30min).

Gela to: Agrigento (4 daily Mon–Sat; 1hr 30min); Caltagirone (5 daily Mon–Sat; 1hr); Caltanissetta (4 daily Mon–Sat, 2 Sun; 2hr); Catania (6 daily Mon–Sat, 2 Sun; 2hr); Enna (1 daily; 1hr 40min); Licata (3 daily Mon–Sat; 45min); Palermo (4 daily Mon–Sat, 3 Sun; 3hr 40min); Piazza Armerina (3 daily Mon–Sat, 1 Sun; 45min); Siracusa (2 daily Mon–Sat, 1 Sun; 2hr); Vittória (6 daily Mon–Sat; 50min).

Sciacca to: Agrigento (11 daily Mon–Sat, 3 Sun; 2hr); Caltabellotta (4 daily Mon–Sat, 3 Sun; 25min); Castelvetrano (3 daily; 1hr 30min); Menfi (7 daily; 35min); Palermo (10 daily Mon–Sat, 5 Sun; 2hr 30min); Trápani (9 daily Mon–Sat, 4 Sun; 3hr).

Catamarans
Licate to: Malta (2 weekly July–Aug; 2hr 15min).

Ferries
Porto Empédocle to: Linosa/Lampedusa (mid-night daily June–Oct; midnight daily except Fri Nov–May; 5hr 45min/8hr 15min).

Lampedusa to: Linosa/Porto Empédocle (mid-night daily June–Oct; midnight daily except Fri Nov–May; 5hr 45min/8hr 15min, departing at 10.15am from Lampedusa, 12.15pm from Linosa).

Planes
Palermo to: Lampedusa (4 daily; 1hr).
Lampedusa to: Palermo (4 daily; 1hr).

CHAPTER NINE

TRÁPANI AND THE WEST

Thanks to the A29 autostrada heading out from Palermo, Sicily's **west** is now more integrated with the rest of the island than it has ever been. Traditionally poor and remote, its economy dependent on fishing and small-scale farming, there's still much here that's different from the rest of the island. Historically, the region has always been distinct, influenced by a strong **Phoenician** and **Arab** culture rather than the prevailing Greek and Norman tradition elsewhere in Sicily. Visually too, the flat land, dotted by white cubic houses, is strongly reminiscent of North Africa, itself only 150km across the Mediterranean and considerably closer than the Italian mainland.

On the northern coast, the **Golfo di Castellammare** is only an hour's train ride from Palermo, and though there are patches of industrial development along the gulf it still manages to offer some empty beaches and a couple of unspoiled villages at its western end. In particular, the coastline between the old tuna-fishing village of **Scopello** and the resort of **San Vito Lo Capo**, encompassing Sicily's first nature reserve, the **Zíngaro**, the least developed and most beautiful on the mainland. **Trápani**, capital of the province that embraces almost this entire area, is a congenial port town within sight of the flat saltpans on which its wealth was based. You could make the city a base for visiting the small, offshore **Égadi** archipelago and, inland, the mountain town of **Érice** – originally a centre of Punic influence, though diverging from the region's dominant trend in its uniform Norman and medieval character. The pattern re-establishes itself a little way down the coast at **Mózia**, Sicily's best example of a Phoenician site, while further south the Moorish imprint is discernible in the secretive alleys and courtyards of **Marsala** and **Mazara del Vallo**.

Although the Greeks never wielded much influence in the area, the Hellenic remains at **Segesta** and **Selinunte** (Selinus) count among the island's most stunning. Between the two, the Valle del Belice delineates the region struck by an earthquake in 1968, which left a trail of destruction still visible in many towns and villages, notably at **Gibellina**, abandoned in its ruined state as a powerful reminder. There could be no greater contrast to this disorder than the peaceful island of **Pantelleria**, a distant outpost, much nearer to Africa than Europe, mountainous and wind-blown, and visited mainly by birds as a stop on their long migrations. It's a lengthy hydrofoil or ferry ride from Trápani, though quick plane connections from Trápani or Palermo make a weekend trip possible if you plan ahead.

You'll find **getting around** the coast a simple matter, as frequent buses and trains cover the short distances between all the towns and villages. There's much less public transport, though, if you strike off **inland**: what interior bus services there are depart from Marsala or Castelvetrano. If you're driving, apart from the two arms of the A29 autostrada there are only two other main roads, the SS115 between Trápani and Marsala and the inland SS188 between Marsala and Salemi.

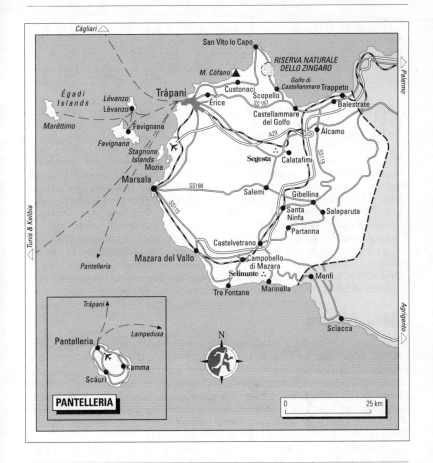

The Golfo di Castellammare

Backed by a forbidding wall of jagged mountains, the wide bowl of the **Golfo di Castellammare** is almost entirely made up of small holiday towns, sometimes uncomfortably close to industrial plants, though these disappear as you progress west. The main train line from Palermo (and the SS187 road) skirts the bay from Trappeto to Castellammare del Golfo, but despite the ease of access and the consequent development the resorts have not entirely shrugged off their original role as fishing villages – though they have completely lost the mean look they had when fishing was the only source of income. If you're after a beach, some of these would make a reasonable morning's halt. Otherwise, the train ride is as fair an entertainment, hugging the coast at the base of massive wedges of rock, often of a raw red colour, echoed by smaller, weathered nuggets poking out of the sea.

If you'd like to see the coast **by boat**, in recent years the *Leonardo da Vinci* (☎0942.34.222) has operated daily tours in summer, leaving Castellammare del Golfo in the morning and visiting Scopello, Zíngaro and San Vito; tickets are L28,000 a head and Trápani tourist office should be able to check if the service is currently operational (see p.338).

Trappeto and Balestrate

The two villages of **TRAPPETO** and **BALESTRATE**, five minutes apart on the train, have a tidy sense of wellbeing in sharp contrast to the poverty that Danilo Dolci found when he came to the region in 1952. His *Sicilian Lives* records his first impressions of Trappeto: "Coming from the North, I knew I was totally ignorant. Looking all around me, I saw no streets, just mud and dust. Not a single chemist – or sewer. The dialect didn't have a word for sewer." Nowadays, things have dramatically improved and the beaches on either side of the villages, backed by orange groves, are regularly visited by Palermitan holiday-makers. There are popular summer pizzerias in both places, and even a couple of **hotels**, cheapest of which is the *Del Golfo* in Balestrate, Via Madonna del Ponte 109 (☎091.878.6328; no credit cards; ①). In Trappeto, *La Sirenella*, Via XXIV Giugno 109 (☎091.878.8356; ②), and, outside town, the *Riviera*, in Contrada Puma Scandaliato (☎091.878.8069; ③, including breakfast), are classier.

Inland: Álcamo

Inland from here, and just inside the Trápani provincial boundary, **ÁLCAMO** is the only large town hereabouts, founded by Frederick II in the early thirteenth century and spread across a low hill overlooking the sea. It'll only be of interest to fans of ecclesiastical architecture, its churches all found around the old town's narrow main street, Corso VI Aprile, though there's an impressive fourteenth-century castle too, just up from the central Piazza Ciullo. To get here at all, though, you really need your own transport as the **train station** (Álcamo Diramazione) lies 5km below town, off the main SS113.

If you get stuck, Álcamo has a rather basic **hotel**, the *Miramare*, Corso Médici 72 (☎0923.21.197; ②), on the edge of town, at the end of the main street away from the central square; the bathroom's a bit scruffy but it's clean enough otherwise. There's a decent **restaurant**, the *Salsaparigua*, at Via Libertà 1, and another, *La Funtanazza*, a few kilometres outside town in the woods on Monte Bonifato (signposted), while the trattoria opposite the station is an acceptable spot.

There is a great incentive in Álcamo never to make it further than the **Stabilimento Termale Gorga** (☎0924.23.842; no credit cards; ①), a thermal spa just a couple of hundred metres from the train station: from the station take the right-hand dirt track and follow its meanderings (don't go down under the bridge) to the spa. The water in the pool is exquisitely hot and for a few thousand lire you can jump in and out to your heart's content; you can stay here too.

Those with a car can also visit a second spa, **Terme Segestane** (☎0924. 530.057), five to ten minutes to the west (though you could also walk there from Álcamo Diramazione station on the country roads).

Castellammare del Golfo

Back on the gulf, **CASTELLAMMARE DEL GOLFO** is the last coastal stop before the train line winds inland to Trápani. It's the biggest of the fishing ports on the gulf, entirely enclosed by high surrounding hills and built on and around a hefty rocky promontory, which is guarded by the squat remains of an Aragonese castle. Beneath the castle walls, on the harbourside, a run of café-restaurants face the fishing-boats, a nice place to kill time and eat lunch. There's a scrappy sand **beach** at the harbour – the writer Gavin Maxwell, who actually lived in the castle for a time in the early 1950s, wrote of watching "Castellammaresi women come down to the sea to bathe and swim fully dressed in their everyday clothes". Today's rather more daring beach-goers prefer the fine sands 2km east of the centre, between the town and train station.

Castellammare's incredible pedigree of bloodshed once gave it one of the worst reputations in Sicily for Mafia violence. Maxwell claimed that in the late 1950s eighty percent of the town's adult males had served prison sentences, and one in three had committed murder: coupled with this are the official statistics for the same period that classify one family in six as destitute. Needless to say, all of this is extremely hard to believe today: strolling down the sloping corso towards the castle and harbour, past handsome *palazzi* interspersed with bars and shops selling beach gear, it seems a most benign place.

There are a couple of **hotels** here, including the *Belvedere Oasi del Golfo* (☎ & fax 0924.33.330; ②), on the main SS187 above town, across the harbour, which has great views and a pizza restaurant. The **campsite**, *Nausicaa*, is 3km east of town (☎0924.33.030, fax 0924.35.173; May–Sept) and handy for the beach. However, you could do much better by moving the 10km west up the coast to Scopello (see below). For a **meal**, *L'Approdo* down at the harbour serves good pizzas in the evening; or try a speciality *cuscus a pesce* at any of the other three or four places here or, in the town itself, at the inexpensive *La Muciara* (closed Mon), just down the steps from the gardens.

The local **train station** is 4km east of town; a bus (L1500) meets arrivals – more or less – and shuttles you into Castellammare, passing the campsite on the way. It drops you at the **bus station** in the upper part of the town on Via della Repubblica, which runs off Via Segesta. From here there are services **to Scopello** and to the beach ("Spiaggia"; at 9.30am and 5.30pm), as well as to San Vito, Palermo, Trápani, Álcamo and Calatafimi/Segesta. Note that there are no buses on Sunday except to Palermo.

You'll find the **tourist office**, whose staff are friendly and eager to give you information in English, up the steps at Via A. de Gasperi 6 (Mon, Wed & Fri 9am–2pm, Tues & Thurs 9am–2pm & 3–6pm; ☎ & fax 0924.592.111), opposite the gardens in Corso Bernardo Mattarella. There is another office on the outskirts of the town, at Viale Umberto I 3 (daily 9am–1pm & 3–7pm; ☎0924.31.320).

Scopello and Zíngaro

The coastline northwest of Castellammare is perhaps the most beautiful in the whole of Sicily, with no shortage of unspoiled coves and gravel beaches, connected by paths to the road above. It culminates in the area around **Scopello**, 10km from Castellammare, a tiny hamlet a little way inland that once serviced an old tuna fishery (*tonnara*) on the coast below. The swimming here is terrific, while the road itself stops 3km beyond Scopello *tonnara*, at a nature reserve, the **Riserva Naturale dello Zíngaro**, where you can proceed on foot through pristine country and past more extremely beautiful coves and beaches. It's not exactly unknown territory, since hundreds of Palermitani descend on Scopello and its surroundings on summer weekends, but at other times – and especially out of season – it's one of the most tranquil places in Sicily. In addition, since the whole area is regulated by building restrictions which actually seem to be enforced, the water quality – and consequently the swimming – is excellent.

The Tonnara di Scopello

The road to Scopello from Castellammare forks just before the village, with one strand running the few hundred metres down to the coast and to the **TONNARA DI SCOPELLO** set in its own tiny cove. This old tuna fishery and its associated outhouses is where the writer Gavin Maxwell lived and worked in the 1950s, basing his *Ten Pains of Death* on his experiences there. It's almost too picturesque to be true – not least the row of abandoned buildings on the quayside, fronted by lines of rusting anchors, and the ruined old watchtowers tottering on knobbly columns of rock above the sea. From the shore, it's still precisely as Maxwell described it forty years ago: "a sea of purple and blue and peacock green, with a jagged cliff coastline and great *faraglioni* [rock towers] thrusting up out of the water as pinnacle islands, pale green with the growth of cactus at their heads". The *tonnara* remained in intermittent use until the 1980s, but although it's still privately owned the gate is always open (free) to allow visitors to wander around the quayside and – more to the point – swim off the tiny shingle beach in the most crystal clear of waters. It's a thoroughly enjoyable spot, made more so by the fact that visitors are tolerated provided they don't bring with them a whole host of proscribed items – dogs, radios, chairs, sunshades "and anything else that would disturb the tranquillity of the place". An injunction like this is usually as a red rag to a bull to a Sicilian, to whom disturbing tranquillity comes as second nature; here, amazingly, peace and quiet appears to hold sway. Don't be surprised if you see a bride and groom turning up for their wedding video.

Scopello

The road past the *tonnara* runs onto Zíngaro (see below), with a loop heading back to the village of **SCOPELLO DI SOPRA** – or simply Scopello – which perches on a ridge a couple of hundred metres above the coastline. This is little more than a paved square and a fountain, off which run a couple of alleys; on one side of the square sits the gateway and enclosed courtyard of the village's eighteenth-century **baglio**, or manor house, now the focus of village life. In here – centred on a huge eucalyptus tree – the courtyard buildings harbour a ceramicist's workshop, artist's studio, craft shop, a couple of bars and a pizzeria-restaurant. With the lights on and the wind rustling the leaves, it's a magical place at night, though at weekends in July and August – when every bar table is full and queues develop at the pizzeria – you could be forgiven for wishing for more solitude. That you'll get if you come anytime other than high summer, when traditional village life is more to the fore: men playing cards at the tables, people gossiping around the fountain and neighbours helping out in each other's fields.

Scopello can be rather an exclusive retreat, given the building restrictions which limit the accommodation choices. In summer, particularly, you'd do well to book in advance if you want to stay here, and be prepared to accept half-board terms in the pensions (which matters little since there's hardly anywhere else to eat anyway). Out of season you'll be able to pick and choose, and the prices drop by a few thousand lire too.

Practicalities

The **bus** from Castellammare drops you in the square, by the fountain; there are four services a day (Mon–Sat) back to Castellammare. All the **places to stay and eat** are within a thirty-second walk, most immediately visible – official street names are a bit pointless, but are given in case you want to write and book. *La Tranchina*, at Via A. Diaz 7 (☎ & fax 0924.541.099; ②, includes breakfast), is run by a friendly family that includes an English speaker, and has comfortable modern rooms with decent plumbing and an open fire in winter (when the nights can get chilly); dinner is served here, too, for L30,000 if you want it. *La Tavernetta,* next door at no. 3 (☎ & fax 0924.541.129; ③), has similarly pleasant rooms, some with distant sea views. The food here isn't bad either, with pasta, fresh fish, local wine and fruit running to around L40,000, though you could eat for less; for example, there's a (not terribly inspired) *menu turístico* for around L18,000. At the *Torre Benistra*, just around the corner at Via Natale di Roma 19 (☎0924.541.128; no credit cards; ⑤), the room price includes half-board and the food here is probably the best in the village; you should aim to eat here anyway. Meals of home-made pasta (with sardines and wild fennel, or tuna roe) and fish caught by the family will come to around L35,000–40,000. There are two other places to eat in the village: *Il Baglio*, in the *baglio* courtyard, an extremely popular place for **pizzas** at the weekend, with attractive outdoor seating and a full menu; and *Al Cantuccio*, on the main road, which does a "flesh" tourist menu for L18,000 and a fish one for L35,000, as well as serving crêpes.

Elsewhere in the village there's an *alimentari*, a bakery, butcher's shop, a couple of other bars, a post office, and phones by the fountain. The nearest **campsite** is *Baia di Guidaloca* (☎0924.541.262; April–Sept), 3km south of Scopello and a stone's throw from the lovely bay of **Cala Bianca**, where there's good swimming; the bus from Castellammare passes right by.

It's also easy to rent **rooms and houses** in Scopello if you fancy staying for a week or so. Dino Barbera (☎0924.541.125), the ceramicist in the *baglio* courtyard, has rooms with and without small kitchen (②); ask in his shop. Alternatively, seek out the *alimentari* in Via P. Gallupi (☎0924.541.135) and ask for Vito Mazzara, who has comfortable pine-clad rooms in a restored farmhouse (②) as well as hammocks in the garden; there's self-catering here as well. Booking is essential in the peak season.

The Riserva Naturale dello Zíngaro

The southern entrance to the **Riserva Naturale dello Zíngaro** is just 2km from Scopello village, along a road affording wonderful views of the *tonnara*'s towers and the gulf beyond, passing reasonably discrete holiday homes, fields of vines and grazing horses.

The Zíngaro was the first nature reserve to have been established in Sicily and comprises a completely unspoiled seven-kilometre stretch of coastline backed by steep mountains. Its genesis was the proposal to force a coast road through from

Scopello to San Vito, an idea that horrified environmentalists, who persuaded six thousand supporters to march in protest in May 1980. The road was scrapped and the reserve established, following which great efforts have been made to attract sympathetic visitors to the site. Most, it's true, come for the isolated cove **beaches**, which provide scintillating swimming, but since there's no vehicle access beyond the entrances it's not hard to escape the crowds by simply walking further into the reserve. There's an excellently maintained network of **paths**, the easiest running close to the coast, though mid- and high-mountain routes are popular with walkers and ornithologists. Around forty different **bird species** nest and mate here, and apart from the wide variety of flora there's also great archeological interest in an area that supported some of Sicily's earliest prehistoric settlements.

At the Scopello entrance, there's a car park and an **information hut**, where you can pick up a simple plan showing the trails through the reserve. There's a water fountain here, too, and in summer a van selling ices and drinks.

It's less than twenty minutes to the first beach, **Punta della Capreria**, which means it can be crowded at weekends and in July and August. When it's not, it's perfect: a tiny cove of white pebbles, azure water, shoals of little fish nibbling at the edge and baby squid darting in and out. There's a **Museo Naturalistico** (daily: summer 9am–7pm; winter 9am–4pm) and visitors' centre (same hours) just above the beach. Sticking with the coastal path, it's 3km to the successive coves of **Disa**, **Berretta** and **Marinella**, which should be a little more secluded, and 7km in total to the **Tonnara dell'Uzzo**, just beyond which is the northern, San Vito Lo Capo, park entrance (see p.348). If you're walking on to San Vito, note it's another 11km from the entrance, and there's no public transport or facilities of any kind along the way.

Trápani

TRÁPANI is the first of three major towns on Sicily's western edge, and, although predominantly modern, has an elegant old centre squeezed into a narrow arm of land pointing out to sea. Lent an end-of-the-line feel by its port, the town's inconspicuous monuments give no great impression of its long history. Nonetheless, Trápani flourished as a Phoenician trading centre and as the port for Eryx, modern Érice, profiting from its position looking out towards Africa. Later, as an important stopover on the sea routes linking Tunis, Naples, Anjou and Aragon, the town was ensured an enduring role throughout the Middle Ages, when Europe's crowned heads virtually passed each other on the quayside. The Navarrese king Theobald died here of typhoid in 1270; two years later Edward I of England touched down after a Crusade to learn he'd inherited the throne, while Peter of Aragon arrived in 1282 to claim the Sicilian throne, following the expulsion of the Angevin French. The city's growth over the last century has been founded on the development of salt, fishing and wine industries, though severe bombardment in World War II has given rise to miles of dull post-war building around Trápani's outskirts.

Still, as a **touring base** for the rest of the west Trápani can't be beaten. There are a good few accommodation possibilities, all in the old-town area, regular trains south to nearby Marsala and Mazara del Vallo, buses to Érice, the resort of San Vito Lo Capo and the more distant site of Segesta – while the nearest of the Égadi Islands is only twenty minutes away by hydrofoil.

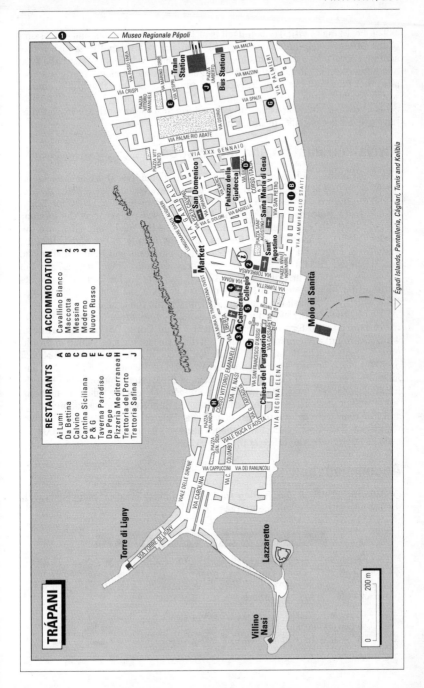

△❶ △ Museo Regionale Pépoli

TRÁPANI

Egadi Islands, Pantelleria, Cágliari, Tunis and Kelibia

RESTAURANTS

Ai Lumi **A**
Da Bettina **B**
Calvino **C**
Cantina Siciliana **D**
P & G **E**
Taverna Paradiso **F**
Da Pepe **G**
Pizzeria Mediterranea **H**
Trattoria del Porto **I**
Trattoria Safina **J**

ACCOMMODATION

Cavallino Bianco 1
Maccotta 2
Messina 3
Moderno 4
Nuovo Russo 5

Train Station
Bus Station
San Domenico
Palazzo della Giudecca
Santa Maria di Gesù
Market
Sant' Agostino
Cattedrale
Collegio
Chiesa del Purgatorio
Molo di Sanità
Torre di Ligny
Lazzaretto
Villino Nasi

0   200 m

The best time to visit Trápani itself is at **Easter**, to see the famous procession of the **Misteri** – eighteenth-century wooden images arranged in scenes representing the last days of Christ's life. If you're aiming to be here then, make sure of a hotel room in advance, though you should have no problem finding space at any other time. You can view the Misteri throughout the year, though the church which contains them has limited opening hours (see p.340); this and Trápani's other churches which are currently closed for restoration work are expected to have greater accessibility in the near future.

Arrival, orientation and information

The **train station** and main **bus station** (for regional buses) are at the edge of the modern part of town, in Piazza Umberto and the adjacent Piazza Malta respectively; the train station has **left-luggage** facilities (8am–9.30pm; L5000 for 12hr). **Buses from Palermo and Agrigento** drop you either here or by the Egatour Viaggi office, Via Ammiraglio Staiti 13, just across the road from which are the docks (Molo di Sanità) for the **ferries and hydrofoils** to the Égadi Islands, Pantelleria, Ústica, Naples, Cágliari (Sardinia), and Tunis and Kelibia in Tunisia; see "Listings" (p.342) for ticket office addresses and "Travel details" for full schedules. Trápani's **airport** (☎0923.549.824), incidentally, has connecting flights to the major Italian cities and Pantelleria, and is 15km south of the city at Birgi, from which you can catch connecting AST buses into the centre.

The **old town**'s narrow and irregular layout occupies around a square kilometre at Trápani's western end, centred on the main **Corso Vittorio Emanuele**, which is around a fifteen-minute walk from the train station. Everything in the old town is easily reachable on foot, though you'll need to catch a **city bus** (#24, #25 or #30) to visit Trápani's museum in the new part of the city: all routes start and finish their journeys at Piazza Generale Scio, at the western end of Corso Vittorio Emanuele. Tickets are L1000, available from *tabacchi*, and are valid for one hour.

For well-produced information written in good English, accommodation listings and free maps, the helpful **tourist office** is at Piazzetta Saturno in the old town (Mon–Sat 8am–8pm, Sun 9am–noon, summer 9am–1pm; ☎0923.29.000 or 0923.29.004); there's an office at the airport too.

Accommodation

Outside the Easter period, finding somewhere to stay is no problem; start with the list opposite or consult the tourist office.

ACCOMMODATION PRICE CODES

These represent the **cheapest available double room in high season**, usually – but not always – without en-suite bathroom or shower. Out of season, you'll often be able to negotiate a lower price than those suggested here. For more information about hotels and room prices, see p.27. The categories are:

① under L60,000	④ L120,000–150,000	⑦ L250,000–300,000
② L60,000–90,000	⑤ L150,000–200,000	⑧ over L300,000
③ L90,000–120,000	⑥ L200,000–250,000	

Hotels

Cavallino Bianco, Lungomare Dante Alighieri (☎0923.21.549). Out of the centre on the lungomare, but a nice place with rooms overlooking the sea. Prices drop by fifteen percent outside July and August. ④.

Maccotta, Via degli Argentieri 4 (☎0923.28.418). Visible off Piazza Sant'Agostino, this has nice, fairly modern rooms and is clean and friendly. ②.

Messina, Corso Vittorio Emanuele 71 (☎0923.21.198). The popular *Messina* occupies the first floor of the eighteenth-century Palazzo Bernardo Ferro, entered through a grand courtyard. The rooms are less impressive and somewhat down at heel, despite a lick of paint, and service is by remote control, but it's the cheapest option in the city. Book ahead if you can. No credit cards. ①.

Moderno, Via Ten. Genovese 20 (☎0923.21.247). As you might imagine, it's no such thing, though it does have more character than the others. It's one block north of the corso. ②.

Nuovo Russo, Via Tintori 4 (☎0923.22.166). Just off the corso, at the bottom end, these are fancier central lodgings, recently renovated, with rooms with and without bath. No credit cards. ②.

Hostel and campsite

Lido Valdérice, Località Cortigliolo (☎0923.573.086). The nearest campsite to Trápani, a 20min bus ride north – five to seven buses daily from the bus terminal. May–Sept.

Ostello per la Gioventù, Contrada Raganzili (☎0923.552.964). Hidden away 3km to 4km out of town, this hostel is not the easiest place to reach under your own steam, nor is it particularly cheap, at L19,000 per bed. Take bus #23 from Via Fardella, three blocks right of the station, and ask to be let off at the Ospedale Villa dei Gerani, a 15min ride; from the stop, take the second on the right and walk 600m uphill. The hostel opens at 6pm. Drivers should take the road to Valdérice and follow signs. There's another hostel outside Érice itself, open summer only and then often fully booked (see p.344).

The City

Corso Vittorio Emanuele, the **old town**'s pedestrianized main street, is dominated at its eastern end by the pinkish marble front of the **Palazzo del Municipio**, the seventeenth-century town hall. It adds a touch of grandeur to the thin promenading strip, otherwise hemmed in by balconied *palazzi*, a couple of Baroque churches, and the **Cattedrale** on the right, with its Baroque portico, cupolas and vast interior. Inside there's a *Crucifixion*, attributed to Van Dyck.

The corso runs to the very tip of the curving promontory from which the town took its Phoenician name of Drepanon (sickle), ending at the seventeenth-century **Torre di Ligny**, an old Spanish fortification whose squat tower has been reconditioned to hold Trápani's collection of prehistoric finds, the **Museo Cívico di Preistoria** (Jan–March Mon, Wed & Fri 9.30am–12.30pm, Tues & Thurs 9.30am–13.30pm & 3–5.30pm, Sat & Sun 9.30am–13.30pm & 4.30–7pm; April–Dec daily 9.30am–12.30pm & 4.30pm–7pm; L2000). It's a surprisingly interesting museum, the two floors holding a quantity of Neanderthal human skulls and bones, fossils, elephant tusks, animal and mineral fragments (including lions' and hippos' teeth), as well as photographs of drawings from the Grotta del Genovese on the island of Lévanzo (see p.352).

Other sights in Trápani's old town are scattered around the maze of streets on the east side of **Via Torrearsa**, back towards the train station. Take time first to walk up to the northern end of Via Torrearsa itself, where there's a good daily **market**: fish, fruit and vegetables are sold from the arcaded Piazza Mercato di Pesce – it's all over by the early afternoon.

Back in the centre of the old town, on Piazzetta Saturno, the church of **Sant'Agostino** (adjacent to the tourist office) has a pretty fourteenth-century rose window of interlocking stone bands; the church is occasionally used as a concert hall (details of performances from the tourist office). Architecturally more appealing is the sixteenth-century church of **Santa Maria di Gesù** (at present undergoing restoration), in Via San Pietro to the east, whose two doors display a diversity characteristic of the town, the right-hand one Gothic, the other defiantly Renaissance, and there's a good relief in the architrave. Step inside, and at the end of the nave there's a terracotta *Madonna degli Ángeli* by Andrea della Robbia, sheltered beneath a graceful marble canopy carved by Antonello Gagini.

There's little more to see in this part of town apart from a few unusual facades, one of them buried in the wedge of hairline streets and alleys north of Corso Italia, at Via della Giudecca 43, where the sixteenth-century **Palazzo della Giudecca** sports a plaque-studded front and some Spanish-style Plateresque windows. The building lies at the heart of Trápani's old **Jewish quarter**, an area dating from Trápani's medieval heyday at the centre of Mediterranean trade.

The Misteri

Trápani's most rewarding church is the **Chiesa del Purgatorio** (Tues 10am–noon, Fri & Lent 10am–noon & 4–7pm), on Via Generale Domenico Giglio, south of the main corso and close to the port. It is the home of the **Misteri**, extraordinary life-size wooden statues depicting scenes from the Passion. Sculpted from cypress wood and cork in the eighteenth century, each of the twenty groups of chocolate-brown figures is associated with one of the town's trades – fishermen, saltworkers, etc – whose representatives undertake to maintain them and, draped in cowls and purple robes, carry them shoulder-high every Good Friday through Trápani's streets. It's one of Sicily's most evocative religious processions, held since the seventeenth century. In *On Persephone's Island*, Mary Taylor Simeti notes how "The procession starts at three in the afternoon and continues, with a brief pause for mass at eight in the evening, until eight the next morning, threading endlessly through the broad avenues and narrow alleyways of the city, changing in character and growing in emotional intensity as the day wears on."

In the church, there's usually a priest around to explain which of the trades are responsible for each of the sculpted groups, and what the particular figures represent – though most of the scenes are familiar enough.

The Santuario dell'Annunziata and the Museo Regionale Pépoli

The only incentive to set foot in the **modern city** is to visit Trápani's most lavishly decorated monument, the **Santuario dell'Annunziata** (daily: summer 7am–noon & 4–8pm; winter 7.30am–noon & 4–7pm; free), a fourteenth-century convent and church whose cloisters also incorporate the town's main museum. Take bus #24, #25 or #30 from Piazza Generale Scio, Corso Vittorio Emanuele, Via Libertà or Via Garibaldi; get off at the park, **Villa Pépoli**, which is just in front of the building.

The sanctuary was rebuilt in 1760 and only the facade, with its Gothic portal and magnificent rose window, is original. Inside (entrance on Via Pépoli), there are a series of sumptuous **chapels**, two dedicated to Trápani's fishermen and seamen – one echoing the facade's shell motif around the sides of the room – and, best of all, the **Cappella della Madonna**, containing Trápani's sacred idol: the beautiful smiling *Madonna and Child*, attributed to Nino Pisano in the fourteenth century. Responsible for a host of miracles, the statue is housed under a grandiose marble canopy sculpted by Antonello Gagini and surrounded by polychrome marble – and generally by a crowd of hushed worshippers.

The **Museo Regionale Pépoli** (Mon–Sat 9am–1.30pm, Sun 9am–12.30pm, plus Tues & Thurs 3–6.30pm; L8000) is adjacent, entered through the Villa Pépoli. Although the museum was designed by one of Italy's foremost architects in the field, it's equipped with abysmal lighting, since it was intended that the exhibits should be seen in full daylight, so come early, preferably in the morning. The wide-ranging collection takes in everything from exemplary Gagini statuary to seventeenth-century coral craftwork. Highlights downstairs include a little-bronze horse and rider by Giacomo Serpotta and a sixteenth-century marble doorway by Berrettaro Bartolomeu, taken from the old church of San Giuliano, which though badly worn in parts displays a lively series of tableaux. Downstairs, too, bizarrely, is a grim wooden guillotine from 1789 with a basket for the head, and a coffin at the ready. The museum houses a good medieval art section – including a powerful *Pietà* by Roberto Oderisio, and a couple of fine fifteenth-century triptychs by the anonymous *Maestro del Políttico di Trápani* (presently under restoration). Other displays include a coin collection, with Greek, Roman, Arab and Italian examples (though this is currently closed for restoration); an eighteenth-century majolica-tiled scene of La Mattanza (tuna slaughter; see p.350), with the fishermen depicted corralling the fish in their boats; a small archeological section with a few finds from Selinunte and Mozia, though nothing outstanding; some intricate coral work, including crib scenes with alabaster and shell decoration, some embroidered altar facings; one of the last rooms has a seventeenth-century map of Trápani showing the harbour to the left, saltpans to the right, and now mostly disappeared buildings in the middle.

Eating and drinking

Eating out in Trápani is one of the city's better attractions. You can get fresh fish and couscous almost everywhere, while the local pasta speciality, *spaghetti alla Trapanese*, is also on most menus – spaghetti served with cold, puréed fresh tomato sauce flavoured with garlic and basil. There are quite a few lively **bars** around, too, good for breakfast and snacks and bustling at night with people stopping off from the rowdy *passeggiata* that fills Via Torrearsa and the bottom end of the corso. The daily **market** is at the northern end of Via Torrearsa. For an explanation of the restaurant price categories, see p.32.

Restaurants

Da Bettina, Via San Christofero 5. Fabulous fish place, just off the Via A. Staiti, not far from *Trattoria del Porto*. Moderate–expensive. Closed Wed.

Calvino, Via N. Nasi 79. An excellent back-street pizzeria, parallel to the corso, the Calvino has some cubbyhole rooms at the back where you can eat superb hot pizza on squares of greaseproof paper, washed down with cold beer. Try the *Rianata*, made with fresh oregano, tomato, garlic, anchovies and pecorino cheese – a local speciality. Inexpensive. No credit cards. Closed Tues.

Cantina Siciliana, Via Giudecca 32. In what was once the old Jewish quarter, this old-town restaurant serves reasonably priced, traditional Sicilian food as well as a fish couscous. Moderate. No credit cards. Closed Mon.

Ai Lumi, Via Emanuele, next to the hotel *Messina*. Specializes in food from the inland countryside, so no fish, but popular with locals. Moderate. No credit cards. Closed Sun & July.

P&G, Via Spalti 1. Close to the station, this rather smart restaurant lays on a fine antipasto selection and good fresh fish or grilled meats. Try the garlicky *spaghetti alla Trápanese*, or *busiate*, a home-made pasta. Moderate–expensive. Closed Sun.

Taverna Paradiso, Via Dante Alighieri 22 (☎0923.22.303). Away from the port along the lungomare, so good for quiet sea ambience. Try the tuna caviar or the noodles with almonds and pine nuts. Expensive. Closed Sun & Aug.

Da Peppe, Via Spalti 52. Locally regarded trattoria on the same strip as *P&G*, with an indoor fountain and a good variety of vegetarian dishes; also specializes in fish, including fish coucous. There's a long list of Sicilian wines too. Moderate–expensive. Closed Mon.

Pizzeria Mediterranea, Corso Vittorio Emanuele 195. Opposite Piazza Jolanda, this is primarily a takeaway joint with a couple of tables at the back (sitting down you'll pay an extra fifteen percent). Again, the *Rianata* is excellent. Tables outside in the square as well. Inexpensive. No credit cards. Closed Thurs.

Trattoria del Porto, Via A. Staiti 45. Family-run trattoria (also known locally as *Da Felice*) opposite the port with booming TV and a succession of large cooks bustling through the dining room to get at the fish cabinet. If you're happy to forgo fish, there's a very good-value *menu turístico* at L25,000; the local wine is rough but cheap. Moderate.

Trattoria Safina, Piazza Umberto I. Opposite the train station, the *Safina* serves abundant portions of pasta, meat, fish and couscous – probably the best bargain in town. Inexpensive. Closed Sun.

Bars, birrerias and cafés

Colicchia, at the corner of Via delle Belle Arti and Via Carosio, just off Via Torrearsa. Fine bar-*pasticceria* with a super array of cakes; a good place to sit and sample a *granita*.

Gino's, Piazza Garibaldi. Make a beeline here for good ice-cream – it's usually bulging with customers. In season you can buy wild strawberries here, too. Closed Wed.

Birreria Italia, Via Torrearsa 5–7. One of several bars at this end of town, the boisterous *Italia* has a couple of dozen types of bottled beer and good snacks and cakes. Closed Sun.

Passa a Taglio, Via Torrearsa 16. Pizza by the slice to take away – with thirty different varieties from which to choose.

Piccadilly, Via Torrearsa 19. Superior bar-*pasticceria* with the best-placed outdoor seats at *passeggiata* time.

Poldo, Piazza Gen. Alberto della Chiesa 9. A noisy *birreria* and *panineria*, busy at night, serving good hot sandwiches and big mugs of beer.

Listings

Air tickets For flights to Pantelleria and the mainland from Agenzia Salvo, Corso Italia 48, (☎0923.545.411); note that they offer their customers a free bus service to the airport.

Banks Banca Populare S. Angelo, Piazza Umberto I 45; Banca di Roma, Corso Italia 38.

Buses Autoservizi Segesta (☎0923.20.066), from Piazza Garibaldi (for Palermo); AST (☎0923.21.021), from Piazza Malta (for destinations within the province, including Érice, Marsala, Mazara del Vallo, Castelvetrano, Gibellina, San Vito Lo Capo, Salemi, Valderice and the airport); S. Lumia (☎0922.20.414), from Piazza Malta (for Agrigento and Sciacca); Tarantola (☎0924.31.024), from Piazza Malta (for Segesta).

Car problems ACI at Via Virgilio 75 (☎0923.27.292).

Car rental Rizzo, Via Passo Enea 38 (☎0923.22.177); Sicily By Car, Via Passo Enea 30 (☎0923.27.251) and airport (☎0923.842.200).

Ferry tickets From offices at the port, Molo di Sanità, or the following agencies: Siremar, Via A. Staiti 61–63 (☎0923.540.515), for the Égadi Islands, Pantelleria and Tunis; Tirrenia, Salvo Viaggi, Corso Italia 48 (☎0923.21.896), for Cágliari and Tunis; Traghetti delle Isole, Via A. Staiti 23 (☎0923.22.467), for the Égadi Islands.

Garages Berretta, Via La Bassi 93, in the new town; Bulgarella, Via Mazzini 17; Serse, Via Passo Enea 30.

Hospital At Via Cosenza (☎0923.809.111); 24hr emergency first aid ☎0923.809.450.

Hydrofoil tickets From offices at the port, Molo di Sanità: Alilauro, Molo di Sanità (☎0923.24.073), for the Égadi Islands; SNAV, Molo di Sanità (☎0923.872.299), for Favignana, Pantelleria, Ústica, Naples and Kelibia (Tunisia); Siremar, Via A. Staiti 63 (☎0923.540.515), for the Égadi Islands; Ústica Lines, Via A. Staiti 31(☎0923.22.200), for the Égadi Islands, Naples, Pantelleria, and Kelibia and Sousse (both Tunisia).

Pharmacy Bianchi, Via Torrearsa 25.

Police Questura at Via Virgilio (☎0923.29.540).

Post office At Piazza Vittorio Véneto, at the bottom of Via Garibaldi. Mon–Fri 8am–7pm, Sat 8am–1pm.

Supermarket Standa, Via Libertà 12.

Taxis Ranks at Piazza Umberto (☎0923.22.808) and Via Ammiraglio Staiti, at the hydrofoil dock (☎0923.23.233).

Telephones Telecom Italia, Via Agostino Pépoli 82, near the Museo Pépoli. Daily 9am–12.30pm & 4.30–8pm.

Travel agent Egatour Viaggi, Via Ammiraglio Staiti 13, Trápani (☎0923.21.754), for information and tickets for getting to Pantelleria; see also Agenzia Salvo, under "Air tickets", opposite.

Érice

Although only a forty-minute bus ride away from Trápani, **ÉRICE** couldn't be further away in spirit. It's a walled mountain town with powerful associations, thoroughly medieval with its creeping hillside alleys, grey stone buildings and silent charm. Founded by Elymians, who claimed descent from the Trojans, the city was known to the ancient world as Eryx, and a magnificent temple, dedicated to Aphrodite Erycina, Mediterranean goddess of fertility, once topped the mountain and was big enough to act as a landmark to sailors. According to legend, it was here that Daedalus landed, unlike his son Icarus who flew too near the sun, after fleeing from Minos; he presented the temple with a honeycomb made of gold as his gift to the goddess. Even though the city was considered impregnable, Carthaginian, Roman, Arab and Norman forces all forced entry over the centuries, but all respected the town's sanctity, the Romans rebuilding the temple and setting two hundred soldiers to serve as guardians of the shrine. Later, the Arabs renamed the town Gebel-Hamed, "Mohammed's mountain", while Count Roger called it Monte San Giuliano, a name that stuck until Mussolini returned its ancient moniker in 1934. Nowadays it's a centre for scientific conferences, and you're as likely to see as many foreigners with labels on their lapels as you are tourists.

The only blots in the town's otherwise homogeneous aspect are twentieth-century ones: the pylons towering above the grey walls and the busloads of tourists that regularly visit during the summer – though, as people have always come to Érice to sightsee and worship, it seems churlish to resent these. In any case, there's little specific to see in town, and enough cobbled alleys and quiet spots to enable you to avoid the tour groups; and as long as the mist keeps off, the **views** from Érice's terraces are superb, taking in Trápani, the slumbering whales of the Égadi Islands and even (allegedly) distant Cape Bon in Tunisia. Scout around the town at random: the most convoluted of routes is only going to take a couple of hours and every street and piazza is a delight.

You enter through the Norman **Porta Trápani**, at the southwestern edge of town: just inside is the battlemented fourteenth-century campanile of the battered, stone **Duomo** (daily 10am–noon & 3–6pm), which did service as a lookout

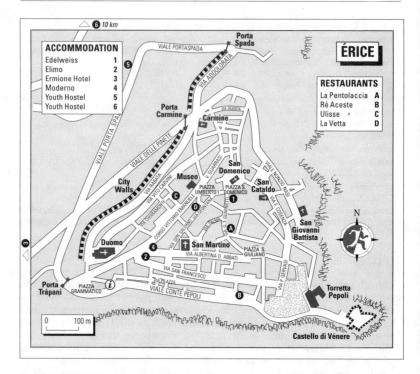

△ 6 10 km

ÉRICE

ACCOMMODATION

Edelweiss	1
Elimo	2
Ermione Hotel	3
Moderno	4
Youth Hostel	5
Youth Hostel	6

RESTAURANTS

La Pentolaccia	A
Ré Aceste	B
Ulisse	C
La Vetta	D

tower for Frederick III of Aragon. From here the main Corso Vittorio Emanuele leads up to the pretty **Piazza Umberto**, with its couple of outdoor bars and the small **Museo Comunale** (Mon–Sat 8.30am–1.30pm, Sun 9am–noon; free), whose main piece is a good *Annunciation* by Antonello Gagini on the ground floor. Further north, the medieval **Porta Carmine** marks the other end of town; from here you can follow the line of the ancient city walls back to the duomo.

Heading east from the Porta Trápani, along Viale Conte Pepoli, you'll eventually come to the ivy-clad, twelfth-century **Castello di Vénere** (daily 8am–2pm & 3–6.30pm; leave a tip under the stone), built on the site of the famed ancient temple of Aphrodite, chunks of which are incorporated into the walls. The castle is built on the most precarious of crags, offering grand views in all directions, while stuck in the middle of the public garden below is a restored fifteenth-century tower, the **Torretta Pepoli**, lived in until the turn of this century.

Arrival and accommodation

Buses from Trápani pull up at the top of Viale Conte Pépoli: walk a few metres down and you'll come to the helpful **tourist office** (June to mid-July & Sept Mon–Sat 8am–2pm, Sun 9am–noon; mid-July to Aug Mon–Sat 8am–2pm & 4–8pm, Sun 9am–noon; Oct–May Mon–Sat 8am–2pm; ☎0923.869.388). If you want to stay in Érice you're probably going to have to pay through the nose and – in summer, or at Easter and Christmas – you'd do well to book in advance. There's a **youth hostel**, at Viale delle Pinete (☎0923.869.144; L20,000 per person), outside the town walls, though this is only open from July to September, and then often booked up by groups, so check first. There's another hostel, open all year, but about 10km further down, so it's not very useful for seeing Érice (see Trápani "Accommodation", p.339).

The least expensive **hotel** is the *Edelweiss*, Cortile Padre Vincenzo (☎0923.869.158 or 0923.869.420; ④), its modern rooms all with bath/shower; it's tucked up a cobbled alley off quiet and central Piazzetta San Domenico. The other two central hotels are both on the main Corso Vittorio Emanuele and rather smarter: the *Elimo* (☎0923.869.377, fax 0923.869.252; ⑥) and the *Moderno* (☎0923.869.300, fax 0923.869.139; ⑤); the *Elimo* is the nicer of the two, and only marginally dearer. If you don't mind staying a few minutes outside town, and you can bear the 1960s architecture, try also the *Ermione* (☎0923.869.138, fax 0923.869.587; ④), at the end of a drive through woods a few minutes' walk below the Porta Trápani. Prices drop outside high season, and the views over Trápani and the islands are magnificent.

Eating

Érice's vastly inflated prices mean that on a day-trip you could do a lot worse than bring your own **picnic**, or there's a *panineria* on Corso Vittorio Emanuele. On the same street, at no. 14, Pasticceria Maria is a speciality **cake shop** selling marzipan fruits, *amaretti* and the like – worth at least pressing your nose against the window.

Some of the **restaurants** do have tourist menus: try *La Pentolaccia*, Via Guarnotti 17 (closed Tues), housed in an old monastery and moderately priced; or the cheaper *La Vetta* – also called *Da Mario* – in Via G. Fontana (closed Thurs), signposted off Piazza Umberto, which does evening pizzas and a good couscous. Slightly more expensive, but worth it, is *Ulisse*, Via Chiaramonte 45 (closed winter & Thurs), reached down the stepped Vico San Rocco, just off the main square. This also has pizzas and full restaurant menu. There are moderately priced meals, too, at the friendly *Ré Aceste*, Viale Conte Pépoli 45 (closed Wed & Nov), which is close to the bus-stop on the road outside the walls and has a terrace overlooking the plain below.

Segesta

Around 30km east of Trápani, in deserted green countryside, are the remains of the ancient city of **SEGESTA** (daily 9am–1hr before sunset; L4000), among the most inspiring on the island. All that still stands is a Doric temple and a brilliantly sited theatre, relics of a city whose roots – like Érice's – lay back in the twelfth century BC. Unlike Érice, though, ancient Segesta was eventually Hellenized and spent most of the later period disputing its border with Selinus (see p.362). The temple dates from a time of prosperous alliance with Athens, but it was never finished – work on it being abandoned when a new dispute broke out with Selinus in 416 BC.

The **temple** itself, started in 424 BC, crowns a low hill, beyond the café and car park. From a distance you could be forgiven for thinking that it's complete: the 36 regular stone columns, entablature and pediment are all intact, and all it lacks is a roof. However, get closer (and for once you're allowed to roam right inside) and you see just how unfinished the building is: stone studs, always removed on completion, still line the stylobate, the tall columns are unfluted and the cella walls are missing. In a way, this only adds to the natural grandeur of the site, and it's not too fanciful to imagine that the temple simply grew here – a feeling bolstered by the birds nesting in the unfinished capitals, the lizards scampering over the pale yellow stone, and the pitted and sun-bleached interior.

Below the car park, a road winds up through slopes of wild fennel to a small **theatre** on a higher hill beyond; if you don't relish the twenty-minute walk – and it's a killer in the heat – you can use the half-hourly summer minibus service (L2000 return). The view from the top is terrific, across green slopes and the plain to the sea, the deep blue of the bay a lovely contrast to the theatre's white stone – the panorama not much damaged by the motorway snaking away below. In odd-numbered years, productions of classical and contemporary **plays** are staged here in the summer: ask at the tourist offices in Palermo and Trápani for details of these and the excursion buses that leave from both cities to carry people to and from the performances.

Practicalities

Coming from Trápani by car, the easiest way to Segesta is along the A29 autostrada. If you don't have your own transport, take one of the four buses a day from Piazza Malta in Trápani, which leave at 8am and 10am, the last one returning shortly after 6pm. Other options all require some walking, though there's nothing off-putting: the **train** from Trápani to Álcamo/Palermo makes a stop at Segesta-Tempio (departing at 12.35pm and arriving at 1pm); it's a twenty-minute walk uphill, the temple up on the right. To return, you'll have to walk from the site car park to the train station of Calatafimi (see below), signposted 4km to the east, from where there are trains back to Trápani roughly every two hours throughout the day.

You can also reach Segesta **from Palermo**. One **train** (departing 7am) stops at Segesta-Tempio, a two-hour ride, returning at 1pm; or there are three daily **buses** from Palermo to Calatafimi (run by Autoservizi Drepanum from Piazza Marina), which pass near the site, also a two-hour journey.

Calatafimi

The small town of **CALATAFIMI** is 4km south of its train station; coming by bus, there are four services daily here from Trápani. This was the site of the first of Garibaldi's victories against the Bourbon forces in 1860, which opened the way to Palermo and hence the rest of Sicily. The battle took place on the Salemi road, around 4km south of Calatafimi, on a hill-top marked by a monument. There are a couple of cheap **hotels** in Calatafimi, most central the *Mille Pini*, Piazza F. Vivona 2 (☎0924.951.260; ①) – a lovely, modern place with good views, and handy if you fancy a night in these quiet surroundings.

North to San Vito Lo Capo

The coastline **north of Trápani** is mainly a rugged, sparsely populated strip, not really suitable for swimming, though making for an attractive bus ride out of the city. The road weaves under some of the gigantic outcrops of rock characteristic of Sicily's west, most spectacular of which is **Monte Cófano** (859m). The village of **CUSTONACI**, 20km from Trápani, nestles under here, slightly inland, famous as a marble-cutting centre and with a smart seaside area lower down on the coast, sprinkled with resort facilities.

The road plunges east and inland here, to re-emerge beside sparkling clear water and more rocky beaches leading up to the resort of San Vito Lo Capo, 40km from Trápani.

San Vito Lo Capo

With its dense ranks of trattorias, hotels and bars, **SAN VITO LO CAPO** is geared to consumers, yet its comparative remoteness has helped to stave off the worst pressures of the tourist industry, even in high season; in winter you won't find a soul. It's a small town, clustered around one of Sicily's finest sand **beaches** – a wide, curving stretch of white sand – framed by the looming cliffs behind and overlooked by jagged slabs of rock. The visitors here are mainly Italian.

San Vito is really just one long shop- and restaurant-lined main strip, **Via Savoia**, which runs away at right angles from the beach; at no. 57 is the small Museo del Mare (Mon–Sat 9am–1pm & 5–7pm; free), though the marine exhibits inside won't grab your attention. A pleasant promenade backs the beach which stretches to the east of town, while in the other direction, past the harbour, it's a twenty-minute walk to the point of **Capo San Vito** itself – a rocky and windswept plain adorned with a fenced-off lighthouse. For views you need to climb above the town (bear left on the way out to the lighthouse), up a steep road leading to the top of the high cliffs and looking down over the Golfo di Castellammare. The other local walk is east to the Riserva Naturale dello Zíngaro, a nature reserve, and a much tougher hike, covered in more detail below.

Arrival and information

Regular daily **buses** run up from Trápani's bus terminal to San Vito Lo Capo, stopping on Via P. Matarella, close to the seafront; the central Via Savoia is three blocks to the right. The last bus back to Trápani leaves at 9.30pm; or you can move on **to Palermo** on the Russo line, buses leaving from San Vito four times daily, and twice on Sundays. The stop for the Palermo bus is next to the church on Via Savoia.

The **tourist office**, in the Museo del Mare, Via Savoia 57 (Mon–Sat 9am–1pm & 5–7pm; ☎0923.972.464), can give information about fishing trips and excursions to Érice and Segesta; they can also help with boat trips to the Riserva Naturale dello Zíngaro (L15,000), Scopello (L28,000 return) and Ústica (L35,000 return) on the *Leonardo da Vinci* and the *Princess* (or contact either directly on ☎0924.34.222). The Commerciale Italiana **bank**, Via Savoia 80, opposite the church, will change travellers' cheques.

Accommodation

Accommodation is plentiful, with most options on and around Via Savoia; though, as with all resorts, the nearer the sea, the more expensive it becomes. There are **rooms to rent** as well, with a clutch of places on Via Mulino – a 500-metre walk from the seafront down Via Savoia, past the Municipio, and on the left. In winter, you're unlikely to find many places open; ask around the bars in the centre.

There are several **campsites** in the area: one of these is very plush, *El Bahira* (☎0923.972.577; April–Sept), 4km south of town, and charges accordingly. The others are more modest and more central: *La Fata*, Via P. Matarella (☎0923.972.133), and *Soleado*, Via della Secca (☎0923.972.166). *La Pineta* (☎0923.972.818) is twenty minutes' walk from town along the seafront (towards

Scopello); here, there's also a bar, pizzeria and rooms to rent. The "No camping" signs on the town beach should be heeded.

Bougainvillea, Via Mulino 51 (☎0923.972.207). Quite a walk from the beach, but a friendly place with climbing plants, decent rooms and a spiral staircase leading to a roof terrace. Cheaper outside high season by L10,000. No credit cards. April–Oct. ②.

Hotel Capo San Vito, Via S. Vito 3 (☎0923.972.284, fax 0923.972.559). Right on the beach, at the end of Via Savoia, this comfortable three-star hotel also has a terrace restaurant. April–Oct. ⑤.

Pensione Costa Gaia, Via Savoia 123 (☎0923.972.268). A good, central first choice, though with only eight rooms it fills quickly. No credit cards. ②.

Eden, Via Mulino 49 (☎0923.972.460). Close to the *Bougainvillea*, with very friendly service. The rooms are clean, and cool in summer; you share a bathroom. No credit cards. ①.

Hotel Miraspiaggia, Via Lungomare 44 (☎0923.972.355). The cheapest hotel on the lungomare, you get decent sea views and a bar-restaurant for your money. Easter–Nov. ②.

Pensione Sabbia d'Oro, Via Santuario 49 (☎0923.972.508). Close to the beach, the spacious rooms are nicely furnished; the separate bathrooms are roomy and with plenty of hot water. The street is behind the church, parallel to the sea. ②.

Eating and drinking

Via Savoia and the lungomare are lined with possibilities: bars, ice-cream parlours, pizzerias and swish restaurants. Most stay open throughout the winter too. There's an explanation of the restaurant price categories on p.32.

Bar Cusenza, Via Savoia, beside the church. Best place for breakfast, with outdoor tables in the square, and good cakes and pastries. Inexpensive.

Al Faro, Via Faro. 10min walk from the centre, by the harbour, on the road to the lighthouse, *Al Faro* overlooks the water and is a real gem. Without a menu being produced, half a dozen tapas-style fish and shellfish dishes are served, followed by seafood spaghetti, risotto and couscous, followed by yet more fresh fish. The meal comes with wine and water, and costs L50,000 a head for an amazing feast. Expensive. Open daily July & Aug and at weekends March–June, Sept & Oct.

Da Peppe, Via Savoia 13. A pizzeria-trattoria on the main street with smoked-fish antipasti, fresh, home-made pasta and a short list of decent pizzas. Inexpensive.

Santareddu, Piazza Marinella 3 (☎0923.974.350). Small, blue and cluttered, this is popular with locals and always busy. The antipasti are overflowing and the fish is good. Booking essential. Closed Wed.

Thaam, Via Duca degli Abruzzi 32–36 (☎0923.972.836). Elaborately decorated restaurant with a marked Tunisian influence – *merguez* and couscous alongside more mainstream dishes. Moderate. Booking advised in summer.

Getting to Zíngaro

The **northern entrance** to the isolated **Riserva Naturale dello Zíngaro** (for full details, see p.335) is 11km southeast of San Vito. Accessible by your own transport or on a day-trip from San Vito Lo Capo (see p.347), it's also a fine walk, initially following the road along the lungomare from San Vito and across the flat headland, before winding up into the mountains. In the higher reaches, the views are exhilarating, with the surrounding scenery almost alpine in character – fir trees, flowers flanking the road, and the clank of bells from goats roaming the hillsides. It's a secluded and dramatic landscape, though sadly with few opportunities for descending from the road to the alluringly deserted coves below.

The **access road** to the reserve is signposted just before the ruined Torre dell'Impiso, around a three-hour walk from San Vito. From the sign to the park entrance itself is about another 1km, following a gravel track and then a path, which runs down into the reserve, past the Tonnara dell'Uzzo. At the San Vito **entrance** there's a car park, hiking information, a beautiful little cove-beach below, translucent water, and glorious peace and quiet all around.

Various well-marked **trails** run through the reserve, with water taps and shelter periodically available. Scopello (see p.334) is a ten-kilometre walk south from the San Vito entrance, though hikers should note that there are no shops, bars or restaurants along the road from San Vito, at the park entrance or in the park itself: take all your own supplies – and take away all the empties.

The Égadi Islands

Moored off the western coast, the three **Égadi Islands** (Isole Égadi) are the easiest of Sicily's offshore islands to visit – something that accounts for the summer crowds swarming over Favignana, the nearest of the Égadis to the Sicilian mainland. The other islands are much less affected, however, and if you come out of season things are noticeably quieter everywhere.

Before the advent of tourism, the economic success of the islands was largely based on a historical relationship with the north Italian city of Genova, whose sailors plied the trading routes on which the Égadis stood throughout the Middle Ages; the seal was formalized in the middle of the seventeenth century, when the Bourbon king Philip IV sold all the islands, in lieu of a debt, to Genovese businessmen. Then, as now, the major element in the local economy was the tuna fish, which congregate here to breed at the end of spring. Channelled through the straits between the two main islands during their migrations around the Sicilian coast, they are systematically slaughtered in an age-old rite known as **La Mattanza**, which has been transformed into a rather obscene tourist attraction.

Favignana, the biggest island and site of the main fishery, is only 25 minutes away from Trápani by hydrofoil. The Genovese link is most apparent in the island of **Lévanzo**, across the strait, which is named after a quarter in the city of Genova and shelters the **Grotta del Genovese**, a cave in which a rich bounty of prehistoric cave paintings was discovered. These days, with the annual tourist influx, the greatest hope for peace and quiet lies in the furthest island, **Maréttimo**, whose rugged coasts are indented with a succession of coves, ideal for clean and secluded swimming. The island also offers a choice of easy **hikes** across its interior and along the rocky coasts.

You could easily see any of the islands as a **day-trip** from Trápani; seeing two on the same day is fairly simple too. If you want to stay longer, be warned that **accommodation** is extremely limited and in summer you should phone ahead to reserve a room. It's certainly worth staying over, though you should also bear in mind that, in general, **prices** for rooms and food are higher than on the mainland.

Getting there
Ferries and hydrofoils depart several times daily from Trápani, and are more frequent between June and September. They generally call at Favignana, Lévanzo and Maréttimo, in that order; the return journey is in reverse, though there are occasional exceptions, and sometimes services don't run as far as Maréttimo. Ferries and hydrofoils **depart** from the terminal in Trápani at Molo di Sanità; buy **tickets** from the agencies mentioned in Trápani's "Listings" (p.342), or else at a booth on the dockside. Ferries are less frequent and take around twice as long as

the hydrofoils, but they're roughly half the price: one-way ferry tickets to Favignana and Lévanzo cost around L6000, and to Maréttimo around L13,000; one-way hydrofoil tickets are around L11,000 and L22,000 respectively; low-season prices are slightly cheaper; all return tickets cost exactly twice as much. See "Travel details" (p.378) for frequencies and journey times.

Favignana

The main island, **FAVIGNANA**, has progressed over the years from prison to tuna centre, and now tourist resort. Looking like a lopsided butterfly, the island is almost split in two, its narrow "waist" holding the port and most of the island's population. To the east are Favignana's best swimming spots, the water accessible from a succession of rocks and inlets, while the western half of the island is only reachable along the southern coastal road and consists mainly of the island's one hill, Monte Santa Caterina (300m). Its peak is occupied by the fortified prison (belonging to the military, and off limits), while Favignana's main tuna fishery is at its base, looking across to the port on the other side of the bay.

The port, **FAVIGNANA TOWN**, is the first stop for ferries and hydrofoils from Trápani, and, as the archipelago's only town, is the focus of most of the tourist traffic. It holds the island's only reasonably priced hotels and various bars and trattorias, but otherwise there's no particular reason to hang around. The town's only distinctive feature is the imposing building near the port, the **Palazzo Florio**. Now the town hall, this was built by Ignazio Florio, an entrepreneur who took over the islands in 1874 and revitalized the fisheries; there's a statue of him in nearby Piazza Europa. His tuna fishery, **Stabilimento Florio**, is similarly impressive, its vaulted nineteenth-century buildings a solid counterpoint across the bay.

The best way to **get around the island** is by bike (see opposite for rentals), since the flat terrain and good road surfaces enable you to see the whole island in an afternoon. It's tidily cultivated, pitted with square white houses built from tufa quarried from curious pits all over the island – an export that has historically provided Favignana with a second source of cash (after fishing).

You can swim at the beach near the town, where you might even see the local children taking their rabbits for a walk, but better is the sandy **beach** at **Cala Burrone**, on the island's south side; otherwise just follow the roads and plunge in off the rocks. Call in at **Cala Azzurra**, below the lighthouse at the island's eastern end, or, just north of here, **Cala Rossa**, whose name – Red Cove – is said to derive from the blood washed ashore after the Roman defeat of the Carthaginians in a fierce sea battle in 241 BC. The road to Cala Rossa in partic-

---

LA MATTANZA

If you're in Favignana in May or June, you may want to watch the bloody spectacle of **La Mattanza**, the slaughter of the local tuna catch. The killings take place two or three times a week, presided over by a *Rais* – a title handed down from the Arabs to indicate the fisherman in charge of the operation. The huge fish are surrounded, netted, impaled, dragged aboard and bludgeoned to death. Most of the meat is sold to the huge Japanese vessels that call in at fishing ports all over the Mediterranean; they transport the cargo back to Japan, where it's put into cans and re-exported back to Europe. For more details ask at the town's tourist office (p.351), or else the fishermen at the port will tell you if a slaughter is scheduled for the next morning.

ular is noted for its tufa quarries, like so many sunken gardens on either side of the road: just before the cove itself is a huge quarry with stacks of tufa and unexcavated pillars rising high from the gloomy depths. If you would like to tour the island's offshore grottoes **by boat**, contact the *Hotel Égadi* (see below), which can usually help.

Arrival, information and accommodation

From the port, you can see the dome of the church: aim for that and you'll reach the main square, Piazza Madrice, with the **tourist office** at no. 8 (Mon–Sat 9am–12.30pm & 4.30–8pm, Sun 9am–noon; ☎0923.921.647). Everything else is contained in the short streets between here and the nearby Piazza Europa, including several **bike-rental** shops – like Isidoro, at Via Mazzini 40: expect to pay about L5000–7000 a day. There's also a **travel agent** in Piazza Europa, and a **bank**, the Banca del Popolo, in Piazza Europa. The **ticket office** for ferries and hydrofoils is down at the port.

The best **hotel** choice is the small *Égadi*, Via Cristóforo Colombo 17 (☎ & fax 0923.921.232; no credit cards; ③; April–Oct), off Piazza Madrice, to the right of the church. Recently renovated, it's modern and comfortable, though you'd be advised to book well in advance here if you're coming in summer, when they're likely to slap an obligatory breakfast charge on your bill. Other possibilities include the slightly cheaper *Bougainvillea*, Via Cimabue 10 (☎0923.922.033; ②), and the plusher *Aegusa*, at Via Garibaldi 11 (☎0923.922.430, fax 0923.922.440; ④; April–Oct).

Campsites lie out of town, an easy walk and well signposted from the port: to the east, the *Camping Egad* (☎0923.921.555; two-berth cabin at L80,000; April–Sept), and, more expensive and much larger, the *Miramare* (☎0923.921.330; four-berth cabins at L26,000 per person; April–Oct), at Località Costicella to the west of town.

Eating and drinking

Piazza Madrice and the surrounding streets are where you'll find all Favignana's bars and **restaurants**. Most renowned is the *Ristorante Égadi*, inside the hotel of the same name, whose house speciality is a splendid *spaghetti all'Aragosta* (lobster spaghetti). Provided you steer clear of the pricier fish choices, it's moderately priced, but it is closed from November to February. The *Ristorante Rais*, Piazza Europa 8 (closed Tues), is a rather scruffy restaurant with fine (if overpriced) food; it remains open all year. Around the bay from the port, the *Nautilus*, Via Amendola 5, is an inexpensive trattoria, while *La Tavernetta*, opposite the church, is pretty and cool; there's no menu but the price is decent. The friendliest **bar** is the *Bar al' 81* on Piazza Madrice; not, as you might expect, at no. 81, but at 65, with indoor seating and large bottles of Messina beer. The *Bar Due Colonne*, nearby at no. 76, also provides good service and does a delicious carrot and lemon juice.

Lévanzo

The other Égadi Islands are remote and primitive after Favignana. **LÉVANZO**, 4km north, is the smallest of the three main islands, most of it used to pasture sheep and goats and, with its turquoise seas and white houses, having very much the feel of a Greek island. Its population is concentrated in **LÉVANZO TOWN**, little more than a cluster of houses around a tiny port, where you'll find the island's two hotels, a bar and a couple of restaurants.

You don't need to stay, though, to see Lévanzo's main attraction, its prehistoric cave paintings in the Grotta del Genovese. The coastline is rocky and largely inaccessible, but you can get around on foot by following the dirt paths along the shore and over the hills. Following the only road twenty minutes west of the port, you'll come to a rocky spire sticking out of the sea – the Faraglione – beyond which there's a rocky path north up the coast to the **Grotta del Genovese** itself. The cave is best approached, though, by following an inland route, shorter and prettier, along a path through the valley in the centre of the island. It's impossible to find on your own and, unless you can persuade one of the local kids in the port to guide you, you'll have to ask the official custodian, Signor Natale Castiglione, who lives at Via Calvario 11 (☎0923.924.032), near the hydrofoil quay. Rates are negotiable, depending on how many you are, and whether you go on foot or by jeep, but you shouldn't have to pay more than L20,000 each; the round-trip is roughly 10km and takes about two hours by jeep, one and a half by boat. Note that in winter tours generally take place only on weekends, and it's always best to telephone ahead.

The cave's walls display some remarkable Paleolithic **incised drawings**, discovered in 1949, as well as later Neolithic pictures; they're mostly of animals, between 6000 and 10,000 years old. Despite their age, the evocative drawings retain their impact, drawn by prehistoric man in an attempt to harness and influence the power of nature: one lovely picture of a deer, kept behind glass near the entrance, dates from when the island was still connected to the Sicilian mainland. The later Neolithic sketches are easy to pick out too; less well drawn, more stylized representations of men and even of tuna fish.

Many of the other grottoes on the island were once used by locals to hide from the corsairs who regularly called on raiding missions. To see the caves, you might bargain for a **boat rental** at the port; again, prices are very flexible. If you want to stretch your legs in the island's lovely **interior**, walk west along the road from the port (towards the Faraglione), turning right up the steep tarmacked road marked as the "Comunale Strada Capo Grosso". It becomes a stone and dirt track once it reaches the upper part of the valley and, if you keep to it, it's around an hour to the lighthouse at **Capo Grosso** at the northeastern point of the island. There's good swimming here, and your peace will only be disturbed by an occasional horse trotting by or the buzzing of passing hydrofoils (though this is less intrusive if you're on the north side of the point).

Practicalities

The port is just below the island's only road, Via Calvario; you can buy Siremar ferry and hydrofoil tickets either at the office at no. 31 or on the vessels and, for Ústica Lines, go to the bar just above the jetty. There are two **hotels**: walk up to the road and, a few metres to the right (past the bar), a sideroad leads up to the left to the newly renovated *Pensione Paradiso* (☎0923.924.080; ②), with marvellous views over the sea. A little further up the sideroad, the *Pensione Dei Fenici* (☎0923.924.083; no credit cards; ②) is much fancier and with the same good views. In summer, both places will usually only take you if you're prepared to eat in their restaurants and pay half-board or full-board, which obviously pushes the price up (from L65,000 per person at the *Paradiso*; and from L80,000 at the *Dei Fenici*); however, as the only other option for food here is an *alimentari* on the main road, these are probably your best bets if you're staying a while. Alternatively, you can sometimes find someone who'll rent you a **room**, if you ask around the port.

Maréttimo

Wildest and furthest out from Trápani, **Maréttimo** was claimed by Samuel Butler, in his *The Authoress of the Odyssey*, as the original Ithaca, home of Odysseus; more far-fetched, Butler also thought that Homer himself was the princess Nausicaa of ancient Trápani. These theories aside, there are compelling reasons to come to Maréttimo. Its spectacular fragmented coastline is pitted with rocky coves sheltering hideaway **beaches**, and there are numerous gentle **walks** to be done which will take you all over the island. Even in high season, you're likely to have much of Maréttimo to yourself, as few tourists can be bothered to visit a place without any hotel and no more than four trattorias.

There's little on Maréttimo to distract you from the natural beauty of the place, though you'll have to get out of the port to see the best of it. Two of the island's **beaches** are conveniently close, one on either side of the town, but you'll find other bathing spots on the way to destinations further afield; at Cala Sarde and

MARÉTTIMO HIKES

• To the Case Romane
The simplest walk takes you to some old Roman defensive works, still in quite good condition. Follow directions in the port to *Pizzeria Filli Pipitone*, turning left up a track on reaching a water tap. Keep to the right over a small iron bridge twenty minutes on, and turn right again after another five minutes. The remains are half an hour on, sitting next to a small and dilapidated church that shows marked Arab characteristics but is thought to have been built by Byzantine monks in the twelfth century.

• To Cala Sarde and Cala Nera
Follow the stony vehicle track south of Maréttimo port, turning inland after about 1km where the path divides. There's a steep climb, with the town's cemetery below you, rising to about 300m. After about half an hour, you'll pass a pine forest and a small outhouse, looking out on views towards Tunisia; below is the **Cala Sarde**, a small bay reachable along a smaller path to the left in another half an hour.
Instead of descending to the bay, continue for about an hour on the main path along the island's rocky west coast. You'll pass a lighthouse and a route down to **Cala Nera**, where you can swim off the rocks in perfect isolation. Continuing along this path on the other side of the inlet, you could meet up with the path across the island's back, taking you up to nearly 500m at Punta Ansini and down to the other side via the Roman remains detailed above, in the first walk.

• To the castle at Punta Troia
This walk follows the footpath all the way to the northeastern tip of the island, a hike that should take you around three hours; you'll need a head for heights in certain stretches. Go past the post office with the sea on your right, and keep to the coast along the path for about ten minutes, until the terrace wall on your left stops. *Don't continue along the path*, but cut up about 10m to find the main path on a small spur above you. This stretches along the whole length of the island about 100m above the sea, ending at some concrete steps that descend to a lovely secluded beach and the foot of the **castle**. This precipitous fortification was originally built by the Saracens, enlarged by Roger II, and further extended by the Spanish in the seventeenth century, when it became a prison, acquiring a dire reputation for cruelty.

Cala Nera on the south coast, or at the Saracen castle at the northeastern point of the island, though these will involve a trek to reach them. The two main footpaths are rarely used, so you'll find the hiking trail (see p.353) helpful: none of the walks are particularly onerous, though you might have to scramble at times – and you should take water with you in the summer if you're planning to stay away from the village for any length of time (around three litres a day per person minimum). Alternatively, you could take a three-hour **boat tour** of the island from the port (around L60,000), letting you see Maréttimo's entire rocky coastline and dive into otherwise inaccessible waters, clean and clear and a joy for snorkellers.

Nobody advertises rooms in **MARÉTTIMO TOWN**, though they do exist, and if you want **to stay** your best bet is to make for the port's main square and ask at the café there. Otherwise, the people at the Siremar agency will point you in the right direction, or you could try the *Torrente* restaurant (☎0923.923.159), which can put you in touch with people with rooms to rent or, if there's a crowd of you (four or five), **apartments** (usually an empty holiday home), which can work out very reasonable indeed. The only place **to eat** that's open all year is the *Torrente*; otherwise there's a summer pizzeria above the town and a bakery near the square.

Mózia and around

Fifteen kilometres down the coast from Trápani lies another, much smaller group of islands, the **Stagnone Islands** (Isole dello Stagnone), uninhabited and mostly given over to salt extraction since the fifteenth century, now commemorated by a **salt museum** on the mainland opposite. The long, thin Isola Grande shelters the only one of the Stagnone group that's visitable: **San Pantaleo**, just offshore in the middle of a shallow lagoon, holding the site of the ancient Phoenician settlement of Motya, or **MÓZIA**. Along with Palermo and Solus (Solunto), Motya was one of the three main Phoenician bases in Sicily, settled some time in the eighth century BC and completely razed to the ground by Dionysius I in 397 BC. It's the only one of the three sites that wasn't subsequently built over, though it remained undiscovered until the seventeenth century, and wasn't properly excavated until the English Whitaker family (one of the Marsala wine dynasties) bought the island in the last century and began digging it up.

You can reach Mózia from either Trápani or Marsala, crossing to the island by ferry – see "Getting There" for the practical details. Once there, you could circle the island's perimeter in 45 minutes, but it's more enjoyable to make a day of it and bring a **picnic** (there are no refreshments available): the site encompasses the whole island, and, as long as you can get a ferry there, it's always open. Don't bother bringing your swimming costume, though: the linguistic link between the islands' name (Stagnone)and our "stagnant" is not entirely coincidental.

The island: the remains of Motya

Only 2.5km in circumference, flat and cultivated, San Pantaleo is one of the most manageable of Sicily's ancient sites, the unique Phoenician ruins spread across the whole island and easily reached by some gentle strolling. The ferry leaves you close to the small **Museo Whitaker** (daily: summer 9am–1pm & 3–6pm; winter 9am–1pm; L5000), its outside adorned by an aristocratic bust of its founder, "Giuseppe" Whitaker. You might as well call in here first to see the finds from the island, two rooms packed with a random collection of jewellery, arrowheads and domestic artefacts, the earliest pieces from the eighth century BC. Pride of place goes to the magnificent fifth-century BC marble sculpture of a youth, *Il Giovanetto di Mozia*: sensual and self-assured in pose, the subject's identity is unknown, but he was likely to have been a high-ranking official, suggested by the subtle indentations round his head, indicating some kind of crown or elaborate headwear.

The remains on the ground start immediately outside the museum: in front and 100m to the left is the **Casa dei Mosaici**, two houses containing some faded black-and-white mosaics made from sea pebbles. One, probably belonging to a patrician, shows animal scenes; the other, thought to be a craftsman's, yielded numerous shards of pottery. Further along the path you come to the **cothon**, a small artificial boat dock built within the ancient town's walls and similar in style to a much larger one at Carthage itself.

The other way, back past the museum, leads along the rough tracks set amongst cobwebbed cacti, once the city's main thoroughfares, most of which end at one of the gates on Motya's formerly well-fortified shore. The once-strong **north gate**, now a ragged collection of steps and ruined walls – up beyond the museum and right – lies at the head of a causeway built by the Phoenicians in the sixth century BC connecting the island with the mainland (and a necropolis) at Birgi, 7km to the north: the road is still there, although these days it's submerged under the water. Just inland of the gate, the **Cappiddazzu** site shows the foundations of a large building, probably a temple, while left along the shore from the gate is the **Tophet** burial ground. Most of the information about day-to-day life in Motya has come from here, the sanctuary revealing a number of urns containing the ashes of animals and people – mainly children – sacrificed to the Phoenician gods, chiefly Baal Hammon.

The salt museum

Near the ferry landing back on the mainland, just opposite Mózia, one of three windmills has been turned into a salt museum, the **Mulino Salina Infersa** (☎0923.966.936; daily 9am–8pm; L4000); if you ring ahead, they'll get the windmill working for you. Inside there's an Archimedes screw, for controlling the flow of water into the pans, and a model of the whole salt-making process, and you can watch an entertaining video. You can also hire a canoe (L8000 per hour) and weave your way around the saltpans and mounds of salt, some of which are encased in tiles, or cross to Mózia itself. There are **rooms** available close by if you're inclined to stay; contact the owner Ennio di Girolamo (☎0923.745.747; ② including breakfast) in person. You can have a traditional home-cooked dinner for an extra L20,000–25,000 per person.

Getting there

If you don't have your own transport, reaching Mózia is easiest **from Marsala**, from where local bus #4 (Mon–Sat; L8000, pay at the bar by the waiting area) leaves hourly in summer (much less frequently in winter) from the central Piazza del Pópolo to the ferry-landing, taking around 25 minutes. **From Trápani**, there is no regular bus service, though the tourist office there may have details of excursions.

The only alternative from either city is to take the local **train** running between Trápani and Marsala and getting off at the small station at Ragattisi, from where it's a four-kilometre walk south down the road to the turnoff for the ferry. Getting off at the station at Spagnuola involves a marginally longer hike northward.

In summer, a steady flow of visitors to the island means that there's usually a **ferry** waiting or on its way; tickets are L5000 return. If there isn't, you'll have to ring the museum custodian (☎0923.712.598; same hours as the Museo Whitaker, see p.354) to arrange to be picked up (the nearest phone is at the *alimentari* back on the main Trápani–Marsala road). In winter the ferry only operates from 9am to 1pm, and before setting out you should really ring first to check.

If you're not on the tour from Trápani, it's easiest to **return** to Marsala. If you've time to kill before the bus arrives, the *Bar-Ristorante Mothia*, next to the *alimentari* on the main road, has coffee and snacks, and an inexpensive *menu turístico*.

Marsala

When the island-city of Motya had been put to the sword by the Syracusans, the survivors founded Lilybaeum, modern **MARSALA**, 10km to the south. The main city of the Phoenicians in Sicily, and the only one to resist the Greek push westwards, Lilybaeum finally succumbed to Rome in 241 BC, and not long after was used as a springboard for an attack against the Carthaginian heartland itself. The town's position at Sicily's western tip later made it the main Saracenic base on the island, and it was renamed Marsah Ali, Arabic for the "port of Ali", son-in-law of the Prophet, from which its modern name derives.

More recently, the town has scored a place in modern Italian history for its role in the saga of the Risorgimento, the struggle for Italian unity in the nineteenth century. It was here that Garibaldi kicked off his campaign to drive out the Bourbons, in the company of his red-shirted "Thousand". Until a planned Garibaldi museum on Marsala's eastern seafront (on Via Scipione Africano) gets

---

THE MAKING OF MARSALA

The Baglio Anselmi, in which Marsala's archeological museum is housed, is one of a number of old *bagli*, or warehouses, conspicuous throughout this wine-making region. Many are still used in the making of the famous dessert wine that carries the town's name. It was an Englishman, John Woodhouse, who first exploited the commercial potential of **Marsala wine**, when he visited the town in 1770. Woodhouse soon realized that, like port, the local wine could travel for long periods without going off, when fortified with alcohol. Others followed: Ingham, Whitaker, Hopps and many more whose names can still be seen on some of the warehouse doors. Interestingly, it was the English presence in Marsala that persuaded Garibaldi to launch his campaign here rather than Sciacca (his first choice), judging that the Bourbon fleet wouldn't dare to interfere so close to Her Majesty's commercial concerns.

Marsala owes much of its current prosperity to the marketing of its wine, still a thriving industry, though no longer in British hands. You can visit some of the *bagli* and **sample** the stuff for free: try the Stabilimento Florio (Mon–Fri 9–11.30am & 3–4.30pm, but worth verifying – ☎0923.781.111), on Lungomare Mediterraneo, to the south of town beyond the port. For enthusiasts, there's also an **Enoteca** (daily 9am–1pm; free) on Via Circonvallazione on the southeastern outskirts of town, and an **Enomuseum** (daily 9am–1pm & 3–6pm; free) at Contrada Berbaro (3km along the road to Mazara del Vallo), where you can look over the old apparatus and techniques for wine-making. Otherwise, you'll find *Marsala* or the sweeter *Marsala all'uovo* (mixed with egg yolks) in every bar and restaurant in town.

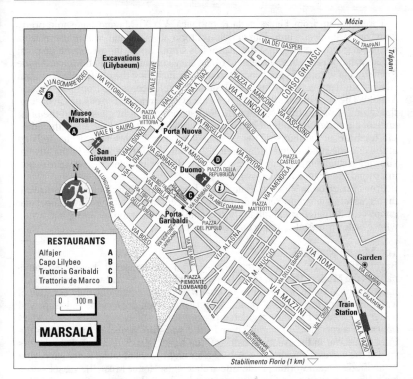

The map shows labels including:
Mózia, VIA TRAPANI, Trapani, VIA DEI GASPERI, Excavations (Lilybaeum), VIA VITTORIO VENETO, VIALE PIAVE, VIALE C. BATTISTI, VIALE A. DIAZ, PIAZZA G. MARCONI, VIA A. LINCOLN, CORSO GRAMSCI, VIA PASCASINO, VIA LUNGOMARE BOEO, Museo Marsala, PIAZZA DELLA VITTORIA, Porta Nuova, VIALE N. SAURO, VIA FRISELLA, VIA XI LUGLIO, San Giovanni, VIALE ISONZO, VIA A. DIAZ, VIA GARRAFFA, VIA XI MAGGIO, VIA PIPITONE, PIAZZA CASTELLO, Duomo, PIAZZA DELLA REPUBBLICA, VIA AMENDOLA, N, VIA LUNGOMARE BOEO, VIA BOTTINO, VIA SIBILLA, VIA GARIBALDI, VIA ABELE DAMANI, PIAZZA MATTEOTTI, VIA FIRRELA, VIA DELLE SIRENE, Porta Garibaldi, PIAZZA DEL POPOLO, VIA ALAGNA, VIA BOEO, VIA SOFONIA L'AFRICANA, VIA DEI MILLE, VIA M. NUCCIO, VIA DELLO SBARCO, VIA ROMA, Garden, VIA GAMBINI, PIAZZA PIEMONTE E LOMBARDO, VIA MAZZINI, C. CALATAFIMI, LUNGOMARE MEDITERRANEO, VIA A. FAZIO, VIA CRISPI, Train Station, Stabilimento Florio (1 km)

RESTAURANTS

Alfajer	A
Capo Lilybeo	B
Trattoria Garibaldi	C
Trattoria de Marco	D

0   100 m

MARSALA

round to opening, memorials to the swashbuckling freedom-fighter are confined to a few statues and street names, and the nearby Porta Garibaldi, at the end of Via Garibaldi, which recalls the hero's entry into the town.

The Town

The town centre is a mainly Baroque assortment of buildings, though there are hints of the older town's layout in the narrow, largely traffic-free streets around the central **Piazza della Repubblica**. The square's elegance is due to its two eighteenth-century buildings: the arcaded **Palazzo Comunale** and the **Chiesa Madre** – dedicated to San Tommaso di Canterbury, patron saint of Marsala – from which four statues peer loftily down. In the large but rather disappointing interior, there are a number of Gagini sculptures, and a plaque near the door commemorating a returned emigrant's donation of funds in 1956 for the completion of the duomo facade. The most central of Marsala's two museums lies behind the duomo, at Via Garraffa 57. The sole display at the **Museo degli Arazzi** (Tues–Sun 9am–1pm & 4–6pm; L2000) is a series of eight enormous hand-stitched wool and silk tapestries depicting the capture of Jerusalem. Made in Brussels in the sixteenth century, they were the gift of the Spanish ambassador, who doubled as the archbishop of Messina, and are beautifully rich, in burnished red, gold and green.

Threading up from Piazza della Repubblica, Via XI Maggio has some pretty courtyards and leads onto Piazza della Vittória at its far end, where there are a couple of good bars. Beyond the piazza lies **Capo Boeo**, the westernmost point of Sicily that was the first settlement of the survivors of annihilated Motya. All the town's major antiquities are concentrated here, including the old **Insula Romana** (daily 9am–1pm & 4pm–1hr before sunset; free), accessible from Via Vittório Véneto. The site contains all that's been excavated so far of the city of Lilybaeum, though most of it is third-century BC Roman, as you might guess from the presence of a *vomitarium*, lodged in the most complete section of the site – the **edificio termale**, or bathhouse. There's some good mosaic-work here: a chained dog at the entrance and, much better, a richly coloured **hunting scene** in the atrium, showing a stag being savaged by a wild beast. If the site's closed, ask at the museum round the corner (see below).

From Piazza della Vittória, Viale Sauro leads to the church of **San Giovanni**, under which is a grotto reputed to have been inhabited by the sibyl Lilibetana, endowed with paranormal gifts. There's another slice of mosaic here, and a well whose water is meant to impart second sight.

The Museo Marsala

Beyond the church, in one of the stone-vaulted warehouses that line the promenade, is the **Museo Marsala** (daily 9am–1pm, plus Wed, Sat & Sun 4–7pm; L4000), most of whose space is given over to what was, until recently, the only example of a warship from the classical period. Surprisingly well preserved, and displayed under a heat- and humidity-regulated plastic tent, it still ranks as the only extant *liburnian*, a specifically Phoenician or **Punic warship**, probably sunk during the First Punic War in the great sea battle off the Égadi Islands that ended Carthage's rule of the waves. Brought here in 1977 after eight years of underwater surveying by an English team working under the archeologist Honor Frost, the vessel – originally 35m long and rowed by 68 oarsmen – has been the source of much detailed information on the period, including what the crew ate and the stimulants they chewed to keep awake. Scattered about the museum is a medley of items found in or around the ship: heaped amphorae and anchors; and various photographs and explanations of the ship's retrieval from the sea. Other rooms have a variety of more mundane finds from Motya and ancient necropoli in the neighbourhood, as well as some colourful examples of Italian and North African pottery.

Practicalities

Buses arrive centrally at Piazza del Pópolo (also known as Piazza Marconi), near Porta Garibaldi. If you're planning to visit Mózia, bus #4 leaves from here for the ferry to the island-site. The **train station** is at the southeastern edge of town, a fifteen-minute walk into the centre. There's a **tourist office** at Via XI Maggio 100, off Piazza Repubblica near the duomo (Mon–Sat 8am–2pm; ☎ & fax 0923.714.097); indeed, sightseers are well catered for here, as at every site and point of interest there is an informative notice in English. You'll find a **post office** at Via Garibaldi, a **bank**, Banco di Sicilia, at Via XI Maggio 83, and a Standa supermarket on Via Cammareri Scurtil.

There's an extremely limited choice of **accommodation** in Marsala. The only central hotel – happily, also the cheapest – is behind the train station, right over the level crossing and right again: the *Garden*, Via Gambini 36 (☎0923.982.320; ②), which is rather bleak, but it's modern and clean enough, and has discounts outside high season. It only has nine rooms, so ring ahead, since the other three or four hotels are all on the outskirts and inaccessible without transport.

In the centre at least, which empties of life after 9pm, **restaurants** are also equally hard to come by, though round the corner from the duomo there is the (unmarked) *Trattoria de Marco* at Via Vaccari 6 (no closing day), providing basic fare with low prices and delicious local wine; get the menu from the obliging proprietor, who has a dead cheroot dangling constantly from his lips. Or try the modern, wood-panelled *Trattoria Garibaldi* at Piazza Addolorata 5 (closed Mon), for something a little more upmarket. Otherwise, head out for the seafront, where the highly rated *Capo Lilybeo* (closed Mon), at Via Lungomare Boeo 40, is housed in a restored warehouse on the westernmost point of town, and also of the Sicilian mainland; you can get cheaper pizzas here, but it's famous for its fish couscous and specializes in local wines. Also in this part of town, close to the Museo Marsala, is *Alfajer*, at Via Lungomare Boeo 3, another ristorante-pizzeria, with sea views over to Favignana and a tourist menu at L25,000. Finish off with a beer or an ice-cream at one of the **bars** outside the Porta Nuova, where you can sit and admire the austere Art Deco front of the Cine Impero, so out of keeping with the Baroque arch opposite. Or, if you are in the centre, the *Bar Repubblica* opposite the duomo is good for *té freddo alla pesca* (peach tea), against a background of earnest discussion over lottery numbers. For general groceries, there is a lively daily **market** just inside the Porta Garibaldi, spilling over into the adjacent Piazza del Pópolo, and for fruit and vegetables at the Lungomare Boeo, at the end of Via S. L'Africanus; if you want to snap up some Marsala, you'll find a couple of **wine shops** back in Via Lungomare Boeo.

Mazara del Vallo

The North African element in the island's cultural melange is stronger than ever at the major fishing port of **MAZARA DEL VALLO**, a half-hour's train or bus ride down the coast from Marsala. Under the Muslims, Mazara was one of Sicily's most flourishing towns and capital of the biggest of the three administrative districts, or *walis*, into which the island was divided, hence the "del Vallo" tag. The first Sicilian city to be taken by the Arabs, and the last they surrendered, Mazara's prosperity lasted for 250 years, coinciding with the height of Arab power in the Mediterranean. Count Roger's anxiety to establish a strong Norman presence in this Muslim powerbase ensured that Mazara's importance lasted long after his conquest of the city in 1087, and it didn't give up its rank as provincial capital until Trápani took over in 1817.

There's little left of Mazara's past glory today, though the Arab links have revived since the lively port became the prime Sicilian destination for Tunisian immigrants flocking across the sea to work in the vast fishing fleet – one of Italy's biggest. Indeed, wandering through the town's casbah-like back-streets, there are moments when you could imagine yourself to be in North Africa, passing Tunisian shops and a café plastered with pictures of the Tunisian president, and Arab music percolating through small doorways. There's also talk of a mosque planned for the families who have stayed to make their homes here.

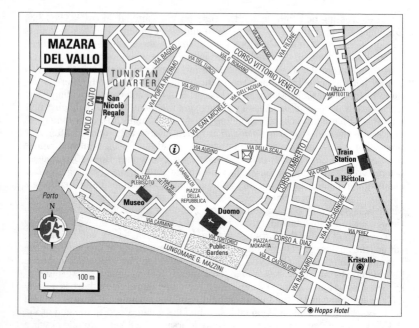

The Town

Mazara's main street, **Corso Umberto I**, ends at the spacious Piazza Mokarta and the ruins of Count Roger's **castello**, magnificently floodlit at night, when the square is the focus of Mazara's youthful crowds. Fronting the garden to one side of the piazza is the **Duomo**, originally Norman but completely remodelled in the late seventeenth century – though the relief over the main door showing a mounted Count Roger trampling a Saracen underfoot was carved in 1584. Inside there's an almost indigestible profusion of stuccoed and sculptured ornamentation, including, behind the altar, a group of seven marble statues depicting the *Transfiguration*, carved by Antonello Gagini. To the right, a niche reveals a newly discovered fragment of Byzantine fresco, dating from the end of the thirteenth century, and there's some excellently chiselled Roman sarcophagi, through the marble doorway on the right side of the nave, with reliefs of a lively hunting scene and a battle, rich with confusion.

Outside the duomo, **Piazza della Repubblica** heralds a harmonious set of Baroque buildings: the square itself is flanked by the double-storey porticoed facade of the **Seminario** and the **Palazzo Vescovile**, both eighteenth-century, while in nearby Piazza del Plebiscito the earlier **Collegio dei Gesuiti** houses the tiny **Museo Cívico** (Mon–Sat 9am–2pm; free) – two rooms off the impressive courtyard displaying a smattering of minor, mainly Roman, finds from the area. You'll find many other Baroque constructions in the intricate network of streets and squares that makes up Mazara's old town, many best seen at night and most built after its teeming Arab population had dwindled to nothing. But it's also around here, especially in the old Pilazza quarter, that their descendants have returned, making up a low-key **Tunisian quarter** centred on Via Porta Palermo and nearby Via Bagno; stroll around here and you'll pass an authentic Tunisian café and shop in Via Goti, and various social clubs resounding to Arab tapes and the clack of backgammon tables. On the edge of the quarter stands the church of **San Nicolò Regale**, a restored Norman church with strong Arab elements – though you'll have to be satisfied with admiring its honey-toned, battlemented exterior, as it's been locked up for years.

The church stands on a platform overlooking the Mázaro river, its waters hidden by the hulls of the two hundred or so trawlers that clog Mazara's brisk **port**. Heavy overfishing and the use of illegal explosives (dropped into the sea to stun the fish) have greatly decreased the catch in recent years, but the rich waters above the continental shelf have ensured that there are enough fish left to make it worthwhile for the fishermen to pursue their trade – at least, given the reduced wages that the Tunisians are prepared to accept.

Out of the centre: the beach and Santa Maria della Giummare

Crossing over the bridge further down the river, you can walk past the docks to Mazara's seafront, mostly sandy **beach**, though a good part of it is choked by seaweed. It gets better the further up you go, but bathers might bear in mind that the stretch between Mazara and the Stagnone Islands was recently found to be one of Sicily's most polluted coastlines. If you're looking for a **swim** you'd be better advised to drive or jump on a bus from Mazara's train station to **TONNARELLA LIDO**, 7km south.

There's one more easy excursion out from the centre of Mazara – walkable this time – a couple of kilometres away on the outskirts of town, though drivers could see it on their way in or out by following Via Circonvallazione, the main SS115 running to Marsala. Signposted "Madonna del Alto", the chapel of **Santa Maria della Giummare** sits on a slight elevation on the right-hand side of the road (looking north). Built as a Basilian convent by a daughter of Count Roger's in 1103, its portal also shows a strong Saracen strain.

Practicalities

Buses stop either outside the **train station** or 200m up at Piazza Matteotti. The **tourist office** is in the old part of town, past the cathedral in Piazza S. Veneranda (Mon–Sat 8am–1.30pm, plus Mon & Wed 3–6pm; ☎0923.941.727).

As usual in this part of Sicily, there's not a lot of choice as far as **accommodation** goes, the cheapest hotel being the *Kristallo* (☎ & fax 0923.932.688; ②) at Via Valeria 36, not far from the station off Corso Armando Diaz. Otherwise you're left with the somewhat exclusive *Hopps Hotel*, Via G. Hopps 29 (☎0923.946.133, fax 0923.932.688; ④), an enormous place at the eastern end of the Lungomare Mazzini; all the rooms here are en suite.

As you might expect in a Sicilian/Tunisian fishing port, you can **eat** well in Mazara. Via Tortorici, leading up from the duomo, has a string of popular **pizzerias and trattorias**, all offering variations of a fish couscous and all with tables outside; *La Béttola* at Corso A. Diaz 20, opposite the train station (closed Sun), is a good place for regional specialities. A good place for **breakfast** is the *Caffè Paradiso* at the junction of Via Francesco Crispi and Corso Umberto, where you'll find pastries and fresh juices.

Selinunte and around

SELINUNTE, the site of the Greek city of Selinus, lies around 30km east of Mazara del Vallo, stranded on a remote corner of the coast in splendid isolation. It's a crucial sight if you're travelling through the west of Sicily, its series of mighty temples lying in great heaps, where they were felled by earthquakes.

Most westerly of the Hellenic colonies, **Selinus** reached its peak in the fifth century BC. A bitter rival of Segesta, whose lands lay adjacent to the north (see p.345), the powerful city and its fertile plain attracted enemies hand over fist, and it was only a matter of time before Selinus caught the eye of Segesta's ally, Carthage. Geographically vulnerable, the city was sacked by Carthaginians, any attempts at recovery forestalled by earthquakes, which later razed the city. However, people continued to live here until 250 BC, when the population was finally transferred to Marsala before the Roman invasion. The Arabs did occupy the site briefly, but the last recorded settlement at Selinunte was in the thirteenth century, after which time it remained forgotten until rediscovered in the sixteenth century. Despite the destruction, the city ruins have exerted a romantic hold over people ever since.

By **public transport**, it's easiest to approach from Castelvetrano (see p.366), which is a twenty-minute ride from Mazara del Vallo by road or rail; Selinunte is another twenty minutes south from there by bus five times a day (Mon–Sat) from Piazza Regina Margherita (tickets from the *tabacchi* in front of San Domenico church), the last departure currently around 5pm. The site is situated just to the west of the tiny village of Marinella (see opposite), a far better base than

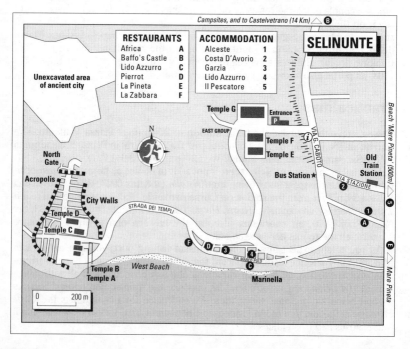

Campsites, and to Castelvetrano (14 Km)

SELINUNTE

RESTAURANTS
Africa	A
Baffo's Castle	B
Lido Azzurro	C
Pierrot	D
La Pineta	E
La Zabbara	F

ACCOMMODATION
Alceste	1
Costa D'Avorio	2
Garzia	3
Lido Azzurro	4
Il Pescatore	5

Unexcavated area of ancient city

Temple G

Entrance

EAST GROUP

Temple F

Temple E

North Gate

Acropolis

City Walls

STRADA DEI TEMPLI

Bus Station ★

Old Train Station

VIA STAZIONE

Temple D

Temple C

VIA MARCO POLO

Temple B
Temple A

West Beach

Marinella

Beach 'Mare Pineta' (500m)

Mare Pineta

0   200 m

Castelvetrano, and where the buses stop. Note, though, that Marinella has few facilities other than hotels and restaurants: the nearest bank, and other services, are in Castelvetrano, though there is an exchange office on Via Marco Polo. You could also approach Selinunte from Sciacca (p.325), an hour to the southeast, the ultimate destination of the bus from Castelvetrano.

Marinella

MARINELLA only has one main road, which winds down to a small harbour, where the fishing-boats are hauled up onto the sands by pulleys, and then runs west to the site of Selinunte. The village is no longer the isolated place it once was, with recent buildings in the centre and new side streets off the main road; the seafront has become slightly top-heavy with trattorias and *pensioni* these days. But it remains an attractive place, certainly if you're planning to use the fine sand **beach** which stretches west from the village to the ruins. The water isn't great to swim in, since it's clogged with seaweed at the sand's edge, though this doesn't deter the kids. However, the surfing here is particularly good, and you can rent equipment in the summer, as well as pedalos, chairs, shades and all the usual beach paraphernalia. There's a less-visited beach east of the village, the **Mare Pineta**; follow the road beyond the port for ten minutes. New construction is sprouting here too, and what was until recently a mere track is now a wide gravel road, but the beach itself remains fairly unspoiled, backed by pine trees stretching into the distance.

Arrival, information and accommodation

The **bus station** is south of the entrance to the temple site, but buses from Castelvetrano or Sciacca will stop right by the entrance as well; the small but obliging **tourist office** (Mon–Sat 8am–9pm, Sun 9am–noon & 3–6pm; ☎0924.46.251) is here, but it can get very busy in summer. Just opposite on this road there's an **alimentari** and, beyond it, in the main residential district, a bigger **supermarket** behind the *Alceste* hotel (see below). The road then descends to the seafront, where the main hotels and restaurants are situated and along which you'll also find **telephones**, an **exchange office**, and a couple of gift shops.

You may well be offered **rooms** as you get off the bus, worth accepting since the **hotels and pensions** in the village fill rapidly in summer. In winter, you should get discounts of a few thousand lire off the price of most rooms. The best places to stay are along the seafront road, close to the beach. First choice here is the *Lido Azzurro*, Via Marco Polo 98 (☎ & fax 0924.46.256; ②, includes breakfast), a charming villa with laid-back staff, prints on the walls, rugs on the floors and attractive rooms with sea-facing balconies. Further along, the *Garzia*, Via Pigafetta 6 (☎0924.46.660, fax 0924.46.196; ③), is more formal and fancier, though also with good sea views.

Cheaper rooms are found in the residential district close to the east group of temples. Opposite the temple car park, the sign pointing to "Chiesa" leads to the old abandoned train station, just before which you'll find the *Pensione Costa D'Avorio* at Via Argonauti 10 (☎ & fax 0924.46.207; no credit cards; ②), comfortable and pleasant, with a charming owner (and the price includes breakfast). On the next parallel street down, the *Alceste*, Via Alceste 21 (☎0924.46.184, fax 0924.46.143; no credit cards; ③), is a larger, more modern choice. Two streets up from here and also signposted, *Il Pescatore*, Via Castore e Polluce 31 (☎ & fax 0924.46.303; no credit cards; ①), is friendly and provides self-catering facilities as well. The fresh-fruit breakfast on the terrace, at an extra L5000 per person, is not to be missed.

There are also two **campsites** virtually next to each other on the main road, though they are a hefty 1.5km north of the village: the *Athena* (☎0924.46.132), with a ridiculous temple facade, and *Il Maggiolino* (☎0924.46.044); the bus to and from Castelvetrano bus passes right by them. No one minds if you camp out in the pinewoods backing the Mare Pineta, east of the village, either, and the beach-bar here will watch your tent during the day.

Eating and drinking

Via Marco Polo, the road above the west beach, is where all the best eating and drinking places are, starting down at the little harbour where a couple of bars put out tables from where you can watch the sun set and the fishermen argue among themselves.

Of the **restaurants**, the *Lido Azzurro* (opposite the eponymous hotel), also known as *Baffo's*, has a huge open dining-room terrace overlooking the sea and does a tasty *spaghetti di frutti di mare*. On the other side of the road, *Pierrot*, no. 108, has a first-floor outdoor terrace and good, large servings of fresh fish and decent pizzas; the Sicilian antipasto plate here is worth ordering. *La Zabbara*, nearest the ruins, is an appealing beach-bar with very reasonably priced drinks, food, umbrellas to rent and showers. On the east beach, Mare Pineta, the *La Pineta* beach-bar has a trattoria at the back (closed in winter) serving wonderfully generous fresh fish meals: a real find, it stays open in the evenings during July and August, but take a torch if you do go at night as the road peters out, becoming an unlit track. In the residential district the ristorante-pizzeria *Africa*, opposite the *Hotel Alceste*, does crispy pizzas in a wood-burning oven, good antipasti and a tourist menu at L15,000. Finally, for entertainment value alone it's hard to beat the experience of dining in *Baffo's Castle*, a bizarre mock-Norman pizzeria-restaurant on the road to Castelvetrano, a couple of kilometres north of the campsites. All these places are moderately priced, at around L20,000 for pizza, salad and wine, and L35,000–45,000 for a full meal.

At night in summer, the locals come in from the surrounding villages to parade along Via Marco Polo on foot, in cars and on Vespas. The **bars** in between the restaurants – like *Agorazein* and *Fire Fly* – turn up the music and put out seats, and a mini street party chugs along quite merrily until well after midnight.

Selinus: the site

The **ruins** of Selinus are back behind the main part of the village, split into two parts with temples in each, known only as Temples A to G and O. After many years of prevarication, the two parts are now enclosed within the same site, with the car park and **entrance** (daily 9am–1hr before sunset; L4000, tickets sold only until 2hr before sunset) lying through the landscaped earthbanks that preclude views of the east group of temples from the road.

Shrouded in the wild celery which gave the ancient city its name, the **East Group** temples are in various stages of reconstructed ruin. The most complete is the one nearest the sea (Temple E), probably dedicated to Hera (Aphrodite) and re-erected in 1958. A Doric construction, almost 70m by 25m, it remains a gloriously impressive sight, its soaring columns gleaming bright against the sky, its ledges and capitals the resting place for flitting birds. Temple F, behind, is the oldest in this group, from around 550 BC, while the northernmost temple (Temple G) is an immense tangle of columned wreckage 6m high in places and crisscrossed by rough footpaths. In Sicily, the only temple bigger than this is the Tempio di Giove at Agrigento.

The road leads down from here, across the (now buried) site of the old harbour, to the second part of excavated Selinus, the **acropolis**, where there's a second car park if you can't face the twenty-minute walk. This contains what remains of the other temples (five in all), as well as the well-preserved city streets and massive stepped **walls** which rise above the duned beach below. These huge walls were all constructed after 409 BC – when the city was sacked by the Carthaginians – in an attempt to protect a limited and easily defensible area of the old city.

Temple C stands on the highest point of the acropolis, giving glorious views out over the sparkling sea. Built in the early sixth century BC (and probably dedicated to Apollo), it was from here that the best of the metopes (decorative panels) were removed; they're now on show in Palermo's archeological museum (see p.79). Its fourteen standing columns were re-erected in the 1920s: other fallen columns here, and at the surrounding temples, show how they were originally constructed – the drums lying in a line, with slots and protrusions on either side which fitted into each other. The buildings immediately behind Temples C and D were shops, split into two rooms and with a courtyard each; while at the end of the main street beyond is the **north gate** to the city – the high blocks of stone marking a gateway that was 7m high. Behind the north gate stood the rest of the **ancient city**, still largely unexcavated, though crisscrossed by little paths through the undergrowth. The agora was probably sited here, as was a necropolis further to the north, though there's no contemporary evidence of either.

Campobello and the Cave di Cusa

If you've got your own transport, it makes some sense to call in at the quarries where the stone for the building of Selinus was extracted in the fifth century BC. They're 3.5km south of the scruffy town of **CAMPOBELLO DI MAZARA**, deep in olive country, which is on a bus route from Castelvetrano and is also a stop on the train between Mazara and Castelvetrano – so if you don't mind the fairly stiff walk you could come by public transport, too. From Selinunte, it's a lovely twenty-kilometre drive, along country roads lined with olive groves and vines: when you reach Campobello, follow the signs ("Cave di Cusa") and keep your fingers crossed.

At the site of the **Cave di Cusa** (always open; free), a path leads into a bucolic setting that owes more to English Romanticism than to ancient Greece. In early summer, workers are forking hay into piles in between the rock ledges and tended shrubs, while behind them stretch shaded groves of olives. Everywhere, you can see the massive column drums and stumps lying randomly about, quarried and chiselled into shape here before being dragged to the ancient city on wooden carts, where they formed part of the great temple complex. There are examples of all the various stages of the process, with unfinished pieces poignantly abandoned, the work interrupted when Selinus was devastated in 409 BC. The most impressive pieces are those stone drums and column sections still in place where they were being excavated: a couple are 6m high and 2m across, with a narrow groove dug all the way around in which the stonemasons had to work – the reflected heat must have been appalling. Other rock sections indicate clearly where drums have already been cut – parts of the site look as though someone has been through with a giant pastry-cutter.

Tre Fontane

If you're looking for a drink or lunch, it's only another 5km or so south from the quarries to the coast at **TRE FONTANE**. The beach here stretches east and west of the road, a long, long sandy stretch with beach-bars, umbrellas, shades and extremely shallow water – you can get 20m out and still only be up to your knees. The small resort itself is basically one long strip of family villas, and not terribly engaging, though there are plenty of "*affitasi* "signs around should you fancy renting a villa, and a **campsite** 1km before the village, *Il Sombrero* (☎0924.80.300). Best place to eat is the *Sabbie d'Oro*, just back from the seafront, a **trattoria-pizzeria** run by a returned American *emigrante*.

Castelvetrano

You might be passing through **CASTELVETRANO**, 15km inland, on your way to Selinunte, or you might be staying overnight in its one cheap hotel, but they're about the only reasons to bring you here. A depressed town, it's saved by an elegant centre, where the **Teatro Selinus** – looking rather like a copy of a Greek temple – boasts a proud plaque commemorating Goethe's visit in 1787. Just around the corner is a good-looking **Chiesa Madre** from the sixteenth century. The church's finely engraved doorway leads into an interior warmly illuminated by stained-glass windows – a rare thing in Sicily – and ornamented by a number of stuccos by Serpotta and Ferraro. Via Garibaldi off the adjacent square, Piazza Garibaldi, holds the **Museo Cívico** (Mon–Sat 9am–1pm & 3.30–7.30pm, Sun 9am–1pm), home of the bronze *Efébo di Selinunte*, a statue of a young man from the fifth century BC.

From behind the church, Via Vittorio Emanuele leads down towards Piazza Matteotti and the train station. Piazza Matteotti marks the end of Via Serafino Mannone, where aficionados of banditry can visit the courtyard in which the body of the island's most notorious outlaw, **Salvatore Giuliano**, was found on July 5, 1950. The courtyard is betweenVia Mannone 92 and 100, though it's a rather less appealing spot than its legend might suggest.

Santíssima Trinità di Delia

Three and a half kilometres west **out of Castelvetrano** is a twelfth-century Norman church that makes a pleasant rural excursion for anyone not in a blazing hurry. Head down Via R. Séttimo from Piazza Umberto, along a country lane fringed by vineyards, keeping left where the road forks. The cupolaed church, **Santíssima Trinità di Delia**, is signposted before you arrive at the artificial lake of Lago Trinità: ring the bell to the right of the church for the key. The small, square building, its four slender columns and triple apse reminiscent of Saracenic styles, was meticulously restored by two brothers, whose mausoleum the church has become. Their tombs, dominating the small interior, rival those of the Norman kings in Palermo for splendour.

Practicalities

To **get to Selinunte**, take the bus for Marinella from outside the train station – there's a timetable posted inside the station – or the more frequent service from Piazza Regina Margherita.

To reach the town centre from the **train station**, in Piazza Améndola, walk up to the main road and turn left: it's just a few minutes to Piazza Matteotti, from where Via Vittorio Emanuele leads all the way to the rear of the church. **Buses** from Marsala or Trápani stop outside the Teatro Selinus, by the central Piazza Garibaldi. There's a **tourist office** in Piazza Gen. Cascilio (Mon–Sat 9.30am–12.30pm & 4–7pm; ☎0924.909.100). Castelvetrano's one **hotel** is nearby, the *Zeus*, at Via Vittorio Véneto 6 (☎ & fax 0924.905.565; ②), and has a **restaurant**, which is about the only decent place to eat in town.

Inland: Salemi and Gibellina

The interior northwest of Castelvetrano is intensely rural, its few small towns little changed by the coming of the A29 autostrada, which cuts across the region. The whole area is green and highly fertile, mainly given over to vine-growing; indeed, the wine around the Salemi district is among Sicily's best. But it still hasn't recovered from the 1968 **earthquake**, which briefly spotlighted western Sicily, sadly more for the authorities' inadequate response to it than for the actual loss of life. Four hundred died and a thousand were injured, no great number by Sicilian standards, but it was the 50,000 left homeless that had the most lingering impact on this already depressed part of the island, and the earthquake's effects are still evident everywhere. Ruined buildings and ugly temporary dwellings being used 25 years on testify to the chronically dilatory response to the disaster, aggravated by private interests and particularly by Mafia contractors capitalizing on the catastrophe. It's an intriguing, little-visited area, and there are a couple of places worth making detours for, also linked by local bus.

Salemi

The town of **SALEMI**, 30km north of Castelvetrano, oddly enjoyed the privilege of being the first capital of a united Italy in 1860, albeit for only three days, as a plaque in front of its thirteenth-century **castello** records. Another plaque marks Garibaldi's declaration of a dictatorship, asserting that "in times of war, it's necessary for the civilian powers to be concentrated in the hands of one man" – namely Garibaldi himself, though King Vittorio Emanuele still gets a mention. The castle contains a **Museo del Risorgimento** (Mon–Sat 8am–2pm & 4–6pm; free) filled with war memorabilia. In the square outside, at the town's highest point, the debris of bricks and broken pillars that litters the place provides copious – and shaming – evidence of the 1968 earthquake. A third of Salemi's population had to abandon their shattered homes; and the castle tower, the town's main monument, is still literally strapped together.

Gibellina

Salemi escaped lightly. Other towns were completely flattened. One of them, Gibellina, on the eastern side of the A29 autostrada, still bears restimony to its decimated state, a distressing monument to the force of the quake. Gibellina's population was moved en masse to a site close to Santa Ninfa: **GIBELLINA NUOVA**, a modern town which has become a symbol of progress in the region, with innovative buildings that deliberately diverge from old styles: weird shapes and forms abound, designed by a handful of modern architects with big budgets. There's a vast petal astride the main SS119, huge white spheres, and giant ploughs, snails and much besides – 47 constructions in all, with a few in the Egyptian style still to come. Many buildings are apparently crumbling already, and the designs themselves are embarrassingly frozen in the images of what appeared modern in the 1970s. You'll see some of it from the road, and those with an aversion to such places won't want to get any closer.

Eighteen kilometres further along the SS119 towards Salaparuta, the old town of **RÚDERI DI GIBELLINA** complements the new: a frightening mountain of rubble from which smashed and mutilated houses poke out, strewn over a green hillside. It's only really a practical destination if you're driving, and it's a macabre stopoff even then. On the way into town, you'll pass what is ironically its best-preserved fragment: a shady cemetery stretching down the side of the valley. Further down, modernism has left its mark here too, in the form of a wide, white mantle of concrete, **Il Cretto**, poured over one slope, and carved through by channels that recall the previous layout of streets. But everything else is as it was after the earthquake struck: only a church has since been restored, and a jumble of scaffolding on a hummock cradles a stage where the new town's inhabitants are supposed to return every year to remember the catastrophe. In reality, though, the event has been co-opted to entice tourists to a very remote spot of the Sicilian countryside to watch a series of **classical dramas**, known as the *Orestiadi*.

As well as works by Euripides, Sophocles and others, there are modern interpretations by the likes of Jean Cocteau, Stravinsky and John Cage. Performances take place from July to September daily at 9pm (Mon–Sat); for more details, phone ☎0924.67.884, or call in at the **tourist office** at Gibellina Nuova, in Piazza XV Gennaio 1968 (Tues–Sat 9am–1pm & 4–7pm; ☎ & fax 0924.67.877), which is helpful and has information on the town in English.

Pantelleria

With the exception of Malta, **PANTELLERIA** is the biggest of the islands surrounding Sicily. Forty kilometres nearer to Tunisia than to Sicily, the island has been occupied since early times by whichever power currently controlled the central Mediterranean. By the Phoenicians, who colonized the island in the seventh century BC, it was called Hiranin, "island of the birds", after the birds who still stop over here on their migratory routes; for the Greeks, it was Kossyra, or "small". But its present name probably derived from the Arabic *bint al-rion* ("daughter of the winds"), after the restless breezes that blow around the island's rocky shores. Currently, the island is one of the main entry points for boatloads of economic migrants from Africa, who are routinely rounded up and transported to the mainland, where they often spend months waiting to be processed.

There are no beaches of any kind in Pantelleria, its rough black coastline mainly jagged rocks, but the swimming is still pretty good in some exceptionally scenic spots. Inland, the largely mountainous country offers plenty of rambling opportunities, all an easy moped or bus ride from the port, where most of the accommodation options are. If you're spending any length of time on Pantelleria, one novel option is to stay in one of the local *dammuso* houses: their strong walls and domed roofs keep the temperature down indoors and many are available for rent.

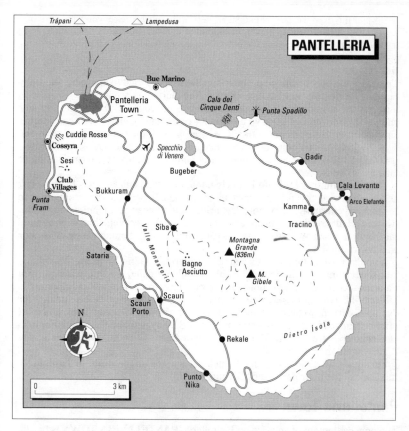

The main drawback to spending time on Pantelleria is the **cost of living**: there are only a few hotels, where the cheapest rooms start at L60,000–80,000 for a double, while food (and water) is mostly imported and therefore relatively expensive. As far as the home-grown **food** is concerned, the island offers some unique gastronomic experiences, as well as some more staple foodstuffs, like lentils, and what are boasted to be the best capers in the Mediterranean. You ought at some point to sample the locally produced ricotta-type cheese known as *tumma*, which is one of the ingredients of *ravioli con menta e ricotta*, a slightly bitter but fresh-tasting dish for which Pantelleria is famous. Pasta often comes served with *pesto pantescho*, a rough sauce of tomatoes, garlic and basil; while an *insalata pantescha* utilizes tomatoes, onions, cubes of boiled potato and local capers and herbs. The **wine** is well thought of too, made from the *zibbibo* grapes that grow well in this volcanic soil. The day-to-day drinking stuff – *vino pantescho* – is mostly white, with a nice fruity fragrance, while for something considerably stronger try the fortified *Moscato*, a sweet, amber-coloured dessert wine. Even better is the raisin wine, known generically as *passito*, which has a rich golden colour and a dry and heady flavour – the best-known variety is *Tanit*.

Despite the expense, a weekend spent here will probably leave you wanting more. Best times are May/June or September/October, to avoid the summer's ferocious heat; try and book your accommodation before you arrive.

Getting there

Trápani is the only mainland port for Pantelleria if you want to arrive by sea. Daily Siremar **ferries** (except Sat Oct–May) do the journey in around five hours, leaving Trápani at midnight, for a deck-class fare of around L40,000 one way. For another L7000 you can reserve a reclining chair, an expense worth considering since the regular seats are difficult to sleep in and uncomfortably close to the TVs. Tickets are on sale in the Siremar office in Trápani, Via A. Staiti 61–63 (☎0923.540.515), right up until departure; book in advance if you're planning to take a car over.

There's a summer **hydrofoil service**, too, from Trápani, which is twice as fast and about twice the price. Ústica Lines (☎0923.27.101) operate from June to September, currently on Wednesday, Friday and Sunday at 8.45am, taking about two and a half hours; tickets are around L60,000 one way. Note that, even in summer, hydrofoil sailings are sometimes cancelled at the last minute because of poor weather conditions.

If you're pushed for time, it's worth considering coming **by plane**: Pantelleria is a thirty-minute flight from Trápani (2–3 flights daily), or fifty minutes from Palermo (2–5 daily). The normal one-way fare from Trápani or Palermo is L90,000–140,000, but there are special deals sometimes on offer: Alitalia, for example, currently charge around L120,000 for a return weekday flight, or a third off the standard fare if you spend Saturday or Sunday night on the island. For tickets, contact Salvo Viaggi in Trápani, Corso Italia 48 (☎0923.545.411), or any Alitalia agent in Trápani or Palermo.

Finally, it's worth knowing that Pantelleria is a stop on the **route to Tunisia** for the Ústica Line hydrofoils (see "Listings", p.373).

Pantelleria Town

The only settlement of any size on Pantelleria, **PANTELLERIA TOWN** is hardly your idyllic island port: most of it was flattened during the last war when Allied bombers pulverized what had become one of the main German bases in the Mediterranean. The scars are still evident, and the numbered blocks of concrete destined for the rebuilding of the harbour are still waiting outside the port.

Consequently, much of the town has an homogenous, modern appearance, its buildings mainly consisting of low-rise concrete cubes spread back two or three streets deep from the harbour. The only building here that predates the war is the morose, black **Castello Barabacane** on the far side of the harbour, a legacy of the Spaniards. The partly restored interior is open daily in summer (6–8pm; free) and for occasional art exhibitions. In case you'd forgotten you're still in Sicily, a plaque on the harbour-facing wall honours assassinated anti-Mafia judge Paolo Borsellino and his five bodyguards.

Yet to call the town unattractive and devoid of interest, as many do, would be to miss the point. It might be small and remote, but it's not as unsophisticated as the other offshore islands – it's long been on the African shipping route and has a distinct liveliness to it, seen best at 6am, when the ferry disgorges its passengers, or at 8pm, when the traffic starts to circle the harbour and the harbourside café-bars fill with perambulating locals. Indeed, arriving here at dawn is rather romantic, as the town lights flick off to reveal a spread of white-painted cubes which – only close up – emerge as modern rather than medieval. Throughout the day delivery vessels and fishing smacks come and go, while the marina sees the manoeuvrings of some uncommonly flash yachts and even the odd schooner or two.

Arrival, information and transport

The **airport** is 5km southeast of town; a bus (L1500) connects with flight arrivals and drops you in the central Piazza Cavour (a 15min journey). **Arriving by sea**, you'll disembark right in the centre of town, just a short walk from most of the bars, restaurants and hotels. In bad weather, you may be deposited instead at Scauri, a smaller port on the island's southwestern side, from where a bus into town picks up foot passengers. Both Siremar and Ústica Lines agencies are on the harbourfront; for ticket agency details, see "Listings", p.373.

There is a **tourist office** (June–Sept Mon–Sat 9.30am–1pm & 5–7pm; ☎0923.911.838) on the main square, Piazza Cavour, or you can usually pick up a rough island **map** from the Siremar office, which – provided it's not too busy – will even entertain a couple of questions about facilities in town.

The little local orange **buses** leave from Piazza Cavour, with regular departures to all the main villages on the island – there are no services on Sundays. Tickets cost L900; buy them in advance from any *tabacchi*, or from *Cicci's Bar* or Alimentari Ugo on the piazza, not on the bus. There's more information about services in the relevant places in the text overleaf. For more independence, you might also consider **renting a moped**; see "Listings" (p.373) for details.

Accommodation

The town has three of the island's **hotels**; other hotels are found at Cuddie Rosse, Punta Fram and Bue Marino and are covered in the relevant places in the text. The price categories given overleaf are in force during July and August, when, depending on demand, there may be a minimum stay of three days or even a

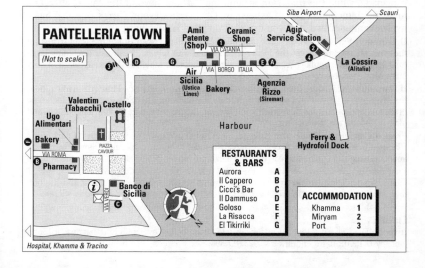

week. There's no **campsite** on the island, and camping rough is impractical given the terrain and the lack of water. If there are two or three of you, a stay in the idiosyncratic *dammuso* houses dotted around the island might be a good idea: try the Call Tour agency, at Via Cágliari 14 (☎0923.911.065), or else check the notices in the bars, hotels and restaurants for local contact numbers.

Khamma, Via Borgo Italia 24 (☎0923.912.680, fax 0923.912.570). Immediately at the end of the dock, on the harbourfront, this offers three-star comforts at fairly reasonable rates. Free pickup from the airport. ⑤.

Miryam, Corso Umberto I (☎0923.911.374, fax 0923.911.777). At the far end of the port, near the castle, this is the cheapest in town and, despite rather glum external appearances, is bright and pleasant inside. Try to get a room with a sea-facing balcony. Breakfast included. ④.

Port, Via Borgo Italia 16 (☎0923.911.299, fax 0923.912.203). Next to the *Khamma* and rather flashier, with a nice covered esplanade-bar overlooking the harbour. Half- or full-board is required in Aug, from L121,000 per person. If you're paying this much, you'll definitely want to secure a harbour-facing room. ⑤.

Eating and drinking

There are several **restaurants and trattorias** in town – all rather flash, though not unaffordable. Most double as pizzerias – and good ones too – so you don't need to spend a fortune every night. Do try at least some of the local specialities though, since the cooking here can be exceptional. Those **self-catering** will find the Alimentari Ugo (8am–1pm & 5.30–8.30pm; closed Wed afternoon & Sun) – selling local cheese, among other things – an adjacent fruit and vegetable shop, and a bakery, respectively on and just off the main Piazza Cavour.

For drinking, the **bars** on the harbourfront are where all the action is, starting at 6am (when they open their doors for the arriving ferry passengers) and finishing any time between midnight and 2am depending on season and inclination. They all have outdoor esplanades (where prices are higher), the nicest belonging to *Goloso*, whose evening drinks come with a dish of olives and other nibbles. *Tikirriki* has good pastries and ice-cream; *Café Aurora* has another fine esplanade; while the *Blue Bar*, around the harbour beyond the castle, attracts a more rambunctious class of fisherman. Off Piazza Cavour, *Cicci's Bar* also has a lively evening crowd, and you can pick up good snacks here.

Il Cappero, Via Roma 31. Probably the best place to eat in town (if not the island), just off the main piazza, this serves the local ravioli stuffed with *tumma*, fresh fish (including large tuna steaks) and popular pizzas. There's a good antipasto table too. Saturday night is very busy. Moderate. No credit cards. Closed Mon in winter.

Il Dammuso, Via Borgo Italia. Trendy little joint that's the best-placed trattoria in town (near the *Miryam*), with windows opening right onto the harbour. There's a long menu, including great fish and pizzas; for dessert, try the *tumma* cheese served here with local capers and olive oil. Moderate. No closing day.

Franco Castiglione, Via Borgo Italia 24. Sleek, air-conditioned restaurant that's part of the *Khamma* hotel. Dip into the excellent (mostly veggie) antipasto table, and follow it with pizza and local wine and you'll escape lightly; full meals are pricier. Moderate–expensive. Closed Fri.

La Risacca, Via Padova 66. Under the same management as *Il Cappero*, and with similar food and prices, but further out from the centre. This place also serves pizzas and has outdoor seating. Moderate. No credit cards. Closed lunchtime in summer & Wed in winter.

Listings

Airport The bus from Piazza Cavour departs 65min before every flight departure, a 15min journey (L1500); flight enquiries ☎0923.911.398.

Bank Banco di Sicilia in Piazza Cavour (Mon–Fri 8.30am–1.30pm & 2.45–3.45pm, plus Aug Mon–Fri 5–6pm & Sat 8.30am–noon); it has a card-taking cash machine. You can also change money at the post office (see below).

Car and bike rental From Autonoleggio Policardo (☎0923.912.844). Bikes from L30,000, scooters from L40,000, and cars from L50,000 (rates vary seasonally).

Ferries and hydrofoils The ferry back to Trápani leaves at 10am (Mon–Thurs & Sun) or 1pm (June–Sept Fri & Sat; Oct–May Fri only). For hydrofoils back to Trápani, from June to Sept, there's a thrice-weekly service at 4.30pm (Wed, Fri & Sun); note, however, that from mid-June to mid-September the Friday departure is at 6.30pm. Hydrofoils also go to Kelibia in Tunisia at 11.30am (June–Sept Wed, Fri & Sun; L30,000 one way), or to Sousse at 10.25am (mid-June to mid-Sept Fri only; L50,000 one way).

First aid and medical matters ☎0923.911.110.

Market Every Tuesday and Friday morning, by the Agip station on the airport road. Fresh fish is sold at stalls on the road to the hospital and lighthouse, on the far side of the harbour from the dock.

Pharmacy Farmacia Greco on Piazza Cavour (Mon–Fri 8.30am–1pm & 4.30–8.30pm).

Police Call ☎0923.912.883.

Post office The island's main post office is off Piazza Cavour on Via Verdi (Mon–Sat 8am–1.20pm); you can change cash and American Express travellers' cheques here.

Shopping There are a couple of good ceramicists working on Pantelleria and shops at the harbour sell decent stuff. For local wines, capers, home-made marmalade, olive paste, preserved seaweed, pasta sauces and much more, visit Amil Patente, a store also marked "Prodotti locali", on Via Catania.

Telephones Phone booths on the corner of Piazza Cavour and on the seafront.

Ticket agencies Cossira, Via Borgo Italia (Mon–Sat 9am–1pm & 5–7pm; ☎0923.911.078), in the *Khamma* hotel, is the Alitalia agent for flights to Trápani and Palermo, and also has local bus timetables posted, as well as those for connecting buses from Trápani and Palermo airports. Siremar tickets are sold by Agenzia Rizzo, Via Borgo Italia 12 (Mon–Fri 5.45am–1pm & 5–6.30pm, Sat 5.45am–1pm, plus Sun in summer 5.45am–1pm; ☎0923.911.104); further along the harbour, the Air Sicilia office sells Ustica Lines hydrofoil tickets before every departure.

Around the island

Surprisingly, most of Pantelleria's population of 8500 are farmers rather than fishermen: with a soil nourished by frequent past eruptions (the last in 1831), the islanders traditionally preferred tilling to risking life and limb in a sea swarming with pirates on the prowl. There are, however, problems relating to farming in Pantelleria, not least the numerous chunks of lava and basalt in the earth that preclude mechanical ploughing, not to mention the incessant wind, scorching sun and almost complete lack of water. But the islanders have evolved methods of minimizing these disadvantages by some ingenious devices that would bring a gleam to an ecologist's eye. The prolific *zibbibo* vines are individually planted in little ridges designed to capture the precious rainwater; and the famous *giardini arabi* – high walls of stone built round orange trees and other plants – give protection from the wind and the salt it carries with it. All over the island, various **co-operatives** (often signposted from the road) sell local produce to visitors and locals – capers, wine, jojoba oil, honey and candles. If you want to buy, look for the words "*azienda agricola*".

Otherwise, it's a blackened landscape, thick with volcanic debris, in which the local **dammuso** houses, when whitewashed, provide some visual relief. Unembellished, these sombre cubic dwellings, unique to the island, blend in perfectly with their environment. These, too, are examples of technological adaptation, the thick walls and shallow-domed roofs designed to maintain a cool internal temperature, while their roofs are ridged to catch the rain.

It's easy enough to get around the island by bus or bike, though to visit the isolated coves of the southeastern Dietro Isola, and other good swimming spots, you'll need to **rent a boat**. There are notices in the agencies along the harbour, in every hotel, and on the boats themselves – it's not hard to track down someone willing to give you a tour, though you'll get a better deal if you can get a small group together.

Along the southwest coast

There are seven daily **buses** along the **southwest coast** to both Scauri and Rekale. If you intend to walk any stretch of this, you're advised to take the bus first to Scauri (25min) and then walk back as far as the Sesi (see below), which, at a couple of hours or so, is more than enough for most people.

The route south of town is initially very unpromising, through an industrial wasteland of noisome and noisy factories, abandoned farmhouses and past a military barracks. Things pick up after a couple of kilometres at the **Cuddie Rosse**, volcanic red rocks that mark the site of a prehistoric cave settlement. There's nothing much to see, though the rocks are overlooked by the *Cossyra Hotel* (☎0923.911.154; ⑤), not bad value given its facilities, which include a pool.

Fifteen minutes' walk further on, a signposted track on the left leads up 300m to the first of the island's strange **Sesi**, massive black Neolithic funeral mounds of piled rock, with low passages leading inside; a second one lies further up to the left. They're thought to be products of Pantelleria's first settlers, possibly from Tunisia. The main one here is 6m high, a striking sight, completely at one with its lunar-like environment. There must have once been scores of these dotting the island, satisfying some primeval fears and beliefs. That so few survive is not so hard to understand when you take a look around at the regular-shaped stones from which the local *dammuso* houses are built – centuries of plunder have taken their toll.

Beyond the Sesi, at **Punta Fram**, the island's poshest resort, the *Club Village Punta Fram* (☎0923.918.075; ⑨; June–Sept) has a tennis court, a fine outdoor swimming pool and steps leading down to its own little rocky cove, from which you can swim happily. There's public access to the coast here, just back down the road a little way towards the Sesi; look for an extremely overgrown footpath, marked "Discesa a mare", opposite a side road to a little tower.

On foot, it's just over an hour all told from the Sesi to **SATARIA**, where concrete steps lead down to a tiny square-cut sea pool, ideal for splashing around in. In the cave behind are more pools where warm water bubbles through, reputed to be good for curing rheumatism and skin diseases: there's usually a handful of people jumping from pools to sea. There's room on the concrete apron around the pool to lay out a towel and it's the only place for kilometres around with any shade; a nice place to eat your picnic.

From the port at **SCAURI**, 2km (30min on foot) further on, you're supposed to be able to see Cape Mustafa in Tunisia on a clear day. There's a commended **restaurant** here, *Zabib*, with a wide terrace right on the portside, though it's only open on summer evenings. The village itself is far removed from its harbour, a steep twenty-minute walk above, and consists of no more than a minuscule church perched on a shelf of land, surrounded by a cluster of houses; there's a bakery and pharmacy, an *alimentari* that does good panini, and – through the hamlet and just beyond the road junction – a sole trattoria, *Trattoria Scauri* (closed Mon & lunchtime in winter).

From here, the only other stop (and end of the bus line) is **REKALE**, an even smaller and more remote hamlet, beyond which the extensive southeastern segment of the island, the **Dietro Isola**, curves round – its most deserted stretch, with the road mostly riding high above the sea with few opportunities for access. There are more hot springs at **Punto Nikà**, which – although you can get there on foot – are better reached by boat.

The northeast coast

There are six daily **buses** along the northeast coast to both Kamma and Tracino, the latter village marking the end of the line, a 25-minute ride from town.

Very early on you'll pass **Bue Marino**, which, though not the most striking part of this coast, does have some more accommodation, in the shape of the *Turistico Residenziale* (☎0923.911.054; ④), and more swimming from the rocks below. The best swimming hereabouts is actually a little further on, from the flat rocks below the road junction to Bugeber (see overleaf).

Really, though, you should stay on the bus, past the **Cala dei Cinque Denti**, whose fantastic-shaped rocks jut out of the sea like monstrous black teeth, hence its name, "Bay of the Five Teeth" – though the rocks are really best seen from the sea. Just beyond, a minor road cuts away to the lighthouse at **Punta Spadillo**, the cliff edges here covered with a carpet of surprising greenery that's somehow taken hold in the volcanic rocks.

There's a fork further on in the road, where the bus can drop you at the top of the smartly engineered route down into **GADIR**, one of the most perfect spots on Pantelleria. It's a small anchorage, with just a few houses hemmed in by volcanic pricks of rock, which – when the wind is up – can be battered and lashed by violent waves. At other times, people desport themselves on the flat concrete harbourside, splashing in the small thermal pools hereabouts.

The lower road from Gadir to Tracino is one of the loveliest on the island, along slopes that are terraced and corralled behind a patchwork of stone walls. Vines grow in profusion; you'll pass capers and blackberry bushes in the hedgerows; and the *Punta Karace* pizzeria-restaurant (☎0923.911.656; June–Sept). It's an easy, fairly flat hour's stroll to the charming **CALA LEVANTE**, a huddle of houses around another tiny fishing harbour. There's a bar here, the *Oasi* (erratic hours) and – provided the sea's not too rough – good swimming from the rocks. Where the road peters out, beyond the *Oasi*, bear right along the path at the second anchorage and keep along the coast for another five minutes until the **Arco dell'Elefante**, or "Elephant Arch", hoves into view, named after the lovely hooped formation of rock that resembles an elephant stooping to drink. Again there's no beach, but it's a good place to swim anyway.

From the harbour, a stupendously steep road climbs all the way up to **TRACINO** in around twenty minutes, passing old *dammusi*, newer holiday homes, and striking gardens of vines and flowers. The top of the road marks the centre of Tracino, where there's a small square, a bar-restaurant, and a parked van selling *tutto per la casa*. There's also a second **restaurant**, *I Mulini* (☎0923.915.398): ask for the *bacci* – waffles wedged together with cream and sugar. It's difficult to see where Tracino ends and adjacent **KAMMA** starts, though it's a matter of supreme indifference once you're on the bus back to town.

Keen **hikers** make Tracino the start of their route into the pretty **Piano Ghirlandia**. The road runs out the other side of Tracino and soon becomes a track, which continues all the way down to meet the road on the south coast near Rekale.

The Specchio di Vénere and Bugeber

From the first road junction on the northwest coast it's a ten-minute walk up and around for the initial stunning views of the island's small lake, **Specchio di Vénere** (Venus Mirror), shimmering below in a former crater. It glistens aquamarine in the middle, though has a muddy-brown edge, deposits of which you're supposed to apply to your body and let bake hard in the sun; then dive in and swim, washing all the mud off in the pleasantly warm water. A path skirts the edge of the lake, around which horse races take place every August as part of the Ferragosto celebrations.

There's a trattoria by the lake shore, *Da Pina*, beyond which the road climbs up for another 2km to the hamlet of **BUGEBER**, set amid tumbling fields of vines and craggy boulders. Just past the white chapel, another **trattoria**, the *Bugeber*, is signposted to the left – it's the house immediately on the left, with a panoramic veranda (closed Tues in winter). The **bus** back to town runs past here twice a day, or walk the 3km past the lake back to the main road, where you can pick up any of the buses from Tracino.

Siba and the Montagna Grande

The other inland destination is up to Pantelleria's main volcano, the Montagna Grande, whose summit is the island's most distinctive feature seen from out at sea. Buses (4 daily) run from the port, turning sharp left past the airport for the crumbly old village of **SIBA**, perched on a ridge below the volcano, with views over the terraced slopes and cultivated plains to the sea. Few of the ancient *dammusi* here are so much as whitewashed, let alone bristling with mod cons; outside, large wooden water barrels sit on the mildewed dry-stone volcanic walls; while the hamlet's only services are an *alimentari* and a *tabacchi*. If time hasn't exactly stood still here, it's in no great hurry to get on with things either.

To climb the peak of **Montagna Grande** (836m), keep left at the telephone sign by the *tabacchi* here, and strike off the main road. The mountain's slopes afford the best views on the island, and are pitted by numerous volcanic vents, the **Stufe de Khazen**, marked by the escaping threads of vapour.

From Siba, another (signposted) path – on the left as you follow the road through the village – brings you in around twenty minutes to a natural sauna, **Sauna Naturale** (or Bagno Asciutto), where you can sweat it out for as long as you can stand. It's little more than a slit in the rock-face, where you can crouch in absolute darkness, breaking out into a heavy sweat as soon as you enter. It's coolest at floor-level; raising yourself up is like putting yourself into a pizza oven, while the ceiling is so hot it's impossible to keep the palm of your hand pressed flat against it. Ten minutes is the most you should attempt the first time – emerging into the midday sun is like being wafted by a cool breeze. Bring a towel.

The road through Siba degenerates into a track which descends back down towards the coast, midway between Scauri and Rekale, running through the so-called **Valle Monastero**. Even locals describe the road as "*brutissima*", but if you're carrying enough water, and tackling the hike early enough in the day, it's a lovely route, past the abandoned monastery that gives the valley its name.

festivals

February
3 Festival of St Biagio in **Salemi**, with pasta figures given to children and a slippery pole competition.

March
19 Festival of St Joseph at **Salemi**, with poetry recitals and sculptures of Jesus, Mary and Joseph made out of bread.

March/April
Good Friday Procession of the Misteri in **Trápani** and **Érice**.

Easter Thursday Enactment of the Passion in **Marsala**, in brightly jewelled processions with gorgeous finery.

Easter Sunday Symbolic meeting of statues of Christ and Mary in **Mazara del Vallo**.

May/June
La Mattanza tuna slaughter in **Favignana**.

June
19–21 Festival of Santa Maria dei Mirácoli at **Álcamo**, with a pilgrimage to Monte Bonifato.
29 Feast of SS Peter and Paul in **Pantelleria**.

July
Music festival in **Trápani** at the Villa Margherita.
10–13 Feast of the Three Maries in **Pantelleria**.

August
Festival of modern Italian art in **Marsala**.
15 Horse race around Specchio di Vénere lake in **Pantelleria**.

September
International couscous festival at **San Vito Lo Capo**.

December
24 Procession of characters from the Nativity story in **Salemi**.

travel details

Trains
Castelvetrano to: Álcamo (8 daily; 45min); Marsala (10 daily; 45min); Mazara del Vallo (10 daily; 20min); Palermo (8 daily; 2hr 15min); Trápani (12 daily; 1hr 10min).
Marsala to: Castelvetrano (11 daily; 45min); Mazara del Vallo (11 daily; 25min); Ragattisi (12 daily; 20min); Trápani (10 daily; 35min).
Mazara del Vallo to: Campobello di Mazara (10 daily; 15min); Castelvetrano (10 daily; 20min); Marsala (12 daily; 25min); Trápani (12 daily; 50min).
Trápani to: Álcamo (10 daily; 40min); Castelvetrano (10 daily; 1hr 10min); Marsala (10 daily; 35min); Mazara del Vallo (10 daily; 50min); Palermo (10 daily; 2hr); Ragattisi (10 daily; 20min); Segesta-Tempio (1 daily; 30min).

Buses
Castellammare del Golfo to: Álcamo (roughly hourly Mon–Sat; 30min); Calatafimi (5 daily Mon–Sat; 40min); Palermo (5 daily; 1hr 30min); San Vito Lo Capo (2 daily Mon–Sat; 1hr); Scopello (5 daily Mon–Sat; 30min); Segesta (5 daily Mon–Sat; 30min); Trápani (3 daily Mon–Sat; 1hr).

Castelvetrano to: Agrigento (4 daily Mon–Sat; 2hr); Gibellina (4 daily Mon–Sat; 30min); Marinella (for Selinunte, 5 daily Mon–Sat; 20min); Marsala (7 daily; 40min); Mazara del Vallo (7 daily; 20min); Palermo (6 daily Mon–Sat, 1 Sun; 2hr); Salemi (4 daily Mon–Sat; 30min); Sciacca (4 daily; 1hr 30min); Trápani (7 daily; 1hr 30min).
Érice to: Trápani (9 daily Mon–Sat, 5 Sun; 40–50 mins).
Marinella/Selinunte to: Menfi/Sciacca (6 daily; 30min/1hr).
Marsala to: Agrigento (5 daily; 3hr 30min); Castelvetrano via Campobello (4 daily; 40min); Mazara del Vallo (7 daily; 30min); Mózia (6 daily Mon–Sat; 15min); Palermo (14 daily Mon–Sat, 5 Sun; 2hr 30min); Trápani (3 daily; 55min).
Mazara del Vallo to: Agrigento (4 daily Mon–Sat; 3hr); Marsala (3 daily; 30min); Palermo (8 daily Mon–Sat, 2 Sun; 2hr 30min); Trápani (3 daily; 1hr 30min).
Pantelleria Town to: Bugeber (2 daily Mon–Sat; 15min); Kamma (6 daily Mon–Sat; 20min); Rekale (7 daily Mon–Sat; 30min); Scauri (7 daily Mon–Sat; 25min); Siba (4 daily Mon–Sat; 20min); Tracino (6 daily Mon–Sat; 25min).

San Vito Lo Capo to: Palermo (4 daily Mon–Sat; 1hr); Trápani (7 daily Mon–Sat, 4 Sun; 1hr 15min).

Scopello to: Castellammare del Golfo (4 daily Mon–Sat; 30min).

Trápani to: Álcamo (6 daily; 40min); Agrigento (4 daily Mon–Sat; 3hr 30min); Castellammare del Golfo (3 daily; 1hr); Castelvetrano (4 daily Mon–Sat; 1hr 30min); Érice (9 daily Mon–Sat, 5 Sun; 40–50min); Marsala (3 daily; 55min); Mazara del Vallo (3 daily; 1hr 30min); Palermo (hourly; 2hr); San Vito Lo Capo (7 daily Mon–Sat, 4 Sun; 1hr 15min).

Ferries

Pantelleria to: Trápani (1 daily June–Sept, 1 daily except Sat Oct–May; 5hr).

Trápani to: Cágliari (1 weekly; 11hr); Civitavecchia (1 weekly; 17hr); Favignana (1 daily; 55min); Lévanzo (3 daily June–Sept, 1 daily Oct–May; 1hr 40min); Maréttimo (1 daily; 2hr 50min); Pantelleria (midnight daily June–Sept, midnight Mon–Sat Oct–May; 5hr 45min); Tunis (1 weekly; 7hr 30min).

Hydrofoils

Pantelleria to: Kelibia, Tunisia (2–3 weekly June–Sept; 1hr 20min); Sousse, Tunisia (1 weekly mid-June to mid-Sept; 2hr 20min); Trápani (3 weekly June–Sept; 2hr 10min–2hr 40min).

Trápani to: Favignana (hourly; 25min); Kelibia, Tunisia (2–3 weekly June–Sept; 4hr); Lévanzo (hourly; 35min); Maréttimo (3 daily; 1hr 5min); Naples (3 weekly June–Sept; 6hr 45min); Pantelleria (3 weekly June–Sept; 2hr 10min–3hr); Sousse, Tunisia (1 weekly June–Sept; 5hr); Ústica (3 weekly June–Sept; 2hr 30min).

Planes

Pantelleria to: Palermo (2–5 daily; 35–50min); Rome (1–2 daily; 30min–1hr 10min); Trápani (2–3 daily; 30min).

Trápani to: Pantelleria (2–3 daily; 30min).

PART THREE

THE

CONTEXTS

SICILY'S HISTORY

Sicily has a richer and more eventful past than any of the other islands dotted around the Mediterranean. Its strategic importance made it the constant prey of conquerors, many of whom, while contributing a rich artistic heritage, also turned Sicily into one of the most desolate war zones in Europe, their greed utterly transforming its ecology and heaping misery onto the vast majority of its inhabitants.

EARLY TIMES

There are numerous remains of the **earliest human settlements** in Sicily, left mainly along the coast by people originally from mainland Europe. The most interesting of these are the cave paintings in Addaura, on the northern face of Monte Pellegrino, and those in the Grotta del Genovese, on Lévanzo in the Égadi Islands, which give a graphic insight into late Ice Age **Paleolithic** culture, from between 20,000 and 10,000 BC.

In the later **Neolithic period**, between 4000 and 3000 BC, there was a new wave of settlers from the eastern Mediterranean, landing on Sicily's east coast and in the Aeolian Islands. Examples of their relatively advanced Stentinello culture – incised and patterned pottery and simple tools – are displayed in the museum on Lípari in the Aeolians. Agricultural advances, the use of ceramics and the domestication of animals, as well as the new tech-

niques of metalworking imported by later waves of Aegean immigrants in the **Copper Age** (3000–2000 BC), permitted the establishment of fixed farms and villages. In turn, this caused an expansion of trade, and promoted greater contact with far-flung Mediterranean cultures. The presence of Mycenaean ware, from the Greek mainland, became more noticeable in the **Bronze Age** (2000–1000 BC), a period to which the sites of Capo Graziano and Punta Milazzese on the Aeolian Islands belong. In about 1250 BC, there were further population movements, this time from the Italian mainland: the Ausonians settled in the Aeolians, and the **Sikels** in eastern Sicily, pushing the indigenous tribes inland. It was the Sikels, from whom Sicily takes its name, who are thought to have first excavated the vast necropolis of Pantálica, near Siracusa. At about the same time, the Sicans, a people thought to have originated in North Africa, occupied the western half of the island. Not much more is known about another tribe in western Sicily, the **Elymians**, who claimed descent from Trojan refugees: their chief city, Segesta, was alleged to have been founded by Aeneas' companion, Acestes.

THE CARTHAGINIANS AND THE GREEKS

After about 900 BC, Mycenaean and Aegean trading contacts began to be replaced by **Carthaginian** ones from North Africa, particularly in the west of the island. The Carthaginians – originally Phoenicians from the eastern Mediterranean – first settled at Panormus (modern Palermo), Solus (Solunto) and Motya (Mózia), during the eighth and seventh centuries BC, their arrival coinciding with the establishment of **Greek colonies** in the east of Sicily. As was the case in previous migrations, the Aegean Greeks who colonized Sicily's eastern coast were driven by a shortage of cultivable land back home. The first Greek settlements had already been made on the Italian mainland in Tuscany and around the bay of Naples, and the colonization of **Naxos** in 734 BC was undertaken primarily for strategic reasons. The possibilities for expansion soon became apparent and the Chalcidinians and Naxians who founded this colony were quickly followed by Megarians at **Megara Hyblaea**, north of Siracusa, Corinthians at **Ortygia** in Siracusa itself, and Rhodians, Cnidians and

Cretans in **Gela**. These cities, while continuing to have close links with their original homes, became independent city-states and founded subcolonies of their own, most important of which were **Selinus** (Selinunte) and **Akragas** (Agrigento). Along with the Greek colonies on the Italian mainland, these scattered communities came to be known as Magna Graecia, "Greater Greece", whose wealth eventually overtook that of Greece itself.

The settlers found themselves with huge resources at their disposal, not least the island's fertility, which they quickly exploited through the widespread cultivation of corn – so much so that Demeter, the Greek goddess of grain and fecundity, became the chief deity on the island: the lake at Pergusa, near Enna, was claimed to be the site of the abduction of her daughter, Persephone. The olive and the vine were introduced from Greece, and commercial activity across the Ionian Sea was intense and profitable. The magnificence of the temples at Syracuse and Akragas often surpassed that of the major shrines in Greece. But the settlers also imported their native rivalries, and the history of Hellenic Sicily is one of almost uninterrupted warfare between the cities, although they generally joined forces in the face of common foes such as the Carthaginians. It was the alliance against Carthage of Gela, Akragas and Syracuse, and the resulting Greek victory at **Himera** in 480 BC, that determined the ascendancy of **Syracuse** in Sicily for the next 270 years. The defeat in about 450 BC of a rebellion led by **Ducetius**, a Hellenized Sikel, extinguished the remnants of any native resistance to Greek hegemony, and the following century has been hailed as the "Golden Age" of Greek Sicily.

The accumulation of power by Syracusan **tyrants** attracted the attention of the mainland Greek states; Athens in particular was worried by the rapid spread of Corinthian influence in Sicily. In 415 BC, Athens dispatched the greatest armada to have ever sailed from its port. Later known as the **Great Expedition**, the effort was in response to a call for help from its ally, Segesta, while at war with Syracuse-supported Selinus. By 413 BC Syracuse itself was under siege, but the disorganization of the attacking forces, who were further hampered by disease, led to their total defeat, the execution of their generals and the imprisonment of 7000 soldiers

in Syracuse's limestone quarries, many destined for slavery. This victory represented the apogee of Syracusan power. Civil wars continued throughout the rest of the island, attracting the attention of the Carthaginian **Hannibal**, who responded to attacks on his territory by sacking in turn Selinus, Himera, Akragas and Gela. A massive counterattack was launched by the Syracusan tyrant **Dionysius I**, or "the Elder" (405–367 BC), which culminated in the complete destruction of the Phoenician base at Motya, its survivors founding a new centre on the western tip of the island at Lilybaeum – modern Marsala.

The general devastation in Sicily caused by these wars was to some extent reversed by **Timoleon** (345–336 BC), who rebuilt many of the cities and re-established democratic institutions with new injections of settlers from Italy and Greece. But the carnage continued under the tyrant **Agathocles** (315–289 BC), who was unrivalled in his sheer brutality. Battles were fought on the Italian mainland and North Africa, and the strife he engendered back in Sicily didn't end until **Hieron II** (265–215 BC) opted for a policy of peacekeeping, and even alliance, with the new power of the day, Rome. The **First Punic War** that broke out in 264 BC – when the mercenary army in control of Messina, the **Mamertines**, appealed to Rome for help against their erstwhile Carthaginian protectors – left Syracuse untouched, though again it led to the ruin of much of the island, before the final surrender of the Carthaginian base at Lilybaeum in 241. For Syracuse and its territories, though, this was a period of relative peace, and Hieron used the breathing space to construct some of the city's most impressive monuments.

ROMAN SICILY

Roman rule in Sicily can be said to have begun with **the fall of Syracuse**, a momentous event that became inevitable when the city, whose territory was by now the only part of Sicily still independent of Rome, chose to side with Carthage in the **Second Punic War**, provoking a two-year siege that ended with the sack of Syracuse in 211 BC. For the next seven hundred years, Sicily was a province of Rome, though in effect a subject colony, since few Sicilians were granted citizenship until the third century AD, when all inhabitants of the Empire were classified as Romans. Much of the island's present appearance was determined during this period.

Large parts of the remaining forests were cut down to make way for the grain cultivation that was to become Sicily's major function. Sicily was Rome's granary or, as Cato had it, "the nurse at whose breast the Roman people is fed". The land was apportioned into large units or *latifondia*, which became the basis for the vast agricultural estates into which Sicily is still to a certain extent divided. Conditions on these estates were so harsh that the second century BC saw two **slave revolts**, in 135–132 BC and 104–101 BC, involving tens of thousands of men, women and children, most of whom had been Greek-speaking citizens from all over Rome's newly won Mediterranean and Asian empire. Far more damaging to the island, however, was the **civil war** between Octavian, the future emperor Augustus, and Sextus Pompey, who seized Sicily in 44 BC. For eight years the island's crucial grain exports were interrupted, and the final defeat of Sextus – in a sea battle off Mylae, or Milazzo – was followed by harsh retribution against the island.

These were isolated incidents, however, and on the whole Sicily benefited from the relative calm bestowed by the Romans. But little of the heavy tribute exacted by Rome was expended on the island itself and, though a degree of local administration existed, all important decisions were taken by the Roman Senate. It was represented on the island by two tax collectors, or quaestors, stationed in Syracuse and Lilybaeum, and a governor (praetor), who normally spent his year-long term extracting as much personal profit from the island as he could. The praetor **Verres** used his three terms of office, from 73 to 71 BC, to strip the countryside and despoil a large part of the treasure still held in the island's lavish temples. **Cicero**'s prosecution of Verres, though undoubtedly exaggerated, constitutes our main source of information on Sicily under the Roman Republic. It gives some idea of the extent of the ruination wreaked by the unscrupulous praetor: "When I arrived in Sicily after an absence of four years, it seemed to me a land in which there had been fought a prolonged and cruel war. Those fields and hills which I had seen bright and green I now saw devastated and deserted, and it seemed as if the land itself wept for its ancient farmers."

With Octavian instated as emperor in 27 BC, Sicily entered a more peaceful period of Roman rule, with isolated instances of imperial splendour, notably the extravagant villa at Casale, near Piazza Armerina. The island benefited especially from its important role in Mediterranean trade, and Syracuse, which handled much of the passing traffic, became a prominent centre of **early Christianity**, supposedly visited by SS Peter and Paul on their way to Rome. Here, and further inland at Akrai, catacombs were burrowed from the third century AD onwards – and in caves throughout Sicily Christian sanctuaries took their place alongside the shrines of the dozens of other cults prevalent on the island.

BARBARIANS, BYZANTINES AND THE ARABS

Rome fell to the Visigoths in 410 AD, though Sicily became prey to another Germanic tribe, the **Vandals**, who launched their invasion from the North African coast. The island was soon reunited with Italy under the Ostrogoth Theodoric, though the barbarian presence in Sicily was only a brief interlude, terminated in 535 AD when the **Byzantine** general Belisarius occupied the island. Although a part of the population had been Latinized, Greek remained the dominant culture and language of the majority, and the island willingly joined the Byzantine fold. In 663, Syracuse even became briefly the centre of the eastern empire, possibly for political reasons but no doubt partly with an eye to the reconquest of barbarian lands and the ultimate revival of the Roman Empire.

But Constantinople was never able to give much attention to Sicily, and the island was perpetually harried by piratical attacks, particularly from North Africa, where the Moors had become the most dynamic force in the Mediterranean. In around 700, the island of **Pantelleria** was taken, and it was only discord among the Arabs that prevented Sicily itself from being next. In the event, trading agreements were signed, Arab merchants settled in Sicilian ports, and it was not until 827 that a fully fledged **Arab invasion** took place, when a Byzantine admiral rebelled against the emperor and invited in the Aghlabid Emir of Tunisia. Ten thousand Arabs, Berbers and Spanish Muslims (known collectively as **Saracens**) landed at Mazara del Vallo, and four years later Palermo fell, though it wasn't until 965 that the invading forces reached the Straits of Messina. As with the Roman invasion, however, the turning point came with the fall of Syracuse in 878, its population massacred and the city plundered of its legendary wealth.

Palermo became the capital of the **Arabs in Sicily**, under whom it grew to become one of the world's greatest cities, wholly cosmopolitan in outlook, furnished with gardens, mosques (more than anywhere the traveller Ibn Hauqal had seen barring Cordoba) and luxurious palaces. The Arabs brought great benefits to the rest of the island, too, resettling rural areas, renovating and extending the irrigation works, breaking down many of the unwieldy *latifondia* and introducing new crops, including citrus trees, sugar cane, flax, cotton, silk, melons and date palms. Mining was developed, the salt industry greatly expanded and commerce improved, with Sicily once more at the centre of a flourishing trade network. Many Sicilian place names testify to the extent of the Arab settlement of the island, with prefixes such as *calta* (castle) and *gibil* (mountain) plentiful; while other terms still in use indicate their impact on fishing, such as the name of the swordfish boats prowling the Straits of Messina (*felucca*), or the tuna-fishing terminology of the Égadi Islands. Taxation was rationalized and reduced, and religious tolerance was greater than under the Byzantines, though non-Muslims were subject to a degree of social discrimination − a factor that probably helped to persuade a large number of Christians to adopt the Muslim faith.

The Arabs were prone to divisive feuding, however, and when in the tenth century the Aghlabid dynasty was toppled in Tunisia and their Fatimid successors shifted their capital to Egypt, Sicily lost its central position in the Arab Mediterranean empire and was left vulnerable to external attack. In 1038, the Byzantine general **George Maniakes** attempted to draw the island back under Byzantine sway, but he was unable to extend his occupation much beyond Syracuse. The real threat came from western Europe, particularly from the **Normans**, some of whom had accompanied Maniakes and seen for themselves the rewards to be gained. One of these, William "Bras de Fer" ("Iron Arm"), who had earned his nickname by his slaying of the Emir of Syracuse with one blow, was the eldest of the Hauteville brothers whose exploits were soon to change the map of southern Europe.

THE NORMANS

The **Hauteville brothers** had long been active in southern Italy by the time the youngest of them, Roger, seized Messina in 1061 in response to a call for help by one of the warring Arab factions. It took another thirty years to take control of the whole island, in a series of bloody and destructive campaigns that often involved the enlistment of Arabs on the Norman side. In 1072 Palermo was captured and adopted as the capital of **Norman Sicily**, and was subsequently adorned with palaces and churches that count among their most brilliant achievements.

The most striking thing about the Norman period in Sicily is its brief span. In little more than a century, five kings bequeathed an enormous legacy of art and architecture that is still one of the most conspicuous features of the island. When compared with the surviving remains of the Byzantines, who reigned for three centuries, or the Arabs, whose occupation lasted roughly two, the Norman contribution stands out, principally due to its absorption of previous styles: the best examples of Arab art to be seen in Sicily are elements incorporated into the great Norman churches. It was this fusion of talent that accounted for the great success of Norman Sicily, not just in the arts but in administration, justice and religious tolerance.

The policy of acceptance and integration was largely determined by force of circumstances: the Normans could not count on having adequate numbers of their own settlers, or bureaucrats to form a governmental class, and instead were compelled to rely on the existing framework. They did, however, considerably streamline and centralize administration, and gradually introduced a Latinized aristocracy and clerical hierarchy from northern Italy and France, so that the Arabic language was largely superseded by Italian and French by 1200.

The first of the great Sicilian-Norman dynasty, **Count Roger**, or Roger I, sustained his power in accordance with Byzantine notions of absolutism and through his retention of a permanent mercenary army and strong fleet. He was a resolute and successful ruler, marrying his daughters into two of the most powerful European dynasties, one of them to the son of the western emperor Henry IV. Roger's death in 1101, followed soon after by the death of his eldest son, left Sicily governed by his widow Adelaide as regent for his younger son, who in 1130 was crowned **Roger II**. This first Norman king of Sicily was also one of medieval Europe's most gifted and charismatic rulers, who consolidated his father's gains by making the island a great melting pot of the most vigorous and creative elements in the Mediterranean world. He spoke Greek, kept a harem and surrounded himself with a medley of advisers, notably **George of Antioch**, his chief minister, or Emir of emirs. As well as being a patron of the arts, Roger extended his kingdom to encompass all of southern Italy, Malta and parts of North Africa, and more enduringly drew up the first written code of law in the island.

His son, William I (1154–1166) – "**William the Bad**" – dissipated these achievements by his enthusiasm for pleasure-seeking and his failure to control the barons, who exploited racial tensions to undermine the king's authority. During the regency that followed, the Englishman Walter of the Mill had himself elected Archbishop of Palermo and dominated the scene for some twenty years, along with two other Englishmen: his brother Bartholomew and Bishop Palmer. This triumvirate preserved a degree of stability, but also encouraged the new king William II (1166–1189), "**William the Good**", to establish a second archbishopric and construct a cathedral at **Monreale** to rival that of Palermo, just 10km away. The period saw a general consolidation of Christianity and a shift away from Muslim influence, though Arabs still constituted the bulk of the rural population and William himself resembled an oriental sultan in his style and habits, building a number of Arab-style palaces.

The death of William, aged only 36 and with no obvious successor, signalled a crisis in Norman Sicily. The barons were divided between **Tancred**, William's illegitimate nephew, and **Constance**, Roger II's aunt who had married the Hohenstaufen (or Swabian) Henry, later to become the emperor Henry VI. Tancred's election by an assembly was the first sign of a serious erosion of the king's authority: others followed, notably a campaign in 1189 against Muslims living on the island, which caused many of them to flee; and a year later the sacking of **Messina** by the English Richard I, on his way to join the Third Crusade. Tancred's death in 1194 and the succession of his young

son, **William III**, coincided with the arrival in the Straits of Messina of the Hohenstaufen fleet. Opposition was minimal, and on Christmas Day of the same year Henry crowned himself king of Sicily. William and his mother were imprisoned in the castle at **Caltabellotta**, never to be seen again.

HOHENSTAUFEN AND THE ANGEVINS

Inevitably, Henry's imperial concerns led him away from Sicily, which represented only a source of revenue for him on the very outer limits of his domain. A revolt broke out against his authoritarian rule, which he repressed with extreme severity, but in the middle of it he went down with dysentery, died, and the throne passed to his three-and-a-half-year-old son, who became the emperor Frederick II, **Frederick I** of Sicily.

At first the running of the kingdom was entrusted to Frederick's mother Constance, but there was little stability, with the barons in revolt and a rash of race riots in 1197. Frederick's assumption of the government in 1220 marked a return to decisive leadership, with an immediate campaign to bring the barons to heel and eliminate a Muslim rebellion in Sicily's interior. The twin aims of his rule in Sicily were to restore the broad framework of the Norman state, and to impose a more authoritarian and imperial stamp on society, indicated by his fondness for classical Roman allusions in his promulgations and coinage. He allowed himself rights and privileges in Sicily that were impossible in his other possessions, emphasizing his own authority at the expense of the independence of the clergy and the autonomy of the cities. As elsewhere in southern Italy, strong **castles** were built, such as those at Milazzo, Catania, Siracusa and Augusta, to keep the municipalities in check. When the most progressive of these, Messina, rebelled in 1232, the port was ruthlessly punished.

A unified legal system was drawn up, embodied in his *Liber Augustales*, while his attempts to homogenize Sicilian society involved the harsh treatment of what had now become minority communities, such as the Muslims. He encouraged the arts, too, championing Sicilian vernacular poetry, whose preeminence was admitted by Petrarch and Dante. A multi-talented ruler, Frederick acquired the name "**Stupor Mundi**" ("Wonder of the World"), reflecting his promotion of science, law and medicine, and the peace that Sicily enjoyed during the half-century of his rule.

However, Frederick's mounting preoccupation with his other territories was to the detriment of the island. The balance of power he achieved within Sicily laid the foundations for many of the island's future woes – for example, the weakening of the municipalities at a time when most European towns were increasing their autonomy. His centralized government worked so long as there was a powerful hand guiding it, but when Frederick died in 1250 decline set in, despite the efforts of his son **Manfred**, who strove to defend his crown from the encroachments of the barons and the acquisitiveness of foreign monarchs. New claimants to the throne were egged on by Sicily's nominal suzerain, the pope, anxious to deprive the Hohenstaufen of their southern possession, and he eventually auctioned it, selling it to the king of England, who accepted it on behalf of his eight-year-old son, Edmund of Lancaster. For ten years Edmund was styled "King of Sicily".

But a new French pope deposed Edmund, who had never set foot in Sicily, and gave the title instead to **Charles of Anjou**, brother of the French king, "St" Louis IX. In 1266 the Angevin forces beat the Hohenstaufen army in a battle on the Italian mainland, in which Manfred was slain, and in 1268 another battle resulted in Manfred's 14-year-old nephew, his heir Conradin, being publicly beheaded. Backed by the papacy and with a degree of popular support, Charles of Anjou embarked on a punitive campaign against the majority of the Sicilian population, who had supported the Hohenstaufen, plundering land to give to his followers and imposing a high level of taxation to recoup the cost of the recent war. The nobility, too, were affected by Charles's draconian measures and some began negotiating with the Ghibelline, anti-papal faction in Aragon, where the king, Peter, had become the champion of the Hohenstaufen cause by marrying Manfred's daughter. But in the end it was a grassroots revolt that sparked off the **Sicilian Vespers**, an uprising against the French that began on Easter Monday 1282; it is traditionally held to have started after the bell for evening services, or Vespers, had rung at Palermo's church of

Santo Spirito. The incident that sparked it all off was an insult to a woman by a French soldier, which led to a general slaughter in Palermo, soon growing into an island-wide rebellion against the French. It was the one moment in Sicilian history when the people rose up as one against foreign oppression – though in reality it was more an opportunity for horrific butchery and the settlement of old scores than a glorious expression of patriotic fervour.

The movement was given some direction when a group of nobles enlisted the support of Peter of Aragon, who landed at Trápani five months after the initial outbreak of hostilities and was acclaimed king at Palermo a few days later. The ensuing **Wars of the Vespers**, fought between Aragon and the Angevin forces based in Naples, lasted for another 21 years, mainly waged in Spain and at sea, while, in Aragonese Sicily, people settled down to over five centuries of Spanish domination.

THE SPANISH IN SICILY

Sicily's new orientation towards Spain and its severance from mainland Italy meant that it was largely excluded from all the great European developments of the fourteenth and fifteenth centuries. There was no liberation from feudalism, and little impact was made by the Renaissance. Rather, the feudal bonds were reinforced at the expense of social mobility, with the granting of large portions of land to a Spanish aristocracy in return for military service, while intellectual life on the island was suffocated by the strictures of the Spanish Inquisition.

Although Peter of Aragon insisted that the two kingdoms of Aragon and Sicily should be ruled by separate kings after his death, his successor James ignored this and even reopened negotiations with the Angevins to sell the island back to them. His younger brother Frederick, appointed by James as Lieutenant of Palermo, convened a "parliament", which elected him king of an independent Sicily as **Frederick II** (1296–1337). As a result of the barons' support for him, Frederick was obliged to increase their feudal privileges, at the expense of his own. Factions arose, growing out of the friction between Angevin and Aragonese supporters and fuelled by Angevin Naples. Open warfare followed until 1372, when the independence of

Sicily – or Trinacria ("three-cornered"), as it was known under the terms of the subsequent treaty, an ancient name revived to distinguish the island from the mainland Regnum Sicilae, ruled by the kngdom of Naples – was guaranteed by Naples in return for an annual tribute and the recognition of the suzerainty of the pope.

It was the populace that suffered most from this feuding, since the policy of both sides was to avoid pitched battles and strike instead at the food sources in the country. This, combined with the effects of the Black Death, led to the interior of Sicily becoming depopulated and unproductive. The feudal nobility spent time mainly in the **towns**, and here at least there is some evidence of wealth in the mansions constructed during this period, in the **Chiaramonte** or the later, richly ornate **Catalan-Gothic** styles. A tradition of artistic patronage grew up, though most of the artists operating in Sicily came from elsewhere – for example, Francesco Laurana and the Gagini family were originally from northern Italy. A notable exception was **Antonello da Messina** (1430–1479), who soaked up the latest Flemish techniques on his continental travels. With the closing off of the eastern Mediterranean by the Ottoman Turks in the fifteenth century, Sicily was isolated from everywhere except Spain – from which, after 1410, it was ruled directly. The ports of Palermo and Messina continued to do a certain amount of business, but most of the merchants were from Genova, Pisa and Lucca. Sicily found itself on the very fringes of Europe, an Aragonese outpost in the firing line from Turkish incursions and raids from North Africa. The unification of Castile and Aragon in 1479, followed soon after by the reconquest of the whole Spanish peninsula from the Moors, meant that Sicily's importance to its Spanish monarchs declined even more, and the island soon became of most use as a source of cash, crucial for the financing of the Riconquista and the wars against the Turks.

Athough **Alfonso II** (1416–1458) made the island the base for his expansion to Naples, the two territories were separated again after his death, and Sicily came under the rule of a succession of **viceroys**, who were to wield power for the next four hundred years. Few of these were Sicilian (none at all after the first fifty years), while the only Spanish king to visit the island during the whole viceregal period was Charles V, on his way back from a Tunisian crusade in 1535.

Little else of note happened in the **sixteenth century**, though the curse of piracy was partially removed by the victory of the combined fleets of Spain, Venice and the Vatican against the Ottomans in 1571, at the Battle of Lépanto. But with the Spanish centres of power removed from the Mediterranean, and mercantile and imperial interest focused instead on the Atlantic, the period saw the utter **stagnation** of Sicily. The island's close bond to Spain meant that its degeneration deepened with Spain's decline in the **seventeenth and eighteenth century**. The aristocracy maintained their power and privileges while they were being eroded everywhere else in Europe, and corruption thrived in the viceroy's court, with offices being bought and sold and political patronage the order of the day. Throughout this period, Sicily still had a parliament, though it was largely symbolic. More far-reaching was the influence of **the Church**, one of the main pillars of the State and mainly non-Sicilian at its highest levels. This was bolstered by the wide powers of **the Inquisition**, both institutions playing a great part in creating and enforcing a sense of loyalty and even veneration to the Spanish Crown, though the overall effect was a docile acceptance of the status quo on the part of Sicilians. Certainly there were few serious attempts at rebellion during this period, apart from a couple of isolated and short-lived uprisings in Sicily's two major towns, Palermo and Messina. There were, too, occasional revolts against the excesses of the zealous Inquisition, though on the whole discontent manifested itself in a resort to **brigandage**, for which the forest and wild *maquis* of Sicily's interior provided an ideal environment. The mixed fear and respect that the brigand bands generated played a large part in the future formation of an organized criminal class in Sicily.

Already burdened by the ever-increasing taxes demanded by Spain to finance its remote religious conflicts (principally, the Thirty Years' War, 1618–1648), the misery of the Sicilians was compounded by sporadic outbreaks of **plague**, and at the end of the seventeenth century by two appalling natural disasters. The **eruption of Etna** in 1669 devastated a large part of the area around Catania, while the **earthquake** of 1693 – also in the east of the island – flattened whole cities, killing around five percent of the island's population. These disasters did at least provide an opportunity for Sicilian craftsmen to show off the latest **Baroque building** techniques when called upon to repair the damage. With the death of Charles II of Spain in 1700 and the subsequent Wars of the Spanish Succession, the island once more took a back seat to mainland European interests, was bartered in the **Treaty of Utrecht** that negotiated the peace, and given to the northern Italian House of Savoy, only to be swapped for Sardinia and given to Austria seven years later.

The **Austrian government** of the island – as usual administered through viceroys – lasted only four years, cut short by the arrival of another Spaniard, Charles of Bourbon, who claimed the throne of the Two Sicilies (the title of the combined southern Italian possessions of the Spanish and Bourbon kings of Naples) for himself. Though he never visited Sicily again after his first landing, **Charles III** (1734–1759) brought a refreshingly constructive air to the island's administration, showing a more benevolent attitude towards his new subjects, to whom he granted significant tax concessions. But, with his succession to the Spanish throne in 1759 and the inheritance of the Neapolitan Crown by his son, **Ferdinand IV**, it was back to the bad old days. Any meagre attempts at reform made by his viceroys were opposed at every turn by the reactionary aristocracy, who were closing ranks in response to the progress of the Enlightenment and the ideas unleashed by the French Revolution. In the ensuing **Napoleonic Wars**, which wracked Europe, Sicily, along with Sardinia, was the only part of Italy unconquered by Napoleon, while the Neapolitan *ancien régime* was further buttressed by the decision of Ferdinand (brother-in-law of Marie Antoinette) to wage war against the revolutionary French. He was supported in this by the British, who sustained the Bourbon state, so that when Ferdinand and his court were forced to flee Naples in 1799 it was **Nelson**'s flagship they sailed in, accompanied by the British ambassador to Naples, Sir William Hamilton, and his wife Lady Emma. Nelson was rewarded for his services by the endowment of a large estate at Bronte, just west of Etna.

Four years later, Ferdinand was able to return to Naples, though he had to escape again in 1806 when Napoleon gave the Neapolitan crown to his brother Joseph. This time he had to stay longer, remaining in Palermo until after the defeat of Napoleon in 1815 – a stay that was accompanied by a larger contingent of British troops and a heavy involvement of British capital and commerce. **Liberalism** became a banner of revolt against the king's continuing tax demands, and Ferdinand's autocratic reaction provoked the British commander **Bentinck** to intervene. Manoeuvring himself into a position where he was the virtual governor of Sicily, Bentinck persuaded the king to summon a new parliament and adopt a **constitution** whereby the independence of Sicily was guaranteed and feudalism was abolished.

Although this represented a drastic break with the past, the reforms had little direct effect on the peasantry, and, following the departure of the British, the constitution was dropped soon after Ferdinand's return to the mainland. He now styled himself "Ferdinand I, King of the Two Sicilies" and repealed all the reforms previously introduced. Renewed talk of independence in Sicily spilled over into action in 1820, when a rebellion was put down with the help of Austrian mercenaries. The **repression** intensified after Ferdinand I's death in 1825, and the island's fortunes reached a new low under Ferdinand II (1830–59), nicknamed Re Bomba for his five-day **bombardment of Messina** following major insurrections there and in Palermo in 1848–49. Another uprising in Palermo in 1860 proved a spur for Garibaldi to pick Sicily as the starting point for his unification of Italy.

UNIFICATION, AND TWO WORLD WARS

On May 11, 1860, five weeks after the Palermo revolt, **Giuseppe Garibaldi**, a professional soldier and one of the leading lights of **Il Risorgimento**, the movement for Italian unification, landed at Marsala with a thousand men, with whom he intended to liberate the island from Bourbon rule, in the name of the Piedmont House of Savoy. His skill in guerrilla warfare, backed by an increasingly cooperative peasantry, ensured that the campaign progressed with astonishing speed. Four days after disembarking, he defeated 15,000 Bourbon troops at **Calatafimi**, closely followed by an almost effortless occupation of Palermo. A battle at **Milazzo** in July decided the issue: apart from Messina (which held out for another year),

Sicily was free of Spain for the first time since Peter of Aragon acquired the crown in 1282.

A **Plebiscite** was held in October, which returned a 99.5 percent majority in favour of union with the new kingdom of Italy under Vittório Emanuele II. The result, greeted by general euphoria, marked the end of Garibaldi's five-month dictatorship, and the official **annexation** of the island to the Kingdom of Savoy. Later, however, many began to question whether anything had been achieved by this change of ruler. The new **parliamentary system**, in which only one percent of the island's population were eligible to vote, made few improvements for the majority of people, with political patronage, as ever, determining voting tendencies. Attempts at opposition – and local uprisings such as that at Palermo in 1866 – were met with ruthless force, sanctioned by a distant and misinformed government convinced that the island's problems were fundamentally ones of law and order. Sicilians responded with their traditional defence of *omertà*, or silent non-cooperation, along with a growing **resentment** of the new Turin government (transferred to Rome in 1870) that was even stronger than their distrust of the more familiar Bourbons.

A series of reports made in response to criticism of the Italian government's failure to solve what was becoming known as "**the southern problem**" found that the lot of the Sicilian peasant was, if anything, worse after unification than it had been under the Bourbons. Power had shifted away from the landed gentry to the middlemen to whom they leased the land, the *gabellotti*. These men became increasingly linked with the **Mafia**, a shadowy, loosely knit criminal association that found it easy to manipulate voting procedures, while simultaneously posing as defenders of the people. Everywhere, liberal programmes of reform were similarly subverted by the deep-rooted power relationships of the rural society onto which they had been superimposed. But at the end of the nineteenth century a new, more organized opposition appeared on the scene in the form of **fasci** – embryonic trade-union groups demanding legislation to protect peasants' interests. Violence erupted and, when landowners called for repressive measures, the Italian prime minister, **Francesco Crispi** – a native Sicilian who had been one of the pioneers of the Risorgimento – dispatched a fleet and 30,000 soldiers to put down the "revolt", making use of an armoury of autocratic measures in the process, such as closing newspapers, censoring postal services and detaining suspects without trial. But, just as rashly, he soon followed repression with a radical series of reforms designed to effect a fairer and more efficient distribution of the land. These proposals, and others to grant partial autonomy to the region, were rejected by conservative Sicilians, who complained of interference in their affairs.

Although there were some signs of progress by the **end of the nineteenth century**, in the formation of worker cooperatives and in the enlightened land-reform programmes of individuals such as **Don Sturzo**, mayor of Caltagirone, the overwhelming despair of the peasantry was expressed in **mass emigration**. Despite their intimate attachment to the land and their close-knit family structure, one and a half million Sicilians decided to leave in the years leading up to 1914, most going to North and South America. Many of these were people who had been left homeless in the wake of the great **Messina earthquake** of 1908, in which upwards of 80,000 lost their lives. The high rate of emigration was a crushing indictment of the state of affairs on the island, though it had many positive effects for those left behind, who became the beneficiaries of huge remittances sent back from abroad and of the wage increases that resulted from labour shortages.

But any advantages were offset by Italy's military adventures. The **conquest of Libya** in 1912 was closely followed by **World War I**, and both were heavy blows to the Sicilian economy. In 1922 **Mussolini** gained power in Rome – largely without Sicilian support – and dispatched **Cesare Mori** to solve "the southern problem" by putting an end to the Mafia. Free of constitutional and legal restrictions, Mori was able to imprison thousands of suspected *mafiosi*. But the effect was only to drive the criminal class deeper underground, while the alliance he forged with the landed classes to help bring this about dissolved all the gains that had been made against the ruling elite, setting back the cause of agrarian reform. In the **1930s** Mussolini's African concerns and his drive for economic and agricultural self-sufficiency gave Sicily a new importance for Fascist Italy, the island now vaunted as "the geographic centre of the empire'. In the much-publicized

"**Battle for Grain**", wheat production increased, though at the cost of the diversity of crops that Sicily required, resulting in soil exhaustion and erosion. Mussolini's popularity on the island is best illustrated by his order, in 1941, that all Sicilian-born officials be transferred to the mainland, on account of their possible disloyalty.

In **World War II**, Sicily was the first part of Europe to be invaded by the Allies, when, in July 1943, Patton's American Seventh Army landed at Gela and Montgomery's British Eighth Army came ashore between Pachino and Pozzallo further east. This combined army of 160,000 men was the biggest ever seen in Sicily, but the campaign was longer and harder than had been anticipated, with the Germans mainly concerned with delaying the advance until they had moved most of their men and equipment over the Straits of Messina. Few Sicilian towns escaped **aerial bombardment**, with Messina itself the most heavily bombed of all Italian cities before it was taken on August 18.

MODERN TIMES

The **aftermath** of the war saw the most radical changes in Sicily since unification, and a series of intense and convoluted struggles between competing interests. With anarchy and hunger widespread, a wave of banditry and crime was unleashed, while the **Mafia** were reinstated in their behind-the-scenes role as adjudicators and power-brokers, now allied to the landowners in the face of large-scale land occupations by a desperate peasantry. **Separatism** became a potent rallying cry for protesters of all persuasions, who believed that Sicily's ills could best be solved by cutting its links with the mainland, and a Separatist army was formed, financed by some of the gentry, though lacking the organization or resources to make any great impact. It was largely in response to this call for independence that, in 1946, Sicily was granted **regional autonomy**, with its own assembly and president – its status comparable to that of Northern Ireland in the UK before the dissolution of Stormont. The same year saw the declaration of a republic in Italy, the result of a popular mandate.

Autonomy failed to heal the island's divisions, however, and brute force was used by the Mafia and the old gentry against what they perceived as the major threat to their position – **Communism**. The most famous bandit of the

time, **Salvatore Giuliano**, who had previously been associated with the Separatists, was enlisted for the anti-communist cause, organizing a campaign of bombings and assassinations, most notoriously at the 1947 May Day celebrations at **Portella della Ginestra**, a mountain pass near Palermo. Giuliano's betrayal and murder in 1950 was widely rumoured to have been carried out to prevent him revealing who his paymasters were, though it all helped to glorify his reputation in the popular imagination.

By the **1950s**, many saw the **Christian Democrat** party, Democrazia Cristiana, as the best hope to defend their interests. Along with the emotional hold it exerted by virtue of its close association with the Church, the DC could draw on many of the Sicilians' deepest fears of change. It became especially important after **Fanfani**'s revitalization of the party after 1954, with Sicily holding about a third of his supporters country-wide. But the party was too closely involved with business and the landowning classes to have any real enthusiasm for reform. All attempts at enterprise were channelled through the party's offices, and favours were bought or bartered. Cutting across party lines, political patronage, or **clientelismo**, grew to be stronger than ever, still today affecting people's lives on all levels, especially in the field of work – from finding a job to landing a contract. The favours system was also evident in the workings of the island's sluggish **bureaucracy**, considered even more contorted than the mainland's, so that the smallest reforms proved complicated to put into practice, often taking years to effect. In 1971 a law was passed to improve the functioning of the bureaucracy, but, though progress has been made, the essential problem is unchanged, with the elaborate machinery of the civil service often exploited to accumulate and dispense personal power.

One area that managed to avoid bureaucratic control or planning of any sort was **construction** – one of Sicily's greatest growth industries, the physical evidence of which is one of the visitor's most enduring impressions of the island. The building boom was inextricably connected with the Mafia's involvement in land speculation, and boosted by the phenomenal rate of **urban growth** all over Sicily. But in both the towns and rural areas, the minimum safety standards were rarely met, as highlighted by the **1968 earthquake**, in which 50,000 were made homeless along the Valle di Belice, although the quake was seismically quite small. But, while large expanses of the countryside have been blighted by rapid and often unsafe development, other areas are badly neglected, for instance Palermo, where, in some areas, bomb damage is still unrepaired after more than fifty years.

Industry, too, has been subject to mismanagement, and, apart from isolated cases, has rarely fulfilled the potential it promised after the discovery of oil near Ragusa and Gela in the 1950s, and the development of refineries and petrochemical plants on the Golfo di Augusta. Despite the huge resources allocated to them, other projects have failed miserably. **Agriculture**, on the other hand, has been deprived of both funds and attention, though investment and the better use of land can produce outstanding results, as shown by the success of citrus cultivation in the north and east of the island, and the draining of the Piana di Catania. Substantial subsidies have helped in these programmes, mainly through a financial agency called the Cassa del Mezzogiorno, set up in 1950 but discontinued in 1983, and from the **European Union**, which Italy joined in 1958. But membership of the European Union, in which Sicily – a "problem region" – is more marginalized than ever, also poses problems for the local economy, with increased competition for farmers following the accessions of Spain, Greece and Portugal.

Subsidy and support, meanwhile, have not prevented Sicilians from complaining of being left out of Italy's great "economic miracle". While Italy claims to be the eighth most industrialized nation in the West, it is the great urban centres of the north of Italy that flaunt their prosperity, while the south of Italy, known as Il Mezzogiorno, is left far behind. The other side of the coin is that the huge financial concessions made to the island have provoked resentment from Italy's more self-sufficient regions, for whom the failure of land-reform programmes and industrial development is chiefly due to corruption and incompetence in the island itself. Few Sicilians would wholly deny this; a longer view, however, points to Sicily's disadvantages being derived principally from the past misuse of resources, coupled with a culture and mentality that have never given much credence to collectivist ideals. But **progress** has been made, and the manifold increase of per capita income in the last fifty years is reflected in greater numbers of newer and bigger cars jamming the island's roads every year, while laws passed relating to land distribution and reform of the bureaucracy show a greater commitment to change. There is more awareness, too, on the part of the state that the fight against **organized crime** requires more than moralistic speeches. Indeed, in **1992**, following the murders of anti-Mafia investigators Falcone and Borsellino (see p.394), the Chief of Police of Palermo was sacked, while 7000 troops were sent to the island to patrol prisons and search towns with a known Mafia presence. There have been significant breakthroughs, though these are mostly connected with a change in the public attitude towards criminality (see "The Mafia in Sicily", p.392).

But beneath the superficial improvements, the deep problems that have always bedevilled Sicily still exist in some form. Unemployment, still high at fifteen to twenty percent, is not helped by the fewer outlets available for **emigration**, though a million still managed to escape the island between 1951 and 1971, along with the majority of Sicily's most outstanding artists and writers. Ironically, the late 1990s have seen the problem of **immigration** hitting the agenda for the first time in several centuries, as economic refugees from North Africa arrive by regular boatloads on the island's southern littoral, particularly the two southernmost islands of Lampedusa and Pantelleria. The *extracomunitari* (literally, "those from non-EU countries") are routinely rounded up and sent to crowded processing centres, where they languish for months, almost all eventually being returned to their countries of origin. Others slip through and join the already strained jobs market. In the long run, perhaps the greatest hope for the island lies in the exploitation of **tourism**: the annual deluge of mainly French, Swiss and Germans is growing in numbers and impact, while more and more Italians are discovering the island's holiday potential, especially its outdoor attractions and wildlife – though the benefits for the island are chiefly concentrated in specific areas so that most Sicilians are missing out.

THE MAFIA
IN SICILY

In Sicily, there is "mafia" and there is "the Mafia". Mafia refers to a criminal mentality, the Mafia to a specific criminal organization. In Italy's deep south, where a man can look mafioso, or talk like a mafioso, meaning he has the aura, or stench, of criminality about him, mafia values are woven into the very fabric of society. The Mafia, on the other hand, operates outside society, and even transcends state boundaries. And, while notions of family solidarity and the moral stature of the outlaw mean that mafia can never be completely extirpated from Sicilian society, the Mafia is an entity whose members can be eliminated and its power emasculated.

What has always prevented this from happening is the shadowy nature of the organization, protected by the long-standing code of silence, or *omertà*, that invariably led to accusations being retracted at the last moment, or to crucial witnesses being found dead with a stone, cork or a wad of banknotes stuffed into their mouths, or else simply disappearing off the face of the earth. As a result, many have doubted the very existence of the Mafia, claiming that it's nothing more than the creation of pulp-thriller writers, the invention of a sensationalist press and the fabrication of an Italian government embarrassed by its inability to control an unusually high level of crime in Sicily.

But in 1982 proof of the innermost workings of the Mafia's organization emerged when a high-ranking member, **Tommaso Buscetta**, was arrested in Brazil, and – after a failed suicide attempt – agreed to prise open the can of worms. His reason for daring this sacrilege, he claimed, was to destroy the Mafia. In its stampede to grab the huge profits to be made from the international heroin industry, the "Honoured Society" (La Società Onorata) had abandoned its original ideals: "it's necessary to destroy this band of criminals", he declared, "who have perverted the principles of Cosa Nostra and dragged them through the mud." He was doubtlessly motivated by revenge: all of those he incriminated – Michele Greco, Pippo Calò, Benedetto Santapaola, Salvatore Riina and many others – were leaders of, or allied to, the powerful Corleonese family who had recently embarked on a campaign of terror to monopolize the drugs industry, in the process eliminating seven of Buscetta's closest relatives in the space of four months, including his two sons.

THE BACKGROUND

Buscetta's statements to Giovanni Falcone, head of Sicily's anti-Mafia "pool" of judges, and later to the Federal Court in Manhattan, were the most important revelations about the **structure** of Cosa Nostra since Jo Valachi – a prominent member of the New York Genovese family – provided the first inside view in 1962. Mafia "families" are centred on areas, he revealed: villages or quarters of cities from which they take their name. The boss (*capo*) of each group is chosen by election, and appoints a lieutenant (*sottocapo*) and one or more *consiglieri*, or counsellors. Larger groups also have officers known as *capodecini*, each in command of ten men. Above the families is the *cupola*, or **Commission**, a governing body that includes representatives from all the major groupings. Democracy and collective interest, Buscetta claimed, had been replaced in the Commission by the greed and self-interest of the individuals who had gained control. Trials of strength alone now decided the leadership, often in the form of bitter feuds between rival factions – or *cosche* (literally, "artichokes", their form symbolizing solidarity).

The existence of the Commission sets the Mafia apart from the normal run of underworld gangs, for without a high level of organization the international trafficking in heroin which they engage in would be inconceivable. The route is a circuitous one, starting in the Middle and Far East, moving on to the processing plants in Sicily, and ending up in New York, where American Mafia channels are said to control sixty percent of the heroin market. This multimillion-dollar racket – known in the US as the **"Pizza Connection"**, because Sicilian pizza parlours were used as covers for the operation – was blown apart chiefly as a result of Buscetta's evidence, and led to the trial and conviction of the leading members of New York's Mafia Commission in September 1986. The trial introduced a significant new note in Mafia cases when the defence lawyers stated at the outset that their clients were self-confessed members of Cosa Nostra – making the issue more one of whether the Mafia was necessarily a *criminal* organization; with most of the American drug profits safely invested in legitimate gambling, construction and high finance, there was little to distinguish it from any other business cartel.

THE HISTORY

The Mafia has certainly come a long way since its rustic beginnings in feudal Sicily. Although Buscetta denied that the word "Mafia" is used to describe the organization – the term preferred by its members is "Cosa Nostra" – the word has been in currency for centuries, and is thought to derive from the Arabic, *mu'afah*, meaning "protection". In 1863, a play entitled *Mafiusi della Vicaria*, based on life in a Palermo prison, was a roaring success among the high society of the island's capital, giving the word its first extensive usage: when the city rose against its new Italian rulers three years later, the British consul described a situation where secret societies were all-powerful: *"Camorre and maffie, self-elected juntas, share the earnings of the workmen, keep up intercourse with outcasts, and take malefactors under their wing and protection."*

Previously, *mafiosi* had been able to pose as defenders of the poor against the tyranny of Sicily's rulers, but in the years immediately following the toppling of the Bourbon state in Italy *mafiosi* were able to entrench themselves in Sicily's new power structure, acting as intermediaries in the gradual redistribution of land and establishing a modus vivendi with the new democratic representatives. There is little or no documentary proof of the rise to power of the "Honoured Society", but most writers agree that between the 1890s and the 1920s its undisputed boss was **Don Vito Cascio Ferro**, who had close links with the American "Black Hand", a Mafia-type amalgam of southern Italian emigrants. Despite numerous homicide charges brought against him, the only man whom Ferro admitted to shooting was an American detective, Jack Petrosino, killed on the same day he docked at Palermo to investigate links between the Sicilian and American organizations.

Ferro's career ended with Mussolini's anti-Mafia purges, instigated to clear the ground for the establishment of a vigorous Fascist structure in Sicily. **Cesare Mori**, the Duce's newly appointed Prefect of Palermo, arrived in the city in 1925 with the declared aim of "clearing the ground of the nightmares, threats and dangers which are paralysing, perverting and corrupting every kind of social activity". This might have worked, but the clean sweep that Mori made of the Mafia leaders (in all, 11,000 cattle rustlers, thieves and "conspirators" were jailed in this period, often on the basis of flimsy hearsay) was annulled after World War II when the prisons were opened and Mafia leaders, seen as unjustly jailed by the Fascist regime, returned to their regular operations. In the confusion that reigned during Italy's reconstruction, crime flourished throughout the south, and criminal leagues regrouped in Naples (the Camorra) and Calabria (*'ndrángheta*), controlling the black market and smuggling rackets. In Sicily, men such as **Don Calógero Vizzini** were the new leaders, confirmed in their power by the brief Anglo-American post-war administration, in return for their contribution towards the smooth progress of the Allied landings and occupation. One of them, **Lucky Luciano**, a founder member of the American Commission, was even flown out from prison in America to facilitate the invasion. Later he was alleged to be responsible for setting up the Sicilian-American narcotics empire, taken over at his death in 1962 by **Luciano Liggio**, who subsequently manoeuvred himself into the leadership of the Corleone family (though he was jailed in 1974).

THE NEW MAFIA

The cycle by now was complete: the Mafia had lost its original role as a predominantly rural organization, and had transformed itself by its post-war "Americanization" through transferring its operations to the cities and moving into entrepreneurial activities like construction, real estate and, ultimately, drug-smuggling. With the growth of the heroin industry, the stakes were raised immensely, as shown by the vicious feuds fought over the division of the spoils. The Italian State responded with an **anti-Mafia Parliamentary Commission** that sat from 1963 to 1976, and posed enough of a threat to the underworld to provoke a change of tactics by the Mafia, who began to target important State officials in a sustained campaign of terror that continues to this day. In 1971, Palermo's chief public prosecutor, Pietro Scaglione, became the first in a long line of **"illustrious corpses"** – *cadáveri eccellenti* – which have included journalists, judges, lawyers, police chiefs and left-wing politicians. A new peak of violence was reached in 1982 with the ambush and murder in Palermo's city centre of **Pio La Torre**, Regional Secretary of the Communist Party in Sicily, who had proposed a special government dispensation to allow lawyers access to private bank accounts.

One of the people attending La Torre's funeral was the new Sicilian prefect of police, **General Dalla Chiesa**, a veteran in the state's fight against the Brigate Rosse, or Red Brigades, and whose dispatch promised new action against the Mafia. The prefect began investigating Sicily's lucrative construction industry, which provided an efficient means of investing drug profits. His scrutiny of public records and business dealings threatened to expose one of the most enigmatic issues in the Mafia's organization: the extent of corruption and protection in high-ranking political circles, the so-called "**Third Level**". But, exactly 100 days after La Torre's death, Dalla Chiesa himself was gunned down, together with his wife, in Palermo's Via Carini. The whole country was shocked, and the murder revived questions about the depth of government commitment to the fight. In his engagement with the Mafia, Dalla Chiesa had met with little local cooperation, and had received next to no support from Rome, to the extent that Dalla Chiesa's son had accused the mandarins of the Christian Democrat party — former prime minister Andreotti among them — of isolating his father. Nando Dalla Chiesa refused to allow many local officials to his father's funeral, including Vito Ciancimino, former mayor of Palermo and a Christian Democrat. Later, Ciancimino was accused, not just of handling huge sums of drug money, but of actually being a sworn-in member of the Corleonese family. Those who were present at the funeral included the Italian president and senior cabinet ministers, all of them jeered at by an angry Sicilian crowd and pelted with coins — an expression of disgust that has since been repeated at the funerals of other prominent anti-Mafia fighters.

To ward off accusations of government inertia or complicity, the law that La Torre had demanded was rushed through Parliament soon afterwards, and was used in the **super-trials**, or *maxiprocessi*, arising from the confessions of Buscetta and the other *pentiti* (penitents) who had followed his lead. The biggest of these tri-

als, lasting eighteen months, started in February 1986, when 500 *mafiosi* appeared in a specially built maximum-security bunker adjoining the Ucciardone prison in the heart of Palermo. The insecurity felt by the Mafia was reflected in continuing bloodshed in Sicily throughout the proceedings, but the worst was to come after the trial closed in December 1986, starting right on the steps of the courthouse with the murder of one of the accused *mafiosi* — many of whom were freed after they had squealed on their accomplices. Of those that were convicted, 19 received life sentences, and 338 others sentences totalling 2065 years.

CONTEMPORARY EVENTS

The **1990s** have seen the violence reach a new level of ferocity, starting in 1992 when a wave of assassinations of high-profile figures splashed over the headlines. In March, Salvatore Lima, a former mayor of Palermo who later became a Euro MP, was shot outside his villa in Mondello. Lima didn't have police bodyguards because he didn't believe he needed them; he had, in fact, been in the Mafia's pocket throughout his political career. His "crime" was his failure to fix the Supreme Court, which had gone ahead and confirmed the convictions of scores of *mafiosi* who had been incriminated in the super-trials of the 1980s.

This murder was followed by two more atrocities in quick succession: in May, the best-known of Sicily's anti-Mafia crusaders, **Giovanni Falcone**, was blown up by half a tonne of TNT on his way into Palermo from the airport, together with his wife and three bodyguards, and two months later his colleague, **Paolo Borsellino** (and five of his police guards), was the victim of a car-bomb outside his mother's house, also in Palermo. These two were the more visible half of the so-called "four musketeers" — judges who refused to be intimidated by death threats routinely made against anti-Mafia investigators. As ever, opinion was divided over what it all meant. There were those who claimed that these murders were public gestures, while others saw in them increasing evidence of the panic percolating through the Mafia's ranks in the face of the growing number of defections of former members who were turning *pentiti*. The carnage certainly mobilized public opinion and propelled the State into action that saw positive results shortly afterwards, with a dramatic break-through: the arrest, in January 1993, of **Salvatore Riina**, the so-called Boss of all the Bosses, and the man held responsible for Falcone's murder. During his televised trial, it emerged that Riina had been ensconced in his native village of Corleone for most of the 24 years that he had been on the run, coming and going pretty much as he liked. Throughout Sicily, there was fury at the political complicity and protection that – presumably – allowed him to remain free, despite being the most wanted man in Europe. See p.290 for more details.

Evidence for the post-war alliance between Italy's former leading party and organized crime had already come to light after November 1991, when Tommaso Buscetta began to implicate politicians for the first time, at last convinced of the state's sincerity in wanting to investigate itself. Allegations inexorably focused on the very highest levels of government, and specifi-cally on the relationship of Mafia stooge Salvatore Lima to his protector, the Christian Democrat leader **Giulio Andreotti**. Italy's most successful post-war politician, Andreotti stepped down as prime minister in 1992 after 45 years in government, during which he had occupied every major position in the cabinet. Formerly considered untouchable, he finally bowed to increasing pressure to relinquish the parliamentary immunity that had hitherto blocked any serious investigation into his role; in September 1995, aged 75, he went on trial in Palermo for complicity and criminal associa-tion. Much fuss was made of the famous *bacio*, a kiss he was reported to have symbolically exchanged with Riina, according to *pentiti* rev-elations in 1994. However, the fact that most of the charges levelled against Andreotti are based on the testimony of Mafia informers (and therefore unreliable witnesses), and his insis-tence that he is the scapegoat for a system thoroughly infiltrated by Cosa Nostra, may yet get the political stalwart – whose nickname, "the fox", recalls his cunning and survival skills – off the hook.

Statements by *pentiti* and others accused of Mafia associations were also at the bottom of investigations into the business dealings of for-mer prime minister **Silvio Berlusconi** and his Fininvest consortium. This time they were con-sidered serious enough to warrant a raid on Berlusconi's Milan headquarters by an elite anti-Mafia police unit in July 1998, and a hasty dash to Sicily by Berlusconi to defend himself against charges of money-laundering for Cosa Nostra. Despite these whiffs of scandal, the interminable delays and legal niceties of the tri-als that, after all, mainly concern past events, have caused many Italians to lose interest in the outcome, and revelations of endemic corruption in northern Italian cities such as Milan and Venice have switched attention away from specifically Sicilian criminality. Since 1992, in the wake of the mass arrests of politicians, businesspeople and crooked contractors, and the resulting confrontation between govern-ment and judiciary, nothing in Italy has seemed stable or predictable any more, and anything is believable, from the detention of the country's top fashion designers to rumours of Mafia infil-tration in far-off Brussels and Strasbourg. The very concept of Mafia involvement has become increasingly irrelevant with each new report of political and business corruption, which have dominated public life in Italy throughout the 1990s; as the mayor of Venice remarked, in response to whispers of Mafia involvement in the fire that destroyed La Fenice opera house in 1996, "Claiming it was burnt by the Mafia is about as useful as saying it was attacked by alien spacecraft."

In Sicily itself, however, the war goes on. In Palermo, **Leoluca Orlando**, the mayor of the city who was forced out of office by his own Christian Democrat party in 1990, has spent the last decade establishing an independent power base from which he has risen to the national stage on an anti-Mafia ticket, at the head of his own Rete (Network) party. Most significantly, Orlando succeeded in dislodging the Christian Democrats and their Partito Popolare heirs as the principal party in Palermo, and regained his post as mayor, since when he and La Rete have polled consistently highly in local and regional elec-tions. Promising to clean up the city, he has presided over a series of important blows against leading Mafia figures, notably the capture in 1995 of **Leoluca Bagarella**, Riina's successor and brother-in-law, and the convicted killer of the chief of the Palermo Flying Squad in 1979. (Bagarella's hideout turned out to be a luxury apartment overlooking the heavily guarded home of two of the judges who had helped catch him.) The following year, another of the Corleonese family, **Giovanni Brusca**, was captured, a particularly gratifying coup for the anti-Mafia forces as Brusca was one of the organization's most ruthless killers; the mastermind behind Falcone's assassination, he was also believed responsible for the strangling of an informant's eleven-year-old son, whose body was then disposed of in a vat of acid – an act that provoked general outrage and a demonstration in the Mafia-ridden town of Altofonte. Elsewhere on the island, **Natale D'Emanuele**, alleged to be the financial wizard behind the Mafia in Catania, was arrested and charged with trafficking arms throughout Italy, using hearses and coffins to transport them in a throwback to 1930s Chicago. Two other bosses, **Vito Vitale** and **Mariano Troia**, were netted in 1998. On the minus side, January 1999 saw one of the worst Mafia massacres in the last half-century, when five people were gunned down in a bar in Vittoria, a town little known for Mafia violence.

The most important development, however, has been the growth of a new open attitude towards the Mafia, in contrast to the previous denial and *omertà*. One of the most watched TV programmes in recent years has been *La Piovra* (*The Octopus*), a drama series which has simultaneously glamorized the Mafia and confronted its reality. Sicilians themselves are now bolder than ever in their public demonstrations of disgust at the killings and intimidation (as witnessed by the angry scenes at the funerals of Falcone and Borsellino). There have been notable individual acts of courage, too, such as that of the wife of one "illustrious" victim, Judge Cesare Terranova (killed in 1979), who has led a women's movement against the Mafia. "If you manage to change the mentality," she has said, "to change the consent, to change the fear in which the Mafia can live – if you can change that, you can beat them."

The strongest weapon in the Mafia's armoury is precisely that element of "consent" among ordinary Sicilians. The product of fear, it is the foundation of the Mafia's existence, bolstered by an attitude that has traditionally regarded the *mafioso* stance as a revolt against the State, justified by centuries of oppression by foreign regimes. Yet, while the corrupt government of foreigners and their acolytes has historically forfeited any deep respect for the law in Sicily, the knowledge that those very authorities have been clinched in a sinister embrace with the Mafia has stirred up general outrage. And it is this, sustained by the revelations of Andreotti's trial, that has damaged the organization where it is most vulnerable: in the public mind. In the long run, no matter how many politicians and businessmen are uncovered for their Mafia associations – and Andreotti's defenders have pointed out that it is impossible for anybody in Italian political life *not* to have had contacts with organized crime – it is the changing attitudes of people at ground level that are more likely to signal the end of the Mafia's hold on Sicilian life. Although the assassinations of *pentiti* and their families, and the feuds within the Mafia clans caused by a new generation jostling for power, suggest that Cosa Nostra is both vigorous and rent with divisions, many Sicilians would now accept that the true Mafia died decades ago, its original altruistic ideals – if they ever existed – long forgotten. Most importantly, the myth of its invincibility has been irreparably dented.

SICILIAN BAROQUE

Most of the church and civic architecture you'll come across in Sicily is Baroque in style, certainly in the east of the island. More particularly, it's of a type known as Sicilian Baroque, and this is a brief introduction to the subject, designed to serve as a handy reference for some of the more important aspects of the style mentioned in the text. It will at least explain the hows and whys of Baroque architecture in Sicily with respect to some of the major towns and sights. For more academic studies, check the recommendations in the "Books" listings, p.407; and for more information about the specific places detailed below, follow up the page references given.

ORIGINS

The qualities that attract art historians to the Sicilian Baroque – the "warmth and ebullience", "gaiety", "energy", "freedom and fantasy"– to some extent typify all **Baroque** architecture. The style grew out of the excesses of Mannerism, a distorted sixteenth-century mode of painting and architecture which had flourished in Italy in reaction to the restraint of the Renaissance. The development of a full-blown, ornate Baroque style followed in the late sixteenth century, again originating in Italy, and it quickly found a niche in other countries touched by the Counter-Reformation. The Jesuits saw in Baroque art and architecture an expression of a revitalized Catholicism, its particular theatrical forms involving the congregation by portraying spiritual ecstasy in terms of physical passion.

The origin of the word "Baroque" is uncertain: the two most popular theories are that it comes either from the seventeenth-century Portuguese *barroco*, meaning a misshapen pearl, or the term *barocco* used by philosophers in the Middle Ages to mean a contorted idea. Whatever its origins, it was used by contemporary critics in a derogatory sense, implying odd or extravagant shapes, as opposed to the much-vaunted classical forms of the Renaissance.

Although Baroque was born in Rome, the vogue quickly spread throughout Europe.

Everywhere, the emphasis was firmly on elaborate ornamentation and spectacle, something that reflected the growing power of the aristocracy, who had begun to challenge the established wealth and tradition of the church. Civic architecture gained in importance, at the expense of formerly pre-eminent religious buildings. The motivating force behind the decoration of the buildings was primarily the need to impress the neighbouring gentry; building to the glory of God came a poor second.

Some of the finest (though least-known) examples of Baroque architecture are to be found in Sicily, although there's some debate as to the specific origins of the **Sicilian Baroque** style. During the eighteenth century alone, Sicily was conquered and ruled in turn by the Spanish Hapsburgs, the Spanish Bourbons, the House of Savoy, the Austrian Hapsburgs and the Bourbons from Naples, lending a particularly exuberant flavour to its Baroque creations – which some say was borrowed from Spain. Others argue that the dominant influence was Italian: Sicilian architects tended to train and to travel in Italy, rather than Spain, and brought home what they learned on the mainland, adapting prevalent Roman Baroque ideas to complement peculiarly Sicilian architectural traditions. Both theories contain an element of the truth, though perhaps more pertinent is Sicily's unique long-term history: two and a half millennia of invasion and domination have produced a very distinct culture and society – one that is bound to have influenced, or even produced, an equally distinct architectural form.

BAROQUE TOWNS

Sicily's seismic instability has profoundly affected its architectural history. The huge **earthquake of 1693** that almost flattened Catania, and completely destroyed Noto, Ragusa, Ávola and Módica, provided a fantastic opportunity for local architects, who began massive rebuilding programmes in the southeast corner of Sicily. To them, as to all contemporary Baroque planners, a **Baroque town** aspired to be, and should have been seen to be, a centre of taste and sophistication: they designed their new towns to please and delight their citizens, to encourage the participation of passers-by and to impress outsiders, with long vistas contriving to focus on the facade of a church or a palace, or an unexpected view of the sea. To enhance the visual effect even more, a building was designed to have multiple, changing views from different angles of approach. This way, a completed plan might include all the buildings in a square or series of squares, and the experience of walking from place to place through varied but harmonious spaces was considered as important as the need to arrive at a destination. Moreover, as much of eighteenth-century Sicilian town-life took place outside, the facade of a building became synonymous with the wealth and standing of its occupant. External features became increasingly elaborate and specialized, and some parts of buildings – windows and staircases, for example – were often merely there for show. Invariably, what seem to be regular stone facades have been cosmetically touched up with plaster to conceal an asymmetry or an angle of less than ninety degrees; a self-conscious approach to town planning that can sometimes give the impression of walking around a stage set. Interestingly, this approach remained confined to the south and east of Sicily; outside the earthquake zone, in the west of the island, local architectural traditions continued to dominate in towns which hadn't had the dubious benefit of being levelled and left for the planners.

Ideally, where there was scope for large-scale planning, an entire city could be constructed as an aesthetic whole. As early as 1615 the Venetian architect and theorist **Vincenzo Scamozzi** published a treatise called *Dell'Idea dell'architettura universale*, in which he stated that the architectural harmony of the ideal city should reflect the perfect relationship between the prince, the judiciary, the Church, the marketplace and the populace.

Noto (p.261) is an almost perfect example of Scamozzi's ideal city. After the 1693 earthquake, the old town was so devastated that it was decided to move its site and rebuild from scratch. The plan that was eventually accepted was nearly an exact replica of Scamozzi's. Noto is constructed on a grid-plan, traversed from east to west by a wide corso crossing a main piazza, which is itself balanced by four smaller piazzas. The buildings along the corso show remarkable balance and grace, while the attention of the Baroque planners to every harmonious detail is illustrated by the use of a warm, golden stone for the churches and *palazzi*.

Neighbouring towns in the southeast were also destroyed by the earthquake and rebuilt

along similar lines, utilizing wide squares and thoroughfares, designed with the possibility of future tremors in mind. **Ávola** (p.261) and **Grammichele** (p.301) were both moved from their hill-top positions to the coastal plain, and their polygonal plans were similarly influenced by Scamozzi. Grammichele, particularly, retains an extraordinary hexagonal layout, unique in Sicily. **Ragusa** (p.266) is more complex, surviving today as two towns, the medieval Ragusa Ibla, which the inhabitants rebuilt after the earthquake, and the Baroque upper town of Ragusa, which is built on a sloping grid-plan, rather similar to Noto. Although Ibla isn't built to any kind of Baroque pattern, it does lay claim to one of the most spectacular of Sicilian Baroque churches (see p.268).

Catania (p.206), unlike the other southeastern towns, was not completely destroyed by the earthquake, and was rebuilt over its old site. New, broad streets were built to link existing monuments and to facilitate rescue operations in case of another earthquake. The city is divided into four quarters by wide streets meeting in Piazza del Duomo, and wherever possible these spaces are used to maximize the visual impact of a facade or monument. The main piazza was conceived as a uniform set piece and, although several different architects collaborated, their intention was to produce a homogenous ensemble. They also went a step further in utilizing the city's natural assets: the main street, Via Etnea, cuts a swath due north from Piazza del Duomo, always drawing the eyes to the volcano, Mount Etna, smoking in the distance.

Over on the other side of the island, Baroque **Palermo** (p.56) evolved differently, without the impetus of any one great natural disaster. There's no comparable city plan, Palermo's intricate central layout owing more to the Arabs than to seventeenth- and eighteenth-century designers; what Baroque character the city possesses is almost entirely to do with its highly individual churches and palaces. They were constructed in a climate of apparent opulence but encroaching bankruptcy; as the Sicilian aristocrats were attracted to Palermo to pay court to the Spanish viceroy, they left the management of their lands to pragmatic agents, whose short-sighted policies allowed the estates to fall into neglect. This ate away at the wealth of the gentry, who responded by mortgaging their lands in order to maintain their living standards.

The grandiose palaces and churches they built in the city still stand, but following the damage caused during World War II many are in a state of terrible neglect and near collapse; wild flowers grow out of the facades and chunks of masonry frequently fall into the street below. Renovation work is hampered by the local Mafia, and minor earthquake tremors always ensure that the need for repair is one step ahead of the builders.

SPECIFIC FEATURES

Eighteenth-century aristocrats in Palermo felt the need for **summer villas** outside the city, to which they could escape in the hottest weather, and many of these still survive around Bagheria (p.104). The villas tend to be quite small and simply designed, but are bedecked with balconies and terraces for afternoon strolling, and were approached by long, impressive driveways. Above all, they are notable for their **external staircases**, leading to the main entrance on the first floor (the ground floor usually contained the kitchen and servants' quarters). It's typical of the Baroque era that an external feature should take on such significance in a building – and that they should show such a remarkable diversity, each reflecting the wealth of the individual owners. Beyond the fact that they were nearly always double staircases, symmetrical to the middle axis of the facade, each one was completely different and, though external staircases can be found elsewhere on mainland Europe, they're rarely of such imaginative construction as in Sicily.

Balconies had always been a prominent feature of Sicilian domestic architecture, but during the eighteenth century they became prolific. The balcony supports, or buttresses, were elaborately carved: manic heads, griffins, horses, monsters and mythical figures all featured as decoration, fine examples of which survive at Noto's **Palazzo Villadorata** (p.263), as well as in Módica (p.269) and Scicli (p.270). The wrought-iron balustrades curved outwards, almost like theatre boxes, to allow room for women's billowing skirts; they still afford the best views of street processions and other festivities at Carnevale.

Church building, too, flourished during this period. Baroque architects could let their imaginations run wild: the facade of the **Duomo** at Siracusa (p.243) was begun in 1728, based on designs by Andrea Palma of Palermo, and the result is highly sophisticated and exciting. Other designs adapted and modified accepted forms for church architecture, as well as inventing new ones. In Palermo especially, typically Sicilian elements – like central circular windows – were used to great effect.

It was in the church **interiors**, however, that Sicilian Baroque came into its own, with tomb sculpture ever more ostentatious and stucco decoration abundant. Inlaid marble, a technique introduced from Naples at the beginning of the seventeenth century, became *de rigueur* for any self-respecting church. It reached its prime in the second half of the century, when whole walls or chapels would be decorated in this way. Palermo fields some of the best examples of all these techniques, most impressive the church of **San Giuseppe dei Teatini** (p.69), designed by Giacomo Besio, a Genovese who lived most of his life in Sicily. For real over-the-top detail, though, the churches of **Santa Caterina** (p.69) and **Il Gesù** (p.72), also in Palermo, conceal a riot of inlaid marble decoration.

Palermo is also distinguished by a series of highly decorative **oratories**, built in the late seventeenth and early eighteenth centuries, when the Spanish viceroys placed much of the city's power in the hands of the local aristocrats, who could afford to endow monasteries with new funds. Much was spent on small private chapels, where local sculptors had the chance to shine. The master of the genre was Giacomo Serpotta (see p.400), and his best works are in the oratories of Santa Zita (see p.80), **San Domenico** (p.78) and **San Lorenzo** (p.81), though he left his mark over much of the west of the island.

ARCHITECTS AND SCULPTORS

Rosario Gagliardi was responsible for much of the rebuilding of Noto and Ragusa, and became known as one of the most important architects in southeast Sicily. Born in Siracusa in 1698, he worked in Noto as a carpenter from the age of 10, and was first acknowledged as an architect in 1726. Between 1760 and 1784 he was chief architect for the city of Noto, and during this time also worked on many different projects in Ragusa and Módica. As far as is known, he never travelled outside Sicily, let alone to Rome, yet he absorbed contemporary architectural trends from the study of books and treatises, and reproduced the ideas with some flair.

Gagliardi's prime interest was in facades and his work achieved a sophisticated fusion of Renaissance poise, Baroque grandeur and local Sicilian ornamentation. He had no interest, however, in spatial relationships or structural innovation, and the interiors of his buildings are disappointing when compared to the elaborate nature of their exteriors. Perhaps his most significant contribution was his development of the belfry as a feature. Sicilian churches traditionally didn't have a separate bell-tower but incorporated the bells into the main facade, revealed through a series of two or three arches – an idea handed down from Byzantine building. Gagliardi extended the central bay of the facade into a tower, a highly original compromise satisfying both the local style and the more conventional notions of design from the mainland. The belfry on the church of **San Giorgio** in Ragusa Ibla (p.268) is an excellent example of this and is Gagliardi's masterpiece.

Giovanni Battista Vaccarini was the principal architect working on the design and rebuilding of Catania after the 1693 earthquake. He was born in Palermo in 1702 but trained in Rome and embraced the current idiom, working with such illustrious figures as Alessandro Specchi (who built the Papal stables) and Francesco de Sanctis (designer of the Spanish Steps). In 1730 he arrived in Catania, having been appointed as city architect by the Senate, and at once began work on finishing the Municipio (p.211); the lower two floors had been designed by a local architect, but Vaccarini completely ignored the original plan and transformed the building by redesigning the *piano nobile* in the Roman style. Outside it he placed a fountain, whose main feature is an obelisk supported by an elephant, the symbol of Catania – reminiscent of Bernini's elephant fountain in Rome.

Giacomo Serpotta, master of the Palermitan oratories, was born in Palermo in 1656. He cashed in on the opulence of the Church and specialized in decorating oratories with moulded plaster work in ornamental frames. He would include life-size figures of Saints and Virtues, surrounded by plaster draperies, trophies, swags of fruit, bouquets of flowers and other extravagances much beloved of the Baroque. One of the most remarkable of his works is the Oratory of the Rosary in the church of **Santa Zita** (p.80), where the end wall is a reconstruction of the Battle of Lépanto. Here three-dimensional representation is taken to an extreme and actual wires are used as rigging.

Other Baroque architects are less well-known, but influential in Sicily all the same. **Giacomo Amato** (1643–1732) was a monk, sent to Rome in 1671 to represent his Order, where he came into contact with the works of Bernini and Borromini. Dazzled by what he'd seen, after his return to Palermo he neglected his religious duties in order to design some of the city's most characteristic churches, **Sant'Ignazio all'Olivella** (p.79) and **San Domenico** (p.78) among them. **Vincenzo Sinatra** had a more traditional career, starting as a stonecutter before working with Gagliardi in the 1730s as his foreman. In 1745 he married Gagliardi's niece, a move which did him no harm at all, since by 1761, when Gagliardi had a stroke, Sinatra was managing all his affairs. For ten years he directed the construction of Noto's Municipio, and during the rest of his life Sinatra worked in collaboration with the other city architects on a variety of projects – a respectable career, but one which makes it difficult to trace any personal architectural method. More important, and certainly with an identifiable style, was **Giovanni Verméxio** who was working in Siracusa at around the same time. His work graces the city's Piazza del Duomo, notably the **Palazzo Arcivescovile**, while he gets a couple of ornate-interior credits, too, in the shape of one of the Duomo's chapels, and the octagonal **Cappella di San Sepolcro** in the church of Santa Lucia in the Achradina quarter of Siracusa.

SICILY
IN FICTION

Some of the most respected modern Italian authors are Sicilian. Extracts from the work of just three – Lampedusa, Vittorini and Sciascia – are reprinted below, and although each author has his own particular viewpoint and style there's a similarity apparent too: each of the extracts touches upon a different aspect of the same theme, namely the intricacies of Sicilian life and the unique problems of the island.

THE LEOPARD

Perhaps the best known of Sicilian novels, The Leopard *is a towering record of a nineteenth-century aristocrat's reactions to the old order crumbling around him as the Bourbon state of Naples and Sicily draws to a close, to be replaced by a new unified Italy. It was the posthumously published masterpiece of* **Giuseppe Tomasi di Lampedusa** *(1896–1957), himself from a Sicilian aristocratic family that claimed descent from a commander of the Imperial Guard of the sixth-century Byzantine emperor Tiberius. Certainly Lampedusa would have had some considerable understanding of the emotions felt by the prince, Don Fabrizio, as he contemplates the destruction of the traditional values he cherishes.* The Leopard *appeared in 1958 to immediate critical acclaim, although Lampedusa wrote little else of note. In the extract below, the prince is out hunting at his country estate with his retainer, Don Ciccio, shortly after the Plebiscite on unification.*

"And you, Don Ciccio, how did you vote on the twenty-first?"

The poor man started; taken by surprise at a moment when he was outside the stockade of precautions in which, like each of his fellow townsmen, he usually moved, he hesitated, not knowing what to reply.

The Prince mistook for alarm what was really only surprise, and felt irritated. "Well, what are you afraid of? There's no one here but us, the wind and the dogs."

The list of reassuring witnesses was not really happily chosen; wind is a gossip by definition, the Prince was half Sicilian. Only the dogs were absolutely trustworthy and that only

because they lacked articulate speech. But Don Ciccio had now recovered; his peasant astuteness had suggested the right reply – nothing at all. "Excuse me, Excellency, but there's no point in your question. You know that everyone in Donnafugata voted 'yes'."

Don Fabrizio did not know this; and that was why this reply merely changed a small enigma into an enigma of history. Before this voting many had come to him for advice; all of them had been exhorted, sincerely, to vote "yes". Don Fabrizio, in fact, could not see what else there was to do: whether treating it as a *fait accompli* or as an act merely theatrical and banal, whether taking it as a historical necessity or considering the trouble these humble folk might get into if their negative attitude were known. He had noticed, though, that not all had been convinced by his words; into play had come the abstract Machiavellianism of Sicilians, which so often induced these people, with all their generosity, to erect complex barricades on the most fragile foundations. Like clinics adept at treatment based on fundamentally false analyses of blood and urine which they are too lazy to rectify, the Sicilians (of that time) ended by killing off the patient, that is themselves, by a niggling and hair-splitting rarely connected with any real understanding of the problems involved, or even of their interlocutors. Some of these who had made a visit *ad limina leopardorum* considered it impossible for a Prince of Salina to vote in favour of the Revolution (as the recent changes were still called in these remote parts), and they interpreted his advice as ironical, intended to effect a result in practice opposite to his words. These pilgrims (and they were the best) had come out of his study winking at each other – as far as their respect for him would allow – proud at having penetrated the meaning of the princely words, and rubbing their hands in self-congratulation at their own perspicacity just when this was most completely in eclipse.

Others, on the other hand, after having listened to him, went off looking sad and convinced that he was a turncoat or half-wit, more than ever determined to take no notice of what he said but to follow instead the age-old proverb about preferring a known evil to an untried good. These were reluctant to ratify the new national reality for personal reasons too; either from religious faith, or from having received favours from the former regime and not being sharp enough to insert themselves into the new one, or finally because during the upsets of the liberation period they had lost a few capons and sacks of beans, and had been cuckolded either freely like Garibaldini volunteers or forcibly like Bourbon levies. He had, in fact, the disagreeable but distinct impression that about fifteen of them would vote "no", a tiny minority certainly, but noticeable in the small electorate of Donnafugata. Taking into consideration that the people who came to him represented the flowers of the inhabitants, and that there must also be some unconvinced among the hundreds of electors who had not dreamt of setting foot inside the palace, the Prince had calculated that Donnafugata's compact affirmative would be varied by about forty negative votes.

The day of the Plebiscite was windy and grey, and tired groups of youths had been seen going through the streets of the town with bits of paper covered with "yes" stuck in the ribbons of their hats. Amid waste paper and refuse swirled by the wind they sang a few verses of *La Bella Gigugin* transformed into a kind of Arab wail, a fate to which any gay tune in Sicily is bound to succumb. There had also been seen two or three "foreigners" (that is from Girgenti) installed in *Zzu* Menico's tavern where they were declaiming Leopardi's lines on the "magnificent and progressive destiny" of a renovated Sicily united to resurgent Italy. A few peasants were standing listening mutely, stunned by overwork or starved by unemployment. These cleared their throats and spat continuously, but kept silent; so silent that it must have been then (as Don Fabrizio said afterwards) that the foreigners decided to give Arithmetic precedence over Rhetoric in the Quadrivium arts.

The Prince went to vote about four in the afternoon, flanked on the right by Father Pirrone, on the left by Don Onofrio Rotolo; frowning and fair-skinned, he proceeded slowly toward the Town Hall, frequently putting up a hand to protect his eyes lest the breeze loaded with all the filth collected on its way should bring on the conjunctivitis to which he was subject; and he remarked to Father Pirrone that the health-giving gusts did seem to drag up a lot of dirt with them. He was wearing the same black frock coat in which two years before he had gone to pay his respects at Caserta to poor King

Ferdinand, who had been lucky enough to die in time to avoid this day of dirty wind when the seal would be set on his own incapacity. But had it really been incapacity? One might as well say that a person succumbing to typhus dies of incapacity. He remembered the king busy putting up dykes against the flood of useless documents: and suddenly he realised how much unconscious appeal to pity there was in these unattractive features. Such thoughts were disagreeable, as are all those which make us understand things too late, and the Prince's face went solemn and dark as if he were following an invisible funeral car. Only the violent impact of his feet on loose stones in the street showed his internal conflict. It is superfluous to mention that the ribbon on his top hat was innocent of any piece of paper; but in the eyes of those who knew him a "yes" and "no" alternated on the glistening felt.

On reaching a little room in the Town Hall used as the voting booth he was surprised to see all the members of the committee get up as his great height filled the doorway; a few peasants who had arrived before were put aside, and so without having to wait Don Fabrizio handed his "yes" into the patriotic hands of Don Calogero Sedàra. Father Pirrone, though, did not vote at all, as he had been careful not to get listed as a resident of the town. Don 'Nofrio, obeying the express desires of the Prince, gave his own monosyllabic opinion about the complicated Italian question; a masterpiece of concision carried through with the good grace of a child drinking castor oil. After which all were invited for a "little glass" upstairs in the mayor's study; but Father Pirrone and Don 'Nofrio put forward good reasons, one of abstinence, the other of stomach-ache, and remained below. Don Fabrizio had to face the party alone.

Behind the Mayor's writing desk gleamed a brand new portrait of Garibaldi and (already) one of King Victor Emmanuel hung, luckily, to the right: the first handsome, the second ugly; both, however, made brethren by prodigious growths of hair which nearly hid their faces altogether. On a small low table was a plate with some ancient biscuits blackened by fly droppings and a dozen little squat glasses brimming with *rosolio* wine: four red, four green, four white, the last in the centre: an ingenious symbol of the new national flag which tempered the Prince's remorse with a smile. He chose the white liquor for himself, presumably because it was the least indigestible and not, as some thought, in tardy homage to the Bourbon standard. Anyway, all three varieties of the *rosolio* were equally sugary, sticky and revolting. His host had the good taste not to give toasts. But, as Don Calogero said, great joys are silent. Don Fabrizio was shown a letter from the authorities of Girgenti announcing to the industrious citizens of Donnafugata the concession of 2,000 lire towards sewage, a work which would be completed before the end of 1961 so the Mayor assured them, stumbling into one of those *lapsus* whose mechanism Freud was to explain many decades later; and the meeting broke up.

Before dusk the three or four easy girls of Donnafugata (there were some others there too, not grouped but each hard at work on her own) appeared on the square with tricolour ribbons in their manes as protest against the exclusion of women in the vote; the poor creatures were jeered at even by the most advanced liberals and forced back to their lairs. This did not prevent the *Giornale di Trinacria* telling the people of Palermo four days later that at Donnafugata "some gentle representatives of the fair sex wished to show their faith in the new and brilliant destinies of their beloved Country, and demonstrated in the main square amid great acclamation from the patriotic population".

After this the electoral booths were closed and the scrutators got to work; late that night the shutters on the balcony of the Town Hall were flung open and Don Calogero appeared with a tricolour sash over his middle, flanked by two ushers with lighted candelabra which the wind snuffed at once. To the invisible crowd in the shadows below he announced that the Plebiscite at Donnafugata had the following results:

Voters, 515; Voting, 512; Yes, 512; No, zero.

From the dark end of the square rose applause and hurrahs; on her little balcony Angelica, with her funereal maid, clapped lovely rapacious hands; speeches were made; adjectives loaded with superlatives and double consonants reverberated and echoed in the dark from one wall to another; amid thundering of fireworks messages were sent off to the King (the new one) and to the General; a tricolour

rocket or two climbed up from the village into the blackness towards the starless sky. By eight o'clock all was over, and nothing remained except darkness as on any other night, always.

From The Leopard *by Giuseppe Tomasi di Lampedusa, translated by Archibald Colquhoun. © Giangiacomo Feltrinelli Editore 1958, © in the English translation Harvill 1961. Reproduced by permission of The Harvill Press.*

CONVERSATION IN SICILY

Elio Vittorini *(1908–1966) was born in Siracusa, a staunch anti-Fascist whose first novel was censored under Mussolini. His best work,* Conversation in Sicily, *written in 1937, initially managed to escape the same fate, as Vittorini wrapped his simple, taut story of a man's visit to his mother in an abstract, almost poetic style. The book deals with the return to Sicily, after fifteen years, of an emigrant who now lives in the industrial – and comparatively wealthy – north of Italy. The "conversations" are the emigrant's encounters with fellow travellers and villagers in Sicily – encounters that lead him to rediscover a humanity in their otherwise downtrodden, despairing existence. The extract reprinted below follows his approach to his former home, a route that today is still redolent with the flavours that Vittorini records.*

Toward midnight I changed train at Florence, then again about six in the morning at the Termini station in Rome, and about midday I reached Naples. There it was not raining, and I sent off a telegraphic money-order of fifty lire to my wife. I wired to her: "Returning Thursday."

Then I took the train for Calabria. It began raining again, and night came on. It all came back to me, the journey, and I as a child on my ten flights from home and Sicily, travelling back and forth through a countryside of smoke and tunnels, the rending whistles of the train halted by night in the jaws of a mountain or by the sea, and the names – Amantea, Maratea, Gioia Tauro – evoking dreams of ancient times. And so, suddenly, the mouse within me was no longer a mouse, but scent, savour, and the heavens, and the pipe no longer played mournfully, but merrily. I fell asleep, awoke, fell asleep again, and awoke once more, until at last I found myself on board the ferry-boat for Sicily.

The sea was black and wintry. Standing on that high plateau of the top deck, I saw myself once again as a boy breathing the air, gazing hungrily at the sea, facing towards the one coast or the other, with all that garbage of coastal town and village heaped at my feet in the rain-swept morning. It was cold, and I remembered myself as a boy feeling cold yet remaining obstinately on that elevated windy platform, with the sea speeding swiftly by below.

We were a tight fit. The boat was full of little Sicilians travelling third-class, hungry, frozen, without overcoats, yet mild-looking, jacket lapels turned up and hands dug into trouser pockets. I had bought some food at Villa San Giovanni, some bread and cheese, and I was munching away on deck at the bread, raw air, and cheese, with zest and appetite, because I recognized the old tang of my mountains, and even their odours – herds of goats and worm-wood – in that cheese. The little Sicilians, bowed with backs to the wind and hands in pockets, watched me eat. They had dark, but mild faces, with beards four days old. They were workers, labourers from the orange groves, and railwaymen wearing grey caps with the thin red piping of the labour gangs. Munching, I smiled at them, and they looked back at me unsmiling.

"There's no cheese like our own," I said.

No one replied. They all stared at me, the women in their voluminous femininity seated on their great bags of belongings, the men standing, small and as if scalded by the wind, hands in pockets.

Again I said: "There's no cheese like our own."

Because I felt suddenly enthusiastic about something – that cheese, its savour in my mouth, with the bread and the sharp air, its flavour clear but acrid, and ancient, its grains of pepper like sudden embers on the tongue:

"There's no cheese like our own," I said for the third time.

Then one of the Sicilians, the smallest and gentlest and darkest of the lot, and the most scalded by the wind, asked me:

"But are you a Sicilian?"

"Why not?" I replied.

The man shrugged his shoulders and said no more. He had what looked like a little girl with him, sitting on a bag at his feet. He bent over her, and taking a great red hand out of his pocket, he seemed to touch her caressingly while he adjusted her shawl to keep her warm.

Somehow this gesture made it clear that she was not his daughter but his wife. Meanwhile Messina drew near, and it was not a heap of garbage on the sea's edge, but houses and moles, white tramcars and rows of dark-hued wagons in the railway sidings. The morning seemed wet, though it was not raining. Everything on the top of the deck was moist, the wind blew moist, the sirens from the ships sounded moist, and the railway engines ashore whistled with a moist note; but it was not raining. And suddenly we saw the lighthouse sailing by in the wintry sea, very high, heading for Villa San Giovanni.

"There's no cheese like our own," I said.

All the men, who were standing, pressed toward the deck rail to gaze at the city, and the women too, seated on their bags, turned their heads. But no one made a move towards the lower deck to be ready to disembark. There was still time. From the lighthouse to the jetty, I remembered, took fifteen minutes or more.

"There's no cheese like our own," I said.

Meanwhile I finished eating. The man with the wife who looked like a child bent down once again: in fact, he knelt; he had a basket at his feet and, watched by her, he began to busy himself with it. It was covered by a piece of wax-cloth sewn with string at the edges. Very slowly he undid a bit of the string, dug his hand under the wax-cloth, and produced an orange.

It wasn't big or very luscious or highly tinted, but it was an orange, and without a word, without rising from his knees, he offered it to his baby wife. The baby looked at me; I could discern her eyes inside the hood of the shawl; and then I saw her shake her head.

The little Sicilian seemed desperate, and remained on his knees, one hand in his pocket, the other holding the orange. Then he rose again to his feet and stood with the wind flapping the soft peak of his cap against his nose, the orange in his hand, his coatless diminutive body scalded by the cold, and frantic, while immediately below us the sea and the city floated by in the wet morning.

"Messina," said a woman mournfully. It was a word uttered without reason, merely as a kind of complaint. I observed the little Sicilian with the baby-wife desperately peel his orange, and desperately eat it, with rage and frenzy, without the least desire; then without chewing he gulped it down and seemed to curse, his fingers dripping with the orange juice in the cold, a little bowed in the wind, the peak of his cap flapping against his nose.

"A Sicilian never eats in the morning," he said suddenly. "Are you American?" he added.

He spoke with desperation, yet gently, just as he had always been gentle while desperately peeling the orange and desperately eating it. He spoke the last three words excitedly, in a strident tense voice, as if it were somehow essential to the peace of his soul to know if I were American.

I observed this, and said: "Yes, I am American. For the last fifteen years."

Reprinted from Conversation in Sicily *by Elio Vittorini, translated by Wilfrid David (Quartet Books).*

THE DAY OF THE OWL

*Widely regarded as one of Italy's finest writers, **Leonardo Sciascia** (1912–1991), from the southwest of Sicily, used the island as a backdrop in all his work – as what he called a "metaphor of the modern world". Both the novels and short stories provide keen insights into the world of the Mafia, the Church in Sicily, the mores of the people and the island's tortuous history – all touched by the same wit and sharp, perceptive characterization.* The Day of the Owl *is at heart a crime story: a Carabinieri inspector arrives from the mainland to investigate a Mafia murder, described below in the book's opening pages.*

The bus was just about to leave, amid rumbles and sudden hiccups and rattles. The square was silent in the grey dawn; wisps of cloud swirled round the belfry of the church. The only sound, apart from the rumbling of the bus, was a voice, wheedling, ironic, of a fritter-seller; fritters, hot fritters. The conductor slammed the door, and with a clank of scrap-metal the bus moved off. His last glance round the square caught sight of a man in a dark suit running towards the bus.

"Hold it a minute," said the conductor to the driver, opening the door with the bus still in motion. Two ear-splitting shots rang out. For a second the man in the dark suit, who was just about to jump on the running-board, hung suspended in mid-air as if some invisible hand were hauling him up by the hair. Then his briefcase dropped from his hand and very slowly he slumped down on top of it.

The conductor swore; his face was the colour of sulphur; he was shaking. The fritter-seller, who was only three yards from the fallen man, sidled off with a crab-like motion towards the door of the church. In the bus no one moved; the driver sat, as if turned to stone, his right hand on the brake, his left on the steering wheel. The conductor looked round the passengers' faces, which were blank as the blinds.

"They've killed him," he said; he took off his cap, swore again, and began frantically running his fingers through his hair.

"The *carabinieri*," said the driver, "we must get the *carabinieri*."

He got up and opened the other door. "I'll go," he said to the conductor.

The conductor looked at the dead man and then at the passengers. These included some women, old women who brought heavy sacks of white cloth and baskets full of eggs every morning; their clothes smelled of forage, manure and wood smoke; usually they grumbled and swore, now they sat mute, their faces as if disinterred from the silence of centuries.

"Who is it?" asked the conductor, pointing at the body.

No one answered. The conductor cursed. Among the passengers of that route he was famous for his highly skilled blaspheming. The company had already threatened to fire him since he never bothered to control himself even when there were nuns or priests on the bus. He was from the province of Syracuse and had had little to do with violent death: a soft province, Syracuse. So now he swore all the more furiously.

The *carabinieri* arrived; the sergeant-major, with a black stubble and in a black temper from being woken, stirred the passengers' apathy like an alarm-clock: in the wake of the conductor they began to get out through the door left open by the driver.

With seeming nonchalance, looking around as if they were trying to gauge the proper distance from which to admire the belfry, they drifted off towards the sides of the square and, after a last look around, scuttled into alley-ways.

The sergeant-major and his men did not notice this gradual exodus. Now about fifty people were around the dead man: men from a public works training centre who were only too delighted to have found such an absorbing topic of conversation to while away their eight hours of idleness. The sergeant-major ordered his men to clear the square and get the passengers back onto the bus. The *carabinieri* began pushing sightseers back towards the streets leading off the square, asking passengers to take their seats on the bus again. When the square was empty, so was the bus. Only the driver and the conductor remained.

"What?" said the sergeant-major to the driver. "No passengers today?"

"Yes, some," replied the driver with an absent-minded look.

"Some," said the sergeant-major, "means four, five or six . . . I've never seen this bus leave with an empty seat."

"How should I know?" said the driver, exhausted from straining his memory. "How should I know? I said 'some' just like that. More than five or six though. Maybe more; maybe the bus was full. I never look to see who's there. I just get into my seat and off we go. The road's the only thing I look at; that's what I'm paid for . . . to look at the road."

The sergeant-major rubbed his chin with a hand taut with irritation. "I get it," he said, "you just look at the road." He rounded savagely on the conductor. "But you, you tear off the tickets, take money, give change. You count the people and look at their faces . . . and if you don't want me to make you remember 'em in the guardroom, you're going to tell me now who was on that bus! At least ten names . . . You've been on this run for the last three years, and for the last three years I've seen you every evening in the Café Italia. You know this town better than I do . . . "

"Nobody would know the town better than you do," said the conductor with a smile, as though shrugging off a compliment.

"All right, then," said the sergeant-major, sneering, "first me, then you . . . But I wasn't on the bus or I'd remember every passenger one by one. So it's up to you. Ten names at least."

"I can't remember," said the conductor, "by my mother's soul I can't remember. Just now I can't remember a thing. It all seems a dream."

"I'll wake you up," raged the sergeant-major, "I'll wake you up with a couple of years inside . . . " He broke off to go and meet the police magistrate who had just arrived. While making his report on the identity of the dead man and the flight of the passengers, the sergeant-major looked at the bus. As he looked, he had an impression that something was not quite right or was missing, as when something in our daily routine is unexpectedly missing, which the senses perceive from force of habit but the mind does not quite apprehend; even so its absence provokes an empty feeling of discomfort, a vague exasperation as from a flickering lightbulb. Then, suddenly, what we are looking for dawns on us.

"There's something missing," said the sergeant-major to *Carabiniere* Sposito, who being a qualified accountant was the pillar of the *Carabinieri* Station of S., "there's something or someone missing."

"The fritter-seller," said *Carabiniere* Sposito.

"The fritter-seller, by God!" The sergeant-major exulted, thinking: "An accountant's diploma means something."

A *carabiniere* was sent off at the double to pick up the fritter-seller. He knew where to find the man, who after the departure of the first bus, usually went to sell his wares at the entrance of the elementary schools. Ten minutes later the sergeant-major had the vendor of fritters in front of him. The man's expression was that of a man roused from innocent slumber.

"Was he there?" the sergeant-major asked the conductor.

"He was," answered the conductor gazing at his shoe.

"Well now," said the sergeant-major with paternal kindness, "this morning, as usual, you came to sell your fritters here . . . As usual, at the first bus for Palermo . . . "

"I've my licence," said the fritter-seller.

"I know," said the sergeant-major, raising his eyes to heaven, imploring patience. "I know and I'm not thinking about your licence. I want to know only one thing, and, if you tell me, you can go off at once and sell your fritters to the kids: who fired the shots?"

"Why," asked the fritter-seller, astonished and inquisitive, "has there been shooting?"

Reprinted from The Day of the Owl *by Leonardo Sciascia, translated by Archibald Colquhoun and Arthur Oliver (Carcanet Press Ltd).*

BOOKS

There are only a few modern writers who have travelled in and written about Sicily, though the island has provided the inspiration for some great literature, by both Sicilians and European visitors. Most of the books listed below are in print and those that aren't shouldn't be too difficult to track down (out-of-print books are indicated by "o/p"). Wherever a book is in print the UK publisher is listed first, followed by the publisher in the US – unless the title is available in one country only, in which case we've specified the country; or if the UK and US editions are the same, when the name is only given once. Where paperback editions are available, these are listed in preference to hardcover.

TRAVEL AND GENERAL

Luigi Barzini, *The Italians* (Penguin; Atheneum). Long the most respected work on the Italian nation, and rightly so. Barzini leaves no stone unturned in his quest to pinpoint the real Italy.

Anthony Blunt, *Sicilian Baroque* (Weidenfeld & Nicolson in UK; o/p in US). The only book specifically on the subject, contains everything you ever wanted to know about Sicilian Baroque, very readable and anecdotal, with pages of black-and-white photos. Out of print in the US, but should be available in large public libraries.

Vincent Cronin, *The Golden Honeycomb* (Harvill). Disguised as a quest for the mythical golden honeycomb of Daedalus, this is a searching account of a sojourn in Sicily in the 1950s. Although overwritten in parts, it manages to combine colourful descriptions of Sicily's art, architecture and folklore with a knowing and erudite commentary.

Duncan Fallowell, *To Noto* (Vintage in UK). Details a trip from London to Baroque Noto in an old Ford – an erudite travelogue, seeping with wit and pithy observations on Sicily and the Sicilians.

Francis M. Guercio, *Sicily: the Garden of the Mediterranean* (Faber in UK; o/p in US). Fairly comprehensive but dated (pre-war) introduction to the island, and with more than a passing sympathy for Mussolini. Interesting as a period piece, though, and the history and archeological site accounts are sound.

Russell King, *Sicily* (David & Charles, o/p). One of the *Islands* series, this is an informed and comprehensive read, with chapters on archeology, industry, bandits, the Mafia, and volcanoes and earthquakes. If you can't track down a copy you'll usually find it in public libraries.

Fiona Pitt-Kethley, *Journeys to the Underworld* (Chatto & Windus in UK). English poet searches Italy for the Sibylline sites, a good third of her time spent in Sicily – though Pitt-Kethley's salacious appetite for sexual adventure often distracts from the real interest.

Mary Taylor Simeti, *On Persephone's Island: A Sicilian Journal* (Penguin, o/p; Vintage). Sympathetic record of a typical year in Sicily by an American who married a Sicilian professor and has lived in the west of the island since the early 1960s. Full of keenly observed detail about flora and fauna, customs, the harvests, festivals and – above all – the Sicilians themselves. Also see "Cuisine" (p.411) for her splendid book on Sicilian food.

SPECIFIC GUIDES

Stefano Ardito, *Backpacking and Walking in Italy* (Bradt, o/p; Hunter, o/p). The only thing there is on serious hiking in Sicily, with a very short eleven-page chapter on the island; walks in the Madonie, Etna region and on Maréttimo.

Paul Duncan, *Sicily: A Travellers' Guide* (John Murray). Recent guide that's strong on architecture in general and Palermo in particular.

HISTORY, POLITICS AND ARCHEOLOGY

David Abulafia, *Frederick II: A Medieval Emperor* (Pimlico; Oxford UP). Definitive account of the Hohenstaufen king, greatest of the medieval European rulers, with much on his rule in Sicily as well as elsewhere in Europe. It's a reinterpretation of the usual view of Frederick, revealing a less formidable king than the omnipotent and supreme ruler usually portrayed.

Brian Caven, *Dionysius I: War-Lord of Sicily* (Yale UP). Detailed but readable account of the life of Dionysius I by a historian who sees him not as a vicious tyrant but as a valiant crusader against the Carthaginians.

M.I. Finley, D. Mack Smith & C.J.H. Duggan, *A History of Sicily* (Chatto & Windus in UK). An updated abridgement of the trilogy first published in 1968, this is the best available history of the island, from the Stone Age to the early 1980s.

Margaret Guido, *Sicily: An Archaeological Guide* (Faber; o/p in US). Indispensable and approachable account of Sicily's prehistoric and Roman remains and the island's Greek sites, comprehensive and with good site-plans. One reservation is that it's not been revised since 1977 – which means there are a few gaps and the practical information is out of date.

John Haycraft, *Italian Labyrinth: Italy in the 1980s* (Penguin; o/p in US). Fine, rambling study of modern Italy, its customs, politics, social problems, economy and arts. There's much on Sicily, with interesting insights into the Church, Mafia and corruption in Palermo.

Christopher Hibbert, *Garibaldi and his Enemies* (Penguin, o/p; Plume, o/p). A popular treatment of the life and revolutionary works of Giuseppe Garibaldi, thrillingly detailing the exploits of "The Thousand" in their lightning campaign from Marsala to Milazzo.

John Julius Norwich, *The Normans in Sicily* (Penguin; o/p in US). Published together for the first time under one title, J.J. Norwich's *The Normans in Sicily* and *Kingdom in the Sun* are the accessible, well-researched story of the Normans' explosive entry into the south of Italy, dealing with their creation in Sicily of one of the most brilliant medieval European civilizations. Full of fascinating anecdotes and background to Sicily's glittering eleventh and twelfth centuries.

Giuliano Procacci, *History of the Italian People* (Penguin in UK). A comprehensive history of the peninsula, charting the development of Italy as a nation-state; there isn't much specifically on Sicily but it puts the island's relationship with the mainland after 1000 AD into perspective.

Steven Runciman, *The Sicilian Vespers* (Cambridge UP). The classic account of Sicily's large-scale popular uprising in the thirteenth century. Dense with information covering the whole Mediterranean region. More entertaining is Runciman's *A History of the Crusades: 1, 2 & 3* (Penguin; CUP), complete with full details of the Norman kings of Sicily, as well as of the crusading Frederick II himself. An essential read if you want to unravel all the intricacies of the period.

CRIME AND SOCIETY

Pino Arlacchi, *Mafia Business* (Oxford Paperbacks; o/p in US). Dry and academic account of how the Mafia moved into big business, legal and illegal, its argument summarized by the book's subtitle *The Mafia Ethic and the Spirit of Capitalism*. The author has served on the Italian government's Anti-Mafia Commission, which makes him supremely qualified to judge accurately the Mafia's cutting edge.

Danilo Dolci, *Sicilian Lives* (Writers and Readers; Pantheon, o/p). Dolci's formidable record of the lives of the Sicilians he met when he moved to Trappeto in the early 1950s. Short accounts told in their own words provide at once a moving and depressing document.

Christopher Duggan, *Fascism and the Mafia* (Yale UP). Well-researched study of how Mussolini put the Mafia in their place. Duggan uses this account to expound his theory that there's no such thing as the Mafia, that it was simply dreamed up by Italians seeking a scapegoat for their inability to control the delinquent society.

Giovanni Falcone, *Men of Honour* (Warner in UK). Judge Falcone's compelling account of what he found out about the Mafia during his time as chief investigator, knowledge that ultimately led to his murder in May 1992. Essential reading for those who still question the existence of the Mafia, or anyone interested in its labyrinthine organization and why the State has failed to curb it, complete with "Commission" membership lists.

Norman Lewis, *The Honoured Society* (Eland; Putnam, o/p). Famous account of the Mafia, its origins, personalities and customs. Certainly the most enjoyable introduction to the subject available, though much of it is taken up with banditry – really a separate issue – and his lack of accredited sources leaves you wondering how much is conjecture.

Clare Longrigg, *Mafia Women* (Chatto in UK). Fascinating look at the new active role of women within organized crime in the 1990s, mainly in Naples and Sicily. Intimidation and fear are shown to be the oil that turns the Mafia wheels, with the supreme place of the family appearing to justify almost any outrage or amount of complicity.

Gavin Maxwell, *The Ten Pains of Death* (Alan Sutton, o/p; Dutton, o/p). Maxwell went to live in Scopello in 1953, and (like Dolci) records the lives of his neighbours in their own words: there's much on Sicilian small-town life and poverty, and sympathetic portraits of traditional festivals and characters. His *God Protect Me From My Friends* (o/p) is a good and sympathetic biography of the notorious bandit Salvatore Giuliano, ripe with intrigue and double-dealing, though its evasiveness about his bloody death begs more questions than it answers.

Peter Robb, *Midnight in Sicily* (Harvill). The Australian Robb spent fifteen years in the Italian south tracing the contorted relations between organized crime and politics. Here, he focuses on the structure of the Mafia, the trials of the bosses in the 1980s, the high-profile assassinations that ensued, and the trial of Andreotti, in a thorough, fast-paced study that provides deep insights into the dynamics of Sicily's society and an authentic portrait of Palermo.

Tim Shawcross & Martin Young, *Men of Honour: The Confessions of Tommaso Buscetta* (HarperCollins in UK). An account of the Sicilian and American Mafia's move into the international narcotics trade, based on the evidence of Buscetta (a former high-ranking Cosa Nostra lieutenant), which kick-started the 1990s' fightback and saw several leaders imprisoned on the basis of his evidence. The various relationships and feuds are contorted enough to require a family tree (which the book lacks) but it's a good, penetrating yarn, if sometimes carelessly constructed. See also Tim Shawcross's *The War Against the Mafia* (Mainstream in UK), an informative background on the ways and workings of the Mafia and the attempts to contain it.

Renate Siebert, *Secrets of Life and Death: Women and the Mafia*, translated by Liz Heron (Verso). History and analysis of the patriarchal nature of Mafia organizations, which are held to be the apotheosis of the masculine society of Italy's south. Poignant first-person narratives give background to the account, exploding the myth of the Mafia as protecting the weak and defending women, who continue to be used as drugs mules and decoys. The author is a German-born professor of sociology at the University of Calabria.

Carl Sifakis, *The Mafia File* (Equation; Facts on File, o/p). An A to Z of organized crime in the United States. All the big Sicilian names are here, alongside intriguing entries for Frank Sinatra, George Raft and a host of other hangers-on.

Claire Sterling, *The Mafia* (HarperCollins; Simon & Schuster, o/p). Thorough piece of Mafia scholarship, showing to a disturbing degree just how little Mafia power has been eroded by the State's onslaught of recent years.

Alexander Stille, *Excellent Cadavers* (Vintage). An important book tracing the modern fight against the Mafia as led by Sicilian magistrates Giovanni Falcone and Paolo Borsellino, both of whom were assassinated in 1992. But, as Stille shows, the work they started led eventually to the imprisonment of Salvatore Riina (see p.290).

NOVELS ABOUT SICILY

Allen Andrews, *Impossible Loyalties* (Deutsch in UK, o/p). Fast-moving, if unevenly paced, narrative of an Anglo-Sicilian family caught up in the turmoil of World War II, containing an authentic portrait of pre-war Messina society.

Tahar Ben Jelloun, *State of Absence* (Quartet in UK, o/p). The French-Moroccan author visited southern Italy and Sicily in 1990, fashioning his notes about daily life into a provoking, realistic novel about the effect of the Mafia on the people of the south.

Norman Lewis, *The March of the Long Shadows* (Secker & Warburg in UK). An affectionate novel set in post-war Sicily, dealing with the Separatist movement, the bandit Giuliano and a whole cast of endearing characters. Good location writing, too, detailing the countryside around Palermo. *The Sicilian Specialist* (Penguin, o/p; Critic's Choice) is a Mafia thriller, full of authentic Sicilian background, which flits from the island to the US to Cuba on the trail of a Mob assassin.

Dacia Maraini, *The Silent Duchess* (Flamingo; Feminist Press). The work of a Florence-born author, but with a Sicilian mother, this is one of the most successful Italian novels of recent years, set in eighteenth-century Sicily. It's a tale of a noble family seen through the eyes of a young duchess; beautifully written and dripping with authentic detail, particularly about the lot of women in those times. *Bagheria* (Peter Owen; Dufour), by the same author, is a delightfully engaging memoir of her childhood in the town of the title, entwining criticism of local corruption with an historical awareness of events and people which figured in her earlier work.

Mario Puzo, *The Godfather* (Mandarin; Signet). The New York Godfather – Don Corleone – was born in Sicily (see p.290) and the book touches on all things Sicilian. In Francis Ford Coppola's three-part film, the first to rehabilitate the Mafia in American eyes, Marlon Brando played an old Don Corleone. The book's a great read, even if you've seen the films (which are pretty faithful to Puzo's novel). Also by Puzo is *The Sicilian* (Bantam, o/p), a novelized life of the bandit Salvatore Giuliano, and the basis of an uninspiring 1988 film starring Christopher Lambert. Better, if you're interested, is to try and catch Francesco Rosi's 1962 film, *Salvatore Giuliano*.

Ann Radcliffe, *A Sicilian Romance* (Oxford Paperbacks). Early Gothic novel, written in 1790, telling of supernatural events haunting an aristocratic family, with much purple description of the Sicilian landscape.

Peter Vansittart, *A Choice of Murder* (Peter Owen in UK). Clever novelized account of the life of Timoleon of Siracusa, based on Plutarch's history of the same. A gripping view of the ancient Greek world in Sicily and beyond.

SICILIAN LITERATURE AND BIOGRAPHY

Gesualdo Bufalino, *The Plague Sower* (Eridanos Press), *Blind Argus* (Harvill in UK), *The Keeper of Ruins* (Harvill in UK), and *Night's Lies* (Harvill). "Discovered" by Sciascia, Bufalino arrived late on the literary scene, publishing his first novel, *The Plague Sower*, when he was into his sixties. Subsequent publications enhanced the reputation made by this remarkable debut, notably *Night's Lies*, which won Italy's most respected literary

award, the Strega Prize, in 1988. Bufalino himself – seeking to explain the Sicilian character – commented, "Don't forget that even our most obscene vices nearly always bear the seal of sullen greatness." He died in 1996.

David Gilmour, *The Last Leopard: A Life of Giuseppe di Lampedusa* (Harvill). First biography in English of Lampedusa, though frankly no more than a readable account of the life of rather a dull man – to whom nothing very much happened except the publication (after his death) of one remarkable novel.

Maria Grammatico & Mary Taylor Simeti, *Bitter Almonds: Recollections and Recipes from a Sicilian Girlhood* (o/p). Maria Grammatico was raised in a convent, where she learned the pastry-cooking skills that she employs in her outlets in Érice. The book, co-authored by Mary Taylor Simeti (see under "Cuisine" opposite), relates her life with the nuns, and includes some of her famous recipes.

Giuseppe di Lampedusa, *The Leopard* (Harvill; Everyman's). The most famous Sicilian novel, written after World War II but recounting the dramatic nineteenth-century years of transition from Bourbon to Piedmontese rule from an aristocrat's point of view. A good character study and rich with incidental detail, including some nice descriptions of the Sicilian landscape, which was put to great effect in Visconti's epic 1963 film – a Sicilian *Gone With the Wind*. There's an extract from the novel on p.401.

Luigi Pirandello, *Six Characters in Search of an Author* (Penguin; Signet), *Henry IV* (Methuen, o/p; Riverrun Press), *The Late Mattia Pascal* (Dedalus), *Short Stories* (Quartet, o/p; Dover, o/p). His most famous and accomplished work, *Six Characters . . .*, written in 1921, and his *Henry IV*, written a year later, contain many of the themes that dogged Pirandello throughout his writing career – the idea of a multiple personality and the quality of reality. *The Late Mattia Pascal* is an early novel (1904), entertainingly written despite its stylistic shortcomings; while the collection of short stories is perhaps the best introduction to Pirandello's work you can buy: abrasive stuff, the dialogue possessing an assured comic touch.

Carmelo Samona, *Brothers* (Carcanet in UK). Palermo-born author of only two novels, Samona here investigates the fraught relationship of two brothers in an eerie work.

Leonardo Sciascia, *Sicilian Uncles* (Carcanet, o/p), *The Wine-Dark Sea* (Carcanet, o/p; Scholarly Book Services), *Candido* (Harvill; Harcourt Brace, o/p), *The Knight and Death* and *Death of an Inquisitor* (both Harvill in UK, o/p), *The Day of the Owl* and *Equal Danger* (Paladin; Godine, o/p; in the US, *The Day of the Owl* is also published on its own as *Il Giorno della Civetta*, by Manchester UP). Economically written, Sciasca's short stories and novellas are packed with incisive insights into the island's quirky ways, and infused with the author's humane and sympathetic view of its people. The best known is *The Day of the Owl*, an extract from which appears on p.405.

Giovanni Verga, *Short Sicilian Novels* (Dedalus; Hippocrene), *Cavalleria Rusticana* (Dedalus; Greenwood, o/p), *Maestro Don Gesualdo* (Dedalus; University of California Press), *I Malavoglia* or *The House by the Medlar Tree* (Dedalus; University of California Press), *A Mortal Sin* (Quartet in UK), *The She-Wolf and Other Stories* (University of California Press; o/p in US) and *Sparrow* (Dedalus; Hippocrene). Verga, born in the nineteenth century in Catania, spent several years in various European salons before coming home to write his best work. Much of it is a reaction against the pseudo-sophistication of society circles, stressing the simple lives of ordinary people, though they're occasionally bestowed with a heavy smattering of "peasant passion", with much emotion, wounded honour and feuds to the death. D.H. Lawrence's translations are suitably vibrant, with excellent introductions. *Sparrow* is a doomed love story set in cholera-ravaged mid-nineteenth-century Sicily, and filmed by Zeffirelli in 1993.

Elio Vittorini, *Conversation in Sicily* (Quartet in UK, o/p). A Sicilian emigrant returns from the north of Italy after fifteen years to see his mother on her birthday. The conversations of the title are with the people he meets on the way, local villagers and his mother, and reveal a pre-war Sicily that is poverty- and disease-ridden – though affectionately drawn. An extract is printed on p.403. New Directions publish a Vittorini omnibus containing the novels *In Sicily*, *The Twilight of the Elephant* and *La Garibaldini*.

CUISINE

Antonio Carluccio, *Southern Italian Feast* (BBC in UK). Glossy TV tie-in by Britain's avuncular Italian master, particularly good on Sicilian fish and snacks – his *arancini* recipe is definitive.

Elizabeth David, *Italian Food* (Penguin in UK). First published in 1954, this was the book that introduced Mediterranean flavours to a UK ravaged by post-war shortages. Although a learned and entertaining stroll through the whole canon of Italian cooking, there are plenty of Sicilian dishes covered. The 1998 edition includes original illustrations by Renato Guttuso.

Valentina Harris, *Southern Italian Cooking* (Trafalgar Square in US). Excellent book with a chapter on Sicilian cooking, including several of the classic recipes. Also covers the related cuisine of Calabria and other southern regions.

Anna Tasca Lanza, *The Flavors of Sicily* (Potter in US). Sicilian summer cooking from the respected owner of a cooking school established at her Sicilian family estate. An anecdotal trawl through the classics and the lesser-known dishes, including several from out-of-the-way places like Pantelleria and Strómboli.

Anna Pomar, *La Cucina Tradizionale Siciliana* (Brancato); **Silvia Trombetta**, *Dolci Tradizionali Siciliani* (Brancato). Published in Italy (in Italian), you'll see these complementary books on sale throughout Sicily. They're extremely comprehensive, the first book detailing recipes from every Sicilian region, the second a wealth of recipes for desserts, sweets and festival food.

Mary Taylor Simeti, *Sicilian Food* (Holt, o/p; published as *Pomp and Sustenance* in US by Ecco Press). Everything a book on food should be: historically and culturally informed, and packed with recipes and fascinating detail about life and food on the island. Thoroughly recommended.

LANGUAGE

The ability to speak English confers enormous prestige in Sicily, but though there's no shortage of people willing to show off their knowledge, particularly returned *emigrati*, few outside the tourist resorts actually know more than some simple words and phrases – more often than not culled from pop songs or films.

SOME TIPS

You'd do well to master at least a little **Italian**, a task made more enjoyable by the fact that your halting efforts will often be rewarded by smiles and genuine surprise that an English-speaker should stoop to learn Italian. In any case, it's one of the easiest European languages to learn, especially if you already have a smattering of French or Spanish, both extremely similar grammatically.

Easiest of all is the **pronunciation**, since every word is spoken exactly as it's written, and usually enunciated with exaggerated, open-mouthed clarity. The only difficulties you're likely to encounter are the few **consonants** that are different from English:

c before **e** or **i** is pronounced as in **ch**urch, while **ch** before the same vowels is hard, as in **c**at.

sci or **sce** are pronounced as in **sh**eet and **she**lter respectively. The same goes with **g** – soft before **e** and **i**, as in **g**entle; hard when followed by **h**, as in **g**arlic.

gn has the **ni** sound of our o**ni**on.

gl in Italian is softened to something like **li** in English, as in vermi**li**on.

h is not aspirated, as in **h**our.

When **speaking** to strangers, the third person is the polite form (ie *Lei* instead of *Tu* for "you"); using the second person is a mark of disrespect or stupidity. It's also worth remembering that Italians don't use "please" and "thank you" half as much as we do: it's all implied in the tone, though if you're in doubt, err on the polite side.

All Italian words are **stressed** on the penultimate syllable unless an **accent** denotes otherwise, although accents are often left out in practice. Note that the ending **-ia** or **-ie** counts as two syllables, hence *trattoria* is stressed on the i. We've put accents in, throughout the text and below, wherever it isn't immediately obvious how a word should be pronounced: for example, in *Maríttima*, the accent is on the first **i**; conversely *Catania* should theoretically have an accent on the second **a.** Other words where we've omitted accents are common ones (like *Isola*, stressed on the I), some names (*Domenico*, *Vittorio*), and words that are stressed similarly in English, such as *Repubblica*.

None of this will help very much if you're confronted with a particularly harsh specimen of the **Sicilian dialect**, which virtually qualifies as a separate language. However, television has made a huge difference and almost every Sicilian can now communicate in something approximating standard Italian.

AN ITALIAN LANGUAGE GUIDE

BASICS

Good morning	*Buon giorno*	Yesterday	*Ieri*
Good afternoon/evening	*Buona sera*	Now	*Adesso*
Good night	*Buona notte*	Later	*Più tardi*
Hello/goodbye	*Ciao* (informal; when speaking to strangers use the phrases above)	Wait a minute!	*Aspetta!*
		In the morning	*Di mattina*
		In the afternoon	*Nel pomeriggio*
		In the evening	*Di sera*
Goodbye	*Arrivederci* (formal)	Here/there	*Qui/là*
Yes	*Sì*	Good/bad	*Buono/cattivo*
No	*No*	Big/small	*Grande/píccolo*
Please	*Per favore*	Cheap/expensive	*Económico/caro*
Thank you	*Grázie*	Early/late	*Presto/ritardo*
(very much)	*(molte/mille grazie)*	Hot/cold	*Caldo/freddo*
You're welcome	*Prego*	Near/far	*Vicino/lontano*
Alright/that's OK	*Va bene*	Vacant/occupied	*Líbero/occupato*
How are you?	*Come stai/sta?* (informal/formal)	Quickly/slowly	*Velocemente/ lentamente*
I'm fine	*Bene*		
Do you speak English?	*Parla inglese?*	Slowly/quietly	*Piano*
I don't understand	*Non capisco*	With/without	*Con/senza*
I haven't understood	*Non ho capito*	More/less	*Più/meno*
I don't know	*Non lo so*	Enough/no more	*Basta*
Excuse me/sorry (informal)	*Scusa*	Mr...	*Signor...*
Excuse me/sorry (formal)	*Mi scusi/Prego*	Mrs...	*Signora...*
Excuse me (in a crowd)	*Permesso*	Miss...	*Signorina...*
I'm sorry	*Mi dispiace*		*(il Signore, la Signora, la Signorina when speaking about someone else)*
I'm here on holiday	*Sono qui in vacanza*		
I live in...	*Abito a...*		
Today	*Oggi*		
Tomorrow	*Domani*	First name	*Primo nome*
Day after tomorrow	*Dopodomani*	Surname	*Cognome*

ACCOMMODATION

Hotel	*Albergo*	Do you have anything cheaper?	*Ha niente che costa di meno?*
Is there a hotel nearby?	*C'è un albergo qui vicino?*	Full-/half-board	*Pensione completa/ mezza pensione*
Do you have a room...	*Ha una cámera...*		
for one/two/three people	*per una persona, due/tre persone*	Can I see the room?	*Posso vedere la cámera?*
for one/two/three nights	*per una notte, due/tre notti*	I'll take it	*La prendo*
for one/two weeks	*per una settimana, due settimane*	I'd like to book a room	*Vorrei prenotare una cámera*
with a double bed	*con un letto matrimoniale*	I have a booking	*Ho una prenotazione*
with a shower/bath	*con una doccia/ un bagno*	Can we camp here?	*Possiamo fare il campeggio qui?*
with a balcony	*con una terrazza*	Is there a campsite nearby?	*C'è un camping qui vicino?*
hot/cold water	*acqua calda/fredda*		
How much is it?	*Quanto costa?*	Tent	*Tenda*
It's expensive	*È caro*	Cabin	*Cabina*
Is breakfast included?	*È compresa la prima colazione?*	Youth hostel	*Ostello per la gioventù*

QUESTIONS AND DIRECTIONS

Where? (Where is/are...?)	*Dove? (Dov'è/Dove sono?)*	Can you tell me when to get off?	*Può dirmi quando devo scendere?*
When?	*Quando?*	What time does it open?	*A che ora apre?*
What? (What is it?)	*Cosa? (Cos'è?)*	What time does it close?	*A che ora chiude?*
How much/many?	*Quanto/Quanti?*	How much does it cost	*Quanto costa?*
Why?	*Perché?*	(...do they cost?)	*(Quantocostano?)*
It is/There is (Is it/Is there...?)	*È/C'è (È/C'è...?)*	What's it called in Italian?	*Come si chiama in italiano?*
What time is it?	*Che ora è?/ Che ore sono?*	Left/right	*Sinistra/destra*
How do I get to...?	*Come arrivo a...?*	Go straight ahead	*Sempre diritto*
How far is it to...?	*Quant'è lontano a...?*	Turn to the right/left	*Gira a destra/sinistra*
Can you give me a lift to...?	*Mi può dare un passaggio a...?*		

TRANSPORT MATTERS

Aeroplane	*Aeroplano*	What time does it leave?	*A che ora parte?*
Bus	*Autobus/Pullman*	When is the next bus/train/ferry to...?	*Quando parte il próssimo pullman/ treno/traghetto per...?*
Train	*Treno*		
Car	*Mácchina*		
Taxi	*Taxi*		
Bicycle	*Bicicletta*	Where does it leave from?	*Da dove parte?*
Ferry	*Traghetto*		
Ship	*Nave*	Which platform does it leave from?	*Da quale binario parte?*
Hydrofoil	*Aliscafo*		
Hitch-hiking	*Autostop*		
On foot	*A piedi*	Do I have to change?	*Devo cambiare?*
Bus station	*Autostazione*	How many kilometres is it?	*Quanti chilómetri sono?*
Train station	*Stazione ferroviaria*		
Ferry terminal	*Stazione maríttima*	How long does it take?	*Quanto ci vuole?*
Port	*Porto*	What number bus is it to...?	*Que número di autobus per...?*
A ticket to...	*Un biglietto a...*		
One way/return	*Solo andata/ andata e ritorno*	Where's the road to...?	*Dov'è la strada a...?*
Can I book a seat?	*Posso prenotare un posto?*	Next stop, please	*La próssima fermata, per favore*

SOME SIGNS

Entrance/exit	*Entrata/uscita*	To let	*Affítasi*
Free entrance	*Ingresso líbero*	Platform	*Binario*
Gentlemen/ladies	*Signori/signore*	Cash desk	*Cassa*
WC	*Gabinetto/bagno*	Go/walk	*Avanti*
Vacant/engaged	*Líbero/occupato*	Stop/halt	*Alt*
Open/closed	*Aperto/chiuso*	Customs	*Dogana*
Arrivals/departures	*Arrivi/partenze*	Do not touch	*Non toccare*
Closed for restoration	*Chiuso per restauro*	Danger	*Perícolo*
Closed for holidays	*Chiuso per ferie*	Beware	*Attenzione*
Pull/push	*Tirare/spingere*	First aid	*Pronto soccorso*
Out of order	*Guasto*	Ring the bell	*Suonare il campanello*
Drinking water	*Acqua potabile*	No smoking	*Vietato fumare*

DRIVING

Parking	*Parcheggio*	No through road	*Vietato il transito*
No parking	*Divieto di sosta/Sosta vietata*	No overtaking	*Vietato il sorpasso*
One way street	*Senso único*	Crossroads	*Incrocio*
No entry	*Senso vietato*	Speed limit	*Límite di velocità*
Slow down	*Rallentare*	Traffic light	*Semáforo*
Road closed/up	*Strada chiusa/guasta*		

PHRASEBOOKS AND DICTIONARIES

The best phrasebook is Rough Guide's own *Italian Phrasebook* (Penguin), which has a large but accessible vocabulary, a detailed menu reader and useful dialogues. As for dictionaries, Collins publish a comprehensive series: their *Gem* or *Pocket* dictionaries are fine for travelling purposes, while their *Concise* is adequate for most language needs.

GLOSSARIES

ARTISTIC AND ARCHITECTURAL TERMS

AGORA Square or marketplace in an ancient Greek city.

APSE Domed recess at the altar-end of a church.

ARCHITRAVE The lowest part of the entablature.

ATRIUM Forecourt, usually of a Roman house.

BOTHROS A pit that contains votive offerings.

CAMPANILE Bell-tower.

CAPITAL Top of a column.

CATALAN-GOTHIC Hybrid form of architecture, mixing elements from fifteenth-century Spanish and northern European building styles.

CAVEA The seating section in a theatre.

CELLA Sanctuary of a temple.

CUPOLA A dome.

DECUMANUS The main street in a Roman town.

ENTABLATURE The part of the building above the capital on a classical building.

EX-VOTO Decorated tablet designed as thanksgiving to a saint.

HELLENISTIC PERIOD 325–331 BC (Alexander the Great to Augustus).

HYPOGEUM Underground vault, often used as an early Christian church.

KOUROS Standing male figure of the Archaic Period (700 BC to early fifth century BC).

KRATER Ancient conical bowl with round base.

LOGGIA Roofed gallery or balcony.

METOPE A panel on the frieze of a temple.

NAUMACHIA Mock naval combat, or the deep trench in a theatre in which it took place.

NAVE Central space in a church, usually flanked by aisles.

ODEON Small theatre, usually roofed, for recitals.

ORCHESTRA Section of the main floor of a theatre, where the chorus danced.

PANTOCRATOR Usually refers to Christ, portrayed with outstretched arms.

POLYPTYCH Painting or carving on several joined wooden panels.

PORTICO The covered entrance to a building.

PUNIC Carthaginian/Phoenician.

SCENE-BUILDING Structure holding scenery in Greek/Roman theatre.

STELAE Inscribed stone slabs.

STEREOBATE Visible base of any building, usually a temple.

STOA A detached roofed porch, or portico.

STYLOBATE Raised base of a columned building, usually a temple.

TELAMON A supporting column in the shape of a male figure.

THERMAE Baths, usually elaborate buildings in Roman villas.

TRIPTYCH Painting or carving on three joined wooden panels.

ITALIAN WORDS

ALISCAFO Hydrofoil.

ANFITEATRO Amphitheatre.

AUTOSTAZIONE Bus station.

AUTOSTRADA Motorway.

BELVEDERE A lookout point.

CAPPELLA Chapel.

CASTELLO Castle.

CATTEDRALE Cathedral.

CENTRO Centre.

CHIESA Church (main "mother" church, Chiesa Matrice/Madre).

COMUNE An administrative area; also, the local council or the town hall.

CORSO Avenue/boulevard.

DUOMO Cathedral.

ENTRATA Entrance.

FESTA Festival, carnival.

FIUME River.

FUMAROLA Volcanic vapour emission from the ground.

GOLFO Gulf.

LAGO Lake.

LARGO Place (like piazza).

LUNGOMARE Seafront promenade or road.

MARE Sea.

MERCATO Market.

MONGIBELLO Italian name for Mount Etna.

MUNICIPIO Town hall.

PALAZZO Palace, mansion or block (of flats).

PARCO Park.

PASSEGGIATA The customary early-evening walk.

PIANO Plain (also "slowly", "gently").

PIAZZA Square.

PINETA Pinewood.

SANTUARIO Sanctuary.

SOTTOPASSAGGIO Subway.

SPIAGGIA Beach.

STAZIONE Station (train station, stazione ferroviaria; bus station, autostazione; ferry terminal, stazione maríttima).

STRADA Road/street.

TEATRO Theatre.

TEMPIO Temple.

TORRE Tower.

TRAGHETTO Ferry.

USCITA Exit.

VIA Road (always used with name, as in Via Roma).

ZONA Zone.

ACRONYMS

AAST Azienda Autonoma di Soggiorno e Turismo (local tourist office).

ACI Italian Automobile Club.

APT Azienda Provinciale di Turismo (provincial tourist office).

DC Democrazia Cristiana; the Christian Democrat Party.

FS Italian State Railways.

IVA Imposta Valore Aggiunto (VAT).

MSI Movimento Sociale d'Italia; the Italian Neo-Fascist party.

PDS Partito Democratico della Sinistra; the former Italian Communist Party.

PSI Partito Socialista d'Italia; the Italian Socialist Party.

RAI The Italian State TV and radio network.

SP Strada Provinciale; a minor road, eg SP116.

SS Strada Statale; a main highway, eg SS120.

INDEX

Small

but perfectly
informed

Every bit as stylish and irreverent as their full-sized counterparts, Mini Guides are everything you'd expect from a Rough Guide, but smaller — perfect for a pocket, briefcase or overnight bag.

Available 1998
Antigua, Barbados, Boston, Dublin, Edinburgh, Lisbon, Madrid, Seattle

Coming soon
Bangkok, Brussels, Florence, Honolulu, Las Vegas, Maui, Melbourne, New Orleans, Oahu, St Lucia, Sydney, Tokyo, Toronto

 Everything you need to know about everything you want to do

the perfect getaway vehicle

low-price holiday car rental.

rent a car from holiday autos and you'll give yourself real freedom to explore your holiday destination. with great-value, fully-inclusive rates in over 4,000 locations worldwide, wherever you're escaping to, we're there to make sure you get excellent prices and superb service.

what's more, you can book now with complete confidence. our £5 undercut* ensures that you are guaranteed the best value for money in holiday destinations right around the globe.

drive away with a great deal, call holiday autos now on **0990 300 400** and quote ref RG.

holiday autos miles ahead

*in the unlikely event that you should see a cheaper like for like pre-paid rental rate offered by any other independent uk car rental company before or after booking but prior to departure, holiday autos will undercut that price by a full £5. we truly believe we cannot be beaten on price.